Horror Film
Festivals
and Awards

ALSO BY THOMAS M. SIPOS

*Horror Film Aesthetics: Creating the
Visual Language of Fear* (McFarland, 2010)

Horror Film Festivals and Awards

Thomas M. Sipos

McFarland & Company, Inc., Publishers
Jefferson, North Carolina, and London

LIBRARY OF CONGRESS CATALOGUING-IN-PUBLICATION DATA

Sipos, Thomas M.
Horror film festivals and awards / Thomas M. Sipos.
p. cm.
Includes bibliographical references and index.

ISBN 978-0-7864-6572-9
softcover : 50# alkaline paper ∞

1. Horror films — History and criticism.   2. Film festivals —
Catalogs.   3. Motion pictures — Awards.   I. Title.
PN1995.9.H6S535   2012   791.43'6164 — dc23   2011025550

British Library cataloguing data are available

© 2012 Thomas M. Sipos. All rights reserved

*No part of this book may be reproduced or transmitted in any form
or by any means, electronic or mechanical, including photocopying
or recording, or by any information storage and retrieval system,
without permission in writing from the publisher.*

Front cover design by Mark Berry (www.hot-cherry.co.uk)

Manufactured in the United States of America

*McFarland & Company, Inc., Publishers
Box 611, Jefferson, North Carolina 28640
www.mcfarlandpub.com*

Table of Contents

Acknowledgments
vii

Preface
1

1 How to Run a Film Festival on Pennies a Day!
5

2 How to Make an Award-Winning Horror Film!
37

3 Working the Film Festival!
65

Directory of Festivals and Awards
95

**List of Award Winners
(by Festival)**
121

Notes
253

Index
257

ACKNOWLEDGMENTS

I thank the following film festival officials for assisting with this book throughout 2010 and into 2011. Some granted interviews, others answered a few questions, or contributed photos or lists of winners, or verified their directory or winners listings. All helped to make this book more complete and accurate.

They are: Gareth "Gaz" Bailey (Abertoir Horror Festival), Jeff Ross (Another Hole in the Head: Two Weeks of Horror, Sci-Fi and Fantasy), David Pike (Arizona Underground Film Festival), Michael Coulombe (Big Bear Horror Film Festival), Brian Kirst (Big Gay Horror Fan Film Festival), Elisabeth Fies (BleedFest), Andrew Rose (Blood Bath Film Festival), Linda Webster (Bloody Harvest and Bloody Valentine), Garen Daly (Boston Science Fiction Film Festival and Boston Terror'thon), Jacqueline Cockerill (British Horror Film Festival), Christoph Foque (Brussels International Fantastic Film Festival), Pablo Sapere and R. Patricio Díaz (Buenos Aires Rojo Sangre), Dorien Eggink (BUT: B-Movies, Underground & Trash Film Festival), Alex Bram (Carnival of Darkness), Robert Nevitt (Celluloid Screams: Sheffield Horror Film Festival), Vivi Amaral (Cinefantasy International Film Festival), Andrew Gurudata (Constellation Awards), Ted Venemann (Creation's Weekend of Horrors), Susana (Cryptshow Festival), Adele Hartley (Dead by Dawn: Scotland's International Horror Film Festival), Shade Rupe (Deep Red International Festival of Fantastic Film), Matthew M. Foster (Dragon*Con Independent Short Film Festival), Bryan Wolford (Drunken Zombie Film Festival), Emiel Labree (Duistere Openbaringen Film Festival), Greg Ropp (Eerie Horror Film Festival), Chris Alexander and Mike Gingold (Fangoria Chainsaw Awards), Alberto Ravaglioli (Fanta Festival), João Fleck (Fantaspoa: Festival Internacional de Cinema Fantástico de Porto Alegre), Tony Tilton (Fargo Fantastic Fest), Daniel Cohen (Festival Européen du Film Fantastique de Strasbourg), Anthony Humbertclaude (Festival International du Film Fantastique de Gérardmer), George T. Marshall (FLICKERS: Rhode Island International Horror Film Festival), Katie Harders (Freak Show Horror Film Festival), Ken Daniels (Fright Night Film Fest), Ian (FrightFest), John Johnson (Frightmares Film Festival), Rhiannon Clifford (Grimm Up North), Andrew Migliore (H.P. Lovecraft Film Festival & CthulhuCon and Zompire: The Undead Film Festival), Sten-Kristian Saluveer (Haapsalu Horror & Fantasy Film Festival), Kelly Jones and Kelly Webster (Halloween Monster Movie Challenge), Alan J. LaFave (Hell's Half Mile Film & Music Festival), Sol Charlotte (Horrorvision: Spanish Horror Trash Film Festival), Phil van Tongeren (Imagine: Amsterdam Fantastic Film Festival), Jason R. Davis (Indy Horror Film Festival), Andrea Beesley-Brown and Jason Carney (International Horror and Sci-Fi Film Festival), Paul Sanchez Yates (International Surrealist Film Festival), Michael Vallier (Killer Film Fest), Rich Peterson (Madison Horror Film Festival), Eric Morgret (Maelstrom International Fantastic Film Festival), Timothy Schultz (Mile High Horror Film Festival),

Alejandro Yamgotchian (Montevideo Fantástico), Pablo Guisa Koestinger (MORBIDO: Festival Internacional de Cine Fantastico y de Terror), João Monteiro (MOTELx — Festival Internacional de Cinema de Terror de Lisboa), Farida Khali (Neuchâtel International Fantastic Film Festival), Jim Carl and Phillip Seib (Nevermore Film Festival), Michael J. Hein (New York City Horror Film Festival), John Gillette and Reyna Young (A Nightmare to Remember San Francisco Horror Film Festival), Alberto Bucci (Ravenna Nightmare Film Festival), Patrick Van Hauwaert (Razor Reel Fantastic Film Festival), David Colton (Rondo Hatton Classic Horror Award), David Daniloff (Rue Morgue Festival of Fear), Tim Meunier (Sacramento Horror Film Festival), Mario DeAngelis (Salty Horror Film Festival), Carlos J. Plaza and Alfonso C. Lopez (San Sebastián Horror and Fantasy Film Festival), Jaime Albornoz (FIXION-STARS: Festival de Cine Fantástico y de Terror de Santiago), Jeff Waldridge (Scare Fest), Tom Carrington (Sci-Fi-London Film Festival), Rena Orocklou (Screamin' Athens Horror Film Festival), G.R. Claveria (Shockfest Film Festival), Denise Gossett (Shriekfest Horror/SciFi Film Festival & Screenplay Competition), Maria Castells (SITGES: Festival Internacional de Cinema Fantàstic de Catalunya), Paul Blom (South African HORRORFEST Film Festival), Katherine Berger (Sydney Underground Film Festival), Claw (Terror Film Festival), Anthony E. Griffin (Thriller! Chiller!), Giovanni Barbo (Science+Fiction), Anne Koester and Matt Manjourides (TromaDance Film Festival), Art Sunday (Underground Horror Filmfest and Underground Horror Fest), Asif Ahmed (Vampire Film Festival), Shannon Lark and Heidi Martinuzzi (Viscera Film Festival), Matthias Engelhardt (Weekend of Fear: Internationales Filmfestival für Horror, Thriller, Science Fiction & Obskure Filme), Kevin Bacon (Winnipeg Horror Cinema), Jim Taylor (Zombie Short Film Festival).

I also thank filmmakers Sharon Reed, J. Neil Schulman, Jon Weimer, Rich Mauro, Christopher Alan Broadstone, Ray Castile, Hanelle Culpepper, Jamie Renee Williams and author S.G. Browne, for contributing their own insights.

Preface

This book lays to rest one myth: that horror films get no respect.

It's a widespread myth, promulgated probably without much thought, repeated because everyone else repeats it. I've heard it at horror conventions. I've heard it from horror artists. I've come across a number of horror film festivals that lament that horror is an ignored, shunned, and disrespected genre — and so such-and-such festival was founded to *finally* give horror its due. For instance, one festival says that it "is dedicated to screening and recognizing the works of filmmakers and screenwriters in the often forgotten genres." Another festival says that its founding goal was "to make film fans and filmmakers aware that there exists a tradition of filmmaking which is often ignored by the mainstream film industry."

Forgotten, by whom? Not by the major studios, which recognize that horror is big box office. Ignored, how? The entertainment news media and academic presses both generously cover horror. Sure, Oscar *usually* overlooks horror, at least for its major award categories. But horror is not starved for awards. Horror has dozens of prizes and plaques and trophies intended to honor the genre. Several of them claim to be "the Oscar of horror," but it would perhaps be more accurate to say that horror has many Oscars. I doubt that any *genre* has as many film festivals devoted to its celebration and promotion. Far fewer festivals are devoted to science fiction or fantasy — and most of *those* welcome (and are sometimes dominated by) horror. *Indie* film festivals outnumber horror festivals. (Probably, I'm actually not certain.) But again, horror is welcome even at the more prestigious indie festivals.

So let's forever end the myth that horror is forgotten, ignored, or unappreciated. Horror has many suitors. She is a darkly alluring lady who's dropped her handkerchief, whereupon a throng of admirers crowd about her to offer assistance. Horror doesn't need any more dance requests, or bouquets, or expensive gifts. She needs help in keeping track of the many she's already received.

Hence this book.

It has three parts. First, a text portion examines horror film festivals from around the world, offering tips and insights to filmmakers and festival directors alike. Second, there is a directory of horror film festivals and awards, past, present, and prospective. And finally, there is a roster of horror's many festival and award winners. It's an extensive list, forming the largest part of this book, and offering overwhelming evidence of all the honors available to horror films (and TV shows) and to those who create them.

Many books have published a roster of Oscar winners from previous years. I'm sure the same is true for Tony and Emmy and Grammy. I believe this is the *first* book to publish the winners of most, if not all, of the horror film festivals and awards contained herein.

Unlike Oscar or Emmy, it's especially important to record horror's many award winners, because, though horror film festivals are numerous, they are also ephemeral. If their winners are not recorded in some permanent form, and soon, they'll begin disappearing down a memory hole. Some of them are already lost to history.

To understand why this is so, you must realize that this book would not have been possible a decade ago, due to lack of material. A few of today's genre film festivals date back to the 1960s,[1] but the real flowering of horror film festivals occurred during the 2000s. Most of the festivals in this book's directory were founded after 1999. Ten years is old for a horror film festival. Screamfest L.A. and Shriekfest—Los Angeles's two most renowned horror film festivals (there are at least seven others in the L.A. area)—were both founded in 2001. Ten years of continuous screenings. Many festivals survive only a few years. Yet for every festival that dies, it seems three new ones arise. A disproportionately large number of horror festivals were founded in just the two years 2009 and 2010.

I suspect several factors contributed to the past decade's horror film festival boom: 1. the rise and success of indie film festivals in the 1990s; 2. the spread of inexpensive production equipment, creating a flood of horror films seeking promotion and distribution; 3. the growth of the internet and social networking, making it easier to promote both films and film festivals.

The internet has both blessed and cursed horror filmmakers. Cyberspace fueled the horror film festival boom, but it was also the sole repository for many of their winners lists, either on festival websites, or as reported by online genre magazines. Cyberspace offers speed and breadth, but not permanence. Festivals and online magazines die. Their urls and web hosting agreements expire; the webpages listing the festival winners vanish.

Adding to the researcher's frustration, some festivals only list their more recent winners online. They update, but don't archive. In some such cases, festival directors helpfully emailed me their lists of past winners. In other cases, I hunted for orphaned webpages listing previous winners, Googling or guessing at the likely urls.[2] Directors of defunct festivals, when I found them, sometimes seemed indifferent about locating their old records, and had to be politely prodded every few months. A director of a festival that was still running had no records of his earlier winners, and could not remember them.

A few former festival directors may have lost interest in their festival's history, but the winning filmmakers (and cast and crew) care deeply. So too the fans, I think. It takes much effort and expense to complete a film, enter a festival, and actually win. The winners deserve to be memorialized in a permanent record. This book is that record.

Why are horror film festivals so ephemeral, their winners so easily forgotten? Partially because horror festivals, like horror films, are a largely indie, grassroots phenomenon. Yes, some festivals have grown up and turned corporate. They are old, well-established, profitable, and professional. They keep good records. But other festivals are young, impoverished, labors of love, run by a group of friends or even one person. If that person feels overwhelmed and quits, the festival dies. It can't happen to Sundance or Cannes, with their big budgets and boards of trustees and directors, but grassroots horror festivals live more tenuously.

I founded the Tabloid Witch Awards in 2004. I run it alone. It turns no profit. People ask why I do it. For the same reason that others take up indie filmmaking, indie music, self-publishing, and blogging. Inexpensive technology and the internet are empowering grassroots artists, journalists, promoters, and critics. Some people make films. Others start a film festival.

This book's text portion incorporates interviews with some two dozen horror film festival directors. This "behind the scenes" look should help horror filmmakers make better films, and take fuller advantage of their festival experiences. It should also assist film festival directors, both current and *aspiring*. I expect many new horror film festivals will be started over the coming years.

If you know of any festivals or award winners that should be included in this book, or know of any changes, updates, or corrections, please contact me at thomas@sipos.org.

A final note. I often say festivals *and* awards because not all horror film awards are presented by film festivals. The Academy of Science Fiction, Fantasy & Horror Films presents the Saturn Award; Spike TV presents the Scream Award; *Fangoria* magazine presents the Fangoria Chainsaw Award. There are others, and their winners too are listed in this book.

1

How to Run a Film Festival on Pennies a Day!

I never intended to create a film festival. It was an accident. In 2004 I founded the Tabloid Witch *Awards*—not the Tabloid Witch *Film Festival*—which grew out of my frustration with genre awards. Like many fans, I am both knowledgeable and opinionated about horror films. That includes sci-fi and suspense films that overlap with horror. I've seen *Alien* and *Psycho* many times. I know next-to-nothing about *Star Trek* or Agatha Christie. The Tabloid Witch was to be a way for me to voice my own opinions about what's good and bad in horror.

Perhaps you've thought along those same lines?

Here are some of the things that put the idea into my head.

Origins of the Tabloid Witch

During the 1990s I had joined several professional and/or genre organizations. Some were hard to get into, requiring professional credits on my part. Some only required that I pay the entry fee. Many of these organizations present awards. They usually offer some high-minded reasons for why they do so—"to promote excellence in the field of... blah, blah, blah, etc."—but mostly it's to publicize the organization. The award recipients also welcome the publicity. Some awards may even turn a profit if the presentations are televised. I suppose every organization hopes that its award may someday interest enough people to be televised. On a major TV network, not some live-streaming webcast.

At one time or another I've been a voting member of the Horror Writers Association (Bram Stoker Award), Science Fiction and Fantasy Writers of America (Nebula Award), Independent Feature Project/West, now Film Independent (Independent Spirit Award), Academy of Science Fiction, Fantasy & Horror Films (Saturn Award), and the Screen Actors Guild (Screen Actors Guild Award).

As with political elections, it's initially exciting to cast a ballot. But one soon notices that one's vote rarely makes a difference. Even worse, one's favorites rarely even appear on the ballot. As an ordinary voting member, I never had a say in selecting the *nominees* for the Independent Spirit, Saturn, or SAG awards. And whatever the award, I was rarely familiar with any of the names or works on the ballot. To rectify such voter ignorance, some Stoker or Nebula nominated authors offer to send free copies of their books or stories to voting members. Others send free copies even if you don't ask. Independent Spirit and SAG Award nominees are also increasingly mailing free DVDs of their films to voting members.

Membership does have its rewards.

In October 2001, I attended my first horror film festival, Screamfest L.A. I was covering it for HorrorFind.com. It was the festival's first year, and Rachel Belofsky (who co-founded the event with Ross Martin) was thrilled to have me. Horror film festivals were rare back then, and few people knew about Screamfest L.A.[1] It was a small affair, attracting a few dozen patrons. It screened at Hollywood's Vogue Theater. An old, rundown theater with sticky floors and wobbly seats. A seedy, grindhouse vibe. A good place for low-budget horror.

Screamfest L.A. has since grown into the largest horror film festival in Los Angeles. It grew fast. I couldn't get a press pass the following year, because, I assume, the websites I represented were no longer deemed important enough. No matter. The seed was planted. Seeing Screamfest L.A. when it was still a baby, I thought, "I can do this. Doesn't seem too hard."

In 2002, Jon Weimer was managing the World Horror Convention's short film festival. WHC is an annual convention, but its film festival isn't. Each year a different group of fans manages WHC, in a different city. Each year the programming is different. In 2002, WHC convened in Chicago. It had a film festival that year because Weimer offered to run a film festival that year.

Weimer felt uneasy about being the sole judge to select the films, so he recruited me as a co-judge. He mailed me a VHS tape containing copies of every short film entry, and I emailed my input. I think he wanted a second opinion partially to lessen any conflict of interest. Weimer is himself a filmmaker. One of the entries was his own film, *Wild*.

That's not unusual. Many festival directors are hyphenates, working (or aspiring to work) in other areas of the entertainment industry. I'm an actor/writer. Belofsky is an actress/producer. Denise Gossett (Shriekfest) is an actress. Shannon Lark and Heidi Martinuzzi (both of Viscera), and Elisabeth Fies (BleedFest), are actress/filmmakers. Michael Coulombe (Big Bear Horror) is "a full time script supervisor." Pablo Guisa Koestinger (Morbido Film Fest) is a producer. Shade Rupe (Deep Red International), Bryan Wolford (Drunken Zombie Film Festival), Eric Morgret (Maelstrom International) and Alex Bram (Carnival of Darkness) are filmmakers. I've met most of them. I'm sure there are *some* festival directors who *don't* want to direct, or act, or write, or produce. I just haven't met them yet.

I first met Morgret at the 2006 Tabloid Witch Awards, where he picked up an Honorable Mention for his feature film, *Strange Aeons*. It may be that Morgret perused the several dozen filmgoers at the Santa Monica Public Library, where the Tabloid Witch screened that year, and thought, "I can do this. Doesn't seem too hard."

I first met Bram at the 2009 Tabloid Witch Awards, where he picked up an Honorable Mention for his short film, *Body of Work*. But his Carnival of Darkness held its inaugural screening a month or two earlier. Winning a Tabloid Witch obviously didn't inspire his festival.

I didn't attend the World Horror Convention in 2002, but previewing its festival entries at home, and emailing my critiques to Jon, was a satisfying experience. Like I said, I'm opinionated. I liked having a say in which films would screen.

The 2003 WHC in Kansas City didn't have a film festival. Instead, a volunteer/fan brought horror films and TV shows from his home video collection, and screened them nearly 24 hours a day. Not quite, but almost. I recall seeing an obscure Canadian horror anthology TV episode at two A.M., after I'd grown bored with the "open bar" partying upstairs. Only two or three filmgoers were in the room. After the screening I thanked the fellow running the event. He seemed very proud of his video collection.

That same year I covered Shriekfest for the HollywoodInvestigator.com. Like Screamfest

L.A., Shriekfest was founded in 2001. I told Shriekfest founder Denise Gossett that I was surprised to learn of Shriekfest, as Screamfest L.A. had claimed (in 2001) to be Los Angeles's only horror film festival.

"Nope," said Gossett. "There's another one."

I'm pretty sure the Tabloid Witch Awards is the third horror film festival to be founded in Los Angeles, though it wasn't the last.

The Blair Witch Project is partially responsible for birthing the Tabloid Witch Awards. During the 1990s I wrote (and kept rewriting) *Hollywood Witches*, a novel in which tabloid reporters discover a cabal of New Age witches operating within the major film studios. *Kolchak: The Night Stalker* meets *The Player*. The filmmakers behind *The Blair Witch Project* had created a cleverly deceptive website to pre-promote their film. The site covered the apparently true Blair Witch phenomenon, making no mention of any film until it was finished and ready for promotion.

Taking inspiration, I founded the HollywoodInvestigator.com and WeeklyUniverse.com websites in 2001 to pre-promote *Hollywood Witches*. The first website parodied the *National Enquirer*, the second parodied the *Weekly World News*. I wrote their fictitious, *Onion*-like articles, giving bylines to the characters from my novel, of which I made no mention.

Hollywood Witches took longer to complete and get published — 2010 — than anticipated. Long before then, I had grown uninterested in writing fake news stories. By 2002 I was publishing real news reports, written by myself and others. The *Hollywood Investigator* covered entertainment, media, celebrities, and current events. The *Weekly Universe* reported on UFOs, the paranormal and bizarre, and alternative health.

Real news websites have advantages over parody sites. They're more likely to be linked, more likely to rank high on Google, and more likely to get you a press pass. I wouldn't have gotten free admittance to Shriekfest were the *Hollywood Investigator* still a parody site.

By 2004 I'd seen enough. I was ready to start my own horror film award. But how to publicize a new contest? How to encourage entries? How to do so on pennies a day?

The *Hollywood Investigator* had become somewhat established. Publishers and publicists were sending me books for review, without my asking. Somebody was reading the site and taking it seriously. And so I had the *Hollywood Investigator* sponsor my horror film award. I hoped this would bring publicity and legitimacy to the new award. Maybe not much, but more than if the award were not affiliated with an established website.

In April 2004, the *Hollywood Investigator* announced the Hollywood Investigator Halloween Horror Film Award, with a call for entries. Winners to be announced in October, to coincide with the Halloween season. The prize was promotion in the *Hollywood Investigator*.

It was a No Entry Fee contest for several reasons. 1. *Legitimacy*. Filmmakers are less likely to suspect a ripoff if there's no fee to rip off. Building legitimacy is especially important for a new contest without a name sponsor. (Yes, some talent contests *are* just money-making scams. It's hard to believe, I know.) 2. *More entries*. Filmmakers are more likely to submit their works if a contest is free. Since my goal was to discover the best in horror, I wanted to encourage everyone to enter. 3. *Less hassle*. If filmmakers are disappointed for any reason, they can't complain (much less sue), because they're not out any money.[2]

Even so, promotion in the *Hollywood Investigator* didn't seem that big a prize. As an *afterthought* I added an additional prize. A *possible* film screening. No guarantees.

I still have the ad copy, written in the *Investigator*'s then-typical panting, tabloid parody style.

Are YOU an unknown or little-known horror filmmaker, writer, actor, musician ... or some other artist involved in horror filmmaking?

These past years, the *Hollywood Investigator* has covered such horror film festivals as Screamfest L.A., Shriekfest, and Screamfest in Florida. We've profiled Christmas horror films, horror writer Ray Bradbury, and horror actors Jonathan Frid, David Drake, Leanna Chamish, and Dee Snider.

Now, in Halloween 2004, we want to discover YOU!—in our Hollywood Investigator Halloween Horror Film Awards!

WHAT TO DO: If you have a finished horror film—short work or feature—that's received little or no distribution (aside from the festival circuit)—then we invite you to send it to us. Between now and mid October, we will be reviewing all submissions, selecting the best of the best. [If we receive your film after we've stopped considering new entries, we will save it for next year's consideration.]

WHAT YOU GET: The best of the best will be profiled in a *Hollywood Investigator* article for Halloween 2004. We plan to highlight at least one short and one feature film, but we may profile additional films, and the people involved (actors, musicians, sfx people, etc.), depending on what we see. Selection of films and artists profiled will be at the exclusive discretion of the *Hollywood Investigator*.

POSSIBLE BONUS: We hope to sponsor a public screening of top films, possibly in spring 2005. But this would be a bonus; there is no guarantee of a screening. Filmmakers will be contacted for permission to screen their films before any such event.

ENTRY FEE: There is NO entry fee! We're not looking to make money off of desperate artists—we're only seeking new discoveries for a story in October 2004! [If this proves more costly than anticipated, we may charge a fee come Halloween 2005—so enter now!]

By "we" I meant the royal we. Why not? I know a filmmaker who's shot several award-winning shorts, each with a long list of names on the end credits roll. Every name was fake. He admitted to me that he'd performed every job behind the camera, from pre-production to post. He invented the names on the credit roll to make his film seem "bigger." I've also met any number of film students who refer to their production companies in the royal we, although it's just that one student.

One nice thing about websites. It helps solo efforts appear bigger.

That "possibly in spring 2005" screening I'd referred to was the WHC, which would meet in New York City that April. I planned to pitch a screening of the *Hollywood Investigator*'s contest winners to WHC, but didn't know if they'd agree to it. They did.

WHC gave me a room with a TV. It wasn't Cannes, but it was a start. Rick Lavon was the only winning filmmaker to show up. He lived in New York and had won the Best Horror Short Film award for *Stiffs by Sid*, a zombie comedy.

A room with a TV doesn't sound like much, but there was also that promotional article in the October 2004 *Hollywood Investigator*. Jamie Thompson of the North Hollywood based MovieBank contacted me in November, asking to be put in touch with Lavon. As a result, *Stiffs by Sid* got a distribution deal, one of four zombie shorts to appear on the *Zombie Collection* DVD set, along with four features: *The Last Man on Earth, White Zombie, King of the Zombies,* and *Night of the Living Dead*.

Tip: Many filmmakers are obsessed with screenings; with the venue, the sound equipment, the size of the crowd. Yes, screenings are fun. You might meet important people. But no matter how large the audience, many more people will read about your film on a website than view it at a festival. It's enough that your film won. Distributors don't have to be at a screening. They can always read about your award on the festival website and ask for your DVD. It happens.

As for distributors (and financiers, agents, managers, producers, etc.) who don't attend the festival or read the website, you can always alert them via press releases and personal emails. "Hey look, I won! Can I send you a free DVD?"

Seven months after the 2005 WHC screening of the *Hollywood Investigator*'s 2004 winners, the 2005 winners were screened at Loscon, a science fiction convention held every Thanksgiving weekend by the Los Angeles Science Fantasy Society. I first visited Loscon in 2002, when they gave a press pass to my *Weekly Universe*. In 2005 they agreed to host the second annual Tabloid Witch Awards screening. They gave me a large room at the Los Angeles airport Marriott Hotel, with a projection DVD player and a screen. Actually, it was two rooms, with the divider pushed aside to create one large room.

I called it the second annual Tabloid Witch Awards, although the name was new. Calling it the Hollywood Investigator Halloween Horror Film Award was a mouthful, too generic, and too tied to the website. The contest was getting entries, screenings, and had a film distribution deal to its credit. It was ready to develop its own identity.

Why Tabloid Witch? *Tabloid*, to recall its sponsor and its past. And *witch*, to evoke the horror genre. I could have called it the Tabloid Vampire, or the Tabloid Ghost, or the Tabloid Monster. But witches are cuter than monsters.

I've thought of creating a Tabloid Sleuth or Tabloid Astronaut award, should mystery or (non-horror) science fiction films ever become as popular among fans and filmmakers as is horror. I don't see that happening. Is there enough material out there for a book about romantic comedy film festivals and awards? I don't think so.

I hired English artist Stuart Smith (GravitonCreations.com) to draw the Tabloid Witch seal: a cute, wholesome witch (no tattoos, piercings, or lewd outfits) reading the *Hollywood Investigator* and looking shocked. She has a backstory. She lives in an alternate universe full of supernatural creatures, where magic is both ubiquitous and boring. She is an ordinary housewife, perhaps married to a vampire. She reads trashy tabloid stories with titles like "I Gave Birth to a Mortal!" and "E.T.'s Shocking Claim: Abducted by Earthlings!" Her hubby gripes about her lowbrow reading tastes.

In 2005 I also introduced lucite trophies bearing the Tabloid Witch seal. I had wanted a heavy, metal statuette of the Tabloid Witch reading her newspaper, much like Oscar's golden eunuch. But custom-sculpted statuettes are prohibitively expensive. Especially for a no entry fee contest with many award categories.

Tip: If you're planning to start a film festival (and who isn't?), consider presenting *physical* awards. Trophies, plaques, whatever. Filmmakers like them. When I gave Kenny Selko (*Alone*) his Honorable Mention trophy in 2006, he told me that he'd won many previous awards, but this was the first time that his award actually came with ... an *award*.

"It feels good," Selko told me. "Feels like I actually won something."

In 2007 I upgraded the award from a lucite trophy to a plaque, with a purple brass plate bearing the Tabloid Witch seal. Alex Bram was impressed enough with his 2009 Tabloid Witch plaque that he later asked me who made it (Maxmedals.com).

The official Tabloid Witch Awards seal. Artist: Stuart Smith. Copyright: Thomas M. Sipos.

Bram wanted a similar plaque for his Carnival of Darkness festival. I like Maxwell Medals partially because they're good about replacing trophies that arrive damaged. Bram did go with them in 2010, but he chose a cup instead.

Happy filmmakers will talk up their awards (and your festival) on their websites and social networks. Every satisfied winner becomes a PR agent for the festival. Low-budget festivals can use all the free promotion they can get.

Festival? I had wanted to create an *award*. But by tossing in a screening as a *potential prize*, the Tabloid Witch was morphing into a film festival. Loscon hosted screenings in 2005, 2007, and 2009. A different committee of fans manages Loscon every year. Some welcome the Tabloid Witch, some don't. Loscon is a *science fiction* convention with a strong fantasy presence. Horror takes a back seat. Every year I offer the Tabloid Witch as a counter-programming event for those attendees who prefer horror to sf/fantasy. Quite by coincidence, I find receptive ears in odd years, never in even years.

Relying on different committee members each year is one of the difficulties of working with a convention. In August 2010, I caught up with Jon Weimer and asked for details about his 2002 WHC film festival experience. Did he approach the convention about doing a festival, or did they approach him?

"I suggested it to them," said Weimer. "Saying that they met the idea with apathy would be generous. They acted like it was an inconvenience and they were doing me a favor. There was concern that there would not be enough room for the film festival and the gross out show. They refused to allow me to screen anything but shorts, and said there was no time for features. It was poorly attended because the WHC didn't promote it. They felt the gross out show was more worthy."

The Gross Out contest is indeed a Very Big Deal at most WHCs. Writers compete to create the most depraved, repulsive, nauseating short story imaginable, which they read before an audience. S.G. Browne previewed his novel, *Breathers: A Zombie's Lament*, at the 2008 WHC Gross Out. "*Breathers* had been sold to Random House the January prior and was already finished," Browne told me in September 2010. "At the WHC, I decided to use some of the elements and narrative style from *Breathers*, and up

Alex Bram (left) presents a cup to Best Film winner Drew Daywalt (director of *Polydeus*) at Carnival of Darkness. Los Angeles Film School, Hollywood. October 28, 2010. (Photograph by the author.)

the disgust factor for the Gross Out. The title I gave to my entry was 'Zombie Gigolo,' which was just published in the John Joseph Adams anthology *The Living Dead 2*."

How gross is the Gross Out? My own entry at the 2006 WHC was entitled "Professional Human Toilet." Use your imagination. Even so, it only ranked fourth place.

The Masquerade Ball is the Very Big Deal at Loscon. That and the Ice Cream Social. Tabloid Witch screenings have always been scheduled opposite the Ball. Like I said, counter-programming. For goths and gorehounds, horror films. And for those of stronger stomach, middle-aged adults dressed up like characters from *Lord of the Rings* and *Doctor Who*.

"If I had to do it all over again," Weimer continued, "I would have solicited features, charged $100 a pop like other festivals, and used the money to reserve my own conference room. That said, I was tremendously pleased with the quality of the short films and the interest of the attendees. There was a lot of enthusiasm. It was a great audience and an example that size doesn't matter."

Weimer later went from festival director to festival winner. "I wrote and produced a non-horror film, called *Change of Life*, distributed by Ariztical Entertainment. It played at a number of domestic and international independent film festivals, and won Best Spiritual/Religious film at the Great Lakes Independent Film Festival."

In 2006, 2007, and 2008, the Tabloid Witch screened at the Santa Monica Public Library's Main Branch. It's a new building, less than a decade old, and features the state-of-the-art Martin Luther King Jr. Auditorium, with stadium seating for 146 people — right next to the library's coffee shop and outdoor patio.

Relaxing in the hotel bar at the 2009 World Horror Convention. Left to right: author Joshua Gee (*Encyclopedia Horrifica*); author S.G. Browne (*Breathers: A Zombie's Lament*); and Gavin Hughes. Across laps, *Batman* illustrator Tommy Castillo. Winnipeg, Canada. May 3, 2009. (Photograph by the author.)

Yes, Tabloid Witch winners were lucky in 2007. They got a premiere screening at the library, and an encore screening at Loscon. The Tabloid Witch goes wherever she's welcome.

The Santa Monica library was a good fit. I live in Santa Monica. Many film industry people and their families live in Santa Monica, so you never know who'll enter the library. All library events must be free and open to the public. (It is a *public* library.) That's a deal-breaker for many festivals, because it means they can't sell tickets. But it's no problem for the Tabloid Witch, which never charges for admission. No entry fees to filmmakers. No admission fees to audiences.[3]

Tip: If you're seeking a free or low-budget venue for your festival (or film), stress *localism* if appropriate. If you live in New York or Los Angeles, where filmmakers are commonplace, stress the *neighborhood* if appropriate. You may not be the only filmmaker in L.A., but perhaps you're the only filmmaker in the Sawtelle district. (Not likely, but give it a shot.)

Even fee-charging festivals can tap into local support. Michael Coulombe of the Big Bear Horror Film Festival says, "Rallying the support of Big Bear was important for us. Big Bear is a vacation destination. People would not only be attending the festival, but they would need to rent rooms, so it made sense to us to talk to local hotel, resort, and cabin chains. Also, by contacting the local chamber of commerce, we were able to attend local chamber meetings and meet business owners. We started advertising with local media, and branched out from there."

Unfortunately, the Tabloid Witch did not return to the library in 2009. With California and its cities suffering from both a budget crunch and the recession, the library experienced cutbacks. It could no longer spare an employee to staff the control booth for a day-long screening. It also seems that rules prohibit non-employees from running the video equipment. When the library had money, it could afford a film festival given to them at no charge. Now that it lacks money, it can't afford a free festival. Ironic, no?

The 2009 Tabloid Witch Award winning films screened at Loscon. In 2010 the Tabloid Witch screened at Santa Monica's Miles Memorial Playhouse, another city-owned, nonprofit venue. As with the library, playhouse director Justin Yoffe was excited to host a *local* horror film festival, especially around Halloween. That I live in Santa Monica, that the *Hollywood Investigator* is based in Santa Monica, and that the Tabloid Witch had previously screened at the local library, were all

Justin Yoffe of the Miles Memorial Playhouse, at the Tabloid Witch Awards's Halloween weekend screening. Santa Monica. October 30, 2010. (Photograph by the author.)

pluses. Yoffe even went to the trouble of buying Halloween decorations and treats for the event. Public arts funding lives on in Santa Monica, even if it struggles at times.

The Tabloid Witch still visits the WHC whenever possible. After its 2005 screening, I pitched the Tabloid Witch to 2006 WHC officials (as with Loscon, a different group every year), but they already had a film event planned. WHC met in San Francisco that year and SF native Shannon Lark, of the Chainsaw Mafia horror film collective, was screening her group's work. I didn't attend the 2007 WHC in Toronto, but the Tabloid Witch held "best of" screenings at the 2008 WHC in Salt Lake City, and the 2009 WHC in Winnipeg, Canada. Several cast and crew members from the Tabloid Witch Award winning film *Dead Noon* live in Salt Lake City, so they dropped by and joined me for a panel discussion on film festivals.

Viscera's Imaginative Zero-Budget Marketing

I first met Shannon Lark at the 2006 WHC. The following year she asked the *Hollywood Investigator* and the Tabloid Witch to sponsor her new Viscera Film Festival, which she'd co-founded with Heidi Martinuzzi. The Viscera had a unique and imaginative business plan. I say unique, because I know of no other festival doing it the Viscera way. Like the Tabloid Witch, the Viscera charges no entry fee. Which means no money to rent screening venues, compelling the festival to rely on the kindness of strangers. But whereas the Tabloid Witch looks to public nonprofits and conventions to host its event, the Viscera piggybacks onto *other* festivals. Each year, the Viscera mails a DVD containing all of its official selections to every sponsoring festival, which then screen at least one Viscera selection, of the sponsor's choice, at their event.

Why would a festival devote precious screening time to a competing festival? Lark had a ready answer. The Viscera was not really competing with other festivals, because its unique mission was to promote horror by women.[4] To win a Viscera Award, a film must be created entirely by women, behind and in front of the camera. Everyone, from director to production assistants to cast, had to be a woman. However, anyone who *identifies* as a woman qualifies (including transgendered folk) because, according to its website, the Viscera is "entirely non-sexist."

Viscera only accepts short films, but that may be because, although "all-women horror" *short* films are rare, all-women horror *features* may be non-existent. I'm sure Viscera would like to include them in the future. Highly specialized festivals exist to promote small and obscure subgenres or filmmakers, to inspire others of like subgenre or demographic to enter the field.

Viscera also honors films in which at least one key person (director, writer, or producer) is a woman. Such films are eligible for other Viscera festival awards, but the Viscera Award itself—along with a $200 cash prize—is reserved for all-women horror. This unique mission means that the Viscera festival does not directly compete against other festivals.

Many festivals agree. Viscera's MySpace page lists the following festivals as sponsors: Chainsaw Mafia Film Festival, Pretty-Scary Film Festival, Dead Channels, South African Horrorfest, A Night of Horror, Shriekfest, Tabloid Witch Awards, Paranoia Horror Film Festival, Madison Horror Film Festival, Terror Film Festival, That's Not Mine Film Festival, Women of Horror Film Festival, Plea for Peace, A Nightmare to Remember, Fantaspoa.

About the first two festivals on that list? Lark runs the Chainsaw Mafia and Martinuzzi owns Pretty-Scary. As I did with my *Hollywood Investigator*, these two ladies were sponsoring their own festival through their websites. You can do that. It's how low-budget, grassroots horror works.

Viscera also enlisted non-festival sponsors, who were asked to help in any way they could. Many of these sponsors were websites or film critics who promoted Viscera. Its MySpace page lists the following non-festival sponsors: The Chainsaw Mafia, Pretty-Scary, Fangoria Entertainment, Ghost Droppings, Cadaver Girls, The Haunted Report, Izabel Grondin, Niki Pretti Photography, Hollywood Investigator, 4321 Films, Ax Wound, Obscure Horror, Scream Queens, Final Girl, Central Valley Horror Club, Cinesploitation, Lipstick Teeth, CutThroat Films, Scars Magazine, The Last Blog on the Left, The Graveyard Show.

Lining up *Fangoria*—the king of horror news reporting—is impressive, albeit not unexpected. *Fangoria* crowned Lark their first Official Spooksmodel in 2008, so Lark had an "in" with them. Even so, it didn't go to Lark's head. She's always accepted any help, big or small. In 2007 the *Hollywood Investigator* ran a promotional article about Lark, as well as free Viscera banner ads. That same year the Tabloid Witch screened the Viscera film, *It's My Birthday*, at Loscon. The following year it screened the Viscera horror music video, *Brains*, at the Santa Monica library.

One nice thing about being a Viscera official selection, it gets you into other festivals without paying the entry fee. Of course, nobody pays an entry fee to the Tabloid Witch, but it does save filmmakers some money at fee-charging events. Another benefit: Viscera official selections are distributed on DVD, sold through the Chainsaw Mafia website. Buyers can screen the entire Viscera Film Festival in the comfort of their own homes.

I'd said horror film festival people tend to be hyphenates, wearing many hats? Even as

Viscera co-founder Shannon Lark (left) and filmmaker Maude Michaud (*Hollywood Skin*) at Lark's "white carpet event." The blood stains would have been harder to see on a *red* carpet. Los Angeles. July 17, 2010. (Photograph by the author.)

she was helping Lark build up the Viscera, co-founder Heidi Martinuzzi was piggybacking yet another award. For three years (2007–09), Martinuzzi's Pretty-Scary.net sponsored the Pretty Scary Award, which was presented at Shriekfest.

Tip: If you want to present an award, but can't afford/don't have time for your own festival, then present your award through an established festival. The festival gets another award to offer filmmakers for their entry fees, and you get promotion for your award/website.

In 2009 at Loscon, horror journalist Eddie McMullen asked me if I'd be interested in him sponsoring a Feo Award at my Tabloid Witch Awards. McMullen runs the FeoAmante.com horror website. The Feo Award's criterion would be "the scariest horror film of the year." McMullen has since refocused his efforts on independent film projects (the man wants to direct), but perhaps someday, somewhere, there will be a Feo Award.

Festivals have a way of growing up, establishing themselves, and leaving their initial sponsoring websites. In 2010 the Viscera Film Festival left TheChainsawMafia.com for VisceraFilmFestival.com. Likewise, the Tabloid Witch was based at the HollywoodInvestigator.com until early 2008, when TabloidWitch.com went online. The parent websites still promote their young, but the kids are living on their own now.

Viscera co-founder Heidi Martinuzzi holds a Viscera Award trophy (painted gold, in her right hand) and an official selection trophy (painted gold, gray, red, in her left hand). Even official selections get a trophy to take home! Los Angeles. July 17, 2010. (Photograph by the author.)

On July 17, 2010, the Viscera Film Festival held its first screening — a screening of its *very own* rather than piggybacked onto another festival — at a public venue: the Downtown Independent theater in Los Angeles. Every Viscera selection from the previous three years was screened, followed by a party. The money came from sponsors and ticket sales. Viscera remains a no entry fee event. Martinuzzi tells me that she's ceased her Pretty Scary Award, and is focusing her festival efforts exclusively on the Viscera. She's even changed the Pretty-Scary.net site to FanGirltastic.com.

Credit these ladies with imagination. While low-budget horror filmmakers are famous for finding ways to stretch a penny (e.g., Roger Corman, Ed Wood), low-budget horror film festival directors are likewise pressed to be financially creative. Not every festival has to be Cannes or Sundance. They don't even have to be Screamfest L.A.

TromaDance's Non-Competitive, Egalitarian Attitude

Viscera attracts sponsoring festivals because its unique "women in horror" mission allows sponsors to support a worthy cause *and* enjoy cross-promotion from Viscera. But Viscera also attracts sponsors because it does not compete against them. This is because 1. Viscera's mission *is* unique (well, until recently); 2. it doesn't have its own screenings (until recently); 3. it doesn't charge entry fees.

This begs the question: *Do horror film festivals compete against one another?*

Festivals have three potential income sources. *Entry fees* from filmmakers. *Ticket sales* to audiences. *Sponsor donations*— money, promotion, a screening venue, free food, or anything the festival director, advertisers, nonprofits, or anyone else cares to contribute.

Festivals do compete for entry fees. Many filmmakers want to screen at every festival. They need the publicity. But indie filmmakers are often poor. They can't afford every festival. They must choose. Using what criteria? *Festival A is bigger and more prestigious if I win there. But Festival B, though less impressive, is smaller, so my chances of winning are better.*

My experience with filmmakers suggests that most will choose Festival A. No matter how ugly a film is, its mother thinks it's the most beautiful horror film in the world, and can't imagine that festival judges won't agree. But either way, if Festivals A and B both charge entry fees, each has a vested interest in not promoting the other.

What about no entry fee festivals? Do they compete with other festivals? The Tabloid Witch doesn't see herself as competing with anyone, but then, she hangs out with nonprofits. Some festivals share her neo-hippie attitude. *It's about art, not fame. It's about the fans, not money. It's about having a good time, not competition.* At Viscera, even official selections get trophies, so every filmmaker feels like a winner. True, only the Viscera Award is painted gold; some trophies are more equal than others. But it still beats a "suitable for framing" paper certificate.

Other festivals take the non-competitive spirit further, eschewing awards entirely. TromaDance presents no awards, charges no entry fees, sells no tickets. Its website proclaims: "Unlike every other film festival, TromaDance does not charge filmmakers to submit their films. Entrance to all screenings is free and open to the public ... there are no VIP reservations

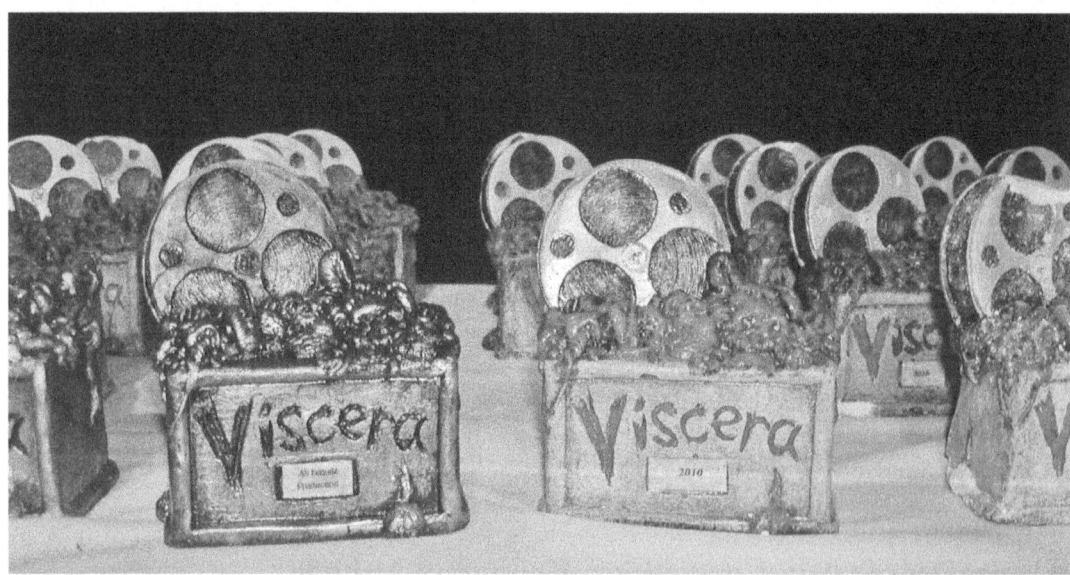

The "All Female Production" golden Viscera Award on the left. The 2010 gold/gray/red Official Selection trophy on the right. Both say "Viscera" on the front, but only the golden trophy is a Viscera Award. (Confusing, no?) Los Angeles. July 17, 2010. (Photograph by the author.)

or preferential treatment regarding films, panels, or parties of any kind given. The organizers of TromaDance believe films are meant to be seen, especially when it comes to new filmmakers. Art — in all its forms — is for the people! Everyone at TromaDance is treated as an equal. The elite and the celebrated are treated no better or worse than the experimental filmmaker or the random moviegoer off the street. Admittance to all screenings, panels, parties, and events is strictly on a first come, first served basis.... TromaDance is proud to be the first and only film festival of the people, for the people, and by the people."

TromaDance is not a horror film festival, but rather, an indie festival — but not the snotty kind. All genres are welcome. Its website (tromadance.com) says: "Films are judged based on artistic merit and originality. Your film need not include sex and violence!" Founded by renowned indie exploitation filmmaker, Lloyd Kaufman, TromaDance relies for funding on the kindness of strangers. Its website explains: "Tromadance is a sponsored project of FracturedAtlas.org, a non-profit arts services organization. Contributions in behalf of Tromadance may be made payable to Fractured Atlas, and are tax-deductible to the extent permitted by law." A 2008 posting on TromaDance's blog adds: "The TromaDance Film Festival is in desperate need of your donations. No donations are too small. Last year our budget was made because of $5, $10, and $20 donations. If you donate more than $100 it can be tax deductible, through Fractured Atlas.... We also accept donations via PayPal. Please support the most idealistic and truly independent film festival. It's all free!!" (TromaDance is spelled with either a big or small D, but big D seems preferred.)

Yes, people do donate online. I have a friend who did fundraising for a nonprofit radio station, and now does fundraising for an antiwar website. She told me a secret to successful fundraising: *If you want someone to give you money, ask them for money.* Many people will donate if asked. TromaDance asks. No shame about it, no false promises, no entry fees for a chance to win. You give because it's a good cause. All you get is a tax deduction and a warm fuzzy.

Tip: If you need money for your film or film festival, then sell it as a worthy cause (it promotes women, minorities, troubled youth, local artists, or sends a positive message) and *ask* for money.

Some potential donors may feel uneasy giving money to a website. What if it's a scam? TromaDance found a way to allay such fears. The festival is sponsored by Fractured Atlas. You can donate to TromaDance through PayPal or Fractured Atlas. The latter's website indicates that they're a legitimate, New York based, nonprofit group.

Tip: If you're an aspiring festival director, or filmmaker, or any kind of artist, you might benefit by perusing FracturedAtlas.org. They offer many services to artists, including liability insurance, online courses, and sponsorship.

Just like Viscera piggybacked onto other festivals' screenings, TromaDance began by piggybacking onto Sundance's presence. A 2008 posting on the TromaDance blog says: "As it does every year, the TromaDance Film Festival will run concurrently with the Sundance Film Festival. On this celebratory year, film screenings and events will take place in Park City and Salt Lake City, Utah, from January 19th–23rd...."

That's clever. Sundance attracts hordes of filmmakers, press, studio executives, distributors, celebrities, and filmgoers, creating a spillover crowd of people who can't get into a Sundance screening. So they instead go to Slamdance. Or to TromaDance. Or to one of the other Dances. (Yes, there is a Horror Dance, but they're in Houston, and they look to be defunct. See horrordance.org.) I know one filmmaker who was rejected by Sundance, but went anyway. Although his film wasn't screening there, he distributed free DVDs of it around Park City.

Where else could he find such a high concentration of studio executives and distributors per square block?

Slamdance was founded in 1995 as a festival for filmmakers rejected by Sundance. Lacking Sundance's fame and promotional budget, Slamdance was situated to receive the spillover crowds generated by Sundance's presence. Over time, Slamdance grew into a prestigious event in its own right. In a sense, TromaDance was piggybacking on both Sundance and Slamdance.

Was that the *intent*? I contacted TromaDance's Anne Koester, who explained: "TromaDance was initially set up as a protest to our view that Sundance was not truly an 'independent film' festival. TromaDance was totally free (and still is) and was a way for everyone who wished to share their vision. It's been over ten years and Sundance has, to some extent, begun to be what Troma views as a truly independent film festival. In the meantime, as TromaDance became more successful, we outgrew Park City, and decided that no place on earth was better suited to celebrating 'reel' independence than New Jersey: the home of our very own Toxic Avenger!"

I also suspect that Asbury Park, NJ, appreciates TromaDance more than had Park City, which takes film festivals for granted. According to TromaDance's Matt Manjourides, "At Park City, a lot of the team has gotten arrested in the past."

The Tromettes (actually audience members) celebrate freedom of expression at the 2010 TromaDance closing party. Asbury Park, New Jersey. (Photograph courtesy TromaDance.)

Here's a curious horror film festival mystery. Wikipedia reports in its entry for Slamdance: "In 2008, Oren Peli's *Paranormal Activity* played its Festival premier [sic] at Slamdance and was acquired by Dreamworks who then passed domestic control of the film onto Paramount." But Screamfest L.A.'s website attributes the following quote to Oren Peli: "When all other festivals were rejecting *Paranormal Activity*, Screamfest was the first and only festival at the time that accepted us. We had a great premiere screening and got positive reviews as a result. Shortly after, we got the attention of CAA and many distributors. The rest, as they say, is history! But it all started at Screamfest!"

So just where was *Paranormal Activity*'s festival premiere?

The next tabloid couple? Film celebrity Toxie (of Troma's *Toxic Avenger* series) puts the move on New York State Film Commissioner (and 2010 "Women in Film Muse Award Winner") Pat Kaufman at TromaDance. Asbury Park, New Jersey. 2010. (Photograph courtesy TromaDance.)

Most festivals grow or die. The Tabloid Witch and Viscera grew. Screamfest L.A. and Shriekfest and Slamdance grew. Even Sundance was humbler when young. TromaDance too has grown. It not only outgrew Park City, as Koester says, but TromaDance has had "satellite" screenings in other U.S. cities, similar to the Tabloid Witch's "best of" screenings outside Los Angeles. As for TromaDance's new Asbury Park location, a 2010 posting on its blog proclaims: "Judging by the packed screenings, lines around the block, and ecstatic reception, the 11th Annual TromaDance also marks the beginning of a long and prosperous relationship between TromaDance and the historic town of Asbury Park."

TromaDance presents no awards of its own, but Manjourides tells me, "With the support of Kodak we present the Kodak Film Award during our AFM Tromadance press conference to an outstanding filmmaker." AFM is the American Film Market, which convenes every November in Santa Monica, CA.

Premiere Bragging Rights

Some festivals promote each other, or are free to filmmakers and fans alike — no entry fees, no admission fees. Other festivals are more yuppie than yippie. They see themselves in a competition for money, prestige, celebrity guests, and the hottest films. They jealousy guard their rankings on industry magazines' "Top Film Festival" lists. If a new festival breaks into the Top 10 or Top 50, another one slips off.

Screamfest L.A. used to require that a film not have screened at any other Los Angeles festival prior to Screamfest, or it was ineligible. Screamfest wanted Los Angeles premiere screening rights. I know of no other L.A. horror film festival that imposed such a demand.

Screamfest could get away with it because they're the biggest horror festival in L.A. (i.e., many filmmakers' first choice, if they could pick only one). I no longer see this restriction on Screamfest L.A.'s website. I *assume* it's no longer in effect. My email asking them about it went unanswered.

Screamfest L.A.'s premiere screening requirement was not unique. Sundance has a similar requirement. A filmmaker told me that he held off on submitting to other festivals until he was rejected by Sundance. (Yes, the same guy who went to Sundance anyway.) Top festivals can demand what amounts to "right of first refusal" because, being rich and prestigious, they can do more to boost a filmmaker's career. Of course, by premiering the best and hottest films (or so they hope), these festivals solidify their top dog status. It's easier to stay on top once you're there.

The downside for filmmakers is that while they're waiting to hear back from the top festivals, they can't enter the smaller ones. This can delay a filmmaker's promotional efforts by a year or more. You wait six months to be rejected by a top festival,[5] and by then the smaller festivals' deadlines have passed. Now you must wait till next year to enter the smaller festivals. This can be especially problematic if your film's story or theme reflects current events or features a hot (but soon to cool) subgenre.

One *solution* is to enter every festival right away. If a top festival selects your film and demands premiere rights, you can always withdraw your film from the smaller festivals (assuming they haven't already screened it, and the entry form/contract you signed permits it). Yes, they will hate you. Yes, they will remember you if you ever submit there again. They might threaten to sue you regardless of what the contract says. Or perhaps they'll just screen your film anyway and tell you to sue them. This "solution" is imperfect.

Top festivals demanding premiere rights also hurts smaller festivals, which miss out on potentially good films. When I heard that a former Tabloid Witch Award winning filmmaker had completed another horror film, I asked to see it. He emailed me: "Much as I'd love to send you [redacted] for this year's awards, I believe that having it screened as part of the TWA's would actually change our premiere status and make us no longer eligible for festivals that insist on World or California Premiere status. I'm checking on that, as I'd love for you to be able to check it out asap."

Most festivals don't care about when, or how often, a film has screened elsewhere. Indeed, many filmmakers brag about their past screenings and awards in the press packets they submit with their DVDs. They hope to sway festival directors with their films' past successes.

It's never swayed me. I don't mind screening a film that's been shown elsewhere[6] but neither do a film's past accolades impress me. If the Tabloid Witch were a rubber stamp on other festivals' tastes, why bother? I've both accepted and rejected award-winning films.[7] And small though it is, the Tabloid Witch has had its share of premiere screenings.

So have most festivals. The top festivals get first pick, but that still leaves lots of rejected films (or films that couldn't afford to enter) seeking their premieres. Besides, one festival's trash may indeed be another festival's treasure. Tastes vary.

On Entry Fees, Volunteers, and Comps

Festivals have three potential income sources: entry fees, ticket sales, and sponsors. Filmmakers wonder about those entry fees. To what extent do filmmakers fund the festival? Do entry fees only cover a token 10 percent of a festival's expenses? Or are filmmakers subsidizing

95 percent of it? Of course, if you've been chosen to screen at a prestigious film festival, then it's worth it. The losing filmmakers have subsidized your limelight. You got a good deal. They did not.

In this book's directory listing, I'd like to have included a breakdown for every festival, stating what percentage of its income was derived from entry fees, ticket sales, and sponsors. For the Tabloid Witch and TromaDance it would be 0/0/100. But I didn't ask. I assumed that many festivals would have either ignored the question or fudged the answers.

Which doesn't prevent filmmakers from speculating. As writer/producer Sharon Reed (*The Sacred*) puts it: "I know the frustration of film festivals. We personally have dropped close to $500 on entry fees alone, with no real results. Today I will drop another $160 into four festivals and see what comes of it.

"Since 2004, there have been over 650 film festivals in the U.S. alone. That's almost two festivals per day. Many of these festivals charge average entry fees of anywhere from $25 to $50. Some are lower (or even free), some are higher (Telluride charges $95 and selects only 20 feature films).

"We recently submitted *The Sacred* to two festivals, Toronto International Film Festival and Toronto After Dark Film Festival. With submission fees and shipping costs, it ended up costing us about $300 to do this. *I don't know about you, but we've spent all our money just finishing the movie.*[8] Toronto International was a long shot, and we got the rejection letter from them at a nice price of $75. Toronto After Dark, with our entry fee of $70, was the surprise. They only selected 17 features and 28 short films, and got well over 700 submissions.

"So I started doing the math. Let's see, 700 × $55 average entry fee = $38,500.

"I remember when we entered into Sundance 2009 (another long shot), and I got the rejection letter from Geoffrey Gillmore. He said they had to whittle down to 200 films from the 9,000 submitted. Yes, 9,000!

"I did the math, and took the average from short films and feature entry fees, and came up with this simple equation: $50 × 9,000 = $450,000.

"Almost a half of million dollars off the backs of independent filmmakers. Where does all this money go? Since I have had the pleasure of volunteering for the Sundance Film Festival, I know it doesn't go to paying many people that actually work the festival. It could go towards paying the full timers or housing the volunteers. When I worked the Sundance festival, I was put on the staff that handled all the 'official' Sundance parties. I was at a different party every night. They had free booze, great catered food, name bands, and famous DJs. That memory comes back to me as I wonder where my entry fee went to in Sundance, Toronto, and After Dark.

"I wonder, how many 'volunteers' played about five minutes of each film before tossing it aside? I know for a fact that a reputable film festival once had a not-so-reputable person in charge. His idea of selection was viewing only the first few minutes of a handful of films, and pawning the rest off to his friends to make the selection. Thankfully, that person has since been removed.

"A number of unscrupulous individuals have jumped on the film festival wagon, and are putting up fraudulent film festivals. They scam a filmmaker, from the entry fee to additional services like marketing materials. It's all a scam, and beware of anyone who invites you to their festival and then wants you to pay. If you ever get an invitation, it should always be free of charge.

"Please learn from our mistakes. Be wise. Do research on the festival. See how many years it's been in business, how many films are selected versus how many get submitted, and enter early to save money. On Withoutabox, you can look up festivals that are specifically under $15 or free to enter. You can also sign up for discounts. With over two film festivals happening per day, there are many choices and many smaller festivals to suit your genre. If you have to try the big dogs (Toronto, Sundance, Cannes, Berlin) know that it is like putting your money on only one number on the roulette wheel in Vegas. Actually, Vegas may have better odds."[9]

I can confirm Reed's observation that festivals rely on unpaid staff. In 2003, I volunteered for the IFP/Los Angeles Film Festival. We received blue, hooded warmup jackets as our festival uniform, which we got to keep. Volunteers also got to see free films, and take home lots of promotional crap that nobody wants. Free pens and kitchen magnets emblazoned with the film's logo, that you put away and forget, then toss out a few years later.

Why do people volunteer for film festivals? It's not for the kitchen magnets. It's not even for the warmup jackets. (Usually, it's not a warmup jacket; just a cheap t-shirt.) When seeking recruits, festivals, like all entertainment or celebrity events, emphasize *the fun* that volunteers will have. Fun is a big selling point. And it can be fun. But I think the main reason people volunteer is to make professional contacts. Most volunteers I met at the L.A. Film Fest, and similar events, are aspiring actors, writers, filmmakers, etc., hoping to meet someone who'll accept their headshot, or screenplay, or business card.

Tip: If you're seeking volunteers for *your* event, tell them (1) that it'll be lots of fun, (2) they'll meet celebrities and/or important people who can advance their careers, (3) it'll be something to put on their résumés. Finally, (4) if there's free stuff to be had, mention it. If not, no big deal. Most volunteers already own a lifetime supply of promotional keychains.

It's a stressful, grueling, thankless job to run a film festival, but somebody must do it. Festival director G.R. Claveria (the gentleman in the silk robe) with three volunteers at the Shockfest Film Festival. Hollywood. November 2010. (Photograph courtesy Shockfest.)

Reed submitted her horror film, *The Sacred*, to both horror and mainstream festivals. Horror filmmakers needn't ignore mainstream festivals. Your chances of being selected are better at horror festivals (not necessarily a whole lot better), but that's not to say the mainstream shuns horror. Many horror festivals say they promote horror because it's disrespected or ignored by the mainstream. Not true. Horror is lucrative. Hollywood respects lucrative.

Filmmaker J. Neil Schulman (*Lady Magdalene's*) echoes some of Reed's gripes: "The third *Shrek* sequel, *Shrek Forever After*, is opening the 2010 Tribeca Film Festival. Thank you, Robert De Niro, for financing your festival with submission fees from thousands of starving independent filmmakers like me, then using our hard-found money to highlight high-budget studio sequels!

"I submitted *Lady Magdalene's* to all the major film festivals — sometimes more than once — which took submission fees ranging as high as a hundred and twenty bucks — some of them from thousands of filmmakers each year — then turned around and used the money to promote major studio releases. This year, it's Tribeca opening with a *Shrek* sequel, but the gone-and-not-missed CineVegas took hundreds of thousands of bucks in submission fees from indie filmmakers like me ... and opened its festival a couple of years back with *Ocean's Thirteen*— the second sequel to a remake. It's disgusting.

"I submitted for the 2007 and 2008 Tribeca Film Festivals, not 2010. After they took my money twice, and sent emails telling me how many swell submissions they got, so they weren't accepting my movie for festival play, I decided not to throw good money after bad. These big 'indie' film festivals take submission money from thousands of indie filmmakers, pick a few to play at their festivals like they're lotto winners, then spend the indie filmmakers' money giving free publicity to major studio releases.

"Let's say more people attend a festival because they get to see a studio release. It does no good for the filmmakers whose money they took and didn't accept their films. If they sell extra tickets to fill the theater, the festival keeps all the money — not a dime of festival box office is shared with the filmmakers. The chances of an indie film making a sale to a distributor because of festival play are minuscule anyway. It's a real sucker play, worthy of Bernie Madoff.

"I've been thinking about how I'd run a film festival. First, I would not charge filmmakers a submission fee. If they wanted to buy an ad for their film in the program book — not a requirement for submitting their film — they could do that. But that's the only thing I'd consider charging a filmmaker for, since they're providing their film to the festival for free, and the festival is selling tickets and not sharing the receipts with them.

"Some festivals find all sorts of things to charge filmmakers for — award banquet tickets, press conferences, premium display of posters, etc. This makes the festival concentrate on squeezing revenue out of the very people it should be supporting — the filmmakers who have already struggled with the costs of making the movie which the festival is going to sell tickets to see!

"The festival should make its money off ticket sales, sales of refreshments, sale of memorabilia. Sponsors and advertisers should pay for the rest, and provide product placements. At the San Diego Black Film Festival all the parties were hosted by Tommy Bahama rum and vodka — which provided both free food and an open bar."[10]

Schulman broaches an issue that most filmmakers don't consider until they begin the festival circuit: complimentary tickets (aka comps, free tickets). Most festivals limit the number of comps given to each film. Some festivals even *charge* filmmakers to attend special events (e.g., the award banquet tickets referred to by Schulman).

Shriekfest is generous with comps. Your entry fee buys you admission into the festival even if your film is rejected. I entered their screenplay contest in 2007, lost, but got free admission for having entered. It meant I didn't need a press pass that year. Explaining Shriekfest's policy, Denise Gossett says, "Everyone who enters can receive a free pass. Everyone who is a finalist receives one pass for themselves and one guest. Cast and crew are not comped."

Carnival of Darkness gives two comps to each selected film.

For the Tabloid Witch, it depends on the venue. The Santa Monica Public Library admits all patrons for free, so comps are not an issue. The Miles Memorial Playhouse allowed four comps per film. One year Loscon gave two comps to each winning filmmaker. This created a problem. One filmmaker felt "insulted" that not everyone in his party, all of whom had worked on the film, could attend for free. He threatened to boycott his own screening and panel discussion. I said the decision was out of my hands. He'd paid no entry fee. The Tabloid Witch prizes he'd won (promotion, plaque, screening, two comp tickets) he got for free. But if he didn't want to come, or even have his film screened, he didn't have to. In the end, he came.

Grateful filmmakers are one of the rewards of running a no entry fee festival. A word of appreciation goes far in making my day. Whiny filmmakers — those who pay nothing, then complain when the venue isn't up to their expectations — are one reason why, each year, I consider changing my policy and charging entry fees. The rejected filmmakers would gripe, but I'd be able to secure cushier digs for the winners.

Some filmmakers entertain unrealistic expectations as to what their entry fees should buy them. A filmmaker using the handle JEV1A posted on Fest21.com: "I have been on the circuits for almost a year now with my new feature doc, and have encountered everything from festival directors asking me to pay for screenings even after I have been selected, to high submission costs where my film was never even pre-juried. Every festival is so different in rules and regulations that I think a Festival Submission Process International Board should be set up to discuss what has truly become a racket. The indie filmmaker puts out thousands of dollars for publicity, your film gets in the program, and then they say, sorry no airfare, no hotel, no drivers, etc. are available ... but we would love to have you attend! How many times have I heard this?"

It's true. Many festivals will not pay for your attendance. Some horror festivals run for several days. We're talking dozens of films. Can you imagine the cost of providing airfare, hotel accommodations, drivers, meals, etc., to dozens of filmmakers flying in from around the world? And also for the cast and crew and family members that some filmmakers would doubtless like to have comped? I sympathize with filmmakers who spend a thousand dollars on entry fees, but my sympathies evaporate when they expect the moon for each $40 fee — or even for no fee.

Reed and Schulman express many filmmakers' anger toward entry fees. Are their points valid? Should every festival be "no entry fee" on principle? From what I've seen, festivals that charge fees are generally bigger and more impressive. Not always, but often so. And significantly so. This suggests that (1) fee-charging festivals derive a significant portion of their income from entry fees, but also that (2) selected filmmakers receive a bargain, buying a single lotto ticket and winning a jackpot, financed by the losers. Not that it's *entirely* luck. It takes work and talent to make a quality film. But it also takes *some* luck. The luck to have encountered a judge whose taste favors your film. Had you submitted your film another year, a different judge may have chosen a different film over yours.

Festival Finances in Europe and Latin America

Patrick Van Hauwaert of Belgium's (no entry fee) Razor Reel Fantastic Film Festival is sympathetic to struggling filmmakers. "It is our belief that a filmmaker who spent a whole lot of money, sometimes his own money, should *not* pay any festival to have his film screened. Moreover, it is my belief that many big festivals who ask for entry fees accept as many fees as possible, but don't take all the films seriously. Many films are entered, without being seen by a selection committee."

Van Hauwaert acknowledges that eschewing entry fees creates challenges. "Having the money to make your festival is difficult, but not impossible. You have to cut costs and work for free. It is hard, but the good part is, we don't need to live from it. We all have our daily work that pay the bills.

"Raising money is the hardest part [of the festival]. We are a recognized cultural event, but that doesn't grant you any government money. It has nothing to do with the amount of films you show, or the ticket prices you ask. It is all up to who you know. We do it without government money (almost none), but with a lot of private money. We do it by selling advertisements, cutting deals with local business partners, and a little bit by pre-selling venues as special events/screenings. Ticket sales once the festival is started is *not* to be seen as a possible income to pay your festival; it must be seen as a possible income to pay your *next* festival. We ask €6 a ticket per film."

Van Hauwaert raises a key difference between American and European festivals. European fests are far likelier to be subsidized by the government—provided you have the contacts. In the U.S., filmmakers and festivals often pander to corporate suits. In Europe, it's to state bureaucrats. Raising money is never easy.

One way to classify film festivals, according to Van Hauwaert, is by its level of government support. "As far as I know, there are three models of film festivals. *Model 1*: Totally sponsored by the government. Scandinavian fests are well known for that, I think. *Model 2*: Totally independent. By totally, I mean the government input is less than 15

Razor Reel founder and program director Patrick Van Hauwaert with actress Amanda Fuller (*CSI* and *Red, White & Blue*) at the 2010 Razor Reel fest. Bruges, Belgium. (Photograph courtesy Razor Reel.)

percent, since every fest profits from *some* use of government resources (e.g., cheap use of locations, etc.). *Model 3*: The mixed bag. Explains it all, I suppose.

"Each model can be seen as one of two categories. A festival that asks for entry fees, and one that doesn't ask for entry fees. The second category is most likely to be found in Europe, on the mainland. The first is a typical Anglo-Saxon festival."

If you're green with envy toward filmmakers in Europe, where no entry fee festivals are the norm, prepare to turn a darker shade of pine. Not only does Razor Reel not charge entry fees — it often *pays* filmmakers for the right to screen their films. That's right —*they* pay *you!*

As Van Hauwaert explains it: "Here in Europe, it is common to pay a *screening fee* to a distributor, and not ask an *entry fee* from a filmmaker or distributor. Many distributors are friendly enough to see a festival as a promotional tool. Some ask a smaller fee of €200–300 to prepare the print (we mostly take care of shipment) and some other extra work. However, some ask €1,000 plus shipment to screen a film once."

These higher fees are beyond Razor Reel's budget. Fortunately, screening fees are negotiable. Says Van Hauwaert, "When we discuss this with the filmmaker, and there is no distributor/sales agent involved, there is mostly *no* screening fee. However, when a distributor/sales agent is involved, screening fees pop up. But sometimes *filmmakers* ask for screening fees. In 2009, the director of *Absurdistan* set Belgian festivals against each other to bid on his film. And [by contrast] some companies see festivals as a promotional tool, and give the films for free. Bigger companies are always asking for money, except if you know the right person, of course.

"It is our goal to find as many films [as possible] for free. Right now, it's 50/50. Every film is a painstaking negotiation. It might sound strange that we even seek out films with distributors, if they ask mostly a high screening fee. But if you want to screen a film with Dutch subtitles, the only place to find it is with the Dutch or Flemish distributors.

"There are far too much film festivals — blame me for starting up another one in 2008. The companies can choose who to work with, and who not!"

Screening fees are also common among Latin American film festivals. Like Razor Reel, Brazil's Fantaspoa: Festival Internacional de Cinema Fantástico de Porto Alegre survives without entry fees. Founded in 2005, its 2010 promotional material states: "So far, we didn't get any financial sponsorship ... the festival was accomplished with the financial resources of the two directors: João Fleck and Nicolas Tonsho. We work under a very tight budget of approximately $10,000. [That's U.S. dollars.] For the 6th edition, in 2010, we decided to double our investment and we'll be receiving a guest for each night of the festival. This wasn't ever done in a film festival in the south of Brazil, so we are anxious to see how that will result.... Fantaspoa is a result of hard and passionate work. Everything in the festival is made by a team of seven persons."

When Fantaspoa says they receive no sponsorship, they mean no *big* sponsors. A business that donates a *small amount* in exchange for a logo in the printed program would be called a sponsor in the U.S., but Fantaspoa calls them "supporters" or "collaborators."

"Here in Brazil, [the word] sponsor is only used when they give 'real' money — something that makes a difference in the festival," said Fantaspoa's João Fleck in our email exchange. "If the festival costs $30,000, a sponsor would be called that if he gives $10,000 or more. Just the cost of subtitles alone would come to a total of more than $40,000.

"We don't get any sponsorship whatsoever, no government and corporate. We get a few collaborations, such as $500 or $1,000. In total, no more than $2,000 per year. Some give us money, others beer, champagne, t-shirts, things like that. We do invest our own pocket money.

Ticket sales help us. We sell around 4,000 tickets at three dollars, and we keep 50 percent of the ticket money, so that's around 6,000 dollars." The other 50 percent goes to the theater.

"We cover the rest [of the expenses] with our own money. In our festival, everybody works as a volunteer. We don't charge entry fees, and we don't pay screening fees. We created a way of making the festival almost sustainable. The only problem is the subtitling process. Last year we exhibited 138 films (74 features), and we subtitled 80 percent of them."

Sponsorship Dollars

Perhaps you're thinking of starting up a film festival, and are wondering what to charge sponsors? Just to give you some general ideas, here are Shriekfest's publicized ad rates from 2010:

Shriekfest Film Festival is in its 10th year and we are offering banner ads on our main page, the opportunity to screen trailers/short commercials at the actual festival, and program ads in this year's festival program, or sponsor a trophy! Reach your target audience of horror and sci-fi fans! We have several options ... if you are interested in a price to do them all, let us know ... we'll be flexible!

Option 1: Premium listing. Your 468 × 60 pixel banner on our main page for 3 months AND a 200 word blurb in our monthly newsletter that goes out to over 5,000 horror/sci-fi fans (3 month listing) AND a full page ad in our program AND your trailer/short commercial aired 2× at the festival: $600.

Option 2: Banner listing. Your 468 × 60 pixel banner on our main page for 2 months: $200; or on our friends page for 2 months: $100.

Option 3: 200 word blurb in our monthly newsletter that goes out to over 5,000 horror/sci-fi fans (3 month listing): $105.

Option 4: Banner listing. Your 468 × 60 pixel banner on our sponsors page for (2 month listing): $150.

Option 5: Have your company sponsor one of our trophies! The trophy will be presented in your company's name with a verbal announcement at the awards show and a logo in our program: $200.

Option 6: Screen your trailer or short commercial for $100 every time we show it! This is a great deal!

Option 7: Program ads. All ads are in black and white or color. *Black & White Pricing.* Business card size: $50; ½ page (4 × 4): $100; Full page (8 × 4): $200. *Color Pricing.* Business Card size: $75; ½ page (4 × 4): $125; Full page (8 × 4): $250.

Here are the Big Bear Horror Film Festival's publicized ad rates from 2010:

SPONSORSHIP OPTIONS:

We are currently offering six levels of sponsorship. Please take a moment to see which of these will best suit your needs, and know that we are available to answer any questions you may have regarding the program.

Level I Sponsor, Business Card Ad (Black & White) $50
Level II Sponsor, Half-page Ad* (Black & White) $100
Level III Sponsor, Half-page Ad (Full Color) $175
Level IV Sponsor, Full-page Ad (Color Only) $300
Level V Sponsor, Inside cover(s) $500
Level VI Sponsor, Back page Ad $1000

Monetary donation(s) of more than $1000 are welcome and will be handled on a case by case basis. Please call for donations of this or greater amounts at: (323) 604-9874.

*This is the same as a ¼ page ad. Ask for specifics when ordering.

EXHIBITORS:

If you are interested in purchasing table space and marketing products or services at the festival, please take a moment to review our exhibitor options:

Option A, Easel $30/day
Option B, Half-table $45/day
Option C, Full table $75/day

Shriekfest is easily the second largest horror film festival in Los Angeles, the film capital of the world.[11] It's long established and widely respected. Big Bear is only in its second year, but it's located in a top resort destination for many Angelinos. Their ad rates may not be realistic for a new festival in Small Town, USA. But who knows? If you attract a large audience, even higher rates may appeal to local businesses. Trial and error (are you deluged with potential sponsors, or can't give away your banner ads?) will guide you as to whether your asking price is realistic.

Reyna Young and John Gillette of A Nightmare to Remember San Francisco Horror Film Festival offer this advice: "Put together a *package deal*! With sponsors, I try to email them, letting them know that for a certain amount of money, they will receive a spot on the website and the program book, and be announced at the fest." Ken Daniels of the Fright Night Film Fest adds, "Sponsors are tougher in these lean times. I wouldn't advise any new shows to start until 2012. It'll be better economically, in my opinion, at that time. At least I hope so."

Europeans are also experiencing sponsorship challenges. Van Hauwaert says, "Attracting sponsors! We always have difficulties for this topic. Any advice is welcome." Robert Nevitt of England's Celluloid Screams Sheffield Horror Film Festival adds, "As we're only in our second year, sponsors are high on the agenda for us. It's a factor we're keen to learn more about."

Tip: Examine the banner ads on *other* film festivals' websites. Some of those entertainment industry companies buy banners on many (horror and non-horror) festival sites. If they'll sponsor other festivals, why not yours? Contact them and ask.

Another tip: If your festival can't compete for *national* sponsors against the bigger festivals, try *local* sponsors. Maybe there's a costume, novelty, candy, or comic books store nearby? Your festival should attract local filmgoers who *like* spooky stuff— the perfect target demographic for local stores that *sell* spooky stuff. Explore your neighborhood. Are any of the businesses especially big on promoting for Halloween? "As for securing locations, sponsors, and guests," says the Eerie Horror Fest's Greg Ropp, "each festival tends to have their own ideas, *best suited to their area, region and budget*."

The Terror Film Festival is based in Pennsylvania, yet even so, they saw an opportunity for *foreign* support after accepting a foreign film. According to Claw, their festival director, "We had a filmmaker fly in from France and bring his actors. We were able to wrangle the French consulate and several people to represent the [filmmaker's] city. It was the filmmaker's first trip to America. When they left, they were filled with love and friendship. It was the best feeling we ever had at our festival."

Withoutabox.com

If you're starting up a film festival, Withoutabox.com can promote it, bringing you plenty of submissions while raking in those entry fees. Withoutabox has a massive online database of film festivals from around the world. Filmmakers need only input their "project profile" once, search the festival database by any criteria (e.g., genre, entry fee, deadline, location), pick their festivals, electronically sign all legal forms, click and pay the entry fee, and you're done! You must still, usually, snail mail your DVD, but some festivals have an electronic option there too. Withoutabox also sends weekly emails to filmmakers, reminding them of upcoming festivals and deadlines, further promoting your event. According to its website:

> Withoutabox helps festival staff to streamline their Call for Entries process and boost their submission outreach and numbers. Festivals and competitions can request submissions globally via the Web and conveniently manage incoming submissions electronically — in the past a very manual and paper-based process. [Hence, "without a box"— get it?] In addition, festivals can promote their event to over 300,000 active filmmakers and screenwriters already on the Withoutabox platform, accept entry forms

and submission fees electronically (if applicable), and automatically notify filmmakers for acceptance into their event.

Filmmakers discover festivals through the Withoutabox Search Engine, weekly Festival Update and Spotlight E-mails, or are referred from festivals' own Websites. *The service is entirely free to filmmakers,* [my italics throughout] save for any entry fees the festival may require. Filmmakers apply via an online entry form, and pay any applicable entry fees securely online. Using Withoutabox's online suite of management tools, festival staff track incoming submission materials and fees via the Withoutabox Festival dashboard, which in turn conveniently notifies filmmakers that their materials have been received....

When filmmakers submit to festivals using Withoutabox, they receive instructions as specified by the festival where to send a screener and in what format (e.g. DVD, VHS, 16mm, 35mm, etc.). Additionally, festivals may opt to accept Secure Online Screeners, Withoutabox's high-quality digital online film submission platform that offers an eco-friendly alternative to receiving hard-copy screeners by mail....

Listing a festival in the Withoutabox Deep Search Engine is entirely free. Setting up a new listing is self-service and can be completed in less than an hour. Having a free listing allows over 300,000 Withoutabox filmmakers to search for your festival and apply though traditional channels.

Activating Withoutabox's online submission capability and unlocking the power of the Festivalsuite *requires a modest setup fee,* providing access to the online management tools for managing incoming submissions electronically. *Festivals that charge entry fees then pay a per-submission commission* and agree to discount their entry fees by at least $5 for Withoutabox submissions. Fees are only charged at the time when filmmakers complete their submission and payment on Withoutabox. All net festival submissions revenue is then paid out monthly as directed by festivals. *Festivals that do not charge entry fees pay a flat fee to access the online submission management tools....* [That flat rate is $2,000.]

Withoutabox is a division of IMDb, and opens many doors to its partner festivals in escalating visibility worldwide via the most trafficked film, television, and entertainment site on the web. With 57 million unique visitors each month, IMDb can be the perfect place for festivals to bolster their presence in the film world, among fans, filmmakers, and industry. Many Withoutabox Festivals are also IMDb-qualifying, granting all eligible submissions an IMDb title page.

Amazon.com owns IMDb, which bought Withoutabox in 2008. The Tabloid Witch Awards is on IMDb's festival listing page, but its awards are not recognized. Tabloid Witch winners cannot add their victories to their films' pages by simply clicking a Tabloid Witch Award button and category on IMDb. However, some winners have found a *solution.* They've written their Tabloid Witch wins onto other areas of their films' pages.

In 2008, I asked IMDb to recognize the Tabloid Witch as an official award. They replied that they were not recognizing *any* new awards "at this time." I tried again in 2009, but it was still "not at this time." I wonder if, were I to use Withoutabox, then now may be "the time."

The Tabloid Witch has yet to use Withoutabox. The $2,000 *flat fee* they charge to "no entry fee" festivals to use their Festivalsuite submission tools is way too much. No entry fee festivals are often strapped for cash. But it's only a $500 *setup fee* were I to charge filmmakers an *entry fee,* from which Withoutabox deducts an 18 percent commission. Withoutabox will accept a smaller 9 percent commission if I pay a $1,200 *flat fee.* (I'm not sure if the $2,000 or $1,200 *flat fees* are *in addition to* the $500 *setup fee.*)

If the cost of screening venues, trophies, and the desire to earn a profit hasn't already convinced a film festival to begin charging entry fees, seeing Withoutabox's rates offers yet another incentive.

Curiously, the *fee-charging* Dark Carnival Film Festival is urging a boycott of Withoutabox. Festival director David E. Pruett writes:

> Withoutabox states that they don't charge any upfront fees for festivals to participate, but this claim is misleading. In fact, they charge a $500 set-up fee that is only refundable after a festival has reached $2500 in submission fees — for which Withoutabox collects an 18 percent commission.
>
> They also require all new festivals to purchase one of their advertising packages, at a minimum of $750. If a festival fails to bring in at least $2500 in submission fees in its first year with the service, they are required to purchase ANOTHER advertising package, again at a minimum of $750.

Those costs end up getting passed on to the filmmakers in the form of higher submission fees.

Many festival directors buy into this arrangement because Withoutabox can funnel hundreds of submissions to their event, creating a very lucrative source of income for both parties.

This creates an environment in which festivals generously broaden their submissions call, to the detriment of filmmakers who find themselves competing with more and more people, wondering if their film even makes it to the festival screening committee.

Withoutabox manages to get by with all this because they have no competition — and have taken active steps to make sure things stay that way.

This past Fall, B-Side Entertainment announced that they would be launching a competing online submission service that would charge roughly half of what Withoutabox charges. [B-Side went online in 2008.] Publicly, a Withoutabox spokesperson said they welcomed the competition, but within weeks they changed their terms of service, forbidding any of their subscribers from using a competing service.

This meant that any festivals that might have wanted to experiment with a new service would have to cancel their subscription to Withoutabox and lose their investment.

Shortly thereafter, B-Side announced that they had abandoned their plans.

Dark Carnival has vowed to boycott Withoutabox, and we look forward to working with any competitor that takes up the challenge.

Our submission fees are among the lowest anywhere [As of 2010, $15 for short films, $20 for features up to 99 minutes, $25 for longer features], and at the same time we offer more to filmmakers than just about any other horror film fest....[12]

Most film festivals like Withoutabox. According to journalist Jen Swanson: "Gen Art was one of the first festivals to accept submissions online through Withoutabox, and in the first year doubled its number of entries to almost 1,000 films.... [Gen Art's Jeff Abramson] would challenge other festival producers to make the same amount of money without using Withoutabox.... Adam Roffman, program director of the Independent Film Festival of Boston ... has subscribed to Withoutabox for more than four years and considers the service to be a good investment. Festival submissions nearly doubled in IFFB's first year using it."[13] George T. Marshall's Rhode Island International Film Festival (RIIFF) has also benefited from Withoutabox. "'We see 100–200 submissions come in after each email blast,' says Marshall of his decision to pay for the marketing.... In 2002, its first year using Withoutabox, RIIFF attracted 206 online submissions, in addition to the 1,000 hard copy submissions sent directly by filmmakers. In 2003, RIIFF processed 486 submissions using Withoutabox. Of the 3,000+ submissions to this year's RIIFF, 1,648 were submitted through Withoutabox."[14]

Swanson cites Ryan Gielen as a filmmaker who likes Withoutabox because it saves time on the submission process. Gielen says it used to "take forever."

But the filmmakers posting at the end of Swanson's article disagree. Anonymous writes: "What none of the festival directors, etc. above have mentioned is that while their submission volume has increased exponentially, how are they facilitating this onslaught of submissions? Sure, they are making more $$$ but now screening committees are bombarded and exhausted with more film to watch — regardless of quality. As a filmmaker, this idea of 'increased submissions' bothers me. This obviously favors the festival (and WOB) but not the filmmaker."[15]

A presumably different Anonymous writes: "Both fests and withoutabox rip off filmmakers. Fests use withoutabox and advertise on withoutabox to increase submissions. That increases cashflow, which is used to pay people and run the fest. Great. But then filmmakers who have no shot waste their money on the submission, because the fest claims 'we just want the best films,' an intentionally vague and visionless call, aimed at getting the most people possible to pay the $45-$100 fee."[16]

And from yet another Anonymous: "It seems that it's been harder to get into festivals that use Withoutabox, because the festivals get so many more submissions than they used to."[17]

And from Australian documentarian Jeni Thornley: "I can see some advantage in not having to fill out many many individual film festival submission forms. BUT on the down side I think it is faceless and impersonal and I sense it may be indirectly causing ALL film festivals to charge applicants submission fees ... WITHOUT A BOX is starting to feel like GAMBLING: tick the box — pay by credit card and BINGO — More DEBT!! and maybe one day the jackpot!!!! that elusive jackpot is a snare and a delusion ... like a gambler chasing the next pokie machine. I have my doubts about this system; when an indie filmmaker has self financed or independently financed a doco, and has no marketing budget, these Film Festival entry fees can be prohibitively expensive. One festival in Australia is charging $400 entry fee for documentaries!"[18]

These filmmakers' complaints boil down to high entry fees and too much competition. And yes, Withoutabox increase both. Festivals must charge higher entry fees to account for Withoutabox's commission, and to earn back the setup and marketing fees. But festivals do earn back this money — and a whole lot more — from more entries. More entries is good for festivals and awards (the more competitive an award, the more prestigious), but is bad for filmmakers who pay and are rejected.

Horror film festivals generally like Withoutabox. Alex Bram of Carnival of Darkness (not to be confused with Pruett's Dark Carnival) tells me: "Withoutabox is amazing and a wonderful tool for filmmakers and festival organizers alike." His site says: "Withoutabox provides cost-saving, online entry to film festivals around the world, with one master entry form, allowing you to enter your film more quickly and with greater accuracy. Filmmakers with an upgraded project on Withoutabox receive discounts on their Entry Fees."

Matthew M. Foster of the Dragon*Con Independent Short Film Festival adds, "Withoutabox is an absolute necessity. The *quality* of films submitted increased massively once we started using Withoutabox. Plus, over and over, filmmakers only realize they need to submit now when Withoutabox tells them — even filmmakers who have had works in the fest in the past."

In other words, not only *more* submissions, but *better* submissions. I believe it. While many Tabloid Witch submissions are as good as any that screen at large, fee-charging festivals (some of them *have* screened at the larger festivals), the Tabloid Witch also attracts many crude films, shot by and starring amateurs. I suspect that *some* of these filmmakers *know* their films aren't very good, and only enter because it's free. So yes, I'm sure Foster is correct. Withoutabox (like entry fees in general) filters out non-serious filmmakers.

Of course, some inept filmmakers are desperately serious about their craft, but are blind to their ineptitude. These budding Ed Woods will continue submitting their masterpieces to every festival, with or withoutabox. No technique can filter out *all* crappy films.

Greg Ropp says, "We use Withoutabox each year and have had incredible success with them. Although they tend to be a bit pricey in terms of joining and the percentage they take from each submission, *I know filmmakers that have told me that they won't even consider submitting to a festival unless they see the Withoutabox logo.* [My italics.] The general vibe is that if a festival has taken the time, the money, and the effort to be a Withoutabox partner, that they have some legitimacy. Withoutabox routinely screens for potential fraudulent activities and is careful about who they chose to work with, turning away, from what I've been told, several potential festival clients each season."

I'm sure Ropp is correct. I suspect some filmmakers don't search beyond Withoutabox, because they assume that all the *real* festivals are already there. Or if they come across a non–Withoutabox festival, the filmmaker assumes that it can't be legit or important. It's ironic.

An awful lot of filmmakers complain about festival entry fees, yet they solely use Withoutabox, thereby encouraging more and higher entry fees.

Robert Nevitt says, "Withoutabox is an excellent resource and we'll be listing on there again for 2010." According to Reyna Young and John Gillette, "Withoutabox is helpful in so many ways of getting the word out. It does help you connect with others to cross-promote, and get to know more people out there doing what you're doing." Michael Coulombe adds, "Withoutabox is a great tool but it's rather expensive. For festivals that are starting up they offer a free service. As long as you're willing to receive and log your own submissions, they will list your festival for free."

I think Coulombe means Withoutabox's Deep Search Engine, which lists festivals but doesn't handle submissions. Much like IMDb lists all festivals on a webpage, but only allows *some* of those festivals' awards to appear on the films' webpages.

A few horror festivals are less enthused. Ken Daniels of Fright Night says, "We personally don't use Withoutabox that much. We prefer to do our own marketing." And Patrick Van Hauwaert of Razor Reel adds, "Withoutabox, way too expensive. We choose to be at the Cannes Market. Also expensive, but much more fun."

Promoting the Festival

Film festivals can be promoted inexpensively online. Greg Ropp says, "Festival directors *must* keep up-to-date with social networking and any online resources to promote their events and network with filmmakers and screenwriters." Michael Coulombe agrees. "One of the biggest ways to promote is using social media. Facebook, Twitter, and MySpace, as well as blogs and forums. They are all free to join and are geared towards specific audiences."

Gareth "Gaz" Bailey of England's Abertoir Horror Festival advises, "Use the internet primarily for promotion. Most fans of horror use the internet constantly for updates and social networking. It's everyone's first port of call for up-to-date news, information, and discussion. It's vital to your festival to have a presence there. It's the best means of advertising and the cheapest. As a second priority, advertise in *genre magazines*. And get *festival flyers* widely distributed. For every 100 flyers, if one person picks it up and considers attending, then it's worth it."

Vivi Amaral of Brazil's Cinefantasy uses social networking to promote his festival to, what he considers to be, an especially tough market. "I believe in USA and Europe it is easier than here, because they already have a great public who loves horror films. It's cultural. Horror in Brazil is still in the underground world. First we have to promote the genre as an attractive, artistic, and — why not? — commercial genre. We use a lot the web to help us on this promotion. Facebook, MySpace, Twitter, Orkut, website, forums, blogs, everything we can use."

Jim Taylor of Canada's Zombie Short Film Festival swears by Twitter. "Don't be annoying about it, but if you twitter regularly, your followers will spread the word and direct folks to your website." Taylor's festival also got a boost from Boingboing.net. "When myself and the other founder (Cory Laffin) came up with the idea, I quickly bought our website domain name, started a simple blog, posted that we had this great idea for a film festival, and asked people to send me an email if they were interested. The next day, I found out that boingboing had picked up the story. We received hundreds of hits on our website, and many, many emails from people wishing to enter. I learned two things from this: 1. It's amazing what a little internet buzz can do; 2. Always have your website up and ready *before* releasing news about your event."

The Tabloid Witch has a website, and a presence on MySpace and Blogger. No Facebook or Twitter. I've read bad things about Facebook. That they abuse private information and refuse to delete sites despite the creator's request. Apparently Facebook owns your posted material, not you. Reporting for Britain's *The Independent* newspaper (not to be confused with the independent film website of the same name) Rhodri Marsden writes that while MySpace also makes leaving difficult, "Facebook presents a knottier problem: according to their terms and conditions, you can't actually delete your account, only 'deactivate' it — and Facebook keeps hold of all your details for perpetuity. They only agree to cancel your account if you manually delete, one by one, every event, message, Mini-Feed entry and so on that's on your profile — and, as regular users will know, that might take several hours."[19] Even so, many people love Facebook. Others think that Facebook is the new Satan. It used to be Microsoft, but now it's Facebook.

A festival that posts a "call for entries" on a *social networking* site should receive some quality films.

Festival director Gareth "Gaz" Bailey at the Abertoir Horror Festival. Aberystwyth, Wales. November 2010. (Photograph courtesy Abertoir Horror Festival.)

Unfortunately, social networking sites also attract lots of teenagers and amateurs playing with a camcorder. A greater percentage of trained and talented filmmakers are found at *professional networking* sites. Kelly Jones and Kelly Webster, coordinators of England's Halloween Monster Movie Challenge, recommend ShootingPeople.com and TalentCircle.org. Horror journalist and filmmaker Eddie McMullen (*Last Call*) networks on Mandy.com. The Tabloid Witch has posted calls for entries at Studentfilmmakers.com and Craigslist.org.

Although Craigslist is not exclusively a filmmaking site, it has filmmaking forums. It also has many visitors, is easy to use, and is free. Craigslist prevents you from posting the same message in different city forums all at once, suspecting that it might be spam. You must wait a week for your post to expire in one city forum before you can post it in another city. Since this prevents you from posting in every city all at once, I recommend focusing on cities with large filmmaker populations. You can also try *rewording* your "call for entry" for each city. If your posts read differently, Craigslist might regard them as different posts, rather than spam.

If you're willing to pay a (currently) $95 annual fee, you can post at Filmindependent.org, a top indie filmmaker website. Membership also allows you to vote for their Independent Spirit Awards, and receive free "for your consideration" DVDs from indie filmmakers begging for your vote.

Google to find other career networking sites. Use experience and word of mouth to determine which are worth paying to join.

Many online *festival directories* will list your event for free. Shortfilmcentral.com, Fest21.com, Filmproposals.com, UnstoppablePacific.com/biglist.html, and Ominous-events.com are some. The latter has an impressive "Horror Fests and Cons Database."

Ultimatefilmfest.com claims to be a "complete film festival database." Well, no. I submitted the Tabloid Witch in late 2009, but as of September 2010, it's still not listed. Shriekfest, Screamfest L.A., and the New York City Horror Film Festival are listed. But not Celluloid Screams, Razor Reel, Cinefantasy, Fantaspoa, Eerie Horror, Terror Film Festival, or Viscera. I eventually stopped searching. Ultimatefilmfest.com lists the bigger horror festivals, but falls short on grassroots horror.

Online *press release services* are helpful. You submit a press release. They distribute it to news organizations (online and paper), who will then, *maybe*, reprint it. News organizations are flooded with PR fluff, rather than *news* that's of interest to their readers. Of course, those readers include horror fans, so maybe your release will qualify as news.

Press release services vary as to what they'll distribute. I-newswire.com rejects releases that promote political candidates or religions, or which defame any religion, or which contain racist or profane material. Some services reject releases which hawk MLM "get rich quick" schemes or online pharmaceuticals. Some reject releases that are *purely promotional* and *lack a news content*, because they don't want news organizations to ignore their releases sight unseen.

A *news content* can be your festival choosing a venue, or announcing nominees or winners, or maybe a colorful celebrity anecdote. Minor celebrities qualify as news when they visit a Starbucks. A-list celebrities qualify as "breaking headline news" whenever they blink. If a celebrity said something nice about your festival, or made a funny face caught on camera, it merits a press release. Some festivals issue releases upon every tiny incident, even if no celebrities were involved, just to keep the festival's name circulating. As in "Only 147 Days Left to Enter Blah Blah Fest!" You can try it. At worst, no news organization will print your release, and you might be out some money.

Press release services vary as to cost. Some charge for every release you submit. Others offer tiered services. I-newswire.com will distribute your release for free, without an image. If you want to attach an image (e.g., a festival photo or logo) you must pay a fee. PRweb.com's Basic Package will distribute your release to all major search engines. But to reach "more than 250,000 PRWeb news subscribers and 30,000+ journalists and bloggers" you must purchase the Standard Package. If you don't write too well, some services will write your release for you — for a fee.

Press release services include I-newswire.com, theopenpress.com, wiredprnews.com, PRweb.com, PRnewswire.com, PRLog.com, and PR.com. I'm sure there are more. You can submit the same release to as many services as you like. Generally, there's no exclusivity.

Websites, MySpace pages, directory listings, and press releases create an online *presence* for your festival, but don't disregard the *direct approach*. I've googled for horror films, found filmmakers' websites, and emailed *personal invites* to them to enter the Tabloid Witch contest. I joined MySpace in 2007 because many horror filmmakers had no websites, just a MySpace page. I *had* to join MySpace to message them.

Then there's old-fashioned, offline marketing in the "meat world." Jones and Webster say, "A lot of the time we spent [on promotion] was approaching filmmakers *in person* at networking events, and talking to them about the challenge."

I've left *promotional flyers* at the various Los Angeles film schools, pinned to bulletin boards or stacked on tables and floors. No film schools in your city? You can email and/or snail mail your festival information to any school in the world. Film professors are generally eager to pass on any opportunities to their students, many of whom will soon graduate to unemployment, burger flipping, or a cubicle job unrelated to the arts.

IMDb provides an extensive list of film school websites at imdb.com/filmschools. When contacting them, you may want to email *and* snail mail. Emails are easily deleted, or prey to spam filters.

Winning filmmakers will often promote your festival, free of charge. Filmmakers love plastering their websites with laurel leaves logos proclaiming: *Winner! 2008 Putrid Pus Award!* Or even *Official Selection! Mosquito Bay Zombie Fest!* Other filmmakers scrutinize those laurel leaves, searching for festivals that haven't rejected them yet.

"The best way to promote your event is to keep in touch with your filmmakers, and keep your website up-to-date," says Taylor. "Filmmakers are used to chatting themselves (and their work) up to anyone who'll listen. Keep them in the loop, make sure they have access to your promotional materials, and you'll be surprised how far-flung your festival's buzz will be."

Young and Gillette offer an example. "Ray Hom, director of *Hubris: A Short Film*, was very eager to have it shown at our fest. He was so excited it was accepted, he did nothing but promote like no tomorrow. He was the only filmmaker we really ever met who helped us get the word out. He had flyers and MySpace ads everywhere. He told everybody he knew. He linked us on his site. When he showed up, he brought so many people with him. Now that's a filmmaker who knows where he's going. We love him. He's awesome."

"Word of mouth promotion is key," says Coulombe. "The more people enjoy your event, the more they'll spread the word. Free advertising is great!" TromaDance's Manjourides advises, "Self promotion is everything. Go to other conventions. *Have a hook.*" I think he means that you should be able to tell filmmakers why your festival is worth entering *in addition to* the many other festivals that they have already spent money on.

One of my hooks: No entry fee! What have you got to lose?

That's actually a pretty good hook. Celebrity filmmakers who routinely screen at Cannes may not care about entry fees, but impoverished, obscure filmmakers welcome no entry fee festivals, even if the event is likewise impoverished and obscure. Fee-charging festivals need other hooks. That your festival has boosted filmmakers' careers. That you're located in a major city, such that entertainment industry leaders and news media will likely attend. That you award really cool prizes.

Filmmakers love wallpapering their websites and DVDs with laurel leaves logos, which can be downloaded for free. Just google "film festival laurel leaves."

But the Terror Film Festival's Claw offers this caveat: "Stop hustling everyone. Start talking straight. It works every time. I can't believe the negative comments I've heard, since we started up, about the other festivals and other companies out there. The worst we've ever been called was honorable and professional. And that was from a member of Bruckheimer's camp."

Festivals can also piggyback upon another event's promotional efforts. Viscera piggybacks on other horror festivals. TromaDance has piggybacked on Sundance's presence. The Tabloid Witch has piggybacked on Loscon and World Horror Con. They bring the crowds, the Tabloid Witch brings the films and filmmakers. Similarly, being part of a convention, the Dragon*Con Independent Short Film Festival isn't burdened with promotional work. Foster says, "We have another department to do promotion for Dragon*Con as a whole. My venue is always set, as well as celebrities."

Finally, festivals (and filmmakers) with money to spare might consider hiring a *publicist*. (A publicist would say: No, you're not *hiring them*—you are *investing in your own career*.) Shop around, and compare their fees and track records. Get referrals. I understand the right publicist, given the right product, can be a big help if you can afford her. The tips in this book are mostly for people who can't.

Entry fees are a big theme in this chapter. Among U.S. film festivals, entry fees are the norm. Some festival directors have told me that entry fees are a *necessity*, without which they could not fund their events. Many filmmakers gripe that fee-charging festivals are a ripoff, but are these the sore losers? Filmmakers who win armloads of trophies on the festival circuit, followed by distribution deals, generally don't complain. Yes, they're the minority. Dems the breaks.

Ripoff can mean two things: a case of *fraud* or a *bad deal*. If a festival delivers on its promises, there is no *fraud*. True, some festivals are so competitive, it's *highly* unlikely that your film will be selected. Such festivals may indeed be a *bad deal* and a waste of your entry fee. Especially if your film isn't that great. But while you may gripe about being *ripped off*, you were not *defrauded*.

Unfortunately, filmmakers are rarely objective about their films' merit. Every mother thinks her horror film is the scariest horror film in the world and *deserves* to win. But festival judges too differ as to their aesthetic criteria and personal tastes. A film that wins an award at one festival might not even make official selection at another.

Even so, festival judges are more likely to agree on certain aesthetic criteria over others. The next chapter should help filmmakers improve their chances of impressing festival judges.

2

HOW TO MAKE AN AWARD-WINNING HORROR FILM!

Horror is competitive. Anyone who's not currently busy managing a horror film festival or award is making a horror film. Hobbyists, film students, and professionals from related creative fields (e.g., theater, commercials, music videos) are all trying their hands at horror. Sadly, some films fail to make it into a single festival, much less win anything, despite the filmmaker spending over a thousand dollars on entry fees. Bummer. Other horror films have their DVD boxes plastered with laurel leaves logos from dozens of festivals and awards.

Why them and not you?

In previewing hundreds of entries to the Tabloid Witch Awards, I keep seeing the same few *recurring* mistakes. The good news is, the worst of them can be fixed *on the cheap*, without busting your budget. All that's required is time and effort. Here are some low-cost tips, culled from both my experience and those of other horror film festival officials.

Acting

In my viewing experience, *acting quality* is the single biggest and most common pitfall among crappy horror films. Actors who are wooden, self-conscious, affectatious, or chew scenery can tank an otherwise decent film. I rejected one film that did a decent job of recreating the 1860s, in costumes and furnishings, only to populate this period piece with some painfully bad acting.

Why do filmmakers cast amateurs? Several reasons, I think.

(1) *Disrespect*. Some filmmakers don't see acting as an art form that requires special talent or training. Only "artsy fartsy" types respect acting. Filmmaking is about equipment; the latest and coolest camera, with the most buttons and menus. That's the meat of filmmaking. Acting is something that anyone can do with a bit of effort. Such as friends and family.

(2) *Ego*. Some filmmakers want to be movie stars. So they cast themselves. Hey, if anyone can act, why not *moi*?

(3) *Sloth*. It's easy to convince friends and family to act in your film, and easy to keep them on set. Apart from having egos of their own, loved ones won't walk off if you're a crappy director, or your shots take too long and they get bored. Sure, they may start goofing off on set. They may not take your film seriously. But at least they're there. Professional actors can

be *so* demanding. They might have *expectations* of you and your film. They might even pressure you to do a good job.

(4) *Insecurity.* Opposite of disrespect. Some filmmakers, being tech-oriented, have no experience with actors, and view the profession as mysterious. They feel inadequate directing trained actors, and worry that their low-budget effort will be disrespected *by the actors.*

(5) *Cheapness.* Trained actors usually want payment. If not money, then a quality production. Naturally, if you disrespect or are intimidated by actors, you're less likely to "waste" effort or money on casting them.

Vivi Amaral of Brazil's Cinefantasy International Film Festival warns, "Don't cast a friend who has never acted before, and doesn't have any talent to do this." Nor is there any excuse for it. Big cities teem with trained actors willing to work cheap or even for free. Small towns often have a community college or theater with trained actors. If you've studied the craft of filmmaking, and you respect your film and your actors, your actors will likely reciprocate.

Rather than expend that effort, some filmmakers *rationalize* their sloth, cheapness, or ego. I've seen horror "parodies" in which, I suspect, the director thought his awful cast was an asset. Wrong. An amateurish cast rarely produces a film that's "so bad it's good," but more often a film that's "so bad it's unwatchable." If you still insist on casting friends and family, insist they get professional training. Otherwise, you're shooting a home movie, and home movies can rarely compete against polished work.

Writing

If it ain't on the page, it ain't on the stage. Poor writing is the second biggest and most common fault among the entries that I've seen. I regret having to reject films that are technically beautiful—embodying much careful and diligent work by the director, cast, and crew—yet which fail because the story is derivative, vapid, vile, or not even a story; just a series of scenes haphazardly strung together. It's sad to see so much talent, effort, and money wasted on crappy scripts.

But while bad acting is my chief complaint, poor writing is the *primary* complaint of many festival officials. Matthew M. Foster of the Dragon*Con Independent Short Film Festival says, "The biggest problem is in writing. Bad scripts, simple scripts, scripts that say nothing and go nowhere. It all starts with a script, and good ones are few and far between. Filmmakers need to put real effort into their scripts. They need to find writers with skills, decide what they want to say, then make sure that actually comes through." Robert Nevitt of England's Celluloid Screams agrees that the script is primary. "Bad acting, dodgy camerawork, poor sound can often be forgiven if the script works. The central idea or concept is key to a film's success."

As with acting, I believe that many tech-oriented filmmakers disrespect writing. Rather than study story-telling (as they would study their cameras), they merely copy their favorite horror scenes, reassembled from a hodgepodge of past horror films. They confuse screenwriting with formatting. All they need is some professional screenwriting software, type some words into it, and out pops a literary masterpiece. *Wow, look how professionally formatted those tabs are—my script must be great!*

Alas, looks can be deceiving. Software only formats. Software doesn't write. Writers write. Great scripts have been written on manual typewriters and even in longhand. You don't need software. You need story-telling skills.

As with acting, if you insist on writing your own script, you must study the art of storytelling as seriously as you would study your lighting gear. And not just storytelling in general (although an understanding of the basic rules of drama helps), but *visual* storytelling. A film's story, characters' traits, and themes are usually better communicated by images than through dialogue or voiceovers. Trim excess dialogue. Use voiceovers sparingly. Then when you're editing, trim excess images.

What's excess? If a line or scene doesn't contribute to the story, characters, or themes, then it's excess. How to determine if a line or scene doesn't contribute? To answer that, the filmmaker must develop an artistic sensibility through study and practice. Over time, you'll know.

Why do some filmmakers write their own scripts when they can't write? Once again, it comes down to *sloth* (it's *hard* to find a writer, or learn storytelling skills), *cheapness* (it costs nothing to write your own script), or *ego*. Many directors want to be "auteurs," which they think requires directing one's own material. Then nobody will dispute that it's *your* film, reflecting *your* artistic vision and no one else's. You'll be recognized as a *real* artist. Not like that obscure hack, Alfred Hitchcock, who directed other writers' scripts.

Seriously, if you're not a writer, find a writer. Successful directors often film others' scripts. To repeat Foster's advice: "Filmmakers need to put real effort into their scripts. They need to *find writers with skills*...." There is no shame in directing someone else's script.

Poor writing creates many problems. Such as?

Tip: *A vignette is not a story.*

Many films confuse the two. "X rises from the grave and kills Y. The End" or "Zombies eat people. The End." Or the film relies on an (often predictable) twist. "X is a serial killer who dates Y who turns out to be a vampire. The End."

I've probably seen thousands of horror films and TV episodes, so I know every "surprise" ending. Festival screeners tend to be well-versed in cinema history, especially in their festival's genre, so don't rely on your film's ending. You need more. Tell a *story*.

A *story* has a beginning, middle, and end. Three parts. *Vignettes* are like *jokes*: no middle. Jokes have two parts: setup — punchline. Vignettes have two parts: setup — surprise twist ending.

TV pilots have no ending. They have a beginning (setting up the forthcoming series), a middle (or at least, the beginnings of a middle), but no end. Why discuss TV pilots? Because sometimes they are submitted to festivals as films. "It's clear the filmmakers don't always know what they're making," says Nevitt. "If your project is a thirty minute TV pilot, it doesn't necessarily function as a short film, and it's unlikely we'd program it."

Want an example? See *Frankenstein*, the 2004 TV movie starring Parker Posey, Vincent Perez, and Michael Madsen. This visually beautiful movie *ends* with Posey and Perez (a police detective and the monster) forming an alliance to fight the evil doctor. Everything so far was exposition. Now the story begins.... But wait, the film is over! We're left hanging, with an unsatisfying ending. Well, of course. This TV movie was merely the start to a series — that was never produced.

Tip: *Do not bite off a bigger story than you can chew.* Greg Ropp of the Eerie Horror Film Festival advises, "Take the time to plot out every move, from the initial idea — is this *original*? is this something I can realistically pull off at this stage in my career and with my budget? do I have the time to put into this? can I depend upon others to help meet deadlines?— to how the final film will be promoted."

Writing is rewriting. An old adage, but Alex Bram of the Carnival of Darkness festival thinks it bears repeating. "Never settle for first draft. Rewrite, re-edit, reshoot. Your first idea is not necessarily a good one. It may lead to a truly *original* and great idea, but don't be lazy and don't settle for anything other than the best. Keep searching. Have a good bullshit meter. Don't allow bullshit into your film. There's already plenty of that." *Keep it short and sweet.* Even a good film can be ruined by fat. Filmmaker Rich Mauro's *Mole* (2001), a story of reporters seeking "mole people" in the abandoned subway tunnels under Manhattan, was initially cut at standard feature film length, but that didn't work. "A ninety-minute *Mole* premiered at the NoDance Film Festival in Park City," Mauro told me in 2005. "After distributors passed on it, instead of killing myself, I went to the editing room to rethink it. When I re-cut *Mole* to one hour, everyone said it was a mistake and would never sell. But I chose to edit the best film, without being confined to a time requirement." *Mole*'s new, nontraditional one-hour length — not quite a feature, not quite a short — proved to be ideal for its story. The film went on to sell in England and Germany, and got U.S. DVD distribution as part of the four DVD *Psychotic Tendencies* horror film package.

I'd never heard of NoDance prior to interviewing Mauro. Just how many Dance fests are there in Park City, Utah, trying to piggyback onto Sundance?

Another example of *short and sweet* is Jamie Renee Williams's *Slinky Milk* (2005), a black and white, surreal film reminiscent of *Un chien andalou*. Offering nightmarish images but no story, *Slinky Milk* is intriguing at its five minutes. Were it a half hour, it would have overstayed its welcome.

"Often films are too long," says Matthias Engelhardt of Germany's Weekend of Fear Film Festival. "Too much dialogue and too many scenes the film's story does not need. Especially at the festival situation — where the audience is watching two, three, four films in a row — there is no patience for boring scenes." Jim Taylor of Canada's Zombie Short Film Festival agrees. "Focus on your story. Take the time you need to tell it — no more, no less. A long film is not a better film unless it's giving us a *reason* to keep watching."

I have seen many films that would have been stronger at half their lengths. Films sabotaged by overlong expository shots, or directors in love with shots that don't contribute to the story, or characters wandering around or engaging in pointless chatter. If a line is unnecessary to the story, don't say it. If a line is necessary, say it in a way that's sharp, funny, clever, intriguing, memorable, or interesting. Dialogue should reveal character or move the story forward. Characters should not sound alike. Vapid chatter that achieves nothing may sound realistic, but banal banter makes for a dull film.

When a film starts to bore, Weekend of Fear's Head of Acquisition, Matthias Engelhardt, takes matters into hand. (There's a reason for Engelhardt's job title.) Erlangen, Germany. (Photograph courtesy Weekend of Fear.)

Characters hook an audience. Readers remember Sherlock Holmes and James Bond even if they forget the story details.

What is character? *Writing + acting = character.* The most memorable characters from classic films and TV shows are created by chemistry. The chemistry that occurs when the right actor meets the right part. This is why it's been said that *90 percent of directing is casting.*

What has this to do with *scripting* a horror film?

When I first saw *Dawn of the Dead* it blew me away. I was in my teens and had never before seen such gore. But after thirty years of horror, I'm bored by gore. Actors in bad makeup eating bloody intestines put me to sleep. I think this is why so many zombie *comedies* are being shot. Hardcore horror fans are jaded. At a certain point, gore *alone* looks silly or sordid, rather than scary or shocking. Filmmakers can try to "push the gore envelop," but I'm not sure there's anywhere left to go.

How then to engage audiences for your latest horror film? *Character.*

Horror films have been compared to roller coasters. To which I'll add: *characters are the car.* A great character engages an audience. Audiences sympathize and empathize with the character, getting into the character's skin so they can "suspend disbelief" and enter the character's world, being shocked and frightened by whatever shocks and frightens the character. Effective characters take audiences for a ride on the coaster. Ineffective characters leave audiences standing on the ground, outside the story and looking up at the coaster. They see it twisting and turning, but they're not on board experiencing the thrill of the ride.

How to create an effective character, one who engages an audience? Audiences should *care* about the character, but that is *not* to say the character *must* be likeable. What then?

Sorry, I have no formula for creating effective characters. If I did, I'd be the richest man in Hollywood. Creating an effective character is an inexact art. Writers and actors who've created great characters in one film, often fail to do so in their next film.

Here is how to become a billionaire: Get a billion dollars. Here is how to create great characters: Write and direct a film with great characters.

Both of these techniques will work. No, I can't provide more details.

"The great failing of horror," says Foster, "is that it is judged differently from other arts by critics, by the general public, and by filmmakers. A horror film needs to tell a good story, and do so in an entertaining way. Big gore shots and 'frights' fade, and what is frightening to some is dull to others. Good film is good film. Horror is a label you put on after the fact for marketing."

Rule are guidelines. Rules can be broken. Christopher Alan Broadstone's *Human No More* (2004) is a vignette rather than a story. *Slinky Milk* has no story and no trained actors. But Broadstone's short film packs a punch because of its artistry and originality; and Williams's avant-garde genre doesn't require a story or acting. Even so, rules are rules because they usually work. Violating them is a risk that rarely pays off.

Production Values

My main complaint is poor acting. For most festival directors it's poor writing. But while I'll forgive a film's mediocre production values if it has a great story with strong performances, Jason Carney and Andrea Beesley-Brown of the International Horror and Sci-Fi Film Festival suggest that "the *hardest* to forgive from a judging and programming view are the technical ones. You might have great writing and acting, but when the technical faults impede the ability to fully appreciate the film, then we have a difficult time placing it into competition. The most important thing is good *sound* and *lighting.* The film may not cost a lot, but if you can make a polished looking product, despite a minimal budget, that is what we are looking for."

I've seen many entries that can do with improved sound and lighting. Again, sloth is partially to blame. Some filmmakers are satisfied with their cameras' built-in mics and automatic exposure controls. Others are ignorant about sound and lighting. But if you're willing to work and learn, don't fret. You needn't attend a pricy film school. You can acquire filmmaking skills *on the cheap* from a community college, volunteer work, trial-and-error, books, DVDs, and talented colleagues.

"Before a shoot, take some basic classes," advises Foster. "Volunteer to work on large films." Reyna Young and John Gillette of A Nightmare to Remember suggest: "Watch the behind-the-scenes making of films [on your DVDs] to get an idea of what goes into making a film. Read scripts. Redo shots over and over until it's perfect." *Effort counts.* "When we receive films, we like to look at who *really got into* making their film. Like, if it was shot with someone running, and it's just someone running, and it's a continuous shot, then that's not very good. But if you have a running scene with parts of the girl's face, her expressions, or different shots, then we can tell you put in more effort. We like to watch horror films where we know people worked really hard at it, and did the best they could."

Eric Morgret of the Maelstrom International Fantastic Film Festival regards "bad story telling" as the weakest link for most entries, but he sees this as both a writing *and* production problem. "Learn to tell a story. I don't just mean the writing. The words, the camera, all tell the story. Storytelling starts on the page, continues on the set, and is finished in the editing room. Watch the great films and learn why they are so compelling."

Kelly Jones and Kelly Webster, coordinators of England's Halloween Monster Movie Challenge, regard bad lighting as their top complaint. "Lighting can make or break a horror film. If there is bad lighting, it affects the production values no matter how much post-production work a filmmaker puts into it."

Others fault poor sound as many entries' biggest flaw. Ken Daniels of Fright Night Film Fest insists, "*Sound, Sound, Sound!* Sound is over 65 percent of the experience. Work on your sound, lighting, and casting. Too many don't take the time to learn the basics. With all the quality equipment available at a fraction of the cost, why give us bad quality? I'd rather see a high-quality short film than an overdone terrible feature." Foster says that among the losing films, "There is a general lack of filmmaking skills, particularly with sound." Morgret agrees. "On a technical side, *bad sound* is my number one problem. I berated the 'shaky-cam' style of filmmaking, but I can watch that if the sound is good. Make the *sound* great and the picture will *look* better. People talk about how bad a movie may look. No one bitches about how bad the sound was, because *if the sound is bad, no one watches.*"

Terror Film Festival director Claw says that his biggest complaint is bad sound. "The sure sign of an amateur film is the *music being too loud.* It needs to complement the moment, not overwhelm it." An excellent point. Many horror films turn up the volume because the director failed to create a frightening story. Cheap, loud shocks try to compensate for scant fear. It's easy to make audiences jump with a sudden BANG! Much harder to instill fear by putting engaging characters in an unsettling story that's dense with creepy atmosphere (e.g., *The Ring*).

Matt Manjourides of TromaDance advises filmmakers to learn every technical element of their art, or just not bother. "Lighting is the most important visual element in a movie. Don't make a movie if you don't know how to light a scene. Sound is on the same level of importance. If you can't capture good sound, don't make a movie. Learn how to edit and make a scene flow. Learn how to shoot coverage."

Amaral believes that most filmmakers' common mistakes change with their level of experience. "Professional films have problems with writing and editing, the *creative part.* Image, sound, and effects are great, but the rhythm and timing sometimes aren't good. The students, young filmmakers, and amateurs have problems with *acting and technical quality*. The creativity is great, but sometimes they don't concern about the quality of the image or effects, and they often forget the sound. They have problems to transfer the script to the screen."

I wouldn't say acting is technical rather than creative, though acting involves technical training. But perhaps something was lost in translation; Amaral is Brazilian, so English is likely not his first language. I think he's saying that professional filmmakers have mastered their equipment, and can capture great images and sound, but perhaps their stories have become stale? Conversely, new filmmakers are more daring and original in story, but production values and acting need improvement.

Unlike Amaral, I haven't found that many new filmmakers are especially original. Every year, I'm inundated with copycat zombies, slashers, torturers, and the occasional Japanese style ghost. I have seen some strikingly original work from both student and seasoned filmmakers, but they're the exceptions.

Filmmaking is collaborative. And thus this tip: *Surround yourself with talented people.* However talented or inept *you* are, skilled people on your project will make you look better, whereas inept people will drag you down. This tip evokes the old Hollywood adage: *It's not what you know; it's who you know.* The former tip is advice for making a quality film; the latter is advice for finding work. The two concepts are not contiguous, but they overlap.

Filmmakers should *delegate* tasks for which they lack skills. "Know what you can't do, and find someone who can," says Foster. "Sound is a skill, and needs someone with training. Next comes lighting. You cannot just look about and figure how to light a scene. And save me from people who think natural lighting lends realism to their project." Michael Coulombe of the Big Bear Horror Film Festival says, "Be flexible when making your movie. Happy mistakes happen on set. It's great to have a vision, but some filmmakers are so focused on that vision, they aren't open to the suggestions of others on set. Movie making is a collaborative process. Utilize your team and you'll find that your movie will be enhanced." Morgret concurs. "The best films come from a combination of a strong vision, and a strong team of talented people. It is the most collaborative art form, and works best when collaboration is embraced." Denise Gossett of Shriekfest advises, "If you can pay your crew and talent, please do. You'll get a higher caliber of work. Surround yourself with really talented people, not so so people."

Because most films draw on the contributions of many people,

Big Bear Horror Film Festival founder and director Michael Coulombe. Big Bear, California. October 2010. (Photograph Scott Brown.)

a corollary rule is: *A film sinks to the level of its weakest link.* Gossett says, "If a story is great, but the film is grainy or poorly acted, it pulls you right out of the film." Gaz Bailey of England's Abertoir Horror Festival laments, "We have had excellent films shot perfectly, but let down by terrible acting. We have had films with excellent acting let down by bad camerawork or sound design. It is vitally important for filmmakers to consider *all* areas of the film, not just concentrate on one area, because major flaws elsewhere will only act against it. There have been countless times when an awful script or poor sound mixing have resulted in a film not being selected when the acting or photography is superb. It makes us feel terrible as a selection committee by turning them down, and equally bad for the individuals who have put so much effort into their work."

I said rules can be broken. Some fine films are not collaborative, or barely so. Remember the filmmaker who confided to me that, despite the many names in the end credit rolls of his three short films, he was the sole crew member. He did everything behind the camera, big and small, on set and in post, then invented the names for his lengthy credit rolls so that his projects would seem "bigger" than they really were. He shot his films on consumer DV (not HD). They did well on the festival circuit, winning awards and DVD distribution. But he's the exception. It usually helps to have help.

Top: Shriekfest co-founder and director Denise Gossett. Raleigh Studios, Hollywood. October 3, 2010. (Photograph by the author.) *Bottom:* Gaz Bailey (left) and Abertoir staffer Nia Edwards-Behi. Aberystwyth, Wales. November 10, 2010. (Photograph courtesy Abertoir Horror Festival.)

Post-Production

Mole, Legion: The Word Made Flesh (2005), and *Human No More* all underwent extensive post-production (e.g., color correction, sound mixing, etc.). *Legion*, a low budget short, resembles such studio fare as *Lost Souls* (2000) in its dark and moody cinematography. Pretty shots won't make up for awful acting and writing, but beautiful footage can sway festival judges on a *close* call. Your film's chances are better if you can avoid that "home video" look: flat, hard, uninspired lighting.

Filmmakers should strive to record clean on-set sound. An attitude of "We'll fix it in post" risks the possibility that you *can't* fix it. However, even *good* sound can often be *improved* in post. *Human No More* achieved both its impressive visuals and densely layered sound with Final Cut Pro. It didn't require much money, only much effort. Multiple award-winning filmmaker Broadstone explained his tools and technique: "The soundtrack was built and mixed entirely in Final Cut Pro. The only production sound used, short of a few stolen and processed sounds, was [actor] Tony Simmons's monologue. Everything else was recorded post-production. Most of what you hear in the film are multiple tracks of multi-layered audio first created independently, then dropped into the master soundtrack as a single-track element for the final film mix. Any dirty or noisy audio was cleaned up with Bias Sound Soap. Audio effects and reverbs were achieved by processing individual sound elements through Bias Peak 4. Equalization of sound elements was achieved by processing through Super Freq, a plug-in package for Peak 4. A tremendous amount of work, but well worth it. Nothing can ruin a movie like a poor soundtrack."

Broadstone never attended film school. He's self-taught and did all of his post-production work with off-the-shelf software. The above is excerpted from my *Hollywood Investigator* interview of him in 2005. Since then computers have gotten more powerful, and post-production software more sophisticated. Now you have still less excuse for crappy sound. However, if you can't be bothered with extensive post-production work, don't complain when the Broadstones of tomorrow are screened at dozens of festivals, and you're staring at a credit card bill for wasted entry fees. At least you'll have the consolation of knowing that your fees are helping other filmmakers promote *quality* work.

Entertain Us

A horror film may fall short in some categories, yet audiences will forgive much so long as the film entertains. Yes, one can *appreciate* a film without being entertained, but such films are of limited appeal. I said rules can be broken. *Entertain Us* is perhaps the least breakable rule. *Blood Feast* (1963) and *Don't Look in the Basement* (1973) have rough productions values and much poor acting, yet they've built cult followings because they entertain.

Engelhardt speaks like a diehard, drive-in schlock fan when he enthuses, "What is always working: a lot of fun and/or a lot of blood. Then bad acting, writing, post-production even can be a plus! [Whereas, on the other hand] 'Serious' films must be convincing in every aspect of filmmaking, otherwise the audience loses interest." However, Amaral qualifies this defense of the bad. "Don't hide behind the trash style. It is different when the trash movie has the truly proposal [done on purpose?] and when it becomes trash because it doesn't work."

Unlike Engelhardt, I hesitate to endorse bad writing, acting, and post-production as ever being "a plus." That only encourages lazy, sloppy filmmaking. And contrary to Amaral's contention, I believe that *intentionally* bad films rarely entertain. *Inadvertently* bad films are more likely to have a modicum of entertainment value. They're endearing because the filmmakers tried their best while remaining clueless to their own ineptitude. Ed Wood is the classic example.

My theory: If you aim for a "so bad it's good" type of cult status, you'll likely fail. A film is usually more entertaining if the writing contains no fat, and the story moves at a good pace, and audiences are not bored or driven off by an amateurish cast. Films that are well-acted, well-written, with beautiful visuals and a clear soundtrack, and are entertaining to boot, will most likely win the awards.

What Do Festival Directors Want?

It's been said that successful artists ignore the market and follow their passion.

Matthias Engelhardt (left) hopes to find "a lot of fun and/or a lot of blood" among the attendees at Weekend of Fear. Erlangen, Germany. (Photograph courtesy Weekend of Fear.)

Okay, but what if you're passionate about *several* story ideas? Are any of your ideas *more likely* to make for a successful horror film — one that sweeps the festivals and awards? Which monsters are currently hot? Which have worn out their welcome? Should you even film what's currently hot — or are your odds better if you submit a ghost film when everyone else is doing zombies?

A few years ago, the Tabloid Witch was deluged with *Hostel* inspired torture films. I'm open to them, but I've yet to see one that didn't leave a bad taste. I wonder what goes through some filmmakers' minds? One film had a man tied to a chair and tortured for 25 of the film's 30 minutes. That was pretty much it. Yes, there was a "surprise ending" in the form of a revelation as to why the torturer hated his victim, but it failed to redeem the film. Then there was that misogynistic mess about a nude woman imprisoned and harvested for organs throughout the entire length of the film. Again, that was pretty much it. One shot depicted her defecating into a pan. Another shot was a close-up of the mad doctor's penis as he masturbated to the woman's agony.

I don't care for misogyny, but I'm also no fan of misandry. I've noticed a double standard. When a man torments a woman in a horror film, audiences are usually invited to revile the man. But a woman tormenting or killing a man is often depicted gleefully; an act of empowerment or justified vengeance. Exceptions exist, but this double standard exists as a general rule. In this sense, horror films echo mystery's noir style, wherein the femme fatale is gleefully celebrated for cheating, lying, stealing, adultery, and spousal murder — it's liberating! — whereas if her husband does likewise, he's considered a controlling sexist. In horror iconography, female villains are often sexually attractive (e.g., scantily clad "scream queens" wielding chainsaws), whereas male killers (vampires excepted) are generally hideous (e.g., Freddy, Jason, Michael Myers, et al.).

But regardless of who's tormenting whom, the Tabloid Witch expects more from a horror film than simply torture or death. "X tortures and kills Y" is a vignette, not a story.

Since the Tabloid Witch's founding in 2004, zombies and slashers have dominated the entries. I'm tired of them, but I honor the rare exceptions that re-envision those subgenres (e.g., 2004's hilarious mocumentary, *Stiffs by Sid*, and 2007's delightful musical comedy, *Zombie Love*), or are especially well made (e.g., 2006's beautifully shot *Zombie Island*, and 2008's visceral slasher gorefest, *100 Tears*). I've yet to see an exceptional torture film.

"Zombie comedies are the largest category [of entries]," says Foster, "with straight zombie films being the second largest grouping. Torture films peaked several years ago, though the level of gore and pain in non-torture films continues to rise." Nevitt agrees. "There's never a shortage of zombie films. The torture cycle seems to have run dry of late. You can never have too much body horror, so I'm always looking for new ways to sicken and terrify in that mold. Too many safe, predictable, generic horror movies that don't offer anything new." Bailey says, "Zombie movies are becoming more common, so they have to be really special to stand out. There's nothing wrong with using a well-known genre type, as long as the film is good and entertaining."

Daniels has received "a glut of zombie movies, as well as just really bad movies in general." Coulombe has no problem with the zombie glut. "Last year [2009] we had a plethora of zombie films. Zombie films are inexpensive to make and are extremely popular. They are my favorite films." But he adds, "I have no opinion either way as to whether we should have more or less of any specific film. The filmmakers' submissions dictate the festival weekend."

Some festivals' selections are dictated by a mission beyond just horror. Just as the Viscera Film Festival and BleedFest focus on horror *by women*, Pablo Guisa Koestinger says that "The main purpose of Morbido is to be a window for all Latin American independent movies." That makes sense, seeing as the Morbido Film Fest is in Mexico. But it's not *exclusively* focused on Latin American indie horror. A secondary mission is "to show international new and classic pictures that are related to each year's main subject. For example, in 2010 the subject was *the mask*." Assuming a film meets the basic criteria, does Morbido prefer any particular sort of horror? Koestinger answers, "In Mexico, ghost stories are always successful. Latin America is a fertile soil for the paranormal. What I would like to see is young directors experimenting with not so common subjects. For example, *Mud Zombies* (2008) from Brazil shows us this beloved monster in the Amazon mangroves, which is something new."

Perhaps new in Mexico, but prevalent in Brazil. Amaral says, "In Brazil, people love to make gore and zombies films. Zombies are the 'Big Star.' Zombies are the creatures who appear the most every year." So too in Belgium. "I noticed the loss of interest in Asian films, and a resurrection of the zombie genre," says Razor Reel's Patrick Van Hauwaert. "Revenge flicks are in again. Probably most important is the rise of a new Australian wave. Films like *The Horseman* and *Animal Kingdom* are much closer to the world we live in than are many U.S. releases. The lack of political correctness in those films make it even scarier. Also, very happy that the cigarette is back in many

Pablo Guisa Koestinger leering morbidly beside the Morbido logo. (Photograph courtesy Morbido Film Fest.)

films. I don't smoke, but notice a lot of people still do. So put it on screen. It adds to your reality factor."

As one may expect, the Zombie Short Film Festival's Jim Taylor relishes the current zombie glut. "The zombie genre is enjoying quite a bit of attention recently. Books like *The Zombie Survival Guide*, *World War Z*, and *Pride & Prejudice with Zombies* are popular with mainstream readers. Major studio pictures like *Zombieland* have pushed the undead into the public eye. We think this is fantastic! But the usual story of the group of misfit survivors holing up and battling hordes of zombies is getting a bit played. We'd love to see zombie movies that push interesting *new* stories or themes. Think outside the box. We enjoy films where zombies are used against the genre, or in a different genre altogether. Innovation, technique, and creativity score big points with our jury."

Ropp is less enthused. "If I have to see one more goddamned zombie movie, I may just have to eat my own brain. Of all the subgenres, none are as tired and overdone (and usually poorly) as zombie movies. Most zombie movies we see each year are the same thing, over and over and over again. Clever titles, which used to be funny, are now red flags to us. Once I see the words '----- *of the Dead*' and the synopsis says something like 'a mysterious plague has caused the dead to come back to life to eat their neighbors and pets,' it's hard to get excited. Here is one genre that needs to go dormant for a while, at least long enough that someone can resurrect it (pun intended) and put a fresh spin on it.

"Torture porn is thankfully disappearing as quickly as it emerged. While I am no prude and love the occasional gorefest, I've yet to see a single film that features torture for 90 minutes that was worth it's weight in ... uh ... blood. And yes, that includes a certain popular horror franchise that inexplicably continues to churn out mindless sequels. While I won't put anyone down for enjoying these films, as a film festival president, one of my jobs is to expose people to the alternatives. Every year, people thank us for screening 'some good horror movies for a change' or 'thank you for showing me that horror movies aren't just dead teenagers and guys in hockey masks.'

"One young fan commented that his generation goes to any horror movie at their local theaters, but added that *big box office returns shouldn't be an indication of what the audience likes*— there were no other choices given to them. Some big shots in Hollywood might think that *Saw Part 38* is what horror fans want, based on the box office. It may have just been the only horror film released at their local cinema.

"I'd like to see more attention given to scripts, better actors, less CGI. Have a *reason* to have the gore and nudity. While I'm not prudish, I'm also not fourteen anymore. Adding blood and boobs to your film isn't going to hide that your film is a piece of shit — especially now that blood and boobs are no longer shock values in horror. I'd like to see a return to more intensely serious horror. There's too many parodies, too many spoofs, and most fall flat in humor and horror. I want to see artistic merit, showing careful attention to mood, lighting, and editing. Even slasher films, gore flicks, and exploitation movies should kick it up a notch."

Echoing Ropp, Rena Orocklou of Greece's Sreamin' Athens Horror Film Festival would like to see "interesting films, not only splatter or full of gore without a reason."

I agree that blood and boobs have become boring. They were shocking in the 1970s, when makeup effects first got graphic on a large scale, but they are no longer. Familiarity breeds mockery. The Frankenstein monster that terrified audiences in the 1930s became the playfully innocuous Herman Munster and Frankenberry cereal by the 1960s. The grotesque, chainsaw-wielding Leatherface of the 1970s has given way to the winsome, chainsaw-wielding scream queens of horror magazines and websites. Although drenched in blood, these ladies are not scary, shocking, or offensive. They are sexually alluring pinups aimed at horror's majority male fan base. Zombies too are losing their bite, hence their displacement by zombie *comedies*. I expect the past decade's J-horror ghost girls are next in line to become playful objects of fun.

Emphasizing that TromaDance is not a horror festival ("most of the films we show are not horror"), Manjourides adds that "everyone has made a zombie movie. When it comes to horror, we like to see something new, not the same old hack and slash. We had a great film last year [2009] called *Lazer Ghosts*. It was really fun. The FX were perfect for it." Even so, he is not averse to blood and boobs. "I would love to see more *commitment* from the director. We get a lot of films that are high school level, low-budget, guy in the woods, etc. But no matter how low-budget—*commit* to the project. Don't show a sex scene if you can't get the girl naked. Don't show a death scene in the house if you can't splatter the walls." He would also "love to see more westerns."

Claw knows what it wants: "More *werewolf* films." Young and Gillette state, "We would like to see more *suspense*. We don't see enough of it. We don't want to get *to the point* in the film; we want to see the *creepiness behind it*. Filmmakers just jump to the conclusion. Watch Hitchcock to see how he goes about creating suspense." David Pike of the Arizona Underground Film Festival says, "We love films that push the boundaries of horror. We love horror cult films, fun B-movies, [and] smart, intelligent films that make audiences think."

Van Hauwaert says, "I like *The Horseman* (thriller/revenge) or *Saw 1* (offscreen horror) above *Saw 2–6* (an orgy of blood and horror) and all those body torture flicks. I don't have any problem with violence, sex, nudity, drugs, or blood onscreen. It adds a certain dimension to a film. But I don't like the stylish body horror, or the political correctness in movies these days. I'm quite conservative and love older flicks from the Seventies more than many younger films, because these films are honest, harsh, and cruel, in contradiction with films from the new millennium. In most cases, offscreen horror (what we hear and imagine going on) is more effective than a full blood-letting onscreen."

Like Ropp, I've seen a rise in comedic horror entries over the years. In my experience, darkly comedic gorefests—especially if energetic, demented, and over-the-top—play better before audiences than does quietly atmospheric horror. The loudest, most exuberant audience reactions at Tabloid Witch screenings have been to comedic horror shorts. I think it's harder for a filmmaker to excel doing a serious horror film (with slowly building suspense and a creepy atmosphere) than with an energetic, funny gorefest.

Even so, comedic horror is no sure-fire winner. It must actually be *funny*. (Duh!) Great comedic horror films thrill more audience members than does great serious horror. But crappy comedic horror is usually "so bad as to be unwatchable," whereas crappy serious horror often retains some redeeming entertainment value. (Ironically, crappy serious horror is usually funnier than crappy comedic horror.)

Bram laments horror's increasing use of comedy and gore. "Unfortunately, everyone has a camera these days, and they think making a horror flick would be fun. The result is a glut of horror comedies and spoofs, or films which just throw buckets of blood at you. My favorite horror films are *The Omen*, *The Shining*, *Rosemary's Baby*, *The Blair Witch Project*, and *Jaws*. There are funny moments in some of these, but there's nothing funny about what is going on in these films. Horror is in danger of becoming a joke. I don't want to see that."

Morgret sees another pitfall to cheap cameras. "Great low-budget films are coming to the festivals. The tools are cheap and readily available. The problem I see is the first-person film. The *Blair Witch effect*, if you will. Too many films are people on a road trip, holding the camera the whole time. This can lead to good films, but it is often lazy filmmaking." Manjourides agrees. "The major problem in indie films right now is that everyone can make a movie, and not everyone should. Most of the movies we see are terrible. Video requires no craft or training." Regarding Morgret's *Blair Witch effect*, Amaral confirms that "movies like *REC* and *Paranormal Activity* have created a trend. Handycams and ghosts are in many movies we've received these years. But the trend depends on the region. Films from the USA are more *REC*'s style. Mockumentaries and black comedies." He adds that while Brazil continues to churn out zombies, European entries are dominated by torture films.

Carney and Beesley-Brown also see torture films as still thriving. "Zombie films will always be popular, but seem to have increased in numbers over the past few years, as have torture films. We don't have a strong preference for themes within the genre, but we are inclined to select films that are creative and re-imagine common themes in a new way, rather than rehashing the same old story."

Speaking for the Tabloid Witch, I'd love to see more creepy, *X-Files* type, horror/sci-fi, particularly grays and alien abductions. Not enough of them around. I'm also a sucker for supernatural horror. Witches, Satanists, and ghosts are all good. Original takes on the paranormal (e.g., the *Final Destination* series) are especially welcome. But vampires are like zombies. A tired subgenre. You'd best either have a fresh take, or if it's the same old, then do it exceptionally well. Ditto slashers.

Bailey agrees. "I'd like to see more supernatural horror films that have the ability to scare, rather than the traditional slasher-type horror, which has really run out of new ideas."

As I write this, *The Twilight Saga: Eclipse* is raking in money. I predict every festival will soon be deluged with vampire romances. Not my favorite subgenre, although I love *Blood and Roses* (1960) and *Bram Stoker's Dracula* (1992). But tastes vary, so if your film loses at one festival, it may yet win at another. I'm eager for more good, Japanese style ghost stories, but Engelhardt says, "Please, no more 'scary' ghost movies with little girls with long hairs in tubes."

Nor does Engelhardt see a zombie glut in Germany. Weekend of Fear's submissions vary in subgenre from year to year. "One year, every second movie has zombies in it. The next year, you find a lot of vampires." He has noticed a *technical* trend. "The gore effects get better and better, especially in small independent films." Shriekfest's experience is similar. Gossett says, "Every year there seems to be a theme in the submissions. Zombie films one year. Werewolves another year. We don't have a preference of types of horror films. We just want sharp ones." Likewise at the Halloween Monster Movie Challenge, where Jones and Webster say, "In 2009 we were lucky, as we had an array of different subgenres. Zombies, werewolves, vampires, ghosts, etc."

Do Audiences Influence Selections?

Festival directors and judges have their personal tastes, which may differ from that of audiences. How to balance the two? When selecting films for a festival, does one try and guess which films will be the crowd-pleasers? Or does one apply some personal aesthetic standard and hope to elevate the audience's taste? Is the festival director a cigar-chomping hack in a Hawaiian shirt, giving the public whatever it wants?—or a snotty critic with a European accent, honoring films the public *should* want? William Castle or Dieter Dieter?

If the festival sells tickets (as most do), programming crowd-pleasers is an important criterion. That may mean accepting films which the festival director doesn't much like. Or it may mean accepting a crappy film that has some stars attached. Then the star will more likely attend your festival, and you'll sell more tickets.

Who selects the films varies. Small festivals may be run entirely by one or two decision-makers. Shannon Lark and Heidi Martinuzzi are the sole judges at Viscera. Large festivals may have a panel of celebrity judges (or jurors) to determine the official selections and/or award winners. The festival director may, or may not, sit on that jury. If not, then there is some "separation of powers" between the festival director's personal tastes and which films get in. This is the case with the Halloween Monster Movie Challenge. As Jones and Webster explain it, "We do not judge ourselves. We approach outside filmmakers and scholars."

Ken Daniels says of Fright Night, "We have a two-step process. Not everyone that is exhibited will be in the running for awards. Three judges initially screen the films to see if they are acceptable or have some value. Maybe they are extremely funny or well written, but lack production values. We may show it at our cult hour times, after midnight, to give our fans fun films to watch. So yes, we do show some films we think our audience will like. The second stage is where we have another set of judges screen the finalists for the awards. They judge them on a 1–100 scale on various qualities: acting, writing, SPFX, editing, cinematography, etc. Winners are picked out of this second group of films. We also have our 'Cinema Showcase,' where the [festival] producer and key staff invite a film to be played because they believe it is worthy of getting more attention."

Engelhardt says, "Our selection committee consists of three persons, and every person has another taste. If one of us likes a film, we assume that (parts of) the audience will like it too. Sometimes you guess wrong. There can be a film all of us like, and the audience is not interested. And there can be a film that is only in the program because we have a free slot — and it wins the audience award! You cannot predict the audience's reaction." Gossett adds, "We have many judges that help with the selection process. There have been some films that have made it into the fest by judges' scores that weren't my top votes."

Morgret doesn't worry about his viewers' tastes. "It would hurt the festival if we tried to figure out what an audience would like. MIFFF strives to find films we hope people will like, but are films we do like." Foster agrees. "I look for quality filmmaking. Guessing what an audience may like is dropping quality in favor of a hopeless attempt to please others. That's the job of a studio marketing department, not a festival director." His judgment carries considerable weight at Dragon*Con. As he describes it, "We have a selection committee, which changes every year, made up of fans, people in the local film community, etc.— but I am the last word with selections. For awards, we have a jury, and is made up of myself and people with film credentials. In past years, the jury has either three or four members — usually four. Each member of the jury has an equal vote."

Foster doesn't try to guess viewers' tastes, but Screamin' Athens does. Orocklou says, "Our goal is to make the audience happy. To screen movies they won't watch anywhere else. We accept films we don't like, but the audience likes them. We try to have films of all horror genres, from horror trash, to mystery, gore, etc." She adds, "The market is not our main concern." However, since she is trying to please her audience, I think she means that Screamin' Athens is not concerned with how well a film performs outside the festival. A film's box office does not necessarily reflect the tastes of Screamin' Athens's audience.

Phillip Seib of the Nevermore Film Festival says, "We program to what we think our audience would like." That makes sense. Seib is Programming and Operations Manager for the Carolina Theatre of Durham, NC, which runs Nevermore. You'd expect a theater to heed the wishes of ticket buyers. As for Big Bear, Coulombe explains, "Official selections and awards are based on the scoring sheets from the festival judges. We try to create a program based on the taste of the audience. They are, after all, the festival patrons." Van Hauwaert agrees. "We do accept films we don't like, for sure! Often, films highly rewarded by audiences around the world turn out to be less than interesting. However, you have to fulfill the need of your clients/audiences."

Koestinger says of Morbido, "It's not a festival that shows only the movies we like. We prefer to show all kind of films and let the audience decide. That's why we have, until now, only the Audience Award. Next year, 2011, we will have a new award, given by all the guest directors presenting movies in the festival: the Directors Award." Claw likewise respects its audience, but is irreverent toward celebrities. "We only select great films that we feel will blow the audience away, regardless of budget, location, or star power. However, great does not mean a $10 million budget.

Who is to judge? At Big Bear Horror, Vincent Delacruz was a judge for the festival's Ultimate Horror Fan contest. Big Bear, California. October 2010. (Photograph Scott Brown.)

Proud daughter Andrea Cardona holds director Rene Cardona III's (center) Golden Sugar Skull Tribute Award. Producer Daniel Birman Ripstein is at right. Tlalpujahua, Michoacan, Mexico. October 2010. (Photograph courtesy Morbido Film Fest.)

We've had $100 films beat out star-driven films, because they were executed better and the story telling was stronger."

Amaral balances his tastes with that of audiences. "Even if we don't like something, maybe the story or the style, we look for the *significance* of the film in the horror genre. The audience is very important. We care about what they like, but this is only one of the things we care about when we select films. One of the functions of a film festival is to show new things to the audience. Something they wouldn't watch usually." Or to repeat Ropp: "As a film festival president, one of my jobs is to expose people to the alternatives."

Carney and Beesley-Brown concur. "When considering films for our competition, we take into consideration what our audience will enjoy and appreciate, but overall, our programmers are looking for films that are the highest quality, and embrace the genre in a way that is innovative and creative. We pick films that are a good balance between our vision of what the festival embodies, and that play well with our audience."

Ropp likewise balances the personal and popular. He seeks original and outstanding films, but also, "I try to keep a finger on the pulse of our audiences, most of whom demand that their horror be a more unique and original experience than what they're used to seeing at the local cineplex. My dream festival would be a celebration of old classic horror and science fiction films prior to 1980. My tastes lie more with Bela Lugosi and Boris Karloff than with the typical dead teenager films of today. [Yet] my own tastes have never dictated what films are shown. We have screened films that I didn't particularly like, but which our judges selected as being worthy. I've hand-picked films which were fiercely original, though they may not have been my cup of tea. We've even had some directors thank us for 'having the balls' to screen their controversial films and/or for showcasing their more somber, more cerebral offerings, which are usually ignored by other festivals."

Other festival directors see no conflict between the personal and the popular, because they believe their tastes reflect that of their audiences. Bram says, "I choose films that satisfy *me* because I think audiences have the same basic desires for horror films. Original ideas, realistic acting, professional level craftsmanship. The film should scare me, or at least have me feeling uneasy or tense." Nevitt agrees. "I've been a horror festivalgoer for over ten years, and a fan since childhood. When it comes to selecting films for our festival, I put myself in that mindset. It was my goal with Celluloid Screams to create an event that I'd want to go to as a fan." His philosophy is echoed by his fellow Brit, Abertoir's Bailey. "Our audiences are hardened horror fans (much like ourselves), so we treat them with the same respect that we do ourselves in terms of what gets shown or not. We don't mind [a low] budget, but we are looking for talent."

How Screenings Hinder Awards

Film festivals are about film *screenings*. Awards are about *honoring the best*. A conflict exists between screenings and awards. Generally, audiences want entertainment, whereas critics seek to discover artistically superior work. A film's entertainment value may factor into a critic's aesthetic judgment, but it's only one factor. If that sounds snobby, so be it.

The Tabloid Witch was intended to be an award, not a film festival. I'm sometimes tempted to ditch the screenings entirely because they hinder the award's artistic purity. (Yes, very snobby indeed.) But I have discovered to my regret that many filmmakers are primarily excited about the prospect of a screening. Screenings mean more to them than "the honor of winning," or promotion in the *Hollywood Investigator*, or even a pretty plaque. Sure, if I gave them an Oscar, they wouldn't care about their film not being screened, but the Tabloid Witch is not Oscar. No horror film festival's trophy is.

The Tabloid Witch too benefits from its screenings. The prize of a screening increases the number of entries, and thus the number of quality films, and thus the award's prestige. (Yes, screenings also increase the number of crappy entries.) Also, I enjoy meeting the filmmakers, some of whom have become friends. And so I continue to offer screenings, albeit with mixed feelings.

How do public screenings hinder the "artistic purity" of an award?

One year I received a film that starred an extraordinary actress. Her performance in the role of a conflicted and complex character was poignant, nuanced, and emotionally multi-layered. She deserved to win Best Actress. Alas, the film was an ugly, mean-spirited, sordid piece of crap. A torture film, featuring a mostly inept supporting cast, and mediocre-to-low production values. I felt dirty watching it.

Had the prize not included a public screening, I would have honored this actress with an award. But then I would have had to screen this crappy film. One crappy film can spark walkouts by disgusted viewers ("How did this piece of shit ever win an award?"), and leave the next film without an audience. When there are screenings to consider, every film must be reasonably entertaining. Every film must keep audiences glued to their seats for the next film.

Should I have awarded this actress, but not screened the film? Imagine my conversation with the director.

"Congratulations," I say. "Your film won for Best Actress."
"Great!" he screams with joy. "When is the screening?"
"Well ... we won't actually be screening your film."
"Huh? What do you mean? I thought the prize included a free screening!"
"Yeeessss. But you see, although your actress was excellent — great casting, by the way! — your film's overall aesthetic quality, that is to say, I don't feel that it resonates artistically in a way that meets those specific criteria by which I would feel comfortable presenting it to the viewing public."
"What do you mean? I don't know what that means."
"I mean ... your film sucks."

Kinda takes the joy out of winning. What director would brag about an award given by someone who said that his film sucked too much to be screened alongside the other winners? As for the actress, how would she feel? Imagine a teacher announcing in class that everyone failed the test, but then adds, "However, I know my test wasn't unreasonably difficult, because while *all the rest of you* got an F, *one person* here got an A+. Congratulations, Mary!"

Imagine how Mary feels, the entire class glaring at her. Probably wishes she'd failed too.

No, the actress's name is not Mary.

And so another talented actress won Best Actress that year. The crappy film won nothing. No, I won't tell you its title. I don't mention losing films, because the Tabloid Witch's goal is to highlight the best, not embarrass the rest. Besides, not all losing films are crappy. Some are quite good, just not as good as the winners. Had no talented actresses been entered that year, I would not have presented that award category.

This problem is not unique to the Tabloid Witch. It hinders every festival. I'll repeat what Gaz Bailey of the Abertoir Horror Festival said: "There have been countless times when an awful script or poor sound mixing have resulted in a film not being selected when the acting or photography is superb. It makes us feel terrible as a selection committee by turning them down, and equally bad for the individuals who have put so much effort into their work."

I wonder. When I read those lists of award winners, how many talented names are missing because their superb work was wasted on a crappy film that never got past a selection committee? Bailey says, "countless times." I doubt that Abertoir is alone in rejecting films that excel in some areas but fail miserably in others. Festivals are about screenings. This means the films must entertain an audience. This is especially true when the audience *pays* for its tickets. Nobody wants to spend money on crap.

Remember our previous tip: *Film is collaborative; surround yourself with talented people.* The Tabloid Witch *wants* to honor the best person. Abertoir "feels terrible" in rejecting superb artists. But screenings are a gun to the head of festival directors, compelling them to consider the audience. Even festival directors who *say* they don't consider the audience probably do to some extent. Nobody screens a film that bores or sickens them, or has an inaudible soundtrack, just because one person working on it was superb.

But while this problem is not unique to the Tabloid Witch, an award (unlike a festival) is especially obligated to resist market pressure. Horror is not just mass entertainment. Horror is an art form. This is true, no matter how snobby it sounds.

For both filmmakers and festival directors, resisting market pressure is easier done with short films than with features. Audiences are less likely to walk out on a difficult or just plain bad film if it doesn't last too long. The longer the film, the more it tries viewers' patience. The crappy torture film with the extraordinary actress was a feature. Had it been a short, I might have presented her with Best Actress and screened the damn thing. The director need never know that I hated his work.

The Tabloid Witch has taken creative risks by honoring "outside the box" horror shorts; films that hardcore horror audiences may not expect to find at a horror festival. In 2007, I presented an Honorable Mention to Shawna Baca's *3:52*, a short film about a Native American girl's struggles with past childhood abuse, alcoholism, and suicide. Was it horror? Vaguely. Two Native American spirits struggled over the girl's soul, but that was less scary than metaphorical. Baca doesn't see *3:52* as horror. She calls her work "magical realism." Close enough for a Tabloid Witch.

In 2008, I introduced the Best Avant-Garde Horror Short Film category specifically for these sorts of "borderline horror" films. That year it went to underground filmmaker Damon Packard's *Chemtrails: An Investigative Report*, a politically satirical mocumentary with hilarious gore scenes, monstrous images, and sci-fi conspiratorial creepiness. In 2009, the award went to Rory Leydier and Deborah Bento's *Bad Friday*, a mixed media film (animation and video, color and black & white) about a woman's return to her past to rectify the harm caused by her attempted suicide. The film's experimental editing requires careful and repeated viewing before one understands its story.

There's room in horror for difficult, experimental works with personal or political messages. But horror audiences come mostly for scary bloodbaths and hilarious gorefests, not PBS, so it's best to keep the avant-garde to a minimum. Short films, not too many, and spaced apart by traditional crowd-pleasers.

The *time constraints* inherent in screenings likewise hinder award selections. When I select the winning films, I must keep in mind how much time the venue has offered that year. If I'm granted six hours, that usually means that two features and a block of shorts can win that year. I can't honor three features, because then one of them couldn't screen. Again, imagine the conversation.

"Good news," I say. "Your film won an Honorable Mention."
"Great!" the director screams. "When is the screening?"
"Well ... your film won't be screening."

"What do you mean? I won, didn't I?"
"Yeeessss. But I only have time to screen two features, and the other two are better than yours. But you still won!"
"What did I win?"
"The honor of having won."
"What a gyp!"

Time constraints are not unique to the Tabloid Witch. All festivals reject worthy films (they say), because the competition for screening slots is so great. But an award (unlike a festival) should not be constrained by time. Oscar distributes a barrelful of trophies every year, unconstrained by having to screen anything. Ditto the Emmys, Grammys, and Saturns. These "pure awards" enjoy the freedom to honor however many recipients they please.

Still, while the constraints imposed by festival screenings are troublesome, they are not unduly onerous. (1) Instances in which a remarkably talented person works on an execrable film are rare. Generally, like attracts like. (2) Time limitations mean that only the best of the best win anything. Good films must be rejected, as there's only room for excellent films. That's not entirely bad for an award. If good is not good enough, then the award becomes that much more competitive, and thus more prestigious and coveted.

This rule holds true for all festivals and awards: *Because of the limited number of screening slots and awards, it's not just how good your film is, but how good the competition is that year.* One year I was deluged with comedy shorts, making Best Comedic Horror Short Film a tough call. Some worthy contenders didn't even get Honorable Mention. The following year, entries in that category were so few and poor, I wasn't going to present the award. Then a great horror short comedy arrived a few days past deadline, winning the award. (Yes, I can ignore deadlines. I have that power.[1]) Had that film arrived the previous year, it might not even have won an Honorable Mention.

Conflicts of Interest in Selections and Awards

One nice thing about running a film festival is that you can screen your own films, and that of friends ... *wait a minute?!*

Screen *your own* films? *Friends'* films? Isn't that a conflict of interest?

As I observed in the previous chapter, many festival directors work, or aspire to work, as film directors, writers, actors, DPs, or in whatnot other film industry jobs. It's only natural that they would hope to utilize their festivals' networking and screening opportunities to advance their own careers. Hollywood abounds with hyphenates. There are writer-directors, director-producers, producer-actors, actor-waiters. Why not festival director-filmmakers?

It's unrealistic to expect people who pursue industry work to put aside their aspirations while running a festival, but they should adhere to some code of ethics.

Any film I'm connected with is *disqualified* for a Tabloid Witch Award. But while the awards are sacred, the screenings are not. If I have the screening time available, I may slip in a "special screening" of a film that hasn't won a Tabloid Witch. In 2007, I screened *It's My Birthday* because I'd agreed to screen a Viscera Festival film. In 2008, I screened *The Ancient Law* because I had an acting role in it. In 2009, I screened *Last Call* because it was shot by a friend.[2]

"Since we're friends, I wouldn't ask you to consider *Last Call* for an award," Eddie had said. "That would be crossing the line."

Every festival director must decide where that line is. Because there is no entry fee, and the awards remain untainted, I have no problem with an occasional special screening. *Festival* festivals typically screen many "official selections," then announce a few winners. The Tabloid Witch *first* announces the winners, *then* screens them, weeks later, with maybe *one* special screening. Most years there haven't been any special screenings. Only in 2009 was there more than one.

Shriekfest charges entry fees, and its official selections are eligible for awards, so festival director/actress Denise Gossett takes a more hands-off approach. "If I'm in the film, it has to be selected by every judge, not me. There are several [films] every year submitted with me in them, and only one has ever made it in." And even then, Gossett did not win the acting award. "It's tough. I want to be fair, so I stay out of it all together."

Michael Coulombe, who runs the Big Bear Horror Film Festival, works as a script supervisor. Like Gossett, he takes a hands-off approach to his festival's selections and winners. "All films are viewed by the judging committee. All movies in the competition are picked based on the judges' scores. The process is completely fair and removed from both myself and my team. This was done to ensure that there would be no conflict of interest."

BleedFest and Viscera have both screened works created by the filmmaker/actresses who run those events. Viscera has two festival director/judges: Shannon Lark and Heidi Martinuzzi. When Martinuzzi's *Wretched* won for Best Cinematography in 2010 (the trophy went to the DP, Jessica Gallant), Lark announced to the theater crowd that Martinuzzi played no role in deciding that particular award; Lark alone decided to award Gallant.

Should *Wretched* have been disqualified from award consideration? Would that have been fair to Gallant? Either way, credit Lark for publicly addressing the issue.

The Drunken Zombie Film Festival presents no awards; the only potential conflicts of interest are in its selections. When festival director/filmmaker Bryan Wolford wanted to screen his short film, *Shadows*, he consulted his co-festival directors. "I run the festival with three other guys. I mentioned that it would be done beforehand, and asked the others about screening it. They were cool with it. So that was easy. We had filmmakers submit films to this year's [2010] festival that we were already friends with, and turned down for one reason or another. We try to be as objective as possible."

Like the Tabloid Witch and Viscera, Drunken Zombie charges no entry fee, which mitigates any unfairness of a festival director screening his or her own works. "We started this festival out of jealousy," says Wolford. "We're a horror podcast, first and foremost. Listening to other horror podcasts, we'd hear about all these people going to film festivals. We were so sad that our home town of Peoria, Illinois, didn't have a horror film festival. I mean, 'If it plays in Peoria....' We figured if we were going to have something like that here, we were going to have to start it."

If you're a filmmaker, and you're beginning to think that horror festivals sound a little too cozy and inbred, here's a *solution*: Start your own festival. *Everybody's* doing it!

Opportunities for self-promotion go beyond screening your own works — often without conflict of interest problems. For instance, running a festival allows you to *network with potential employers*. Actors and writers normally pursue directors and producers. Directors and producers pursue financiers and distributors. But if you run a film festival, suddenly, everyone is banging on *your* door.

I've never sold a script to a Tabloid Witch Award winning filmmaker, but I have been cast in a film by one. Again, I have a code of ethics. *After* I announce the award winners, I sometimes offer my headshot or screenplay to winning filmmakers. *Never* before the awards are announced. It's sleazy to tell an entrant, "I haven't decided about your film yet, but I understand you're casting your next project, so, if you'd like to see my headshot...?"

Similarly, Coulombe founded his film festival partially to boost his own career. "When Jamie and I started the festival, the economy was bad and the U.S. was in a recession. Work in the industry was slow. It [the festival] was a way for us to help the industry, as well as local business in Big Bear, as well as *introduce ourselves to others in the industry*. It helps *us* find work, as well as those involved, and those that attend. It is definitely a great resource." My emphasis.

Wolford too enjoys the networking opportunities that come from running a festival. "It's nice to know other filmmakers for bouncing ideas off of, and asking advice from."

Networking at Morbido helped festival director Pablo Guisa Koestinger's producing career. "In the 2008 edition, I got to know Argentine director Adrián García Bogliano. We spoke about a possible co-production." They later corroborated on *Masacre esta noche* (A.K.A. *Massacre, Tonight*). Bogliano was a co-director/co-writer on that film. Koestinger served as a co-executive producer. And since Morbido birthed the film, it was only natural that Morbido promote it. "In the 2009 edition, we made the world premier of this movie," says Koestinger. "Morbido is always looking for projects to help, in any way we can."

Morbido boosted Koestinger's producing career, but didn't start it. He had previous credits, including *Saori* (executive producer, 2006), *Free Tibet* (assistant producer, 2005), and *Aire* (associate producer, 2005).

Shriekfest aggressively promotes its participants long after their screenings and awards. Gossett distributes a monthly e-newsletter (with sponsorship ads) promoting participants' current projects (and, occasionally, her own).[3] According to Gossett, her e-newsletter goes to over 5,000 recipients, including filmmakers, fans, screenwriters, agents, and press. "We get a lot of compliments on it and people requesting to be interviewed. Other press sites request to reprint portions too."

Shriekfest also sponsors monthly networking socials, usually in some eatery or nightclub in the Hollywood area. You needn't have submitted anything to Shriekfest. The socials are geared to the Los Angeles horror filmmaking community but *anyone can come!* "We average 50–60 [people] a month," says Gossett, "sometimes way more. They are a lot of fun. We mingle without the pretentiousness of some other networking events in Hollywood.[4] Tons of positive results. People are planning their projects together, and casting and hiring from these events." A great place for anyone to network (including Gossett).

Screamfest L.A. boosted festival director Rachel Belofsky's filmmaking career. Five years after co-founding her festival, she produced and co-wrote *Going to Pieces: The Rise and Fall of the Slasher Film* (2006).[5] This documentary interviews prominent horror film directors and actors, many of whom Belofsky doubtless met, directly or indirectly, through her festival.[6] Certainly, running Los Angeles's largest horror film festival gives Belofsky the credibility to have her calls returned.

Other festival director/filmmakers include Eric Morgret (Maelstrom International), Alex Bram (Carnival of Darkness), and Shade Rupe (Deep Red International). Deep Red first screened in 2009, then announced plans for 2010 which never materialized. On September 22, 2010, I asked Rupe if Deep Red will continue. He replied, "It could. I've gotten extraordinarily busy. I was at Cannes and Toronto this year. I wrote a 3-D horror film, and I'm working on this new film with Harvey Keitel. I do talk about [Deep Red], and it will most likely happen again. I just can't say when yet."

That's one filmmaker who, for the time being at least, doesn't need to network.

Every festival offers networking opportunities. Can the prospect of such opportunities give rise to conflicts of interest? I can imagine one scenario. If a powerful studio executive (or producer, director, celebrity) submits a crappy film, I suppose a festival director may be tempted to screen it, solely to meet the power brokers behind it.

It's a possibility, but I don't think it's a major concern. 1. *Every* talented filmmaker is a potential future Peter Jackson (i.e., a potential future employer). If a festival director wants to meet talented filmmakers, and thus screens talented filmmakers, well, that's what the festival should be doing anyway. 2. Festivals may screen films directed by or starring celebrities, not because the film is good, but because celebrities have fans (i.e., ticket buyers). That's a legitimate reason to screen a celebrity film, if not a reason to award it. I don't endorse screening celebrity crap, but I can't condemn festivals who cater to public tastes. 3. A-list celebrities are unimpressed by most events or awards. Unless you have an A-list event (e.g., Sundance, the Oscars), it's pointless to select or award an A-list celebrity's film *solely* to tempt them to come. Select or award their films if it's deserved. If not, then not.[7]

Some festival directors aspire to add "consultant" to their hyphenated job titles. Several told me that they were available for hire as "film festival consultants," ready to help *you* establish or grow *your* film festival! I won't give their names, because I'm sure that *every* festival director is available for paid, professional consulting work. Most artists (filmmakers, writers, actors, musicians, etc.) are available for *paid* consulting or teaching work. So if you're looking to *hire* a film festival consultant, pick whoever you like. If you want *free* advice, pick whoever will return your call.

Submission Materials

When submitting a film, naturally, you should follow the festival's rules. But provided the festival doesn't say otherwise, are there any materials that can, if placed in the submission package, induce a festival to accept your film?

Most filmmakers submitting to the Tabloid Witch only send a DVD, and perhaps a letter or business card. But some filmmakers send elaborate and expensive submission packages, tossing in promotional t-shirts, posters, pop-up displays, spooky toys and merchandising tie-ins (e.g., a peace sign medallion for a film set at an evil commune), and heavy binders containing actors' headshots, slides from the film, a budget breakdown, the film's festival history to date, local newspaper stories and reviews, and bios of the entire cast and crew. Other filmmakers include some of this material on DVD press kits. Still others, just to play it safe, will submit everything in *both* paper and electronic formats.

It's not necessary. None of it sways me. The t-shirts are nice, but don't improve your odds. And if you win, I'll interview you myself. I prefer to ask my own questions, so that the *Hollywood Investigator* will contain original material, and not the same talking points that you've mailed to other publications. If I did want to research a film before deciding anything, I can usually find loads of information about it on IMDb and the film's website, MySpace page, etc. No need to include all that press material. Robert Nevitt agrees. "In terms of submissions, the one recommendation I'd make is for filmmakers not to send full, printed press kits. The film should (initially) speak for itself. A professionally presented DVD screener is all we need. Any info about past screenings or awards can be included on the DVD sleeve."

Reading about your past awards on a DVD's sleeve may raise my hopes, but not your chances. I didn't start the Tabloid Witch to rubber stamp others' opinions. And because it's an award rather than a festival, its primary goal is not to please audiences, but to recognize talent. Or even better, to discover talent. While I don't hold previous wins against a film, when faced with two films of *equal* merit, I'm inclined to favor the more obscure film. To recognize the unrecognized. Discovering unknown talent is one of the joys of presenting an award.

I also prefer to use my own screen captures of a film, rather than whatever images are included in a press kit. The reason, once again, is so the images in the *Hollywood Investigator* are not the same as those which appear in other publications. Although that's changing. I'm increasingly using YouTube clips to illustrate articles.

YouTube clips of a film's trailer, scenes from the film, and/or "making of" interviews are important promotional tools. Or if not YouTube, then some other site that allows for *easy embeds*. If you want your clips to "go viral," it's important that film review websites and blogs can easily embed them. It also helps if your clips are entertaining and intriguing, leaving viewers excited but unsatisfied; wanting to see more.

Matthias Engelhardt says, "The best marketing is *the film itself*. If you have a great poster, a great title, etc., but the film is garbage, we will not screen it." Matt Manjourides adds, "Make a good movie. That's the most important thing. You can send a good movie in a Ziploc bag, and it will get in."

He's right. In 2006, I received a copy of *Zombie Island*, its DVD box wrapped in a brown paper bag, bearing a hand-written title. Writer/director William Whirity later told me the film was newly finished, and there was no time to create a nice poster for the DVD box before the Tabloid Witch's deadline. *Zombie Island* is a beautifully stylized, energetic, and entertaining short film (and I'm generally sick of zombies) that deserved its Honorable Mention. Conversely, I've gotten beautifully packaged films that were crap.

An awful lot of crappy films have visually resplendent opening title sequences, set to gorgeous music soundtracks. These opening titles enthrall me, raise my hopes and expectations — and then there follows an inept camcorder film starring amateur "actors."

I have a theory. These filmmakers did not create their films' title sequences. There must be production companies that will create opening titles for any film, for a fee. Some filmmakers contract out the creation of the poster art; others contract out production of the title sequence. I've seen lots of alluring posters and stunning title sequences attached to amateurish home movies.

Never judge a film by its cover art. Nor by its opening title sequence.

Tip: *It's not a good idea to have a title sequence that's overly superior to the film*. The contrast makes the film look that much shabbier. Imagine showing a superb crystal sculpture of a soaring eagle to an audience, followed by a misshapen lump of clay that's supposed to be ... a three-legged cat? Well, maybe the clay cat-thing wouldn't look *that* bad if the image of the crystal eagle wasn't still lodged our memories.

Unlike most festival directors I spoke to, Patrick Van Hauwaert likes elaborate submission packages. "If you don't have a neat package, DVD cover, or promotional art, that's okay. Send it without. But if you have something worthwhile, *use* it. We receive about 150 films over a short period of four months. We have to choose where to start. Tell me in four lines something that makes me want to watch your film *now*. Not tomorrow, not next week, but *now*. Those who present their films well attract our attention."

And *include your contact information*. Van Hauwaert explains: "Over the years, we found many filmmakers sending large packets with t-shirts, promotional material, posters. But *they neglected to fill out a simple contact form!* Please keep sending me t-shirts and films, but don't forget to introduce yourself."

In 2009 a creepy little film won a Tabloid Witch Award, but the filmmaker had not included a phone number or email address. I mentioned this when announcing the winners on the *Hollywood Investigator*. Fortunately, the filmmaker read it and quickly responded.

I prefer that all contact information be professionally printed (by a machine) on the DVD itself. Many filmmakers hand-write their contact info on the DVD, and that's okay too. Others include the information on the DVD box, or in a letter, or a business card. Just don't forget to include it *somewhere*.

I don't require promotional material, but I would like filmmakers to include their films' *credits list*, naming everyone who worked on the film and their job functions. Festivals differ as to award categories. Directors and actors are commonly honored. The Tabloid Witch also has a Best Sound award. Sound is important. Which is why I'm amazed at the many films (short films, especially) that don't list sound credits. *Somebody* must have recorded, mixed, and edited the sound—but not according to the film's end credits roll.

Sure, I can ask the filmmaker. *Who did your sound?* Sometimes I've done so. But I don't like to, because it's a tip-off that the film is being considered for Best Sound.

One year I couldn't decide on Best Sound. I'd narrowed the choice to two films, repeatedly replaying them while listening carefully to their soundtracks. It was a tough choice. But then I saw that one film listed no sound credits. That was the tie-breaker. I awarded the other film. Why not? The director knew, better than I did, how his film's sound was created. If he didn't think his sound person deserved recognition, who was I to second guess?

Van Hauwaert echoes one of my pet peeves when he says, "Don't *beg* in a letter how important it is to see your film screened."

Yes, indeed. Do not beg. And do not apologize for your film. Not even implicitly. It's bad form for filmmakers to make excuses, or seek sympathy by going on about how little money there was, and how hard everyone worked, and how cold or hot or rainy it was on location, and what a "hardcore horror fan" they are, and how they hope the festival will understand, and view their film "in the proper spirit." *Hint, hint, I know it sucks, but please have mercy!*

I dislike letters of introduction that sound like letters of apology, implying that a festival should overlook a film's flaws because of all the hardships it suffered in getting made. Most filmmakers, especially low-budget indie filmmakers, suffer hardships. There's nothing special about your pains. A letter of apology warns me that the film I am about to see is no good. Letters that boast of past awards raise my expectations. Letters of apology lower them. Neither affects my judgment. Every film is judged on its merits. There is no point in begging to be judged by a lower standard.

After your film is selected, and you're being interviewed for publication, or are discussing your work before an audience, *then* it's perfectly fine to relate your hardships. Readers and filmgoers love to hear filmmakers' war stories. At this point, you're not a beggar displaying your sores. You're a victorious general explaining your brilliant campaign.

Engelhardt offers another tip. "Important is a screener DVD that works. We often get burned CDs/DVDs that do not run in our DVD players, or have poor picture quality. We wanna have fun, too, when we watch the movies filmmakers send us!"

Good point. The Tabloid Witch receives many low-budget films whose DVDs were apparently home-burned off a laptop. Their quality is often inferior to DVDs manufactured by a professional production house. Home-burned DVDs will more likely skip and/or freeze in a dedicated DVD player. When that happens, I try the DVD on my laptop. Computers generally have higher quality DVD players, and can sometimes play DVDs that dedicated players cannot. Yet a few DVDs even freeze in my laptop.

Tip: *If you burn a DVD on your computer, test to see how it plays on a dedicated DVD player, not on a computer.* If possible, test it on several DVD players. DVDs that only play well on a computer do not make for a professional submission.

Only submit *recently* home-burned DVDs. Filmmaker Ray Castile says, "Some home-burned DVDs start developing playback problems after a year or so." You don't want to submit a DVD that plays fine before a festival's selection committee, only to have it crap out before the audience. Yes, I've seen it happen.

Why are professionally manufactured DVDs more reliable than home-burned DVDs? According to James Grimmelmann:

> There are two ways to make readable DVDs, and they use completely different technology. The large-scale industrial method is to "press" the DVD: that involves encoding the data as a series of tiny three-dimensional bumps on a mold used to stamp a corresponding pattern of pits into metal blanks, which are then encased in a layer of lacquer to make DVDs. This process, as you might imagine, has high fixed costs; the equipment alone will run you upwards of a million dollars. In contrast, the home method is to "burn" the DVD. Here, the blank disc comes from the factory pre-lacquered and containing an optically sensitive dye on the surface of the metal. Focus the right kind of laser on the dye and its transparency changes. From the perspective of the DVD player that will later read the disc's patterns of opaque and transparent regions, the results are much the same as if the disc had pits and non-pits. Some areas reflect; others don't. Ones and zeroes, more or less.[8]

If a DVD submitted to the Tabloid Witch freezes, and I haven't seen enough of the film to form an opinion, or if it looks promising, I'll ask the filmmaker for a better copy. Some home-burned DVDs play better than others, even if burned by the same computer. But if what I've seen so far does not look promising, I won't request a replacement DVD. I'll never learn if the film gets any better.

A few poorly burned DVDs have gone on to win, once I saw the film in its entirety. Still, it's annoying to see part of a film, then have to wait to see the rest.

I wonder how many festival staffers don't bother to request a clean copy of a DVD that freezes partway? I wonder how many *fee-charging* festivals don't bother to do so? I wonder how much money *you've* wasted by submitting poorly burned DVDs that nobody could see, or be bothered to ask for a replacement? Now there's a spooky thought!

Regarding DVDs, Van Hauwaert advises, "Do not hesitate to

They're filmmakers (*The Commune: A New Cult Classic*), festival co-founders (BleedFest), and sisters: Brenda and Elisabeth Fies. Los Angeles. December 2010. (Photograph courtesy BleedFest.)

put a watermark on it. We do understand the reasons. But please don't fill the screen with a watermark. Don't put a watermark above the subtitles."

I dislike watermarks, but I can live with a small mark in the screen's corner. Or an occasional scroll across the bottom of the screen (not really a watermark) every 20 or 30 minutes, reminding me that this DVD is the property of so-and-so, and is not for resale, and not to steal it.

But Van Hauwaert is right. Some watermarks are unreasonably annoying. One year I received two feature films with a huge watermark spread across the entire screen, and which remained onscreen throughout the length of the film. Such watermarks "take me out of the story." They make it difficult to discern onscreen objects that match the watermark's color, and hinder my overall viewing experience.

There is a better way. As a voting member of the Screen Actors Guild Awards and Independent Spirit Awards, I've gotten screener DVDs from the big studios. Some of these DVDs come with warnings that the DVD is *encrypted with a unique code*, and that *the studio knows who was mailed which code*. If the DVD, or any copies struck from it, are found for sale anywhere on the planet, the studios can trace back the pirated DVDs to their original recipient.

Some nice things about encrypted DVDs are that (1) they don't mar the film with unsightly watermarks, and (2) they're more secure. The chance of getting caught should deter some recipients from selling or copying encrypted DVDs. By contrast, watermarks won't stop pirates. Crappy copies, especially in certain parts of the world, still have some market value.

The bad thing about encrypted copy protection, for filmmakers, is that it's more expensive than watermarking. I haven't checked. Just a hunch.

It's not either/or. Some studio screener DVDs come with encrypted codes, and watermarks, and additional warnings about how the FBI will arrest, waterboard, and kill you if you so much as lend your DVD to anyone. I've received DVDs that warned me to destroy the disc after viewing it (as in *Mission Impossible*). Just in case, I suppose, the DVD was ever stolen from me, making me criminally liable if it resurfaced on the market. (No, I am not joking. Several screener DVDs I received in 2009 did indeed advise me to cut up the DVD immediately after viewing it.)

Despite all the fuss, there may be no foolproof copy protection technology. Google and you'll find many websites hawking programs that claim to remove watermarks and "rip" any DVDs out there. I don't know which programs work. I'm sure the pirates do.

Low-budget indie filmmakers struggling for recognition on the festival circuit shouldn't worry about piracy. Pirates steal what's popular, not what's available. As novelist Cory Doctorow said about eBooks, "I really feel like my problem isn't piracy. It's obscurity."

Filmmakers should be aware of TV/DVD region codes and submit appropriately. North America and Japan use NTSC. The United Kingdom and Australia use PAL. France and Russia use Secam. Other nations also use one or another of those three codes. Before submitting, check if the festival requires screener DVDs of a particular region code. Some filmmakers erroneously assume that festival venues can screen DVDs of any code. My DVD player is region-free, so yes, I can. But one year a winning filmmaker could only provide a PAL DVD to the Tabloid Witch Awards, and neither Loscon nor the Santa Monica Public Library were able to screen it.

Abertoir's Gaz Bailey adds, "We will never turn down a film based on supplied format. The selection for getting screened is 100 percent down to the film itself."

Filmmakers should also be aware of language barriers. The Tabloid Witch requires that all submitted films play in English, or be dubbed or subtitled in English, or have so few spoken foreign words that an English-speaking audience can still understand the film. Likewise for Morbido, Koestinger says, "Since we are in Mexico, and we have lots of guests and media from Latin America, having the trailer and movie with Spanish subtitles is a must."

If you're submitting to a foreign festival, pay attention to their language requirements. Americans have a reputation for assuming that everyone understands English. Yes, it's a widespread language throughout much of the world, but it's by no means universal.

Finally, a word about *submission deadlines*. I am amazed at the flood of submissions that arrive during the final weeks before the Tabloid Witch's deadline. Many filmmakers wait until the last minute to enter. Some offer excuses, especially if they worry that their films will arrive late. "I just now literally finished editing my film this morning before burning a copy to drop off at the post office this afternoon!"

I wonder, why do so many fee-charging festivals have *tiered* submission fees? A cheaper *early bird fee*, a pricier *standard fee*, and a really pricey *late fee*? Is it to discourage late submissions? Or to create a filmmaker-friendly image by offering a cheaper option, while knowing that many filmmakers, however broke, will submit late anyhow?

Filmmakers should naturally submit as early as possible — without compromising their film's quality. It may be wiser to let the deadline pass, and submit next year, if it means your film will be that much better. Some festivals let you *resubmit* the same film, year after year, provided you pay an entry fee each time.

A tip for filmmakers: *Save your money, and wait till your film is its best before submitting.*

And a tip for festival directors: *Leave plenty of time between the entry deadline and the screenings.* Cinefantasy's Vivi Amaral says, "I have realized that almost all the problems we had (subtitling, Custom House, 35mm copies delays, film's material for our website and catalogue) on last editions, we could have solved with *more time* between the end of the submission period and the event. So, we have enlarged this meantime from this edition on, and this is working."

My experience is similar to Amaral's. For 2011, I changed the Tabloid Witch Awards's entry deadline from September 30th to August 31st. This means I'll have a list of the winning films a month earlier. It's easier to promote film screenings if you know which films are to be screened.

3

WORKING THE FILM FESTIVAL!

The Zombie Short Film Festival's Jim Taylor observes that when winning filmmakers promote the festival, they promote themselves. "The best way for a filmmaker to maximize the promotional benefits of being in our festival is to *spread the word!* The more people that know about our festival, the more popular it's going to be."

Because the Tabloid Witch is a contest, not a festival, I don't regard the screenings as a big deal. The award is the thing. The screenings are just for fun. Many filmmakers disagree. For filmmakers and festivals alike, the screening is the thing.

Just to be chosen for a screening is an honor. It means your film is an *Official Selection*. To be a festival *Winner* is better, but being an official selection counts for something. It's *like* winning an award because it's *competitive*—and thus *impressive*. It's a consolation prize for films that didn't win an actual award. Look at all the DVD boxes plastered with laurel leaves logos bragging about being an Official Selection at Sundance. Or even an Official Selection at the Dogpatch Junction Slimy Fest. Never mind that the film failed to win their Putrid Pus Plaque.

Of course, just being an Official Selection at Sundance or Cannes is more impressive than actually *winning* the Pus Plaque. There is a hierarchy to festivals and awards, some more prestigious (and thus more competitive) than others. Celebrity filmmakers normally only enter the top festivals. For obscure filmmakers, the odds of winning are better at smaller fests. Yet all filmmakers enter for the same reasons: to promote their films and their careers.

Awards can lead to bigger and better things. Winning an award, or just being an official selection, validates your film and your talents. An objective third party (either a film-savvy judge or an audience of hardcore genre fans) has announced: "This film is good!" It may not guarantee that a distributor will pick up your film, or an agent will represent you, or investors will finance your next project—but it raises your film and résumé above the competition. Now that you've won, distributors, agents, and investors will actually *look* at your DVD before rejecting it.

The Eerie Horror Fest's Greg Ropp says, "A win at *any* festival is a feather in the cap of a filmmaker. The more wins, the less likely you are to be brushed off when you go talk to the big boys about distribution. A win, or even being selected for screening, shows a potential distributor that their target audience has 'approved' your project. That it has legs. The more wins the better, but I would guess that a win at an established festival, maybe one that's gone on for more than five years, means more than from one just starting out. That doesn't mean filmmakers should ignore the younger festivals. A win is a win. Sometimes it's easier to be selected, and even win, at those, than at the older, established ones, due to the smaller volume of films received."

Promoting at the Festival

Screenings aren't just about bragging rights. Attending a festival enables you to meet people who can advance your career. You might run into a big shot studio executive who can hire you. But don't dismiss fellow filmmakers who might collaborate with you on future projects. And don't disregard fans. Passionate genre fans blog about their favorite films, post on film sites (including IMDb), and can generate positive "buzz."

In 2005, the Tabloid Witch screened at Loscon. The producer of one winning film arrived, apparently expecting a red carpet event with a bevy of photographers. He was certainly well dressed. He peeked into the screening room at the LAX Marriott Hotel, saw the assembled film geeks and nerds, no celebrities or photographers in sight, and left, saying, "Sorry, this really isn't my scene." The film's director later apologized, explaining that his producer didn't understand the value of promoting to grassroots fans.

How *should* filmmakers promote their work at festivals? You've busted your bank account on your film and entry fees. Now that you're in, how to make the most of this brief window of opportunity? And it *will* be brief. Other festivals are coming up, showcasing other filmmakers. You won't be a "hot, new discovery" for long. Andy Warhol promised you fifteen minutes. Yes, you might get more — but only if you make the most of your first fifteen.

Have a marketing budget. Ropp says, "Each season I hear from filmmakers about how they have spent every last dime on their projects, but didn't leave anything for the promotion of it — including entering it into film festivals. Budgeting the project should be top priority. A large amount should be set aside for festival entries, websites, advertising, press kits, etc. This is lost on many filmmakers just starting out." Ken Daniels of the Fright Night Film Fest agrees. "Most filmmakers neglect a marketing budget of any kind. It would be foolish to do this."

Several times a year, filmmakers tell me how grateful they are that the Tabloid Witch doesn't charge entry fees, because they've spent all their money on making the film. I don't doubt they're low on funds. Even so, I'm sure I can squeeze a few extra pennies from them, were I so inclined. Filmmakers (like all artists generally) are notorious for making desperate financial and personal sacrifices so they can create and promote their work. That's why they are easy to exploit. And why there are so many scams in Tinseltown.

If you have a marketing budget, what to spend it on? Terror Film Festival's Claw suggests promoting your screening *before* the event. "Invest in postcards that contain the venue address and screening times/dates. And at least one poster. Filmmakers should also contact the local radio, TV, and television networks, and inform them they are in town and available for interviews."

Michael Coulombe of the Big Bear Horror Film Festival is ready to help filmmakers on both counts. "We provide a table near the entrance, where filmmakers can set up postcards of their film with the date and screening time. We also provide filmmakers with contacts to the local press to help them promote."

Alas, once accepted into a festival, some filmmakers expect to relax and be treated like royalty. But small festivals have small budgets. And bigger festivals, while they do spend more on promotion, also have many attending filmmakers, making it easy for your film to get lost in the crowd. In either case, filmmakers are wise to do their own promotion — before, during, and after the event.

Reyna Young and John Gillette of A Nightmare to Remember advise, "It's all about promotion. Filmmakers leave it up to me, to do it all. But there's only one of me. [Actually, there are two of them.] Any little thing can help, like telling your friends and family, spreading the word, putting up fliers." Maelstrom's Eric Morgret concurs. "Tell everyone you know that the film is showing. Spread the word. Contact local media. Get them interested. I promote individual films when I can, but it is much better for the filmmaker to engage in the process." Carnival of Darkness's Alex Bram dittos Morgret. "Tell everyone you know. Mailing lists are great, but one-on-one invitations are usually more effective." Ken Daniels says, "Promote on your social networking sites and your own website. Do as many podcasts as possible. Send out to your email list, many, many times."

Well, not *too* many. You don't want to come off as a spammer. Or a conceited egomaniac. Yes, promotion is good. Spamming is bad. Use your judgment at finding the delicate balance between the two. Bram's tip is helpful. The personal invite is usually less offensive than repeated mass emailings.

Shriekfest works hard on promotion. "We send out tons of press releases leading up to the fest," says Denise Gossett. She only wishes she'd get more *cooperation*. "When we set you up for interviews, go on them. Return the calls or emails. At the festival, do all of the interviews with the press. If we request a Q&A with you, please do it. All of this can only help you. Prepare for our fest by having flyers, posters, press packets all ready to go. You never know who may be asking. Some filmmakers do themselves a disservice by not marketing their films in general. There's no excuse nowadays with all of the social networking out there."

Jason Carney and Andrea Beesley-Brown of the International Horror and Sci-Fi Film Festival suggest that "the filmmaker actively engage with the staff of the festival. Attend any networking and mixing functions. Common mistakes are a lack of marketing, and being inaccessible to the public." The Abertoir Horror Festival assists filmmakers in their marketing. Gaz Bailey says, "If filmmakers supply posters and trailers, they *will* get displayed. Postcards increase a title's presence in the festival. It's important that filmmakers provide publicity materials to make their films stand out among the rest." Brazil's Cinefantasy also encourages filmmakers to send promotional materials. Vivi Amaral says, "We ask everyone who is selected to send us the marketing material, with release,

Siren's posters were prominently displayed for its world premiere at Abertoir — pleasing actress Tereza Srbova and producer Christopher Granier-Deferre. Aberystwyth, Wales. November 11, 2010. (Photograph courtesy Abertoir Horror Festival.)

Above: A 2009 Weekend of Fear poster, autographed by filmmakers and guests. (Image courtesy Weekend of Fear.) *Opposite:* Does the Tabloid Witch have a Welsh cousin? Abertoir's 2010 poster. (Image courtesy Abertoir Horror Festival.)

3. Working the Film Festival!

stills, posters, trailer, director's bio, curiosities, awards. All information is important to publicize the film. Some filmmakers don't have this material or part of it."

Dragon*Con's Matthew M. Foster is less bullish about traditional promotional items. "Printing cards and producing expensive banners is a waste of time. Filmmakers need to market *themselves* with their work. *Talk to people*. If it is a bloody film, or one with a monster, a bit of makeup doesn't hurt, so people will ask what that is for." In other words, *create an impression*. Wear an outlandish costume. Get noticed. Then launch your pitch.

Daniels thinks that promotional materials enhance the personal approach. "Go up to as many people as possible. Let them know what your film is about, and when it's screening. Bring plenty of promotional materials to hand out." Coulombe adds, "I'm a big believer in word-of-mouth. Talk to festival attendees and filmmakers. Tell them about your movie. Attend *their* screenings and/or parties. You can't expect people to support your project, if you don't support theirs."

To summarize, *it helps to be there*. Robert Nevitt of Celluloid Screams says, "For filmmakers looking to maximize the potential of their screening — come to the festival! Our audiences are passionate and committed to the genre. When filmmakers attend screenings, it shows they care about their work. Audiences respond to that. It adds value for everyone. We aim to make our guests feel welcome and valued, and try our damnedest to guarantee a good time." Carney and Beesley-Brown agree. "Festival patrons love to meet filmmakers. The more you can interact with your potential viewers, the more you will get out of the experience." Daniels advises that you "get a table at a film festival or convention. They can get a very inexpensive booth at ours." Morgret adds, "If you can afford it, it's always good to be at the festival in person. If your film is showing, be ready to answer questions and talk in front of people."

Yes, *if you can afford it*. This raises a point of frustration for some filmmakers. Recall the filmmaker posting as JEV1A on Fest21.com,

The South African HORRORFEST's 2010 poster. (Photograph Dr. Benway.)

who said: "The indie filmmaker puts out thousands of dollars for publicity, your film gets in the program, and then they say, sorry no airfare, no hotel, no drivers, etc. are available ... but we would love to have you attend! How many times have I heard this?"

It's a bummer not being able to attend your own film screening. But here's a tip: *If you can't attend, send a representative.* Preferably someone who worked on your film, and can talk intelligently about it. Three Tabloid Witch Award winning films were regional efforts (shot in Wyoming, Montana, and Florida) whose directors couldn't come to Los Angeles. But actors from each film was in L.A. at the time, so they represented their films at the audience Q&As.

Another tip: While you should always hire for talent, *it doesn't hurt if every cast and crew member happens to live in a different major festival city, just in case....*

Screening Venues

Tabloid Witch Awards screenings have always had only one screen. One audience, viewing one block of films, on that one screen. This is typical of smaller festivals. Bigger festivals may offer *multi-track screenings*; two or more screening rooms that run (usually) different films, simultaneously. Some festivalgoers like this, as it gives them more choices. Others dislike it; they may wish to see both films, but can see only one. This problem may be mitigated if a festival runs each film several times over the course of the fest.

Filmmakers generally don't like multi-track screenings (unless *their* film appears on all screens simultaneously, which can happen with popular or eagerly anticipated films). Filmmaker J. Neil Schulman believes that "there should only be one track of film programming. Films at a festival shouldn't have to compete for audience with other films. Run the festival extra days if necessary."

Extra days, of course, cost extra money. I sympathize with filmmakers. But I also sympathize with festival directors. Filmmakers don't want to pay entry fees, but they want to be flown to festivals, and have them extended for additional days. Good luck with that.

Shriekfest always screens at Raleigh Studios, in Hollywood, California. Not in a public theater, or a hotel convention room, or a library — but the backlot of an authentic, Hollywood film studio.[1] In 2009, Shriekfest had three screening rooms at Raleigh. A sizeable auditorium for feature films. Two smaller rooms for short films. The smaller rooms ran identical shorts, almost simultaneously, so the short films did not compete against *other shorts* for viewers. Having two rooms ensured that, though the rooms were smaller, there'd be enough seats for everyone who wanted to see the shorts.

There were more than enough seats. The short films were competing against the *features* which were screening down the hall. You could see shorts or features, your choice. I opted for shorts. Before each short film block, Denise Gossett introduced the filmmakers, who stood up to applause. It seemed most of the audience was composed of filmmakers and their entourages. Where were all the ticket buyers? The fans?

After six hours of shorts, I watched my first feature at Shriekfest: *Dark House*, an excellent supernatural horror film starring Jeffrey Combs. The large auditorium was packed. *Here* is where most of the hardcore fans had been all day. In the auditorium, watching features.

When I attend a festival, I prefer to watch shorts. This partially stems from my affection for horror anthology films (a collection of shorts), but it's also because festivals are the only place I'll ever see most of these shorts. I can always see horror features in the outside world.

I am the exception. Most fans prefer features. Don't rely on my anecdotal example. Check

Downstairs from the screening rooms, Shriekfest volunteers sell snacks and festival t-shirts. Raleigh Studios, Hollywood. October 3, 2010. (Photograph by the author.)

out the DVDs selling on Amazon. Not too many short films or short film collections. I've seen *award-winning* short films posted on YouTube. Short film directors are *giving away* their work because they can't sell them.

There's rarely any money in shorts. Short films are generally a "calling card" to the industry. A work sample, which filmmakers (and cast and crew) hope will lead to paying jobs. Some filmmakers also hope that their shorts will be expanded into features. These shorts are not just a work sample, but a sample of the proposed feature. If the short film version performs well on the festival circuit, investors may be enticed to fund the feature version.

Sometimes this intent is obvious. The short film feels incomplete. Its story is unresolved, or has an intriguing "high concept" that invites further exploration. Whenever I spot such a film, and suggest that it would make for a great feature, the filmmaker always confirms that that indeed is the plan. (Am I especially good at spotting such films, or do some filmmakers simply jump at my idea?) Yet despite the best laid plans, shorts rarely blossom into features. So many award-winning shorts, so few investors for the feature versions. But it *can* happen. In 2006, Paul Solet's horror short, *Grace*, won a Tabloid Witch. It also won at the Rhode Island International Horror Film Festival. In 2009, *Grace* was released as a feature.

Even after your film makes it into a festival, it still competes for attention. Not only against other films, but against other events. Shriekfest has both a snack bar and café outside its screening rooms, where fans, filmmakers, and journalists can rest their eyeballs after watching too many films. "The Eerie Horror Film Festival hosts an Expo," says Greg Ropp, "or mini-convention, where fans can meet celebrity guests and purchase horror merchandise. We present panels and workshops on topics ranging from filmmaking techniques to paranormal research." The Big Bear Horror Film Festival runs seminars hosted by horror film experts and celebrities.

Conventions are even more likely than film festivals to program competing events against the film screenings: parties, hospitality suites, art shows, dealer rooms, and special events (e.g., Loscon's Masquerade Ball, or World Horror Con's Gross Out Contest). And just like festivals, conventions sometimes have multi-track screenings. At Loscon, the Tabloid Witch's horror fare has always competed against animie films, screening just a few rooms away.

Filmmakers can be bummed about having to compete for attention at a festival. They overcame so many hurdles to become an Official Selection. Aren't they now entitled to ninety lousy minutes during which everyone focuses on *them*?

According to Matthias Engelhardt of Germany's Weekend of Fear, if the films are effectively counter-programmed, they're not really competing. "We have two cinemas. We try to run two very different films against each other. For example, cinema 1 shows a gory, funny zombie flick. Cinema 2 shows a dark, intense psychological drama. If you show two films *of the same kind*, fans of that genre are angry ('We wanna watch both!'), and fans of the other genre are going home."

According to this theory, different horror subgenres attract different audiences. The feature film fans at Shriekfest weren't about to watch shorts anyway. Call this the *counter-programming theory of multi-track film screenings*. Yes, some filmmakers believe that *their* film appeals to *all* horror fans — indeed, to all humanity — if only festivalgoers would give the film a chance and watch it. But as I said, filmmakers are rarely the best judges of their own works.

Razor Reel's Patrick Van Hauwaert believes that less popular films benefit from counter-programming. "We have created two different paths in our festival. A bigger screening room, with more accessible feature films. And a smaller screening room, with my personal favorites, films from new filmmakers, hardcore horror, short films, anything off the beaten path. We hope to lure in people new to horror with a big name movie, and in the same time, we hope to lure regular visitors into something more daring."

By this theory, the "big name movies" attract people who might otherwise not attend the festival. Some of them will then wander into the smaller screening room. The A-list films don't steal viewers from the B-list. Rather, the A-list sends a few extra viewers to the B-list. The A-list bakes the loaf. The B-list gets the crumbs. B-list filmmakers may gripe, but without A-list films, there wouldn't be a loaf, or even crumbs. Call this the *trickle down theory of multi-track films screenings*.

This phenomenon (of B-listers feeding off of A-listers' audiences) is analogous to all those "Dance" festivals opening up near Sundance, hoping to attract Sundance's overflow crowds.

Filmmakers should not expect everyone to see their film. Ken Daniels of the Fright Night Film Fest says, "Very few people come to sit through all of the films. They come to network, and be around like-minded people. We also have around twenty celebrities from the movies come to our show to sign autographs. Build your festival up with alternate programming to make it fun. We go till 3 A.M. showing movies. Some will be packed at that time, others won't."

How to ensure that your screening is packed? Jason Carney and Andrea Beesley-Brown advise, "By bringing ample promotional products (fliers, posters, giveaways), you'll have a better chance at enticing the public to choose your film over others." Filmmakers needn't work so hard at Maelstrom. Eric Morgret says, "Right now MIFFF is a fun, one theater film-going experience. That makes it very easy to prepare for. Just show up."

That's currently the case with Shriekfest, which in 2010 only rented the large auditorium. Shorts and features no longer compete for viewers. Gossett told me that some viewers had complained in 2009 about not being able to see every film, so now there's only one screen. She says she'd received no complaints from filmmakers about having to compete for viewers.

Even so, on the Sunday I attended, the short films attracted fewer viewers than did the features. It may partially be due to scheduling. Shorts ran from 12 noon to 4 P.M., then three features, then the awards show at 10 P.M. The crowd was light in the afternoon, but heavy by 8 P.M. I suppose every filmmaker, from all three days of screenings, came for the awards, hoping to win. Awards also attract more journalists than do short film screenings.

Why did the shorts attract fewer viewers than the features? Was it the afternoon scheduling, or are shorts just less popular? Probably a bit of both, but I think more the latter.

What technical elements should a screening venue provide? As a filmmaker, Schulman knows what he wants. "A movie theater setting isn't required, but there should be theater quality projection of films. High-definition players and projectors should be used. Nowadays, Blu-Ray as well as standard-def DVD should be the main projection formats, in addition to 16mm and 35mm film. Seating needs to be comfortable, when you have people sitting for entire days. One big advantage of existing theater seating is that it can be raked—that is, you don't have a flat floor where people can't see over the heads of the people in front of them. Or the screen can be raised, but that means people will get stiff necks from looking up."

A venue should also have *multi-region* DVD players. Not all of them do. I've had problems when filmmakers sent me PAL DVDs, which neither Loscon nor the Santa Monica library could play. I forewarn filmmakers that it's best to submit NTSC DVDs, but not everyone heeds my advice.

Some festival directors emphasize the importance of the venue's staff. Nevitt says, "A top-class technical team is one of the most important factors, and we're lucky in this respect. [They] pay close attention to sound, aspect ratio, all elements of the presentation." Engelhardt adds, "The most important thing is that you have a cinema that is looking forward to the event. If the crew of the cinema has fun, the audience will have fun too." Bailey suggests, "Find a venue with passion for the event. Abertoir is run by the venue itself, meaning that we have easy access to the concert hall and theatre, as well as the cinema. For organizers who don't have a venue, it's important that [the venue] support what the festival is doing, as dedication by everyone really pays off."

Jon Weimer's experience, running the film festival at the 2002 World Horror Con, is instructive. "Saying that [WHC] met the idea with apathy would be generous. They acted like it was an inconvenience and they were doing me a favor. There was concern that there would not be enough room for the film festival and the gross out show. They refused to allow me to screen anything but shorts, and said there was no time for features. It was poorly attended because the WHC didn't promote it. They felt the gross out show was more worthy."

Staff enthusiasm matters. Some Loscon committees have been more enthusiastic about hosting the Tabloid Witch than have others, and it showed in the room, equipment, and promotional support provided. But also recall Gossett's advice to filmmakers: "If you can pay your crew and talent, please do. You'll get a higher caliber of work." I'll extend that rule to festival and venue staffers: *Paid staff will more likely work enthusiastically than will volunteers.* Unlike paid professionals, volunteers at a convention or festival expect to have fun. Why not? They're *told* that volunteering will be fun.

Many festivals use both paid staff and volunteers. When you rent a theater or screening room, paid technicians are often included. Some theaters (and their insurance carriers) forbid anyone *other* than their employees from touching the equipment, no matter how skilled your volunteers. Perhaps a corollary rule (to my above rule) should be: *If a job is important and requires skill, it's a good idea to pay the person; otherwise, a volunteer will suffice.* Shriekfest, Screamfest L.A., the Los Angeles Film Festival, and Sundance all use volunteers. No matter how big the festival gets, I don't know of one that doesn't welcome volunteers.

Coulombe says that a good venue should have "ample parking, room for screenings, a space for exhibitors to set up tables, and rooms for seminars." Engelhardt adds, "A nice ambiance is important. You have to feel comfortable during two movies, and to have the possibility to buy some drinks or a small snack." Morbido Fest provides a nice *horror* ambiance, its theater spookily decorated to reinforce the onscreen horrors. Young and Gillette advise building a long-term relationship with your venue. They've been with theirs for three years now. "It's good to have the same location where regulars know where to go every year." Schulman wants, "Plenty of bathrooms. Plenty of water. And decent security so people don't steal the filmmakers' posters."

Ropp agrees. "Have security on hand at all times. And by security, I mean professional, law enforcement types — not some fat dude who's getting paid with beer, which could open up a whole different kind of legal issue should something go horribly awry. The Eerie Horror Film Festival employs local law enforcement officers each year.

"Always expect something to go wrong. If you go in thinking otherwise, you will be in for a rude wakeup call when things fall apart. I've had headlining guests pull out at the last minute, literally while people are standing in line at the box office to buy tickets to meet them.

Demonic and ghostly effigies, spookily lit, haunt either side of the theater's screen. October 2010. Tlalpujahua, Michoacan, Mexico. (Photograph courtesy Morbido Film Fest.)

I've had films malfunction, microphones go dead on stage during a Q&A, and the occasional drunk or stoned person who is getting out of hand. I could supply a list of horror stories — but an even longer one with the successes and the righting of such situations. Each year I learn more about what to repeat, what went gloriously well, what went hellishly wrong, and go from there.

"Be prepared for the worst and know that the show must go on. Every ticket holder, guest, filmmaker is there because they trust us to provide the best experience possible. Handle with respect each issue as it arises. Try to defuse the situation no matter how grim. Be honest always. Show that you are willing to go the extra mile to set things straight, that you are willing to work with filmmakers and attendees to correct any problems that arise. They will thank you. They will let others know."

Diffusing problems can require improvisation. At the 2009 Loscon, the DVD equipment failed before the Tabloid Witch's screening of *Parasomnia* (2008). It took ten minutes to locate a hotel staffer to fix the problem. Not wanting bored attendees to wander off to other Loscon events, I asked the film's director, William Malone, to introduce his film and entertain audience questions. He kept the audience in their chairs until the technical problem was resolved.

Tip: *Always have backup entertainment.* This can mean an interesting speaker. Or extra copies of the scheduled films in case a DVD freezes. Or if the filmmaker didn't provide a backup DVD, then the DVD to an entirely different, unscheduled film. ("Due to technical difficulties we will not be screening *Zombie Horror Bloodbath*—but we're thrilled to instead present the equally brilliant *Slasher Terror Massacre*!")

Live entertainment is a good idea. A standup comic or scream queen can give festivalgoers a change of pace between screenings, but also provide a fun diversion should a DVD player suddenly need to be repaired. Kelly Jones and Kelly Webster of England's Halloween Monster Movie Challenge report that in 2009 they had "a few bands playing" prior to the screenings and during the breaks. Engelhardt enlivened Weekend of Fear with spooky performance art.

Zombina and the Skeletones perform at Abertoir. Aberystwyth, Wales. November 12, 2010. (Photograph courtesy Abertoir Horror Festival.)

"In 2006, we had a guy with a chainsaw. He was masked, like a weird slasher killer, had a lot of tattoos, and ran during a screening into the cinema. Unfortunately, the room was not too big, and it was a chainsaw that ran on gas [rather than on electricity]. It stank a lot, and the whole night through."

Bring friends to help you through any problems and improvised solutions. Young and Gillette advise, "It's very stressful running a film festival, so it's always good to have some friends there to help you with passing out program books, or getting prizes passed out, or just moral support." And if that's not enough, these Californians have another tip for reducing festival stress: "Before doing any event *meditation* is very helpful."

"Listen to your audience," says Bailey. "After a while, you get a feel for what works and what doesn't. Talk with your customers. Listen to suggestions. Atmosphere is important. We offer a friendly atmosphere, where guests are not separated from fans. A place where everyone will know everyone else by the end of five days. Make sure every person feels welcome."

The Tabloid Witch welcomes everyone — even the homeless!

The city of Santa Monica is circumscribed by Los Angeles on three sides, and the Pacific Ocean on its west. Home to the American Film Market and to many entertainment companies, employees, and celebrities, Santa Monica also has a large homeless population, attracted by the city's warm climate and generous social services programs. The Santa Monica Public Library reflects these economic extremes. Its main branch has a lavish new building with an outdoor café, garden, and state-of-the-art theater that can seat 146. But because it's open to the public, it's also open to homeless patrons.

Following the Tabloid Witch's 2008 screening at the library, an attending journalist complained to me, "Tom, you have *homeless people* in the audience!"

Yes, I know. That was also the case in 2006 and 2007. Admission is free and homeless people enjoy horror films too.

Actually, there weren't all *that many* homeless in the audience. Maybe a half dozen. There's no need to fret. The library has security guards (paid professionals, not fat dudes paid with beer) in case anyone causes trouble. No one ever has.

Not everyone was upset. Playwright/critic Ben Pleasants, formerly with the *Los Angeles Times*, was also there in 2008. When I mentioned the journalist's complaint about the homeless, Pleasants exclaimed, "No, it's wonderful! It's a people's event!"[2]

Pleasants was especially enamored with a German short film, *Vadata*, which reminded him of Luis Buñuel's work. I put Pleasants in touch with the filmmaker, Manuel Lebelt. Pleasants in turn put Lebelt in touch with Buñuel's nephew, Rafael. You never know who'll see your film at any festival's screening — even if there *are* homeless fans in the audience.

On rare occasions, filmmakers are ruder than any homeless person. At a 2007 Loscon screening, some audience members began making snide remarks about the film being screened, much like they do on *Mystery Science Theater 3000*. Turning around, I was surprised to see the rude remarks coming from a filmmaker and his/her friends. Filmmakers are *supposed* to support each others' work, and they usually do, but not always.

The Tabloid Witch hasn't screened at the library since 2008, so it no longer has homeless fans, but I'm glad some of them saw and enjoyed the screenings. Halloween is my favorite holiday. Were I ever homeless, I'd still like to be able to participate in the season's dark festivities. Horror films offer us a brief refuge from our daily woes. Most people don't understand how one can find relief in horror, but those reading this book know what I'm talking about.

TromaDance's philosophy bears repeating: "Art — in all its forms — is for the people! Everyone at TromaDance is treated as an equal. The elite and the celebrated are treated no better or worse than the experimental filmmaker or the random moviegoer off the street. Admittance to all screenings, panels, parties, and events is strictly on a first come, first served basis."

So too at the Tabloid Witch.

Festival directors should also consider *nontraditional screening venues.* Cinespia is a Los Angeles film program that screens at the Hollywood Forever Cemetery. Filmgoers bring their own lawn chairs, pillows, and blankets to spread out among the tombstones, then watch films that are projected onto "the white marble wall of Rudolph Valentino's tomb."[3] Yet despite its graveyard screening venue, Cinespia is not an exclusively horror event. They show everything.

Morbido Film Fest screens at traditional theatrical venues in the cities of Tlalpujahua, Mexico City, Oaxaca, and Merida—but like Cinespia, Morbido also screens at cemeteries. How do the ghosts feel about film people disturbing their peace? According to Pablo Guisa Koestinger, "In the past two editions, there have been encounters with ghosts. The first year, our Spanish guest director, Sergio Blasco, ran out from the Cofradia, a small 18th century chapel in which we [would] screen. He arrived to the production office, pale, and told us about this. I went with him to the chapel, walked with him inside. Then I ran out and lock the door with him inside. His screams were very, very loud."

Screening Schedules

The *sequence* in which films are shown should not be determined randomly. Some films work better following another film, than visa versa. There's an art to finding the sequence that is most pleasing to an audience. "We give a lot of thought to the schedule," says Gossett. "It's important. It's hard to explain how we do it, though."

The first chapter is crucial in a novel. By hooking the reader early, the author wins the reader's trust. The reader will thus endure the slower chapters, assuming they're there for a reason, and that the story will end on an entertaining and meaningful note.

Likewise, when programming a short film block, I begin with a crowd pleaser (i.e., something of great appeal to the largest number of fans). Usually I pick an energetic, comedic gorefest that's not too long. Say, under 15 minutes. Something to excite and surprise the audience. Something to convince them that *there are great films to be seen here, so stick around.* The first film should hook everyone, so that everyone will be patient if one of the later films does not please this or that particular viewer.

I like to *hammock* films, those with popular appeal supporting the more obscure.[4] To *alternate* between comedic and dramatic horror, with the rarer avant-garde or animated film dropped amid them. Between long and short films, energetically gory and quietly atmospheric films, and films of different subgenres. You don't run two zombie films back-to-back. Favorite subgenres vary among horror fans, so variety is nice.

Abertoir's Gaz Bailey agrees. "We show old and new films. We like to vary the program by not having too many similar films so close to each other." Jim Taylor adds, "You might think there's little room for variation at the Zombie Short Film Festival, but we're big on variety. Last year we had films from all over the world, and in a variety of styles. We made sure that every film offered something a little bit different for our audience. That way, even if they didn't like the film they were currently watching, there'd be something they'd enjoy coming right around the corner."

Aside from wanting to give audiences variety, another reason I wouldn't run two zombie films back-to-back is because it would reflect poorly on the weaker one. A weak zombie film should be hammocked between two strong non-zombie films.

Weaker films in general should be hammocked between stronger films. A succession of weak films drive off audiences. Of course, most festivals won't admit to screening weak films. Bailey says, "We don't like to think that some films are weaker than others. That's why we have our selection committee." According to TromaDance's Matt Manjourides, "If you have good films, the audience will stay. Our last TromaDance had only four walks-outs in eight hours." Dragon*Con's Foster adds, "You shouldn't have weak films in a fest." Fright Night's Daniels says, "No, we don't alternate between weaker and stronger films." The Terror Film Festival's Claw insists, "We don't screen weak films. If it's not great, it doesn't get selected." Nevertheless, some films are more popular than others with horror audiences. That's a weaker film. I don't mean a crappy film. I've seen films that I enjoy and whose artistry I appreciate, yet which are long, quiet, even self-indulgent. Select viewers appreciate such films, but others are bored. Read the Amazon.com reviews for the prestigious and internationally acclaimed *Picnic at Hanging Rock* (Australia 1975). One reviewer raves: "One of my favorite 'horror' movies. Even with no on screen deaths or bodies, it remains one [of] the most frightening PG rated films." But another disagrees: "Reviewers mention the oppressive heat of the landscape as a metaphor for the oppression of this class-conscious, sexually repressed Victorian setting. No, it's a warning of the oppression, lethargy, and boredom you'll feel at having to sit though this nonsense."

Such films are not artistically bad — I admire *Picnic at Hanging Rock*—but they are weaker in that they appeal to fewer hardcore horror fans.

Alternating between types of films within a short film block creates a sense of unpredictability. This is good. If audiences feel that they don't know what's coming up next, they may want to stay and find out. Like Forrest Gump's box of chocolates, you never know what kind of horror you're gonna get next.

A short film block should end with a bang. The last film must be another crowd-pleaser. That may mean a comedic gorefest, or perhaps a film that's especially poignant, unusual, or creative. Since the last film needn't hold over the audience, you can be more experimental in your selection. Use your instincts as to which film will most "wow" viewers. You won't always be right, but your programming skills will improve with successive screenings and festivals.

Foster advocates hammocking up to a point. "A block should have a spectacular moment early on, with long, slower pieces broken up with fast-pasted fx works." But he qualifies that by adding, "A horror block should all be of films of the *same intensity*, or the extreme films will get a poor reception, and the light films will seem silly. But then there needs to be a break from pure horror. I split horror blocks with a comedy or action block. Straight horror can drain an audience."

Dragon*Con is not an exclusively *horror* film festival, but a horror/sci-fi/fantasy convention. Its schedule has room for non-horror films. This is also true of Cinefantasy. "We are a fantastic film festival," says Amaral. "It is not only horror. But my advice is to schedule *as many kinds* of horror movies as you can. From gore to black comedy. The Brazilian horror scene is new and weak when we talk about public opinion — that's why film festivals are so important here — so I always alternate Brazilian works with foreign films in the short programme."

The Eerie Horror Fest strives for *thematic unity*. "We usually program two shorts and one feature per screening block," says Ropp. "Similarly themed films are programmed together. Sometimes fans have fun trying to figure out the theme, if it's not obvious at first glance. One year, even though the storylines were different, all three films in one block featured 'weird girls' and another block featured 'political dread.' It's fun. It also makes sense. To just throw a bunch of random movies together is lazy on the part of the programmer."

Jones and Webster of the Halloween Monster Movie Challenge disagree. "There was no real order in which the films were screened, as there was no favoritism."

Careful film scheduling prioritizes the *audience's* viewing pleasure, but an argument can be made for the Movie Challenge's random schedule. From a *filmmaker's* perspective, some spots in the schedule are more desirable than others. One year a filmmaker complained to me that I'd scheduled his feature for last. He worried that by the time his film was shown, the audience's brains would be fried. He had a point. But as I explained to him, somebody has to be last.

I've read a theory that, if you're ever part of a political candidates' forum, or any forum in which you're trying to sell yourself or a message, the first and last spots are considered the best. All things being equal, the first speaker makes the strongest impression. The last speaker lingers longest in the audience's memory. The other speakers risk getting "lost in the middle."

The same may hold true for a block of films. Yet all films are not equal. A film's position in the schedule may give it an edge when it comes time to vote for Audience Favorite, but many other factors — more important factors — will influence the audience. Such as the films' merit. Yes, if two films are of identical aesthetic quality and entertainment value, their spots in the schedule may give one film the advantage in the audience vote. But it's rare that two films will hold an identical appeal to fans. Hardcore horror fans are a passionate and opinionated bunch. We know which films we like best.

Time of day is another scheduling consideration. Recall how Shriekfest attracted more viewers for its Sunday evening features than for its afternoon shorts. Of Eerie Horror, Ropp says, "We schedule our screenings to reflect what kind of audiences we may attract at a specific time. We may program a foreign language film in the afternoon as opposed to prime time. We have our harder R-rated films at night, so parents can feel better about earlier shows." Amaral's approach is similar. "Cinefantasy has three screening places, and we usually have three sessions. The first ones are lighter, maybe for children." Bailey adds, "We are considerate of timing with each film, and program accordingly. Japanese splatter films traditionally get a midnight slot. If we have a famous celebrity guest Q&A, they might be in a premium time slot to appeal for audiences outside of the horror festival."

"We put weaker films earlier," says Van Hauwaert. "Hard or gore films at midnight. Mainstream films on prime time. Just like everyone, I suppose."

Finally, an honest man! Razor Reel admits to screening weaker films. Why not? We all do.

At Celluloid Screams, Robert Nevitt takes hammocking, thematic unity, and time of day all into consideration. "Scheduling can get a little stressful when it comes to the overall flow of the event. *Pacing* is the key. We try to match similarly themed shorts to features, but equally, there's no sense in putting a run of similar films in a row. In our 2009 festival, we'd got two Japanese gore movies that I was determined to program on different days. We also had two similarly themed films in *Lake Mungo* and *Paranormal Activity*. It would be a disservice to either film to show them too close together. It's almost a balancing act to ensure all films have room to breathe. Overall, it's a case of knowing your programme inside out. A movie like Juan Piquer Simón's *Pieces* (1982) is made for a midnight slot, whereas it simply wouldn't work at three in the afternoon."

However much filmgoers love horror, brains can fry from watching too many films in a row. I've attended festivals where I've declined seeing yet another feature, though it looked promising, because I'd already seen six or eight hours worth of films that day.

Scheduling non-film activities can mitigate audience burnout. "We break up the day with events such as talks, or theatre or music performances, to allow a diverse and never boring schedule," says Bailey. "We show a whole history of horror films. Not just indies. Not just studio films. We show classic films, cult films, silent films with live accompaniment, music performances, theatre. We offer master classes, Q&As, book events, talks, and five days of films."

Michael Coulombe does likewise. "Mixing up the schedule is important. That allows everyone a chance to watch a film, attend a seminar, take a break, go into town and support the local fare. It also allows the chance to network, socialize, and enjoy the weekend." Since the Big Bear Horror Film Festival is situated in a beautiful California resort area, going into town is an attractive option. So too in Mexico. Koestinger says, "One of Morbido's hits is to have other activities, and not only movies. We have literary events, art exhibits, music concerts. We alternate indoor and outdoor activities, and audiences don't get bored." But he adds a warning. "One recommendation is not to have many parties, because that makes everybody not to arrive at the early screenings. The purpose of the festival is to watch films, not to get drunk."

Getting drunk till 4 A.M., then waking up late the next morning might happen at film festivals, but I suspect it's more common at conventions. Late night parties (some with open bars) are among the World Horror Con's more popular events. I suspect the early morning panels and readings are lightly attended, but I wouldn't know. I'm not a morning person. *Tip*: If you do screen films at a convention, best you don't schedule them too early.

Morbido's Koestinger warns against too much drinking, but just try prying these beer steins away from Weekend of Fear's Mike Neun (second from left) and the filmmaking team behind *Skeleton Crew* (aka *Snuff Massacre — Skeleton Crew*, 2009) (from left): Tero Molin (co-director); Tommi Lepola (co-director), Ilkka Niemi (co-producer). Erlangen, Germany. (Photograph courtesy Weekend of Fear.)

Not every festival is situated in a resort area, or can afford ancillary events. Luckily, there are cheaper ways to prevent audience burnout. Keep the festival short. Young and Gillette of A Nightmare to Remember explain, "Our fest is three hours long. Two hours of short films. A twenty minute break. Then our host, Miss Misery, gives out awards and raffle and prizes to the audience, and has guests come up, speak, and gives them awards. We usually have a guest of honor, and a local horror achievement award winner. Three hours is short and sweet!"

Jim Taylor offers another, low-budget suggestion: "An intermission always helps."

Is there an ideal *time of year* to schedule a horror film festival? Many American festivals favor the Halloween *season*, screening anywhere from early October to mid November. Yes, Halloween has grown into a season. I've seen spooky merchandise on store shelves by August. I've seen creepy lawn displays crop up in September. Long before October 31st, American mass media and corporate marketing turn people's thoughts to horror, putting them in the mood for frightful fun.

Horror festivals piggyback onto this seasonal zeitgeist, though in Los Angeles, they don't screen on Halloween itself (or even during the last weekend in October, which can substitute for Halloween when the holiday falls on a weeknight). A big city offers too many competing Halloween happenings: parades, parties, haunted houses, live shows, and the usual trick-or-treating. These are once-in-a-year events, whereas one can always watch a horror film. This is not just theory. In 2010, for the first time, the Tabloid Witch screened on Halloween weekend, to one of its sparser audiences. Afterwards, past midnight, I ate with a friend at a 24-hour-diner, crowded with people in costumes, coming from parties, the parade in West Hollywood, and who knows where else. Certainly not from a film festival.

In a small town, your horror festival may be the biggest thing going on, in which case, it may make sense to schedule it on Halloween. I've also heard that Halloween is not such a big deal in some foreign countries; there is no Halloween season. Either way, you should assess your locale's seasonal zeitgeist, and the strength of competing events, when picking days on the calendar.

Q&A Panels

Film fans like to meet famous actors and filmmakers. If no celebrities are available, then *non*-famous actors and filmmakers are the next best thing. Even with the prevalence of camcorders, webcams and YouTube, a certain *glamour* still attaches to someone who is associated with a professional looking film. Seeing the actress you just now saw on screen, sitting before you in the flesh, is an almost thrilling experience. She may not be Angelina Jolie, but she's kinda, sorta, *like* Angelina Jolie. Both women read lines in front of a camera.

At every screening, I try to ensure that at least *some* people from *some* of the films show up for a Q&A panel discussion. Panel discussions with actors and filmmakers help differentiate film festivals from the ordinary movie-going experience. Panels are an "added value" which I trumpet on my Tabloid Witch promotional flyers: "Meet the Actors and Filmmakers!" Otherwise, why come? Why not just wait for the feature film's DVD release? Or watch the short film on YouTube?

Apart from attracting star-struck fans and genre geeks, panel discussions also appeal to aspiring actors and filmmakers seeking advice from panelists on how to "make it" in Hollywood. This is no small group. The Los Angeles area is full of aspiring actors and filmmakers, some of whom may want to meet the filmmakers on your panel. That was certainly true at the 2010 Carnival of Darkness, which screened at the Los Angeles Film School. Alex Bram, while moderating the panel, asked audience members how many of them aspired to work in film. Quite a few hands went up. That's what happens when you screen at a film school.

Even so, filmmakers' panels alone won't guarantee huge turnouts for your festival. Throughout Los Angeles (and other major cities, I assume) film panels are always convening. Festivals, adult education classes, industry events — everyone's paneling. People are interested in filmmakers, but there are so many panels to choose from, why attend *yours*? Whereas, if your festival is located in a small town, it may be the only game around. Even if the actors and filmmakers on your panel aren't famous, they might attract a bigger crowd than some panels in Los Angeles or New York.

Celebrity panelists are always a big attraction in any city. This is why celebrities sometimes get paid to attend. How much depends on how big a celebrity. For some, you need only pay their expenses. Bigger celebrities may want a fee. But big celebrities make it easier to sell more (and more expensive) tickets to your event, so a celebrity fee might pay for itself.

When seeking panelists, two contrary problems arise: 1. Assuming you don't pay them, can you find *anyone* for your panel? 2. Have you found *two many* people?

The Tabloid Witch Awards recognizes films from around the world, yet no foreign film winner has ever flown in to Los Angeles to attend a screening. Winners have flown in from Illinois and Washington state, but from no farther. Even so, I've never had trouble filling up the panels, because several L.A. based filmmakers win every year. Despite runaway production, L.A. teems with filmmakers. Even when a regional film wins, I later discover that many of the film's actors live in Los Angeles, or will be in town on business, or that the filmmaker has since moved to Los Angeles. Thus, I've never had problems recruiting panelists.

Small or new festivals that screen in more isolated areas will have greater difficulty attracting filmmakers to serve on panels. One *solution* is to create some categories for films from the festival's home state or region. Louisville's Fright Night Film Fest has a "Kentucky Filmmaker of the Year" award category. Orlando's Freak Show Horror Film Festival has a "Best Florida Horror Film" category. Honoring local talent increases the likelihood that at least *some* winners live close enough to attend your event, and in turn, attract local fans. "One of *ours* made a movie? I gotta meet the guy!" Localism also attracts local sponsors (who sell products to your local festivalgoers) and nonprofits (who may be required by their charters to support only local artists).

While I've not had trouble filling up my panels, I've sometimes been burdened with having *too many* panelists. A functioning panel can only have so many talking heads. Two people (an interviewer and a guest) can work nicely; it may create an intimate, artsy, Charlie Rose style of discussion. A moderator and up to four guests is better. With five people (moderator in the middle, two panelists on either side) there's less chance of the conversation petering out. You're more likely to have at least one chatty guest, or perhaps an intriguing guest who inspires questions from the audience. You don't want a panel that turns silent after five minutes.

But beyond a certain point, as the number of panelists rises, the discussion becomes increasingly unwieldy. With too many panelists, and too little time, *in-depth* discussion and follow-up on any one topic becomes impossible. The panel becomes less a discussion than a round robin, with the moderator asking a question, then going down the line so everyone can contribute a sound bite.

With too many panelists, there's also a risk that a few will dominate the conversation, pushing more timid panelists into the background. That's unfair to the timid, and unfair to the audience. Every panelist is up there because he or she made a great film. Each may have something interesting to say, if given the chance. But that's hard to do lost in a crowd, dominated by a few talkative alpha personalities.

It's the moderator's job to keep the conversation going, by asking provocative questions. It's also the moderator's job to ensure that everyone has a chance to speak, by shifting the conversation to whoever has not yet spoken. All this becomes harder to do as the number of panelists grows.

I once moderated a panel with eight guests. It was doable, but becoming more of a round robin Q&A than a discussion. At the 2010 Viscera Film Festival, I counted *twenty-one* guests on one panel, plus moderator Heidi Martinuzzi, who walked past the line of panelists with a microphone, giving everyone a chance to speak. I understand why. She wanted every filmmaker to enjoy their moment of glory. Every panelist had a film screened earlier that day. Martinuzzi wanted to honor them all.

Filmmakers have egos. That's the root of my "too many panelists" problem. I always ask winning filmmakers if they'd like to sit on the Q&A panel after the screenings. I can't remember any filmmakers *not* wanting to serve on a panel, provided they were in town and could attend the screenings. Even more problematic, sometimes cast and crew members want to join in.

Overly large panels don't serve anyone. The panelists don't get much attention, and it's less interesting for audiences. Film buffs want to get to know the filmmakers on a panel, learn the details of how they made their films, and not just hear quick sound bites.

To limit the number of panelists, I have a rule. Only one guest per film has *a right* to sit on the panel. I'll allow more guests from the same film if there's room, but I grant a right to no more than one. I let the director decide who will be The One to represent the film. I can't think of an instance when the director hasn't chosen himself (if available).

Occasionally, a filmmaking team ignores my rule and crashes the panel. I stress the rule beforehand, emphasizing that it's only fair to everyone to have only one person per film. Yet

Filmmakers gather *en masse* for a Viscera Film Festival Q&A. Heidi Martinuzzi with the microphone. Los Angeles. July 17, 2010. (Photograph by the author.)

Panel discussions do *not* require chairs! The filmmaking team behind *Dead Hooker in a Trunk* (2009) participate in an informally staged panel at BleedFest. Los Angeles. December 2010. (Photograph courtesy BleedFest.)

when it's time to go up on stage, two or more people from one film come up. Not wanting unpleasantries, I say nothing and begin the discussion. (I wonder if cast and crew members from the other films, sitting in the audience, are thinking, *Hey.... But he said.... But there are two people from one film up there!*)

A *solution* to discourage panel crashers may be to have a table up on stage, with only so many chairs, and a name card before each chair. But some venues are more casual. At the Santa Monica library, we just sit along the edge of the stage. No chairs. No table. At Loscon, we just grab folding chairs from the audience and come on up.

A *solution* to accommodate more panelists would be to break up a big panel into several smaller panels. Whether this is feasible depends on the available time. From 2005 to 2008, after the short film block and two features were screened, the Tabloid Witch only had time for one panel discussion. Every guest from every film shared that one panel. Three panels (one for the short film block, one for each feature) would have been nicer. But a low budget limits how much time the venue can donate, or you can rent. I suppose the Viscera Festival (another no entry fee event) was similarly constrained.

In 2009 and 2010, the Tabloid Witch Awards ran for two days, allowing time for multiple panels. *Within* (2009) enjoyed a panel all to itself, with four guests from that one feature. The short film block also had four guests. Four plus the moderator makes five — a nice, well-balanced number.

Perhaps you've noticed that when I speak of panels, I speak of actors and filmmakers serving on such panels. What about cinematographers, composers, or sound engineers? Alas, audiences are less interested in technicians or stagehands than in actors, directors, and even writers. True, there may be an aspiring gaffer in the audience, bursting with questions for the film's head gaffer on how to break into professional gaffing, eager for "behind the scenes" gaffing anecdotes from the film just screened, and wondering about the classic gaffing techniques used in *Citizen Kane*. But such is the exception. Most people don't care.

If I can't book a film's director on the panel, I try to get an actor. The Tabloid Witch has award categories for cinematography, sound, music soundtrack composition, visual effects, make-up effects, and acting. They all win plaques, but the actors have dibs on the panels.

A moderator should prepare questions before a panel discussion begins. Not the sort of questions that can be answered with a simple yes or no. The goal is to spark discussion, not just to get answers.

It can be helpful to pre-interview panelists at least a day before the panel convenes. Then you'll know which questions have interesting answers. I first interviewed filmmaker CJ Johnson about a month before the 2007 Tabloid Witch screenings, for the *Hollywood Investigator*'s article about the winners. Much of Johnson's short horror/sci-fi film, *The Signal*, was shot in the desert. It looked uncomfortably hot, so I asked Johnson about it. He had some colorful anecdotes about his actors' travails under the scorching heat, so I asked him the same question during the post-screening panel discussion. He related the same anecdotes, without missing a beat.

Frequent panelists get good at repeatedly answering the same questions, and repeatedly relating the same stories and jokes and talking points. Public speaking is a form of public performance. You're not there so much to provide answers, as to entertain. Authors who frequently do public readings eventually learn this.[5] Filmmakers who frequently pitch projects and serve on panels eventually learn this. Actors are among *the first* to learn this, because they're "always on stage" (an attitude that is ingrained into them). It also helps if they've trained in comedy improv. Their attitude and training are additional reasons why actors make for more entertaining panelists than do crew members.

Skilled panelists are like standup comics. They know how to handle embarrassing questions and rude remarks. With humor. "When we were fielding questions after one of our UK premiere screenings in 2009," says Robert Nevitt, "there was one audience member who clearly didn't like the film, and bluntly informed the producer. This culminated in the attendee describing the film as '*Funny Games* for morons,' which thankfully the producer took in good humour. Later we joked that they should use that quote on the poster."

Don't worry that pre-interviews may lessen your panel's spontaneity. The moderator can still go off on tangents, shift the conversation toward fresh directions, or ask unexpected questions if the discussion grows stale.

The questions you ask will naturally depend to some extent on the film. Here are some good generic starter topics:

(1) Why did you choose to tell this story? What were your film's influences? Your film evokes XYZ film/TV show. Was that an inspiration?

(2) How did you find your actors? What was the casting process?

(3) What's your educational and professional background? Why led you into filmmaking?

(4) Where did you shoot your film? How did you gain access to the locations?

(5) What format(s) did you shoot in? What film/video or editing equipment and programs did you use?

(6) How did you find your DP? Who composed the music?

(7) What's been the film's distribution history so far? What has its reception at other festivals been like?

(8) Do you have any advice for people wanting to break into film?

That last question is extremely popular — if you don't ask it, someone from the audience probably will. Alas, the answer always disappoints. Filmmakers usually repeat the same stuff about "Write every day," and "if you want to be a filmmaker, you have to make films," and the importance of networking. Good advice, but not what audiences really want to hear. What they want to hear is "Call up Jon Brickmeyer over at Paramount. I'll give you his number. He'll buy your screenplay for $500,000 tomorrow, with you attached to direct. Good thing you asked, because Jon is searching for a new screenplay, and neither of us knew where to find one."

I hate those promotional "making of" documentaries included in some DVD's special features. I hate the insincere, boilerplate, mutual praise that everyone involved in the film heaps on each other. If a panel devolves into a mutual admiration society, try steering the discussion to the film's story, themes, politics, philosophy, ethics, and influences. Horror is a genre rich in metaphor and symbolism. That's way more interesting than "When I saw Sarah's past work, I knew that she was the only person in the world I could ever hire as my boom operator. It was either Sarah on the boom, or give up filmmaking entirely and go to law school."

You may have noticed that I didn't include any questions about money. I think many festivalgoers are interested in how much a film cost, but even more so in *how the money was raised*. Other filmmakers in the audience are especially eager for fundraising tips, so they can do likewise.

Filmmakers sometimes brag about how little their films cost, though they don't always tell the truth. I've known filmmakers who've claimed widely different budgets for the same film, in different interviews. Filmmakers are even more cagey if I ask, "*How* did you raise the money?" I get vague answers. "I found some people who had confidence in me." Or sometimes I'm told "the investors wish to remain confidential." I dunno. I thought some people invested in films precisely to see their names in the credits. That and the chance to meet pretty actresses.[6]

I have a theory. Filmmakers dislike revealing the names of their investors, or even how their investors were found, because they plan to pitch more projects to these investors. But if other filmmakers learned about these film-friendly investors, they'd swoop in to pitch their own projects. There's only so much investment capital available. The goose can lay only so many golden eggs. So if you've found a golden goose, you keeps its whereabouts a secret.[7]

Celebrity Guests

How do you attract celebrity guests to your festival and its panels? Celebrities will more likely come if: 1. You're giving them an award; 2. They're already in town; 3. They're promoting a new project; 4. You're paying them to come; and/or 5. They're not *that* big a celebrity. An actress with only a few direct-to-DVD credits to her name, who lives within driving distance, will likely show up to accept her Bloody Torso Trophy for her work in *Facebook Friends Massacre* even if you don't pay her "standard" $100 event fee. Angelina Jolie probably won't come even if you offer her $200.

Carnival of Darkness attracted several local writers and artists by setting up sales and promotional tables outside the screening room, as conventions often do. Los Angeles writer/illustrator Angus Oblong (*Creepy Susie and 13 Other Tragic Tales for Troubled Children* and TV's *The Oblongs*) drew cartoons, sold books, and signed autographs for festivalgoers. "Some were paid a small fee for travel/expenses," says Alex Bram of his guests, "but most just came for the opportunity to expose their products and wares." Los Angeles film festivals are lucky in that the town is full of celebrities for every budget (A-list to Z-list), and, being locals, their travel expenses are modest.

A celebrity can incur expenses that are unexpected. Razor Reel's Patrick Van Hauwaert relates this funny tale: "Director Paco Plaza and his girlfriend came over to visit our festival [in 2009] and the screening of *REC 2*. We provided food and lodging. One night the twosome went to bed, quite tired, and for some reason stayed in bed talking, reading, we don't know, *but* they had a candle burning. (Our romantic city of Bruges [in Belgium] maybe gave them the right mood.) As you can suspect, they fell asleep, the candle burned completely and set fire to a small cabinet. A lot of smoke was produced. Fortunately, the fire alarm did work well. Nothing was damaged in a serious way, and everybody was healthy. Neither Paco or his wife dared to tell us anything about what happened. We found out only days later, when we went paying the bills."

Some festivals create an award for a celebrity who makes himself available. In 2006, the New York City Horror Film Festival presented actor Tony Todd with an Excellence in Acting Award, the first and only year for that award. According to festival director Michael J. Hein, "Tony was given a special award that year because he was in town for the entire festival, took the time to talk with all the attending filmmakers, and paneled with us, and basically is an actor we thought should be recognized for his outstanding work in genre pictures. We never really intended it to be an annual award. It's hard enough organizing the Lifetime Achievement Award each year!"

Although Todd is familiar to horror fans primarily for his work on the *Candyman* film series, I am especially impressed by his portrayal of a taxi driver in Michael Shoob's *Driven* (1996), one of my favorite indie (non-horror) films of the 1990s.

The Big Bear Horror Film Festival one-upped New York City Horror. They didn't just present Kerry O'Quinn (founder of *Fangoria* and *Star Log* magazines) with an award — they *named the award after him!* In 2009, Kerry O'Quinn was the first recipient of Big Bear Horror's O'Quinn Award, given "for excellence and cutting edge creativity." O'Quinn must have been pleased, because he emceed for Big Bear in both 2009 and 2010. And in case you're wondering, 2010's O'Quinn Award went to Victor Miller.

"To attract celebrity guests," advises Gaz Bailey, "we have found that our unique variety of events and interesting location (mid Wales) helps to attract people, as it offers something different from the usual major cities. *Look for a USP* [unique selling point] and use it." Robert Nevitt suggests, "With celebrity guests, we've found that approaching them with an invite *well in advance* is the best course of action."

How do you contact a celebrity? Where do you find them? You can begin with an on-

Angus Oblong at Carnival of Darkness. Los Angeles Film School, Hollywood. October 28, 2010. (Photograph by the author.)

line search. Celebrities have websites and social network pages too, though the bigger they are, the less likely that they personally manage their own sites. You'll have to go through "their people" managing the site. Acting unions are another source of information. In the U.S., the Screen Actors Guild (sag.org) and American Federation of Television and Radio Artists (aftra.org) keep many of their members' contact information (e.g., publicist, agent, manager) on file. The information is free for the asking. Foreign countries have their own acting unions, which I assume are similarly helpful.

The only actors I've sought for panels were those who appeared in Tabloid Witch Award winning films. The director usually provides the contact information. I don't care if the actors aren't famous; they're talented nonetheless.

Cast members Jessica Blackmore, Lauren Brown, Jordan Wall (*The Sacred*) at the 2010 Tabloid Witch Awards. The Tabloid Witch found and contacted Ms. Brown through MySpace. She brought the others. Santa Monica. October 30, 2010. (Photograph by the author.)

Yet there is something to be said for inviting celebrities. They can enliven a festival's atmosphere. According to Reyna Young, "I had Tony Moran (original Michael Myers) at our fest in 2009. So many people came out to see him, it was amazing. I couldn't believe how many people freaked over him being there. John [Gillette] and I were so proud of ourselves for giving the opportunity to locals to meet him and experience A Nightmare to Remember!"

Legal Issues

Many legal issues confront filmmakers and festivals, including laws pertaining to contracts, employment, corporations, securities, personal injury, copyright, trademark, libel, privacy, publicity, *et al.* Indie filmmakers and grassroots film festivals often ignore potential legal pitfalls. Budgets are low and there's rarely a profit. Everyone is working toward the same, shared goal: to make a great film or run a great festival. Many of the people involved in the project are friends, or friends of friends, or volunteers hoping to build professional contacts (i.e., to make friends). The reigning attitude is to "just do it" and hope that if everyone works in good faith, then everything will work out.

"Our biggest legal issues come from filmmakers not knowing the law," says Dragon*Con's Matthew M. Foster. "We've had entertainment lawyers speak [on panels] for that reason. Every year we get film after film where the filmmaker *does not have rights* to the characters they are using, the names, etc. But the worst is music. Filmmakers routinely put music into their films just because they liked it."

Directors of "fan films" (i.e., films based on *other people's* famous films, TV shows, or characters) rarely bother to secure any rights. Instead, they rely on the Fair Use exemption in copyright law, reasoning that the film is "just for fun" and not for profit. That's nice, but if you don't own the characters, you're limited to how or where you can distribute your film. You can screen it for your friends at home, sure. Beyond that, it becomes dicey.

Curiously, in all the festivals I've attended, I've not seen any horror fan films. I suppose some may exist, but fan films are more of a sci-fi/fantasy phenomenon. I've seen a few fan films screen at Loscon, featuring characters from *Doctor Who* and (yes) *Star Trek*. Fan films are typically of home movie quality, with the characters portrayed not by trained actors, but by fans.

Because popular music (such as a hit or classic song) is expensive to license for use in a film, many student and indie filmmakers only license the *festival rights*. The film can now screen with that hit music on the festival circuit, but nowhere else. Such filmmakers figure that they'll be able to afford the much pricier *commercial license fee* after the film finds a distributor. Because the distributor will pay for it. Sometimes that happens. Other times, a distributor may insist that the filmmaker reedit the film with cheaper music.

At least the expensive, hit music got the distributor's attention, right? But that's not always a good thing. The distributor may love the film *with* the expensive music, and cannot imagine the film *without* that music, and so, because the music is so expensive, rejects the film entirely.

Tip: If you can't afford a commercial hit song for your film, either license some cheap canned music, or hire an unknown composer. Many talented composers will grant you a *nonexclusive worldwide sync license* for little money, just to have their music showcased in a film.[8]

Consider originality over some popular but overused hit song. It's cheaper, and often better. I've seen several horror films over the past few years that played Karen Carpenter's "Only Just Begun," and several others that played Tammy Wynette's "Stand by Your Man." Yes, familiar songs provide a reliable emotional punch, but they rarely compensate for a mediocre film. Licensing original music, composed especially for your film, avoids the *aesthetic risk* of your film's story being overwhelmed by familiar *and superior* music, and the *financial risk* of buying festival rights to a song whose commercial rights you can't afford.

Regarding the aesthetic risk, I once saw a slipshod student video synced to John Lennon's "Imagine." Because the video was so sloppily shot and edited, Lennon's beautiful song failed to enhance the images, but rather, created a *contrast* that made the images appear that much crappier by comparison.

Music is most indie films' biggest legal pitfall. But a film's distribution potential can also be hindered because some of the items shown onscreen fall under copyright or trademark protection (e.g., book covers, movie posters, sports logos, famous dolls or plush toys, brand names, familiar landmarks). Did you know that New York City's Chrysler building is a registered trademark? If you feature the building too prominently in your film, you'll need permission. Read the end credits roll to M. Night Shyamalan's *Unbreakable* (2000). Or read the end credits to *Ghost Dog: The Way of the Samurai* (1999), which thanks Tor Books for allowing the film to show the cover to Tor's edition of *Frankenstein*, a public domain work. The end credits to *Ghost World* (2001) is also noteworthy for all the permissions the film secured.

I think that filming many of these objects *should* be allowed under Fair Use, and indeed *are* allowed if Fair Use is properly interpreted. But expensive lawyers and federal judges may disagree with me. Filmmakers wishing to avoid distribution problems — or lawsuits — might want to consult with an attorney *before* shooting their films.

What if you've already shot your film, and then an attorney says that your film shows an item onscreen that you can't, and thus, you won't secure a distribution deal? Normally, you'd have four options: 1. seek permission from the rights-holder *after* your film is shot (potentially expensive); 2. edit out the offending shots (creatively problematic); 3. digitally erase the offending item (expensive *and* creatively problematic); 4. self-distribute your film and hope you don't get sued. Perhaps you won't, if you're poor and your film flops. If your film is a hit, at least you'll have money for lawyers.

It's not just filmmakers who need permissions. Festivals are also legally liable if they screen a film that has music, or anything else, for which the filmmaker doesn't have permission.

"Festivals should clear permissions and rights for all the films they show," says Celluloid Screams's Robert Nevitt. "It takes a lot of work in some cases, but it has to be done." Michael Coulombe of Big Bear Horror agrees. "The best answer is CYA. [Cover your ass.] Make sure that the filmmakers own the rights to the movie, including the music they use in the movie. Part of the submission process includes the filmmaker signing terms and conditions stating that they, in fact, have obtained all licenses and clearances."

Eerie Horror Fest's Greg Ropp says, "*Festivals* need all the proper copyright clearances for their event and any screenings. They should be aware of BMI and ASCAP laws in regards to music being played either *between screenings* or *in the films* being shown. We have our entrants certify that they have secured the rights to use music within their films. Festivals should have a disclaimer on their entry forms and/or on Withoutabox covering the terms, should some legal issue arise."

Alas, *disclaimers* offer only limited protection to festivals. Normally, by signing the disclaimer (or *release form*, or whatever name the agreement goes by), the filmmaker agrees to reimburse the festival for any losses caused by the film infringing on the rights of others. Unfortunately, a disclaimer is only worth as much money as the filmmaker has — and many filmmakers at least claim to be broke by the time they finish their films.

Here's a possible scenario: Festival screens Filmmaker's *Slasher Terror*. Afterward, Jason claims he owns the copyright to the mask used in *Slasher Terror*. Jason sues *both* Festival and Filmmaker. The court awards Jason a million dollars. Legally, *both* Festival and Filmmaker owe a million dollars to Jason. This is called "joint and several liability." It means that Festival and Filmmaker jointly share in the debt. Each must pay as much as they can afford until Jason gets his full million. Jason can't get more than a million, but it doesn't matter who pays —*whoever has the money, pays*. No, a disclaimer cannot protect you from "joint and several liability."

Here's what a disclaimer does: Festival pays a million dollars to Jason. Then Festival sues Filmmaker for reimbursement of the million. *Because of the disclaimer*, Festival wins! The court awards a million dollars to Festival! Alas, Filmmaker is broke and pays nothing. Well, of course — this is why Festival paid the *full* million to Jason in the first place. (Of course, if *both* Festival and Filmmaker are broke, Jason gets no money, in which case he goes on a murder rampage at Festival's next event, or on Filmmaker's next production, whichever comes first.)

Some festival entry forms/disclaimers require that all disputes be settled by *private arbitration*, which is cheaper and faster than going to court. But only people who sign such an agreement are bound by it. Since Jason didn't sign, he can sue in court.

Although disclaimers offer only limited protection, they are not worthless: 1. Some filmmakers actually have money. If not a million dollars, then an old car, or perhaps some nice camera equipment. 2. The disclaimer's legalese may scare some filmmakers into thinking, *Do I really own all the rights in my film?* If not, or if they're unsure, they may reconsider submitting their film, sparing legal problems for the festival.

Festivals can obtain additional legal protection by: 1. *Incorporating themselves.* Then when Jason sues, he might still end up owning the festival, but at least he won't own the festival director's house. 2. *Buying insurance.* An "errors and omissions" policy offers protection against claims for copyright or trademark infringement, libel, invasion of privacy, and related matters.[9]

Ropp recommends that festivals hire a lawyer and buy insurance. Lawyers can help festivals avoid lawsuits. And apart from "errors and omissions," if a theater patron slips and falls in the aisle, and sues, liability insurance will cover their damages.

Many public venues already have music performance licenses and insurance policies that will cover your festival screenings. But ask and make sure. In some cases, the festival may have to buy its own music performance license and/or insurance policy.

Whatever the issue, Van Hauwaert advises to *get it in writing.* "A given word is worth nothing these days. Better sign a contract. If the signed contract doesn't come in, something is not right."

Finally, *nothing in this book is intended as legal advice. Neither the author, publisher, nor any of the people interviewed for this book guarantee the accuracy of, or assume any legal liability for, anything contained herein. If you require legal advice, consult an attorney.* (In English: No matter how much you paid for this book, you can't sue us, so don't even try.)

Do Film Festivals *Really* Help?

Filmmakers enter festivals for two main reasons. They seek *distributors* for their films and *promotion* for their careers. A festival selection or award guarantees nothing, but there are success stories.

Gaz Bailey of Abertoir says, "The £45 zombie film, *Colin*, directed by Marc Price, was shown here. We saw past the limitations of budget, and realized here was a talented filmmaker with a fresh idea — a film from a zombie's point of view. We screened the film and recommended it to a sales agent, Helen Grace from Left Films. She took it on and got it screened in Cannes 2009, where it got worldwide recognition for being the '£45 zombie movie.' It has since been sold around the world, both on DVD and in cinemas. There have been two other films that Left Films have taken on after our recommendations, *Resurrecting the Street Walker* and *Umbrage.* The latter screened at Cannes 2010 for the world market. Our festival has a good track record of helping indie movies find a sales agent."

Weekend of Fear has its own success stories. Matthias Engelhardt says, "A lot of movies found German distributors at our festival. *Dead & Breakfast*, a U.S. production, won the jury award in 2004 and found a distributor. A lot of German directors — Olaf Ittenbach, Joerg Buttgereit, Andreas Schnaas, Timo Rose — were at our festival from the beginning of their careers." That's also the case with international directors. "Weekend of Fear was the first German festival that screened *Braindead.* Peter Jackson and Timothy Balme were among our guests."

Shriekfest has "tons" of success stories, according to Denise Gossett. "We have a success page and a testimonial page [on the website]. Ninety-five percent of all features that have screened at Shriekfest have gotten distribution. Screenplays get sold every year, and often come back to compete in film form the next year. We do not give out filmmaker or screenwriter private info. We give tons of referrals every year, but we always let the filmmaker or screenwriter decide if they want to contact the interested party."

Ken Daniels relates Fright Night's successes: "*Nightmare Man*, with Tiffany Shepis, went on to play at 8 Films to Die For After Dark Horrorfest. *Bad Reputation* was distributed through Maverick Entertainment and shown at Blockbuster. Gary Ugarek, director of *Deadlands Rising 1* and *2*, is in negotiations for a one million [dollar] deal for his third picture. *Miyuki* was picked up by R2 distribution. *Dead Moon Rising*, directed by Mark Poole, was picked up internationally — number six bestseller at Best Buy and played at several theatres."

Nightmare Man is a great film — tense, energetic, and full of surprises. In 2006, it won Tabloid Witch Awards for Best Feature Film, Best Cinematography, Best Music Soundtrack, Best Actress, and Best Supporting Actress (which went to Tiffany Shepis).

Vivi Amaral of Brazil's Cinefantasy says, "There are some filmmakers who could be recognized by media and public through the festival. Joel Caetano is one. He sent his first short film to the first edition of the festival. Since then, he has always sent short films to Cinefantasy. Last year [2009], he won the Audience Award for short films. This year, a PhD in Brazilian horror movies made a study about Joel's films."

According to the Terror Film Festival, "When a film wins a Claw Award, it usually picks up distribution within the next three months. All of our best feature winners were picked up right after the festival." Matt Manjourides of TromaDance adds, "We found the team that is now shooting *Father's Day*, produced by Troma, through the TromaDance film festival."

Other festivals' claims are more modest. "We are a very young festival," says Razor Reel's Van Hauwaert, "so we can't claim any fame. However, a nice part of the films we have selected — and were not on any other Belgium festival before — found some distributors. Of course, it all could be coincidence." Dragon*Con's Foster concurs. "We've had numerous filmmakers who have gone on to bigger things, but I cannot say how much of that was from our fest."

Greg Ropp adds, "I'm not sure anyone has gotten a deal or distribution based solely on our event, but I know we've had our palm leaves and name featured on several DVD releases over the years. Our fest was definitely a part of the journey for these people, but not the end game. Every win helps. In that regard, we are confident that we've played a small role in helping these folks get noticed."

The Tabloid Witch has had its own modest successes. In 2007, *Dead Noon* won two Tabloid Witches (and promotion in the *Hollywood Investigator*), which actor Robert Bear credits for the film's DVD deal with Lion's Gate. Bear posted his gratitude on his MySpace page: "The Tabloid Witch Awards was a huge help in getting our movie picked up by a studio. Thanks again for getting our film out there. Anyone with a great independent horror film [should] submit it to these guys. Pure Gold!"

Hanelle Culpepper's *Within* secured a distribution deal (DVD and broadcast on the Lifetime network) after back-to-back wins at the Big Bear Horror Film Festival and Tabloid Witch Awards in fall 2009. Director Culpepper emailed me: "Since there are so many independent horror films made, winning awards helps to legitimize a movie. *Within* had no major stars and no gore/sex — so the awards provided a marketing hook to get the attention of potential buyers. It's always better to have outside sources say your film is great, rather than just saying it yourself — and awards say that."

Awards can even help find distribution for *short* films, which are generally harder to place. Paul Carty, a Tabloid Witch Honorable Mention winner in 2006, emailed me: "Thank you for the heads-up on the distribution opportunities. I just signed a licensing/distribution agreement for *The Kooky Kastle* with The Crypt Club Productions."

Not that any distribution deal is better than none. According to Ropp, "I urge filmmakers to take time and have patience when trying to find a distributor. I've seen many rush to get a deal just to boast that they were successful in getting distribution for their project, only to learn later on that the deal wasn't as good as they thought. I even know one case where the filmmaker now owes the distributor money! Get an attorney. Don't take the first offer just to get your project out there. Keep a lid on your ego."

Horror journalist Eddie McMullen (of FeoAmante.com) advises filmmakers to avoid distributors whose only plan is to release your film on Amazon.com's CreateSpace. *Anyone* can upload and distribute films on CreateSpace. If that's to be your film's only distribution, you should do-it-yourself and get 100 percent of the proceeds (after Amazon takes its cut), rather than let a "distributor" upload your film and get only 50 percent. Some distributors *promise* to promote your film to earn their 50 percent, but McMullen warns that this often amounts to nothing. Many unscrupulous indie distributors will toss a few dozen films up on CreateSpace a year, and barely promote them for their 50 percent.

McMullen also advises filmmakers to reject royalties-only contracts. Get an advance payment. Royalties-only distributors will tell filmmakers: "There is no advance. This means we're *both* taking a risk." McMullen disagrees. "No, the filmmaker *already* took the risk in financing the film. The film might have turned out badly. If a distributor is interested in a film, that means the film didn't turn out badly. Now it's the *distributor's turn* to take a risk by paying for the distribution costs — including paying an advance to the filmmaker."

Of course, just how badly does anyone want your film? A royalties-only contract for *nonexclusive* distribution rights might make some sense for *short* films. Short films are harder to distribute. Many award-winning short films are tossed up on YouTube because the filmmaker couldn't find a paying audience for it beyond the festival circuit.

I've heard several indie filmmakers say nice things about Netflix. That they are effective in getting a film "out there" before the public, to be seen by many. Netflix sometimes picks up films that have no other distributor, so that the film becomes "exclusive to Netflix," at least for a limited time. Amazon has a similar "exclusive for a limited time" program. I don't know if either Netflix or Amazon pay advances.

Naturally, you should shop around for the best deal. Start with the top studios, TV networks, and DVD distributors, then lower your expectations as the rejections pile up. Heed Ropp's advice: get an attorney to research the *terms of your contract*. But also *research the distributor*. Which retailers (brick-and-mortar, and online) carry their films? Have they heavily promoted other filmmakers? Have you *seen* their promotional efforts? Ask around.

Directory of Festivals and Awards

New film festivals are always starting up, even as old ones die. Some festivals endure for decades, some fold after one year, some never live to see their first screening. All that remains of them is an abandoned MySpace account. This is why I list each festival's founding year. A festival that's been around for a while will likely be around a while longer. *Longevity indicates stability.* No guarantees, but an older festival is less likely to fold and keep your entry fee. So if money is tight, you might want to bypass a new festival. Unlike the Oscars, most horror film festivals don't care when you completed or first publicly screened your film, so waiting another year to enter won't harm its eligibility. (However, new festivals are *usually* less competitive, so your chances of being selected may be better.)

This directory emphasizes currently active horror film festivals that accept new films. But I've also included dormant festivals (because "sometimes they come back"); genre conventions that screen new horror films; sci-fi/fantasy festivals that welcome horror films; and horror (and sci-fi/fantasy) film and TV awards that are unconnected to film festivals.

If you know of a festival, award, or organization that should be listed, or know of any changes, updates, or corrections, please contact me at thomas@sipos.org.

Argentina

BARS: Buenos Aires Rojo Sangre

Casilla de Correo 19, Correo Argentino, Sucursal 2- Martínez, CP 1640 Buenos Aires. Director: Pablo Sapere. Ph: +54-11-4733-0890. Email: correo@quintadimension.com. Web: rojosangre.quintadimension.com, MySpace.com/buenosairesrojosangre, Facebook.com/BuenosAiresRojoSangre, Twitter.com/rojosangre. First screening 1999. Awards first presented 2004.

Australia

Beg, Scream and Shout!

2 Maghull St East Brunswick, Melbourne Vic 3057. Email: mikey@begscreamandshout.com. Web: begscreamandshout.com. Not a film festival, but a monthly film screening at the Workers Club in Melbourne's Fitzroy neighborhood. "We don't care if your piece is 30 seconds or 4 hours, if we like it we'll figure out some way to show it: short film, music clip, feature or some weird ass piece of video art you and a friend cooked up over a weekend of no sleep." Not specifically horror, but appears to welcome horror. Apparently there's **no entry fee**.

Melbourne Underground Film Festival

PO Box 822, South Yarra, VIC 3141. Director: Richard Wolstencroft. Email: info@muff.com.au. Web: muff.com.au, Facebook.com/group.php?gid=254554504486, Twitter.com/MUFFXI. First screening 2000. Not a horror festival, but welcomes horror.

A Night of Horror International Film Festival

PO Box 143, Beecroft NSW 2119. Contacts: Dean Bertram, Lisa Mitchell. Email: info@anightofhorror.com. Web: anightofhorror.com, MySpace.com/nightofhorror, Facebook.com/group.php?gid=4301147862, Twitter.com/anightofhorror. First screening 2007. Screening location Sydney, Australia. Screenplay contest.

Scary Brains Horror Film Festival — defunct?

SBHFF/Rigby Transmedia, 6256 Caves Road, Margaret River, Western Australia 6285. Claims to also screen in New York, USA. Web: MySpace.com/scaryfilmfest. As of December 2010, their MySpace page has not been logged into since June 2009.

Schlockfest

PO Box 2002, Fortitude Valley B.C., Qld 4006. Contact: Zillah Hose. Web: myspace.com/schlockfest, shadowtheory.com. Email: schlockfest@hotmail.com. A roving horror show, with live music, burlesque performance, and **short** films (7 minutes max) by **local** filmmakers. Films "must adhere to the schlock horror genre.... Schlockfest is a beast without a home, roaming Fortitude Valley and appearing at The Troubadour and The Globe Theatre among other homes!" Fortitude Valley is in Brisbane, Queensland.

Sydney Underground Film Festival

PO Box 202, Summer Hill NSW 2130, Australia. Directors: Katherine Berger, Stefan Popescu. Ph: +61-2-9797-9428 and +61-430-471-598. Email: info@suff.com.au. Web: suff.com.au, sydneyundergroundfilmfestival.com. Supports "alternative film culture through the promotion of independent and experimental films ... [and] filmmakers who operate outside established film industry infrastructures, by providing a platform for exhibition, exposure and critical discussion." Not a horror festival, but should be open to horror. Calls its trophy the "Suff Dead Oscar."

Belgium

BIFFF: Brussels International Fantastic Film Festival

Peymey Diffusion A.S.B.L., Rue de la Comtesse de Flandre 8 Gravin van Vlaanderenstraat, 1020 Brussels. Contact: Christoph Foque. Ph: 02-201-17-13. Fax: 02-201-14-69. Email: info@bifff.net. Web: bifff.org, MySpace.com/fantasticfilmfestival, Facebook.com/group.php?gid=6228548591.

European Fantastic Film Festivals Federation

Rue de la Comtesse de Flandre 8, B-1020 Brussels. Ph: +32-2-201-1713. Fax: +32-2-201-1469. Web: melies.org. Not a film festival. The EFFFF presents the Méliès d'Or (Golden Méliès) for Best European Fantastic Feature Film and Best European Fantastic Short Film. Feature films have been honored since 1996, short films since 2002. The EFFFF has 20 member festivals, not all in Europe. Membership levels include Affiliated, Adherent, and Supporting. Depending on their membership level, festivals present the Méliès d'Argent (Silver Méliès), a "nomination award," to feature films.

Razor Reel Fantastic Film Festival

St.-Arnolduslaan 47, B-8200 Brugge, Belgium. Contacts: Yves Ballegeer, ph: +32-0-498-841399; Patrick Van Hauwaert, +32-0-497-532314; Kristof De Vestele, +32-0-476-799987. Fax: +32-0-50-82 6799. Email: info@razorreel.be. Founded 2008. Accepts films "situated in an unrealistic world and/or the situation is so uncommon or extreme that this never happens." Wants horror, science fiction, thriller, manga, fantasy, absurdist comedy, and "enchanting fairylike stories." **No entry fee.**

Brazil

Cinefantasy International Film Festival

Espada Street, 73, Alphaville, Stna. de Parnaiba, São Paulo, 06540395. Founder and director: Vivi Amaral. Ph: 55-11-8754-9383, skype: vivi.cine fantasy. Email: contact@cinefantasy.com.br. Web: cinefantasy.com.br, cinefantastico.com.br, MySpace.com/curtafantastico, Facebook.com/cinefantasy, Twitter.com/cinefantasy. Founded 2005. First screening 2006. Features and shorts. In addition to horror accepts sci-fi, fantasy. Screenplay contest, also no entry fee, for features and shorts. And "a screenplay contest for very scary 'minishort' films (no more than 5 minutes long), The Master of the Scream Contest." **No admission fee** for audiences. "We are trying to work with Brazilian audiences in order to strengthen it for fantastic film genre. So, for now, we will not charge tickets." Presents The Dry Corpse Trophy. "It's about a Brazilian legend." **No entry fee.**

Fantaspoa: Festival Internacional de Cinema Fantástico de Porto Alegre

Rua Dom João VI, 246, CEP: 90660-020, Porto Alegre, RS, Brasil. Contact: João Fleck. Ph: 5551-8436-2968. Email: fantaspoa@fantaspoa.com. Web: Fantaspoa.com. Founded 2005. **No entry fee.**

RIOFAN: Rio Fantastic Film Festival — defunct?

RIOFAN, Rua Senador Dantas 80, sala 1301, Centro, Rio de Janeiro, RJ, CEP 20031-201. Rio de Janeiro, RJ. Contact: Fernando Verissimo. Email: info@riofan.com.br. Web: riofan.com.br, MySpace.com/riofantasticfilmfestival. Website down throughout 2010. MySpace not logged into since April 2009. Email bounces throughout 2010. On August 10, 2010, João Fleck of Fantaspoa emailed me: "RioFan, in Rio de Janeiro only had one edition and they decided to cancel the festival." **No entry fee.**

SP Terror — Festival Internacional de Cinema Fantástico

Reserva Cultural, Av Paulista, 900, São Paulo. Ph: 11-3287-3529. Or: CineSesc, Rua Augusta, 2075, São Paulo. Ph: 11 3082-0213. Contact: Fernando Henrique. Email: info@spterror.com, fehenrique77@hotmail.com. Web: spterror.com, Facebook.com/pages/SP-TERROR/132371243446334, Twitter.com/spterror.

Trash: Mostra Goiana de Filmes Independentes

Email: Mostratrash@gmail.com. Web: mostratrash.com.br. João Fleck of Fantaspoa describes Trash as "a small festival, dedicated to trash films."

Canada

Calgary Underground Film Festival

#212, 223-12 Avenue SW, Calgary, Alberta T2R 0G9. Ph: 403-852-0279. Email: cuff@calgaryundergroundfilm.org. Web: calgaryundergroundfilm.org. Founded 2003. Screening location Calgary, Alberta. Not specifically a horror festival. Seeks "films that defy convention ... feature, documentary, animation, short, experimental ... all genres, from horror, sci-fi and fantasy to comedies, thrillers and music-related films."

Constellation Award

PO Box 7097, Station A, Toronto, Ontario, M5W 1X7. Ph: 416-410-8266. Email: constellations@tcon.ca. Web: constellations.tcon.ca. Facebook.com/pages/The-Constellation-Awards/126413587420834, Twitter.com/CDNSciFiAwards. Not a film festival. "...Canada's annual science fiction awards focused on rewarding excellence in science fiction film and television. Now in its fifth year [2011], the Constellation Awards celebrate and honor the actors, writers, and technical artists behind the best of today's science fiction film and TV works — with an added focus on Canadian contributions to science fiction film and television. The Constellation Awards are also the only Canadian science fiction film and TV awards where YOU, the Canadian viewing public, get to select the nominees and winners in all categories."

Danse Macabre International Horror Film Festival — defunct?

Kingston, ON. Web: dansemacabre.ca, MySpace.com/dansemacabrefilmfest. First screening 2007. As of October 2010, this festival's site is expired. Its MySpace page indicates that they only accepted short films.

Dark Bridges Film Festival

920 7th Street, Saskatoon, SK, S7H 0Y6. Contact: John Allison. Email: john@darkbridges.com. Web: darkbridges.com, Facebook.com/DarkBridges. First screening 2010. Accepts "cool independent and foreign genre films." **No entry fee.**

Exofest — defunct?

Edmonton, Alberta. Contact: David Bond. Email: dbond@exophagy.com. Web: exofest.com. In January 2010 Exofest's David Bond emailed me: "We haven't decided if we will continue with the festival." As of June 2010 their website was still "last updated" in May 2007.

Fantasia International Film Festival

Montreal. Co-director of international programming: Mitch Davis. Email: mitch@fantasiafestival.com. Web: fantasiafest.com, MySpace.com/fantasiafest, facebook.com/group.php?gid=2312858507, Twitter.com/FantasiaFest. Founded 1996. "While predominantly a fantastic film festival, Fantasia has always embraced films whose sheer individuality puts them in a genre of their own ... we've showcased captivating dramas, eccentric comedies, provocative documentaries, mind-blowing experimental works, musicals, atypical children's films.... Any work produced in the past 18 months is eligible for official jury competition and our Public's Prize." **No entry fee for Canadian films.** Non-Canadian films can submit, but are charged a fee.

Indie Horror Film Festival — defunct?

Vancouver. Web: Facebook.com/topic.php?uid=31491046993&topic=7599. Apart from some 2009 postings on Facebook by "The Gory Hole: Miss.Gory-Rae" [sic], I can't find a trace of this festival anywhere. Not to be confused with the Indy Horror Film Festival in the United States.

Midnight Madness — Toronto International Film Festival

Toronto. Ph: 416-968-FILM or 1-877-968-FILM. Email: submissions@tiff.net. tiff.net/filmsandschedules/programmes/midnightmadness, MySpace.com/midnightmadness_tiff, Facebook.com/group.php?gid=2583935211. Midnight Madness is the horror portion of the greater Toronto International Film Festival.

Rue Morgue Festival of Fear

2926 Dundas Street West, Toronto ON, M6P 1Y8. Contact: David Daniloff. Ph: 416-651-9675. Fax: 416-651-6085. Email: daniloff@rue-morgue.com. Web: rue-morgue.com/rmp_fof.php. Well-known horror magazine *Rue Morgue* runs this "horror expo." Daniloff tells me: "David Cronenberg was the recipient of the Rue Morgue Lifetime Achievement Award at this year's [2010] Festival of Fear. Other than that we don't present any awards normally. FoF was founded in 2004. FoF is not a film festival but rather a horror convention." Nevertheless, their site indicates that they've screened new horror films in the past, including shorts. Not a major screening opportunity (obviously), but you can always ask.

Spacey Award — defunct

SPACE, CTVglobemedia, 299 Queen Street West, Toronto, Ontario, M5V 2Z5. Email: space@

spacecast.com. Web: Spacecast.com/spaceys, Facebook.com/SPACEchannel, Twitter.com/SPACEchannel. Not a film festival. According to Wikipedia, this award is "presented by the Canadian cable network Space. Awards are presented in the areas of sci-fi, fantasy and horror films, television series and video games. Some of the awards are voted on by the viewers choice and the others by Space employees.... It's unknown whether there will be any more Spacey Awards since CTV took over the Space channel." Unknown no more. The Space Channel emails me that they "no longer have the Spaceys." Apparently, 2007 was their last year. Aka The Spaceys.

Toronto After Dark Film Festival

3219 Yonge Street, Suite 346, Toronto, Ontario M4N 3S1. Contact: Chris Emery. Ph: 416-995-8448. Fax: 416-481-7028. Email: info@torontoafterdark.com. Web: torontoafterdark.com, MySpace.com/torontoafterdark, Facebook.com/torontoafterdark, Twitter.com/TADFilmFest. Founded/first screening 2006. Accepts feature and shorts. Lower entry fees for Canadian filmmakers.

Winnipeg Horror Cinema

71 Bonin Bay, Winnipeg, Manitoba R3V 1P8. Organizer: Kevin Bacon (no relation to the actor). Ph: 204-293-3959. Email: winnipeghorrorcinema@gmail.com. Web: Facebook.com/pages/Winnipeg-Horror-Cinema/124122860974540. Founded/first screening 2010. Shorts only.

Winnipeg Short Film Massacre—defunct

Web: winnipegshortfilmmassacre.com. MySpace.com/winnipegshortfilmmassacre. Website indicates that this "Canadian only" short film festival ran from 2004–2009. "After six years of bringing you homegrown horror, the Winnipeg Short Film Massacre is disbanding." The farewell message continues, and is signed by Jenn Jozwiak and Jeremy Gillespie, and is dated September 2010.

Zombie Short Film Festival

The Revue Cinema, 400 Roncesvalles Avenue, Toronto, ON, M6R 2M9. Co-founder and coordinator: Jim Taylor. Ph: 1-647-291-4774. Email: zombieshortfilmfestival@gmail.com. Web: zombieshortfilmfestival.com, Facebook.com/pages/The-Zombie-Short-Film-Festival/146096955201, Twitter.com/ZombieFilmFest. Founded/first screening 2009. Screening locations: Toronto; tentative for New York City. Accepts shorts only; no longer than 20 minutes. Any genre, "provided the film features zombies." $500 cash prize and Z'omb D'or Award.

Chile

FIXION-SARS: Festival de Cine Fantástico y de Terror de Santiago

Contact: Jaime Albornoz. Web: fixionsars.com, Facebook.com/FIXIONSARS, Twitter.com/fixion_sars. Founded 2007. They ran in 2007, 2008, then skipped 2009. They were to return in 2010. On October 21, 2010, Mr. Albornoz emailed me: "Due to a problem with the Consejo de Calificacion Cinematografica (the chilean MPAA), we had to change the dates of our festival. This change in the engagement book, as far as possible, does not alter the works and movies already selected, nor some of the activities that were planned and ready to be published." Although they skipped 2010, as of July 2011, they're all set up for their October 2011 event.

Colombia

Zinema Zombie Fest

Web: zinemazombie.com, MySpace.com/zinemazombie. Their sites give little information, but it seems they're a convention, with conferences in addition to any film screenings.

Estonia

Haapsalu Horror & Fantasy Film Festival

HOFF/Tallinna Pimedate Ööde Filmifestival, Telliskvi 60A 10143 Tallinn Estonia. Ph: +372-6-314-640. Fax: +372-6-314-644. Director: Sten-Kristian Saluveer. Email: sten.saluveer@poff.ee. Web: hoff.ee, poff.ee, Facebook.com/hoffestival, Twitter.com/@h6ff. Founded 2006. "A three day independent festival focusing of screening best films from the darker side of cinema from fantasy to horror, forgotten classics, filmmaker and country retrospectives, extreme films and celebrated guests ... takes place either on late March or April usually coinciding with full moon." Winners received the White Lady Award.

Finland

Espoo Ciné International Film Festival

PO Box 95, 02101 Espoo, Finland. Director: Timo Kuismin. Ph: +358-9-466-599. Fax: +358-9-466-458. Email: office@espoocine.fi. Web: espoocine.fi. "Espoo Ciné is a general film festival focusing on new European cinema, with special sections as e.g. fantastic films and gay films." They are an EFFFF member.

France

Festival Européen du Film Fantastique de Strasbourg

Les Films du Spectre, 18, rue du vieux marché aux poisons, 67000 Strasbourg, France. Directeur Artistique: Daniel Cohen. Directrice Adjointe: Consuelo Holtzer. Ph: +33-(0)-607-104-758. Email: spectrefilm@gmail.com. Web: strasbourgfestival.com, spectrefilm.com. Mr. Cohen emails me: "In 2006 and 2007, the festival had no competition. We only screened classics. In 2006, the festival's name was Hammer Film Festival.... In 2007, the festival's name was Spectre Film Festival, and we made a panorama of different sub-genre in science fiction [again, all older classics] ... in 2008 we changed the name of the festival to Strasbourg European Fantastic Film Festival when we started to show *new* productions and created an European fantastic film competition for shorts and feature films. Since the 2009 edition we are adherent member of the European Fantastic Film Festival Federation (www.melies.org) and we became affiliated member since 2010. That's why the awards changed every year (Golden Octopus, Méliès d'Argent etc)." A.K.A. Strasbourg European Fantastic Film Festival.

Festival International du Film Fantastique de Gérardmer

Festival de Gérardmer, 29 avenue du 19 Novembre — BP 105, 88403 Gérardmer Cedex. Coordinateur Général: Anthony Humbertclaude. Ph: 03-29-60-1142 (standard 9821). Fax: 03-29-60-9814. Email: ahumbertclaude@festival-gerardmer.com, info@festival-gerardmer.com. Web: festival-gerardmer.com, Facebook.com/pages/Festival-International-du-Film-Fantastique-de-Gerardmer-Officiel/138285092886150. Accepts features and shorts. "Dedicated to the fantasy genre under all its forms: science-fiction, horror, supernatural, etc...."

Gorenight

Email: gorenight@free.fr. Web: gorenight.free.fr, MySpace.com/gorenight. First screening 2004. Welcomes "trash" films and work by "amateurs."

Utopiales — Festival International de Science-Fiction de Nantes

5 rue de Valmy, BP 24102, 44 041 NANTES Cedex 1. President: Pierre Bordage. Ph: +33 (0) 2 51 88 20 54. Fax: +33 (0) 2-4035-5723. Email: organisation@utopiales.org. Film Section Contact: Marie Masson. Ph: +33 (0) 2-5188-2054. Email: info@nantes. Web: utopiales.org, http://fr.facebook.com/people/Utopiales-Nantes/100001690299870, Twitter.com/utopiales2010. Founded 1998. Seems more of a convention than a film festival, but they do screen films. "A multimedia festival featuring whole sections devoted to literature, comics, science, video games and, of course, film.... [T]he most important SF cultural event in Europe and one of the biggest SF writers' conventions in the world. The film section at Utopiales organizes yearly international feature and short film competitions as well as retrospectives and special programs."

Germany

Amberg Horror Fest—defunct

Amberg, Bavaria. Web: amberghorrorfest.com, MySpace.com/amberghorrorfest, Facebook.com/group.php?gid=26589786115. Website is down. On December 2010 their MySpace page still says: "Hell Nights Tour 2008 kicks off in Amberg on the 28th of October."

Fantasy Film Fest

Rosebud Entertainment, Andreas Bernauer, Herzog-Wilhelm-Str. 27, 80331 München. Email: fans@rosebud-entertainment.de. Web: fantasyfilmfest.com, MySpace.com/fantasyfilmfest. Screenings in cities throughout Germany.

Weekend of Fear: Internationales Filmfestival für Horror, Thriller, Science Fiction & Obskure Filme

c/o Mike Neun, 9 Films International, Glueckstr. 1, DE-91054, Erlangen. Contacts: Mike Neun, director; Matthias Engelhardt, head of acquisition. Ph: 0049-(0)9131-209384. Fax: 09131-125803. Emails: mike@weekend-of-fear.com (Neun's), maze@weekend-of-fear.com (Engelhardt's). Web: Weekend-of-Fear.com, MySpace.com/weekendoffear, Twitter.com/WOFFILMFESTIVAL.

Founded/first screening 1990. Screening location Erlangen, Germany. Accepts features and shorts. In addition to horror accepts sci-fi, dark comedy, fantasy, thriller, action, weird, obscure. Plaques and an audience award, The Golden Glibb (among other colors), a two-foot high, edible jelly baby. Not to be confused with *Fangoria*'s Weekend of Fear. **No entry fee.**

Weekend of Horrors

CC Entertainment, Ferdinands Höh 22, 22587 Hamburg. Contact: Thomas Hartz. Email: info@weekendofhorrors.com. Web: weekendofhorrors.com, MySpace.com/189864451. A convention rather than a film festival, but they screen a few films.

Greece

Screamin' Athens Horror Film Festival

101A Voutsina Street, 15561 Holargos, Athens. Founder and director: Rena Orocklou. Ph: 003

06942575548. Email: rena.orocklou@gmail.com. Web: MySpace.com/screaminathensfest, Facebook.com/group.php?gid=34858258574. Founded 2007. First screening 2008. Screening location Athens, Greece. Accepts features and shorts. In addition to horror accepts thrillers and documentaries. No prizes. **No entry fee.**

Ireland

Horrorthon

Irish Film Institute, 6 Eustace Street, Temple Bar, Dublin 2. Director and programmer: Ed King. Ph: +353-1-679-5744 or 01-679-3477. Email: info@irishfilm.ie. Web: horrorthon.com, irishfilm.ie/horrorthon2010. Founded in 1997.

Italy

Fanta Festival

25 Maggio — 6 Giugno, Roma. Directors: Adriano Pintaldi, Alberto Ravaglioli. Their emails: a.pintaldi@immaginestrategia.com and albertorav@libero.it. Also: info@fanta-festival.it. Ph: 06-8841246 or 06-8413721. Fax: 06-8841310. Web: fanta-festival.it, MySpace.com/fantafestival, Facebook.com/pages/Fantafestival/101013713273620, Twitter.com/fantafestival. Primarily a science fiction and fantasy festival, but they are open to horror. Roger Corman was a guest attendee.

Ravenna Nightmare Film Festival

ST/ART, via Mura di Porta Serrata 13, 48100 Ravenna, Italy. Director: Franco Calandrini. Ph: +39-0544-684242. Fax: +39.0544.682970. Email: ravenna@melies.org and ravennanightmare@gmail.com. Web: ravennanightmare.it. First screening 2003.

Science+Fiction

via Economo 12/9, 34123 Trieste. Contact: Giovanni Barbo. Ph: +39-040-3220551. Email: giovanni.barbo@scienceplusfiction.org, info@scienceplusfiction.org. Web: scienceplusfiction.org. This festival is, at least in spirit, a continuation of the old Trieste International Science Fiction Film Festival. Barbo tells me: "That was a different festival, and lasted from 1963 to 1982. Then there was a gap, to be filled starting from year 2000 by our new festival.... You could call it a resurrection, I guess." Founded 2000. Presents the Urania d'Argento (Silver Urania), a career achievement award, and the Asteroide Award, for the best film in competition. The Urania d'Argento was first presented in 2002. Claims to be "a showcase for new trends in sci-fi, fantasy and horror film." Despite their sci-fi name, this festival's past guests and honorees include such horror icons as Dario Argento, Lamberto Bava, John Landis, Joe Dante, Roger Corman, and Christopher Lee. A.K.A. scienceplusfiction.

Trieste International Science Fiction Film Festival — defunct

See entry for Science+Fiction.

Latvia

Riga International Fantasy Film Festival

Marstalu iela 14, Riga LV-1050, Latvia. Director: Augusts Sukuts. Ph: +371-7221620. Fax: +371 782 0445. Email: fff@arsenals.lv and sarlote@arsenals.lv. Web: arsenals.lv. First screening 2003. "The Festival proceeds once in two years in the spring.... Full length films enter the FFF competition to be assessed by a jury of film theoreticians, filmmakers, those fond of fantasy film." The festival showcases "latest productions from fantasy film, Sci-Fi, horror and thriller genres." They present The Golden Tooth to the best film, and a "special jury prize" called The Silver Tooth.

Japan

Yubari International Fantastic Film Festival

(city of) Yūbari, Sorachi, (on the island of) Hokkaidō, Japan. Web: yubarifanta.com. Founded 1990. As the name implies, this is not primarily a horror festival, but horror films are welcome. "The Yubari International Fantastic Film Festival was the first of its kind to be held in a resort-like environment.... The film festival is not only about the movies, it's also about the delightful foods of Hokkaido, skiing and snowboarding. It's also a chance for locals to meet celebrities from around the world."

Mexico

Aurora: Cuarta Muestra de cine de Horror

Guanajutao, Mexico. Director general: Alejandro Montes Santamaria. Ph: 01-473-73-23971 (para mensajes) and 45-473-1030407 (cel). Email: aurora.horror@gmail.com. Web: mictlan.envy.nu, aurorahorror.blogspot.com. Website in Spanish.

Macabro: Festival de Horror en Cine y Video

PO Box 77-A, Centro Cívico, Cd. Satélite, 53100. Email: festivalmacabro@yahoo.com.mx, Web: macabro.mx/Festival_Macabro/Festival_Macabro.html, My-

Space.com/festivalmacabro, Facebook.com/pages-/Macabro-Film-Festival/55401035969, Twitter.com/festivalmacabro. Founded 2002. Accepts features and shorts. Screens in locations throughout Mexico. Non-competition, but that may change beginning in 2010. "Produced by the nonprofit Organization Arte Audiovisual Alternativo."

MORBIDO Festival Internacional de Cine Fantastico y de Terror / Morbido Film Fest

Tabasco 93-A, Col Roma, CP 06700, Mexico DF. CEO/director: Pablo Guisa Koestinger. Ph: (52) 55-52-087-225 Mexico City, and (52) 55-52-088-007 Mexico City. Emails: pguisa@spiderland.tv, pguisa@morbidofest.com, info@morbidofest.com. Web: MorbidoFest.com, Twitter.com/morbidofest. Founded 2007. First screening 2008. Screening at four locations: primarily in Tlalpujahua, Michoacan; also in Mexico City, Oaxaca, Oaxaca and Merida, Yucatan. Also screens at local cemeteries. Accepts features and shorts. In addition to horror accepts fantasy. Presents the Golden Sugar Skull and Silver Sugar Skull trophies. **No entry fee.**

Netherlands

BUT: B-Movies, Underground & Trash Film Festival

Stichting Idee-fixe, tav. BUT 2011, Markendaalse weg 36, 4811 KC Breda. Email: post@butff.nl. Web: butff.nl, Myspace.com/butff, Facebook.com/group.php?taal=1&gid=141389281038, Twitter.com/butfilmfestival. First screening 2006. Seeks "films made on a small budget, independent of big studio productions. Underground-films are films pioneering at the borders of admissibility. Often they contain explicit features. Trash-films are over-the-top films with an extravagant content and imagery." Not a horror festival, but obviously open to horror. Event includes "performances, lectures, workshops, art." **No entry fee.**

Duistere Openbaringen (Dark Revelations) Film Festival

Postbus 857, 5700 AW Helmond. Festival Organisator: Emiel Labree. Email: info@duistere-openbaringen.net. Web: duistere-openbaringen.net. Website lists winners going back to 2005. In addition to horror accepts thriller, suspense, crime, mystery, dark drama.

Imagine: Amsterdam Fantastic Film Festival

Timorplein 52, 1094 CC Amsterdam. Ph: +31-0-20-679-4875. Contact: Phil van Tongeren. phil@imaginefilmfestival.nl or info@imaginefilmfestival.nl. Web: imaginefilmfestival.nl, Facebook.com/group.php?v=wall&gid=355050928011, Twitter.com/ImagineAFFF. Van Tongeren emails me: "Imagine started in 1984. It started out as 'The Weekend of Terror,' but nowadays we're a ten-day festival, where other fantastic genres are equally important as horror." That is, they began as a horror festival, but now also welcome sci-fi, fantasy, animation, animie, cult, exploitation, and trash. European Fantastic Film Festivals Federation affiliate.

North America

North American Fantastic Festival Alliance

Web: fantasticalliance.org. According to their website: "NAFFA was founded by Montreal's Fantasia, Alamo Drafthouse's Fantastic Fest in Austin and Dead Channels: the San Francisco Festival of Fantastic Film." Okay, but Dead Channels appears to be *dead*. The NAFFA website also says that they aim to "provide emerging and established imaginative artists with access to an Alliance of acclaimed festivals that actively support the discovery and promotion of thrillingly unique independent film from all over the world. NAFFA is recognized by the European Fantastic Film Festivals Federation." Okay. I don't know how valuable or active these people are, but check them out if you're so inclined.

Poland

Horror Fiesta Film Festival — defunct

Warsaw. Appears to have screened only once, in 2004. I've found no complete list of winners. I have found several films on the web claiming to have won this or that award at Horror Fiesta. But as I have reason to doubt some of those films' past claims regarding their wins at other festivals, I haven't included them in this book's award listings. I wish someone can provide me with a complete, reliable list of this festival's winners.

Portugal

Fantasporto

Rua Aníbal Cunha, 84 sala 1.6, 4050-046, Porto. Ph: +351-222-058-819. Fax: +351-222-058-823. Email: info@fantasporto.com. Web: fantasporto.com. In 2011 they will run their 31st edition, so their first screening was likely in 1980. While the name "Fantas" implies fantasy, Wikipedia says they screen "commercial feature films, auteur films and experimental projects from all over the world.... In spite of being organized by a private entity, the event is mostly state funded...." Their award winners include horror films like *Cube*, and they present a Méliès d'Argent, but they also award plenty of non-genre indie films like *Bad Lieutenant* and *Happiness*. So while they welcome horror films (as do many mainstream festivals), this is not primarily a horror/sci-fi/fantasy festival.

MOTELx — Lisbon International Horror Film Festival

R. Filipe Folque 30, 6B, 1050-113 Lisboa, Portugal. Contact: João Monteiro. Ph: +351-91-63-622-96. Fax: +351-21-31-745-05. Email: info@motelx.org. Web: motelx.org, MySpace.com/motelxinternational, Facebook.com/pages/MOTELx/57389992230. First screening 2007. They have three categories: Room Service (recent horror films from around the world), Doc Horror (documentaries about horror films or themes), and Short Films. "The festival encourages and will consider other cinematic proposals oùtside the scope of these sections, for eventual retrospectives or special screenings." They present the "MOTELx Award for the Best Portuguese Horror Short Film" open to Portuguese productions and co-productions. Prize is € 2,000. A.K.A. MOTELx — Festival Internacional de Cinema de Terror de Lisboa.

South Africa

Celludroid Sci-Fi, Anime, Fantasy Film Festival

Web: Celludroid.net. See the entry for South African Horrorfest.

South African HORRORFEST Film Festival

602 Summerways, Hofmeyr Road, Three Anchor Bay, 8005, Cape Town. Organizers, Paul Blom, Sonja Ruppersberg, coordinator and co-founder. Ph: +27 (0)21 434 3825. Email: info@flamedrop.com. Web: Horrorfest.info, ShadowRealMinc.com, MySpace.com/SAhorrorfest, Facebook.com/group.php?gid=6575356874, Twitter.com/SAhorrorfest. Founded 2004. First screening 2005. Screening location Cape Town. Accepts features and shorts. In addition to horror accepts dark, experimental, and documentaries with extreme subjects. Charges late fee if past deadline. "Best locally produced short film wins a R20,000 production prize from two video services companies." Other categories receive official certificates. Screenplay contest possible in future, but not for now. Paul Blom also manages X Fest, which "focuses on movies that are extreme, but not necessarily horror. X Fest was created when some movies sent to HorrorFest didn't fit the format but were still scary, shocking, or generally crazy flicks. People can submit for either, but if we feel a film may fit better in one of the others, we suggest that." In 2009, Blom founded Celludroid Sci-Fi, Anime, Fantasy Film Festival. He plans to launch a documentary festival focusing on "daring subjects": Flamedrop.com/daringdoccies. A.K.A. The Horror Festacular. **No entry fee.**

X Fest Extreme Film Festival

Web: XFest.org, facebook.com/group.php?gid=7939698591. See the entry for South African Horrorfest.

South America

Latin American Alliance of Fantastic Film Festivals

Web: fantafestivales.org, Facebook.com/group.php?gid=19827376149. Most of the top South American horror film festivals appear to members of this group. A.K.A. Alianza Latinoamericana de Festivales de Cine Fantástico.

South Korea

Puchon International Fantastic Film Festival

Pifan Organizing Committee Office 1F, Comic Business Center, Korea Manhwa Contents Agency (KOMACON), 529-2 Sang-Dong, Wonmi-Gu, Bucheon City, Gyeonggi Province, 420-030, Korea. Ph: 032-327-6313. Fax: 032-322-9629. Web: pifan.com. Features and shorts. Presents the Puchon Choice Award.

Spain

Cryptshow Festival

Barcelona. Contact: Toni Benages i Gallard. Ph: +34653529910. Email: premsa@cryptshow.com. Web: cryptshow.com, Facebook.com/people/Cryptshow-Apologia-del-Terror/1652467431. Founded 2007. Accepts shorts and features. **No entry fee.**

Horrorvision: Spanish Horror Trash Film Festival

C/. Martinez de la Rosa 38, 08012, Barcelona. Director: Sol Charlotte. Ph: +34-93-368-4856. Email: laoscuraceremonia@gmail.com. Web: laoscuracermonia.com/horrorvision, Facebook.com/pages/HORRORVISION-Spanish-Horror-Trash-Film-Festival/173384512039. First screening 2009. Accepts trash, horror, monsters, gore, or sci-fi. Short films only (15 minutes maximum length). Soundtrack or subtitles must be in Spanish or Catalan, or a silent film. First prize is € 200 and a statue. Second prize is € 100 and a certificate. Charlotte says: "The festival is organized by The Dark Ceremony, Sub-Films and The Monster Museum." **No entry fee.**

San Sebastián Horror and Fantasy Film Festival

Donostia Kultura, Cinema Dept., Teatro Victoria Eugeni, Reina Regente, 8 — 4th Floor, 20003 San Sebastián. Director: Josemi Beltrán; print traffic: Alfonso C. López; press and publications: Carlos J. Plaza. Ph: (34) 943-48-1538, or (34) 943-48-11 57/97. Fax: (34) 943-43-0621. Email: cinema_cinema@donostia.org. Web: SanSebastianHorrorFestival.com. Founded 1990. First screening 1990. Screening location San Sebastián. Accepts features and shorts. In addition to horror accepts fantasy, science fiction, animation. Trophies, cash prize of € 6,000 (for best feature), and nomination for the Golden Méliès (for best short). A.K.A. Semana de Cine Fantástico y de Terror. **No entry fee.**

SITGES: Festival Internacional de Cinema Fantàstic de Catalunya

C/ Joan Maragall 36, 08870 Sitges. Responsable de Premsa: Maria Castells. Email: premsa@sitgesfilmfestival.com, festival@sitgesfilmfestival.com. Ph: +34 93-811-2232, +34-93-894-9990. Fax: +34-93-894-8996. Web: sitgesfilmfestival.com, cinemasitges.com, Facebook.com/sitgesfilmfestival. Twitter.com/sitgesfestival. Founded/first screening 1968. Features and shorts. A journalist (who's interviewed many horror filmmakers over the years) tells me that *their* consensus opinion is that SITGES is *the most important* horror film festival in the world (as of now) for marketing a horror film. True? I don't know. Take it for what it's worth.

Sweden

Fantastisk Filmfestival

See entry for Lund International Fantastic Film Festival.

Lund International Fantastic Film Festival

Västra Mårtensgatan 12, 223 51 Lund. Web: fff.se. Director: Johan Barrander. Ph: +46-0-7358 22704. Email: johan@fff.se. Web: fff.se. Founded 1995. First screening 1996. "Fantastic film is usually used as a collective term for film genres like science fiction, fantasy and horror. But Lund International Fantastic Film Festival does not set narrow limits ... fantastic cinema is about imagination. The aim of the festival is to help stretch the limits of the imagination." A.K.A. Fantastisk Filmfestival.

Switzerland

Neuchâtel International Fantastic Film Festival

NIFFF — Neuchâtel International Fantastic Film Festival, Passage Max-de-Meuron 6, CH- 2000 Neuchâtel. Press office: Farida Khali. Ph: +41-0-32-730-5031, +41-0-79-796-2215. Fax: +41-0-32-731-0775. Email: info@nifff.ch, press@nifff.ch. Web: nifff.ch. Founded 2000. Not really a horror festival, but open to it.

United States

Academy of Science Fiction, Fantasy & Horror Films

334 West 54th Street, Los Angeles, CA 90037. Contact: Robert Holguin. Ph: 323-752-5811. Email: scifiacademy@ca.rr.com. Web: saturnawards.org. Not a film festival. Presents the Saturn Award. Founded 1972. For $150 you can purchase a one-year regular membership, entitling "you to vote in the annual Saturn Awards as well as to attend (with a guest) all of the Academy screenings held in the Los Angeles area. We average 130 film screenings every year." If you live too far away, you can buy a $40 membership entitling you to vote, but not attend screenings.

AdventureCon Horror Film Festival — defunct?

Ph: 800-608-6494, 865-365-1073. Email: info@adventurecon.net. Web: adventurecon.com, indiehorrornet.com/filmfest.html. Short films only. In addition to horror accepts sci-fi and fan films. Presents certificates, cash. In 2009, AdventureCon was at Knoxville, TN, but in 2010 it's at Pigeon Forge, TN. The film festival seems to have been a one-time event. In May 2010, the con website was promoting the May 2010 con, but no film festival. As of October 2010, festival site still touts the June 2009 event.

After Dark Horrorfest: 8 Films to Die For

8967 Sunset Blvd, Los Angeles, CA 90069. Ph: 310-270-4260. Fax: 310-270-4262. Web: horrorfestonline.com. Not a film festival, but an annual DVD package of horror films from After Dark Films and Lionsgate. I list them in case you've heard the name and were wondering.

Akron Screams — defunct

Civic Theatre Box Office, 182 South Main Street, Akron, Ohio 44308. Ph: 330-253-2488. Fax: 330-535-9828. Web: akroncivic.com, MySpace.com/akronscreams. Appears to be a project of the Akron

Civic Center. Akron Screams described itself as a "horror film and music festival." Its 2010 event was canceled, but it promised to return in 2011. Then its MySpace page disappeared. It's unclear whether they were open to new horror films, or only previously released films. My guess is, it no longer matters. There's an Akron Screams website and Facebook page which seem unrelated to this former film festival: akronscreams.com, Facebook.com/pages/Akron-Screams/119096381473137.

All Nite Scream-O-Rama — defunct

Tucson, Arizona. Email: screamorama@hotmail.com. MySpace.com/screamorama, MySpace.com/screamoramaaz. Apparently took place at Tucson's Loft Cinema. The former MySpace page has not been updated since 2007, the latter not since 2008. Its hotmail bounces.

Annie Award

Gretchen Houser, Annie Awards Events Director, 1827 Ximeno Avenue, No. 370, Long Beach, CA 90815. Ph: 562-209-9900. Email: Gretchen@annieawards.org. Web: annieawards.org. The Annie Awards are presented by the International Animated Film Society, ASIFA-Hollywood, 2114 W. Burbank Blvd, Burbank, CA 91506. Ph: 818-842-4691 or 818-842-8330. Email: info@asifa-hollywood.org. Web: asifa-hollywood.org. Honors all animation, not just genre. But many animated works are fantasy, horror, or science fiction, so you may want to contact these people.

Another Hole in the Head

530 Divisadero Street # 183, San Francisco, CA 94117. Founder and director: Jeff Ross. Ph: 415-820-3907. Email: info@sfindie.com. Web: sfindie.com, MySpace.com/sfindie, Facebook.com/sfindie, Twitter.com/sfindie. Founded/first screening 2004. Screening location San Francisco, CA. Accepts features and shorts. In addition to horror accepts science fiction, grindhouse, animation, bizarre, extreme. Audience Awards for best feature and best short. "SF IndieFest is the parent organization. We produce the SF Independent Film Fest, the SF Documentary Festival and Another Hole in the Head (plus two music festivals)."

Arizona Underground Film Festival

PO Box 692, Tucson, AZ 85702. Founder and director: David Pike. Ph: 520-730-2131. Email: info@azundergroundfilmfest.com, davidpike@azundergroundfilmfest.com. Web: azundergroundfilmfest.com, MySpace.com/azundergroundfilmfest, Facebook.com/pages/Arizona-Underground-Film-Festival/350046847637, Twitter.com/AZUndergroundFF. Founded/first screening 2008. Accepts features and shorts. In addition to horror accepts narrative, documentary, experimental, exploitation. They pay for filmmakers' hotel rooms and "sometimes airfare." Screened at Tucson's Loft Cinema, as has the All-Nite-Scream-O-Rama. David Pike explains, "We work with The Loft to bring films to them to screen. No, we are not affiliated with the Scream-O-Rama." For 2010 expanded to "screenings in both Tucson and Phoenix." Presents awards for best horror feature and short. Presents trophies as of 2010.

Ashtoberfest Horror Film Festival

Asheville, NC. Web: ashtoberfest.com, MySpace.com/ashevillezombiewalk, Facebook.com/people/Asheville-Zombiewalk/100000020694272, Twitter.com/ZombiesAshevill. Not just a film festival, but a music festival, zombie walk, parties, etc.

Atlanta Horror Fest — defunct?

Atlanta, GA. Contacts: Lucas Godfrey, Blake Myers. Email: atlantahorrorfest@yahoo.com (Godfrey) or blakemyers1977@yahoo.com (Myers). Web: atlhorrorfest.com, MySpace.com/atlantahorrorfest. Accepts features and shorts. Not just a film festival, but horror music, art, zombie walks, more. Its website has not been updated since 2009, its MySpace page since March 2010. The event has morphed into the Buried Alive Horror Film Festival (see entry).

Atlanta Horror Film Festival

1132 Virginia Ave. NE Ste. 19, Atlanta, GA 30306. Staff: Beth Cunningham, Jose Gross, Lisa Highfill, Joseph McClelland, Matt Newman, Eric Panter. Email: (first name of staffer) @festivalleague.com. Web: atlantahorrorfest.com, atlantahorrorfilmfest.com. First screening 2006. First awards 2007. Accepts shorts and features.

B Movie Celebration

111 East Monroe Street, Franklin, IN 46131. Contact: William Dever. Ph: 317-225-9767. Email: info@indyfilmco–op.org. Web: bmoviecelebration.com. "For the past five years, fans of the often misunderstood genre of B-Movies gather in Franklin, Indiana — not just to watch classic films, but to, as the name implies, celebrate them!" They screen many old classics, but also some new indie films.

B-Movie Film Festival

Syracuse, New York. Ph: (315) 652-3868. Email: webmaster@b-movie.com. Web: bmoviefest.com, b-movie.com/bmoviefest. Accepts features and shorts.

Big Bear Horror Film Festival

PO Box 3168, Burbank, CA 91508. Contacts: Michael Coulombe, director of programming; Jamie Kristen, founder and co-producer. Ph: 323-604-9874. Fax: 714-447-4506. Email: info@bigbearhorrorfilmfest.com. Web: bigbearhorrorfilmfest.com, Myspace.com/BBHFF, MySpace.com/bigbearlakehorrorfilmfest, Facebook.com/pages/Burbank-CA/Big-Bear-Horror-Film-Festival/87412533174, Twitter.com/bbhff. Founded/first screening 2009. Screening location: Big Bear Lake Performing Arts Center, 39707 Big Bear Boulevard, Big Bear Lake, CA 92315. Accepts shorts and features. Does not share proceeds with filmmakers "but that could change as the festival begins to turn a profit." Trophies. Also presents the O'Quinn Award.

Big Gay Horror Fan Film Festival — prospective

Contact: Brian Kirst. Email: biggayhorrorfan@gmail.com. In December 2010, Kirst emailed me that this festival "is something I'm planning to do in the next year or so." Not every festival gets off the ground, but you may want to check back to see if this one does. Kirst runs queerfearscarewithatwist.blogspot.com. He was once involved with the Horror Society. See their entry in this directory.

Black Swamp International Film Festival — defunct?

Toledo, OH. Web: blackswampfilmfestival.com. First screening October 2009. As of October 2010, their site is down. Based on information from other sources, and despite its name, Black Swamp seems to be [have been?] a mainstream festival. However, they screened some horror in 2009, so they were open to it.

BleedFest

8380 Waring Avenue #108 West Hollywood, CA 90069. Co-founders: Elisabeth and Brenda Fies. Ph: 310-990-5875. Email: lisfies@gmail.com, brendafies@aol.com. Web: bleedfest.com. First screening July 2010. Elisabeth Fies emails me: "We are a monthly genre film festival featuring shorts and features by women.... We waive the submission fee and ask it only of those films accepted to play. We are currently raising money for our 2011 monthly screenings...." Website says: "Shorts in competition will be eligible to win the Audience Award, which is our exclusive bronze statue, the Inanna, (A.K.A. the Bleedy).... All features screened will receive the Inanna Award." Trophies for all feature film selections, monthly, is financially ambitious, especially if only selected films pay entry fees. They screened twice in 2010. How monthly they'll be in 2011 likely depends on how successfully they raise funds. Not to be confused with Bled Fest, which appears to be a non-horror event: MySpace.com/bledfest.

BlobFest

The Colonial Theater in Phoenixville, PA, hosts many horror screenings, including an event called BlobFest. Focus is on classics, rather than new films. But the theater also sponsors an annual **short film contest**, called The Shorty's Contest, described as "our way of paying homage to the late, great Shorty Yeaworth, Jr., director of *The Blob*." Entry films must be "centered on *The Blob* and/or BlobFest. If you'd like, you can use the winning script from last year's script contest as the basis for your short film." Yes, they have a **script contest**. Theater office: 227 Bridge St, Phoenixville, PA 19460. Ph: 610-917-1228. Email: kirsten@thecolonialtheatre.com. Web: thecolonialtheatre.com.

Blood Bath Film Festival

Texas. Contact: Andrew Rose. Email: info@doabloodbath.com. Web: doabloodbath.com, texasbloodbath.com, MySpace.com/texasbloodbath, Facebook.com/group.php?gid=158915055116. Produces several festivals, including one-time events. In 2009: Texas Blood Bath Film Festival. In 2010: Pretty Scary Blood Bath Film Festival (Feb); Fears for Queers GLBT Film Festival (June); Blood Bath 2: The Film Festival (Nov). Pretty-Scary.net founder Heidi Martinuzzi says, "My website, Pretty/Scary, was a sponsor of this screening event, which took place as part of Women in Horror Month (womeninhorrormonth.com). We didn't organize the festival, we just sponsored it. There were no awards given out." See entry for Pretty Scary.

Bloody Harvest Film Festival — defunct

Contact: Linda Webster. Email: jl@bloodyharvest.com. Web: bloodyharvest.com, myspace.com/bloodyharvestfest. Website says "This event has been canceled." Bloody Harvest was to screen in October 2009 in Las Vegas, then changed plans to Seattle. Its affiliated Bloody Valentine Film Festival was to screen in Los Angeles in February 2009. None of which happened. But Linda Webster emailed me on May 19, 2010: "There may be something similar being planned for February of 2011." But by 2011 the website is dead.

Bloody Valentine Film Festival — defunct?

See Bloody Harvest Film Festival.

Boston Fantastic Film Festival — defunct

First screening 2003. Last event seems to have been 2007. A project of The Brattle Theatre, 40 Brattle St. Cambridge, MA 02138. Ph: 617/876-6837. Email: info@brattlefilm.org. The festival's page on the theater's site — brattlefilm.org/bfff — is gone and redirects to the theater's homepage. Their other page — www.fantastic.brattlefilm.org — is dead.

Boston Science Fiction Film Festival

Contact: Garen Daly, Zeotrope Media, Inc. Ph: 603-593-3610 or 617-901-7280. Web: bostonsci-fi.com, Facebook.com/pages/Boston-Sci-Fi-Fest/143431763533. Founded 1975. Screens in Somerville, which "is right next to Boston." Presents the Gort Award. Affiliated with the Boston Terror'thon.

Boston Terror'thon

Email: j.cannibal@gmail.com. Web: jcannibal.com. Affiliated with Boston Science Fiction Film Festival.

Boston Underground Film Festival

Email: info@bostonunderground.org. Web: bostonunderground.org, MySpace.com/bostonunderground, Facebook.com/bostonunderground, Twitter.com/BOSunderground. Not a horror festival, but likely friendly to horror. Their MySpace page says they're "committed to the celebration of alternative vision and cultivation of independent, provocative and experimental filmmaking ... work that pushes the envelope in form, style and content ... provocative and experimental features, shorts, animation, music videos, and documentaries ... seeks the alternative, the confrontational, the political and the controversial." Founded 1998. Presents the Bacchus Awards. Affiliated with the Boston LGBT Film Festival.

Bram Stoker Award

Horror Writers Association, 244 5th Ave., Ste 2767, New York, NY 10001. Email: hwa@horror.org. Web: horror.org. The HWA primarily comprises novelists, short story writers, and poets, though they accept horror writers working in any medium (e.g., scripts, video games, comic books, etc.). They had an award category for screenwriters from 1998 to 2004. Then they dropped it. Then they revived it in 2011.

Buffalo Screams Horror Film Festival

1824 Kensington Avenue, Cheektowaga, New York, 14215. Co-founders/co-directors: Emil Novak, Gregory Lamberson. Email: enovak3178@aol.com. Web: buffaloscreams.com. First screening: 2010. Accepts features and shorts. Screenplay contest.

Buried Alive Film Fest

Atlanta, GA. Email: blakemyers1977@gmail.com. Web: buriedalivefilmfest.com, Facebook.com/pages/Atlanta-GA/Buried-Alive-Horror-Film-Festival/254131212591 "The Buried Alive Film Fest comes from the same group of twisted minds and horror film buffs that have brought you the Atlanta HorrorFest for the past five years." See entry for Atlanta Horror Fest.

California International Animation Film Festival

PO Box 580450, Modesto, CA 95358. Ph: 209-537-5221. Fax: 209-531-0233. Email: festival@calanifest.com. Web: calanifest.com. Founded 2005. First screening 2006. They are "dedicated to a recognition that animation, gaming and film making are not separate businesses, but fingers on the same hand." Affiliated with the Fireside Foundation, which also runs Shockerfest.

Cape Fear Independent Film Festival

Cape Fear, NC. President: Rich Gehron. Email: info@cfifn.org. Web: cfifn.org. Despite their name, this is not a horror festival. They just happen to be located in Cape Fear, North Carolina.

Carnage Film Festival

Wilmington, NC. Contacts: Matt & Sarah Mizell. Email: info@carnagefilmfestival.com. Web: carnagefilmfestival.com, MySpace.com/carnagefilmfestival, Facebook.com/pages/Carnage-film-festival/345585352318, Twitter.com/carnagefilmfest. Founded 2009. They say their first event will be in late fall 2011. Films "must contain blood" and "bodies or formally [sic] dead bodies." Films must be "90 minutes or less in length." Accepts horror, thriller, supernatural, sci-fi, gore.

Carnival of Darkness

10153 Riverside Drive, Ste. 693, Toluca Lake, CA 91602. Director: Alex Bram. Email: bram@ladirector.com. Web: carnivalofdarkness.net. Founded/first screened 2009. Screens in Los Angeles. Accepts shorts only. In addition to horror accepts sci-fi, suspense, thriller. Presents the Thrill Ride Award, a trophy.

Chainsaw Mafia Film Festival

PO Box 724, Carlsbad, NM, 88221-0724. CEO: Shannon Lark. Ph: 510-207-1418. Email: shannon@thechainsawmafia.com. Web: thechainsawmafia.com/filmfestival.html, MySpace.com/thechainsawmafia. The Chainsaw Mafia is a San Francisco–based collective of horror filmmakers and actors, founded in 2004. Lark says, "We used to throw film festivals, but it was simply officially selected films. No awards were presented." Lark ran the horror film screenings at the World Horror Con when it convened in San Francisco in 2006. Her film festival efforts are currently focused on the Viscera Film Festival.

Chicago Horror Film Festival

Gatlin Pictures, PO Box 167, Somers WI 53171. Director: Jason R. Davis. Email: chicagohorrorfest@yahoo.com. Web: chicagohorrorfest.com, MySpace.com/chicagohorrorfest. Founded 2003.

Chiller Eyegore Award

See entry for Eyegore Award.

Chiller Theatre Convention

Hilton Parsippany, Parsippany, N.J. Ph: 973-267-7373. Email: webmaster@chillertheatre.com. Web: chillertheatre.com. They describe themselves as a "toy, model and film expo." I see no film festival on their website. Even so, this could be a place for filmmakers to promote and sell their DVDs.

Cincinnati Horror Film Festival—defunct

Email: admin@horrorsociety.com. Web: cincinnati.horrorsociety.com. As of December 2010 its website still promotes its June 2008 screening, apparently held at the Fairfield Community Arts Center-Theater, 411 Wessel Drive, Fairfield, OH 45014. Ph: 513-867-5348.

Cinefamily Halloween Horror Film Fest

611 N. Fairfax Avenue, Los Angeles, CA 90036. Ph: 323-655-2510. Email: events@cinefamily.org. Web: cinefamily.org. "The Cinefamily is an organization of movie lovers devoted to finding and presenting interesting and unusual programs of exceptional, distinctive, weird and wonderful films.... Our home is the Silent Movie Theatre, one of Hollywood's most beloved and beautiful cultural landmarks." The Halloween Horror Film Fest is what this theater calls its horror film program every October. Emphasis is on old features (lots of 1980s films), but also includes student shorts. Because 2010 was this festival's third year, it likely first screened in 2008. Despite their focus on old features, they sound open-minded. You might call them and see if they'll consider your work.

Cinema Edge Award—defunct

Web: wickedpixel.com/cinemaedge, Facebook.com/note.php?note_id=130177934498. Wicked Pixel is an indie horror film company. In December 2010, I saw no mention of this award on Wicked Pixel's site, but the award's Facebook page is still up. It says: "The movie that wins Best Feature will receive a distribution contract from ... VCI Entertainment. All profits from sales of your movie will be split between you and VCI Entertainment. That's right, you're not just competing for bragging rights and a plastic trophy. This is one film contest that holds real profit *potential* [my italics] for the winner!" Sounds like a *royalties only* contract (i.e., no advance). Not the best of deals. An August 25, 2009 posting on Fearnet.com says that the just launched Cinema Edge has two award categories: Best Feature and Best Short. However, in December 2010, I saw a filmmaker's DVD box (for a short film) covered with laurel leaf logos claiming to have won *three* Cinema Edge Awards: Best Actor, Best Story Concept, Best Visual Presentation. Emails to Wicked Pixel and the filmmaker have both gone unanswered. I don't know what's accurate, but by 2011 the website is dead.

Cinespia

6000 Santa Monica Boulevard, Hollywood, CA 90038. Web: cinespia.org, Facebook.com/cinespia, Twitter.com/CINESPIA. "Cemetery Screenings Saturdays and Sundays All Summer Long!" Not a film festival, but rather, a film program screened at the Hollywood Forever Cemetery and projected onto "the white marble wall of Rudolph Valentino's tomb." Founded 2002. They screen older classics, and not just horror. However, because they screen in a cemetery, some people confuse them for a horror only event.

Circus of Terror—defunct

New Orleans, LA. Web: circusofterror.com, MySpace.com/circusofterror. As of July 2010, its site says: "Due to the negative impact the British Petroleum oil spill is currently causing on the local ecology, economic assets and tourism market, Terror Enterprises is forced at this time to postpone the 'Circus of Terror' scheduled for October 29–31, 2010.... It is our intent to re-examine local conditions for a possible return in Halloween 2011." Yet its website was dead by 2011. I think 2010 was to be its first event.

Comic-Con International Independent Film Festival

PO Box 128458, San Diego, CA 92112-8458. Ph: 619-491-2475. Fax: 619-414-1022. Email: cci-info@comic-con.org. Web: comic-con.org/cci/cci_iff.shtml. "accepts genre-related films in the following categories: action/adventure, animation, comics-oriented, pop culture–related documentary, horror/suspense, humor, and science fiction/fantasy." Awards and prizes.

Con Nooga

5251-C Hwy 153, Box 280, Hixson, TN 37343. Email: info@connooga.com. Web: connooga.com. Event held at Chattanooga, TN. "A convention for fans of science fiction, horror, fantasy, gaming, anime, paranormal, costuming, films, artist, celebrities, comics, haunting ... so much more!" They're seeking "fan and indie films" and promise awards for 2011.

Crypticon

Minneapolis, MN. Email: count_kaufman@hotmail.com. Web: crypticonminneapolis.com, MySpace.com/crypticonmn, Facebook.com/Crypticon-Minnesota. A convention rather than a festival.

Crypticon Horror Convention

331 Andover Park E # 330, Tukwila, WA 98188. Ph: 206-276-8122. Email: info@crypticonseattle.com. Web: crypticonseattle.com, MySpace.com/crypticonseattle, Twitter.com/crypticon. Event location Seattle, WA. A convention rather than a festival. "The Maelstrom International Festival of Fantastic Films is handling all Crypticon film submissions." See

entry for Maelstrom International Fantastic Film Festiva.

Dark Carnival Film Festival

1824 E. Thornton Dr., Bloomington, IN 47401. Contact: David E. Pruett. Ph: 812-720-9185. Email: info@darkcarnivalfilmfest.com. Web: darkcarnivalfilmfest.com, MySpace.com/darkcarnivalfilmfest. Accepts shorts, features, trailers. Accepts "horror, dark fantasy, sci-fi and every sub-genre in between."

Dark Woods Con

Kentucky. Web: darkwoodscon.com, Facebook.com/home.php#/pages/Dark-Woods-Con/11 4704353191. A convention rather than a film festival. They describe themselves as "a horror movie/paranormal convention." Also: "The DarkWoods Con venues *typically* include a film festival and an awards presentation." My italics.

Dead Channels Film Festival—defunct

San Francisco, CA. Director: Bruce Fletcher. Email: info@deadchannels.com. Web: deadchannels.com, Myspace.com/dead_channels, Facebook.com/pages/Dead-Channels/15875055815. Founded 2007. All three sites still tout their October 2008 event. Accepts "science fiction, fantasy, horror, experimental, 'sploitation and offbeat genre movies."

Deep Red International Festival of Fantastic Film—defunct?

465 West 51st Street, No. 1E, New York, NY 10019-6317. Contact: Shade Rupe. Emails: shade@shaderupe.com, shaderupe@gmail.com, shade@deepredfilmfest.com. Web: deepredfilmfest.com. Founded/first screening 2009. Screening locations Portland, OR; Seattle, WA. Shade Rupe is affiliated with Cloud Zero, "The first international film festival that starts at Sundance and continues in the palm of your hand" (see Cloud-Zero.com). Deep Red accepts features and shorts, horror, science fiction, fantastique, bizarro, cult, and exploitation. No awards/non-competitive. There was no screening in 2010. In September 2010, Rupe told me that Deep Red "will most likely" screen again in the future, but by 2011 the website was down.

Doorways Unhinged Horror Film Festival—defunct

Web: doorwaysmagazine.com. Apparently had its first and last screening in 2007. Sponsored by *Doorways Magazine*. Website is dead, so I assume the magazine has folded.

Dragon*Con Independent Film Festival

PO Box 16459, Atlanta, GA 30321-0459. Director: Matthew M. Foster. Ph: 770-909-0115. Emails: matthew@fosteronfilm.com, filmfestival@dragoncon.org, filmfest@fosteronfilm.com. Web: filmfest.dragoncon.org, dragoncon.org, MySpace.com/dcifilmfest, Facebook.com/pages/DragonCon-Film-Festival/89634118595. Founded/first screening 1987. Screening location Atlanta, GA. Features and shorts. In addition to horror accepts science fiction, fantasy, action, suspense, comedy, animation. Charges admission to Dragon*Con, but all attendees may see all screenings without additional charge. Two $500 awards for Best of Fest, plaques for first place in genre categories.

Drunken Zombie Film Festival

Bryan Wolford, 4010 N. Brandywine Dr., Apt. 208, Peoria, IL 61614. Web: drunkenzombiefilmfestival.com, Facebook.com/group.php?gid=8582811641, Twitter.com/drunkenzombie. Founded/first screening 2008. Non-competitive. Despite the name, they accept all sorts of horror, not just zombies. Shorts and features. **No entry fee.**

Eerie Horror Film Festival

PO Box 98, Edinboro, PA 16412. Founder and president: Greg Ropp. Ph: 814-873-2483. Emails: info@eeriehorrorfest.com, greg@eeriehorrorfest.com. Web: eeriehorrorfilmfestival.com, eeriehorrorfest.com, MySpace.com/eeriehorrorfest, Myspace.com/eeriehorrorfilmfestival, Facebook.com/pages/Eerie-Horror-Film-Festival/251865626815, Twitter.com/EHFF. Founded/first screening 2004. Screening location Erie, PA. Features and shorts. In addition to horror accepts science fiction, suspense, documentaries about horror. Donates some proceeds to local charities (e.g., Make-A-Wish; Food Bank of NW Pennsylvania). Plaques, sponsored awards (usually software), cash for best screenplays. Screenplay contest.

Eyegore Award

Universal City, CA. Not a film festival. Currently A.K.A. Chiller Eyegore Award, and co-sponsored by Universal Studios and the Chiller TV cable channel. Previously A.K.A. Eyegore Horror Award. According to LAsThePlace.com the "Eyegore Horror Awards ... celebrates the triumphant accomplishments made by directors, actors, and writers in the horror film genre." See Halloween Horror Nights Scary Film Competition.

Fangoria Chainsaw Award

250 W. 49th Street, Ste. 304, New York, NY 10019. Web: Fangoria.com. Award founded 1991. Not a film festival, but a horror film award voted on by readers of *Fangoria*. Ballots are published in the magazine.

Fangoria's Weekend of Horrors

Creation Entertainment, 217 S. Kenwood St., Glendale, CA 91205. Creative director/producer: Ted Venemann. Ph: 818-409-0960 ext. 235. Email: ted@

creationent.com. Web: weekendofhorrors.net, fangocon.com, creationent.com/cal/woh.htm, MySpace.com/weekendofhorrors. A convention rather than a film festival. In 2010 they ran a "Grindhouse Film Festival." Says Ted Venemann: "Our film programs are not competitions, just screenings with talent Q & A sessions."

Fantastic Fest

Austin, Texas. Contact: Tim League. Email: info@fantasticfest.com. Press contacts: brandy@fonspr.com or ryan@fonspr.com. Web: fantasticfest.com, Facebook.com/fantasticfest, Twitter.com/fantasticfest. Accepts "new sci-fi, horror, fantasy and genre films, as well as classic and obscure cult titles." Most screenings held at The Alamo Drafthouse Cinema, South Lamar, 1120 South Lamar Blvd., Austin, TX 78704. Ph: 512-476-1320 or 512-912-0529. Fax: 630-839-7663. Although based in Austin, "Fantastic Fest is a member of the European Fantastic Film Festivals Federation which is composed of 20 festivals — on the European continent as well as in Asia and North America — with a joint audience of approximately 600,000 spectators."

Fargo Fantastic Film Festival

PO Box 7202, Fargo, ND 58106. Chairman: Tony Tilton. Email: conchairs@valleycon.com. Web: valleycon.com/filmfest.html. "The FFFF takes place during the ValleyCon 36: The Fargo Entertainment Expo." Not a standalone film festival, but rather, part of a larger genre convention. FFFF "exists to showcase the ambitious and creative independent filmmaker. To make a good 'genre' film takes real creativity, craftsmanship and — yes, artistic merit. We show professional and amateur productions as both can learn from the other. Any lengths, formats and styles accepted!" ValleyCon 29 was this festival's first year. Tilton tells me that "FFFF4 and FFFF6 were based at the Fargo Theatre, but since then we've kept it with ValleyCon. We may be expanding into a local theatre chain this fall (2011) though!"

Fear Fiesta

Casa 0101 Theater, 2009 East First Street, Los Angeles, CA 90033. Casa0101 Theater ph: 323-263-7684. Email info@casa0101.org, info@latinhorror.com. Web: latinhorror.com, casa0101.org, Myspace.com/latinhorror, Facebook.com/group.php?gid=46005877292, Twitter.com/latinhorror. Founded/first screening 2010. "Latin Horror joins with Casa 0101 Theater, screenwriter/author Josefina Lopez, and filmmaker/curator Tyger Torrez to proudly present Fear Fiesta 2010 ... devoted specifically to celebrating Latino filmmakers and performers in the horror genre."

FearFest

See: Texas FearFest.

Fearless Tales Genre Fest — defunct

San Francisco, CA. Director: Michael Davidson. Email: ace@fearlesstales.com. Web: fearlesstales.com, MySpace.com/fearlesstales. The latest news on its website is dated January 2009. A July 2006 posting says: "Fearless Tales Genre Fest 3 is to be postponed." Its MySpace page hasn't been logged into since August 2007.

Fears for Queers GLBT Film Festival

See: Blood Bath Film Festival.

Festival of Fear

See entry for Rue Morgue's Festival of Fear.

Freak Show Horror Film Festival

8533 Fantasia Park Way, Riverview, Florida 33578. Festival coordinator: Katie Harders. Ph: 407-536-7406. Email: contact@freakshowfilmfest.com. Web: freakshowfilmfest.com, MySpace.com/fearfilmmovies, Facebook.com/freakshowhorrorfest, Twitter.com/freakshowhorror. Accepts shorts and features. Presents the Freaky Award.

Fright Night Film Fest

4621 Outer Loop # 310, Louisville, KY 40219. Founder and director: Ken Daniels. Ph: 502-338-2137. Email: frightnightfilmfest@yahoo.com. Web: frightnightfilmfest.com, MySpace.com/frightnightfilmfest, Facebook.com/pages/Fright-Night-Film-Fest/63772024471. Founded/first screening 2005. Screenings in Louisville. Features and shorts. In addition to horror accepts sci-fi, cult, comedy, drama, documentaries. Presents the Silver Scream Award trophy and prizes. In 2010 they began presenting several Corman Awards in honor of Roger Corman. Screenplay contest.

Frightmares Film Festival — defunct?

Darkstone Entertainment, PO Box 4585, Charlottesville, VA 22905. Contact: John Johnson. Ph: 866-445-7114. Email: darkstone@darkstone-ent.com. Web: darkstone-ent.com. In 2007 Darkstone (a low-budget production and distribution entity) announced a shorts only horror film festival, but by 2010 the festival has disappeared from the website. Its MySpace page promotes the Graveyard Shift radio show: MySpace.com/frightmaresfest. On January 7, 2011, John Johnson emailed me: "Sadly the Firghtmares film fest is on hold at the moment. Hopefully we will be able to bring it back soon!"

Gasparilla Film Festival

See Halloween Horror Picture Show.

Grim Reaper Award

See Reaper Award.

Grimmy Award

See Reaper Award.

Halloween Horror Nights Scary Film Competition

Universal City, CA. Web: halloweenhorrornights.com/hollywood/2010/film_contest.html. Sponsored by Universal Studio's Halloween Horror Nights. That's Universal's annual horror show/haunted house extravaganza, held on the Universal backlot every Halloween season. In 2010, this horror film contest "started with well over 100 hopeful filmmakers, then to the final ten. Now, it's down to one. Elizabeth Schieffer ... [whose] film *Jasper* was selected as this year's winner by online voters who picked their favorite from the 10 finalists. *Jasper* will premiere on Chiller TV, and is posted on SyFy.com. Schieffer receives a $1,000 cash prize and an exclusive invitation to the opening night Eyegore Awards." A.K.A. Halloween Horror Nights–Rob Zombie Film Competition. Universal often alters/builds upon/renames their annual Halloween events. I worked there in 1996, when it was called Chamber of Chills. See Eyegore Award.

Halloween Horror Picture Show — defunct?

Tampa, FL. Web: halloweenhorrorpictureshow.com. As of July 2011, its website is still promoting its October 2008 event. Also says it's presented by the Gasparilla Film Festival, but this indie fest makes no mention of Halloween Horror on its site: gasparillafilmfestival.com. The Halloweenapalooza horror con lays claim to Halloween Horror on MySpace: MySpace.com/halloweenapalooza (last updated March 2010), but its halloweenapalooza.net site is dead.

Halloweenapalooza

See entry for Halloween Horror Picture Show.

HAuNTcon Amateur Horror Film Festival

Scott Morrow, 222 Rodman Ave., Jenkintown, PA 19046. Email: fearlessghosthunter@yahoo.com. Web: hauntcon.com/hauntcon-horror-film-contest, Myspace.com/hauntcon, Facebook.com/HAuNTcon, Twitter.com/hauntcon. Accepts shorts and features. "Movies can be 'R rated' but any film deemed pornographic will be removed from the competition without refund." Not really a film festival, but rather a contest sponsored by the Haunted Attraction National Tradeshow & Convention.

Haunted Newport Horror Film Festival — defunct?

Web: hauntednewport.net. Website is dead. Kenny Selko's MySpace page has an October 13, 2006, posting which says that his short film, *Alone*, is an official selection at this film festival. Seems they were around in 2006, but no longer.

Hell's Half Mile Film and Music Festival

Bay City, Michigan. Director: Alan J. LaFave. Email: info@hhmfest.com. Web: baycityhhmfest.com, Facebook.com/group.php?gid=27897958928, Twitter.com/HHMFEST. Founded 2006. Despite the name, this is a non-genre, indie film festival. LaFave emails me: "HHM is not a horror fest, although we do tend to show some horror films each year. We tend to be perceived as a horror fest due to the month the fest takes place and the name."

Hollywood Horror Film Festival

Hollywood Network, Inc., 433 N. Camden Drive, Suite 600, Beverly Hills, CA 90210. Ph: 310-288-1882. Fax: 310-288-0060. Email: info@hollywoodawards.com. Web: hollywoodawards.com/horror.html, MySpace.com/hollywoodfilmfestival. Features and shorts. Part of the greater Hollywood Awards, encompassing every genre.

Horrific Film Fest

330 Kitty Hawk Rd #705, Universal City, TX 78148. Contact: George L. Ortiz. Email: info@thehouseofthedemon.com. Web: horrificfilmfest.com. Founded 2007. First screening 2008. In August 2010 it was held at La Quinta Inn & Suites, San Antonio Convention Center, 303 Blum, San Antonio, TX 78205-3303. Ph: 1-210-222-9181. Fax: 1-210-228-9816. They also sponsor a zombie walk. Their email bounced in October 2010, but I think this festival's still active.

Horror Dance — defunct?

3262 Westheimer Rd. #511, Houston, TX. 77098. Owner, founder, CEO: Kevin Devil. Email: info@horrordance.org. Web: horrordance.org. Founded in 2005. Features and shorts. As of July 2011, its website still says, "Selections for the 2009 festival are still being processes and finalized." **No entry fee.**

Horror Gathering Film Festival

Cleveland, OH. Web: MySpace.com/horrorgathering. A convention, but with a film festival.

Horror Realm

Pittsburgh, PA. Email: Info@horrorrealmcon.com. Web: horrorrealmcon.com, MySpace.com/horrorrealmconvention, Facebook.com/group.php?gid=12 9691239865, Twitter.com/HorrorRealmCon. A convention, but they include a "zombie & horror film festival." They screen both features and shorts, and have a shorts only (under 20 minutes) contest. "Your prize is: we show your short horror film at our little event at Horror Realm 2010 and talk about it. Please show up at the convention so we can even introduce you to the hardcore horror movie fans! We'll review the film and post it on bastardsofhorror.com beforehand and it will be included in the next *Gross Movie Reviews* book!" **No entry fee.**

Horror Society Film Festival

Chicago, IL. Contact: Mitchell Wells. Email: admin@horrorsociety.com. Web: horrorsociety.com/festivals, MySpace.com/horrorsocietyfilmfestival. Features and shorts. Also runs other horror film festivals under different themes and titles; e.g., Women of Horror, B-Movie Madness, Zombie Disco, Zombie Outbreak, Summer of Slaughter, Holiday of Horrors. Some are popular enough to have grown into a series (e.g., Women of Horror 2, B-Movie Madness 2).

Horrorfind Weekend Film Festival

9722 Groffs Mill Drive, Ste 109, Owings Mills, MD 21117. Contact: Joe Ripple. Email: filmfest@horrorfind.com. Web: horrorfindweekend.com/filmfest.html, MySpace.com/horrorfindweekend, Facebook.com/pages/Horrorfind-Weekend-Convention/108153785888647, Twitter.com/HorrorFilmFest. Features and shorts. Business address is in Maryland, but the event location varies year to year, though always in the eastern U.S. In 2010 it will be Gettysburg, PA. In the past this has been a convention only (with a short film contest in 2006), but beginning in 2010 they expect to include an annual film festival.

H.P. Lovecraft Film Festival & CthulhuCon

1827 NE 44th Ave Ste 340, Portland, OR 97213 (current); 2626 NE 31st Ave, Portland, OR 97212 (long term). Founder and director: Andrew Migliore. Ph: 503-734-8822. Email: andrew@zompire.com, andrew@hplfilmfestival.com. Web: hplfilmfestival.com, MySpace.com/hplfilmfestival. Founded 1995. First screening 1996. Screenings have been held in Portland, OR; Salem, MA; Los Angeles, CA; Austin, TX; Vancouver, BC, Canada. Features and shorts. In addition to horror, accepts fantasy and appropriate documentaries. Awards statues, prizes. "The H.P. Lovecraft Award (or 'Howie'), is awarded annually to filmmakers, directors, writers, scholars, and other people or organizations that have produced significant contributions to the genre of cosmic horror, weird tales, and the promotion of Lovecraft and his work in particular." Affiliated with Zompire: The Undead Film Festival. Screenplay contest.

Hugo Award

World Science Fiction Society, PO Box 1270, Kendall Square Station, Cambridge, MA 02142. Web: thehugoawards.org, Facebook.com/pages/The-Hugo-Awards/206080968187, Twitter.com/thehugoawards. Presented by the World Science Fiction Society, which organizes the annual World Science Fiction Convention (A.K.A. Worldcon). Convention attendees (A.K.A. members) nominate and vote for the winners from works released the previous year. This means the 2010 winners were all released in 2009, etc. The Hugos are primarily a literary award, but they also have a Best Dramatic Presentation award for films, TV episodes, and "other" dramatic works. Despite Hugo's reputation as science fiction's most prestigious award, horror works do sometimes win. There's also a Retro Hugo for older dramatic works.

Indy Horror Film Festival

Dekalb, IL. Webmaster: Jason R. Davis. Email: indyhorrorfilmfest@yahoo.com Web: indyhorrorfilmfest.com, MySpace.com/indyhorrorfilmfest. Facebook.com/pages/Indy-Horror-Film-Festival/218339325379. Founded 2005. Features and shorts. Not to be confused with the Indie Horror Film Festival in Canada.

International Horror and Sci-Fi Film Festival

1700 N 7th Ave, Suite 250, Phoenix, AZ 85007. Senior director: Jason Carney. Ph: 602-955-6444. Fax: 602-955-0966. Email: office@phxfilm.com. Web: horrorscifi.com, MySpace.com/horrorscifi, Facebook.com/horrorscifi. Founded/first screening 2005. Features and shorts. In addition to horror accepts sci-fi. Affiliated with the Phoenix Film Festival. Screenplay contest. "We are a non-profit organization." Presents plaques.

International Surrealist Film Festival

PO Box 3863, Los Angeles, CA 90078. Contact: Paul Sanchez Yates. Ph: 914-907-6851. Email: oniongod@gmail.com. Web: theinternationalsurrealistfilmfestival.com, Facebook.com/pages/The-International-Surrealist-Film-Festival/196158843035. Founded 1990. Some horror films are surrealistic, so they may be open to your film. Their last screening was in Los Angeles in March 2010. As of November their website still touts that 8-months-old event, yet apparently they're still alive. On November 8, 2010, Yates emailed me that "we give out several types of awards. Trophies like The Duchamp award or The Nusch. We also give out a grand prize of a Bolex 16mm camera and film, but this year we gave out a Digital Hirenazumi camera."

It Came from Lake Michigan—defunct

Milwaukee, Wisconsin. Contact: Wayne Clingman. Web: itcamefromlakemichigan.com, MySpace.

com/itcamefromlakemichigan. Email bounces. Website dead. Its MySpace page offers no info beyond 2007.

Killer Film Fest

Foxboro, MA. Director: Michael Vallier. Ph: 617-391-8001. Email: mvallier@killerfilmfest.com. Web: killerfilmfest.com, Facebook.com/group.php?gid=109461405743384, Twitter.com/killerfilmfest. First screening 2009.

Knoxville Horror Film Fest

Knoxville, TN. Email: info@knoxvillehorrorfest.com. Web: knoxvillehorrorfest.com, Facebook.com/pages/Knoxville-Horror-Film-Fest/322137305194, Twitter.com/KnoxHorrorFest. Founded 2009. Screenplay contest.

Madison Horror Film Festival

549 D'Onofrio Drive, Suite 3, Madison, WI 53719. Director: Rich Peterson. Ph: 608-338-3064. Email: madisonhorror@gmail.com. Web: madisonhorror.com, MySpace.com/madisonhorror, Facebook.com/profile.php?id=1348624889, Twitter.com/madisonhorror. Founded/first screening 2008. Features and shorts. "Strictly horror." Presents plaques. Screened in 2009, but no apparent activity in 2010 and the website looks dead. I'm tempted to tag this one **defunct**, but Mr. Peterson emailed me in June 2010 and gave no indication of the festival shutting down.

Maelstrom International Fantastic Film Festival

PO Box 50205, Bellevue WA 98015. Director and co-programmer: Eric Morgret. Ph: 425-269-9150. Email: info@mifff.org. Web: www.mifff.org, MySpace.com/maelstromfestival, Facebook.com/group.php?gid=18959875871, Twitter.com/mifff. Founded/first screening in 2007 as the Zombiebot Film Festival. Screenings in Seattle. Features and shorts. In addition to horror accepts sci-fi, fantasy, action. "We are working on starting some online distribution deals for the award winners from each year." Also, a "physical award is in the works."

Master of Macabre — defunct?

Fort Lauderdale, FL. Contact: John Skinner. Web: projectbreakout.com/shortfilm2, MySpace.com/horrorshortfilmz, Facebook.com/people/John_Skinner/5203055. A "Project Breakout" horror **short film** online contest. Seems to have been a one-time event.

Mile High Horror Film Festival

Denver, CO. Director: Timothy Schultz. Ph: 303-728-9279. Fax: 303-450-7670. Email: info@milehighhorrorfestival.com. Web: milehighhorrorfestival.com. Founded 2010. Shorts and features. Has a special categories for student films and Colorado filmmakers.

Monster-Mania Con

Cherry Hill, NJ, and Hunt Valley, MD. Contact: Dave Hagan. Email: dave@monstermania.net. Web: monstermania.net, MySpace.com/officialmonstermaniacon, MySpace.com/monstermaniaconvention, MySpace.com/monstermania, Facebook.com/pages/-/Monster-Mania-Convention/46231714170. A convention, not a festival. Its film screenings are devoted to (exclusively?) horror classics with large fan bases.

Monsterpalooza

Burbank, CA. Email: therubberroom101@aol.com. Web: rubberroom101.com, Myspace.com/monsterpalooza, Facebook.com/pages/monsterpalooza/117236381628233. This convention emphasizes horror makeup, artists, and special effects. Film screenings, mostly indie shorts, are a small part of this con, but it's been known to happen.

Motor City Nightmares

Novi, MI. Email: motorcitynightmares@gmail.com. Web: motorcitynightmares.com, MySpace.com/motorcitynightmares. A convention, not a film festival. But for 2010 they have a horror film festival, a short film contest, and an "R-Squared Film Distribution Contest." These are three separate events. For the short film contest, you're given a word to build a film around. In both contests, the films need not be horror-related.

Nebula Award

Presented by the Science Fiction and Fantasy Writers of America. Web: nebulaawards.com, sfwa.org. The Nebula is primarily a literary award, founded in 1965. Its recognition of screenplays and films has been spotty, featuring occasional awards by various names. In 2009, its Best Script award category was replaced by the **Ray Bradbury Award for Outstanding Dramatic Presentation**. Some say that this is technically not a Nebula Award. Even so, it's presented at the Nebula Awards ceremony, and follows the Nebula rules and procedures for nomination and voting.

Nevermore Film Festival

c/o Carolina Theatre of Durham, 309 West Morgan Street, Durham, NC 27701. Contacts: Jim Carl, founder and senior director; Phillip Seib, film programming and operations manager. Ph: 919-560-3040 ext 229, or 919-560-3030. Fax: 919-560-3065. Emails: jim@carolinatheatre.org, phil@carolinatheatre.org. Web: festivals.carolinatheatre.org/nevermore, carolinatheatre.org, MySpace.com/nevermorefilmfestival. Founded/first screening 1999. Screening location Durham, NC. Features and shorts. In addition to horror accepts mystery, sci-fi, cult, animation. "We accept almost everything." **Shares proceeds with filmmakers**. "We pay royalties to distributors as well as guarantees to filmmakers, if requested." No winners. "We're a non-competition festival." Formerly The Nevermore Horror, Gothic and Fantasy Film Festival. Name shortened in 2006. Jim Carl is senior director of the Carolina Theatre of Durham. **No entry fee.**

New York City Horror Film Festival

PO Box 8582, Woodcliff Lake, NJ 07677. Director: Michael J. Hein. Ph: 201-666-6729. Email: nychorrorfest@aol.com. Web: nychorrorfest.com, MySpace.com/nychff, Facebook.com/pages/NYC-Horror-Film-Festival/83287509660. Founded 2001. First screening 2002. Screening location: New York, NY. Accepts features and shorts. Plaques, trophies, products. Screenplay contest. Hein died on July 9, 2011.

A Nightmare to Remember San Francisco Horror Film Festival

Last Doorway Productions, 2936 Acton Street, Apt B, Berkeley, CA 94702. Contacts: John Gillette, Reyna Young. Emails: j_r_gillette@sbcglobal.net, john@lastdoorwayproductions.com, reyna@lastdoorwayproductions.com. Web: anightmaretoremember.com, lastdoorwayproductions.com, thelastdoorwayshow.com, MySpace.com/lastdoorwayproductions, Facebook.com/profile.php?ref=profile&id=1247196875, Twitter.com/lastdoorwayshow. Founded/first screening 2008. Screening location San Francisco, CA. Accepts only shorts; no longer than 20 minutes. Presents the Coffin Award. Reyna Young and John Gillette are co-founders and co-directors of the festival, and co-owners of Last Doorway Productions. **No entry fee.**

Oklahoma Horror Film Festival & Convention

Tulsa, OK. Web: oklahomahorrorfilmfest.com, http://www.facebook.com/oklahomahorrorfilmfest. Features and shorts. Founded 2010. In 2011 this event was "expanded" into the mainstream Tulsa International Film Festival, with a "Nightmare Division" for horror films.

Paranoia Horror Film Festival—defunct?

Paranoia Horror Festival, 137 N Larchmont Blvd. #139, Los Angeles, CA 90004. Email: james@paranoiafest.com. Web: paranoiafest.com, MySpace.com/paranoiafest. Features and shorts. In addition to horror accepts sci-fi, crime, thriller, suspense, cult, bizarre, genre-defying, experimental. As of September 2010 their website has been down for at least two months, the domain name still awaiting renewal.

Phoenix Fear Film Festival

PO Box 13653, Scottsdale, AZ 85267. Contact: Chris McLennan. Ph: 602-399-9500. Email: director@phxfearfilmfestival.com. Web: phxfearfilmfestival.com, MySpace.com/phoenixfearfilmfestival. Features and shorts.

Phoenix International Horror and Sci-Fi Film Festival

See entry for International Horror and Sci-Fi Film Festival.

Pittsburgh Horror Film Festival

209 Mall Blvd., Monroeville, PA 15146. Also: 39 55 Ralph Drive, Glenshaw, PA 15116. Web: Pittsburgh HorrorFilms.com, Facebook.com/pages/Pittsburgh PA/Pittsburgh-Horror-Film-Festival/160952297262 214, Twitter.com/PGHHorrorFest. Announced in 2010. They intend to hold their first event in June 2011. Audience award in several categories.

Pretty Scary

Contact: Heidi Martinuzzi. Email: superheidi@msn.com. Martinuzzi founded Pretty-Scary.net (now fangirltastic.com) to promote women in horror. Through Pretty-Scary, Martinuzzi sponsored the Pretty Scary Blood Bath Film Festival in Feb. 2010. She also "sponsored an award for excellence in female horror filmmaking" at Shriekfest for three years (2007–09), but "I am not doing so in 2010 as now I am involved in the Viscera Film Festival." See entries for BleedFest, Blood Bath Film Festival, Shriekfest, and Viscera Film Festival.

Puerto Rico Horror Film Fest

214 Casa Magna Ave., San Patricio, esq Caobo Guaynabo, PR 00968, or PO Box 10937, San Juan, PR 00922-0937. Contact: Zoilo Rodríguez. Ph: 787-532-1212. Email: zrod@horrorpr.com. Web: horror-pr.com.

QuatreCon Film Festival—defunct

1341 H Street, Napa, CA 94559. Contact: Craig Appel. Ph: 707-773-4589. Web: quatrecon.com, MySpace.com/sf.paracon, Facebook.com/pages/San-Francisco-Paranormal-Conference/119217747650, Twitter.com/QuatreCon. QuatreCon's website, MySpace, Facebook, and Twitter accounts are dead. Craig Appel tells me that he's working on another, upcoming horror convention.

Ray Bradbury Award

See entry for Nebula Award.

Reaper Award

Not a film festival, but a "horror on home video" award. Judges pick the nominees; the fans (or anyone else) vote for the winners online. Web: reaperawards.com, Twitter.com/reaperawards. Run by *Home Media Magazine* and DreadCentral.com. First award year 2009. A.K.A. the Grim Reaper Award, or the Grimmy Award.

Rhode Island International Horror Film Festival

PO Box 162, Newport, RI 02840. Contact: Demetria J. Carr. Ph: 401-861-4445. Fax: 401-490-6735. Email: info@film-festival.org. Web: film-festival.org/Horror_ri.php, rihorrorfilmfest.blogspot.com, Facebook.com/group.php?gid=12095499454, Twitter.com/RIFIlmFest. Affiliated with the greater Rhode Island International Film Festival. Features and shorts. Also accepts documentaries. A.K.A. FLICKERS: Rhode Island International Horror Film Festival.

Rock and Shock Film Festival

The Palladium, 261 Main Street, Worcester, MA 01608. Ph: 508-797-9696 x11. Email: Palladium Email@aol.com. Web: rockandshock.com, MySpace.com/rockandshock, MySpace.com/rockandshockfilms, Twitter.com/MassConcerts. Seems to be a convention (with a heavy emphasis on rock bands), with a growing film festival portion. "While fans can meet their favorite horror film stars, directors, writers and bands during the day — at night we have well-known national bands performing each night next door at The Palladium."

Rondo Hatton Classic Horror Award

A.K.A., the Rondo. Not a film festival, but an online award presented by fans (or whoever cares to vote online). Web: rondoaward.com. "The Rondo Hatton Classic Horror Awards were created by David Colton and Kerry Gammill at the Classic Horror Film Boards in 2002. Anyone in fandom can vote or propose nominees." The award is a bust "sculpted by Kerry Gammill and cast by modeler Tim Lindsey ... a miniature version of the bust of Hatton seen in *House of Horrors* (1946).... Nominees are suggested by horror fans, pros and enthusiasts ... and finalized by David Colton (taraco@aol.com), with the help of more than 20 classic horror fans from around the world, and with expertise in all parts of fandom. Voting is by an electronic ballot or by email to taraco@aol.com."

Sacramento Horror Film Festival

7 Caruso Island Court, Sacramento CA 95823. Founder and director: Tim Meunier. Ph: 916-869-8954. Email: admin@sachorrorfilmfest.com. Web: sachorrorfilmfest.com, MySpace.com/sachorrorfilmfest. Accepts features and shorts. In addition to horror accepts suspense, thriller, sci-fi, documentaries, music videos. Also has an annual "filmmaker challenge" (with a $500 cash prize) in which you create a film "around a theme."

Salem Independent Horror Film Festival — defunct?

83 Essex St. #2, Salem, MA 01970. Contact: Scott Masterson. Email: salemfilm@yahoo.com. Web: salemfilm.com. Formerly the Salem "Amateur" Horror Film Festival. Website down throughout 2010.

Salty Horror Film Festival

1070 East 300 South Apt. 307, Salt Lake City, UT 84102. Founder and director: Mario DeAngelis. Ph: 801-637-0622. Email: mariopd65@hotmail.com, info@saltyhorrorfilmfestival.com. Web: saltyhorrorfilmfestival.com, Facebook.com/people/Mario-De Angelis/816932845, Twitter.com/SaltyHorrorFest. Founded 2009. First screening 2010. Screenings in Salt Lake City. Features and shorts. Winners receive a trophy and "there may be cash prizes at the end of the festival." Screenplay contest. They also have a Demon Chaser challenge in which contestants complete a film that has salt in it, within 36 hours, and is 6 minutes, 66 seconds (i.e., 7 minutes, 6 seconds) long.

Saturn Award

See entry for: Academy of Science Fiction, Fantasy & Horror Films.

Scare Fest

Lexington, KY. Contact: Jeff Waldridge. Email: thescarefest@hotmail.com. Web: scarefestcon.com, MySpace.com/thescarefest, Facebook.com/thescarefest, Twitter.com/thescarefest. A "horror & paranormal convention" rather than a film festival, but they do screen new, indie horror films. They present **no awards**. I found one film on the web claiming to have won for "Best Sound Design and Effects" at the 2003 Scare Fest, but Waldridge tells me: "Sometimes these films get creative. We only select films and allow them to put official selection. They [the films] do not receive any award. The films we show are winners because they are an official selection." No, it wasn't a different Scare Fest. Waldridge confirmed that the filmmaker was referring to Waldridge's Scare Fest.

Science Fiction + Fantasy Short Film Festival

EMP | SFM, 330 6th Avenue North, Suite 200, Seattle, WA 98109. Ph: 206-770-2700. Web: empsfm.org/programs. Founded 2005. First screening 2006. Originally the Science Fiction Short Film Festival, with Fantasy added later. Not a horror event, but some horror qualifies as "dark fantasy," so they may be open to it. EMP | SFM stands for Experience Music Project | Science Fiction Museum.

Scream Award

Not a film festival. Latest web address: spike.com/event/scream2010. According to Wikipedia this is "an award show dedicated to the horror, sci-fi, and fantasy genres of feature films. Originally only having Scream Queen and Heroic Performance awards for actors, the personnel awards have expanded to include actors and actresses of all three recognized genres. In addition, comic books awards were also given and have been recently expanded. It is broadcast on Spike TV and has been branded in the past as the Spike TV Scream Awards. Recently, the show has become labeled simply Scream with the respective year, i.e., Scream 2009. The show was created by executive producers Michael Levitt, Cindy Levitt, and Casey Patterson."

Screamfest L.A.

8840 Wilshire Blvd., 3rd Floor, Beverly Hills, CA 90211. Founder and director: Rachel Belofsky. Ph: 310-358-3273. Fax: 310-358-3272. Email: info@screamfestla.com. Web: Screamfestla.com, MySpace.com/screamfestla, Facebook.com/pages/Screamfest-Horror-Film-Festival/100351747266, Twitter.com/screamfest. Founded/first screening 2001. Features and shorts. Winners receive trophies, cash, products. Screenplay contest.

ShockerFest

PO Box 580450, Modesto CA 95358. Co-directors: George and Louise Baker. Ph: 209-537-5221. Fax: 209-531-0233. Web: shockerfest.com, MySpace.com/shockerfest. Founded 2002. Features and shorts. Their 2010 festival selections were aired throughout October 2010 on a local TV station. Shockerfest estimates that 25,000 viewers saw all or some of the films. Sponsored by the Fireside Foundation, a non-profit corporation promoting independent film which also runs the California International Animation Film Festival. Not to be confused with Shockfest. A.K.A. **Firelight Shocks Film Festival.**

Shockfest Film Festival

PO Box 93095, Hollywood, CA 90093. Contact: G.R. Claveria. Ph: 626-576-8803. Email: contactus@ShockFilmFest.com. Web: shockfilmfest.com. Claveria emails me: "Our small festival started as a school endeavor to showcase the fun of horror and shock. We have been working our best to make it grow year by year." Not to be confused with ShockerFest (see previous entry).

Shriekfest Horror/SciFi Film Festival & Screenplay Competition

PO Box 920-444, Sylmar CA 91392. Co-founder and director: Denise Gossett. Email: shriekfest@aol.com. Web: shriekfest.com, MySpace.com/shriekfest, Facebook.com/shriekfest, Twitter.com/shriekfest. Founded 2001. Screening location Hollywood, CA. Features and shorts. In addition to horror accepts thriller, sci-fi, fantasy. Presents Shriekfest Tombstone trophy, cash, products, services. Screenplay contest for shorts and features.

Silicon

1009 E. Capitol Expressway, # 415, San Jose, CA 85121-2415. Web: siliconventions.com, MySpace.com/siliconventions, Facebook.com/group.php?gid=13387 8152147. A "multi-media, sci-fi, comic, anime convention," but they also have a film festival. "SiliCon is a family friendly convention, so please keep contents to a G or PG level rating. We may accept some R rated material to be shown at later hours of the screening." Shorts only (20 minutes or less). Website says there will be no Silicon in 2010, due to the economy, but they vow to return in 2011, so I've not yet tagged them as *defunct*. In 2009 I met a man at Loscon who said that Silicon's festival had **no entry fee**, but that's unconfirmed.

Spooky Movie: The Washington D.C. International Horror Film Festival

PO Box 4059, Arlington, VA 22204. Email: spookyfests@gmail.com. Web: thespookymovie.com, MySpace.com/spookymovie, Facebook.com/pages/-Spooky-Movie-The-Washington-DC-International-Horror-Festival/35142648410, Twitter.com/spookymovie. First screening 2006. As of 2009 they present a DarkHart Screenplay Award (sponsored by DarkHart Press) to unproduced scripts (i.e., they have a screenplay contest). Accepts features and shorts. In addition to horror accepts documentaries, "silly fan films."

Tabloid Witch Award

PO Box 1903, Santa Monica, CA 90406-1903. Founder and director: Thomas M. Sipos. Ph: 310-458-6048. Email: editor@hollywoodinvestigator.com. Web: tabloidwitch.com, MySpace.com/tabloidwitch. Founded 2004. First screening 2005. Screenings in Santa Monica and Los Angeles; has held special screenings in New York City, Salt Lake City, and Winnipeg, Canada. Features and shorts. In addition to horror accepts sci-fi, avant-garde, experimental, music videos. Winners receive plaques. **No entry fee.**

Telluride Horror Show

PO Box 182, 135 W. Pacific Ave, Telluride, CO 81435. Director: Ted Wilson. Ph: 970-708-3906. Fax: 970-369-5198. Email: info@telluridehorrorshow.com. Web: Telluridehorrorshow.com, Facebook.com/pages/Telluride-Horror-Show/124124550958173, Twitter.com/telluridehorror. Founded 2010. Shorts and features. Accepts "horror, thriller, dark fantasy, and dark sci-fi." Their site says that they're a "3-Day horror film festival in world-famous Telluride, Colorado" and that the Telluride Film Commission is a sponsor. Not affiliated with the famous Telluride Film Festival. They email me: "We're a non-competitive festival at this time, so no list of winners."

Terror Film Festival

PO Box 823, Frazer, PA 19355. Founder and director: Claw. Ph: 610-889-4928. Email: terrorfilm fest@aol.com. Web: terrorfilmfestival.net, MySpace.com/terrorfilmfestival, Twitter.com/terrorfilmfest. Founded/first screening 2006. Screening location Philadelphia, PA. Features and shorts. In addition to horror accepts fantasy, sci-fi, thriller, dark, drama. Sometimes shares proceeds with filmmakers. "Depends on the particular situation." Winners receive the Claw Award, cash prizes. Screenplay contest.

Terror'thon
See entry for Boston Terror'thon.

Texas Blood Bath Film Festival
See: Blood Bath Film Festival.

Texas FearFest
Email: admin@gutsandgory.com. Web: txfearfest.com, myspace.com/txfearfest. A convention rather than a film festival. Most recently (2010) held at Sneaky Pete's Sports Bar, in Lewisville, Texas.

Texas Frightmare Weekend
Texas. Contact: Loyd Cryer. Email: loyd@texasfrightmareweekend.com. Web: texasfrightmareweekend.com, MySpace.com/texasfrightmareweekend, Facebook.com/pages/Texas-Frightmare-Weekend/13624001797, Twitter.com/txfrightmare. A convention, but they include a film festival. Seems to occur throughout Texas. One year they were in Irving. For 2011 they'll be in Dallas.

That's Not Mine Film Festival
Contact: Nick Karner. Email: Nick@prankfilms.com. Web: prankfilms.com. Appears to be a personal project of filmmaker/actor Karner. Not a horror festival, but open to horror (and most everything else, it seems).

Thriller! Chiller!
Grand Rapids, MI. Directors: Anthony E. Griffin, Chris Randall. Email: info@thrillerchiller.com. Web: thrillerchiller.com, Facebook.com/thrillerchiller, Twitter.com/thrillchill. Founded 2006. In addition to horror, accepts action, sci-fi, suspense.

Thrillerfest
ITW, PO Box 311, Eureka, CA 95502. Web: thrillerfest.com and thrillerwriters.org. Not a film festival, but a thriller writers convention focusing on books. Sponsored by the International Thriller Writers. ITW founded 2004. First awards presented 2006. Their Thriller Award is currently presented only to novelists and short story writers, but they had a screenplay category in 2006 and 2007. Not to be confused with the other Thrillerfest (see below entry).

Thrillerfest—defunct?
Grand Center, Inc., 3526 Washington Avenue, St. Louis, MO 63103. Contact: Eddie Dee. Ph: 314-289-1500 or 314-437-4378. Email: thrillerfest2009@gmail.com. Web: grandcenter.org. Founded 2009. Posted on an unofficial site: "Screen Jewels Productions is hosting the First Annual Horror Film Festival on October 30th & 31st at the Grand Center Intersection for Life and Arts: Thrillerfest 2009." The Grand Center seems to have been the venue, but not necessarily the organizers behind Thrillerfest. As of October 2010 (a year after the first Thrillerfest), there is no sign of its return. The "first annual" Thrillerfest may also have been the last. Not to be confused with the other Thrillerfest (see above entry).

Tribeca Film Festival: Midnight Section
375 Greenwich Street, New York, NY 10013. Ph: 212-941-2003. Email: trosen@tribecaenterprises.com. Web: tribecafilmfestival.org, MySpace.com/tribecafilmfestival, Facebook.com/TribecaFilm, Twitter.com/TriBeCaFilmFest. This festival emphasizes indie and studio films, but they have a Midnight Section for horror. And even much non-horror, as their 2009 screening schedule indicates: tribecafilm.com/festival/features/TFF_09_Midnight.html.

TromaDance
The Troma Building, 36–40 11th Street, Long Island City, NY 11106. Contact: Anne Koester. Email: anne@troma.com or volunteer@tromadance.com. Web: tromadance.com, MySpace.com/tromadance, Twitter.com/lloydkaufman. Screens in Asbury Park, New Jersey. Founded 2004. Accepts features and shorts. Not a horror film festival, but open to all indie fare. **No entry fee**.

25-Hour Horror Feast
The Little Theatre, 240 East Avenue, Rochester, NY 14604. Contact: Karen van Meenen. Email: info@thelittle.org. Web: thelittle.org/filmfest.php, MySpace.com/littletheatrefilmsociety, Facebook.com/pages/Rochester-NY/The-Little-Theatre/45000244066, Twitter.com/TheLittleRoch. This festival is run by a movie theater every Halloween. Most of their films are famous horror classics, but they've accepted short film submissions from new filmmakers in the past.

Underground Horror Fest
See entry for Underground Horror Filmfest. They're separate events, but both are run by Art Sunday, who says, "Show films at both, but one more of a filmfest, the other just got screening rooms. Plus I do four shows a year." Founded Oct. 28, 2009. First screening Feb. 6, 2010.

Underground Horror Filmfest
Tulsa, OK. Founder/director: Art Sunday. Ph: 918-402-8540. Email: undergroundhorror@yahoo.com. Web: MySpace.com/undergroundhorrorfest, Face-

book.com/UndergroundHorrorFest. Twitter account: Uhorrorfest. Founded Dec. 31, 2009. First screening July 10, 2010. Accepts shorts, features, music videos. Winners receive cash, trophies, plaques. **No entry fee.**

Vampire Film Festival

Reel Energy Entertainment, 563 N. Marengo Ave. Ste. #1, Pasadena, CA 91101. Director: Asif Ahmed. Ph: 504-298-VAMP. Web: vampirefilmfestival.com. Email: asif@reelenergy.com. Founded 2003. Not just a film festival, but a vampire fan and lifestyle convention, featuring panels, parties, and "living art." Ahmed emails me: "We accept new films, old films, any language, format, etc. Our festival looks at vampire films, voodoo films, gothic films, mythic horror films, music videos and documentaries covering any of the areas." Despite their California address, their 2009 and 2010 events were held in New Orleans. They also have a "regional director" for Sarasota, Florida. A.K.A. Vampire Film Series & Festival, and International Vampire Film Festival.

Viscera Film Festival

PO Box 724, Carlsbad, NM 88221-0724. Co-directors: Shannon Lark, Heidi Martinuzzi. Ph: 510-207-1418. Emails: shannon@thechainsawmafia.com, superheidi@msn.com. Web: viscerafilmfestival.com, MySpace.com/viscerafilmfestival, Facebook.com/pages/Viscera-Film-Festival/103276146381373, Twitter.com/VisceraFilmFest. Women only festival. One category for films in which *everyone* involved (pre-production, cast, post-production) is a woman. Another category for films in which either the *producer, director, or writer* is a woman. Also: "Transgendered women or those who identify strongly with the female gender are encouraged to apply." Short films and feature film trailers only. Winners receive cash prize, trophies, and DVD distribution. Founded 2007, in San Francisco. Viscera had its first screening in July 2010, in Los Angeles. **No entry fee.**

Weekend of Horrors

See entry for "Fangoria's Weekend of Horrors."

Wonder Award

Web: cinefantastiqueonline.com. Not a film festival. Cinefantastique Online (formerly *Cinefantastique* magazine) says that their award is their "answer to the Oscars — a chance to recognize the great science fiction, fantasy, and horror films that are denied Academy Award nominations because of their genre affiliation." Award founded 2009. I presume it's called the Wonder Award because science fiction (especially), horror, and fantasy all evoke a "sense of wonder."

Zompire: The Undead Film Festival

Web: zompire.com, Myspace.com/zompirefilmfestival. See entry for H.P. Lovecraft Film Festival & CthulhuCon. Andrew Migliore of that festival founded Zompire. It was canceled for 2010, but it plans to return in 2011.

United Kingdom

Abertoir: Aberystwyth Horror Festival

Aberystwyth Arts Centre, Aberystwyth, SY23 3DE, Wales. Founder and director: Gaz Bailey. Ph: 44-1970-628682. Emails: gaz@abertoir.co.uk, Rhys@abertoir.co.uk. Web: abertoir.co.uk, Facebook.com/#!/group.php?gid=13305853204, Twitter.com/abertoirfest. Founded/first screening 2006. Screening location: Aberystwyth, Wales. Accepts horror features, and horror and fantasy shorts. No fantasy features. Audience award for best feature film, plus best short film. A physical trophy was introduced in 2010. **No entry fee.**

Bram Stoker International Film Festival

PO Box 666, Skelton, North Yorkshire, TS12 1HY, England. Ph: (office) 44-05602-722983, (cell) 44-07500-926530, Email: info@bramstokerfilmfestival.com. Web: bramstokerfilmfestival.com. Screening location: Whitby, North Yorkshire. Founded 2009. They screen horror and Hammer classics as well as new films.

British Fantasy Award

Presented by the British Fantasy Society. Web: britishfantasysociety.org. The BFS was founded in 1971; their award first presented in 1972. It's primarily a literary award, their recognition of scripts and films being spotty. The BFS also runs the annual FantasyCon (web: fantasycon2011.org) where they sometimes screen films. The film and TV BFAs generally go to major releases, but they might screen your short or long film at FantasyCon. It's worth asking.

British Horror Film Festival

Social Media Manager: Jacqueline Cockerill. Info: info@thefilmfestivalguild.com. Old web: britishhorrorfilmfestival.com. New web: thefilmfestivalguild.com, Twitter.com/ukfilmfestivals. Affiliated with the British Independent Film Festival and the Newport International Film Festival. First screening 2010, held at The Pier Theatre, Bournemouth.

Celluloid Screams: Sheffield Horror Film Festival

Showroom Cinema, Paternoster Row, Sheffield, S1 2BX. Director: Robert Nevitt. Ph: +44 (0)114-275 7727. Email: info@celluloidscreams.co.uk. Web: celluloidscreams.co.uk, Facebook.com/group.php?gid=

24446229634, Twitter.com/sheffhorrorfest. Founded 2009. Screening location Sheffield. Accepts features and shorts. **No entry fee.**

Dead by Dawn: Scotland's International Horror Film Festival

88 Lothian Road, Edinburgh EH3 9BZ, Scotland. Director: Adele Hartley. Email: info@deadbydawn.co.uk. Web: deadbydawn.co.uk. "Scotland's International Horror Film Festival, in association with Filmhouse" (filmhousecinema.com). **No entry fee.**

Fanomenon

Leeds International Film Festival, Town Hall, The Headrow, Leeds, LS1 3AD. Director: Chris Fell. Ph: +44-0-0113-247-8398. Email: chris.fell@leeds.gov.uk. Web: leedsfilm.com. Fanomenon is the "horror programme" portion of the Leeds International Film Festival. They accept shorts and features, new and previously released (i.e., old classics take up some of the screen time).

Fantastic Films Weekend

Bradford, West Yorkshire, England. Contact: Tony Earnshaw. Email: tony.earnshaw@nationalmediamuseum.org.uk. Web: www.nationalmediamuseum.org.uk/fantastic/2010. Founded 2002. "Dedicated to horror, fantasy and sci-fi cinema and television ... celebration of old, new, bloody and obscure is hosted by the National Media Museum in Bradford ... showcasing classic chillers, sci-fi shockers, fantasy epics, vintage TV shows and rarely seen gems from the vaults. FFW runs the gamut from the stark monochrome classics of the silent era through to the latest digital epics."

FantasyCon

See entry for the British Fantasy Award.

Festival of Fantastic Films

Manchester. Contact: Gil Lane-Young. Email: gil@glaneyoung.freeserve.co.uk. Web: fantastic-films.com. First screening 1995. "In addition to the retrospective film programme that is the backbone of the event, the Festival of Fantastic Films has become the premiere UK venue for new genre movies. We showcase an amazing selection of independently produced feature and short films from all over the world."

Film4 FrightFest

See entry for FrightFest.

FrightFest

London FrightFest Ltd., 10 Wiltshire Gardens, Twickenham, London, TW2 6ND. Ph: 00-44-20-8296-0555. Email: frightfest@mac.com. Web: frightfest.co.uk, MySpace.com/94650103, Facebook.com/group.php?gid=2361328675. Founded in 2000. Ian, a festival representative, tells me: "We don't award prizes."

Glastonbury Horror Festival

See entry for Horror UK.

Grimm Up North

Manchester. Director: Simeon Halligan. Email: info@grimmfest.com. Web: grimmfest.com, Twitter.com/grimmfest. In addition to horror films, they also feature sci-fi and gaming. First screening 2009. Awards first presented 2010. A.K.A. Grimmfest.

Halloween Monster Movie Challenge

Birmingham, Midlands. Festival coordinators: Kelly Webster, Kelly Jones. Email: hmmc-uk@hotmail.com. Web: halloweenmonstermoviechallenge.co.uk, MySpace.com/monstermoviechallenge, Facebook.com/group.php?gid=118163970906, Twitter.com/moviechallenge. Founded/first screening 2009. Shorts only. Kelly Webster says: "We ask independent filmmakers to make a new horror film within the space of two months. The movie has to be between 3–10 minutes long and include a monster, e.g., Frankenstein, werewolf, swamp monster, zombie, or a monster of their own imaginings. It also has to include a line of dialogue which we give them so we know their film was made for the challenge." Seems to be a United Kingdom only event: "Open to all UK based filmmakers to celebrate monster movies, promote the independent scene." Winners receive trophies. **No entry fee,** but "just £3 to get into the venue."

Horror Fest UK—defunct?

Portsmouth, England. Email: info@horrorfest.co.uk. Web: horrorfest.co.uk, MySpace.com/horrorfestuk, Facebook.com/people/Horror-Fest-UK/541176836. First screening in 2006. Email bounces. MySpace last logged into on April 2008. Website is a blank page with the words: "This page has been reserved for future use."

Horror UK

Ph: +44-1329-312847. Web: horroruk.com. They apparently sponsored the **28 Hours Later** film festival on October 30, 31, 2009, and next month, **Portsmouth Scream** (web: Facebook.com/note.php?note_id=175647807217), on November 12, 2009, at: 49 Barnfield Court, Fareham, PO14 1NF. They also sponsor the **Glastonbury Horror Festival** (Web: http://eventful.com/events/horror-uk-glastonbury-horror-fest-/E0-001-027939714-5). I suspect these are all one-time events. The HorrorUK.com site offers little details, and no contact info.

Leeds Anime Horror Film Festival — defunct?

Leeds, England. Contact: Boyd Christopher. Web: leedsanimehorrorfilmfestival.co.uk, MySpace.com/leedshorror. Website down. MySpace still up.

London International Festival of Science Fiction and Fantastic Film

See entry for Sci-Fi-London Film Festival.

Mayhem Horror Festival

Mayhem, c/o Broadway Media Centre, 14–18 Broad Street, Nottingham, NG1 3AL. Contact: Steven Sheil, Chris Cooke, Gareth Howell. Email: info@mayhemhorrorfest.co.uk. Web: mayhemhorrorfest.co.uk, Facebook.com/group.php?gid=3445629987, Twitter.com/mayhem_festival. Founded 2004. Screens classic horror features, but seems to accept new short films.

Portsmouth Scream — defunct?

See entry for Horror UK.

Sci-Fi-London Film Festival

Sci-Fi-London, c/o FestivalBiz, 2nd Floor, 145–157 St John Street, London EC1V 4PY. Contacts: Esther Hookman, Louis Savy. Ph: +44(0)20 3239 9277. First screening 2002. Email: info@sci-fi-london.com. Web: sci-fi-london.com, MySpace.com/scifilondon, Facebook.com/scifilondon, Twitter.com/scifilondon. A.K.A. London International Festival of Science Fiction and Fantastic Film.

28 Hours Later — defunct?

See entry for Horror UK.

Uruguay

Montevideo Fantástico

Joaquín Requena 1077 — Apto 101 (CP: 11200), Montevideo, Uruguay. Contact: Alejandro Yamgotchian. Ph: 598-2409-2123. Email: organizacion@montevideofantastico.com.uy. Web: montevideofantastico.com.uy, Facebook.com/people/MontevideoFantastico/100001546146518, Twitter.com/montevideofan. Features and shorts.

List of Award Winners (by Festival)

In compiling this material, I always began my research with primary sources: directly contacting the festival or going to their website. Whenever that proved unhelpful, I relied on secondary sources: Wikipedia, the Internet Movie Database (IMDb), online genre magazines and blogs (some of which still carry old press releases), filmmakers' websites, etc.

I've found Wikipedia's listings to be usually more complete than those of the IMDb. I've also learned to be wary of filmmakers' claims; some stretch the truth. One filmmaker claimed on a website that his film had won for "Best Sound Design and Effects" at the 2003 Scare Fest. Yet when I checked with Scare Fest's Jeff Waldridge, he confirmed that his festival was noncompetitive, adding, "Sometimes these films get creative. We only select films and allow them to put official selection. They [the films] do not receive any award. The films we show are winners because they are an official selection."

I caught another filmmaker claiming on her website that her film was a "Winner" at Scotland's Dead by Dawn. But when I asked Dead by Dawn's Adele Hartley about it, she explained that the filmmaker had won *second* place. (Hartley doesn't list second place recipients on her site.) The filmmaker had committed a half-lie. Yes, she "won" second place. But when you say "winner" without qualifications, people assume you mean first place. I'm sure the filmmaker knows this.

Some festivals sponsor contests for unproduced screenplays. I've marked such winning scripts as "unproduced," to distinguish them from winning screenplays for produced films. Of course, a script that was unproduced when it won a festival's contest, might by now be produced. Shriekfest's Denise Gossett says, "[Contest winning] screenplays get sold every year, and often come back to compete in film form the next year."

Some festival websites' awards listings contain omissions or misspellings. I've corrected those that were obvious to me. When I read that "Abgela Bettis" had won a festival's acting award, I assumed it was Angela Bettis. (How could I forget her performance in *May*?) But I'm sure I've missed some mistakes.

Tip for creative talent: If you've won an award, check your listing on the festival's website. If you see a problem, contact the festival and politely request that they correct it.

If any readers know of an award that should be included below, or know of any changes, updates, or corrections, please contact the author at thomas@sipos.org.

Abertoir: Aberystwyth Horror Festival

2010

Best Short Film ..... *Manual practico del amigo imaginario* (Ciro Altabas)
Audience Award for Best Feature ..... *Rare Exports* (Jalmari Helander)
Méliès d'Or Short Film Nomination ..... *The Elemental* (Robert Sproul-Cran)

2009

Best Short Film ..... *Wheelchair Werewolf* (dir: Joe Avella)
Audience Award .... *The Tingler* (dir: William Castle)

2008

Best Short Film ..... *Vadata* (dir: Manuel Lebelt)

Arizona Underground Film Festival

2010

Best Narrative Feature ..... *Machotaildrop* (dir: Corey Adams, Alex Craig)
Best Narrative Short ..... *Guignol* (dir: Dana Turken)
Best Horror Feature ..... *Beyond the Grave* (dir: Davi de Oliveira Pinheiro)
Best Horror Short ..... *The Sleuth Incident* (dir: Jason Kupfer)
Best Documentary Feature ..... *Roll Out, Cowboy* (dir: Elizabeth Lawrence)
Best Documentary Short ..... *Extreme Nature of Bats* (dir: Greg Passmore)
Best Experimental ..... *Window on Your Present* (dir: Cinqué Lee)
Best Animation ..... *DemiUrge Emesis* (dir: Aurelio Voltaire)
Best Exploitation ..... *Nude Nuns with Big Guns* (dir: Joseph Guzman)
Best of the Fest ..... *Phasma Ex Machina* (dir: Matt Osterman)
Audience Award ..... *The Last Lovecraft: Relic of Cthulhu* (dir: Henry Saine)
Director's Choice Award ..... *Quit* (dir: Dick Rude)

2009

Best Narrative Feature ..... *Modern Love Is Automatic* (dir: Zach Clark)
Best Narrative Short ..... *My Cousin's Keeper* (dir: Tom Woodruff, Jr.)
Best Horror Feature ..... *Evil Angel* (dir: Richard Dutcher)
Best Horror Short ..... *Kagamiko* (dir: Mathieu Arsenault)
Best Exploitation ..... *Run! Bitch Run!* (dir: Joseph Guzman)
Best Documentary Feature ..... *Oh My God! It's Harrod Blank!* (dir: David Silberberg)
Best Documentary Short ..... *Severing the Soul* (dir: Barbara Klutinis)
Best Experimental ..... *The Soil's Soft Horizon* (dir: Adam Petke)
Best Animation ..... *Seven Corners* (dir: Todd Hemker)
Best Music Video ..... *Everything Burns* (dir: Aram Kouyoumdjian)
Best of Fest ..... *I'm Gonna Do It Until the Day I Die!* (dir: Dale Peterson, Coleman Weinberg)
Audience Award ..... *La Funcionaria Asesina*, A.K.A. *The Slayer Bureaucrat* (dir: Sergio Kardenas)
Special Jury Award ..... *Someone's Knocking at the Door* (dir: Chad Ferrin)

Honorable Mention: *Doctor "S" Battles the Sex Crazed Reefer Zombies* (dir: Bryan Ortiz)
Director's Choice Award ..... *Cigarette Girl* (dir: Michael McCarthy)

2008

Best Narrative ..... *Altamont Now* (dir: Joshua Von Brown)
Best Narrative Short ..... *The Heart Is a Hidden Camera* (dir: Gabriel Judet-Weinshel)
Best Horror Feature ..... *Bonnie & Clyde vs. Dracula* (dir: Timothy Friend)
Best Horror Short ..... *Excision* (dir: Robert Bates, Jr.)
Best Documentary ..... *Unspeakable: The Life & Art of Reverend Steven Johnson Leyba* (dir: Marc Rokoff)
Best Animation ..... *Puppet* (dir: Patrick Smith)
Best Music Video ..... *Mission Creeps "Creepy"* (dir: Gene Torres)
Best Experimental ..... *Death of the Reel* (dir: Benjamin Meade)
Best of the Fest ..... *Dark Reel* (dir: Josh Eisenstadt)
Audience Award ..... *Left/Right* (dir: Matthew Wolfe)
Juror Award ..... *AM1200* (dir: David Prior)

Atlanta Horror Fest

Seems to have morphed into the Buried Alive Film Fest (see its awards list for 2009 and 2010). Not to be confused with the Atlanta Horror Film Festival.

2008

Best Feature ..... *Chainsaw Cheerleaders* (dir: Donald Farmer)
Honorable Mention, Feature ..... *Bikini Bloodbath Carwash* (dir: Jonathan Gorman and Thomas Edward Seymour)
Best Short ..... *Urine Trouble* (dir: Sam Thompson)
Honorable Mention, Short ..... *There's a Werewolf in My Attic* (dir: Sam Thompson)

Atlanta Horror Film Festival

No awards presented in 2009. Not to be confused with the Atlanta Horror Fest.

2010

Best Feature Film ..... *Cyrus—Mind of a Serial Killer* (dir: Mark Vadik)
Best Writer/Director Feature ..... *God Thinks You're a Loser* (dir/writ: Gary Chason)
Best Foreign Feature ..... *Strigoi* (dir: Faye Jackson)
Best Dramatic Horror Feature ..... *Kiss the Abyss* (dir: Ken Winkler)

Best Thriller Feature ..... *True Nature* (dir: Patrick Steele, prod: Ann Rotolante)
Best Horror Anthology Feature ..... *Drive-In Horrorshow* (dir: Michael Neel, prod: Greg Ansin)
Best Erotic Horror Feature ..... *Sculpture* (dir: Pete Jacelone)
Best Special FX in a Feature ..... *El Monstro del Mar!* (dir: Stuart Simpson)
Best Experimental Feature ..... *Wanderlust* (dir: David Kabler)
Best Horror Comedy Feature ..... *Werewolf Fever* (dir: Brian Singleton)
Best Short Film ..... *Zombies and Cigarettes* (Rafael Martinez and Inaki San Roman)
Best Sci-Fi Short ..... *Maya* (dir: Ron Johnson)
Best Thriller Short ..... *Night* (dir: Brian Elkins)
Best Comedy Horror Short ..... *Tombstone Brides* (dir: Victor Mathieu)
Best International Short ..... *St. Christophorus: Roadkill* (dir: Gregor Erler)
Best Experimental Short ..... *The Tell Tale Heart* (dir: Lynn Cohen)
Best Animated Short ..... *Death Row Diet* (dir: Mike Salva and Tom Snyder)
Best Horror Anthology Short ..... *Monster on My Mind* (dir: Chris Miller)
Best Supernatural Short ..... *The Devil's Toy* (dir: Alex Lugones)
Best Drama Short ..... *A+Positive* (dir: Chris Bamford and Serge Ou)
Best Local Short ..... *May Hell Keep Her* (dir: Brian McQuilkin)
Best Short Short ..... *DemiUrge Emesis* (dir: Aurelio Voltaire)
Most Disturbing Short ..... *Eyes Beyond* (dir: Daniel Reininghaus)

2008

Best Feature Film ..... *Blood on the Highway* (dir: Barak Epstein, Blair Rowan)
Best International Feature ..... *Maldito Bastardo!*, A.K.A. *Damn Bastard!* (dir: Javi Camino)
Best Director (Feature) ..... Bryce Fridrik Olson (*The Caretaker*)
Best Screenplay (Feature) ..... Graham Reznick (*I Can See You*)
Best Short Film ..... *See the Dead* (dir: Robert W. Filion)
Best Director (Short) ..... *Peekers* (dir: Mark Steensland)
Best International Short ..... *Because There Are Things You Never Forget* (dir: Lucas Figueroa)
Best Sci-Fi ..... *Attackazoids!* (dir: Brian Lonano)
Best Screenplay (Short) ..... Ryan Spindell, Bradford Hodgson (*Kirksdale*)
Best Special FX ..... *Eel Girl* (dir: Paul Campion)
Best Animated Horror ..... *A Break in the Monotony* (dir: Damien Slevin)

2007

Best Feature Film ..... *Evil Keg* (dir: Allen Wilbanks)
Best Local Feature ..... *Bad Land* (dir: Ron McLellen)
Best Director ..... Yfke van Berckelaer (*Zombie Love*)
Best Documentary ..... *Blood, Boobs, and Beast* (dir: John Paul Kinhart)
Best Horror-Comedy Feature ..... *Blood Car* (dir: Alex Orr)
Best Schlock-Horror Film ..... *Come Get Some More* (dir: Steven Grainger)
Best International Feature ..... *Gritos en el Pasillo*, A.K.A. *Going Nuts* (dir: Manuel Cristobal)
Best Short Film ..... *Of Darkness* (dir: Gary Irwin)
Best Horror-Comedy Short ..... *Zombie Love* (dir: Yfke van Berckelaer)
Best Local Short ..... *Jump Rope with Gutz* (dir: Blake Myers)
Best International Short ..... *Happy Birthday to You* (dir: David Alcalde)
Best Animation ..... *Cannibal Flesh Riot* (dir: Gris Grimly)
Best Cinematography ..... *Of Darkness* (dir: Gary Irwin)
Best Special FX ..... *W.O.R.M.* (dir: Anthony Sumner)

B Movie Celebration

Although this Midwest horror film festival primarily screens old classics, it also screens new films. Presents the Golden Cob Award.

4th — 2009 (presented in 2010)

Best B Movie Release ..... *Dead Snow*
Runner-Up for Best B Movie Release ..... *Mega Shark vs. Giant Octopus*
Best B Movie Director ..... Tommy Wirkola (*Dead Snow*)
Runner-Up for Best B Movie Director ..... Albert Pyun (*Bulletface*)
Best Scream Queen ..... Brooke Lewis (*Slime City Massacre*)
Runner-Up for Best Scream Queen ..... Debbie Rochon (*Slime City Massacre*)
Best Leading Man ..... Jim O'Rear (*The Dead Matter*)
Runner-Up for Best Leading Man ..... Bill Moseley (*Repo: The Genetic Opera*)
Best Soundtrack ..... Chuck Cirino (*Bone Eater*)
Runner-Up for Best Soundtrack ..... Tony Riparetti (*Bulletface*)
Bill Cothron Best Emerging Filmmaker Award ..... Elisabeth Fies (*The Commune*)
Runner-Up for Bill Cothron Best Emerging Filmmaker Award ..... Darin Wood (*Monster from Bikini Beach*)

Best Rising B Movie Actress ..... Jessica Cameron (*Absolution*)
Runner-Up for Best Rising B Movie Actress ..... Kayla Gill (*Monster Cruise*)
Best Rising B-Movie Actor ..... Shay Baker (*Monster Cruise*)
Runner-Up for Best Rising B-Movie Actor ..... Chris Massoglia (*The Vampire's Assistant*)
Best Documentary ..... *Popatopolis* (dir: Clay Westervelt)
Runner-Up for Best Documentary ..... *Blood, Boobs & Beast* (dir: John Paul Kinhart)
Best Special Effects ..... Kristin Hellebust (*Dead Snow*)
Runner-Up for Best Special Effects ..... Switch VFX (*Repo: The Genetic Opera*)
Bob Wilkins Award for Best Horror Host ..... Ms. Monster (*Hel on Ice*)
Runner-Up for Bob Wilkins Award for Best Horror Host ..... Wolfman Mac (*Chiller Drive-In*)
Superfan of 2009 ..... Daniel Roebuck
Runner-Up for Superfan of 2009 ..... Duane L. Martin (*Rogue Cinema*)
Lifetime Achievement Award ..... Herschell Gordon Lewis
Members of the B Movie Hall of Fame ..... Earl Owensby, Dick Miller, William Castle

B-Movie Film Festival

Based in Syracuse, New York, the festival's website appears incomplete. It invites entries for its 2010 festival, lists 2009 nominees but no winners, makes no mention of 2008, prominently displays 2007 winners, and buries its 2006 winners in the archives. Emails to them go unanswered.

2007

Best Doc ..... *Blood, Boobs & Beast*
Best Short ..... *Ivory Bastards Against Extinction*
Best Celebrity Cameo ..... Dick Miller (*Trail of the Screaming Forehead*)
Best Editing ..... *Summer School*
Best Set Design ..... *Speed Freak*
Best Make-Up/Special Effects ..... *Brain Dead*
Best Digital Effects ..... *Dead Wood*
Best Photography/Cinematography ..... *Devil Girl*
Best Music ..... *Thicker Than Water: The Vampire Diaries Part 1*
Best Supporting Actress ..... Fay Masterson (*Trail of the Screaming Forehead*)
Best Supporting Actor ..... Gabriel Diani (*The Little Documentary That Couldn't*)
Best Actress ..... Jamie Newell (*Treadmill*)
Best Actor ..... Adrian Di Giovanni (*Treadmill*)
Best Foreign Feature ..... *East of Euclid*

Best Writer ..... Shawn Brazeau, Matt Lambro, Ken Saba (*The Little Documentary That Couldn't*)
Best Director ..... Phil Messerer (*Thicker Than Water: The Vampire Diaries Part 1*)
Best Movie ..... *Werewolf in a Women's Prison*

2006

Best Animated Short ..... *Flyaway*
Best Short ..... *Bon Appetit*
Best Documentary ..... *Pawns of Paradise*
Best Set Design ..... *Borrowing Time*
Best Music ..... *Big Fish in Middlesex*
Best Cinematography ..... *The Last Eve*
Best Digital/Special Effects ..... *Borrowing Time*
Best Make-Up ..... *Big Foot*
Best Editing ..... *Borrowing Time*
Best Supporting Actress ..... Axelle Red (*Ellektra*)
Best Supporting Actor ..... Michael Wingfield (*Big Fish in Middlesex*)
Best Actress ..... Jackie Parker (*Both*)
Best Actor ..... Ray Wise (*Cyxork 7*)
Best Writer ..... Jonathan Straiton (*Big Fish in Middlesex*)
Best Director ..... Webster Crowell (*Borrowing Time*)
Best Foreign B-Movie ..... *Ellektra* (Belgium)
Best B-Movie ..... *Big Fish in Middlesex*

Big Bear Horror Film Festival

Their O'Quinn Award is "presented for excellence and cutting edge creativity." It was named to honor Kerry O'Quinn, co-publisher of *Starlog, Fangoria, Cinemagic, Future Life*, and *Comics Scene*. O'Quinn is also the award's first recipient.

2010

Outstanding Feature Film ..... *Pelt*
Outstanding Director ..... Kevin McGuiness (*Red*)
Outstanding Short Film ..... *Devil's Creek*
Outstanding Animation ..... *Red*
Fan Favorite ..... *Pelt*
Outstanding Performance ..... the cast of *Clemency*
Outstanding Sound ..... *The Unfun House*
Outstanding Special Effects Make-up ..... *Clemency*
Outstanding Special Visual Effects ..... *Red*
O'Quinn Award ..... Victor Miller

2009

Outstanding Feature Film ..... *Within*
Outstanding Director ..... Stian A. Schie (*Palazzo Massacre*)
Outstanding Short Film ..... *Psycho Hillbilly Cabin Massacre*
Outstanding Animation ..... *Sebastian's Voodoo*

Outstanding Special Effects Make Up ..... *The Open Door*
Outstanding Special Visual Effects ..... *Gay Zombie*
Outstanding Sound (effects and creep factor) ..... *Psycho Hillbilly Cabin Massacre*
Fan Favorite ..... *Phantasm* (1979)
O'Quinn Award ..... Kerry O'Quinn

Blood Bath Film Festival

Produced by DOA Blood Bath Entertainment. In 2009 it was known as the Texas Blood Bath Film Festival. In 2010 it was Blood Bath 2: The Film Festival.

2010

Best Feature ..... *The Super* (dir: Brian Weaver, Evan Makrogiannis)
Best Performance in a Feature ..... Jeff Dylan Graham (*Fell*)
Best Short Film ..... *Ready Teddy* (dir: Jerod Costas)
Best Performance in a Short Film ..... Shannon Lark (*Lip Stick*)
Lou Perryman Audience Award ..... *Kodie* (dir: Abel Berry)

2009

Best Feature ..... *Sweatshop* (dir: Stacy Davidson)
Best Short ..... *Rekindled* (dir: Jack Daniel Stanley)
Critics Choice ..... *Sweatshop* (dir: Stacy Davidson)
Directors Choice ..... *Vindication* (dir: Bart Mastronardi)
Lou Perryman Audience Award ..... *Sweatshop* (dir: Stacy Davidson)

Boston Fantastic Film Festival

First screened in 2003. The last screening appears to have been in 2007.

2006 (Audience Award) ..... *Severance*
2005 (Audience Award) ..... *Three: Extremes*
2004 Audience Award) ..... *Infernal Affairs*
2004 (First Runner-Up) ..... *Ong-bak*
2004 (Second Runner-Up) ..... *Freeze Frame*
2003 (Audience Award) ..... *Robot Stories*

Boston Science Fiction Film Festival

Founded in 1975, yet 2010 was the year of their "SF33 Award Winners." The festival's Garen Daly tells me: "We began giving awards away in 2010. The award is The Gort, an especially designed sculptured representation of Gort from the original *Day the Earth Stood Still*. There were other awards in recent years, but last year [2010] was the first where we had an actual statue to give people." Daly, of Zeotrope Media, Inc., also runs the Boston Terror'thon.

33rd—2010

Best Independent Feature Film ..... *Puzzlehead* (dir: James Bai)
Audience Award, Best Short ..... *The Grandfather Paradox* (dir: Jean-François De Sylva)
First Runner-Up, Best Short ..... *The Professor's Daughter* (dir: Luke Pebler)
Second Runner-Up, Best Short ..... *Microgravity* (dir: David Sanders)
Honorable Mention, Best Short ..... *Rangressions* (dir: Valerie Weiss)
Judge's Award, Best Short ..... *The Professor's Daughter* (dir: Luke Pebler)
Judge's Award, Best Special Effects ..... *Mizar* (dir: Hseuh Yuting)
Judge's Award, Best Artistic Vision (tie) ..... *The Grandfather Paradox* (dir: Jean-François De Sylva) and *The Professor's Daughter* (dir: Luke Pebler)
Judge's Award, Best Music ..... *Spaceboy* (dir: Ransom Riggs)
Judge's Award, Best Editing ..... *The Professor's Daughter* (dir: Luke Pebler)
Judge's Award, Best Cinematography ..... *The Professor's Daughter* (dir: Luke Pebler)
Judge's Award, Best Acting ..... *The Professor's Daughter* (dir: Luke Pebler)
Judge's Award, Most Creative ..... *The Professor's Daughter* (dir: Luke Pebler)

Boston Terror'thon

From the same people who run the Boston Science Film Festival.

2010

Best Film ..... *Tucker & Dale vs. Evil*
Best Director ..... Kerry Prior (*The Revenant*)

Bram Stoker Award

The Horror Writers Association primarily serves novelists, short story writers, and poets. For a few years, their Bram Stoker Award also had a category for screenwriters (winners below), which ended after 1998, but was resurrected in 2011.

2004 (tie) ..... *Eternal Sunshine of the Spotless Mind* (Charlie Kaufman, Michel Gondry, Pierre Bismuth) and *Shaun of the Dead* (Simon Pegg, Edgar Wright)

2003 ..... *Bubba Ho-Tep* (Don Coscarelli)
2002 ..... *Frailty* (Brent Hanley)
2001 ..... *Memento* (Christopher & Jonathan Nolan)
2000 ..... *Shadow of the Vampire* (Steven Katz)
1999 ..... *The Sixth Sense* (M. Night Shyamalan)
1998 (tie) ..... *Gods and Monsters* (Bill Condon) and *Dark City* (Alex Proyas, David Goyer, Lem Dobbs)

Bram Stoker International Film Festival

2010

Best Picture ..... *Red Victoria* (dir: Anthony Brownrigg)
Best Director ..... Caroline du Potet, Éric du Potet (*Dans ton sommeil*, A.K.A. *In Their Sleep*)
Best International Picture ..... *The Commune* (dir: Elisabeth Fies)
Best Short Film ..... *The Familiar* (dir: Kody Zimmermann)
Audience Award ..... *Red Victoria* (dir: Anthony Brownrigg)
Best Screenplay ..... *Trippin'* (writer/dir: Devi Snively)
Award for the Most Iconic & Influential British Horror Movie ..... *The Wicker Man*
Award for Services to the Horror Genre ..... Hammer Films
Best Special Effects ..... *Axed* (dir: Joshua Long)

British Fantasy Award

The BFA honors works released the previous year (i.e., the 2009 awards are presented in 2010, etc.). The BFA is primarily a literary award, first presented in 1971. Its recognition of dramatic works has been spotty (1973–90, 2009–present). Below is a complete list of their film and TV award winners. They also present Special Awards, on occasion. I've included them only when the winners were clearly film or TV people. The below list does not include the BFA's many non-dramatic categories.

2010 (Best Film) ..... *Let The Right One In* (dir: Tomas Alfredson)
2010 (Television) ..... *Doctor Who* (head writer, Russell T. Davies)
2009 (Best Film) ..... *The Dark Knight* (dir: Christopher Nolan)
2009 (Best Television) ..... *Doctor Who* (head writer, Russell T. Davies)
2008 (Special Award) ..... Ray Harryhausen
2004 (Special Award) ..... Peter Jackson (for *The Lord of the Rings*)

1990, *Indiana Jones and the Last Crusade*
1989, *Beetlejuice*
1988, *Hellraiser*
1987, *Aliens*
1986, *Nightmare on Elm Street*
1985, *Ghostbusters*
1984, *Videodrome*
1983, *Blade Runner*
1982, *Raiders of the Lost Ark*
1981, *The Empire Strikes Back*
1980, *Alien*
1979, *Close Encounters of the Third Kind*
1978, *Carrie*
1977, *The Omen*
1976, *Monty Python and the Holy Grail*
1975, *The Exorcist*
1974, *Legend of Hell House*
1973, *Tales from the Crypt*

British Horror Film Festival

2010

Best Feature ..... *Devil's Playground*
Best Short Film ..... *Mutantland*
Best Student Film ..... *Roadkill*
Best Director ..... Mark McQueen (*Devil's Playground*)
Best Producer ..... Jonathan Sothcott, Freddie Hutton Mills, Bart Ruspoli (*Devil's Playground*)
Best Actor ..... Danny Dyer (*Devil's Playground*)
Best Actress ..... Marysia Kay (*Short Lease*)
Best Supporting Actor ..... John Noble (*Voodoo Lagoon*)
Best Supporting Actress ..... Jessica Marais (*Needle*)
Best Cinematography ..... Stephen Windon (*Needle*)
Best Special Effects ..... *Needle*
British Horror Award ..... *Short Lease*
Audience Award ..... *Nursery Crimes*
Best Screenplay (unproduced) ..... *Unseen* (Kristi Barnett)

Brussels International Festival of Fantastic Film

2010

Golden Raven ..... *Orphan* (dir: Jaume Collet-Serra)
Silver Raven ..... *Thirst* (dir: Chan-wook Park)
Silver Raven ..... *Symbol* (dir: Hitoshi Matsumoto)
Méliès d'Argent ..... *The Door* (dir: Anno Saul)
7th Orbit Award ..... *Symbol* (dir: Hitoshi Matsumoto)
Thriller Award ..... *Cell 211* (dir: Daniel Monzon)
Audience Award ..... *Vampires* (dir: Vincent Lannoo)

2009

Golden Raven ..... *Let the Right One In* (dir: Tomas Alfredson)

Silver Raven ..... *Sauna* (dir: AJ Annila)
Silver Raven ..... *The Last House on the Left* (dir: Dennis Iliadis)
Méliès d'Argent ..... *Sauna* (dir: AJ Annila)
7th Orbit Award ..... *Dream* (dir: Ki-duk Kim)
Thriller Award ..... *The Chaser* (dir: Hong-jin Na)
Audience Award ..... *Sexykiller* (dir: Miguel Marti)

2008

Golden Raven ..... *13 Beloved* (dir: Chukiat Sakveerakul)
Silver Raven ..... *Stuck* (dir: Stuart Gordon)
Silver Raven ..... *[Rec]* (dir: Jaume Balaguero)
Méliès d'Argent ..... *Frontière(s)* (dir: Xavier Gens)
7th Orbit Award ..... *The Aerial* (dir: Esteban Sapir)
Audience Award ..... *[Rec]* (dir: Jaume Balaguero)

2007

Golden Raven ..... *The Host* (dir: Joon-ho Bong)
Silver Raven ..... *The Restless* (dir: Dong-oh Cho)
Silver Raven ..... *Black Sheep* (dir: Jonathan King)
Méliès d'Argent ..... *Dead in 3 Days* (dir: Andreas Prochaska)
7th Orbit Award ..... *Brand Upon the Brain!* (dir: Guy Maddin)
Audience Award ..... *Death Note* (dir: Shusuke Kaneko)

2006

Golden Raven ..... *Adam's Apples* (dir: Anders Thomas Jensen)
Silver Raven ..... *Storm* (dir: Marlind & Stein)
Méliès d'Argent ..... *Adam's Apples* (dir: Anders Thomas Jensen)
7th Orbit Award ..... *Sigaw* (dir: Yam Laranas)
Audience Award ..... *Adam's Apples* (dir: Anders Thomas Jensen)

2005

Golden Raven ..... *Marebito* (dir: Takashi Shimizu)
Silver Raven ..... *Night Watch* (dir: Timur Bekmambetov)
Silver Raven ..... *Vital* (dir: Shinya Tsukamoto)
Méliès d'Argent ..... *Hipnos* (dir: David Carreras)
7th Orbit Award ..... *The Taste of Tea* (dir: Katsuhito Ishii)
Audience Award ..... *Saw* (dir: James Wan)

2004

Golden Raven ..... *Save the Green Planet!* (dir: Joon-hwan Jang)
Silver Raven ..... *A Tale of Two Sisters* (dir: Jee-woon Kim)
Silver Raven ..... *Gozu* (dir: Takashi Miike)
Méliès d'Argent ..... *The Green Butchers* (dir: Anders Thomas Jensen)
Audience Award ..... *The Butterfly Effect* (dir: Eric Bress & J. Mackye Gruber)

2003

Golden Raven ..... *Cypher* (dir: Vincenzo Natali)
Silver Raven ..... *May* (dir: Lucky McKee)
Silver Raven ..... *Aragami* (dir: Ryuhei Kitamura)
Méliès d'Argent ..... *Dead End* (dir: Jean-Baptiste Andrea, Fabrice Canepa)
Audience Award ..... *Dead End* (dir: Jean-Baptiste Andrea, Fabrice Canepa)

2002

Golden Raven ..... *Dog Soldiers* (dir: Neil Marshall)
Silver Raven ..... *Fausto 5.0* (dir: Alex Ollé)
Silver Raven ..... *Dark Water* (dir: Hideo Nakata)
Méliès d'Argent ..... *Thomas est Amoureux* (dir: Pierre-Paul Renders)
Audience Award ..... *Dog Soldiers* (dir: Neil Marshall)

2001

Golden Raven ..... *The Isle* (dir: Ki-duk Kim)
Silver Raven ..... *The Gift* (dir: Sam Raimi)
Silver Raven ..... *Vampire Hunter D* (dir: Yoshiaki Kawajiri)
Méliès d'Argent ..... *The Art of Dying* (dir: Alvaro Fernandez Armero)
Audience Award ..... *Terror Tract* (dir: Lance W. Dreesen)

2000

Golden Raven ..... *The Nameless* (dir: Jaume Balaguero)
Silver Raven ..... *Galaxy Quest* (dir: Dean Parisot)
Silver Raven ..... *Eye of the Beholder* (dir: Stephan Elliott)
Méliès d'Argent ..... *Possessed* (dir: Anders Ronnow Klarlund)
Audience Award ..... *Galaxy Quest* (dir: Dean Parisot)

1999

Golden Raven ..... *Ringu* (dir: Hideo Nakata)
Silver Raven ..... *Cube* (dir: Vincenzo Natali)
Silver Raven ..... *In Dreams* (dir: Neil Jordan)
Méliès d'Argent ..... *The Wisdom of Crocodiles* (dir: Po-chih Leong)
Audience Award ..... *Dark City* (dir: Alex Proyas)

1998

Golden Raven ..... *Lawn Dogs* (dir: John Duigan)
Silver Raven ..... *Arcane Sorcerer* (dir: Pupi Avati)
Silver Raven ..... *8 Heads in a Duffel Bag* (dir: Tom Schulman)
Méliès d'Argent ..... *Lawn Dogs* (dir: John Duigan)
Audience Award ..... *Event Horizon* (dir: Paul Anderson)

1997

Golden Raven ..... *Luna e l'Altra* (dir: Maurizio Nichetti)

Silver Raven ..... *Karmina* (dir: Gabriel Pelletier)
Silver Raven ..... *Retroactive* (dir: Louis Morneau)
Méliès d'Argent ..... *Tesis* (dir: Alejandro Amenabar)
Audience Award ..... *Karmina* (dir: Gabriel Pelletier)

1996

Golden Raven ..... *El Dia de la Bestia* (dir: Álex de la Iglesia)
Silver Raven ..... *Haunted* (dir: Lewis Gilbert)
Silver Raven ..... *Angela* (dir: Rebecca Miller)
Méliès d'Argent ..... *El Dia de la Bestia* (dir: Álex de la Iglesia)
Audience Award ..... *Over My Dead Body* (dir: Rainer Matsutani)

1995

Golden Raven ..... *Accumulator 1* (dir: Jan Sverak)
Silver Raven ..... *Second Sight* (dir: Ola Solum)
Silver Raven ..... *Half Spirit: Voice of the Spider* (dir: Henri Barges)
Audience Award ..... *Nightwatch* (dir: Ole Bornedal)

1994

Golden Raven ..... *Frauds* (dir: Stephan Elliott)
Silver Raven ..... *Cronos* (dir: Guillermo del Toro)
Silver Raven ..... *Younger & Younger* (dir: Percy Adlon)
Audience Award ..... *12:01* (dir: Jack Sholder)

1993

Golden Raven ..... *Army of Darkness* (dir: Sam Raimi)
Silver Raven ..... *Matinee* (dir: Joe Dante)
Silver Raven ..... *Simeon* (dir: Euzhan Palcy)
Audience Award ..... *Army of Darkness* (dir: Sam Raimi)

1992

Golden Raven ..... *Timescape* (dir: David N. Twohy)
Silver Raven ..... *Highway 61* (dir: Bruce McDonald)
Silver Raven ..... *Tetsuo: The Iron Man* (dir: Shinya Tsukamoto)
Audience Award ..... *The People Under the Stairs* (dir: Wes Craven)

1991

Golden Raven ..... *A Paucity of Flying Dreams* (dir: Eizo Sugawa)
Silver Raven ..... *Henry: Portrait of a Serial Killer* (dir: John McNaughton)
Silver Raven ..... *Warlock* (dir: Steve Miner)
Audience Award ..... *Hardware* (dir: Richard Stanley)

1990

Golden Raven ..... *La Banyera* (dir: Jesus Garay)
Silver Raven ..... *Society* (dir: Brian Yuzna)
Silver Raven ..... *The Discarnates* (dir: Nobuhiko Obayashi)

1989

Golden Raven ..... *Paperhouse* (dir: Bernard Rose)
Silver Raven ..... *Waxwork* (dir: Anthony Kickox)
Silver Raven ..... *Shadow of Death* (dir: Robert Kirk)

1988

Golden Raven ..... *Anguish* (dir: Bigas Luna)
Silver Raven ..... *The Monster Squad* (dir: Fred Dekker)
Silver Raven ..... *Near Dark* (dir: Kathryn Bigelow)

1987

Golden Raven ..... *Radioactive Dreams* (dir: Albert Pyun)
Silver Raven ..... *Street Trash* (dir: Jim Muro)
Silver Raven ..... *De Wisselwachter* (dir: Jos Stelling)

1986

Golden Raven ..... *Piccoli Fuochi* (dir: Peter del Monte)
Silver Raven ..... *Maxie* (dir: Paul Aaron)

1985

Golden Raven ..... *Dreamscape* (dir: Joseph Ruben)
Silver Raven ..... *Looker* (dir: Michael Crichton)

1984

Golden Raven ..... *Nightmares* (dir: Joseph Sargent)
Silver Raven ..... *Children of the Corn* (dir: Fritz Kiersch)
Silver Raven ..... *Videodrome* (dir: David Cronenberg)
Silver Raven ..... *Bloodbath at the House of Death* (dir: Ray Cameron)

1983

Golden Raven ..... *Savage Hunt of King Stakh* (dir: Valeri Rubinchik)
Silver Raven ..... *Le Dernier Combat* (dir: Luc Besson)
Audience Award ..... *Galaxina* (dir: William Sachs)

Buenos Aires Rojo Sangre

2010

Best Film ..... *The Life and Death of a Porno Gang*
Best Director ..... Faye Jackson (*Strigoi*)
Best Actor (tie) ..... Andrew Howard (*Pig*) and Nicanor Loreti (*Nunca mas asistas a este tipo de fiestas*)
Best Actress ..... Roxana Guttman (*Strigoi*)
Best Writing ..... Mladen Djordjevic (*The Life and Death of a Porno Gang*)
Best FX ..... Tomoo Haraguchi (*Death Kappa*)
People's Choice Award ..... *Nunca mas asistas a este tipo de fiestas*

Best Iberoamerican Film (by popular vote) ..... *Trash*
Special Mention ..... *MyM Matilde y Malena*
Special Mention ..... *Nunca mas asistas a este tipo de fiestas*
Special Mention ..... *Molina's Ferozz*
Best Short Film ..... *Cabine of the Dead*
Best Director, Short Film ..... Sebastian Marka (*Interview*)
Best Argentine Short Film ..... *La vuelta del malón*
People's Choice Award, Short Film ..... *Umiko*
Special Mention, Short Film ..... *Copia A*
Special Mention, Short Film ..... *Working Day*
Special Mention, Short Film ..... *Zombie Burger Attack*

2009

Best Film ..... *Masacre esta noche*
Best Direction ..... Marc Price (*Colin*)
Best Writing ..... Demian Rugna (*They Want My Eyes*)
Best Actor ..... Diego Cremonese (*Masacre esta noche*)
Best Actress ..... Mariana Zanette (*Morgue Story*)
Best FX ..... *Yesterday*
People's Choice Award ..... *Recortadas*
People's Choice, Best Iberoamerican Film ..... *Operación Cannabis*
Special Mention, Breakthrough Actresses ..... Noelia Antunez and Mariana Levy (*Recortadas*)
Special Mention, Breakthrough Actor ..... Jorge Pinarelo (*Masacre esta noche*)
Special Mention, Scream Queen ..... Natacha Mendez (*Masacre esta noche*)
Best Short Film ..... *Die Schneider Krankheit*
Best Argentine Short Film ..... *La extravagante y poco práctica venganza de la momia*
Best Direction, Short Film ..... María Laura Casabé (*Sabrosura, Violín y Perico*)
People's Choice, Best Short Film ..... *La villa seca*
Special Mention for Post-production, Short Film ..... *Ataque de Pánico*
Special Mention for Writing, Short Film ..... *La menace vient de l'espace*
Special Mention for Adaptation, Short Film ..... *The Raven*
Best Zombie Short Film ..... *Evacuación*

2008

Best Film ..... *Tokyo Gore Police*, A.K.A. *Tôkyô zankoku keisatsu* (Yoshihiro Nishimura)
People's Choice Award ..... *Mud Zombies*, A.K.A. *Mangue Negro* (Rodrigo Aragao)
Best Iberoamerican Film ..... *Nadie Inquietó Mas* (Gustavo Leonel Mendoza)
Best Director ..... Bill Plympton (*Idiots & Angels*)
Best Writing ..... *The Man from Earth*
Best FX ..... Yoshihiro Nishimura (*Tokyo Gore Police*, A.K.A. *Tôkyô zankoku keisatsu*)
Best Actor ..... Chris Sharp (*Murder Party*)
Best Actress ..... Josefina Sanz (*Nocturnos*)
Special Mention for General Production ..... Paco Limón (*Doctor Infierno*)
Special Mention for Production Design ..... *Tokyo Gore Police*, A.K.A. *Tôkyô zankoku keisatsu*
Best Short Film ..... *ELA in Love at First Byte* (Fernando Sarmiento)
People's Choice Award, Short Film ..... *Maldito Sean 1º episodio* (Demián Rugna)
Best Argentine Short Film ..... *Aquellos ojos brujos* (Cesar Leonardo Delgado Brog)
Best Direction, Short Film ..... Alfons Casal, Hector Mas (*El Comte Yácula*)
Best Comedy, Short Film ..... *División Bahia* (Laura Casabé)
Best Animation, Short Film ..... *Piscis* (Juan Camardella)
Best Production Design, Short Film ..... *The Container* (Diego Melo)

2007

Best Film ..... *On Evil Grounds*, A.K.A. *Auf bösem Boden*
Best Director ..... Peter Koller (*On Evil Grounds*, A.K.A. *Auf bösem Boden*)
Best Writing ..... Demián Rugna (*The Last Gateway*)
Best Actress ..... Victoria Maurette (*Left for Dead*)
Best Argentine Film ..... *Masacre Marcial IVX* (Matías Lojo, Pablo Marini)
Best Short Film ..... *Droomtijd*, A.K.A. *Dreamtime* (Tom Van Avermaet)
Best Director, Short Film ..... Gabe Ibañez (*Máquina*)
Best Argentine Short Film ..... *Naturaleza muerta* (Romina Caramagna)
People's Choice Award, Best Film ..... *Filmatrón* (Pablo Parés)
People's Choice Award, Best Short Film ..... *Sucesión* (Pablo Baltera)

2006

Best Film ..... *Mondo Psycho* (Mad Crampi)
Best Director ..... Marcus Widegren (*Kraftverk 3714*)
Best Writing ..... Ramiro and Adrián García Bogliano (*36 pasos*)
Best Actor ..... Emil Jonsson (*Kraftverk 3714*)
Best Actress ..... Mapi Romero (*Belcebú*)
People's Choice Award ..... *Song of the Dead* (Chip Gubera)
Best FX ..... Martin Frías, Iru Landucci (*36 pasos*)
Best Short Film ..... *El cojonudo* (Federico Álvarez)
Best Short Film Director ..... Sacha Whitehouse (*The City Eats Its Weak*)
Best Fantasy Argentine Short Film ..... *Asterión* (Juan Carlos Camardella)
People's Choice Award, Short Film ..... *El cojonudo* (Federico Álvarez)
Honorable Mention, Short Film ..... *Griscelda* (Gabriel Grieco)

2005

Best Film ..... *Beneath the Cogon*, A.K.A. *Sa Ilalim ng cogon* (Rico Maria Ilarde)
Best Director ..... Jennifer Kroot (*Sirens of the 23rd Century*)
Best Writing ..... Bill Marks, Sean K. Robb (*Zombie King and the Legion of Doom*)
Best Actor ..... David Muyllaert (*Dead Meat*)
Best Actress ..... Paula Guía (*De noche van a tu cuarto*)
Best Argentine Film ..... *Grité una noche*, A.K.A. *Scream the Night* (Adrián García Bogliano)
People's Choice Award ..... *De noche van a tu cuarto* (Sebastián de Caro)
Best Short Film ..... *Retruc* (Francesc Talavera)
Best Short Film Director ..... John Dunstan, Michael Pazt (*Battle Chess*)
Best Fantasy Argentine Short Film ..... *Después de Recién* (Ignacio Laxalde, Bernardo Francese)
People's Choice Award, Short Film ..... *Alex, Vampire Slayer* (Al Katrina)

2004

Best Film ..... *The Last Horror Movie* (Julian Richards)
Best Director ..... Greg Pak (*Robot Stories*)
Best Writing ..... Greg Pak (*Robot Stories*)
Best Actor ..... Kevin Howarth (*The Last Horror Movie*)
Best Actress ..... Elena Siritto (*Habitaciones para turistas*)
People's Choice Award ..... *Habitaciones para turistas* (Adrian García Bogliano)
Best Short Film ..... *Redrat, la rata retobada* (Guillermo Kloetzer)
Best Short Film Director ..... Daniel Greaves (*Little Things*)
People's Choice Award, Short Film ..... *Gorgonas* (Salvador Sanz)

Buffalo Screams Horror Film Festival

The city of Buffalo is in western New York state, so I assume "WNY" (e.g., Best WNY Horror Feature) stands for Western New York.

Best Horror Feature ..... *El monstro del mar!*
Best WNY Horror Feature ..... *House of Horrors: The Movie*
Best Horror Short ..... *The Familiar*
Best WNY Horror Short ..... *Davis*
Best More Than Horror Short ..... *Damn Your Eyes* (western)
Best More Than Horror Feature ..... *Triptosane* (science fiction)
Best Director ..... Stuart Simpson (*El monstro del mar!*)
Best Screenplay ..... Kody Zimmermann (*The Familiar*)
Best Actor ..... Daniel Reininghaus (*Eyes Beyond*)
Best Actress ..... Marianne Porter (*True Nature*)
Best Editing ..... Aaron Doolittle, Dominic Luongo, Chris Santucci (*Davis*)
Best Cinematography ..... Marco Fagnoli, Evan A. Nesbitt (*True Nature*)
Best Special Make-Up Effects ..... Emma Julia Jacobs (*M*)
Best Special Visual Effects ..... Carl Caprino (*The Black Cat*)
Original Screenplay Competition (unproduced) ..... Weston Ochse (*Desert Dogs*)
Dedication to Excellence in Independent Filmmaking Award ..... Debbie Rochon
Genre Spirit Award ..... Brett Kelly
Local Hero Award ..... Michael O'Hear
Best WNY Special Make-Up Artist ..... Andrew Lavin
Filmmakers to Watch ..... Sam Qualiana and Kash Costner
Local Grindhouse Award ..... John Renna and Jay Mager

Buried Alive Film Fest

Formerly the Atlanta Horror Fest (see its awards list, above), which is not to be confused with the Atlanta Horror Film Festival.

2010

Best Feature ..... *Herschell Gordon Lewis: The Godfather of Gore* (dir: Frank Henenlotter)
Honorable Mention, Feature ..... *Robogeisha* (dir: Noboru Iguchi)
Best Short Comedy ..... *Tub* (dir: Bobby Miller)
Honorable Mention, Short Comedy ..... *The United Monster Talent Agency* (dir: Greg Nicotero)
Best Short Drama ..... *Off Season* (dir: Jonathan van Tulleken)
Honorable Mention, Short Drama ..... *Sadness* (dir: Andre Paim)
Visionary Award ..... Ashley Thorpe
"What the Fuck?" Award ..... *The Demonology of Desire* (dir: Rodrigo Gudino)

2009

Best Feature ..... *The Hagstone Demon* (dir: Jon Springer)
Best Short ..... *The Tell-Tale Heart* (dir: Robert Eggers)
Honorable Mention ..... *Beast of Burden* (dir: Sam Carter)

BUT: B-Movies, Underground & Trash Film Festival

BUT's Dorien Eggink informs me that while their first screening was in 2006, their first awards presentation was in 2009, and that this is their complete winners list.

2010

BUT Feature Award ..... *Earthling* (dir: Clay Liford)
BUT Short Film Award ..... *The Terrible Thing of Alpha-9* (dir: Jake Armstrong)
BUT Student Film Award ..... *Super Seiserzauger*

2009

BUT Feature ..... *Hora* (dir: Reinert Kiil)
BUT Short Film Award ..... *I Live in the Woods* (dir: Max Winston)
BUT Student Film Award ..... *The Return of the Milkman* (dir: Jonas Ott)

Carnival of Darkness

Short films only. First screened in 2009. First award presented in 2010.

2010

(Best Short Film) ..... *Polydeus* (dir: Drew Daywalt)

Celluloid Screams

Both of their award categories are audience awards (i.e., voted on by the audience).

2010

Best New Feature Film ..... *The Revenant* (dir: Kerry Prior)
Best Short Film (tie) ..... *AM1200* (dir: David Prior) and *Bobby Yeah* (dir: Robert Morgan)

2009

Best New Feature Film ..... *Lake Mungo* (dir: Joel Anderson)
Best Short Film ..... *Mama* (dir: Andres Muschietti)

Chicago Horror Film Festival

2010

Best Feature Film ..... *The Man Who Collected Food*
Best Short Film ..... *Clemency*
Best Experimental Short Horror Film ..... *Demi-Urge Emesis*
Best Director ..... Mark Vadik (*Cyrus: Mind of a Serial Killer*)
Best Actor ..... Mike N. Kelly (*The Man Who Collected Food*)
Best Actress ..... Adrienne Barbeau (*Alice Jacobs Is Dead*)
Best Screenwriting ..... *Devil's Creek*
Best Special Effects ..... *Contagion* (dir: John Lechago)

Cinefantasy

This Brazilian festival presents the Dry Corpse Award. Founded in 2006. First presented awards in 2009, for short films only. They expanded to include features in 2010.

5th — 2010

Best Horror Feature ..... *Christopher Roth* (Max Sender)
Best Sci-fi Feature ..... *1* (Pater Sparrow)
Best Fantasy Feature ..... *Strigoi* (Faye Jackson)
Audience Winner, Feature, 1st Place ..... *Strigoi* (Faye Jackson)
Audience Winner, Feature, 2nd Place ..... *Dead Hooker in a Trunk* (Jen and Sylvia Soska)
Audience Winner, Feature, 3rd Place ..... *Death Waltz* (Krisztián Károly Köves)
Best Direction, Feature ..... *Dark Souls* (César Ducasse, Mathieu Peteul)
Best Screenplay, Feature ..... *Recortadas* (Sebastián Rotztein, Sebastián De Caro)
Best Creature, Feature ..... *Evil Angel*
Best Victim, Feature ..... *Popatopolis* (Julie K. Smith)
Best Villain, Feature ..... *Christopher Roth*
Best Make-Up, Feature ..... *Christopher Roth* (Giannetto De Rossi)
Best Special Effects, Feature ..... *Christopher Roth* (Giovanni Corridori and Stefano Corridori)
Best Soundtrack, Feature ..... *Christopher Roth* (Claude Samard Polikar)
Best Horror Short Film ..... *Quiropterofobia* (Fernando Mantelli)
Best Sci-Fi Short Film ..... *La Revelacion* (Vincent Diderot)
Best Fantasy Short Film ..... *Coda* (Marcos Camargo)
Best Short Animation ..... *Os Anjos do Meio da Praça* (Alêxandre Camargo, Camila Carrossine)
Short Film Audience Winner, 1st Place ..... *Deus Irae* (Pedro Cristiani)
Short Film Audience Winner, 2nd Place ..... *Deriva* (Ángel Tirado)
Short Film Audience Winner, 3rd Place ..... *Quiropterofobia* (Fernando Mantelli)
Best Short Film Director ..... *A História de Lia* (Rubens Mello)

Best Short Film Screenplay ..... *A Língua das Coisas* (Alan Minas)
Student Incentive Award ..... *Sorria* (Marcos Gonzalez)
Beginner Incentive Award ..... *Aqueles Olhos* (Fabiana Sevilha)
Best Short Film Creature ..... *Deus Irae*
Best Short Film Victim ..... *Um Animal Menor*
Best Short Film Villain ..... *Shrove Tuesday*
Best Short Film Make-Up ..... *Deus Irae*
Best Short Film Special Effects ..... *Shrove Tuesday*
Best Short Film Soundtrack ..... *Tudo Por Um Fio* (Ricardo Gilly)

4th — 2009

Best Horror Short Film ..... *El Hombre de la Bolsa* (Pedro Cristiani)
Best Sci-Fi Short Film ..... *Forecast* (Erik Courtney)
Best Fantasy Short Film ..... *DVD* (Ciro Altabás)
Audience Award ..... *Gato* (Joel Caetano)
Student Incentive Award ..... *Romance .38* (Vinícius Casimiro, Vitor Brandt)
Amateur Incentive Award ..... *A Última Noite* (Guilherme Rezende)
Best Director ..... *Porque Hay Cosas Que Nunca Se Olvidan* (Lucas Figueroa)
Best Creature ..... *El Hombre da la Bolsa* (Pedro Cristiani)
Best Make-up ..... *Fun on Earth* (Jesse Gordon)
Best VFX ..... *Silêncio e Sombras* (Murilo Hauser)
Best Soundtrack ..... *Next Floor* (Denis Villeneuve)
Best Screenplay ..... *Manual Práctico Del Amigo Imaginário* (Ciro Altabás)
Horror Honor Mention ..... *A Break the Monotony* (Damien Slevin)
Screenplay Honor Mention ..... *Romance .38* (Vinícius Casimiro, Vitor Brandt)
Master of the Scream Contest ..... *Mamá* (Andres Muschietti)

Comic-Con International Independent Film Festival

Comic-Con has many events, and presents many awards. This is only a listing of their film festival awards, for their two most recent years. I was unable to obtain more from Comic-Con.

2010

Best Action/Adventure Film ..... *The Action Hero's Guide to Saving Lives*
Best Science Fiction/Fantasy Film ..... *Stingray Sam*
Best Documentary Film ..... *Marwencol*
Best Comics-Related Film ..... *The Legacy*
Best Horror/Suspense Film ..... *The Window*
Best Humor Film ..... *Herpes Boy*
Best Animation Film ..... *The Mouse That Soared*

2009

Best Action/Adventure ..... *Al's Beef*
Animation ..... *The Hidden Life of the Burrowing Owl*
Comics-Oriented ..... *The Book of Tomorrow*
Documentary ..... *Dig Comics*
Horror/Suspense ..... *Alice Jacobs Is Dead*
Humor ..... *Animated American*
Science Fiction/Fantasy ..... *Hirsute*
Judges' Choice Award ..... *The Hidden Life of the Burrowing Owl*

Constellation Award

Honors works from the previous year (i.e., 2010 winners were released in 2009).

2010

Best Male Performance in a 2009 Science Fiction TV Episode ..... David Tennant (*Dr. Who*, "The Waters of Mars")
Best Female Performance in a 2009 Science Fiction TV Episode ..... Lena Headey (*Sarah Connor Chronicles*, "Some Must....")
Best Science Fiction TV Series of 2009 ..... *Supernatural*
Best Male Performance in a 2009 Science Fiction Film, TV Movie, or Mini-Series ..... Karl Urban (*Star Trek*)
Best Female Performance in a 2009 Science Fiction Film, TV Movie, or Mini-Series ..... Zoe Saldana (*Avatar*)
Best Science Fiction Film, TV Movie, or Mini-Series of 2009 ..... *Star Trek*
Best Technical Accomplishment in a 2009 Science Fiction Film or TV Production ..... Weta Digital, visual effects (*Avatar*)
Best Overall 2009 Science Fiction Film or TV Script ..... *FlashForward*, "No More Good Days"
Outstanding Canadian Contribution to Science Fiction Film or TV in 2009 ..... Bruce Greenwood

2009

Best Male Performance in a 2008 Science Fiction TV Episode ..... Michael Hogan (*Battlestar Galactica*, "Revelations")
Best Female Performance in a 2008 Science Fiction TV Episode ..... Catherine Tate (*Doctor Who*, "Turn Left")
Best Science Fiction TV Series of 2008 ..... *Doctor Who*
Best Male Performance in a 2008 Science Fiction Film, TV Movie, or Mini-Series ..... Robert Downey, Jr. (*Iron Man*)
Best Female Performance in a 2008 Science Fiction Film, TV Movie, or Mini-Series ..... Claudia Black (*Stargate: Continuum*)

Best Science Fiction Film, TV Movie, or Mini-Series of 2008 ..... *WALL-E*
Best Technical Accomplishment in a 2008 Science Fiction Film or TV Production ..... *WALL-E*, animation (Pixar Animation Studios)
Best Overall 2008 Science Fiction Film or TV Script ..... *Doctor Who*, "Silence in the Library" (Steven Moffat)
Outstanding Canadian Contribution to Science Fiction Film or TV in 2008 ..... the *Stargate* franchise

2008

Best Male Performance in a 2007 Science Fiction TV Episode ..... David Tennant (*Doctor Who*, "Human Nature/The Family of Blood")
Best Female Performance in a 2007 Science Fiction TV Episode ..... Carey Mulligan (*Doctor Who*, "Blink")
Best Science Fiction TV Series of 2007 ..... *Doctor Who*
Best Male Performance in a 2007 Science Fiction Film, TV Movie, or Mini-Series ..... Will Smith (*I Am Legend*)
Best Female Performance in a 2007 Science Fiction Film, TV Movie, or Mini-Series ..... Emma Watson (*Harry Potter and the Order of the Phoenix*)
Best Science Fiction Film, TV Movie, or Mini-Series of 2007 ..... *Transformers*
Best Technical Accomplishment in a 2007 Science Fiction Film or TV Production ..... *Transformers*, transformation effects (Industrial Light & Magic)
Best Overall 2007 Science Fiction Film or TV Script ..... *Supernatural*, "What Is and What Should Never Be" (Raelle Tucker)
Outstanding Canadian Contribution to Science Fiction Film or TV in 2007 ..... Tanya Huff, writer/creative consultant (*Blood Ties*)

2007

Best Male Performance in a 2006 Science Fiction TV Episode ..... David Tennant (*Doctor Who*, "The Girl in the Fireplace")
Best Female Performance in a 2006 Science Fiction TV Episode ..... Claudia Black (*Stargate SG-1*, "Memento Mori")
Best Science Fiction TV Series of 2006 ..... *Doctor Who*
Best Male Performance in a 2006 Science Fiction Film, TV Movie, or Mini-Series ..... Hugo Weaving (*V for Vendetta*)
Best Female Performance in a 2006 Science Fiction Film, TV Movie, or Mini-Series ..... Natalie Portman (*V for Vendetta*)
Best Science Fiction Film, TV Movie, or Mini-Series of 2006 ..... *Pan's Labyrinth*
Best Technical Accomplishment in a 2006 Science Fiction Film or TV Production ..... *Battlestar Galactica*, visual effects (Zoic Studios)
Best Overall 2006 Science Fiction Film or TV Script ..... *Stargate SG-1*, "200" (Brad Wright, Robert C. Cooper)
Outstanding Canadian Contribution to Science Fiction Film or TV in 2006 ..... *Doctor Who*

Cryptshow Festival

2010

Best Short Film ..... *Delaney* (Carles Torrens)
Audience Award ..... *Zombie: le documental* (Maurice Vadeboncoeur, Mathieu Handfield)
Special Mention, Short Film ..... *Danse Macabre* (Pedro Pires)
Special Mention, Short Film ..... *The Horribly Slow Murderer with the Extremely Inefficient Weapon* (Richard Gale)
Special Mention, Best Motion Picture ..... *The Terrible Thing of Alpha 9!* (Jake Armstrong)
Best Actor ..... Paul Clemens (*The Horribly Slow Murderer with the Extremely Inefficient Weapon*)
Best Actress ..... Delaney Manning (*Delaney*)
Best Script ..... Víctor Palacios (*Turno de Noche*)
Best Cinematography ..... Pedro Pires (*Danse Macabre*)
Best Special Effects ..... Fede Álvarez (*Ataque de Pánico*)
Best Original Soundtrack ..... J. Oskura Nájera (*Torbellino de hostias* and *Yo fui un Fredy Kruger adolescente*)

2009

Best Short Film ..... *Treevenge* (Jason Eisener)
Audience Award ..... *Spider* (Nash Edgerton)
Special Mention, Short Film ..... *Coming Home* (Éric Falardeau)
Special Mention, Short Film ..... *El Mal de Schneider* (Javier Chillón)
Special Mention, Short Film ..... *La Casa Brown* (Issac Berrokal)
Best Actor ..... Nash Edgerton (*Spider*)
Best Actress ..... Mirrah Foulkes (*Spider*)
Best Script ..... *The Facts in the Case of Mr. Hollow* (Rodrigo Gudiño, Vincent Marcone)
Best Specials Effects ..... *Next Floor* (Denis Villeneuve)
Best Soundtrack ..... *The Facts in the Case of Mr. Hollow* (Johnny Hollow)

Dark Carnival Film Festival

2010

Best Feature Film ..... *El monstro del mar!*
Best Short Film ..... *Enter the Dark*

Best Actor ..... Scott Anthony Leet (*The Prometheus Project*)
Best Actress ..... Tiffany Shepis (*The Prometheus Project*)
Best Supporting Actor ..... Alan Rowe Kelly (*Hychondriac*)
Best Supporting Actress ..... Toya Turner (*Slices of Life*)
Best Director ..... Anthony Sumner (*Slices of Life*)
Best Screenplay ..... *Satan Hates You*
Best Special Effects ..... *The Taint*
Best Cinematography ..... *The Extreme Nature of Bats*
Best Editing ..... *El monstro del mar!*
Best Score ..... *DemiUrge Emesis*
Outstanding Achievement ..... Patrick Rea

2009

Best Feature Film ..... *Vindication* (dir: Bart Mastronardi)
Best Short Film ..... *Seance* (dir: Robin Kasparik)
Best Actor ..... William Tulin (*Shellter*)
Best Actress ..... Raine Brown (*Sculpture*)
Best Supporting Actor ..... Jerry Murdock (*Vindication*)
Best Supporting Actress ..... Tiffany Shepis (*Thirsty*)
Best Special Effects ..... *The Tower* (Dan Falzone)
Best Cinematography ..... *Aqua ad lavandum — in brevi* (Benjamin Bayer)
Best Editing ..... *Cottonmouth* (Christopher P. Garetano)
Best Feature Screenplay (unproduced) ..... *Fear the Reaper* (Dave Campfield)
Best Short Screenplay (unproduced) ..... *Roses* (Terry Dellinger)

2008

Best Feature Film ..... *Dark Reel* (dir: Josh Eisenstadt)
Best Short Film ..... *The Room* (dir: Andres Meza-Valdes, Diego Meza-Valdes)
Best Screenplay ..... *It's My Party and I'll Die If I Want To* (Tony Wash)
Best Special Effects ..... *Eel Girl* (Paul Campion)
Best Cinematography ..... *The Season* (Pedja Radenkovic, Adam Brooks)
Best Editing ..... *Peekers* (Mark Steensland)

2007

Best Feature Film ..... *The Blood Shed* (dir: Alan Rowe Kelly)
Best Short Film ..... *Of Darkness* (dir: Gary Irwin)
Best Documentary ..... *The Scare* (Javier C. Rivera)
Best Special Effects ..... *W.O.R.M.* (Anthony Sumner)
Best Cinematography ..... *Nympha* (Ivan Zuccon)
Best Music Video ..... *Rain un Thunder* (Medusa)

Dead by Dawn

A.K.A. Dead by Dawn: Scotland's International Horror Film Festival. Founded 1993. Festival director Adele Hartley confirmed to me that this is a complete list of their award winners. In 2010 they held a small, impromptu event (they'd almost canceled that year), rather than their regular event, so there was "no Cutting Edge programme" that year. They plan to return to full size in 2011.

17th — 2010

Audience Award, Best Feature ..... *5150, Rue des Ormes*, A.K.A. *5150 Elm's Way*
Audience Award, Best Short (tie) ..... *Tufty* and *Danse Macabre*

16th — 2009

Audience Award, Best Feature ..... *Cold Storage* (dir: Tony Elwood)
Audience Award, Best Short ..... *Next Floor* (dir: Denis Villeneuve)
Cutting Edge Short Film ..... *Kirksdale* (dir: Ryan Spindell)

15th — 2008

Audience Award, Best Feature ..... *Stuck* (dir: Stuart Gordon)
Audience Award, Best Short ..... *Spider* (dir: Nash Edgerton)
Cutting Edge Short Film ..... *Criticized* (dir: Richard Gale)

14th — 2007

Audience Award, Best Feature ..... *End of the Line* (dir: Maurice Devereaux)
Audience Award, Best Short ..... *Monster* (dir: Jennifer Kent)
Cutting Edge Short Film ..... *The Fifth* (dir: Ryan Levin)

13th — 2006

Audience Award, Best Feature (tie) ..... *Broken* (dir: Simon Boyes and Adam Mason), *Blood Trails* (dir: Robert Krause)
Audience Award, Best Short ..... *Oculus* (dir: Mike Flanagan)
Cutting Edge Short Film ..... *Los Ojos de Alicia* (dir: Hugo Sanz)

12th — 2005

Audience Award, Best Feature ..... *The Dark Hours* (dir: Paul Fox)
Audience Award, Best Short ..... *The Ten Steps* (dir: Brendan Muldowney)

Cutting Edge Short Film ..... *The French Doors* (dir: Steve Ayson)

11th — 2004

Audience Award, Best Feature ..... *Shallow Ground* (dir: Sheldon Wilson)
Audience Award, Best Short ..... *Ward 13* (dir: Peter Cornwell)
Cutting Edge Short Film ..... *Buried* (dir: Tim Bullock)

Dead Channels Film Festival

2008

Best Feature Film, Audience Award ..... *Let the Right One In*, A.K.A. *Låt den Rätte Komma In*
Best Short Film, Audience Award ..... *The Horribly Slow Murderer with the Extremely Inefficient Weapon*

2007

Best Feature Film, Audience Award ..... *The Devil Dared Me To*
Best Short Film, Audience Award (tie) ..... *Criticized*
Best Short Film, Audience Award (tie) ..... *The Handyman*

Dragon*Con Independent Film Festival Awards

Festival director Matthew M. Foster says, "Our awards go to the film, and therefore, the rights holders of the film. We choose a 1st place in genre categories (exact genres can change from year to year, based on the films we accept), and then choose the Best Short Film and the Best Animated Film from the winners in the genre categories." The Spirit of Dragon*Con Award is presented to an individual.

2010

Best Animated Film ..... *Yamasong*
1st Place Animated Comedy ..... *The Bolt Who Screwed Christmas*
1st Place Animated Fantasy ..... *Yamasong*
1st Place Animated Science Fiction ..... *Tales from the Afternow: Little Rocks*
1st Place Animated Short-Short ..... *The Sacrifice*
Best Short Film ..... *Sunday Punch*
1st Place Comedy ..... *Whaling and the Inherent Dangers Therein*
1st Place Dark Comedy ..... *Self-Inflicted*
1st Place Documentary ..... *The Pledge*
1st Place Drama ..... *The Tea Master*

1st Place Thriller ..... *Sunday Punch*
1st Place Magic Realism ..... *Lorelei*
1st Place Fantasy ..... *Bottles*
1st Place Horror ..... *Alice Jacobs Is Dead*
1st Place Horror Comedy ..... *The Necronomicon*
1st Place Science Fiction ..... *Mnemosyne Rising*
1st Place Feature ..... *Doctor 'S' Battles the Sex Crazed Reefer Zombies: The Movie*
Best Cult Film ..... *Frank DanCoolo: Paranormal Drug Dealer*
Honorable Mention ..... *Elusive Man*
Best Screenplay ..... *Bottles*
Spirit of Dragon*Con Comcast Award ..... Mike Salva (*Death Row Diet*)

2009

Best Short Film ..... *Hector Corp.*
Best Animated Film ..... *Mythic Journeys: The Bone Orchard*
Honorable Mention ..... *Animated American*
Honorable Mention ..... *The Price to Pay*
Honorable Mention ..... *Rosfeld*
1st Place Action ..... *Interpretation*
1st Place Animated Comedy ..... *Chroma Chameleon*
1st Place Animated Fantasy ..... *Mythic Journeys: The Bone Orchard*
1st Place Animated Science Fiction ..... *Theosaurology*
1st Place Animated Short-Short ..... *X-Mess Detritus*
1st Place Comedy ..... *The Action Hero's Guide to Saving Lives*
1st Place Dark Comedy ..... *Hector Corp.*
1st Place Documentary ..... *Striking Metal*
1st Place Fantasy ..... *Bathtub to Happiness*
1st Place Horror ..... *On Edge*
1st Place Horror Comedy ..... *Death in Charge*
1st Place Magic Realism ..... *That's Magic!*
1st Place Science Fiction ..... *Enigma*
1st Place Thriller ..... *SHADOWNET*
The Spirit of Dragon*Con Award ..... Devi Snively (*Death in Charge*)

2008

Best Short Film ..... *Al's Beef*
Best Animated Film ..... *Paper Shepherd*
Honorable Mention ..... *Centigrade*
Honorable Mention ..... *The Procedure*
1st Place Animated Comedy ..... *Max the Hero*
1st Place Animated Fantasy & Science Fiction ..... *Paper Shepherd*
1st Place Animated Horror ..... *The Book Dealers*
1st Place Comedy ..... *Lowenstein's a Terrorist*
1st Place Dark Comedy ..... *3 Stories About Evil*
1st Place Dark Fantasy ..... *Winter's Tale*
1st Place Drama ..... *Verboten*
1st Place Experimental Animation ..... *Transrexia*
1st Place Fantasy ..... *The Delivery*
1st Place Horror ..... *Reflections*
1st Place Horror Comedy ..... *Harvest Moon*

1st Place Machinima ..... *The Demise*
1st Place Science Fiction ..... *Outsource*
1st Place Short Shorts ..... *The Diary of Anne Frank of the Dead*
1st Place Suspense ..... *By Appointment Only*
1st Place Thriller ..... *Al's Beef*

2007

Best Short Film ..... *Jakob and the Angels*
Best Animated Film ..... *Operation: Fish*
Honorable Mention ..... *Thanksgiving With the Kranzes*
1st Place Action & Suspense ..... *Forged*
1st Place Animated Comedy ..... *Whale*
1st Place Animated Drama ..... *When the World Goes Dark*
1st Place Animated Fantasy & Science Fiction ..... *Operation: Fish*
1st Place Animated Horror ..... *Puppet*
1st Place Asian-Themed ..... *Lullaby Crossing*
1st Place Comedy ..... *Monster Job Hunter*
1st Place Dark Comedy ..... *The Fifth*
1st Place Fantasy ..... *Jakob and the Angels*
1st Place Horror ..... *Para-Normal*
1st Place Horror Comedy ..... *Zombie Love*
1st Place Magic Realism ..... *Enter the Dragonfly*
1st Place Parody *07*
1st Place Science Fiction ..... *D-I-M, Deus in Machina*
1st Place Short Shorts ..... *A Little Night Fright*

2006

Best Short Film ..... *Oculus*
Best Animated Film ..... *Dragon*
Honorable Mention ..... *The Call of Cthulhu*
1st Place Animated Comedy ..... *Hazel's Hips*
1st Place Animated Fantasy ..... *Dragon*
1st Place Animated Horror ..... *From Beyond*
1st Place Comedy ..... *The Wright Stuff*
1st Place Documentary ..... *Pulp Fiction Art: Cheap Thrills and Painted Nightmares*
1st Place Drama ..... *The Analyst's Goodbye*
1st Place Fantasy ..... *The Greatest Story of All Time*
1st Place Horror ..... *Oculus*
1st Place Horror Comedy ..... *Raven Gets a Life*
1st Place Parody ..... *Bon Appetit*
1st Place Science Fiction ..... *Helix*
1st Place Thriller ..... *Now You See Me, Now You Don't*

2005

Best Short Film ..... *Apartment 206*
Best Animated Film ..... *The Mysterious Geographic Explorations of Jasper Morello*
Honorable Mention ..... *Turn*
1st Place Animated Comedy ..... *Rattus Pistofficus*
1st Place Animated Fantasy & Science Fiction ..... *The Mysterious Geographic Explorations of Jasper Morello*

1st Place Animated Horror ..... *Little Dead Girl*
1st Place Comedy ..... *Final Sale*
1st Place Extreme Horror ..... *Means to an End*
1st Place Fantasy ..... *Apartment 206*
1st Place Horror ..... *Colour Blind*
1st Place Horror Comedy ..... *Pee Shy*
1st Place Parody ..... *Confederate Zombie Massacre!*
1st Place Science Fiction ..... *Cost of Living*
1st Place Thriller ..... *D*

Duistere Openbaringen (Dark Revelations)

Festival Organisator Emiel Labree emails me: "There was no 2008 edition of the festival."

2010

Beste Film ..... *Het Snoepmonster* (Ruwan Heggelman)
Beste Scenario ..... Ruwan Heggelman (*Het Snoepmonster*)
Beste Cinematografie ..... Addie Reiss (*Vogelvrij*)
Beste Montage ..... Sander Kuipers (*Iedereen Die Iets Betekent*)
Beste Acteur ..... Jurriaan Fuchs (*Schoft*)
Beste Actrice ..... Mareille Labohm (*Birdday*)
Beste VFX ..... Tom Jacobs, Jeroen Groen & Gijs van Broekhoven (*Strike*)
Beste Make-up FX ..... Kayah Kolodziejczyk (*De Kat, De Kast en De Krijsende Vrouw*)
Beste Geluid ..... Marc Lizier & Floris Schönfeld (*Akiko*)
Beste Muziek ..... Stan Koch (*Papier Hier*)
Beste Promotie ..... *Papier Hier*

2009

Beste Film ..... *Brother's Keeper* (Martijn Smits)
Beste Scenario ..... Bart van Dekken (*Vleesdag*)
Beste Cinematografie ..... Luuk Zonnenberg (*Taxandria*)
Beste Montage ..... Roy Jacobs and Marc van den Boom (*Morgana*)
Beste Acteur ..... Victor Löw (*Popo*)
Beste Actrice ..... Tamar Tieleman and Sophie Jonker (*Lenteveld*)
Beste Make-up FX ...... Suzi Terror
Beste VFX ..... Shosho
Beste Geluid ..... Renko Koppe (*Inversus*)
Beste Muziek ..... Bernard Martens (*Mijn Mooiste Creatuur*)
Beste Promotie ..... *Horizonica*
Eervolle juryvermelding ..... *Horizonica*
Publieksfavoriet ..... *Harry Doright's Prelude to Hell*

2007

Professioneel ..... *De Bug* (Martijn Smits)
Semi-Professioneel ..... *De Overkant* (Iván López Núñez)

Amateur ..... *De Vrucht Van Uw Schoot, Vers Van de Boom* (Danny de Jager)
Publieksfavoriet ..... *Amicus Mortis* (Video Entertainment Team)

2006
Professioneel ..... *Dilemma* (Boris Paval Conen)
Semi-Professioneel ..... *The End* (Eldar Gross)
Amateur ..... *Yurei* (Sandesh de Rijk)
Publieksfavoriet ..... *Amicus Mortis* (Video Entertainment Team)
Eervolle Vermelding ..... *Solex* (Wolfgang Hollaar, Alex Pitstra)

2005
Professioneel ..... *Dokter Vogel* (Lodewijk Crijns)
Semi-Professioneel ..... *Vandaag* (Mark Weistra)
Amateur ..... *Acrofobia* (Peter Hoogendoorn)
Publieksfavoriet ..... *No. 0014* (Brian and Jeffrey De Vore)

Eyegore Award

Currently A.K.A. Chiller Eyegore Award. Previously A.K.A. Eyegore Horror Award. It's tough to find a complete list of winners or categories on the internet. The below list was pieced together from the Internet Movie Database, Dreadcentral.com, and LAsThePlace.com. The IMDb and LAsThePlace.com indicate that 1997 was this award's first year, and no awards were presented in 2001–06. I contacted Universal's PR Dept about the Eyegore, via email and fax, but got no reply. Presented in October. In 2010, their Short Film Competition was called the Halloween Horror Nights Scary Film Competition

2010
Winners ..... Eli Roth, Christopher Lloyd, Sid Haig, Betsy Russell, Gina Holden.
Short Film Competition Winner ..... Elizabeth Schieffer (*Jasper*)

2009
Filmmaker of the Year ..... Rob Zombie
Best Villain in a Film Series ..... Tobin Bell (the *Saw* series)
Best Villain ..... Noah Segan (*Deadgirl*)
Short Film Competition Winner ..... Drew Daywalt (*Bedfellows*)
Jack Pierce Lifetime Achievement Award ..... Rick Baker

2008
Winners ..... Bill Moseley, Tobe Hooper, Julie Benz, Gunnar Hansen

2007
Winners ..... Roger Corman, Patricia Arquette, Sheri Moon Zombie, Shawnee Smith, Corey Feldman, Michael Berryman, Don Mancini

2000
Winners ..... Joss Whedon, the cast of *Buffy the Vampire Slayer*, the cast of *Angel*, Karen Black, Gloria Stuart, The Undertaker

1999
Winners ..... Rob Zombie, Stephen Sommers, Arnold Vosloo, Lupita Tovar

1998
Winners ..... Janet Leigh, Clive Barker, Jennifer Tilly

1997
Winner ..... Alice Cooper

Fangoria Chainsaw Award

Michael Gingold of *Fangoria* magazine explains: "The years listed are those for the years the awards were given out/announced, honoring films and talent *from the previous year.* Nominees were selected by the editors of *Fangoria*, and the winners voted on by the readers via ballots in the mag and online. (There were no nominees for Worst Film, which was left to the readers' open vote.)

"Awards were given out from 1992–1996 at Fangoria/Creation Weekend of Horrors conventions in Los Angeles, in ceremonies produced by myself with guest presenters from the horror filmmaking field. Thereafter, the winners were announced in *Fangoria* only."

There were no awards in 2007 and 2008.

There were *two* sets of awards in 2006. One was the usual award, with nominees chosen by *Fangoria*'s editors and voted on by readers. However, later in 2006, "*Fangoria* and the Fuse Channel teamed up for a *different* Chainsaw Awards show with *fresh* categories, with nominees drawn from films released between summer 2005 and summer 2006. These nominees were announced online for fan voting in late summer 2006, with the awards ceremony taking place that October. Plans for more Fangoria/Fuse Chainsaw Awards shows never materialized, so we went back to doing the awards in the previously established manner beginning in 2009."

2010

Best Wide-Release Film ..... *Drag Me to Hell*
Best Limited-Release/Direct-to-DVD Film ..... *Trick 'R Treat*
Best Actor ..... Jesse Eisenberg (*Zombieland*)
Best Actress ..... Morjana Alaoui (*Martyrs*)
Best Supporting Actor ..... Dylan Baker (*Trick 'R Treat*)
Best Supporting Actress ..... Lorna Raver (*Drag Me to Hell*)
Best Screenplay ..... Pascal Laugier (*Martyrs*)
Best Score ..... Christopher Young (*Drag Me to Hell*)
Best Makeup/Creature FX ..... Justin Raleigh, Ozzy Alvarez (*Splinter*)
Worst Film ..... *Friday the 13th* (2009)
Fangoria Hall of Fame Inductees ..... Tom Atkins, Tobin Bell

2009

Best Wide-Release Film ..... *Hellboy II: The Golden Army*
Best Limited-Release/Direct-to-DVD Film ..... *Let the Right One In*
Best Actor ..... Ron Perlman (*Hellboy II: The Golden Army*)
Best Actress ..... Lina Leandersson (*Let the Right One In*)
Best Supporting Actor ..... Doug Jones (*Hellboy II: The Golden Army*)
Best Supporting Actress ..... Beatrice Dalle (*Inside*)
Best Screenplay ..... John Ajvide Lindqvist (*Let the Right One In*)
Best Score ..... John Soderqvist (*Let the Right One In*)
Best Makeup/Creature FX ..... Mike Elizalde, Cliff Wallace, David Martí, Montse Ribé (*Hellboy II: The Golden Army*)
Worst Film ..... *Prom Night* (2008)
Fangoria Hall of Fame Inductees ..... Doug Jones, Roger Corman, Forrest J Ackerman

2006

(Fangoria/Fuse Chainsaw Awards)

Killer Movie ..... *The Devil's Rejects*
Most Thrilling Killing (Best Death Scene) ..... Emmanuelle Vaugier (*Saw II*)
Relationship from Hell (Best Couple or Duo) ..... Bill Moseley and Sheri Moon Zombie (*The Devil's Rejects*)
Best Butcher (Villain) ..... Tobin Bell (*Saw II*)
Creepiest Kid ..... Seamus Davey-Fitzpatrick (*The Omen*)
Bloodiest Beatdown ..... Michael Bailey Smith (*The Hills Have Eyes*)
Best with Less (limited release or budget) ..... *Zombie Honeymoon*
Looks That Kill (Best Makeup) ..... *The Hills Have Eyes*
Killer Television ..... *Masters of Horror*
Killer Video ..... The Red Hot Chili Peppers ("Dani California")
Best Video Inspired by a Movie ..... 30 Seconds to Mars ("The Kill")
Prince of Darkness (darkest male in a music video) ..... Jared Leto ("30 Seconds to Mars")
Femme Fatale (most evil female in music video) ..... Avenged Sevenfold ("Beast and the Harlot")

2006

Best Wide-Release Film ..... *The Devil's Rejects*
Best Limited-Release/Direct-to-Video Film ..... *Toolbox Murders*
Best Actor ..... Sid Haig (*The Devil's Rejects*)
Best Actress ..... Cecile de France (*High Tension*)
Best Supporting Actor ..... William Forsythe (*The Devil's Rejects*)
Best Supporting Actress ..... Leslie Easterbrook (*The Devil's Rejects*)
Best Screenplay ..... Rob Zombie (*The Devil's Rejects*)
Best Score ..... Tyler Bates (*The Devil's Rejects*)
Best Makeup/Creature FX ..... Greg Nicotero, Howard Berger (*Land of the Dead*)
Worst Film ..... *The Fog*
Fangoria Hall of Fame Inductees ..... KNB EFX, Eli Roth

2005

Best Wide-Release Film ..... *Shaun of the Dead*
Best Limited-Release/Direct-to-Video Film ..... *Ginger Snaps 2: Unleashed*
Best Actor ..... Simon Pegg (*Shaun of the Dead*)
Best Actress ..... Emily Perkins (*Ginger Snaps 2: Unleashed*)
Best Supporting Actor ..... Nick Frost (*Shaun of the Dead*)
Best Supporting Actress ..... Tatiana Maslany (*Ginger Snaps 2: Unleashed*)
Best Screenplay ..... Simon Pegg, Edgar Wright (*Shaun of the Dead*)
Best Score ..... Christopher Young (*The Grudge*)
Best Makeup/Creature FX ..... Chad Waters, Matt Rose, Mike Elizalde (*Hellboy*)
Worst Film ..... *The Village*
Fangoria Hall of Fame Inductees ..... Emily Perkins, Ron Perlman

2004

Best Wide-Release Film ..... *28 Days Later*
Best Limited-Release/Direct-to-Video Film ..... *Bubba Ho-Tep*
Best Actor ..... Bruce Campbell (*Bubba Ho-Tep*)
Best Actress ..... Angela Bettis (*May*)
Best Supporting Actor ..... Sid Haig (*House of 1000 Corpses*)

Best Supporting Actress ..... Karen Black (*House of 1000 Corpses*)
Best Screenplay ..... Alex Garland (*28 Days Later*)
Best Score ..... Nathan Barr, Angelo Badalamenti (*Cabin Fever*)
Best Makeup/Creature FX ..... Bill Terezakis (*Freddy vs. Jason*)
Worst Film ..... *House of the Dead*
Fangoria Hall of Fame Inductees ..... Don Coscarelli, Sid Haig, Bill Moseley

2003

Best Wide-Release Film ..... *The Ring*
Best Limited-Release/Direct-to-Video Film ..... *Dog Soldiers*
Best Actor ..... Robin Williams (*One Hour Photo*)
Best Actress ..... Naomi Watts (*The Ring*)
Best Supporting Actor ..... Ralph Fiennes (*Red Dragon*)
Best Supporting Actress ..... Monica Bellucci (*Brotherhood of the Wolf*)
Best Screenplay ..... Brent Hanley (*Frailty*)
Best Score ..... Hans Zimmer (*The Ring*)
Best Makeup/Creature FX ..... Steve Johnson, Tippett Studio (*Blade II*)
Worst Film ..... *Feardotcom*
Fangoria Hall of Fame Inductees ..... Bill Paxton, Rob Zombie

2002

Best Wide-Release Film ..... *Jeepers Creepers*
Best Limited-Release/Direct-to-Video Film ..... *Ginger Snaps*
Best Actor ..... Anthony Hopkins (*Hannibal*)
Best Actress ..... Nicole Kidman (*The Others*)
Best Supporting Actor ..... Jonathan Breck (*Jeepers Creepers*)
Best Supporting Actress ..... Adrienne Barbeau (*The Convent*)
Best Screenplay ..... Karen Walton (*Ginger Snaps*)
Best Score ..... Hans Zimmer (*Hannibal*)
Best Makeup/Creature FX ..... KNB EFX (*Thir13en Ghosts*)
Worst Film ..... *Valentine*
Fangoria Hall of Fame Inductees ..... Mario Bava, Guillermo del Toro

2001

Best Wide-Release Film ..... *American Psycho*
Best Limited-Release/Direct-to-Video Film ..... *Cherry Falls*
Best Actor ..... Christian Bale (*American Psycho*)
Best Actress ..... Ellen Burstyn (*Requiem for a Dream*)
Best Supporting Actor ..... Vincent D'Onofrio (*The Cell*)
Best Supporting Actress ..... Parker Posey (*Scream 3*)
Best Screenplay ..... Steven Katz (*Shadow of the Vampire*)
Best Score (tie) ..... Howard Shore (*The Cell*), and Wojciech Kilar (*The Ninth Gate*)
Best Makeup/Creature FX (tie) ..... Michele Burke (*The Cell*), and Pauline Fowler, Julian Murray, Amber Sibley (*Shadow of the Vampire*)
Worst Film ..... *Book of Shadows: Blair Witch 2*
Fangoria Hall of Fame Inductees ..... Udo Kier, Joe Dante

2000

Best Wide-Release Film ..... *The Sixth Sense*
Best Limited-Release/Direct-to-Video Film ..... *The Day of the Beast*
Best Actor ..... Johnny Depp (*Sleepy Hollow*)
Best Actress ..... Heather Donahue (*The Blair Witch Project*)
Best Supporting Actor ..... Haley Joel Osment (*The Sixth Sense*)
Best Supporting Actress ..... Toni Collette (*The Sixth Sense*)
Best Screenplay ..... M. Night Shyamalan (*The Sixth Sense*)
Best Score ..... Danny Elfman (*Sleepy Hollow*)
Best Makeup/Creature FX ..... Kevin Yagher (*Sleepy Hollow*)
Worst Film ..... *The Haunting*
Fangoria Hall of Fame Inductees ..... Tim Burton, Paul Naschy

1999

Best Wide-Release Film ..... *Dark City*
Best Limited-Release/Direct-to-Video Film ..... *The Night Flier*
Best Actor ..... James Woods (*Vampires*)
Best Actress ..... Jamie Lee Curtis (*Halloween: H20*)
Best Supporting Actor ..... Udo Kier (*Blade*)
Best Supporting Actress ..... Sheryl Lee (*Vampires*)
Best Screenplay ..... David Goyer, Lem Dobbs, Alex Proyas (*Dark City*)
Best Score ..... John Carpenter (*Vampires*)
Best Makeup/Creature FX ..... Kevin Yagher (*Bride of Chucky*)
Worst Film ..... *I Still Know What You Did Last Summer*
Fangoria Hall of Fame Inductees ..... Brad Dourif, Dick Miller

1998

Best Wide-Release Film ..... *Scream 2*
Best Limited-Release/Direct-to-Video Film ..... *Lost Highway*
Best Actor ..... Al Pacino (*The Devil's Advocate*)
Best Actress ..... Sigourney Weaver (*Alien: Resurrection*)
Best Supporting Actor ..... Robert Blake (*Lost Highway*)
Best Supporting Actress ..... Courteney Cox (*Scream 2*)

Best Screenplay ..... Kevin Williamson (*Scream 2*)
Best Score ..... Angelo Badalamenti (*Lost Highway*)
Best Makeup/Creature FX ..... Phil Tippett, Kevin Yagher (*Starship Troopers*)
Worst Film ..... *Spawn*
Fangoria Hall of Fame Inductees ..... Kevin Williamson, Sigourney Weaver, Lucio Fulci

1997

Best Wide-Release Film ..... *Scream*
Best Limited-Release/Direct-to-Video Film ..... *Cemetery Man*
Best Actor ..... George Clooney (*From Dusk Till Dawn*)
Best Actress ..... Neve Campbell (*Scream*)
Best Supporting Actor ..... Jeffrey Combs (*The Frighteners*)
Best Supporting Actress ..... Drew Barrymore (*Scream*)
Best Screenplay ..... Kevin Williamson (*Scream*)
Best Score ..... Danny Elfman (*The Frighteners*)
Best Makeup FX ..... KNB EFX (*From Dusk Till Dawn*)
Worst Film ..... *The Crow: City of Angels*
Fangoria Hall of Fame Inductees ..... Jamie Lee Curtis, Stuart Gordon

1996

Best Wide-Release Film *Se7en*
Best Limited-Release/Direct-to-Video Film ..... *Castle Freak*
Best Actor ..... Christopher Walken (*The Prophecy*)
Best Actress ..... Jada Pinkett (*Tales from the Crypt: Demon Knight*)
Best Supporting Actor ..... Kevin Spacey (*Se7en*)
Best Supporting Actress ..... Virginia Madsen (*The Prophecy*)
Best Screenplay ..... Andrew Kevin Walker (*Se7en*)
Best Score ..... Simon Boswell (*Lord of Illusions*)
Best Makeup FX ..... Todd Masters, Kevin Yagher (*Tales from the Crypt: Demon Knight*)
Worst Film ..... *Halloween: The Curse of Michael Myers*
Fangoria Hall of Fame Inductees ..... Christopher Lee, Christopher Walken

1995

Best Wide-Release Film ..... *The Crow*
Best Limited-Release/Direct-to-Video Film ..... *Phantasm III*
Best Actor ..... Brandon Lee (*The Crow*)
Best Actress ..... Heather Langenkamp (*Wes Craven's New Nightmare*)
Best Supporting Actor ..... Antonio Banderas (*Interview with the Vampire*)
Best Supporting Actress ..... Kirsten Dunst (*Interview with the Vampire*)
Best Screenplay ..... Wes Craven (*Wes Craven's New Nightmare*)
Best Score ..... Graeme Revell (*The Crow*)
Best Makeup FX ..... Stan Winston (*Interview with the Vampire*)
Worst Film ..... *Leprechaun 2*
Fangoria Hall of Fame Inductees ..... Heather Langenkamp, Peter Cushing

1994

Best Wide-Release Film ..... *Army of Darkness*
Best Limited-Release/Direct-to-Video Film ..... *Dead Alive*
Best Actor ..... Bruce Campbell (*Army of Darkness*)
Best Actress ..... Mindy Clarke (*Return of the Living Dead III*)
Best Supporting Actor ..... Jeff Goldblum (*Jurassic Park*)
Best Supporting Actress ..... Embeth Davidtz (*Army of Darkness*)
Best Screenplay ..... George A. Romero (*The Dark Half*)
Best Score ..... Joseph Loduca, Danny Elfman (*Army of Darkness*)
Best Makeup FX ..... Tony Gardner, KNB EFX (*Army of Darkness*)
Worst Film ..... *Leprechaun*
Fangoria Hall of Fame Inductees ..... Peter Jackson, Angus Scrimm

1993

Best Studio/Wide-Release Film ..... *Bram Stoker's Dracula*
Best Independent/Direct-to-Video Film ..... *The Resurrected*
Best Actor ..... Gary Oldman (*Bram Stoker's Dracula*)
Best Actress ..... Virginia Madsen (*Candyman*)
Best Supporting Actor ..... Anthony Hopkins (*Bram Stoker's Dracula*)
Best Supporting Actress ..... Alice Krige (*Sleepwalkers*)
Best Screenplay ..... James V. Hart (*Bram Stoker's Dracula*)
Best Soundtrack ..... Wojciech Kilar (*Bram Stoker's Dracula*)
Best Makeup FX ..... Greg Cannom (*Bram Stoker's Dracula*)
Worst Film ..... *Dr. Giggles*
Fangoria Hall of Fame Inductees ..... Anthony Hopkins, Linnea Quigley

1992

Best Studio/Big-Budget Film ..... *The Silence of the Lambs*
Best Independent/Low-Budget Film ..... *Bride of Re-Animator*
Best Actor ..... Anthony Hopkins (*The Silence of the Lambs*)
Best Actress ..... Jodie Foster (*The Silence of the Lambs*)

Best Supporting Actor ..... Brad Dourif (*Body Parts*)
Best Supporting Actress ..... Christina Ricci (*The Addams Family*)
Best Screenplay ..... Ted Tally (*The Silence of the Lambs*)
Best Soundtrack ..... Brad Fiedel (*Terminator 2: Judgment Day*)
Best Makeup FX ..... Stan Winston (*Terminator 2: Judgment Day*)
Worst Film ..... *Freddy's Dead: The Final Nightmare*
Fangoria Hall of Fame Inductees ..... Lance Henriksen, Jeffrey Combs

Fanta Festival

Alberto Ravaglioli emails me: "Fanta Festival just awards Best Feature. The 2008 and 2009 editions were noncompetitive." Its first edition was in 1981; the 30th in 2010. This Italian festival used to participate in the Méliès Awards [see entry], but Ravaglioli tells me that Fanta Festival has chosen to withdraw from the EFFFF. IMDb.com reports that "Alan Smithee," credited as the director for the 1996 winner, *Hellraiser: Bloodline*, is really Kevin Yagher, and that Joe Chappelle was an additional "uncredited" director on that film.

2010 ..... *La horde*, A.K.A. *The Horde* (dir: Yannick Dahan, Benjamin Rocher)
2009 ..... noncompetitive
2008 ..... noncompetitive
2007 ..... *Asylum*, A.K.A. *Follia* (dir: David Mackenzie)
2006 ..... *Le mele di Adamo*, A.K.A. *Adam's Apples* (dir: Anders Thomas Jensen)
2004 ..... *Evilenko* (dir: David Grieco)
2003 ..... *28 Days Later*, A.K.A. *28 giorni dopo* (dir: Danny Boyle)
2002 ..... *Sleepwalker* (dir: Johannes Runeborg)
2001 ..... *Versus* (dir: Ryuhei Kitamura)
2000 ..... *Los sin nombres*, A.K.A. *The Nameless* (dir: Jaume Balagueró)
1999 ..... *Ravenous*, A.K.A. *L' insaziabile* (dir: Antonia Bird)
1998 ..... *Perdita Durango* (dir: Álex de la Iglesia)
1997 ..... *La lengua asesina* (dir: Alberto Sciamma)
1996 ..... *Hellraiser: Bloodline* (dir: Alan Smithee)
1995 ..... *Nattevagten*, A.K.A. *Nightwatch* (dir: Ole Bornedal)
1994 ..... *Dellamorte Dellamore*, A.K.A. *Cemetery Man* (dir: Michele Soavi)
1993 ..... *Accion Mutante*, A.K.A. *Azione mutante* (dir: Álex de la Iglesia)
1992 ..... *The People Under the Stairs*, A.K.A. *La casa nera* (dir: Wes Craven)
1991 ..... *The Pit and the Pendulum* (dir: Stuart Gordon)
1990 ..... *Witches*, A.K.A. *Chi ha paura delle streghe* (dir: Nicholas Roeg)
1989 ..... *Bad Taste*, A.K.A. *Fuori di testa* (dir: Peter Jackson)
1988 ..... *Monkey Shines: An Experiment in Fear*, A.K.A. *Monkey Shines: Esperimento nel terrore* (dir: George A. Romero)
1987 ..... *The Hitcher*, A.K.A. *La lunga strada della paura* (dir: Robert Harmon)
1986 ..... *Re-Animator* (dir: Stuart Gordon)
1985 ..... *Demoni* (dir: Lamberto Bava) and *The Company of Wolves*, A.K.A. *In compagnia dei lupi* (dir: Neil Jordan)
1984 ..... *Evil Dead*, A.K.A. *La casa* (dir: Sam Raimi)
1983 ..... *Alone in the Dark* (dir: Jack Sholder)
1982 ..... *Wolfen*, (dir: Michael Wadleigh)
1981 ..... *Monster Club*, A.K.A. *Il club dei mostri* (dir: Roy W. Baker)

Fantasia International Film Festival

Offers juried and public prizes, the latter voted for by the audience. Some of the 2006 and 2007 awards that are for "short feature" are apparently for "short film." Their DIY short film awards (which likely stands for Do It Yourself) honors "the growing pool of local filmmakers who ignore budgetary restraints to offer us pure gems of imagination and talent."

2010 Jury Prizes

Best Feature Film ..... *Sawako Decides* (dir: Yuya Ishii)
Special Jury Prize, Feature ..... *Castaway on the Moon* (dir: Lee Hae-jun)
Best Actor, Feature ..... Noah Taylor (*Red, White & Blue*)
Best Actress, Feature ..... Hikari Mitsushima (*Sawako Decides*)
Best Director, Feature ..... Lee Jun-ik (*Blades of Blood*)
Best Screenplay, Feature ..... Mladen Djordjevic (*Life and Death of a Porno Gang*)
Best First Feature ..... *Tucker and Dale vs. Evil* (dir: Eli Craig)
Special Mention, First Feature ..... *A Serbian Film* (dir: Srdjan Spasojevic)
Best Animated Feature Film ..... *Mai Mai Miracle* (dir: Sunao Katabuchi)
Special Mention, Animated Feature Film ..... *Oblivion Island* (dir: Shinsuke Sato)
Best Animated Short Film ..... *Madagascar* (dir: Bastien Dubois)

Special Mention, Animated Short Film ..... *Wisdom Teeth* (dir: Don Hertzfeldt)
Grand Prize, International Short Film ..... *The Adder's Bite* (dir: Firas Momani)
Special Mention, International Short Film ..... *Heal* (dir: Mian Adnan Ahmad)
Best Quebec Short Film ..... *The Greens* (dir: Serge Marcotte)
Best Direction for a Quebec Short Film ..... *À Vif* (dir: Cynthia Tremblay)
Best Cinematography for a Quebec Short Film ..... *Danse Macabre*
Best Performance in a Quebec Short Film (tie) ..... Laurence Leboeuf (*Sans Titre*) and Brent Marrale (*The Greens*)
Best Screenplay for a Quebec Short Film ..... *Le Technicien* (Simon Olivier Fecteau)
Jury's Pick for a Quebec Short Film ..... *Marius Borodine* (dir: Emanuel Hoss-Desmarais)
Best DIY Quebec Short Film ..... *Le Tiroir et le Corbeau* (dir: Frédérick Tremblay)
Best Direction for a DIY Quebec Short Film ..... *Windigo* (dir: Kris Happyjack-McKenzie)
Best Screenplay for a DIY Quebec Short Film ..... *Hero* (Carnior)
Best Special Effects for a DIY Quebec Short Film ..... *Astuko's Legend*
Jury's Pick for a DIY Quebec Short Film ..... *Les Quebecers Contre les Zombies 2* (dir: Louis Allard)
AQCC Prize (for Best Asian Film) ..... *Air Doll* (dir: Hirokazu Kore-eda)
AQCC Prize, Honorable Mention ..... *The Executioner* (dir: Choi Jin-ho)
Séquences Prize for Best International Feature Film (tie) ..... *Somos lo que Hay*, A.K.A. *We Are What We Are* (dir: Jorge Michel Grau), and *Red, White & Blue* (dir: Simon Rumley)
Écran Fantastique Prize ..... *Tears for Sale* (dir: Uros Stojanovic)

2010 Public Prizes

Best Asian Film, Gold ..... *IP Man 2*
Best Asian Film, Silver ..... *Sell Out!*
Best Asian Film, Bronze (tie) ..... *Castaway on the Moon* and *Dream Home*
Best European, North American, or South American Film, Gold ..... *A Serbian Film*
Best European, North American, or South American Film, Silver ..... *At World's End*
Best European, North American, or South American Film, Bronze ..... *Rec 2*
Best Animated Film, Gold ..... *Summer Wars*
Best Animated Film, Silver ..... *Technotise: Edit and I*
Best Animated Film, Bronze (tie) ..... *King of Thorns* and *Space Battleships Yamato: Resurrection*
Best Canadian or Quebecois Feature, Gold ..... *The Shrine*
Best Canadian or Quebecois Feature, Silver ..... *Suck*
Best Canadian or Quebecois Feature, Bronze (tie) ..... *Frankenstein Unlimited* and *Neverlost*
Guru Prize for Most Energetic Film, Gold ..... *IP Man 2*
Guru Prize for Most Energetic Film, Silver ..... *Rec 2*
Guru Prize for Most Energetic Film, Bronze ..... *Symbol*
Most Innovative Film, Gold (tie) ..... *Symbol* and *A Serbian Film*
Most Innovative Film, Silver ..... *Sell Out!*
Most Innovative Film, Bronze ..... *Rubber*
Best Documentary ..... *Marwencol*
Best International Short Film, Gold ..... *Clean Carousel*
Best International Short Film, Silver (three-way tie) ..... *Jack* and *Ninjas* and *Tous les Hommes s'Appellent Robert*
Best International Short Film, Bronze ..... *Lambs*
Best DIY Quebec Short Film ..... *L' Histoire du Méchant Dragon* (dir: Francis Gélinas)

2009 Jury Prizes

Best Feature Film ..... *Breathless* (Yang Ik-june)
Jury Special Prize, Feature ..... *Love Exposure* (Sion Sono)
Best Male Performance, Feature ..... Yang Ik-June (*Breathless*)
Best Female Performance, Feature ..... Hikari Mitsushima (*Love Exposure*)
Best Director, Feature ..... David Russo (*The Immaculate Conception of Little Dizzle*)
Best Screenplay, Feature ..... Nicolas Alberny and Jean Mach (*8th Wonderland*)
Best Cinematography, Feature ..... Hideho Urata (*The Clone Returns Home*)
Technical Prize, Feature ..... *IP Man*
Special Mention for Best Direction of Child Actors ..... Tom Shankland (*The Children*)
Best First Feature ..... *White Lightnin'* (Dominic Murphy)
Special Mention, First Feature ..... Debut Performance of Actress Eline Kuppens (*Left Bank*)
Best Live Action International Short Film ..... *Hold Your Fire* (Wes Benscoter)
Best Animated International Short Film ..... *The Control Master* (Run Wrake)
Best Quebec Short Film ..... *Les Outils* (Simon Laganière)
Best Director of a Quebec Short Film ..... *Kagamiko* (Mathieu Arsenault)
Best Screenplay for a Quebec Short Film ..... *Un Court Sans Titre* (Alexandre Gibault)
Best Performance in a Quebec Short Film ..... Pierre-Luc LaFontaine (*Déraciné*)
Special Jury Prize for a Quebec Short Film ..... *Fantasme* (Izabel Grondin; also for her body of work)

Best DIY Short Film ..... *Panorama: Seeking Voïvod* (Jean-Marc E. Roy)
Best DIY Short Film Screenplay ..... *Chers Parents* (Sébastien Godron)
Special Jury Prize for a DIY Short Film (tie) ..... *Massacrator* (Pierre Ayotte) and *Simonac* (Sylvain Lavigne)
Séquences Award ..... *Rough Cut* (Jang Hun)
L' Écran Fantastique Award ..... *Paco and the Magic Book* (Tetsuya Nakashima)

2009 Public Prizes

Best Asian Film, Gold ..... Love Exposure (Sion Sono)
Best Asian Film, Silver ..... IP Man (Wilson Yip)
Best Asian Film, Bronze ..... Thirst (Park Chan-wook)
Best International Film, Gold ..... 8th Wonderland (Nicolas Alberny, Jean Mach)
Best International Film, Silver (tie) ..... *Embodiment of Evil* (Jose Mojica Marins) and *Must Love Death* (Andreas Schaap)
Best International Film, Bronze ..... Black (Pierre Laffargue)
Best Quebec Film, Gold ..... Sans Dessein (Caroline Labrèche, Steeve Léonard)
Best Quebec Film, Silver ..... The Ante (Max Perrier)
Best Quebec Film, Bronze ..... Crawler (Sv Bell)
Best Animated Film ..... Hells (Yoshiki Yamakawa)
Guru Prize for Most Energetic Film, Gold ..... Yatterman (Takashi Miike)
Guru Prize for Most Energetic Film, Silver ..... IP Man (Wilson Yip)
Guru Prize for Most Energetic Film, Bronze (tie) ..... *Vampire Girl vs. Frankenstein Girl* (Naoyuki Tomomatsu, Yoshihiro Nishimura) and *Fireball* (Thanakorn Pongsuwan)
Most Innovative Film, Gold ..... Love Exposure (Sion Sono)
Most Innovative Film, Silver ..... 8th Wonderland (Nicolas Alberny, Jean Mach)
Most Innovative Film, Bronze (tie) ..... *Genius Party Beyond* (Mahiro Maeda, Koji Morimoto, Kazuto Nakazawa, Shinya Ohira, Tatsuyuki Tanaka) and *Must Love Death* (Andreas Schaap)
Best Documentary ..... Best Worst Move (Michael Paul Stephenson)
Best Short Film, Gold ..... *The Horribly Slow Murderer With the Extremely Inefficient Weapon* (Richard Gale)
Best Short Film, Silver ..... *Hidden Life of the Burrowing Owl* (Mike Roush)
Best Short Film, Bronze (tie) ..... *Cencoroll* (Atsuya Uki) and *Mortified* (Robert Nevitt)

2008 Jury Prizes

Best Feature Film ..... Let the Right One In (Tomas Alfredson)
Best Director, Feature ..... Tomas Alfredson (Let the Right One In)
Best Script, Feature ..... Satoshi Miki (Adrift in Tokyo)
Best Photography, Feature ..... Hoyte Van Hoytema (Let the Right One In)
Best Actor, Feature ..... Ben Siegler (Rule of Three)
Special Mention of the Jury, Feature ..... actors Jô Odagiri and Tomokazu Miura (Adrift in Tokyo)
Best Actress, Feature ..... Jin-hie Park (Shadows in the Palace)
Best First Feature, Gold ..... Ex-Drummer (Koen Mortier)
Best First Feature, Silver ..... Timecrimes (Nacho Vigalondo)
Best First Feature, Bronze ..... From Inside (John Bergin)
Best International Live Action Short Film (tie) ..... *With a Little Patience* (Laszlo Nemes) and *I Love Sarah Jane* (Spencer Susser)
Best International Animated Short Film ..... *The Facts in the Case of Mister Hollow* (Rodrigo Gudiño, Vincent Marcone)
Special Mention for an Animated Short Film ..... *Yellow Sticky Notes* (Jeff Chiba Stearns)
Best Quebec Short Film ..... À Mère et Marées (Alain Fournier)
Best Director of a Quebec Short Film ..... Mathieu Denis (Code 13)
Best Acting in a Quebec Short Film ..... Claude Despins (Papillons Noirs)
Special Jury Prize for a Quebec Short Film ..... L' Astronaute (Christian Laurence)
Best DIY Quebec Short Film ..... 1888 (Simon Bérubé)
Best Direction of a DIY Quebec Short Film ..... Simon Lehembre (Cheveux Blanc)
Special Jury Prize, DIY Quebec Short Film ..... Superhuman (Dagan Taylor)

2008 Public Prizes

Best Asian Film, Gold ..... Tokyo Gore Police (Yoshihiro Nishimura)
Best Asian Film, Silver ..... Sukiyaki Western Django (Takashi Miike)
Best Asian Film, Bronze ..... 4BIA (Youngyooth Thongkonthun, Banjong Pisanthanakun, Parkpoom Wongpoom, Paween Purikitpanya)
Best European, North or South American Film, Gold ..... Let the Right One In (Tomas Alfredson)
Best European, North or South American Film, Silver ..... [REC] (Jaume Balagueró, Paco Plaza)
Best European, North or South American Film, Bronze (tie) ..... *Pig Hunt* (James Isaac) and *Midnight Meat Train* (Ryuhei Kitamura)
Best Animation Film ..... Idiots and Angels (Bill Plympton)
Most Innovative Film, Gold ..... Repo! The Genetic Opera (Darren Lynn Bousman)

Most Innovative Film, Silver ..... *[REC]* (Jaume Balagueró, Paco Plaza)
Most Innovative Film, Bronze ..... *La Antena* (Esteban Sapir)
Best Documentary, Gold ..... *I Think We're Alone Now* (Sean Donnelly)
Best Short Film, Gold ..... *Treevenge* (Jason Eisener)
Best Short Film, Silver ..... *Superhuman* (Dagan Taylor)
Best Short Film, Bronze ..... *Rojo Red* (Juan Manuel Betancourt)

2007 Jury Prizes

Best Feature Film ..... *Memories of Matsuko* (Tetsuya Nakashima)
Best Director, Feature ..... Feng Xiaogang (*The Banquet*)
Best Script, Feature ..... Han Jae-rim (*The Show Must Go On*)
Best Photography, Feature ..... Li Zhang (*The Banquet*)
Best Actor, Feature (tie) ..... Song Kang-ho (*The Show Must Go On*) and Ryu Deok-hwan (*Like a Virgin*)
Best Actress, Feature ..... Mary McCormack (*Right at Your Door*)
Best Quebec Short Feature ..... *Flutter* (Howie Shia)
Special Jury Mention, Quebec Short Feature ..... *Moi* (Yan England)
Special Jury Mention, Quebec Short Feature ..... the photography of Claudine Sauvé (*Hotel* and *Moi*)
Best International Short Feature (tie) ..... *The Last 15* (Antonio Campos) and *Maquina* (Gabe Ibanez)
Best Animated Short Feature ..... *Everything Will Be OK* (Don Hertzfeldt)
Special Jury Mention, Animated Short Feature ..... *The Runt* (Andreas Hykade)
Best DIY Quebec Short ..... *L' Écervelé* (Benoît Desjardins)
Special Mention, DIY Quebec Short ..... *20 Secondes* (Patrick Rozon)
Special Mention, DIY Quebec Short ..... *Flush!* (Jef Grenier)
Special Mention, DIY Quebec Short ..... *Jihad Joe II* (Simon Bouchard)
Séquences Magazine Award ..... *Wool 100%* (Mai Tominaga)
Info Culture Award, Best Documentary ..... *Ghosts of Cité Soleil* (Asger Leth)
L'Écran Fantastique Award ..... *Right at Your Door* (Chris Gorak)
Special Mention ..... Rory Cochrane and Mary McCormack

2007 Public Prizes

Best Asian Film, Gold ..... *13 Beloved* (Chookiat Sakveerakul)
Best Asian Film, Silver ..... *Exiled* (Johnnie To)
Best Asian Film, Bronze (tie) ..... *City of Violence* (Ryoo Seung-wan) and *Memories of Matsuko* (Tetsuya Nakashima)
Best European, North or South American Film, Gold ..... *Hatchet* (Adam Green)
Best European, North or South American Film, Silver ..... *End of the Line* (Maurice Devereaux)
Best European, North or South American Film, Bronze (tie) ..... *Mulberry Street* (Jim Mickle) and *The Signal* (David Bruckner, Dan Bush, Jacob Gentry)
Best Animated/Stop Motion Film, Gold ..... *Tekkon Kinkreet* (Michael Arias)
Best Animated/Stop Motion Film, Silver ..... *We Are the Strange* (M dot Strange)
Best Animated/Stop Motion Film, Bronze ..... *Aachi & Ssipak* (Joe Bum-jin)
Most Groundbreaking Film, Gold ..... *We Are the Strange* (M dot Strange)
Most Groundbreaking Film, Silver ..... *Exte: Hair Extentions* (Sion Sono)
Most Groundbreaking Film, Bronze ..... *Memories of Matsuko* (Tetsuya Nakashima)
Best Documentary, Gold ..... *King of Kong* (Seth Gordon)
Best Documentary, Silver ..... *Your Mommy Kills Animals* (Curt Johnson)
Best Documentary, Bronze (tie) ..... *Ghosts of Cité Soleil* (Asger Leth) and *Zoo* (Robinson Devor)
Best Short Film, Gold ..... *The Fifth* (Ryan Levin)
Best Short Film, Silver ..... *Angel* (Paul Hough)
Best Short Film, Bronze (tie) ..... *Criticized* (Richard Gale) and *The Morning After* (Daniel Knight)
Best Putain D'Court! ..... *Gratte-Papier* (Guillaume Martinez)

2006 Jury Prizes

Best Feature Film ..... *Strange Circus* (Sion Sono)
Best Director, Feature ..... Nicolas Winding Refn (*Pusher 3*)
Best Script, Feature ..... David Mamet (*Edmond*)
Best Photography, Feature ..... Ji-yong Kim (*A Bittersweet Life*)
Best Actor, Feature ..... Zlatko Buric (*Pusher 3*)
Best Actress, Feature ..... Masumi Miyazaki (*Strange Circus*)
Best Quebec Short Feature ..... *L'Étranger* (Guillaume Fortin)
Best International Short Feature ..... *Before Dawn* (Balint Kenyeres)
Best Animated Short Feature ..... *Zéro Degree* (Omid Khoshnazar)
Special Award, Visual Accomplishment, Short Feature ..... *Rabbit* (Run Wrake)
Best DIY Short, Francophone ..... *Easy Living* (Berge Kasparian, Martin Tremblay)
Best DIY Short, Anglophone ..... *A Date with the Dead* (Chris Smith)

Séquences Award ..... *Behind the Mask: The Rise of Leslie Vernon* (Scott Glosserman)
L'Écran Fantastique Award ..... *Behind the Mask: The Rise of Leslie Vernon* (Scott Glosserman)

2006 Public Prizes

Best Asian Film, Gold ..... *Great Yokai War* (Takashi Miike)
Best Asian Film, Silver ..... *A Bittersweet Life* (Kim Ji-Woon)
Best Asian Film, Bronze ..... *Citizen Dog* (Wisit Sasanatieng)
Best European, North or South American Film, Gold ..... *Behind the Mask: The Rise of Leslie Vernon* (Scott Glosserman)
Best European, North or South American Film, Silver ..... *Wilderness* (Michael J. Bassett)
Best European, North or South American Film, Bronze ..... *The Descent* (Neil Marshall)
Best Animated/Stop Motion Film, Gold ..... *Full Metal Alchemist* (Seiji Mizushima)
Best Animated/Stop Motion Film, Silver ..... *Blood Tea and Red String* (Christiane Cegavske)
Best Animated/Stop Motion Film, Bronze ..... *Worlds of Wounded Clay* (Robert Morgan)
Most Groundbreaking Film, Gold ..... *Funky Forest: The First Contact* (Katsuhito Ishii, Hajime Ishimine, Shinichiro Miki)
Most Groundbreaking Film, Silver ..... *Citizen Dog* (Wisit Sasanatieng)
Most Groundbreaking Film, Bronze ..... *Wild Blue Yonder* (Werner Herzog)
Best Short Film, Gold ..... *Terreur Au 3918* (Mathieu Fontaine)
Best Short Film, Silver ..... *The Big Empty* (Lisa Chang, Newton Thomas Sigel, Alison Smith)
Best Short Film, Bronze ..... *Bugcrush* (Carter Smith)

2005 Jury Prizes

Best Feature Film ..... *Mind Game* (Yuasa Masaaki)
Best Director (tie) ..... Gen Sekiguchi (*Survive Style 5+*) and Yuasa Masaaki (*Mind Game*)
Best Script ..... Yuasa Masaaki (*Mind Game*)
Best Cinematography ..... Kosuke Matushima (*The Taste of Tea*)
Best Actor ..... Choi Min-sik (*Crying Fist*)
Best Actress ..... Kate Greenhouse (*Dark Hours*)
Special Award, Visual Accomplishment ..... Yuasa Masaaki (*Mind Game*)
L'Écran Fantastique Award ..... *Survive Style 5+* (Gen Sekiguchi)
Séquences Award, Best Asian Film ..... *Shutter* (Banjong Pisanthanakun, Parkpoom Wongpoom)
Séquences Award, Special Mention ..... *One Nite in Mongkok* (Derek Yee)
Séquences Award, Special Mention, Guilty Pleasure ..... *Godzilla: Final Wars* (Ryuhei Kitamura)

2005 Public Prizes

Best Asian Film, Gold (tie) ..... *Survive Style 5+* (Gen Sekiguchi) and *The Taste of Tea* (Katsuhito Ishii)
Best Asian Film, Silver ..... *Crying Fist* (Ryoo Seung-wan)
Best Asian Film, Bronze (tie) ..... *Arahan* (Ryoo Seung-wan) and *Godzilla: Final Wars* (Ryuhei Kitamura)
Best European, North or South American Film, Gold (tie) ..... *El Lobo* (Miguel Courtois) and *Trouble* (Harry Cleven)
Best European, North or South American Film, Silver ..... *The Devil's Rejects* (Rob Zombie)
Best European, North or South American Film, Bronze ..... *Night of the Living Dorks* (Matthias Dinter)
Best Animated Film, Gold ..... *Mind Game* (Yuasa Masaaki)
Best Animated Film, Silver ..... *The Place Promised in Our Early Days* (Makoto Shinkai)
Best Animated Film, Bronze ..... *Live Freaky! Die Freaky!* (John Roecker)
Most Groundbreaking Film, Gold ..... *Survive Style 5+* (Gen Sekiguchi)
Most Groundbreaking Film, Silver ..... *Mind Game* (Yuasa Masaaki)
Most Groundbreaking Film, Bronze ..... *The Taste of Tea* (Katsuhito Ishii)
Best Short Film, Gold ..... *Kakurenbo* (Shuhei Morita)
Best Short Film, Silver ..... *Flat Life* (Jonas Geirnaert)
Best Short Film, Bronze ..... *Redrat: La Rata Retobada* (Guillermo Kloetzer)
Best Quebec DIY Short Film, Gold ..... *Alex, Vampire Slayer* (Al Kratina)
Best Quebec DIY Short Film, Silver ..... *Cogne Fou* (Donald Caron)
Best Quebec DIY Short Film, Bronze ..... *Séquestrée* (Denis-Steve Giguère)

Fantaspoa

A.K.A. International Fantastic Film Festival of Porto Alegre. The festival's first year, 2005, was noncompetitive. They say their 2006 festival was "the first competition in the history of Brazil of national genre short films." Awards are juried, unless they are Public Awards (i.e., Audience Award).

2010

Best Film, Feature ..... *The Life and Death of a Porno Gang* (dir: Mladen Djordjevic)
Best Film, Feature, Audience Award ..... *I Sell the Dead* (Glenn McQuaid)
Best Director ..... Eli Craig (*Tucker & Dale vs. Evil*)

Best Actor ..... Peter Marshall (*The Horseman*)
Best Actress ..... Olga Fedori (*Mum & Dad*)
Best Screenplay ..... Konstantin Lopushansky, Vyacheslav Rybakov (*Ugly Swans*)
Best Special FX ..... Reyes Abades (*La Herencia Valdemar*)
Best Brazilian Live-Action Short Film ..... *Mapa-Múndi* (dir: Pedro Zimmermann)
Best Brazilian Animation Short Film ..... *O Jumento Santo* (dir: Léonardo Domingues, William Paiva)
Best International Live-Action Short Film ..... *El Nunca lo Haría* (dir: Anartz Zuazua)
Best International Animation Short Film ..... *Alma* (dir: Rodrigo Blaas)
Best Brazilian Live-Action Short Film, Audience Award ..... *Animal Menor* (dir: Pedro Harres, Marcos Contreras)
Best Brazilian Animation Short Film, Audience Award ..... *Anjos no Meio da Praça* (dir: Alêxandre Camargo, Camila Carrossine)
Best International Live-Action Short Film, Audience Award..... *Cabuleros* (dir: Damian Slipoi)
Best International Animation Short Film, Audience Award..... *Le Petit Dragon* (dir: Bruno Collet)

2009

Best Film, Feature ..... *Zibahkhana*
Best Direction, Feature ..... Vadim Jean (*The Colour of Magic*)
Best Screenplay, Feature ..... Chris Gardner, Blair Rowan (*Blood on the Highway*)
Best Special Effects, Feature ..... *Tokyo Gore Police*
Best Actor in a Leading Role, Feature ..... Marc Senter (*The Lost*)
Best Actress in a Leading Role, Feature (tie) ..... Maria Inez Alonso, Veronica Mari (*Breaking Nikki*)
Best Film, Feature, Public Award ..... *The Machine Girl*
Best Animated Short Film ..... *The Separation*
Best Live-Action Short Film ..... *The Basket Case*
Best Brazilian Animated Short Film (tie) ..... *Dossiê Rê Bordosa* and *O menino que plantava invernos*
Best Brazilian Live-Action Short Film ..... *Bicho*
Best Animated Short Film, Public Award ..... *Dans la téte*
Best Live-Action Short Film, Public Award ..... *Porque hay cosas que nunca se olvidam*
Best Brazilian Animated Short Film, Public Award ..... *Dossiê Rê Bordosa*
Best Brazilian Live-Action Short Film, Public Award ..... *Bicho*

2008

Best Film, Feature ..... *Hogfather* (Vadim Jean)
Best Direction, Feature ..... Richard Schenkman (*The Man from Earth*)
Best Screenplay, Feature ..... Guillem Morales (*El habitante incierto*, A.K.A. *The Uncertain Guest*)
Best Special Effects, Feature ..... *Jack Brooks: Monster Slayer*
Best Actor in a Leading Role, Feature ..... Norman Briski (*Los chicos desaparecen*)
Best Actress in a Leading Role, Feature ..... Jimena Anganuzzi (*El propietario*)
Best Animated Film, Feature ..... *Sword of the Stranger* (Masahiro Andô)
Best Animated Short Film ..... *Viaje a Marte* (Juan Pablo Zaramella)
Best Live-Action Short Film ..... *Missing* (Matthieu Donck)
Best Brazilian Short Film ..... *Casa da luz vermelha* (Bernardo Mangaravite)
Best Animated Short Film, Public Award ..... *Viaje a Marte* (Juan Pablo Zaramella)
Best Live-Action Short Film, Public Award ..... *Missing* (Matthieu Donck)
Best Brazilian Short Film, Public Award ..... *Fraulein Gertie*, A.K.A. *Señorita Gertie* (Tomás Creus, Lavinia Chianello)

2007

Best Short Film (tie) ..... *Sete Vidas* (dir: Zé Mucinho and Marcelo Spomberg), and *Maquina* (dir: Gabe Ibanez), and *A Ninja Pays Half My Rent* (dir: Steven K. Tsuchida)

2006

Best Short Film (tie) ..... *Green Vinyl* (dir: Kleber Mendonça Filho), and *Historietas Assombradas (para Crianças Mal Criadas)* (dir: Victor-Hugo Borges)
Lifetime Achievement Award ..... Coffin Joe

Fantasporto

This is a hybrid festival. They have a large fantasy section (as "Fantasporto" implies) and they participate in the Méliès awards. But they also honor many non-genre films. The winners' lists on their website's history page is incomplete, so the below material was supplemented with information from the IMDb.

2010

INTERNATIONAL FANTASY FILM AWARDS
Best Film ..... *Heartless* (Phillip Ridley)
Jury's Special Award ..... *Deliver Us from Evil* (Ole Bornedal)
Best Direction ..... Philip Ridley (*Heartless*)
Best Actor ..... Jim Sturgess (*Heartless*)
Best Actress ..... Neve McIntosh (*Salvage*)
Best Screenplay ..... Arnaud Bordas, Yannick Dahan, Stéphanie Moissakis, Benjamin Rocher (*La horde*)
Best Special Effects or Cinematography ..... Yannick Dahan, Benjamin Rocher (*La horde*)

Best Short Film ..... *La carte* (Stefan le Lay)
Special Mention of the Jury ..... *Valhalla Rising* (Nicolas Winding Refn)
Special Mention of the Jury ..... *Embargo* (António Ferreira)

20TH DIRECTORS WEEK/MANOEL DE OLIVEIRA AWARDS
Best Film ..... *Fish Tank* (Andrea Arnold)
Jury's Special Award ..... *Ward nº 6* (Karen Shakhnazarov)
Best Director ..... Pater Sparrow (*I*)
Best Screenplay ..... Andrea Arnold (*Fish Tank*)
Best Actor ..... Zóltan Mucsi (*I*)
Best Actress ..... Elena Anaya (*Hierro*)

ORIENT EXPRESS AWARDS
Best Film ..... *Thirst*, A.K.A. *Bakjwi* (Chan-wook Park)
Special Award ..... *A Frozen Flower* (Yoo Ha)

OTHER AWARDS
Critics Award ..... *T.M.A.* (Juraj Herz)
Audience Award ..... *Solomon Kane* (Michael J. Bassett)
Homage of the Year ..... French Cinema
Career Award ..... Samuel Hadida, Colin Arthur, Luís Galvão Teles
Inspiration Award of the International Film Guide ..... *First Squad* (Yoshiharu Ashino)

2009

INTERNATIONAL FANTASY FILM AWARDS
Best Film ..... *Idiots and Angels* (Bill Plympton)
Special Award of the Jury ..... *Hansel & Gretel* (Phil-Sung Yim)
Best Direction ..... *Eden Lake* (James Watkins)
Best Actor ..... Jack O'Connell (*Eden Lake*)
Best Actress ..... Macarena Gómez (*Sexykiller*, A.K.A. *Sexykiller, morirás por ella*)
Best Screenplay ..... Bill Plympton (*Idiots and Angels*)
Best Cinematography ..... James Hawkinson (*The Unborn*)
Best Fantasy Short ..... *Next Floor* (Denis Villeneuve)
Special Mention of the Jury ..... *Astropia* (Gunnar Gudmundsson)

19TH DIRECTORS WEEK/MANOEL DE OLIVEIRA AWARDS
Best Film ..... *Moscow, Belgium* (Christhope van Rompaey)
Special Prize of the Jury ..... *Palermo Shooting* (Wim Wenders)
Best Director ..... Bent Hamer (*O'Horten*)
Best Actor ..... Brian Cox (*The Escapist*)
Best Actress ..... Mamatha Bhukya (*Vanaja*)
Best Screenplay ..... Sergey Rokotov, Yevgeniy Nikishow (*The Vanished Empire*)

ORIENT EXPRESS AWARDS
Best Film ..... *Hansel & Gretel* (Phil-Sung Yim)
Special Jury Award ..... *The Chaser* (Hong-Jin Na)

OTHER AWARDS
Méliès D'Argent, Feature ..... *Absurdistan* (Veit Helmer)
Méliès D'Argent, Short Film ..... *Mamá* (Andres Muschiette)
Homage of the Year ..... Galician Cinema
Critics Award ..... *Delta* (Kornél Mundruczó)
Audience Award ..... *The Wrestler* (Darren Aronofsky)
Career Award ..... José Fonseca e Costa, Wim Wenders, Paul Schrader

2008

INTERNATIONAL FANTASY FILM AWARDS
Best Film ..... *REC* (Jaume Balagueró, Paco Plaza)
Special Prize of the Jury ..... *How to Get Rid of Others* (Anders Ronnow Klarlund)
Best Direction ..... Juan Antonio Bayona (*El Orfanato*)
Best Actor ..... Marc Borkowski (*The Ungodly*)
Best Actress ..... Belén Rueda (*El Orfanato*)
Best Screenplay ..... *La habitación de Fermat*, A.K.A. *Fermat's Room* (Luis Piedrahita, Rodrigo Sopeña)
Best Cinematography ..... Gábor Medvigy (*Dolina*)
Best Fantasy Short ..... *Rojo Red* (Juan Manuel Betancourt)
Special Mention of the Jury ..... *I'm a Cyborg, But That's OK* (Chan-wook Park)

18TH DIRECTORS WEEK AWARDS
Best Film Award ..... *Opium, Diary of a Madwoman*, A.K.A. *Ópium: Egy elmebeteg nö naplója* (János Szász)
Special Prize of the Jury ..... *The Lovebirds* (Bruno de Almeida)
Best Director ..... Roy Andersson (*You, The Living*)
Best Actor ..... Sasson Gabai (*The Band's Visit*, A.K.A. *Bikur Ha-Tizmoret*)
Best Actress ..... Kirsti Stubø (*Opium, Diary of a Madwoman*, A.K.A. *Ópium: Egy elmebeteg nö naplója*)
Best Screenplay ..... Steve Buscemi, Theodor Holman, David Schechter (*Interview*)

ORIENT EXPRESS AWARDS
Best Film ..... *Triangle* (Ringo Lam, Johnnie To, Tsui Hark)
Special Jury Award ..... *Breath* (Kim Ki Duk)

OTHER AWARDS
Méliès D'Argent, Feature ..... *La habitación de Fermat*, A.K.A. *Fermat's Room* (Luis Piedrahita, Rodrigo Sopeña)

Méliès D'Argent, Short Film ..... *The Ark*, A.K.A. *Arka* (Grzegorz Jonkajtys)
Homage of the Year ..... Danish Cinema
Critics Award ..... *The Band's Visit*, A.K.A. *Bikur Ha-Tizmoret* (Eran Kolirin)
Audience Award ..... *REC* (Jaume Balagueró, Paco Plaza)
Career Award ..... Max Von Sydow, Fernando Lopes

2007

INTERNATIONAL FANTASY FILM AWARDS
Best Film ..... *El Laberinto del Fauno*, A.K.A. *Pan's Labyrinth* (Guillermo del Toro)
Special Prize of the Jury ..... *Historias del Desencanto* (Alejandro Valle, Felipe Gómez)
Best Direction ..... Bong Joon-Ho (*The Host*)
Best Actor ..... Sergi Lopez (*El Laberinto del Fauno*, A.K.A. *Pan's Labyrinth*)
Best Actress ..... Ariadna Gil (*Ausentes*)
Best Screenplay ..... James Moran (*Severance*)
Best Special Effects ..... *Re-Cycle* (Danny & Oxide Pang)
Best Fantasy Short ..... *The Listening Dead* (Phil Mucci)
Special Mention of the Jury ..... *The Bothersome Man* (Jens Lien)

17TH DIRECTORS WEEK AWARDS
Best Film ..... *Un Franco, 14 Pesetas*, A.K.A. *Crossing Borders* (Carlos Iglésias)
Special Prize of the Jury ..... *Suicídio Encomendado* (Artur Serra Araújo)
Best Director ..... *Un Franco, 14 Pesetas*, A.K.A. *Crossing Borders* (Carlos Iglésias)
Best Actor ..... Jung-Woo Ha (*Time*)
Best Actress ..... Isabella Leong (*Isabella*)
Best Screenplay ..... Kim Fupz Aakeson (*Pure Hearts*)

ORIENT EXPRESS AWARDS
Best Film ..... *Isabella* (Ho Cheung Pang)
Special Jury Award ..... *The Promise* (Chen Kaigé)

OTHER AWARDS
Méliès D'Argent, Feature ..... *Renaissance* (Christian Volckman)
Méliès D'Argent, Short Film ..... *Finkle's Odyssey* (Barney Clay)
Homage of the Year ..... Greek Cinema
Critics Award ..... *Paprika* (Satoshi Kon)
Audience Award ..... *Taxidermia* (György Pálfi)
Career Award ..... Henry Thomas, Rosanna Arquette, Ruy de Carvalho

2006

INTERNATIONAL FANTASY FILM AWARDS
Best Film ..... *Frostbitten* (Anders Banke)
Best Actor ..... Jaume García Arija (*Zulo*)
Best Actress ..... Orsolya Tóth (*Johanna*)
Best Director ..... Robin Aubert (*Saint Martyrs of the Damned*)
Best Screenplay ..... *Animal* (Roselyne Bosch)
Best Cinematography ..... *Die blaue Grenze* (Manuel Mack)
Best Short ..... *Home Delivery*, A.K.A. *Servicio a domicilio* (Elio Quiroga)
Special Jury Prize ..... *Johanna* (Kornél Mundruczó)
Special Mention ..... *Shadow Man* (David Benullo)

16TH DIRECTORS WEEK AWARDS
Best Film ..... *Adam's Apples* (Anders Thomas Jensen)
Best Actor ..... Ulrich Thomsen (*Adam's Apples*)
Best Actress ..... Victoria Abril (*Swindled*)
Best Director ..... Pieter Kuijpers (*Off Screen*)
Best Screenplay ..... *Adam's Apples* (Anders Thomas Jensen)
Special Jury Prize ..... *Be with Me* (Eric Khoo)

ORIENT EXPRESS AWARDS
Best Film ..... *Lady Vengeance* (Chan-wook Park)
Special Jury Award ..... *Hwal* (Ki-duk Kim)

OTHER AWARDS
Méliès D'Argent, Feature ..... *Animal* (Roselyne Bosch)
Méliès D'Argent, Short Film ..... *The Legend of the Scarecrow* (Marco Besas)
Critics Award ..... *Die blaue Grenze* (Till Franzen)
Audience Award ..... *The Other Half* (Richard Nockles, Marlowe Fawcett)
Career Award ..... Christiane Torloni, Bill Plympton, Manoel de Oliveira

2005

INTERNATIONAL FANTASY FILM AWARDS
Best Film ..... *Nothing* (Vincenzo Natali)
Special Prize of the Jury ..... *Bubba Ho-Tep* (Don Coscarelli)
Best Direction ..... Robin Campillo (*Les revenants*, A.K.A. *They Came Back*)
Best Actor ..... Bruce Campbell (*Bubba Ho-Tep*)
Best Actress ..... Karen Black (*Firecracker*)
Best Screenplay ..... *Saw* (James Wan)
Best Visual Effects ..... *Natural City* (Byung-chun Min)
Best Fantasy Short ..... *La dernière minute* (Nicolas Salis)

15TH DIRECTORS WEEK AWARDS
Best Film ..... *Oldboy* (Chan Wook Park)
Special Prize of the Jury ..... *Sideways* (Alexander Payne)
Best Director ..... Naoto Kamazawa ("Birthday" episode in *Tokyo Noir*)
Best Actor ..... Paul Giamatti (*Sideways*)

Best Actress ..... Kate Elliot (*Fracture*)
Best Screenplay ..... *Oldboy* (Hwang Jo-yun, Lim Jun-hyeong, Park Chan-wook)

ORIENT EXPRESS AWARDS

Best Film ..... *My Mother the Mermaid* (Heung-shik Park)
Special Award of the Jury ..... *Vital* (Shinya Tsukamoto)

OTHER AWARDS

Méliès D'Argent, Feature ..... *Les revenants* (Robin Campillo)
Méliès D'Argent, Short Film ..... *La dernière minute* (Nicolas Salis)
TMN Award for Best Portuguese Short ..... *Abraço do Vento* (José Miguel Ribeiro)
Homage of the Year ..... German Cinema
Critics Award ..... *Vinzent* (Ayassi)
Audience Award ..... *Constantine* (Francis Lawrence)
Career Award ..... Karen Black, Guillermo del Toro, Doug Bradley, Tino Navarro, Claudio Simonetti, Brian Yuzna, Vincenzo Natali, John Hurt, Dario Argento, GNR (rock band)

2004

INTERNATIONAL FANTASY FILM AWARDS

Best Film ..... *A Tale of Two Sisters* (Kim Ji-woon)
Special Award of the Jury ..... *Killing Words*, A.K.A. *Palabras encadenadas* (Laura Mañá)
Special Mention ..... *La fin de notre amour* (Hélène Cattet, Bruno Forzani)
Best Director ..... Kim Ji-woon (*A Tale of Two Sisters*)
Best Actor ..... Dario Grandinetti (*Killing Words*, A.K.A. *Palabras encadenadas*)
Best Actress ..... Lim Soo-jeong (*A Tale of Two Sisters*)
Best Screenplay (tie) ..... Fernando de Felipe, Jordi Galceran, Laura Mañá (*Killing Words*, A.K.A. *Palabras encadenadas*) and Hubert Selby, Jr., Nicolas Winding Refn (*Fear X*)
Best Visual Effects ..... Michael O'Brien, Wayne Toth (*House of the 1000 Corpses*)
Best Short ..... *I'll See You in My Dreams* (Miguel Ángel Vivas)

14TH DIRECTORS WEEK AWARDS

Best Film ..... *The Green Butchers* (Anders Thomas Jensen)
Special Award of the Jury ..... *El otro lado de la cama*, A.K.A. *The Other Side of the Bed* (Emilio Martínez Lázaro)
Best Director ..... Anders Thomas Jensen (*The Green Butchers*)
Best Actor ..... Mads Mikkelsen (*The Green Butchers*)
Best Actress ..... Rachael Blake (*Perfect Strangers*)
Best Screenplay ..... David Serrano (*El otro lado de la cama*, A.K.A. *The Other Side of the Bed*)

ORIENT EXPRESS AWARDS

Best Film ..... *Acacia* (Park Ki-hyeong)
Special Award of the Jury ..... *A Tale of Two Sisters* (Kim Ji-woon)

OTHER AWARDS

Méliès D'Argent, Feature ..... *Killing Words*, A.K.A. *Palabras encadenadas* (Laura Mañá)
Méliès D'Argent, Short Film ..... *I'll See You in My Dreams* (Miguel Ángel Vivas)
Homage of the Year ..... Julio Fernandez
Critics Award ..... *The Last Horror Movie* (Julian Richards)
Audience Award ..... *See Grace Fly* (Pete McCormack)

2003

INTERNATIONAL FANTASY FILM AWARDS

Best Film ..... *Intacto* (Juan Carlos Fresnadillo)
Special Prize of the Jury (tie) ..... *Cypher* (Vincenzo Natali) and *A Snake of June* (Shinya Tsukamoto)
Best Direction ..... Danny Boyle (*28 Days Later*)
Special Mention ..... Robert Schwentke (*Tattoo*)
Best Actor ..... Jeremy Northam (*Cypher*)
Best Actress ..... Asuka Kurosawa (*A Snake of June*)
Best Screenplay ..... Juan Carlos Fresnadillo, Andrés Koppel (*Intacto*)
Best Visual Effects ..... *Cypher* (Bret Culp, Bob Monroe)
Best Fantasy Short ..... *Atraksion* (Raoul Servais)

13TH DIRECTORS WEEK AWARDS

Best Film ..... *L.I.E.* (Michael Cuesta)
Special Prize of the Jury ..... *The Last Minute* (Stephen Norrington)
Best Director ..... Michael Cuesta (*L.I.E.*)
Best Actor ..... Paul Franklin Dano (*L.I.E.*)
Best Actress ..... Maggie Gyllenhaal (*Secretary*)
Best Screenplay ..... Matt Manfredi (*Bug*)

OTHER AWARDS

Méliès D'Argent, Feature ..... *28 Days Later* (Danny Boyle)
Méliès D'Argent, Short Film ..... *Atraksion* (Raoul Servais)
Homage of the Year ..... the New Austrian Cinema
Critics Awards (tie) ..... *Cube 2: Hypercube* (Andrzej Sekula) and *Nos miran*, A.K.A. *They're Watching Us* (Norberto López Amado)
Audience Award ..... *Toy Love* (Harry Sinclair)

2002

INTERNATIONAL FANTASY FILM AWARDS

Best Film ..... *Fausto 5.0* (Isidro Ortiz, Álex Ollé, Carles Padrissa)
Best Actor (tie) ..... Eduard Fernández, Miguel Ángel Solá (*Fausto 5.0*)
Best Actress ..... Jin-young Jang (*Sorum*)
Best Director ..... Jong-chan Yun (*Sorum*)

Best Screenplay ..... *Das Experiment* (Mario Giordano, Christoph Darnstädt, Don Bohlinger)
Best Special Effects ..... *Vidocq* (Pascal Giroux)
Best Short Film ..... *7337* (Sergio G. Sánchez)
Special Jury Award ..... *Sorum* (Jong-chan Yun)

12TH DIRECTORS WEEK AWARDS
Best Film ..... *Bloody Sunday* (Paul Greengrass)
Best Actor ..... Tim Pigott-Smith (*Bloody Sunday*)
Best Actress ..... Sarah Peirse (*Rain*)
Best Director ..... Christoph Stark (*Julietta*)
Best Screenplay ..... *Nine Queens* (Fabián Bielinsky)
Special Jury Award ..... *Dog Days* (Ulrich Seidl)

OTHER AWARDS
Méliès D'Argent, Feature ..... *Vidocq* (Pitof)
Méliès D'Argent, Short Film ..... *Venus Velvet* (Jorge Cramez)
Onda Curta Award (tie) ..... *The Cat with Hands* (Robert Morgan) and *À donf* (Lolo Zazar)
Critics Award (tie) ..... *The Living Forest*, A.K.A. *El bosque animado* (Ángel de la Cruz, Manuel Gómez) and *Suzhou River*, A.K.A. *Suzhou he* (Ye Lou)
Audience Award ..... *Bloody Sunday* (Paul Greengrass)
Career Award ..... Carlos Saura, Oswaldo Caldeira, Julien Temple, Alex Cox

2001

INTERNATIONAL FANTASY FILM AWARDS
Best Film ..... *Amores Perros* (Alejandro González Iñárritu)
Best Actor ..... Willem Dafoe (*Shadow of the Vampire*)
Best Actress ..... Jung Suh (*The Isle*)
Best Director (tie) ..... Harry Cleven (*Why Get Married the Day the World Ends?*) and Alejandro González Iñárritu (*Amores Perros*)
Best Screenplay ..... *Amores Perros* (Guillermo Arriaga)
Best Special Effects ..... *Heart of the Warrior*
Best Short Film (tie) ..... *The Rain* (David Beatty) and *L'homme, est-il bon?* (Roman Barthonieu)
Special Jury Award ..... *The Isle* (Ki-duk Kim)
Special Mention ..... *Audition* (Takashi Miike)

11TH DIRECTORS WEEK AWARDS
Best Film ..... *Purely Belter* (Mark Herman)
Best Director ..... Julian Simpson (*The Criminal*)
Best Screenplay ..... *Better Housekeeping* (Frank Novak)
Special Jury Award ..... *Scoutman* (Masato Ishioka)
Special Mention ..... *Magik and Rose* (Vanessa Alexander)

OTHER AWARDS
Critics Award ..... *The Price of Milk* (Harry Sinclair)
Audience Award ..... *Quills* (Philip Kaufman)
Career Award ..... Vasilis Mazomenos, Julian Grant

2000

INTERNATIONAL FANTASY FILM AWARDS
Best Film ..... *Siam Sunset* (John Polson)
Best Actor (tie) ..... Tom Fisher (*The Nine Lives of Tomas Katz*) and Konstantin Prochorowski (*Holgi*)
Best Actress ..... Danielle Cormack (*Siam Sunset*)
Best Director (tie) ..... Jaume Balagueró (*The Nameless*, A.K.A. *Los sin nombre*) and Ben Hopkins (*The Nine Lives of Tomas Katz*)
Best Special Effects ..... *Animal Farm* (Sue Rowe, Jonathan Privett, Jim Henson's Creature Shop)
Best Short Film ..... *The Periwig-Maker* (Steffen Schäffler)
Special Jury Award ..... *Tuvalu* (Veit Helmer)

10TH DIRECTORS WEEK AWARDS
Best Film ..... *East Is East* (Damien O'Donnell)
Best Director (tie) ..... Les Bernstien (*Night Train*) Erik Poppe (*Schpaaa*)
Best Screenplay ..... *Sugar Town* (Allison Anders, Kurt Voss)
Special Jury Award ..... *Schpaaa* (Erik Poppe)
Special Mention ..... *Two Hands* (Gregor Jordan)

OTHER AWARDS
Méliès D'Argent, Feature ..... *La mujer más fea del mundo*, A.K.A. *The Ugliest Woman in the World* (Miguel Bardem)
Onda Curta Award ..... *The Periwig-Maker* (Steffen Schäffler)
Onda Curta Award ..... *The Tale of the Rat That Wrote* (Billy O'Brien)
Onda Curta Award ..... *A Noite* (Regina Pessoa)
Onda Curta Award ..... *A Suspeita* (José Miguel Ribeiro)
Critics Award ..... *The Nameless*, A.K.A. *Los sin nombre* (Jaume Balagueró)
Audience Jury Award ..... *Tuvalu* (Veit Helmer)
AMC Audience Award ..... *Exhuming Mr. Rice* (Nicholas Kendall)
Career Award ..... José Mojica Marins, Danny Elfman

1999

INTERNATIONAL FANTASY FILM AWARDS
Best Film ..... *Cube* (Vincenzo Natali)
Best Actor (tie) ..... Kevin McKidd, Gary McCormack (*The Acid House*)
Best Actress ..... Sofie Gråbøl (*Sekten*)
Best Director ..... Lars von Trier (*The Kingdom II*)
Best Screenplay ..... *The Kingdom II* (Lars von Trier, Morten Arnfred)
Best Special Effects ..... *Cube* (Bob Munroe, John Mariella)
Best Short Film ..... *Trigon* (Niklas Roy)
Special Jury Award (tie) ..... *To hrima—Mia mythologia tou Skotous* (Vasilis Mazomenos) and *Jin Roh: The Wolf Brigade* (Hiroyuki Okiura)

Special Mention ..... actress Dalila Carmo (*O Anjo da Guarda*)

9TH DIRECTORS WEEK AWARDS
Best Film ..... *Happiness* (Todd Solondz)
Best Director ..... Don McKellar (*Last Night*)
Best Screenplay ..... *Divorcing Jack* (Colin Bateman)
Best Cinematography ..... *Love Is the Devil: Study for a Portrait of Francis Bacon* (John Mathieson)
Special Jury Award ..... *When It Thunders* (Manuel Mozos)
Special Mention ..... *High Art* (Lisa Cholodenko)

OTHER AWARDS
Fantasia Section Award, Best Film, Live Action ..... *Choyonghan kajok* (Ji-woon Kim)
Fantasia Section Award, Best Film, Animation ..... *Jin Roh: The Wolf Brigade* (Hiroyuki Okiura)
Méliès D'Argent, Feature ..... *The Acid House* (Paul McGuigan)
Critics Award ..... *Divorcing Jack* (David Caffrey)
Audience Jury Award ..... *Cube* (Vincenzo Natali)
AMC Audience Award ..... *The Acid House* (Paul McGuigan)
Career Award ..... Júlio Bressane, Bill Plympton

1998

INTERNATIONAL FANTASY FILM AWARDS
Best Film ..... *Retroactive* (Louis Morneau)
Best Actor ..... Nancho Novo (*Dame algo*)
Best Actress ..... Rebecca Hobbs (*The Ugly*)
Best Director ..... Héctor Carré (*Dame algo*)
Best Screenplay ..... *The Fifth Province* (Nina Fitzpatrick, Frank Stapleton)
Best Special Effects ..... *Photographing Fairies* (Ron Mueck, John Markwell)
Best Short Film ..... *Flying Saucer Rock'n'Roll* (Enda Hughes)
Special Jury Award (tie) ..... *Funny Games* (Michael Haneke) *Fudoh: The New Generation* (Takashi Miike)
Special Mention ..... *The Oath* (Tjebbo Penning)
Special Mention ..... *The Ugly* (Scott Reynolds)

8TH DIRECTORS WEEK AWARDS
Best Film ..... *Character* (Mike van Diem)
Best Director ..... Giuseppe M. Gaudino (*Round the Moons Between Earth and Sea*)
Best Screenplay ..... *Kings for a Day* (François Velle, Mariusz Pujszo)
Best Cinematography ..... *Budbringeren* (Kjell Vassdal)
Special Jury Award ..... *Dribbling Fate* (Fernando Vendrell)

OTHER AWARDS
Fantasia Section Award, Best Film, Live Action ..... *Fudoh: The New Generation* (Takashi Miike)
Fantasia Section Award, Best Film, Animation ..... *Perfect Blue* (Satoshi Kon)

Méliès D'Argent, Feature ..... *Photographing Fairies* (Nick Willing)
Méliès D'Argent, Special Mention ..... *The Fifth Province* (Frank Stapleton, George Sluizer)
RTP Jury Award ..... *Taxi de nuit* (Marco Castilla)
RTP Jury Award, Special Mention ..... *The Oath* (Tjebbo Penning)
Critics Award ..... *Funny Games* (Michael Haneke)
Audience Jury Award ..... *Topless Women Talk About Their Lives* (Harry Sinclair)
AMC Audience Award ..... *Ulee's Gold* (Victor Nunez)
Special Award ..... Ivan Cardoso
Career Award ..... Paul Naschy

1997

INTERNATIONAL FANTASY FILM AWARDS
Best Film ..... *Bound* (Andy Wachowski, Lana Wachowski)
Best Actor ..... Juan Inciarte (*Sólo se muere dos veces*)
Best Actress ..... Jennifer Tilly (*Bound*)
Best Director ..... Robert Tinnell (*Frankenstein and Me*)
Best Screenplay ..... *Darklands* (Julian Richards)
Best Special Effects ..... *La lengua asesina* (Image Animation)
Best Short Film ..... *L'enchanteur* (Richard G. Wright)
Special Jury Award (tie) ..... *Darklands* (Julian Richards) and *Sweet Angel Mine* (Curtis Radclyffe)
Special Mention ..... *Ghost in the Shell* (Mamoru Oshii)

7TH DIRECTORS WEEK AWARDS
Best Film ..... *Unhook the Stars* (Nick Cassavetes)
Best Director ..... Scott Hicks (*Shine*)
Best Screenplay ..... *The Daytrippers* (Greg Mottola)
Best Cinematography ..... *The Empty Mirror* (Frederick Elmes)

OTHER AWARDS
Méliès D'Argent, Feature ..... *Darklands* (Julian Richards)
Méliès D'Argent, Special Mention ..... *Mortinho por Chegar a Casa* (Carlos da Silva, George Sluizer)
Critics Award ..... *Darklands* (Julian Richards)
Audience Jury Award ..... *Forgotten Silver* (Peter Jackson)
Career Award ..... Raoul Servais

1996

INTERNATIONAL FANTASY FILM AWARDS
Best Film ..... *Se7en* (David Fincher)
Best Actor ..... Rupert Everett (*Cemetery Man*)
Best Actress ..... Helena Bonham Carter (*Margaret's Museum*)
Best Director (tie) ..... Philip Ridley (*The Passion*

of *Darkly Noon*) and Kazuyoshi Okuyama, Rintaro Mayuzumi (*Rampo*)
Best Screenplay ..... *Se7en* (Andrew Kevin Walker)
Best Special Effects ..... *Taxandria*
Best Short Film (tie) ..... *The Wild Heels*, A.K.A. *Les escarpins sauvages* (Didier Poiraud, Thierry Poiraud) and *The Bitch Is Back* (Tjebbo Penning)
Special Jury Award (tie) ..... *Taxandria* (Raoul Servais) and *Institute Benjamenta, or This Dream That One Calls Human Life* (Stephen Quay, Timothy Quay)

6TH DIRECTORS WEEK AWARDS
Best Film (tie) ..... *To mand i en sofa* (Amir Rezazadeh) and *Madagascar Skin* (Chris Newby)

OTHER AWARDS
Méliès D'Argent, Feature ..... *Taxandria* (Raoul Servais)
Critics Award ..... *Denise Calls Up* (Hal Salwen)
Audience Jury Award ..... *Denise Calls Up* (Hal Salwen)
Career Award ..... André Delvaux

1995

INTERNATIONAL FANTASY FILM AWARDS
Best Film ..... *Shallow Grave* (Danny Boyle)
Best Actor ..... Karra Elejalde (*La madre muerta*)
Best Actress ..... Rena Owen (*Once Were Warriors*)
Best Director ..... Juanma Bajo Ulloa (*La madre muerta*)
Best Screenplay ..... *New Nightmare* (Wes Craven)
Best Special Effects ..... *Faust* (Jan Svankmajer)
Best Short Film ..... *Bout d'essai* (Frédéric Darie)
Special Jury Award ..... *Clean, Shaven* (Lodge Kerrigan)

5TH DIRECTORS WEEK AWARDS
Best Film ..... *Clean, Shaven* (Lodge Kerrigan)
Special Mention ..... *Loaded* (Anna Campion)

OTHER AWARDS
Critics Award ..... *In the Mouth of Madness* (John Carpenter)
Critics Award, Special Mention ..... *Once Were Warriors* (Lee Tamahori)
Audience Jury Award ..... *La madre muerta* (Juanma Bajo Ulloa)
Career Award ..... Ben Kingsley

1994

INTERNATIONAL FANTASY FILM AWARDS
Best Film ..... *Cronos* (Guillermo del Toro)
Best Actor ..... Federico Luppi (*Cronos*)
Best Actress ..... Sarah Smuts-Kennedy (*Jack Be Nimble*)
Best Director ..... Dave Borthwick (*The Secret Adventures of Tom Thumb*)
Best Screenplay ..... *Jack Be Nimble* (Garth Maxwell)
Best Special Effects ..... *Necronomicon: Book of Dead*
Best Short Film ..... *The Temptation of Sainthood* (Simon Pummell)
Special Jury Award ..... *The Forbidden Quest* (Peter Delpeut)

4TH DIRECTORS WEEK AWARDS
Best Film ..... *Bodies, Rest & Motion* (Michael Steinberg)
Special Mention ..... *The Elementary School* (Jan Sverák)

OTHER AWARDS
Critics Award ..... *Yiu sau dou si* (Tai Kit Mak)
Critics Award, Special Mention ..... *The Secret Adventures of Tom Thumb* (Dave Borthwick)
Audience Jury Award ..... *Cronos* (Guillermo del Toro)

1993

INTERNATIONAL FANTASY FILM AWARDS
Best Film ..... *Dead Alive* (Peter Jackson)
Best Actor ..... Harvey Keitel (*Bad Lieutenant*)
Best Actress ..... Evangelina Sosa (*Ángel de fuego*)
Best Director ..... Jean-Claude Lauzon (*Léolo*)
Best Screenplay ..... *One False Move* (Billy Bob Thornton, Tom Epperson)
Best Special Effects ..... *Dead Alive* (Steve Ingram)
Best Short Film ..... *Cat's Cradle* (Liz Hughes)
Special Jury Award ..... *Ángel de fuego* (Dana Rotberg)

3RD DIRECTORS WEEK AWARDS
Best Film ..... *Swoon* (Tom Kalin)

OTHER AWARDS
Critics Award ..... *Army of Darkness* (Sam Raimi)
Audience Jury Award ..... *Léolo* (Jean-Claude Lauzon)

1992

INTERNATIONAL FANTASY FILM AWARDS
Best Film ..... *Toto the Hero* (Jaco Van Dormael)
Best Actor ..... Jeff Daniels (*Timescape*)
Best Actress ..... Juliet Stevenson (*Truly Madly Deeply*)
Best Director ..... Lars von Trier (*Europa*)
Best Screenplay ..... *Toto the Hero* (Jaco Van Dormael)
Best Special Effects ..... *Sien nui yau wan II yan gaan do*
Best Short Film ..... *The Midas Touch* (Enric Folch)
Special Jury Award ..... *Tetsuo II: Body Hammer* (Shinya Tsukamoto)

2ND DIRECTORS WEEK AWARDS
Best Film ..... *Trys dienos* (Sharunas Bartas)

OTHER AWARDS
Critics Award ..... *Poison* (Todd Haynes)
Audience Jury Award ..... *Delicatessen* (Jean-Pierre Jeunet, Marc Caro)

1991

INTERNATIONAL FANTASY FILM AWARDS
Best Film ..... *Henry: Portrait of a Serial Killer* (John McNaughton)
Best Actor ..... Michael Rooker (*Henry: Portrait of a Serial Killer*)
Best Actress (tie) ..... Tracy Arnold (*Henry: Portrait of a Serial Killer*) and Billie Whitelaw (*The Krays*)
Best Director ..... Richard Stanley (*Hardware*)
Best Screenplay ..... *Henry: Portrait of a Serial Killer* (Richard Fire, John McNaughton)
Best Special Effects ..... *Es ist nicht leicht ein Gott zu sein* (Sergei Brzhestovsky)
Best Short Film ..... *Á bas l'éternité* (Philippe Rony)
Special Jury Award ..... *Chrome Hearts* (Dan Hoskins)

1ST DIRECTORS WEEK AWARDS
Best Film ..... *Rosencrantz & Guildenstern Are Dead* (Tom Stoppard)
* Other Awards
Critics Award ..... *Nightbreed* (Clive Barker)
Audience Jury Award ..... *Es ist nicht leicht ein Gott zu sein* (Peter Fleischmann)

1990

Best Film ..... *Black Rainbow* (Mike Hodges)
Best Actor ..... Bernard-Pierre Donnadieu (*The Vanishing*)
Best Actress ..... Rosanna Arquette (*Black Rainbow*)
Best Director ..... George Sluizer (*The Vanishing*)
Best Screenplay ..... *La luna negra* (Imanol Uribe)
Best Cinematography ..... *Ghost Town* (Mac Ahlberg)
Best Short Film ..... *Kitchen Sink* (Alison Maclean)
Special Jury Award ..... *La banyera* (Jesús Garay)
Critics Award ..... *A Nightmare on Elm Street 5: The Dream Child* (Stephen Hopkins)
Critics Award, Special Mention ..... *Étoile* (Peter Del Monte)
Critics Award, Special Mention ..... *Troma's War* (Michael Herz, Lloyd Kaufman)
Audience Jury Award ..... *La luna negra* (Imanol Uribe)

1989

Best Film ..... *Monkey Shines* (George A. Romero)
Best Actor ..... Jeremy Irons (*Dead Ringers*)
Best Actress ..... Charlotte Burke (*Paperhouse*)
Best Director ..... José Luis Cuerda (*El bosque animado*)

Best Cinematography ..... *The Navigator: A Mediaeval Odyssey* (Geoffrey Simpson)
Best Short Film ..... *Ei* (Danniel Danniel)
Special Jury Award ..... *Paperhouse* (Bernard Rose)
Critics Award ..... *Monkey Shines* (George A. Romero)
Audience Jury Award ..... *The Navigator: A Mediaeval Odyssey* (Vincent Ward)

1988

Best Film ..... *De wisselwachter* (Jos Stelling)
Best Actor ..... Jim van der Woude (*De wisselwachter*)
Best Actress ..... Charlotte Rampling (*Mascara*)
Best Director ..... Jack Sholder (*The Hidden*)
Best Screenplay ..... *Mannequin* (Michael Gottlieb)
Best Special Effects ..... *Masters of the Universe*
Best Short Film ..... *Bartakiáda* (Oldrich Haberle)
Special Jury Award ..... *Kin-Dza-Dza* (Georgi Daneliya)
Critics Award ..... *Hellraiser* (Clive Barker)
Critics Award, Special Mention ..... *A Nightmare on Elm Street 3: Dream Warriors* (Chuck Russell)
Audience Jury Award ..... *De wisselwachter* (Jos Stelling)
Special Award ..... Abi Feijó

1987

Best Film ..... *Defense of the Realm* (David Drury)
Best Actor ..... Gabriel Byrne (*Gothic* and *Defense of the Realm*)
Best Actress ..... Julieta Serrano (*Matador*)
Best Director ..... Pedro Almodóvar (*Matador*)
Best Screenplay ..... *Defense of the Realm* (David Drury)
Best Special Effects ..... *Gothic*
Best Short Film ..... *Street of Crocodiles* (Stephen Quay, Timothy Quay)
Critics Award ..... *Defense of the Realm* (David Drury)
Audience Jury Award ..... *Cujo* (Lewis Teague)

1986

Best Film ..... *Fuego eterno* (José Ángel Rebolledo)
Best Actor ..... Ian Holm (*Dreamchild*)
Best Actress ..... Domiziana Giordano (*Zina*)
Best Director ..... Lars von Trier (*The Element of Crime*)
Best Screenplay ..... *Zina* (Ken McMullen, Terry James)
Best Cinematography ..... *Fuego eterno* (Javier Aguirresarobe)
Best Short Film ..... *Na dnie szafy* (Jerzy Kopczynski)
Special Jury Award (tie) ..... *Karnabal* (Carles Mira) and *Matador* (Pedro Almodóvar)
Critics Award ..... *Dreamchild* (Gavin Millar)

Critics Award, Special Mention ..... *Zina* (Ken McMullen)
Critics Award, Special Mention ..... *Fright Night* (Tom Holland)
Audience Jury Award ..... *Blood Simple* (Joel Coen)
Audience Jury Award, Special Mention ..... *Zina* (Ken McMullen)
Audience Jury Award, Special Mention ..... *The Musician and Death* (Lubomir Benes)

1985

Best Film ..... *The Company of Wolves* (Neil Jordan)
Best Actor (tie) ..... John Hurt (*Nineteen Eighty-Four*) and Eddy Mitchell (*Frankenstein 90*)
Best Actress ..... Adriana Herrán (*Carne de tu carne*)
Best Director ..... Carl Schenkel (*Abwärts*)
Best Screenplay ..... *Frankenstein 90* (Paul Gégauff, Alain Jessua)
Best Special Effects ..... *The Company of Wolves*
Best Short Film (tie) ..... *Necrofilia* (Vítor Silva) and *Après rasage* (Hugues Desmichelle, J.P. Huguet, F. Robbes)
Special Jury Award ..... *Dicht hinter der Tür* (Mansur Mahdavi)
Critics Award ..... *The Company of Wolves* (Neil Jordan)
Critics Award, Special Mention ..... *Dicht hinter der Tür* (Mansur Mahdavi)
Critics Award, Special Mention ..... *Kyvadlo, jáma a nadeje* (Jan Svankmajer)
Audience Jury Award ..... *The Company of Wolves* (Neil Jordan)
Audience Jury Award, Special Mention ..... *Abwärts* (Carl Schenkel)

1984

Best Film ..... *Le Dernier Combat*, A.K.A. *The Last Battle* (Luc Besson)
Best Actor (four-way tie) ..... Vincent Price, Peter Cushing, Christopher Lee, John Carradine (*House of the Long Shadows*)
Best Actress ..... Anny Duperey (*Demon Is on the Island*)
Best Director ..... Luc Besson (*Le Dernier Combat*, A.K.A. *The Last Battle*)
Best Screenplay (tie) ..... *The Mysterious Castle in the Carpathians*, A.K.A. *Tajemství hradu v Karpatech* (Oldrich Lipsk, Jirí Brdecka) and *Gosti iz galaksije* (Dusan Vukotic, Milos Macourek)
Best Special Effects ..... *Demon Is on the Island*
Best Short Film ..... *Au nom du fil* (Luc Noorbergen)
Special Jury Award ..... *The Outcasts* (Robert Wynne-Simmons)
Special Jury Award, Special Mention ..... *Processo Andrómeda* (Vítor Silva)
Critics Award ..... *The Outcasts* (Robert Wynne-Simmons)
Critics Award, Special Mention ..... *Kamikaze 89* (Wolf Gremm)

Critics Award, Special Mention ..... *Czule miejsca* (Piotr Andrejew)
Audience Jury Award ..... *Elle voit des nains partout!* (Jean-Claude Sussfeld)
Audience Jury Award, Special Mention ..... *Le Dernier Combat*, A.K.A. *The Last Battle* (Luc Besson)
Audience Jury Award, Special Mention ..... *Inferiority Complex* (Milos Macourek, Adolf Born, Jaroslav Doubrava)

1983

Best Film ..... *Scanners* (David Cronenberg)
Best Actor ..... Fabijan Sovagovic (*Ritam zlocina*)
Best Actress ..... Isabelle Adjani (*Possession*)
Best Director ..... Bigas Luna (*Caniche*)
Best Screenplay ..... *Ritam zlocina* (Pavao Pavlicic)
Best Special Effects (tie) ..... *Xtro* and *The Fridays of Eternity*
Best Short Film ..... *Mrlja na savjesti* (Dusan Vukotic)
Critics Award ..... *Caniche* (Bigas Luna)
Critics Award, Special Mention ..... *Chronopolis* (Piotr Kamler)
Audience Jury Award ..... *Britannia Hospital* (Lindsay Anderson)
Audience Jury Award, Special Mention ..... *Possession* (Andrzej Zulawski)
Audience Jury Award, Special Mention ..... *Stalker* (Andrey Tarkovskiy)

1982

Best Film ..... *Izbavitelj* (Krsto Papic)
Best Actor ..... Eusebio Poncela (*Rapture*)
Best Actress ..... Julie Christie (*Memoirs of a Survivor*)
Best Director (tie) ..... David Gladwell (*Memoirs of a Survivor*) and Piotr Szulkin (*Wojna swiatów — nastepne stulecie*)
Best Screenplay ..... *Rapture* (Iván Zulueta)
Special Mention ..... *Night of the Werewolf* (Paul Naschy)
Special Mention ..... *Beauty and the Beast* (Juraj Herz)
Critics Award ..... *Rapture* (Iván Zulueta)
Critics Award, Special Mention ..... *Night of the Werewolf* (Paul Naschy)
Audience Jury Award ..... *Memoirs of a Survivor* (David Gladwell)

Fantastic Fest

This Austin, Texas event has no winners listing on their website, so this material comes from Wikipedia.

2010

The Dell/AMD Next Wave Award, Best Feature ..... *We Are What We Are*

The Dell/AMD Next Wave Award, Best Director ..... Thomas Cappelen Malling (*Norwegian Ninja*)
The Dell/AMD Next Wave Award, Best Screenplay ..... Jorge Michel Grau (*We Are What We Are*)
The Dell/AMD Next Wave Award, Best Actor ..... Mads Ousdal (*Norwegian Ninja*)
The Dell/AMD Next Wave Award, Best Actress ..... Ji Sung Won (*Bedevilled*)
Horror Jury Award, Best Horror Feature ..... *Kidnapped*
Horror Jury Award, Best Horror Director ..... Miguel Angel Vivas (*Kidnapped*)
Horror Jury Award, Best Horror Screenplay ..... Simon Barrett (*A Horrible Way to Die*)
Horror Jury Award, Best Horror Actor ..... A J Bowen (*A Horrible Way to Die*)
Horror Jury Award, Best Horror Actress ..... Amy Seimetz (*A Horrible Way to Die*)
Fantastic Fest Jury Award, Best Fantastic Feature ..... *The Sound of Noise*
Fantastic Fest Jury Award, Best Fantastic Director ..... Pablo Trapero (*Carancho*)
Fantastic Fest Jury Award, Best Fantastic Screenplay ..... Sion Sono and Yoshiki Takahashi (*Cold Fish*)
Fantastic Fest Jury Award, Best Fantastic Actor ..... Stellan Skarsgard (*A Somewhat Gentle Man*)
Fantastic Fest Jury Award, Best Fantastic Actress ..... Martina Gusman (*Carancho*)
Horror Shorts Award, Best Horror Short ..... *Legend of Beaver Dam* (Jerome Sable)
Horror Shorts Award, Special Mention ..... *Deus Irae* (Pedro Cristiani)
Best Fantastic Short ..... *Sorry ... I Love You* (Leticia Dolera)
Best Animated Short ..... *Teclopolis* (Javier Mrad)
Audience Award, Best Feature ..... *Bedevilled* (Jang Cheol-so)
Audience Award, Honorable Mention ..... *IP Man 2*
Audience Award, Honorable Mention ..... *Rubber*
Audience Award, Honorable Mention ..... *Golden Slumber*

2009

Next Wave Award, Best Feature ..... *Down Terrace* (Ben Wheatley)
Next Wave Award, Best Director ..... Yang Ik-Joon (*Breathless*)
Next Wave Award, Best Screenplay ..... Robin Hill, Ben Wheatley (*Down Terrace*)
Next Wave Award, Best Actor ..... Jeong-min Hwang (*Private Eye*)
Next Wave Award, Best Actress ..... Shera Bechard (*Sweet Karma*)
Horror Jury Award, Best Horror Feature ..... *Human Centipede* (Tom Six)
Horror Jury Award, Best Horror Director ..... Kerry Prior (*The Revenant*)
Horror Jury Award, Best Horror Actor ..... Dieter Laser (*Human Centipede*)
Horror Jury Award, Best Horror Actress ..... Neve McIntosh (*Salvage*)
Fantastic Fest Jury Award, Best Fantastic Feature ..... *Mandrill* (Ernesto Diaz-Espinoza)
Fantastic Fest Jury Award, Best Fantastic Director ..... Kim Nguyen (*Truffe*)
Fantastic Fest Jury Award, Best Fantastic Screenplay ..... Tamio Hayashi adapted from Kotaro Isaka (*Fish Story*)
Fantastic Fest Jury Award, Best Fantastic Actor ..... Marko Zaror (*Mandrill*)
Fantastic Fest Jury Award, Best Fantastic Actress ..... Chiaki Kuriyama (*Kamogawa Horumo*)
Horror Shorts Award, Best Horror Short ..... *Full Employment* (Thomas Oberlies, Matthias Vogel)
Horror Shorts Award, Special Mention ..... *Excision* (Richard Bates, Jr.)
Best Fantastic Short ..... *Terminus* (Trevor Cawood)
Special Jury Award ..... *Next Floor* (Denis Villeneuve)
Animated Shorts Award, Best Animated Short ..... *I Am So Proud of You* (Don Hertzfeldt)
Animated Shorts Award, Special Mention ..... *Alma* (Rodrigo Blaas)
Audience Award, Best Feature ..... *A Town Called Panic* (Stephane Aubier, Vincent Patar)
Audience Award, Honorable Mention ..... *Fish Story*
Audience Award, Honorable Mention ..... *Breathless*
Audience Award, Honorable Mention ..... *The Revenant*
Audience Award, Honorable Mention ..... *Merantau*

2008

AMD Next Wave Award, Gold Medal ..... *Tokyo Gore Police*
AMD Next Wave Award, Silver Medal ..... *Deadgirl*
AMD Next Wave Award, Bronze Medal ..... *La Creme*
AMD Fantastic Fest Online, Best Feature Film ..... *South of Heaven*
AMD Fantastic Fest Online, Best Short Film ..... *Treevenge*
Horror Feature, Gold Medal ..... *Let the Right One In*
Horror Feature, Silver Medal ..... *Acolytes*
Horror Feature, Bronze Medal ..... *Donkey Punch*
Special Jury Award for Most Politically Incorrect Gore ..... *Feast 2*
Special Jury Award for Best Use of Latex ..... *Jack Brooks: Monster Slayer*
Fantastic Feature, Gold Medal ..... *How to Get Rid of The Others*
Fantastic Feature, Silver Medal ..... *Cargo 200*
Fantastic Feature, Bronze Medal ..... *Ex Drummer*

Special Jury Award for Originality and Vision ..... *Santos*
Horror Short, Gold Medal ..... *Electric Fence*
Horror Short, Silver Medal ..... *I Love Sarah Jane*
Horror Short, Bronze Medal ..... *El Senor Puppe*
Special Jury Award for Sheer Enjoyability ..... *The Horribly Slow Murderer with the Extremely Inefficient Weapon*
Fantastic Short, Gold Medal ..... *The Object*
Fantastic Short, Silver Medal ..... *Spandex Man*
Fantastic Short, Bronze Medal ..... *Stagman*
Special Jury Award for Visual Invention ..... *Rojo Red*
Animated Short, Gold Medal ..... *Bernie's Doll*
Animated Short, Silver Medal ..... *Muto*
Animated Short, Bronze Medal ..... *Violeta*
Special Jury Award for Technical Merit ..... *The Facts in the Case of Mr. Hollow*

2007

AMD Next Wave Award, Gold Medal ..... *Los cronocrímenes*, A.K.A. *Timecrimes*
AMD Next Wave Award, Silver Medal ..... *Spiral*
AMD Next Wave Award, Bronze Medal ..... *Mirageman*
Special Jury Prize for Innovative Vision ..... *End of the Line*
Horror Jury Award, Gold Medal ..... *Exte*, A.K.A. *Hair Extensions*
Horror Jury Award, Silver Medal ..... *Alone*
Horror Jury Award, Bronze Medal ..... *The Devil's Chair*
Fantastic Fest Jury Award, Gold Medal ..... *Offscreen*
Fantastic Fest Jury Award, Silver Medal ..... *Never Belongs to Me*
Fantastic Fest Jury Award, Bronze Medal ..... *Aachi and Ssipak*
Fantastic Fest Jury Award, Special Jury Prize for Most Original Scenario ..... *Never Belongs to Me*
Horror Short Award, Gold Medal ..... *In the Wall*
Horror Short Award, Silver Medal ..... *The Fifth*
Horror Short Award, Bronze Medal ..... *Far Out*
Animated Short Award, Gold Medal ..... *Everything Will Be OK*
Animated Short Award, Silver Medal ..... *Raymond*
Animated Short Award, Bronze Medal ..... *X-Pression*
Fantastic Shorts Award, Gold Medal ..... *Waiting for Yesterday*
Fantastic Shorts Award, Silver Medal ..... *Sniffer*
Fantastic Shorts Award, Bronze Medal ..... *Suityman*
Audience Award, Gold Medal ..... *Mirageman*
Audience Award, Silver Medal ..... *Timecrimes*
Audience Award, Bronze Medal ..... *Jack Ketchum's The Girl Next Door*

2006

Horror Jury Award, Best Picture ..... *Isolation*
Horror Jury Award, Best Director ..... Billy O'Brien (*Isolation*)
Horror Jury Award, Best Script ..... Dylan Bank and Morgan Pehme (*Nightmare*)
Horror Jury Award, Best Actor ..... Kane Hodder (*Hatchet*)
Horror Jury Award, Best Actress ..... Nicole Roderick (*Nightmare*)
Horror Jury Award, Best Supporting Actor ..... Lance Henriksen (*Abominable*)
Horror Jury Award, Best Supporting Actress ..... Kristen Bell (*Roman*)
Horror Jury Award, Best Art Direction ..... Alex Boynton (*Unrest*)
Horror Jury Award, Best Cinematography ..... Robby Ryan (*Isolation*)
Horror Jury Award, Best Special Effects ..... *Hatchet*
Horror Jury Award, Best Make-Up ..... *Broken*
Short Film Jury Award, Best of Show ..... *The Listening Dead*
Short Film Jury Award, Best Short Form ..... *Cost of Living*
Short Film Jury Award, Best Long Form ..... *Rogairi*, A.K.A. *Villains*
Short Film Jury Award, Best Animated ..... *If I Had a Hammer*
Short Film Jury Award, Best Comedy ..... *They're Made Out of Meat*
Fantastic Fest Jury Award, Best Film ..... *The Living and the Dead*
Fantastic Fest Jury Award, Best Director ..... Simon Rumley (*The Living and the Dead*)
Fantastic Fest Jury Award, Best Script ..... Larry Kent and Daniel Williams (*The Hamster Cage*)
Fantastic Fest Jury Award, Best Actor ..... Leo Bill (*The Living and The Dead*)
Fantastic Fest Jury Award, Best Actress ..... Jodie Jameson (*Venus Drowning*)
Fantastic Fest Jury Award, Best Supporting Actor ..... Alan Scarfe (*The Hamster Cage*)
Fantastic Fest Jury Award, Best Supporting Actress ..... Kate Fahy (*The Living and the Dead*)
Fantastic Fest Jury Award, Best Art Direction ..... *Starfish Hotel*
Fantastic Fest Jury Award, Best Cinematography ..... *A Quiet Love*
Fantastic Fest Jury Award, Best Special Effects ..... *Puzzlehead*
Fantastic Fest Jury Award, Best Make-up ..... *The Living and the Dead*
Fantastic Fest Jury Award, Special Jury Mention ..... *Blood Tea and Red String*
Audience Award, 1st Place ..... *Hatchet*
Audience Award, 2nd Place ..... *Isolation*
Audience Award, 3rd Place ..... *Firefly*

Fargo Fantastic Film Festival

Affiliated with the ValleyCon genre convention. ValleyCon 29 was this festival's first screening. Chairman Tony Tilton tells me that "No awards were given for FFFF3 (VC 31). FFFF4 and FFFF6 were based at the Fargo Theatre, but since then we've kept it with the genre convention. We may be expanding into a local theatre chain this fall [2011] though!"

VC 36— 2010

Best Thriller Feature ..... *True Nature*
Best Thriller Short Film ..... *Clemency*
Best Fan Production (webisodes) ..... *League of STEAM*
Best Science Fiction Short Film ..... *Nickel Children*
Best Fantasy ..... *Cornerboys*
Best Action, Pro Film ..... *Red Princess Blues*
Best Action, Student Film ..... *Pack of Pain*
Best Comedy Short Film ..... *The Action Hero's Guide to Saving Lives*
Best Comic Adaptation Film ..... *Street Angel*
Best Foreign Language Film (Spain) ..... *Because There Are Things You Never Forget*

VC 35— 2009

Best Horror Feature ..... *Shellter* [sic]
Best Sci-Fi/Comedy Feature ..... *Mutant Swingers from Mars*
Best Action/Adventure Feature ..... *Target Practice*
Best Horror Short Film ..... *Dead Creek*
Best Humorous Short Film ..... *Death in Charge*
Best Animated Short Film ..... *Botnik!*

VC 34— 2008

Best Feature ..... *Yesterday Was a Lie*
Best Horror/Comedy ..... *Brain Dead*
Best Comics Oriented Film ..... *The Crusaders #357—Experiment in Evil!*
Best Documentary ..... *Lovecraft: Fear of the Unknown*
Best Short Fantasy ..... *The Light*
Best SF Short ..... *Omega 35*
Best Cinematography ..... *Yesterday Was a Lie*
Best Visual Effects ..... *Omega 35*
Best Special Makeup Effects ..... *Brain Dead*

VC 33— 2007

Best Short Horror/Comedy ..... *They Walk Among Us*
Best Horror/Comedy/Musical ..... *Zombie Love*
Best SF Short ..... *Agnieszka*
Best Short Comedy (Caper/Heist) ..... *Senior Moments*
Best Documentary ..... *Blood, Boobs & Beast*
Best Visual Effects ..... *Agnieszka*

VC 32— 2006

Best Feature, Horror/Comedy ..... *Stomp! Shout! Scream!*
Best Short Subject, Thriller ..... *Alone*
Best Short Subject, Comedy/SF ..... *Prequel Apology Syndrome*
Best Short Subject, Comedy/Horror ..... *Mime Massacre*
Best Short Subject, Spaghetti Western/Horror ..... *Sunset*

VC 30— 2004

Best Feature, Student ..... *The Adventures of Eon Delevan/The Making of the Adventures of Eon Delevan*
Best Short Subject ..... *Can of Paint*
Best Short Subject, Student ..... *Spank*
Best Fan Film, Almost Pro ..... *World's Finest*
Best Fan Film, Novice ..... *The Green Goblin's Last Stand*
Best Star Wars Fan Film ..... *KnightQuest*

VC 29— 2003

Best Independent Feature ..... *Ghost Rock*
Best Horror Comedy ..... *Rex Havoc and the Ass-Kicker's of the Fantastic*
Best Fantasy Fan Film ..... *Batman: Dead End*
Best Comedy Short ..... *Breaking the Code*
Best Thriller Short ..... *Virus*
Best Horror Short ..... *Province of Twilight*
Best Sci-Fi Fan Film ..... *Troops*

Fearless Tales Genre Fest

Not much information on this defunct San Francisco fest. The below winners list comes from *London Voodoo*'s promotional material. The list is obviously incomplete. The festival's "Michael and Jeff" told Ugtv.com that "the theme of the festival this year is 'Filmmaking In the Age of Terror.'" (ugtv.org/fearless.php). Actually, that's likely *every* year's theme, since this festival appears to have only run in 2004.

2004

Best Director ..... *London Voodoo*
Best Acting ..... *London Voodoo*

Festival Européen du Film Fantastique de Strasbourg

2010

Méliès d'Argent for Best Feature Film ..... *Buried* (Rodrigo Cortes)
Jury's Special Mention ..... *Two Eyes Staring*, A.K.A. *Zwart Water* (Elbert Van Strien)
Audience's Choice ..... *Buried* (Rodrigo Cortes)
Nomination for Méliès d'Or ..... *Mr. Foley* (D.A.D.D.Y)

Audience's Choice ..... *Mr. Foley* (D.A.D.D.Y)
Student Jury Prize ..... *Fard* (David Alapont, Luis Briceno)

2009

Golden Octopus for Best Feature Film ..... *Moon* (Duncan Jones)
Jury's Special Mention ..... *The Children* (Tom Shankland)
Audience's Choice ..... *Dead Snow* (Tommy Wirkola)
Nomination for Méliès d'Or ..... *Full Employment*, A.K.A. *Arbeït fur alle* (Thomas Oberlies, Matthias Vogel)
Audience's Choice ..... *Full Employment*, A.K.A. *Arbeït fur alle* (Thomas Oberlies, Matthias Vogel)
Student Jury Prize ..... *The Knot*, A.K.A. *Liten Knute* (Jersti Steinsbo)

2008

Golden Octopus for Best Feature Film ..... *Vinyan* (Fabrice Du Welz)
Jury's Special Mention ..... *Shiver*, A.K.A. *Eskalofrio* (Isidro Ortiz)
Audience's Choice ..... *The Substitute*, A.K.A. *Vikaren* (Ole Bornedal)
Golden Octopus for Best Short Film ..... *Scary* (Martijn Hullegie)
Jury's Special Mention ..... *The Insomniac*, A.K.A. *L'insomniaque* (Mathieu Mazzoni)
Audience's Choice ..... *Scary* (Martijn Hullegie)
Student Jury Prize ..... *Cold and Dry*, A.K.A. *Tort Og Kjolig* (Kristoffer Joner, Bjørn Arne Odden)

Festival of Fantastic Films

This British festival's Delta Award goes to amateur films. Their website variously refers to the Delta Award, the Delta Film Award, or sometimes just says that a film won for Best Amateur Film. If the latter, the film is probably a Delta Award winner.

21st— 2010

Delta Award ..... *Pigeon: Impossible* (dir: Lucas Martell)
Delta Award, Highly Commended ..... *Back in the Woods* (dir: Liam Engle)
Delta Award, Commended ..... *Short Lease* (dir: Prano Bailey-Bond, Jennifer Eiss)

20th— 2009

Best Feature Film ..... *Kirk* (dir: Michael Ferns)
Runner-Up Feature Film ..... *Lodo* (dir: Karlos Alastruey)
Highly Commended Feature Film ..... *Evil Angel* (dir: Richard Dutcher)
Highly Commended Feature Film ..... *Dreamscape* (dir: Daniel J Fox)
Best Short Film (tie) ..... *Enchanted Island* (dir: Noel Kearns) and *Under My Garden* (dir: Andrea Lodovichetti)
Highly Commended Short Film ..... *Mark Macready and the Archangel Murders* (dir: Sean Candon)
Highly Commended Short Film ..... *Babylon 2084* (dir: Christian Schleisiek)
Best Amateur Film ..... *McDonough* (dir: Kyle Stephens)
Runner-Up Amateur Film ..... *Home* (dir: Francesco Filippi)
Highly Commended Amateur Film ..... *He Dies at the End* (dir: Damian McCarthy)
Highly Commended Amateur Film ..... *La vie de la mort* (Brandyn Bold)
Highly Commended Amateur Film ..... *Monster Movie* (dir: Stephen Hammond)

19th— 2008

Best Independent Feature Film ..... *The Devil's Music* (dir: Pat Higgins)
Best Independent Short Film ..... *Alicja Wonderland* (dir: Martin Gavreau)
Best Amateur Film ..... *Small Things* (dir: Matt Bloom)
Highly Commended Amateur Film ..... *Oberschule* (dir: Amanda Beggs)
Commended Amateur Film ..... *Under the Bed* (dir: Stephen Hammond)
Commended Amateur Film ..... *Schrodinger's Biro* (dir: Caroline Eccles)

18th— 2007

Best Independent Feature Film ..... *Fallen Angels* (dir: Jeff Thomas)
Highly Commended Independent Feature Film ..... *Chill* (dir: Serge Rodnunsky)
Highly Commended Independent Feature Film ..... *Something Beneath* (dir: David Winning)
Highly Commended Independent Feature Film ..... *The Planet* (dir: Mark Stirton)
Commended Independent Feature Film ..... *Death Knows Your Name* (dir: Daniel de la Vega)
Commended Independent Feature Film ..... *Kreating Karloff* (dir: Vatche Arabian)
Commended Independent Feature Film ..... *Hellbride* (dir: Pat Higgins)
Commended Independent Feature Film ..... *Dreamscape* (dir: Daniel J Fox)
Commended Independent Feature Film ..... *Insanity* (dir: Richard T. Celenza)
Best Independent Short Film ..... *D'Entre les Morts* (dir: Alain Basso)
Highly Commended Independent Short Film ..... *Colour Blind* (dir: Bryan Tyrell)
Commended Independent Short Film ..... *Paraffin* (dir: Laurence Easeman)

Best Amateur Film ..... *Contretemps* (dir: Jean Luc Baillet)
Highly Commended Amateur Film ..... *Flyer* (dir: Helmi Yusof)
Commended Amateur Film ..... *Halfway* (dir: Karl Holt)
Commended Amateur Film ..... *The Morality Game* (dir: Jim Walker)

17th — 2006

Best Independent Feature Film ..... *The Toybox* (dir: Paolo Sedazzari)
Highly Commended Independent Feature Film ..... *Dark Night* (dir: Daniel Grant)
Highly Commended Independent Feature Film ..... *The Slaughter* (dir: Jay Lee)
Best Independent Short Film ..... *Oculus* (dir: Mike Flanagan)
Highly Commended Independent Short Film ..... *Tell Tale Art* (dir: Jeremy Dylan Lanni)
Highly Commended Independent Short Film ..... *Psychiatric Channel* (dir: Louis Segal)
Commended Independent Short Film ..... *Survivor* (dir: Christoph Warrack)
Independent Short Film ..... *Purgatory* (dir: Christopher Chow)
Delta Award, Best Amateur Film ..... *Eddie Loves You* (dir: Karl Holt)
Delta Award, Special Commendation/Amateur Film ..... *The Call of Cthulhu* (dir: Andrew Leman)
Delta Award, Special Commendation/Amateur Film ..... *Guy's Guide to Zombies* (dir: Daniel Austin)
Delta Award, Special Commendation/Amateur Film ..... *The Spell* (dir: Pablo Millán)

16th — 2005

Best Independent Feature Film ..... *A Year in the Death of Jack Richards* (dir: Benjamin Paquette)
2nd Place, Independent Feature Film ..... *The Naked Monster* (dir: Ted Newsome)
3rd Place, Independent Feature Film ..... *Experiment* (dir: Daniel Turner)
Best Independent Short Film ..... *Der Beste* (dir: Arne Jysch, Rasmus Borowski)
2nd Place, Independent Short Film ..... *Las Viandas* (dir: Jose-Antonio Bonet)
3rd Place, Independent Short Film ..... *Don't Look in the Attic* (dir: Andrew Harrison)
Delta Award, Best Amateur Film ..... *The Kingdom of Shadows* (dir: Ross Shepherd)
Delta Award, Commended Amateur Film ..... *Feathers* (dir: Sam Rogers)
Delta Award, Commended Amateur Film ..... *Alexander* (dir: Rafa Dengra)
Delta Award, Commended Amateur Film ..... *Inside* (dir: Brian Philip Davis)

15th — 2004

Best United Kingdom Independent Feature Film ..... *London Voodoo* (dir: Robert Pratten)
Best Foreign Independent Feature Film ..... *Tempus Fugit* (dir: Enric Folch Highly)
Highly Commended Independent Feature Film ..... *Freak Out* (dir: Christian James)
Highly Commended Independent Feature Film ..... *Lovesick: Sick Love* (dir: Wolfgang Buld)
Highly Commended Independent Feature Film ..... *Crash Test* (dir: Sam Voutas)
Best United Kingdom Independent Short Film ..... *Half Life* (dir: Luke Jacobs)
Best Foreign Independent Short Film (3-way tie) ..... *U43* (dir: Anna Kuczynski, Wolf Mocikat) and *The Visage* (dir: Kirk Henderson) and *E.D.E.N.* (dir: Fabio Guaglione, Fabio Resinaro)
Highly Commended Independent Short Film ..... *Bitch* (dir: Cristina Read)
Highly Commended Independent Short Film ..... *A Can of Paint* (dir: Robi Michael)
Highly Commended Independent Short Film ..... *The Affidavit* (dir: Pil Pilegaard)
Highly Commended Independent Short Film ..... *The Shoe Collector* (dir: Justin Smith)
Highly Commended Independent Short Film ..... *Cash Flow* (dir: Shaun Andrews)
Highly Commended Independent Short Film ..... *Time & Space* (dir: Michael Barnes)
Highly Commended Independent Short Film ..... *The Seller* (dir: Matthew Humphreys)
Highly Commended Independent Short Film ..... *The Measure of My Days* (dir: Caradog James)
Highly Commended Independent Short Film ..... *The Crypt Club* (dir: Miguel Gallego)
Highly Commended Independent Short Film ..... *If I Could Only...* (dir: Marc Wyn Jones)
Highly Commended Independent Short Film ..... *The Hairy Fairy* (dir: Armando Garci)
Highly Commended Independent Short Film ..... *Conceptual* (dir: Owen Tooth)
Highly Commended Independent Short Film ..... *Monster of 11.05* (dir: Mark Loughman)
Highly Commended Independent Short Film ..... *TV Conspiracy* (dir: Consuela Giorgi)
Highly Commended Independent Short Film ..... *Natural Cures for Common Ailments* (dir: Zoe & Christabel Gingell)
Highly Commended Independent Short Film ..... *Detained* (dir: Jason Tammemagi)
Highly Commended Independent Short Film ..... *Rubber* (dir: David Dupont)
Highly Commended Independent Short Film ..... *Y* (dir: Frances Poltera)
Commended Independent Short Film ..... *Pope Leo Electrocutes an Elephant* (dir: John Hansen)
Best Amateur Film ..... *The Curse* (dir: Brett Harvey)

Highly Commended Amateur Film ..... *Dark Visions* (dir: Jackson Sharp Highly)
Highly Commended Amateur Film ..... *Too Much Time* (dir: Damien Kelly)

14th — 2003

Best Independent Feature Film ..... *The Last Horror Movie* (dir: Julian Richards)
Best Independent Animated Feature Film ..... *Dominator* (dir: Tony Luke)
Best Independent Documentary ..... *Frazetta — Painting With Fire* (dir: Lance Laspina)
Highly Commended Independent Feature Film ..... *Ghost of the Needle* (dir: Brian Avenet Bradley)
Highly Commended Independent Feature Film ..... *The Late Twentieth* (dir: Hadi Hajaig)
Highly Commended Independent Feature Film ..... *13 Seconds* (dir: Jeff Thomas)
Highly Commended Independent Feature Film ..... *Requiem* (dir: Mitchell Morgan, Jon Kirby)
Commended Independent Feature Film ..... *Numb* (dir: Michael Ferris Gibson)
Best Independent Short Film ..... *Mrs. Meitlemeihr* (dir: Graham Rose)
Best Animated Independent Short Film ..... *Glitch* (dir: Damien Slevin)
Highly Commended Independent Short Film ..... *Toss of the Coin* (dir: Patrick Steele)
Highly Commended Independent Short Film ..... *Gabriel's Word* (dir: David Bjerre)
Highly Commended Independent Short Film ..... *Another Flush* (dir: Sam Hurwitz)
Highly Commended Independent Short Film ..... *Project Gamma* (dir: David Sarrio)
Highly Commended Independent Short Film ..... *Treasure* (dir: Neasa Hardiman)
Highly Commended Independent Short Film ..... *Red Lines* (dir: Frazer Lee)
Commended Independent Short Film ..... *Beneath the Frost Line* (dir: Andy Davis)
Commended Independent Short Film ..... *Crosstalk* (dir: Stsampani P. Kolkovalis)
Commended Independent Short Film ..... *Hallucinations in Croissant Sauce* (dir: Jude Talmor)
Commended Independent Short Film ..... *Eskimo Hill* (dir: Max Evry)
Best Amateur Film ..... *Tilted Love* (dir: Robin Burke)
Highly Commended Amateur Film ..... *Blinkers* (dir: Jake Major)
Highly Commended Amateur Film ..... *In the Dark* (dir: Tristan Goligher)

13th — 2002

Best Independent Feature Film (tie) ..... *Dr. Jekyll & Mr. Hyde — The RockNRoll Musical* (dir: Andre Champagne) and *Dr. Jekyll & Mr. Hyde* (dir: Mark Redfield)
3rd Place, Independent Feature Film (tie) ..... *Dark Heaven* (dir: Douglas Schulze) and *Saul's Pupils* (dir: Andrew Harrison)
Highly Commended Independent Feature Film ..... *Breakfast With the Colonel* (dir: John Harden)
Highly Commended Independent Feature Film ..... *One Blood Planet* (dir: Jerry Decker)
Commended Independent Feature Film ..... *Hell's Highway* (dir: Steven Lee Taylor)
Commended Independent Feature Film ..... *Incredibly Strange People* (dir: Jason Delorme)
Best Independent Short Film ..... *Timmy's Wish* (dir: Patrick Cannon)
2nd Place, Independent Short Film ..... *Time 2 Save the World* (dir: Adam Trotman)
3rd Place, Independent Short Film (3-way tie) ..... *Reconcilers* (dir: Pil Pilegaard) and *Mindfield* (dir: Gary Andrews) and *Dr. Crosier* (dir: Owen Matthews)
Highly Commended Independent Short Film ..... *Fusion 21* (dir: Andy Bittner)
Commended Independent Short Film ..... *Daredevil (The Teaser)* (dir: David Sarrio)
Commended Independent Short Film ..... *First Light* (dir: Alexander Galant)
Commended Independent Short Film ..... *Nebulous Dawn* (dir: Omar Hassan)
Special Judges' Award ..... *Jack Pierce — The Man Behind the Monsters* (dir: Scott Essman)
Delta Award, Best Amateur Film ..... *I Am Peter Cushing* (dir: Al Lougher)

12th — 2001

Best Independent Feature Film ..... *Alien Rampage* (dir: Don Dohler)
Runner-Up Independent Feature Film ..... *Le Rat* (dir: Christophe Ali, Nicolas Bonilauri)
Highly Commended Independent Feature Film ..... *Dark Eyes* (dir: Andrew Spencer)
Best Independent Short Film (tie) ..... *Encounter at Black Ridge* (dir: Andrew Harrison) and *The Tell Tale Heart* (dir: Alfonso S. Suarez)
Runner-Up Independent Short Film ..... *Playing Truant* (dir: Jason Wilcox)
Highly Commended Independent Short Film ..... *Harry's Joint* (dir: Mark Holmes)
Highly Commended Independent Short Film ..... *Meine Heimatstadt* (dir: Gili Dolev)
Highly Commended Independent Short Film ..... *Creepy Crawly* (dir: John Carr)
Highly Commended Independent Short Film ..... *Avenging Angel* (dir: Gary Andrews)
Best Amateur Film ..... *Jesabelle* (dir: Bryn Jones)
Runner-Up Amateur Film ..... *Time* (dir: Ben Campbell)
Highly Commended Amateur Film ..... *Eden* (dir: Tamara Maloney)
Highly Commended Amateur Film ..... *893 Pike Street* (dir: Jonathan Ameli)

Highly Commended Amateur Film ..... *The Sandman* (dir: David Teague)

11th — 2000

Best Independent Feature Film ..... *The Last Man* (dir: Harry Ralston)
Best Independent Short Film ..... *La Dernier Reve*, A.K.A. *The Last Dream* (dir: Emmanual Jespers)
Best Amateur Film ..... *Schrodinger's Cat* (dir: Nova Jacobs, John Sinclair)
Special Commendation ..... Leo Nicholson for his stop-motion *Run Monkey Run*
Commendation ..... Katie Koskenmaki for *The Windigo*

10th — 1999

Best Independent Short Film ..... *Succubus: The Motion Picture* (dir: Harry Weinmann)
Delta Award, Best Amateur Film ..... *Abduction* (dir: Ben Campbell)

9th — 1998

Best Independent Feature Film ..... *Long Twilight* (dir: Attila Janisch)
Highly Commended Independent Feature Film ..... *The Last Roadstop* (dir: Tyler Tharpe)
Highly Commended Independent Feature Film ..... *Demagogue* (dir: Thomas Lawes, Adam Trotman)
Highly Commended Independent Feature Film ..... *Weird Ones* (dir: John Meagher)
Highly Commended Independent Feature Film ..... *I, Zombie: The Chronicles of Pain* (dir: Andrew Parkinson)
Best Independent Short Film ..... *Domino* (dir: Ori Savan)
Highly Commended Independent Short Film ..... *Striker Bob* (dir: Lars Damoiseaux)
Highly Commended Independent Short Film ..... *Cupid's Arrow* (dir: Marinelli & Marinucci)
Highly Commended Independent Short Film ..... *Winged* (dir: Val Keller)
Delta Award, Best Amateur Film ..... *The Gift* (dir: Shane Hannafey)
Delta Award, Highly Commended Amateur Film ..... *'Till Death* (dir: Sean Hogan)
Delta Award, Highly Commended Amateur Film ..... *PU 239* (dir: Christian Lajarescu)
Certificate of Merit ..... *Hypnos* (dir: Bryan Turell)
Certificate of Merit ..... *The Magic Umbrella* (dir: Ian Rintoul)
Certificate of Merit ..... *The Magician* (dir: Tim Clague)
Certificate of Merit ..... *Millennium Bug* (dir: Lee Lanier)
Certificate of Merit ..... *Mother & Son* (dir: Barbar Ahmed)

Freak Show Horror Film Festival

Presents the Freaky Award.

2010

Best Feature ..... *Kiss the Abyss*
Best Florida Feature ..... *Parasitic*
Best Short ..... *Murderabillia*
Best Florida Short ..... *Grave Reality*
Best Actor ..... Brooke McCarter (*Emerging Past*)
Best Actress ..... Tiffany Shepis (*She Wolf Rising*)
Best Cinematography ..... *Body of Work*
Best Special FX Makeup ..... *Doomsday County*

2009

Best Feature ..... *The Sky Has Fallen*
Best Florida Horror Film ..... *Scare Zone*
Best Short Film ..... *Thirsty*
Best Actor ..... Kristopher Shepard (*Evil Angel*)
Best Actress ..... Ginny Weirick (*Dark Moon Rising*)
Best Cinematography ..... *The Sleuth Incident*
Best Special FX Makeup ..... *Dark Moon Rising*
Audience Choice Award ..... *The Black Waters of Echo's Pond*
Lifetime Achievement Award ..... Herschell Gordon Lewis

2008

Best Feature ..... *Alien Raiders*
Best Florida Horror Film ..... *The Curse of Dr. Mongoo*
Best Short Film ..... *Cam 2 Cam*
Best Actor ..... Carlos Benard (*Alien Raiders*)
Best Actress ..... Caitlin McIntosh (*Shadowland*)
Best Cinematography ..... *Shadowland*
Best Special FX Makeup ..... *Vlog*
Audience Choice Award ..... *Battle of the Bone*

2007

Best Feature ..... *Deadwood Park*
Best Florida Horror ..... *Zombies, Zombies, Zombies*
Best Short ..... *Nothing Face*
Best Actor ..... Matt Carmody (*Carver*)
Best Actress ..... Bethany Newell (*Redsin Tower*)
Best Cinematography ..... Eric Stanze (*Deadwood Park*)
Best Special FX Makeup ..... Jerami Cruise (*Redsin Tower*)
Audience Choice Award ..... *100 Tears*
Lifetime Achievement Award ..... Harry Mandfredini (composer, *Friday the 13th*)

2006

Best Feature ..... *The 8th Plague*
Best Florida Horror Film ..... *Delivery*
Best Short ..... *The Listening Dead*
Best Actor ..... Matt Nelson (*Delivery*)

Best Actress ..... Laura Bach (*The Slaughter*)
Best Cinematography ..... *The Listening Dead*
Best Special FX Makeup ..... Patrick Magee (*The Slaughter*)
Audience Choice Award ..... *Date of the Dead*
Lifetime Achievement Award ..... Lloyd Kaufman

Fright Night Film Fest

Presents the Silver Scream Award.

2010

Best Short ..... *Alice Jacobs Is Dead* (dir: Alex Horwitz)
Best Feature ..... *Shadowland* (dir: Wyatt Weed)
Best Soundtrack ..... *Danger, Zombies, Run* (dir: Brian Wimer)
Scream Queen of the Year ..... Heather Langenkamp
Best Special FX Practical ..... *The Taken* (Brian Sipe Special Effects)
Best Special FX CGI ..... *Guardian of the Realm*
Best Screenplay ..... *The Ripper* (Joe Randazzo)
Best Action ..... *God of Vampires*
Best Sci Fi ..... *Flying Saucer Exodus* (dir: Jerry Williams)
Best Zombie ..... *Revelation* (dir: Will Graver)
Best Comedy ..... *Danger, Zombies, Run*
Best Director ..... Morgan Mead (*My Bloody Wedding*)
Best Fan Film ..... *Hell Raiser: Deader Winters Lament* (dir: Jonathan S. Kui)
Best Documentary ..... *Graphic Sexual Horror* (dir: Barbara Bell)
Kentucky Filmmaker of the Year ..... Jacob Ennis
Best Cinematography ..... *The Prometheus Project*
Best Actor ..... Kane Hodder (*Old Habits Die Hard*)
Best Actress ..... Jessica Von (*The Taken*)
Horror Icon of the Year ..... Tom Atkins
Best of the Fest ..... *The Taken* (dir: Richard Valentine)
Audience Pick ..... *My Bloody Wedding* (dir: Morgan Mead)
Honorable Mention ..... *Gun Town* (dir: Lee Vervoort)
Honorable Mention ..... *Get Off My Porch* (dir: Patrick Rea)
Honorable Mention ..... *The Survivors* (dir: Soham Mehta)
Honorable Mention ..... *Moon-Lite* (dir: Kenneth Dowell)
Honorable Mention ..... *Nightmare at Bunnyman Bridge* (dir: Robert Elkins)

2009

Best Short ..... *Double*
Best Foreign Short ..... *The Gynecologist*
Best Foreign Feature ..... *Family Demons*
Best Soundtrack/Score ..... *Eat Me: The Musical*
Best SPFX Practical ..... *Devil's Grove*
Best Action ..... *The Dogs of Chinatown*
Best Sci Fi ..... *Fun on Earth*
Best Zombie ..... *Deadlands 2: Trapped*
Best Comedy ..... *Auburn Hills BreakDown*
Best Director ..... Jack Daniel Stanley
Best Fan Film ..... *Indiana Jones and the Mummies Skull*
Best Feature ..... *Mantra*
Best Animated ..... *Night of the Invisible Man*
Best Cinematographer ..... *Huneman Brown Eagle for Mrs. Brummetts Garden*
Best Actor ..... Ron Palillo (*Curse of Micah Rood*)
Best Actress ..... Cassandra Kane (*Family Demons*)
Best of the Fest ..... *Sea of Dust*
Honorable Mention ..... *Angels and Fire*
Honorable Mention ..... *Ceaser and Otto's Summer Camp Massacre*
Honorable Mention ..... *Shellter*
Honorable Mention ..... *Alone*
Honorable Mention ..... *The Revenant*
Honorable Mention ..... *I Don't Sleep I Dream*
Honorable Mention ..... *Run Bitch Run*
Honorable Mention ..... *Blood on the Highway*
Honorable Mention ..... *Bikini Girls on Ice*
Honorable Mention ..... *Thirsty*
Honorable Mention ..... *Dead Sucks*

2008

Best Action ..... *Razor Sharp*
Best Actor ..... Trent Haaga
Best Actress ..... Monica Knight (*Windcroft*)
Best of the Fest ..... *Bonnie and Clyde vs. Dracula*
Best Cinematography ..... *Lily* (Daniel Boneville)
Best Feature ..... *Windcroft* (dir: Evan Meszaros)
Best Comedy ..... *Shh! It's Alive* (dir: Ryan Cadima)
Most Original Film ..... *Gunther Toody's Happy Time Fun Show* (Jimmy Humphrey)
Best Sci Fi *O2*
Best Director ..... Evan Meszaros
Best Short ..... *Of Darkness* (dir: Gary E. Irwin)
Best One Liner ..... *Zombie Apocalypse*
Best Zombie Film ..... *Zombthology* (dir: Elias Dancey, Chris Kiros, Robert Elkins)
Best Soundtrack ..... *Zombie Love*
Best Special Effects ..... *Curse of the Flesh*
Kentucky Filmmaker of the Year ..... George Bonilla
Horror Icon of the Year ..... Angus Scrimm
Honorable Mention ..... *Paper Dolls*
Honorable Mention ..... *Liar's Pendulum*
Honorable Mention ..... *Alone*
Honorable Mention ..... *Taste of the Flesh*
Honorable Mention ..... *The Conjurer*
Honorable Mention ..... *The Vagrant*
Honorable Mention ..... *Miyuki*

2007

Best Feature ..... *Scrapbook*
Best Short ..... *Woman's Intuition*

Best Soundtrack ..... *Gimme Skelter*
Best Special Effects ..... *Horrors of War*
Best Zombie ..... *Dead Moon Rising*
Best Foreign Horror Film ..... *Bad Dreams* (Sweden)
Most Original Idea ..... *The Guardian* (dir: Aaron Marshall)
Horror Icon of the Year ..... Tony Moran
Honorable Mention ..... *9 Lives of Mara* (Balaji K. Kumar)
Honorable Mention ..... *Salvation* (J.A. Steel)
Honorable Mention ..... *Burial Party* (Joseph Dodge)
Honorable Mention ..... *The Day They Came Back* (Scott Goldberg)

2006

Best Feature ..... *The Hazing*
Best Short (tie) ..... *Fangs for the Memories* and *Disconnected*
Best Soundtrack ..... *Silence of Isbella*
Best Cinematography ..... *Nightmare Man*
Best of the Fest Audience Award (tie) ..... *Katie Bird* and *Bad Reputation*
Most Original Film ..... *Secret Life of Sarah Sheldon*
Best Zombie Film ..... *Deadlands: The Rising*
Best Special Effects ..... *Edison Death Machine*
Honorable Mention ..... *Joshua*

Festival International du Film Fantastique de Gérardmer

Their Prix Littéraire (A.K.A. Literary Prize) goes to a fantasy novel, not to a film. Winners of the Prix du Jury Jeunes (Youth Jury Award) are chosen by selected students from France's Lorraine region. The Grand Prix du Court Métrage is a Best Short Film Award. The Prix du Public L'Est Républicain—Vosges Matin is an Audience Award. Winners of the Sci-Fi award (sometimes spelled Syfy) are chosen by viewers of TV's Sci-Fi Channel. The Prix 13ème Rue may be translated as the 13th Street Award.

The Prix Première is "pour le film le plus innovant" (the most innovative film). Mad Movies is a sponsor, not an award category.

2010

Grand Prix du Festival ..... *The Door*, A.K.A. *Die Tür* (Anno Saul)
Prix du Jury ..... *Moon* (Duncan Jones)
Prix de la Critique Internationale ..... *Moon* (Duncan Jones)
Prix du Jury Jeunes ..... *Possessed*, A.K.A. *Bulshinjiok* (Lee Yong-ju)
Prix du Public L'Est Républicain—Vosges Matin ..... *5150, Rue des Ormes*, A.K.A. *5150 Elm's Way* (Éric Tessier)
Prix Syfy Universal ..... *La Horde*, A.K.A. *The Horde* (Yannick Dahan, Benjamin Rocher)
Grand Prix du Court Métrage ..... *La Morsure*, A.K.A. *The Bite* (Joyce A. Nashawati)
Prix Prix du Public Mad Movies—Inédits Vidéo ..... *Inside* (Phedon Papamichael)

2009

Grand Prix du Festival ..... *Morse*, A.K.A. *Let the Right One In* (Tomas Alfredson)
Prix du Jury ..... *Grace* (Paul Solet)
Prix de la Critique Internationale ..... *Morse*, A.K.A. *Let the Right One In* (Tomas Alfredson)
Prix du Jury Jeunes ..... *Sauna* (Antti Jussi Annila)
Prix du Public L'Est Républicain—Vosges Matin ..... *The Midnight Meat Train* (Ryuhei Kitamura)
Prix Sci-Fi ..... *The Midnight Meat Train* (Ryuhei Kitamura)
Grand Prix du Court Métrage ..... *Dix*, A.K.A. *Ten* (Bif)
Prix Prix du Public Mad Movies—Inédits Vidéo ..... *Timecrimes*, A.K.A. *Los cronocrímenes* (Nacho Vigalondo)

2008

Grand Prix du Festival ..... *L'Orphelinat*, A.K.A. *The Orphanage*, A.K.A. *El Orfanato* (Juan Antonio Bayona)
Prix du Jury (tie) ..... *REC* (Jaume Balaguero, Paco Plaza) and *Teeth* (Mitchell Lichtenstein)
Prix de la Critique Internationale ..... *Diary of the Dead* (George A. Romero)
Prix du Jury Jeunes ..... *REC* (Jaume Balaguero, Paco Plaza)
Prix du Public L'Est Républicain—La Liberté de l'Est ....., *REC* (Jaume Balaguero, Paco Plaza)
Prix Sci-Fi ..... *L'Orphelinat*, A.K.A. *The Orphanage*, A.K.A. *El Orfanato* (Juan Antonio Bayona)
Grand Prix du Court Métrage ..... *Dans leur peau*, A.K.A. *In Their Skin* (Arnaud Malherbe)
Prix du Public Mad Movies—Inédits Vidéo ..... *Détour Mortel 2*, A.K.A. *Wrong Turn 2* (Joe Lynch)

2007

Grand Prix du Festival ..... *Den brysomme mannen*, A.K.A. *The Bothersome Man* (Jens Lien)
Prix du Jury (tie) ..... *Black Sheep* (Jonathan King) and *Fido* (Andrew Currie)
Prix de la Meilleure Musique de Film (Best Film Music) ..... *Fido*
Prix de la Critique Internationale ..... *Den brysomme mannen*, A.K.A. *The Bothersome Man* (Jens Lien)
Prix du Jury Jeunes ..... *Den brysomme mannen*, A.K.A. *The Bothersome Man* (Jens Lien)

Prix du Public L'Est Républicain — La Liberté de l'Est ..... *Black Sheep* (Jonathan King)
Prix Sci-Fi ..... *Den brysomme mannen*, A.K.A. *The Bothersome Man* (Jens Lien)
Grand Prix du Court Métrage ..... *Echo* (Yann Gozlan)
Prix du Public Mad Movies — Inédits Vidéo ..... *Alien Apocalypse* (Josh Becker)

2006

Grand Prix du Festival ..... *Isolation* (Billy O'Brien)
Prix du Jury ..... *Fragile* (Jaume Balaguero)
Prix de la Critique Internationale ..... *Isolation* (Billy O'Brien)
Prix du Jury Jeunes ..... *Fragile* (Jaume Balaguero)
Prix du Public L'Est Républicain — La Liberté de l'Est ..... *Fragile* (Jaume Balaguero)
Prix 13ème Rue ..... *Fragile* (Jaume Balaguero)
Grand Prix du Court Métrage ..... *Le Baiser*, A.K.A. *The Kiss* (Stefan Le Lay)
Prix du Public Mad Movies — Inédits Vidéo ..... *Shutter* (Parkpoom Wongpoom, Banjong Pisanthanakum)

2005

Grand Prix du Festival ..... *Trouble* (Harry Cleven)
Prix du Jury (tie) ..... *Saw* (James Wan) and *Calvaire*, A.K.A. *Calvary* (Fabrice du Welz)
Prix de la Critique Internationale ..... *Calvaire*, A.K.A. *Calvary* (Fabrice du Welz)
Prix du Jury Jeunes ..... *Saw* (James Wan)
Prix Première ..... *Calvaire*, A.K.A. *Calvary* (Fabrice du Welz)
Prix 13ème Rue ..... *Trouble* (Harry Cleven)
Grand Prix du Court Métrage ..... *Organik* (David Morlet)
Prix du Public Mad Movies — Inédits Vidéo ..... *Into the Mirror*, A.K.A. *Geoul sokeuro* (Seong-Ho Kim)
Prix Littéraire ..... *Le mort-homme*, A.K.A. *Dead Man* (Denis Bretin)

2004

Grand Prix du Festival ..... *A Tale of Two Sisters*, A.K.A. *Deux Soeurs* (Kim Jee-Woon)
Prix du Jury ..... *Happiness of the Katakuris*, A.K.A. *La mélodie du Malheur*, A.K.A. *The Melody of Woes* (Takeshi Miike)
Prix de la Critique Internationale ..... *Love Object* (Robert Parigi)
Grand Prix Anim'arts ..... *Wonderful Days* (Moon-Saeng Kim)
Prix du Jury Jeunes ..... *A Tale of Two Sisters*, A.K.A. *Deux Soeurs* (Kim Jee-Woon)
Prix Première ..... *Love Object* (Robert Parigi)
Prix 13ème Rue ..... *A Tale of Two Sisters*, A.K.A. *Deux Soeurs* (Kim Jee-Woon)

Grand Prix du Court Métrage ..... *La collection de Judicaël* (Corinne Garfin)
Prix du Public Mad Movies — Inédits Vidéo ..... *My Little Eye* (Marc Evans)
Prix Littéraire ..... *Immortalis*, A.K.A. *Immortal* (Elias Jabre)

2003

Grand Prix du Festival ..... *Dark Water* (Hideo Nakata)
Prix du Jury (tie) ..... *Maléfique* (Eric Valette) and *The Gathering* (Brian Gilbert)
Prix de la Critique Internationale ..... *Dark Water* (Hideo Nakata)
Prix du Jury Jeunes ..... *Dark Water* (Hideo Nakata)
Prix Première ..... *May* (Lucky McKee)
Grand Prix du Court Métrage ..... *Bloody Christmas* (Michel Leray)
Prix du Public Mad Movies — Inédits Vidéo ..... *2009: Lost Memories* (Si-myung Lee)
Prix Littéraire ..... *Le 5 ème règne* (Maxime Williams)

2002

Grand Prix du Festival ..... *Fausto 5.0* (Isidro Ortiz, Carles Padrissa, Alex Olle)
Prix du Jury ..... *L'Echine du diable*, A.K.A. *El espinazo del diablo*, A.K.A. *The Devil's Backbone* (Guillermo del Toro)
Prix de la Critique Internationale ..... *L'Echine du diable*, A.K.A. *El espinazo del diablo*, A.K.A. *The Devil's Backbone* (Guillermo del Toro)
Prix du Jury Jeunes ..... *L'Echine du diable*, A.K.A. *El espinazo del diablo*, A.K.A. *The Devil's Backbone* (Guillermo del Toro)
Prix Première ..... *Donnie Darko* (Richard Kelly)
Grand Prix du Court Métrage ..... *A Louer* (James L. Frachon)
Prix Canal + du Court Métrage Fantastique ..... *A Louer* (James L. Frachon)
Prix Mad Movies — Inédits Vidéo ..... *Jack et le haricot magique* (Brian Henson)
Prix du Vidéo Clip ..... *Where's Your Head At?* (Felix Buxton for Basement Jaxx)
Prix Littéraire ..... *Wonderlantz* (Jean-Luc Bizien)

2001

Grand Prix du Festival ..... *Thomas est amoureux* (Pierre-Paul Renders)
Prix du Jury ..... *Chasing Sleep*, A.K.A. *Insomnies* (Michael Walker)
Prix de la Critique Internationale ..... *Tales of the Unusual* (Masayuki Ochiai, Masayuki Suzuki, Mamoru Hoshi, Hisao Ogura)
Prix du Jury Jeunes ..... *Thomas est amoureux* (Pierre-Paul Renders)
Grand Prix du Court Métrage ..... *Quand on est amoureux c'est merveilleux* (Fabrice du Welz)

Prix Canal + du Court Métrage Fantastique ..... *Epidermique* (Célia Canning)
Prix Télé K7 du Public — Inédits Vidéo ..... *They Nest*, A.K.A. *Eclosion* (Ellroy Elkayem)
Prix du Vidéo Clip ..... *Sabrina* (John Hillcoat for Einsturzende Neubauten)
Prix du Jeu Vidéo ..... *Resident Evil Code: Veronica* (sur console Dreamcast)
Prix des Lecteurs Ciné Live ..... *Thomas est amoureux* (Pierre-Paul Renders)
Prix Littéraire ..... *Le templier* (François Angelier)

2000

Grand Prix du Festival ..... *Stir of Echoes*, A.K.A. *Hypnose* (David Koepp)
Prix du Jury ..... *Los sin nombres*, A.K.A. *The Nameless*, A.K.A. *La secte sans nom* (Jaume Balaguero)
Prix de la Critique Internationale ..... *Los sin nombres*, A.K.A. *The Nameless*, A.K.A. *La secte sans nom* (Jaume Balaguero)
Prix de la Découverte Ciné Live ..... *Los sin nombres*, A.K.A. *The Nameless*, A.K.A. *La secte sans nom* (Jaume Balaguero)
Prix du Film Publicitaire ..... *AMD K6* (pour l'agence Hill Holiday)
Grand Prix du Court Métrage ..... *L'homme est-il bon?* (Romain Berthomieu)
Prix des Inédits Vidéo ..... *Razor Blade Smile* (Jake West)
Prix du Vidéo Clip ..... *Aphex Twin* (Chris Cunningham for Come to Daddy)
Prix du Jeu Vidéo ..... *Silent Hill* (sur console Playstation)
Prix du Jury Jeunes ..... *Los sin nombres*, A.K.A. *The Nameless*, A.K.A. *La secte sans nom* (Jaume Balaguero)
Prix Littéraire ..... *Les mémoires de l'homme-éléphant* (Xavier Maumejean)

1999

Grand Prix du Festival ..... *Cube* (Vincenzo Natali)
Prix du Jury (tie) ..... *The Wisdom of Crocodiles*, A.K.A. *La sagesse des crocodiles* (Po-Chih Leong) and *Bride of Chucky*, A.K.A. *La fiancée de chucky* (Ronny Yu)
Prix de la Critique Internationale ..... *Cube* (Vincenzo Natali)
Prix du Public ..... *Cube* (Vincenzo Natali)
Grand Prix du Court Métrage ..... *Opus 66* (Lionel Delplanque)
Prix des Inédits Vidéo ..... "Coronation" (*Profiler*)
Prix du Vidéo Clip ..... *Alarm Call* (Alexander McQueen for Björk)
Prix du Jeu Vidéo ..... *Zelda* (sur console Nintendo)
Prix Littéraire ..... *La maison usher ne chutera pas*, A.K.A. *The House of Usher Does Not Fall* (Pierre Stolze)

1998

Grand Prix du Festival ..... *An American Werewolf in Paris*, A.K.A. *Le loup-garou de paris* (Anthony Waller)
Prix du Jury (tie) ..... *Photographing Fairies*, A.K.A. *Forever* (Nick Willing) and *Gattaca*, A.K.A. *Bienvenue à gattaca* (Andrew Niccol)
Prix de la Critique Internationale ..... *Photographing Fairies*, A.K.A. *Forever* (Nick Willing)
Prix du Public ..... *An American Werewolf in Paris*, A.K.A. *Le loup-garou de paris* (Anthony Waller)
Grand Prix du Court Métrage ..... *Le bal du minotaure* (Lorenzo Recio)
Prix des Inédits Vidéo ..... "Redux" (*The X-Files*)
Prix du Vidéo Clip (tie) ..... *Excalibur* (William Sheller) and *Nomenklatura* (No One Is Innocent)
Prix du Jeu Vidéo ..... *Oddworld*
Prix Spécial Frissons du Jury Jeux Vidéo ..... *Resident Evil* (Virgin Interactive)
Trophée Fun Radio (tie) ..... *Gattaca*, A.K.A. *Bienvenue à gattaca* (Andrew Niccol) and *An American Werewolf in Paris*, A.K.A. *Le loup-garou de paris* (Anthony Waller)
Prix Littéraire ..... *Les mères noires* (Pascal Françaix)

1997

Grand Prix du Festival ..... *Scream* (Wes Craven)
Prix du Jury ..... *Nur über meine Leiche*, A.K.A. *Tuez-moi d'abord* (Rainer Matsutani)
Mention Spéciale du Jury ..... *Ghost in the Shell* (Mamoru Oshii)
Prix de la Critique Internationale ..... *Nur über meine Leiche*, A.K.A. *Tuez-moi d'abord* (Rainer Matsutani)
Prix du Public ..... *Scream* (Wes Craven)
Grand Prix du Court Métrage ..... *L'illusion* (Gabriela Greeb)
Prix des Inédits Vidéo ..... *Le Dentiste*, A.K.A. *The Dentist* (Brian Yuzna)
Prix du Vidéo Clip ..... *Au commencement* (Philippe Gauthier for Etienne Daho)
Mention Spéciale du jury Vidéo Clips ..... *Personne* (Vidal and Durand for Pascal Obispo)
Trophée Fun Radio ..... *Nur über meine Leiche*, A.K.A. *Tuez-moi d'abord* (Rainer Matsutani)
Prix Littéraire ..... *La qualité du silence* (Max Dorra)

1996

Grand Prix du Festival ..... *El dia de la bestia*, A.K.A. *Le jour de la bête* (Álex de la Iglesia)
Prix du Jury ..... *Mute Witness*, A.K.A. *Témoin muet* (Anthony Waller)
Mention Spéciale du Jury pour l'interprétation ..... Marina Sudina (*Mute Witness*, A.K.A. *Témoin muet*)

Prix de la Critique Internationale ..... *The Secret of Roan Inish* (John Sayles)
Prix du Public ..... *Powder* (Victor Salva)
Grand Prix du Court Métrage ..... *A l'arraché* (Christophe Smith)
Mention Spéciale du Jury Courts Métrages ..... *J'ai échoué* (Philippe Donzelot)
Prix des Inédits Vidéo ..... "Le dossier secret" (*Aux frontières du réel*, A.K.A. *The X-Files*) (R.W. Goodwin, Rob Bowman)
Prix du Vidéo Clip ..... *Earth Song* (Michael Jackson)
Trophée Fun Radio ..... *Nadja* (Michael Almereyda)
Prix Littéraire ..... *Les mécaniques des ombres* (Benjamin Legrand)

1995

Grand Prix du Festival ..... *Heavenly Creatures*, A.K.A. *Créatures célestes* (Peter Jackson)
Prix du Jury ..... *Dellamorte Dellamore*, A.K.A. *Cemetery Man* (Michele Soavi)
Prix Spécial du Jury ..... *Akumulátor 1* (Jan Sverak)
Prix de la Critique Internationale ..... *Akumulátor 1* (Jan Sverak)
Prix du Public ..... *Dellamorte, Dellamore*, A.K.A. *Cemetery Man* (Michele Soavi)
Grand Prix du Court Métrage ..... *J'veux qu'on m'aime* (Patrick Contre)
Mention Spéciale du Jury Courts Métrages ..... *Ovo*, A.K.A. *Eggs*, A.K.A. *Oeufs* (Pierre Bouchon, José Miguel Ribeiro, Yvon Guillon)
Prix des Inédits Vidéo (tie) ..... *La cité des monstres*, A.K.A. *Freaked* (Alex Winter, Tom Stern) and *Le crépuscule des aigles*, A.K.A. *Fatherland* (Christopher Menaul)
Prix du Vidéo Clip ..... *Jurassic Park*
Prix Littéraire ..... *Le chien qui rit* (Anne Dugüel)

1994

Grand Prix du Festival ..... *Jiang Hu: Between Love and Glory*, A.K.A. *La fiancée aux cheveux blancs*, A.K.A. *Bai fa mo nu zhuan* (Ronny Yu)
Prix du Jury ..... *La ardilla roja*, A.K.A. *L'Ecureuil rouge* (Julio Medem)
Prix Spécial du Jury ..... *Man's Best Friend* (John Lafia)
Prix de la Critique Internationale ..... *La ardilla roja*, A.K.A. *L'Ecureuil rouge* (Julio Medem)
Prix du Public ..... *Return of the Living Dead 3* (Bryan Yuzna)
Grand Prix du Court Métrage ..... *M. Foudamour, la lune promise* (Kram, Plof)
Mention Spéciale du Jury Courts Métrages ..... *Deus ex machina* (Vincent Mayrand)
Prix des Inédits Vidéo ..... *12h01—prisonnier du temps*, A.K.A. *12:01* (Jack Sholder)
Prix du Vidéo Clip (tie) ..... *Steam* (Peter Gabriel) and *Savoure le rouge* (Indochine)

Prix du Meilleur Ouvrage BD, Jeunes Auteurs ..... Stan and Vince for the *Vortex* series
Prix du Meilleur Ouvrage BD, Auteurs Confirmés ..... *L'histoire du corbac aux baskets* (Fred)

Frightmares Film Festival

A defunct, shorts only event. John Johnson confirms this is a complete list of winners.

2008

Best Picture ..... *Callous Sentiment*
Chupacabre Surprise Award ..... *Dirth*

Grimm Up North

A.K.A. Grimmfest. Rhiannon Clifford emails me: "This is the first year [2010] Grimm Up North is having an awards ceremony." Presents the Golden Scythe Award. First screened in 2009.

2010

Best British Film ..... *13 Hrs* (dir: Jonathan Glendening)
Best International Film ..... *Bedevilled* (dir: Cheolso Jang)
Best Low Budget Film ..... *Opstandelsen* (dir: Casper Haugegaard)
Best Short Film ..... *Click*
Best Direction ..... Hélène Cattet, Bruno Forzani (*Amer*)
Best Actor ..... Francisco Barreiro (*We Are What We Are*)
Best Actress ..... Hanna Stanbridge (*Outcast*)
Best British Newcomer ..... Colm & Tom McCarthy (*Outcast*)
Best Production Design ..... *13 Hrs*
Best SFX ..... *The Pack*

Haapsalu Horror & Fantasy Film Festival

"The White Lady Award, and accompanying glass statuette portraying the symbol of Haapsalu—the ghost of the White Lady appearing on full moon nights to the chapel window of Haapsalu's bishops castle—is presented jointly by the festival and the City of Haapsalu [in Estonia]. The award was initiated in 2008 with the aim of recognizing selected filmmakers for their contribution to fantastical, horror or genre cinema, as well as celebrating films premiering at HOFF."

2011 ..... Stephen Manuel (director) for European sneak preview of *Iron Doors*
2011 ..... Axel Wedekind (actor) for European sneak preview of *Iron Doors*
2011 ..... Shinya Tsukamoto (director) for Lifetime Achievement in Fantastic Cinema with *Tetsuo* series
2010 ..... Adam Mason (director) for the World Premiere of *Pig*
2010 ..... Andrey Iskanov (director) for the World Premiere of *Ingression*
2009 ..... Simeon Halligan (director) for the International premiere of *Splintered*
2008 ..... Brian Yuzna (producer-director) for Lifetime Achievement in Fantastic Cinema
2008 ..... Marek Piestrak (director) for Lifetime Achievement in Fantastic Cinema

Halloween Horror Nights Scary Film Competition

Sponsored by Universal Studio's Halloween Horror Nights. Over 100 entered their 2010 contest, which was whittled down to one winner. See Eyegore Award.

2010 ..... *Jasper* (Elizabeth Schieffer)
2009 ..... *Bedfellows* (Drew Daywalt)

HAuNTcon Amateur Horror Film Festival

2010

1st Place, Feature Length ..... *Horrid* (dir: James Pronath)
2nd Place, Feature Length ..... *The Haunting of North 3rd Street* (dir: Jon Hyers)
1st Place, Short Film ..... *Knicker Knockers* (dir: Robert Kreh)
2nd Place, Short Film ..... *Dissimulation* (dir: Rob Winfrey)
3rd Place, Short Film ..... *Hellraiser: Deader—Winter's Lament* (dir: Jonathan S. Kui)

2009

Best Feature Film ..... *Fistful of Brains* (dir: Christine Parker)
Best Short Film ..... *Crotch Rot* (dir: Robert Kreh)

Horrific Film Fest

2010

Best Feature ..... *Naked Horror*
Best Short Film ..... *Freaky Friday the #13*
Best Special Effect ..... *Scum*

Best Actress ..... Christine Holder
Best Actor ..... Tom Long (*Cutting Room*)

2009

Best Feature ..... *No Exit*
Best Short Film ..... *Psycho Killer Attack!*
Best Actress ..... Allyn Carrell (*Fright Flick*)
Best Actor ..... Jerome Scott (*The Inherited*)
Best Special Effects ..... *Echo*

2008

Best Feature ..... *It's My Party and I'll Die If I Want To*
Best Short ..... *Host*
Best Actress ..... Géraldine Bazán (*La hacienda del terror*)
Best Actor ..... George H. Russell (*Long Pig*)
Best FSX ..... *Scorned*

Horror Dance

2008

Best Film of the Year ..... *Nothing Face* (dir: Mitch Csanadi)
Director's Choice ..... *Dead Noon* (dir: Andrew Wiest)
Best International Film ..... *Anatomy* (dir: Vincenzo Pandolfi)

2007

Best Film ..... *The Sisters* (dir: Yap Jen Huey)
Director's Choice ..... *A Four Course Meal* (dir: Clay Liford)
Best New Director ..... *Chicken Ass 2* (dir: Joe Weaver)
Honorable Mention ..... *Peri'l* (dir: J.D. Hawkins, Corey Shields, Errol Anthony Wilks)
Honorable Mention ..... *H.P. Lovecraft's The Other Gods* (dir: Peter Rhodes)
Honorable Mention ..... *Yard Work* (dir: Brian Razzano)

2006

Best Film ..... *Nothing In the Dark* (dir: John Correl, Jr.)
Director's Choice ..... *Bloodspit* (dir: D. Hendrix)
Honorable Mention ..... *Snow Day, Bloody Snow Day* (dir: Faye Hoerauf, Jessica Baxter)

2005

Best Villain ..... *Trick or Treat* (dir: Oliver Pearce)
Best Make-Up/Special Effects ..... *My Skin!* (dir: Christopher Alan Broadstone)
Best Screenplay ..... *Pervula* (dir: Armando D. Muñoz, Justin Mapes)
Best Production ..... *The Crypt Club* (dir: Miguel Gallego)
Kat Cresswell Memorial Scream Queen Award ..... *Siege of Evil* (dir: Jeff Carney)

Director's Choice Award ..... *Street Tales of Terror* (dir: J.D. Hawkins, Corey Shields)
Best Film ..... *Herbie!* (dir: Drew Barnhardt)

Horrorvision: Spanish Horror Trash Film Festival

Short films only.

2010

Horrorvision First Prize ..... *Santiago Martínez, cazador de ovnis y alienígenas* (Manuel Ortega Lasaga)
Monstermania Second Prize ..... *Blarghaaahrgarg* (dir: Nuria Leon Bernardo; prod: Fernando Alle)
Sangre Award for Best FX ..... *Brutal Relax* (dir: Adrián Cardona, Rafa Dengrá, David Muñoz; FX by Adrián Cardona, Eva Ayats)

2009

Horrorvision First Prize ..... *Space Monster* (dir: J. O. Romero)
Monstermania Second Prize ..... *Chucladores de Cerebros*, A.K.A. *Brain Suckers* (dir: Paulo Morgue)
Sangre Award for Best FX ..... *Papa Wrestling* (dir: Fernando Alle)

H.P. Lovecraft Film Festival & CthulhuCon

Their site promises that "2004 and all previous year" is coming soon, so this list is incomplete. Their site is also confusing as to whether their Audience Awards are a kind of Brown Jenkin Award, or a separate award.

2010

Brown Jenkin Award for Best Weird Tale ..... *Derailed* (Nicolas Simonin)
Brown Jenkin Award for Best Lovecraftian Film ..... *Fyren* A.K.A. *Keeper of the Light* (Robert P. Olsson)
Special Audience Award for Most Disturbing Film ..... *To My Mother and Father* (Can Evrenol)
Brown Jenkin Award for Best Comedy ..... *Frank DanCoolo: Paranormal Drug Dealer* (Andrew W. Jones)
Deep One Award for Best Screenplay ..... Brian R. Hauser
Howie Award for Lovecraftian Cinema ..... The H.P. Lovecraft Historical Society, Andrew Leman, Sean Branney
Special Jury Award for Spirit of the Festival ..... *The Call of C'Thulu*
Special Jury Award for Spirit of the Festival ..... *Dunwich*
Special Jury Award for Spirit of the Festival ..... *Rats in the Wall*
Special Jury Award for Spirit of the Festival ..... *Dagon*

2009

Howie Award ..... Dan O'Bannon's.
Brown Jenkin Award, Best Feature ..... *Colour from the Dark*
Brown Jenkin Award, Best Comedy ..... *Relic of Cthulhu*
Brown Jenkin Award, Best Short ..... *Dirt Dauber*
Audience Award, Best of Show ..... *Relic of Cthulhu*
Audience Award, Best Adaptation ..... *Pickman's Muse*
Deep One Award, Best Screenplay ..... *Effulgence* (Andrew Fuller)

2008

Howie Award ..... Brian Lumley
Howie Award ..... Mike Mignola
Brown Jenkin Award, Best of Festival ..... *AM 1200* (David Prior)
Brown Jenkin Award, Best Cosmic Horror Film ..... *AM 1200* (David Prior)
Brown Jenkin Award, Best Short Film ..... *Eel Girl* (Paul Campion)
Brown Jenkin Award, Best Special Effects ..... *Eel Girl* (Paul Campion)
Brown Jenkin Award, Best Comedy ..... *Eel Girl* (Paul Campion)
Brown Jenkin Award, Best Dramatic Reading ..... Doug Bradley (*The Outsider*)
Audience Award for Best Feature ..... *Alien Raiders* (Ben Rock)
Deep One Screenwriter Award, 1st Prize ..... Jeffrey Blake Palmer (*The Sleeping Deep*)
Deep One Screenwriter Award, Runner-Up ..... Faisal A. Qureshi (*In Bright Darkness*)

2007

The H. P. Lovecraft Award ..... Bernie Wrightson
The H. P. Lovecraft Award ..... Richard Band
The H. P. Lovecraft Award ..... John Carpenter
The Brown Jenkin Award, Audience Pick for Best Short ..... Gary Irwin (*Of Darkness*)
The Brown Jenkin Award ..... Daniel Gildark (*Cthulhu*)
The Brown Jenkin Award ..... Balaji K. Kumar (*9 Lives of Mara*)
The Brown Jenkin Award ..... Shawn Linden (*Nobody*)

2006

The H. P. Lovecraft Award ..... Ramsey Campbell
The H. P. Lovecraft Award ..... Robert Price

The Brown Jenkin Award ..... Raymond Zablocki (*Binding Silence*)
The Brown Jenkin Award ..... Paul von Stoetzel (*Asleep in the Deep*)
The Brown Jenkin Award ..... Michael Granberry (*From Beyond*)

2005

The H. P. Lovecraft Award ..... Christopher Heyerdahl
The Brown Jenkin Award, Best of Festival ..... H. P. Lovecraft Historical Society (*The Call of Cthulhu*)
The Brown Jenkin Award, Audience Pick ..... H. P. Lovecraft Historical Society (*The Call of Cthulhu*)

Hugo Award

Hugo honors works released the previous year (i.e., 2010 winners were released in 2009, etc.) The Hugos are primarily a literary award. The below winners list is for the Best Dramatic Presentation and Retro award categories. It does not include Hugo's many non-dramatic categories. There have been three Retro Hugos to date: in 2004, 2001, and 1996. Unless a listing says Retro Hugo, it's a Best Dramatic Presentation winner, either Long Form or Short Form. This distinction between Long and Short did not exist prior to 2003. By "sc" I mean screenplay.

2010 (Long Form) ..... *Moon* (dir/story: Duncan Jones; sc: Nathan Parker)
2010 (Short Form) ..... *Doctor Who*, "The Waters of Mars" (dir: Graeme Harper; sc: Russell T. Davies, Phil Ford)
2009 (Long Form) ..... *WALL-E* (dir: Andrew Stanton; sc: Andrew Stanton, Jim Reardon; story: Andrew Stanton, Pete Docter)
2009 (Short Form) ..... *Dr. Horrible's Sing-Along Blog* (dir: Joss Whedon; sc: Joss Whedon, Zack Whedon, Jed Whedon, Maurissa Tancharoen)
2008 (Long Form) ..... *Stardust* (dir: Matthew Vaughn; sc: Matthew Vaughn, Jane Goldman; original novel: Neil Gaiman)
2008 (Short Form) ..... *Doctor Who*, "Blink" (dir: Hettie MacDonald; sc: Steven Moffat)
2007 (Long Form) ..... *Pan's Labyrinth* (dir/sc: Guillermo del Toro)
2007 (Short Form) ..... *Doctor Who*, "The Girl in the Fireplace" (dir: Euros Lyn; sc: Steven Moffat)
2006, (Long Form) ..... *Serenity* (dir/sc: Joss Whedon)
2006 (Short Form) ..... *Doctor Who*, "The Empty Child"/"The Doctor Dances" (dir: James Hawes; sc: Steven Moffat)
2005 (Long Form) ..... *The Incredibles* (dir/sc: Brad Bird)
2005, (Short Form) ..... *Battlestar Galactica*, "33" (dir: Michael Rymer; sc: Ronald D. Moore)
2004 (Long Form) ..... *The Lord of the Rings: The Return of the King* (dir: Peter Jackson; sc: Peter Jackson, Fran Walsh, Philippa Boyens; original novel: J. R. R. Tolkien)
2004 (Short Form) ..... Gollum's acceptance speech at the 2003 MTV Movie Awards (dir/sc: Peter Jackson, Fran Walsh, Philippa Boyens)
2004 (Retro Hugo) ..... *The War of the Worlds*, 1954 (dir: Byron Haskin; sc: Barré Lyndon; original novel: H.G. Wells)
2003 (Long Form) ..... *The Lord of the Rings: The Two Towers* (dir: Peter Jackson; sc: Peter Jackson, Fran Walsh, Philippa Boyens, Stephen Sinclair; original novel: J. R. R. Tolkien)
2003 (Short Form) ..... *Buffy the Vampire Slayer*, "Conversations with Dead People" (dir: Nick Marck; sc: Jane Espenson, Drew Goddard)
2002 ..... *The Lord of the Rings: The Fellowship of the Ring* (dir: Peter Jackson; sc: Peter Jackson, Fran Walsh, Philippa Boyens; original novel: J. R. R. Tolkien)
2001 ..... *Crouching Tiger, Hidden Dragon* (dir: Ang Lee; sc: Wang Hui-Ling, James Schamus, Tsai Kuo Jung; original novel: Wang Dulu)
2001, (Retro Hugo) ..... *Destination Moon*, 1951 (dir: Irving Pichel; sc: Alford Van Ronkel, James O'Hanlon, Robert A. Heinlein; original novel: Robert A. Heinlein)
2000 ..... *Galaxy Quest* (dir: Dean Parisot; sc: David Howard, Robert Gordon; story: David Howard)
1999 ..... *The Truman Show* (dir: Peter Weir; sc: Andrew Niccol)
1998 ..... *Contact* (dir: Robert Zemeckis; sc: James V. Hart, Michael Goldenberg; story: Carl Sagan, Ann Druyan; original novel: Carl Sagan)
1997 ..... *Babylon 5*, "Severed Dreams" (dir: David Eagle; sc: J. Michael Straczynski)
1996 ..... *Babylon 5*, "The Coming of Shadows" (dir: Janet Greek; sc: J. Michael Straczynski)
1996, (Retro Hugo) ..... *The Picture of Dorian Gray*, 1946 (dir/sc: Albert Lewin; original novel: Oscar Wilde)
1995 ..... *Star Trek: The Next Generation*, "All Good Things..." (dir: Winrich Kolbe; sc: Ronald D. Moore, Brannon Braga)
1994 ..... *Jurassic Park* (dir: Steven Spielberg; sc: David Koepp, Michael Crichton; original novel: Michael Crichton)
1993 ..... *Star Trek: The Next Generation*, "The Inner Light" (dir: Peter Lauritson; sc: Peter Allan Fields, Morgan Gendel; story: Morgan Gendel)

1992 ..... *Terminator 2: Judgment Day* (dir: James Cameron; sc: James Cameron, William Wisher, Jr.)
1991 ..... *Edward Scissorhands* (dir: Tim Burton; sc: Caroline Thompson; story: Tim Burton, Caroline Thompson)
1990 ..... *Indiana Jones and the Last Crusade* (dir: Steven Spielberg; sc: Jeffrey Boam; story: George Lucas, Menno Meyjes)
1989 ..... *Who Framed Roger Rabbit* (dir: Robert Zemeckis; sc: Jeffrey Price, Peter S. Seaman; original novel: Gary K. Wolf)
1988 ..... *The Princess Bride* (dir: Rob Reiner; sc/original novel: William Goldman)
1987 ..... *Aliens* (dir/sc: James Cameron; story: James Cameron, David Giler, Walter Hill)
1986 ..... *Back to the Future* (dir: Robert Zemeckis; sc: Robert Zemeckis, Bob Gale)
1985 ..... *2010* (dir/sc: Peter Hyams; original novel: Arthur C. Clarke)
1984 ..... *Star Wars, Episode VI: Return of the Jedi* (dir: Richard Marquand; sc: Lawrence Kasdan, George Lucas; story: George Lucas)
1983 ..... *Blade Runner* (dir: Ridley Scott; sc: Hampton Fancher, David Peoples; original novel: Philip K. Dick)
1982 ..... *Raiders of the Lost Ark* (dir: Steven Spielberg; sc: Lawrence Kasdan; story: George Lucas, Philip Kaufman)
1981 ..... *Star Wars, Episode V: The Empire Strikes Back* (dir: Irvin Kershner; sc: Leigh Bracket, Lawrence Kasdan; story: George Lucas)
1980 ..... *Alien* (dir: Ridley Scott; sc: Dan O'Bannon; story: Dan O'Bannon, Ronald Shusett)
1979 ..... *Superman* (dir: Richard Donner; sc: Mario Puzo, David Newman, Leslie Newman, Robert Benton; story: Mario Puzo; original character: Jerry Siegel, Joe Shuster)
1978 ..... *Star Wars Episode IV: A New Hope* (dir/sc: George Lucas)
1977 ..... no award
1976 ..... *A Boy and His Dog* (dir: L.Q. Jones; sc: L.Q. Jones, Wayne Cruseturner; original story: Harlan Ellison)
1975 ..... *Young Frankenstein* (dir: Mel Brooks; sc/story: Mel Brooks, Gene Wilder; original novel: Mary Shelley)
1974 ..... *Sleeper* (dir: Woody Allen; sc: Woody Allen, Marshall Brickman)
1973 ..... *Slaughterhouse-Five* (dir: George Roy Hill; sc: Stephen Geller, original novel: Kurt Vonnegut, Jr.)
1972 ..... *A Clockwork Orange* (dir/sc: Stanley Kubrick; original story: Anthony Burgess)
1971 ..... no award
1970 ..... news coverage of Apollo 11 (multiple sources)
1969 ..... *2001: A Space Odyssey* (dir: Stanley Kubrick; sc: Stanley Kubrick, Arthur C. Clarke; original story: Arthur C. Clarke)
1968 ..... *Star Trek*, "The City on the Edge of Forever" (dir: Joseph Pevney; sc: Harlan Ellison)
1966 ..... no award
1967 ..... *Star Trek*, "The Menagerie" (dir: Marc Daniels; sc: Gene Roddenberry)
1965 ..... *Dr. Strangelove or: How I Learned to Stop Worrying and Love the Bomb* (dir: Stanley Kubrick; sc: Stanley Kubrick, Terry Southern, Peter George; original novel: Peter George)
1964 ..... no award
1963 ..... no award
1962 ..... *The Twilight Zone* (creator/sc: Rod Serling)
1961 ..... *The Twilight Zone* (creator/sc: Rod Serling)
1960 ..... *The Twilight Zone* (creator/sc: Rod Serling)
1959 ..... no award
1958 ..... *The Incredible Shrinking Man* (dir: Jack Arnold; sc/story: Richard Matheson)

Imagine: Amsterdam Fantastic Film Festival

The Sp!ts (sic) Silver Scream Award is an audience award. The Méliès d'Argent is a jury prize. The Black Tulip is a jury prize for best fantastic feature of the festival (except in 2006). The Imagine Time Capsule is for online fantastic shorts.

2010

Sp!ts Silver Scream Award ..... Adam Elliot (*Mary and Max*)
Méliès d'Argent ..... Roland Vranik (*Transmission*)
Black Tulip, Best Feature ..... Arpad Sopsits (*The Seventh Circle*)
Imagine Time Capsule ..... Suzi Terror (*The Vegan Vampire*)
Career Achievement Award ..... Dick Maas

2009

Sp!ts Silver Scream Award ..... Tomas Alfredson (*Let the Right One In*)
Méliès d'Argent ..... F. Javier Gutiérrez (*Before the Fall*)
Black Tulip, Best Feature ..... Tomas Alfredson (*Let the Right One In*)

2008

Sp!ts Silver Scream Award ..... Jaume Balagueró & Paco Plaza (*[REC]*)
Méliès d'Argent ..... Gonzalo López-Gallego (*King of the Hill*)
Black Tulip, Best Feature ..... Nacho Vigalondo (*Timecrimes*, A.K.A. *Los cronocrímenes*)
Career Achievement Award ..... Tim Burton

2007

Sp!ts Silver Scream Award ..... Anders Thomas Jensen (*Adam's Apples*)
Méliès d'Argent ..... David Moreau & Xavier Palud (*Them*, A.K.A. *Ils*)
Black Tulip, Best Feature ..... Jens Lien (*The Bothersome Man*)
Career Achievement Award ..... Terry Gilliam

2006

Sp!ts Silver Scream Award ..... Vincent Lannoo (*Ordinary Man*)
Méliès d'Argent ..... Måns Mårlind & Björn Stein (*Storm*)
Black Tulip, Best Feature ..... Pål Sletaune (*Next Door*)
Black Tulip, Best Feature Debut ..... Dave McKean & Neil Gaiman (*MirrorMask*)
Black Tulip, Best Short ..... András Dési & Gábor Móray (*Doll No. 639*)
Career Achievement Award ..... Roger Corman

2005

Sp!ts Silver Scream Award ..... Stephen Chow (*Kung Fu Hustle*)
Méliès d'Argent ..... Fabrice Du Welz (*Calvaire*)
Career Achievement Award ..... Ray Harryhausen, Paul Naschy

2004

Sp!ts Silver Scream Award ..... Enric Folch (*Tempus Fugit*)
Méliès d'Argent ..... Anders Thomas Jensen (*De Grønne Slagtere*)

2003

Sp!ts Silver Scream Award ..... Hayao Miyazaki (*Spirited Away*)
Méliès d'Argent ..... Marc Evans (*My Little Eye*)
Career Achievement Award ..... Lloyd Kaufman

2002

Sp!ts Silver Scream Award ..... Richard Kelly (*Donnie Darko*)
Méliès d'Argent ..... Guillermo del Toro (*El Espinazo del Diablo*)
Career Achievement Award ..... Paul Verhoeven

2001

Sp!ts Silver Scream Award ..... Daniel Monzón (*El Corazón del Guerrero*)
Méliès d'Argent ..... Daniel Monzón (*El Corazón del Guerrero*)
Career Achievement Award ..... Dario Argento

2000

Sp!ts Silver Scream Award ..... Dean Parisot (*Galaxy Quest*)
Career Achievement Award ..... Wes Craven

1990–1999

1999, Sp!ts Silver Scream Award ..... David Cronenberg (*Existenz*)
1998, Sp!ts Silver Scream Award ..... Alex Proyas (*Dark City*)
1997 ..... No awards this year.
1996, Sp!ts Silver Scream Award ..... Robert Rodriguez (*From Dusk Till Dawn*)
1995, Sp!ts Silver Scream Award ..... Michele Soavi (*Dellamorte Dellamore*, A.K.A. *Cemetery Man*)
1994, Sp!ts Silver Scream Award ..... Brian Yuzna (*Return of the Living Dead 3*)
1993, Sp!ts Silver Scream Award ..... Peter Jackson (*Braindead*)
1992, Sp!ts Silver Scream Award ..... Katsuhiro Otomo (*Akira*)
1991, Sp!ts Silver Scream Award ..... Jonathan Demme (*The Silence of the Lambs*)
1990, Sp!ts Silver Scream Award ..... Clive Barker (*Nightbreed*)

Indy Horror Film Festival

2010

Best Feature Film ..... *Michael Morlock's Supernatural World*
Best Director ..... Matthew Roth (*The Man Who Collected Food*)
Best Short Film ..... *Devil's Creek*
Best Actor ..... Robert O. Berdahl (*Bind*)
Best Actress ..... Melinda Messenger (*Exposure*)
Best Screenwriter ..... Patrick Rea (*Next Caller*)
Best Special Effects ..... *Devil's Creek*
Best Death Scene ..... *Bind*

International Horror and Sci-Fi Film Festival

2010

Best Horror Feature ..... *Rage*
Best Horror Feature Screenplay ..... *Ashes*
Best Sci-Fi Feature ..... *Everything's Eventual*
Best Sci-Fi Feature Screenplay ..... *Lunopolis*
Best Horror Short ..... *The Furred Man*
Best Student Horror Short ..... *Abra Cadaver*
Best Sci-Fi Short ..... *Cockpit: The Rule of Engagement*
Best Student Sci-Fi Short ..... *Kontakt*
Horror and Sci-Fi Hall of Fame Inductees ..... Lance Henriksen, Charles Cyphers
Screenplay Competition, 1st Place (unproduced) ..... *Plantation* (Ryan Gilmore)
Screenplay Competition, 2nd Place (unproduced) ..... *Ripper* (Joe Randazzo)
Screenplay Competition, 3rd Place (unproduced) ..... *Tatt* (Rob Ingalls)

Screenplay Competition, 4th Place (unproduced) ..... *Serial* (Patrick Kevin Day, Andrew Hanson)
Screenplay Competition, 5th Place (unproduced) ..... *Dome* (Lawrence Garcia)
Screenplay Competition, 6th Place (unproduced) ..... *Dead of Night* (Alexander Hilhorst)
Screenplay Competition, 7th Place (unproduced) ..... *Sunny's Nights* (Jerel Damon)
Screenplay Competition, 8th Place (unproduced) ..... *Hoax* (Matt Allen, Scott Park)
Screenplay Competition, 9th Place (unproduced) ..... *Walk In* (Jeffrey Sherman)
Screenplay Competition, 10th Place (unproduced) ..... *Dead Crows* (Chris Todd)

2009

Best Horror Feature ..... *XII*
Best Horror Screenplay ..... *Neighbor*
Best Horror Short ..... *Jack the Reaper*
Best Student Horror Short ..... *Void*
Best Sci-Fi Feature ..... *Eyeborgs*
Best Sci-Fi Screenplay ..... *8th Wonderland*
Best Sci-Fi Short ..... *Schizofredric*
Best Student Sci-Fi Short ..... *Bohemibot*
Hall of Fame Inductees ..... Casper Van Dien, Marilyn Burns, Judith O'Dea
Screenplay Competition, 1st Place (unproduced) ..... *2058* (Louis Rosenberg)
Screenplay Competition, 2nd Place (unproduced) ..... *House of Wolves* (Joseph Gumbs)
Screenplay Competition, 3rd Place (unproduced) ..... *The Untitled Zombie Project* (Suzanne Kelly)
Screenplay Competition, 4th Place (unproduced) ..... *Macau Twilight* (Tony Shyu)
Screenplay Competition, 5th Place (unproduced) ..... *Upgrade* (Louis Rosenberg)
Screenplay Competition, 6th Place (unproduced) ..... *Five Thousand Years* (Jim Grieco)
Screenplay Competition, 7th Place (unproduced) ..... *White Rabbit* (David Lawrence)
Screenplay Competition, 8th Place (unproduced) ..... *Dimensions, Part 1* (David Sheperd)
Screenplay Competition, 9th Place (unproduced) ..... *Man Monkey* (Michaele Lyons, Dennis Mahoney)
Screenplay Competition, 10th Place (unproduced) ..... *Ashes to Ashes* (Jon Stout)

2008

Best Horror Feature ..... *Farmhouse*
Best Horror Short ..... *Kirksdale*
Best College Horror Short ..... *Zombie Gets a Date*
Best Sci-Fi Feature ..... *Ray Bradbury's Chrysalis*
Best Sci-Fi Short ..... *D-I-M, Deus in Machina*
Best Horror Screenplay ..... *Alien Raiders*
Best Sci-Fi Screenplay ..... *Man from Earth*
Special Achievement in Cinematography ..... *Probed*
Hall of Fame Inductees ..... Adrienne King, Jeffrey Combs

2007

Best Horror Feature ..... *Long Pigs*
Best Cinematography, Horror Feature ..... *Frayed*
Best Visual Effects, Horror Feature ..... *Brain Dead*
Best Sci-Fi Feature ..... *11 Minutes Ago*
Best Screenplay, Sci-Fi Feature ..... *11 Minutes Ago*
Best Cinematography, Sci-Fi Feature ..... *Nobody*
Best Horror Short ..... *Coming to Town*
Best Horror Micro Short ..... *Gourmet*
Creepiest Horror Short ..... *Anesthesia*
Best Cannibalism, Horror Short ..... *The Butcher*
Goriest Horror Short ..... *The Lycanthrope*
Creative Vision Award, Horror Short ..... *Nightmare*
Best Demon, Horror Short ..... *The Sitter*
Best Production Design, Horror Short ..... *The First Vampire*
Best Horror Short Screenplay ..... *Summer Job*
Best Zombie Film, Horror Short ..... *Gay Zombie*
Best Revenge, Horror Short ..... *Criticized*
Breakout Talent, Horror Short ..... *Harbinger*
Best Arizona Horror Short ..... *Revelation Nine*
Best Visual Effects, Horror Short ..... *Revelation Nine*
Best Ghost Story, Horror Short ..... *Para-Normal*
Best International Horror Short ..... *Dara*
Best Splatter, Horror Short ..... *Psycho Hillbilly Cabin Massacre*
Best Visual Effects, Horror Short ..... *Itsy Bitsy*
Best Animation, Horror Short ..... *Toll*
Best Cinematography, Horror Short ..... *We're Closed*
Short Film Hall of Fame, Horror ..... *Pig Tale*
Short Film Hall of Fame, Horror ..... *The Descendant*
Best Actor, Horror Short ..... David Morse (*AWOL*)
Most Promising Filmmaker, Horror Short ..... *Of Darkness*
Best Sci-Fi Short ..... *Epicac*
Best Dark Future Sci-Fi Short ..... *The Un-Gone*
Best Dystopic Future, Sci-Fi Short ..... *The Nothing Pill*
Best Alternate Reality, Sci-Fi Short ..... *Haunted Planet*
Best Animated Sci-Fi Short ..... *Glitch*
Best Director, Sci-Fi Short ..... *Face Machine*
Best Dark Future Screenplay, Sci-Fi Short ..... *Eli*
Best Screenplay, Sci-Fi Short ..... *Other Worlds*
Best Short Fantasy Film ..... *Victor Y La Maquina*
Best Fandom Fantasy Film ..... *Maklar, Anyone?*
Best Foreign Language Sci-Fi Short ..... *La lluvia*
Best Humorous Sci-Fi Short Film ..... *Auto Da Fe*
Best Set Design, Sci-Fi Short ..... *Mogadon 7*
Hall of Fame Inductees ..... Linda Blair, Ken Foree, Ted V. Mikels

2006

Best Science Fiction Feature ..... *Firefly*
Best Director ..... *Firefly*
Best Documentary ..... *Pulp Fiction Art: Cheap Thrills and Painted Nightmares*

Best Animated Sci-Fi Feature ..... *Robotech: Shadow Chronicles*
Best Science Fiction Short Film ..... *The Grandfather Paradox*
Best Science Fiction Animated Short ..... *I Must Destroy You*
Best Alternate Reality Featurette ..... *Assumption*
Best Surreal Short Film ..... *Reality Check*
Best Science Fiction Musical ..... *Alien Rose*
Best Alternate Reality Short ..... *Outside In*
Best Science Fiction Tragedy ..... *Microgravity*
Best Cinematography ..... *Model Man*
Best Story in an SF Short Film ..... *The Futurist*
Best Set Design ..... *Adidas—"Adicolor Green"*
Best Surreal Future Short Film ..... *Last Man in Brooklyn*
Best Fantasy Short Film ..... *Say That You Love Me...*
Best Horror Feature ..... *Unrest*
Best Actress ..... Corri English (*Unrest*)
Best Screenplay ..... *In Memorium*
Best Splatter ..... *The Slaughter*
Best Short ..... *Penny Dreadful*
Best College Sound Design ..... *Penny Dreadful*
Best Editing ..... *Penny Dreadful*
Best Actress College Short ..... Emily Vacchiano (*Penny Dreadful*)
Creepiest Micro Short ..... *No. 12*
Best Zombie Comedy ..... *Zombies in Love*
Most Disturbing Short ..... *Faceless*
Atomic Comics Fright Fest Award ..... *Zomburrito*
Best Zombie Film ..... *Recently Deceased*
Creepiest College Short ..... *Watcher*
Best Foreign Short ..... *Akai*
Goriest Micro Short ..... *Deadly Tantrum*
Best Dark Future Drama ..... *A Through M*
Best Screenplay ..... *A Through M*
Best Dark Fantasy Short Film ..... *Scribble*
Best Science Fiction Satire ..... *Passion to the Max*
Best Distopic Future Short Film ..... *Bartholomew's Song*
Best Special Effects ..... *Man vs. Woman*
Best Dark Future Foreign Film ..... *Missing Pages*
Best Dark Future Short Film ..... *The Salesman*
Best Superhero Short Film ..... *Dial 'A' for Alphaman*
Best Accidental Apocalypse ..... *Genesis Antipode*
Best Science Fiction Short Drama ..... *NIA*
Best Black and White Science Fiction Short *36*
Best Story in a Dark Future Short Film ..... *Robots Are Blue*
Creepiest Short ..... *Room to Breathe*
Micro Short Hall of Fame ..... *Ghost Busted*
Best Micro-Short Cinematography ..... *The Cobbler's Daughter*
Best Adaptation ..... *Pit and the Pendulum*
Most Promising Filmmaker ..... *Schattenkind*
Best Comedy/Horror, Micro Short ..... *Movie Monster Insurance*
Best Documentary ..... *Horror Fans*
Best Micro Short Zombie Film ..... *Cannibal Grave Yard*
Best Sound Design, Foreign Short ..... *Bad Dreams*
Creative Vision Award ..... *Siniestro*
Goriest Short ..... *A Terrorist Ate My Brain*
Best Comedy/Horror ..... *Zombie American*
Best Animated Short ..... *If I Had a Hammer*
Best Cinematography, Foreign Short ..... *Devilwood*
Best Costumes, Foreign Short ..... *Devilwood*
Best High School Short ..... *Snowmaniac*
Best Actress, Horror Short ..... Lea Moreno (*The Need*)
IHSFF Alumni Award, Best Returning Filmmaker ..... *The Resurrectionist*
Best Music ..... *The Resurrectionist*
Best Short Screenplay ..... *The Resurrectionist*
Best Short Film Cinematography ..... *The Listening Dead*
Best Effects ..... *The Listening Dead*
Best Production Design ..... *The Listening Dead*
Hall of Fame Inductee ..... Mick Garris

2005

Best Picture, Horror Feature ..... *The Dark Hours*
Best Director, Horror Feature ..... Paul Fox (*The Dark Hours*)
Best Creature Feature, Horror Feature ..... *Insecticidal*
Best Screenplay, Horror Feature ..... Wil Zmak (*The Dark Hours*)
Best Performance, Horror Feature ..... Aidan Devine (*The Dark Hours*)
Best Cinematography, Horror Feature ..... Rudy Harbon (*The Passing*)
Best Visual Effects, Horror Feature ..... *The Curse of El Charro*
Best Picture, Sci-Fi Feature ..... *Experiment*
Best Director, Sci-Fi Feature ..... Daniel Turner (*Experiment*)
Best Documentary, Sci-Fi Feature ..... *The Phoenix Lights*
Best Screenplay, Sci-Fi Feature ..... Charles Hall, Ryan Neill, Adam MacLean (*Messengers*)
Best Horror Short ..... *Herbie!*
Best College Horror Short ..... *The Boarder*
Best Sci-Fi Short ..... *No Sanctuary*
Best College Sci-Fi Short ..... *The Promethean*
Special Achievement in Sci-Fi Films ..... Peter Mayhew
Hall of Fame Inductees ..... Tobe Hooper, Lloyd Kaufman

It Came from Lake Michigan

Festival website is down. Its MySpace page offers nothing other than the 2007 winners. A genre news site reports that this festival first screened in 2006. Filmmaker Devi Snively (whom I trust) tells me that she won the Lizzie Borden Award in 2006 and that "My friend Don Gerron and his team won the big main award, though I don't know what it was called." I found it after some Googling. As best I know, the below 2007 list is complete, the 2006 list is incomplete, and there are no other award years.

2007

Best Sci-Fi Film ..... *The Edison Death Machine*
Best Fantasy Film ..... *Dork of the Rings*
Best Horror Film ..... *Witches' Night*
Best Screenplay (unproduced) ..... *Pulp Science Fiction* (Ron Podell)

2006

Best Sci-Fi Film ..... *Diabolical Tales: Part I* (Brandon Kane)
Lizzie Borden Award ..... *Confederate Zombie Massacre!* (Devi Snively)

Killer Film Fest

2010

Best Picture ..... *President's Day*
Best Short Film *2:22*
Best Director ..... Alex Horwitz (*Alice Jacobs Is Dead*)
Best Screenplay ..... *President's Day*
Best Editing ..... *Ouvert 24/7*
Best Sound Design ..... *Shellter*
Best Cinematography ..... *The Sacred*
Best Original Score ..... *Able*
Best Actor ..... Daniel Reininghaus (*Eyes Beyond*)
Best Actress ..... Morgane Housset (*Ouvert 24/7*)
Best SFX ..... *The Sacred*
Best Killer/Monster ..... *Papá Wrestling*
Best Death Scene ..... *Papá Wrestling*
Best Scare ..... *Survivors*
Best Use of a Former President ..... *President's Day*
Pointless Nudity Award ..... *Bring It Up*
Father of the Year Award ..... *Papá Wrestling*
Employee of the Month Award ..... *The Unfun House*
Most Frequent Use of One F@#$ing Phrase ..... *Sled* ("You know you're off the trail, right?")

Knoxville Horror Film Fest

They have two film competitions. A local/regional competition, and a "touring competition" for films that are not local/regional. All U.S. and international films vie in the touring competition.

2010

Best Local/Regional Longer Film ..... *Nightmare at Bunnyman Bridge*
Best Local/Regional Shorter Film ..... *Nightmare at Number 92*
Audience Award for Local/Regional Longer Film ..... *Nightmare at Bunnyman Bridge*
Audience Award for Local/Regional Shorter Film ..... *The Next*
Best Performance, Local/Regional Film ..... James Fritz (*Father's Day*)
Best Cinematography, Local/Regional Film ..... *Tumbleweed Holocaust*
Best Gore Effects, Local/Regional Film ..... *Tumbleweed Holocaust*
Best U.S. Film ..... *Death in Charge*
Best International Film (tie) ..... *Deus Irae* and *Off Season*
Audience Award for U.S. Film ..... *Death in Charge*
Audience Award for International Film ..... *Off Season*
Best Performance, Touring Film ..... Marina Benedict (*Death in Charge*)
Funniest Touring Film ..... *The Horror of Our Love*
Scariest Touring Film ..... *Off Season*
Weirdest Touring Film ..... *Tub*
KHFF Screenplay Contest Winner (unproduced) ..... Philip Tatler (*Eyepole*)

2009

Best U.S. Film, Jury Award ..... *Excision*
Best U.S. Film, Audience Award ..... *Excision*
Best International Film, Jury Award ..... *My Love Lives in the Sewer*
Best International Film, Audience Award ..... *My Love Lives in the Sewer*
Best Local Film, Jury Award ..... *Flesh of My Flesh*
Best Local Film, Audience Award ..... *Flesh of My Flesh*
Best Performance, Jury Prize ..... ensemble cast (*Flesh of My Flesh*)
Best Gore Effects, Jury Prize ..... *Road to Oblivion*

Lund International Fantastic Film Festival

A.K.A. Fantastisk Filmfestival.

2010

Siren Award for Best International Film ..... *The Loved Ones* (Sean Byrne)
Méliès d'Argent for Best European Fantastic Film ..... *Red White & Blue* (Simon Rumley)
Méliès Jury Special Mention ..... *Vampires*
Nomination for the a Méliès d'Or for Best European Fantastic Short Film ..... *Out of a Forest* (Tobias Gundorff Boesen)
Audience Choice Award, Best Feature Film ..... *Scott Pilgrim vs. the World*
Audience Choice Award, Best Short Film ..... *The Horribly Slow Murderer with the Extremely Inefficient Weapon*

2009

Méliès d'Argent (three-way tie) ..... *A Town Called Panic* and *The Siren* and *Van Diemen's Land*
Audience Choice Award, Best Feature Film ..... *Moon*
Audience Choice Award, Best Short Film ..... *Virtual Dating*

2008

Audience Choice Award, Best Feature Film ..... *The Fall*
Audience Choice Award, Best Short Film, Live Action ..... *The Auburn Hills Breakdown*
Audience Choice Award, Best Short Film, Animation ..... *Something Never Seen Before*
Nomination for a Méliès d'Or, Best European Short Film ..... *Because There Are Things You Never Forget*
Méliès d'Argent ..... *Left*

2007

Audience Choice Award, Best Short Film ..... *Raymond* (Fabrice Le Nezet, Francois Roisin, Jules Janaud)
Nomination for a Méliès d'Or, Best European Short Film ..... *Raymond* (Fabrice Le Nezet, Francois Roisin, Jules Janaud)
Audience Choice Award, Best Feature Film ..... *Severance* (Christopher Smith)

2006

Méliès d'Argent ..... *A Quiet Love*, A.K.A. *Die Blaue Grenze* (Till Franzen)
Nomination for a Méliès d'Or, Best European Short Film ..... *Mebana* (Daniel Wallentin)
Audience Choice Award, Best Feature Film ..... *The Kovak Box* (Daniel Monzón)
Audience Choice Award, Best Short Film, Animation ..... *Bendito Machine* (Jossie Malis)
Audience Choice Award, Best Short Film, Live Action ..... *Dupe* (Chris Waitt)

2005

Méliès d'Argent ..... *The Descent* (Neil Marshall)
Honorary Mention ..... *MirrorMask* (Dave McKean)
Audience Choice Award, Best Feature Film ..... *Antikörper* (Christian Alvart)
Audience Choice Award, Best Short Film, Live Action ..... *Der Beste* (Arne Jysch, Rasmus Borowski)
Audience Choice Award, Best Short Film, Animation ..... *One D* (Mike Grimshaw)
Nomination for a Méliès d'Or, Best European Short Film ..... *Der Beste* (Arne Jysch, Rasmus Borowski)

2004

Audience Choice Award, Best Feature Film ..... *Tempus Fugit* (Enric Folch)

Méliès d'Argent ..... *Tempus Fugit* (Enric Folch)
Honorary Mention ..... *Blueberry* (Jan Kounen)
Nomination for a Méliès d'Or, Best European Short Film ..... *Daddy's Boy* (Toni Harman)
Audience Choice Award, Best Short Film, Animation ..... *The God* (Konstantin Bronzit)
Audience Choice Award, Best Short Film, Live Action ..... *7h35 in the Morning* (Nacho Vigalondo)

2003

Audience Choice Award, Best Short Film, Live Action ..... *The Holiday Plan* (Allan Gustafasson)
Audience Choice Award, Best Short Film, Animation ..... *Love Tricycle* (Andrew Goode)
Honorary Mention ..... *Inside Out* (Oliver Knott)
Audience Choice Award, Best Feature Film ..... *Robot Stories* (Greg Pak)
Nomination for a Méliès d'Or, Best European Short Film ..... *My Bearded Mother* (Maria Hedman)
Méliès d'Argent ..... *Beyond Re-Animator* (Brian Yuzna)

2002

Méliès d'Argent ..... *Doctor Sleep* (Nick Willing)
Nomination for a Méliès d'Or, Best European Short Film ..... *Verboden Ogen*, A.K.A. *Forbidden Eyes* (Elbert Van Strien)
Audience Choice Award, Best Feature Film ..... *Series 7: The Contenders* (Daniel Minahan)
Audience Choice Award, Best Short Film, Animation ..... *Das Rad*, A.K.A. *Rocks* (Chris Stenner, Heidi Wittlinger, Arvid Uibel)
Audience Choice Award, Best Short Film, Live Action ..... *Fait d'Hiver*, A.K.A. *Gridlock* (Dirk Beliën)
Honorary Mention ..... *Dans la nuit*, A.K.A. *At Night* (François Reumont)
Honorary Mention ..... *Tattoo* (Robert Schwentke)

2001

Jury Grand Prize ..... *Chasing Sleep* (Michael Walker)
Jury Short Film Prize ..... *Argent content*, A.K.A. *Easy Money* (Philippe Dussol)
Audience Choice Award, Best Feature Film ..... *Donnie Darko* (Richard Kelly)
Audience Choice Award, Best Short Film, Animation ..... *Granny & Death* (Dimitri Vysotsky)
Audience Choice Award, Best Short Film, Live Action ..... *Argent content*, A.K.A. *Easy Money* (Philippe Dussol)
Honorary Mention ..... *Visitor Q* (Takashi Miike)

2000

Audience Choice Award, Best Feature Film ..... *Tuvalu* (Veit Helmer)

Audience Choice Award, Best Short Film ..... *Familjen Jacobssons Öden och Äventyr* (Anders Gustafsson)

1999

Jury Grand Prize ..... *Les Mille merveilles de l'Univers*, A.K.A. *The Thousand Wonders of the Universe* (Jean-Michel Roux)
Jury Short Film Prize ..... *Bryllupsnatten*, A.K.A. *The Wedding Night* (Mads Tobias Olsen)
Audience Choice Award, Best Feature Film ..... *Sieben Monde*, A.K.A. *Night Time* (Peter Fratzscher)
Audience Choice Award, Best Short Film ..... *Staevnemödet*, A.K.A. *The Date* (Mads Tobias Olsen)

1998

Jury Grand Prize ..... *Bullet Ballet* (Shinya Tsukamoto)
Honorary Mention ..... *Razor Blade Smile* (Jake West)
Jury Short Film Prize ..... *A Alma do Negócio*, A.K.A. *The Soul of Business* (José Roberto Torero)
Audience Choice Award, Best Feature Film ..... *Tetsuo*, A.K.A. *The Iron Man* (Shinya Tsukamoto)
Audience Choice Award, Best Short Film ..... *Días sin luz*, A.K.A. *Days Without Light* (Jaume Balagueró)

1997

Jury Grand Prize ..... *Face/Off* (John Woo)
Honorary Mention ..... *Retroactive* (Louis Morneau)
Audience Choice Award, Best Feature Film ..... *Retroactive* (Louis Morneau)
Audience Choice Award, Best Short Film ..... *Larger Than Life* (Ellory Elkayem)

1996

Jury Grand Prize ..... *The Dentist* (Brian Yuzna)
Audience Choice Award, Best Feature Film ..... *Crying Freeman* (Christophe Gans)

Madison Horror Film Festival

All awards are presented to the director, even the Cinematography and Special FX categories.

2009

Best Feature Film ..... *Murder Loves Killers Too* (Drew Barnhardt)
Best Short Film ..... *Death in Charge* (Devi Snively)
Best Cinematography ..... *Doctor "S" Battles the Sex Crazed Reefer Zombies: The Movie* (Bryan Ortiz)
Best Special FX ..... *Deadland* (Damon O'Steen)

2008

Best Feature Film ..... *Blood on the Highway* (Barak Epstein)
Best Short Film ..... *Initiation* (Stéphane Beaudoin)
Best Cinematography ..... *Initiation* (Stephen Beaudoin)
Best Special FX ..... *Brain Dead* (Kevin S. Tenney)

Maelstrom International Fantastic Film Festival

2010

Best Feature ..... *The Presence*
Best Horror Short ..... *The Familiar*
Best Sci-Fi Short ..... *Babylon 2084*
Best Fantasy Short ..... *Manual Práctico del Amigo Imaginario (abreviado)*
Best Animation Short ..... *A Complex Villainelle*
Best Action Short ..... *Street Angle*
Audience Favorite Horror ..... *The Familiar*
Audience Favorite Sci-Fi ..... *3rd Letter*
Audience Favorite Fantasy ..... *Manual Práctico del Amigo Imaginario (abreviado)*
Audience Favorite Animation ..... *Ducked and Covered*
Audience Favorite Action ..... *Street Angel*

2009

Best Feature ..... *Strigoi*
Best Animation Short ..... *Enter the Sandbox*
Best Fantasy Short ..... *Hart*
Best Horror Short ..... *Death in Charge*
Best Sci-Fi Short ..... *The Kirkie*

Melbourne Underground Film Festival

2010

Best Australian Film ..... *El monstro del mar!*
Runner-Up, Australian Film ..... *Bad Behaviour*
Best Australian Director ..... Joseph Sims (*Bad Behaviour*)
Best Australian Male Actor ..... Lindsay Farris (*Bad Behaviour*)
Best Australian Female Actor ..... Nelli Scarlet (*El monstro del mar!*)
Best Australian Supporting Male Actor ..... Roger Ward (*Bad Behaviour*)
Best Australian Supporting Female Actor ..... Ellen Grimshaw (*Bad Behaviour*)
Best Foreign Film ..... *The Wild and Wonderful Whites of West Virginia*

Best Foreign Director ..... Bruce La Bruce (*L.A. Zombie*)
Best Male Actor, Foreign Film ..... Morten Rudå (*Dark Souls*)
Best Female Actor, Foreign Film ..... Ingrid Schram (*Blondes in the Jungle*)
Special Jury Prize ..... *Road Train*
Best Guerrilla Film ..... *Burlesque*
Best Documentary ..... *Lanfranchi's Memorial Discotheque*
Best Cinematography ..... Stuart Simpson (*El monstro del mar!*)
Best Screenplay ..... Joseph Sims (*Bad Behaviour*)
Best Short Film ..... *Dark Horse & The Zimmer Gang*
Runner-Up, Short Film ..... *Carrot*
Best Male Actor in a Short Film ..... Miles O'Neill (*Carrot*)
Best Female Actor in a Short Film (tie) ..... Alin Sumarwata (*Dark Horse*) and Vanessa De Largie (*Crazy in the Night*)
Best International Short ..... *The Dandy Doctrine*

2009

Best Australian Film (tie) ..... *Into the Shadows* and *Eraser Children*
Runner-Up, Australian Film ..... *The Tumbler*
Best Australian Director ..... Marc Gracie (*The Tumbler*)
Best Australian Male Actor ..... Gary Sweet (*The Tumbler*)
Best Australian Female Actor (tie) ..... Sandra Casa (*Bad Habits*) and Kristen Condon (*The Beautiful & Damned*)
Best Australian Supporting Male Actor ..... Shane Nagle (*Eraser Children*)
Best Australian Supporting Female Actor ..... Georgii Speakman (*Carmilla Hyde*)
Special Jury Prize ..... *Seeking Wellness: Suffering Through Four Movements*
Special Jury Prize, Short Film ..... *Herman: Am I Proud*
Best Guerrilla Film ..... *Carmilla Hyde*
MUFF Producers Award ..... *Prey* (Robert Galinsky, Elizabeth Howatt-Jackman)
Best Documentary (tie) ..... *The Nigel Diaries* and *Burn City*
Best Cinematography ..... Justin Brickle (*The Tumbler*)
Best Screenplay (tie) ..... Jack Ketchum (*Offspring*) and Dominic Deacon (*Bad Habits*)
Best Short (tie) ..... *The Marina Experiment* and *Matinee*
Runner-Up, Short Film ..... *Higher Plane*
Best Foreign Film ..... *Impolex*
Best Foreign Director ..... Zach Clark (*Modern Love Is Automatic*)
Best Foreign Male Actor ..... Riley O'Brien (*Impolex*)

Best Foreign Female Actor ..... Melodie Sisk (*Modern Love Is Automatic*)
Lifetime Achievement ..... Frank Howson, John La Monde

2008

Best Australian Film (tie) ..... *Acolytes* (Jon Hewitt) and *The Horseman* (Steven Kastrissios)
Runner-Up, Australian Film ..... *No Through Road* (Sam Barrett)
Best Australian Director ..... Steven Kastrissios (*The Horseman*)
Best Australian Male Actor ..... Joel Edgerton (*Acolytes*)
Best Australian Female Actor ..... Alexandra Weaver (*The Run*)
Best Australian Supporting Male Actor ..... Michael Piccirilli (*Devil's Gateway*)
Best Australian Supporting Female Actor ..... Megan Palinkas (*No Through Road*)
Special Jury Prize ..... *The Gates of Hell* (dir: Kelly Dolen)
Best Guerrilla Film ..... *Cannibal Suburbia* (Jean-Luc Syndikas, D.A. Jackson)
Best Documentary ..... *Xaviera Hollander* (prod: John Patti)
Best Cinematography ..... Mark Pugh (*Acolytes*)
Best Screenplay ..... *Dead Girl* (Trent Haaga)
Best Short Film (tie) ..... *Sin Shoes* (Raul Palomar) and *Garden of Earthly Delights* (Stuart Simpson)
Runner-Up, Short Film ..... *Jumping Jack* (Julian Costanzo)
Best Foreign Film ..... *Tin Can Man*
Best Foreign Director (tie) ..... Ivan Kavanagh (*Tin Can Man*) and Thomas Clay (*Soi Cowboy*)
Best Foreign Male Actor ..... Michael Parle (*Tin Can Man*)
Best Foreign Female Actor ..... Pimwalee Thampanyasan (*Soi Cowboy*)

2006

Best Film ..... *Darklovestory* (dir: Jon Hewitt)
Best Director ..... Stefan Popescu (*Roseberry 7470*)
Best Male Actor (tie) ..... Aaron Pedersen (*Darklovestory*) and Christian Poppi (*Welcome Stranger*)
Best Female Actor (tie) ..... Belinda McClory (*Darklovestory*) and Alice Ansara (*Roseberry 7470*)
Best Supporting Male Actor ..... Adam Royall (*Blue Notes*)
Best Supporting Female Actor ..... Katy Manning (*When Darkness Falls*)
Special Jury Prize ..... *Blue Notes* (dir: Bill Mousoulis)
Best Use of the Guerrilla Aesthetic ..... *Demonsamongus* (dir: Stuart Simpson)

Most Gratuitous Use of Pets and Boobs ..... *Pornstar Pets* (dir: Margie Schnibbe)
Most Gratuitous Use of Violence ..... *When Evil Reigns* (dir: Luke and Alix Jackson)
Most Gratuitous Use of Sex ..... *Jupiter Love* (dir: Michael Andre)
Best Documentary (tie) ..... *Damon and Hunter: Doing it Together* (dir: Tony Comstock) and *Plagues and Pleasures on the Salton Sea* (dir: Chris Metzler, Jeff Springer)
Best Cinematography ..... Jason Turley (*Blue Notes*)
Best Screenplay ..... Christopher Folino (*Gamers*)
Best Sound ..... *Demonsamongus* (dir: Stuart Simpson)
Best Editing ..... Jason Turley (*Welcome Stranger*)
Best Short Film (tie) ..... *Remembering Nigel* (dir: Frank Howson) and *Penny* (dir: John King)
Runner-Up, Short Film ..... *Glass* (dir: Ivan Duzel)

2005

Best Film ..... *Wait Means Never* (dir: Andrew Groves)
Best Director (tie) ..... Brownfield & Petrie (*The Money Shot*) and Rachel Lucas (*Bondi Tsunami*)
Best Screenplay ..... Anna Brownfield and Lance Petrie (*The Money Shot*)
Best Male Actor ..... Peter Stefanou (*The Money Shot*)
Best Female Actor ..... Caitlin Higgins (*The Actress*)
Special Jury Prize ..... *Spring Rhapsody* (dir: Bill Mousoulis)
Best Guerrilla Film ..... *Welcome to Greensborough* (dir: Tom McEvoy)
Best Cinematography ..... Bryan Donnell (*Wait Means Never*)
Best Sound ..... *Spring Rhapsody*
Best Editing ..... *Welcome to Greensborough*
Most Gratuitous Use of Violence ..... *In Blood*
Most Gratuitous Use of Sex ..... *Sex and Sensitivity*
Best Short Film (tie) ..... *Grim* (dir: John-Paul Nickel, Joanna Lowe) and *Clown* (dir: Karl Hirsch)
Runner-Up, Short Film (tie) ..... *Smacked Out Kisses* (dir: David Mazzarella) and *Wooden Heart* (dir: Jason Turley)
Best Animated Short Film ..... *Herman the Legal Labrador* (dir: David Blumenstein)
Best Documentary, Short Film ..... *Fritz Niedsone Is the New Black* (dir: Andrew Iser)
Best Experimental, Short Film ..... *Esmeralda Video* (dir: Yasmin Sabuncu)
Best Comedy Short Film ..... *1982s* (dir: Despain & Vainwad)
Best Action/Violence Short ..... *Honour* (dir: Dale Reeves)

2004

Best Female Actor ..... Susanne Hausschmid (*Defenceless: A Blood Symphony*)
Best Male Actor ..... Gregory Pakis (*The Garth Method*)
Special Jury Prize ..... *The Raspberry Reich* (dir: Bruce La Bruce)
Best Director ..... *The Garth Method* (dir: Gregory Pakis)
Best Film ..... *Defenceless: A Blood Symphony* (dir: Mark Savage)
Best Cinematography ..... *Defenceless: A Blood Symphony*
Best Screenplay ..... *The Garth Method* (Gregory Pakis)
Best Sound ..... *Lost: Black Earth*
Best Editing ..... *The Garth Method*
Best Feature-Length Documentary ..... *R.I.P., Rest in Pieces: A Portrait of Joe Coleman* (dir: Robert-Adrian Pejo)
Best Short Film ..... *Scab a Smoke* (dir: Jason Turley)
Best Animated Short Film ..... *After Dolly* (dir: Mick Elliott)
Best Short Documentary ..... *Escape from the Planet of the Tapes* (dir: Anthony Mullins, Kris Kneen)
Best Experimental Short Film ..... *Who Killed Target 1967?* (dir: Angie Kwong)
Best Use of the Guerrilla Aesthetic ..... *Exquisite Corpse* (dir: David Fishel)
Most Gratuitous Violence ..... *Get Rich Quick* (dir: Samuel Genocchio)
Most Gratuitous Sex ..... *The Raspberry Reich* (dir: Bruce La Bruce)
MUFF Encouragement Award ..... *Why We Had to Kill Bitch* (dir: John-Paul Nickel)
Honorary Mention (Silver MUFF Award) ..... *Voice* (dir: George Beshir)
Honorary Mention (Silver MUFF Award) ..... *Meat Market* (dir: Remo Camerota)

2003

Best Film ..... *The Magician*
Best Director ..... Scott Ryan (*The Magician*)
Best Male Actor ..... Scott Ryan (*The Magician*)
Best Female Actor ..... Asia Argento (*Scarlet Diva*)
Best Cinematography (tie) ..... *A Bullet in the Arse* and *Lovesick*
Best Screenplay ..... *Black Coffee*
Best Sound (tie) ..... *A Bullet in the Arse* and *Reign in Darkness*
Best Editing ..... *Black Coffee*
Best Documentary ..... *Horns and Halos*
Runner-Up, Documentary ..... *Reverend Billy and the Church of Stop Shopping*
Best Short Film ..... *Scenes from an Endless War* (dir: Norman Cowie)

Runner-Up, Short Film (tie) ..... *The Distance Between* (dir: Andrew Hickinbotham) and *Larry in Relation to the Ground* (dir: Ted Fisher)
Best Innovation in Underground Cinema ..... *Lovesick*
Best Use of the Guerrilla Aesthetic ..... *Razor Eaters*
Most Gratuitous Violence ..... *A Bullet in the Arse*
Most Gratuitous Sex ..... *Trail of Passion*
Most Judicious Use of the Word "Lesbo" in the Title ..... *Lesbo-A-Go-Go*
Special Jury Prize ..... *Razor Eaters*

Méliès Award

A Méliès d'Or (Golden Méliès) is presented by the European Fantastic Film Festivals Federation (EFFFF) for Best European Fantastic Feature Film and Best European Fantastic Short Film. The short film Méliès d'Or was founded in 2002. Nominees for a feature film Méliès d'Or must first win a Méliès d'Argent (Silver Méliès), which is a "nomination award." Short film nominees are simply called nominees. Méliès d'Argent winners (and Méliès d'Or short film nominees) are chosen by the EFFFF's member festivals. Méliès d'Or winners are determined by an EFFFF jury. If you're still confused, see Méliès.org. (Also, by Fantafestival, they mean Fanta Festival. I've seen it spelled both ways.)

2010

Méliès d'Or/Best European Fantastic Feature Film ..... *Buried*
Méliès d'Or/Best European Fantastic Short Film ..... *The Attack of the Robots from Nebula 5*, A.K.A. *El ataque de los robots de Nebulosa 5*
Brussels International Fantastic Film Festival/Méliès d'Argent ..... *The Door*, A.K.A. *Die Tur*
Brussels International Fantastic Film Festival/Short Film Nomination for Méliès d'Or ..... *Echo*
Espoo Ciné International Film Festival/Méliès d'Argent ..... *Amer*
Espoo Ciné International Film Festival/Short Film Nomination for Méliès d'Or ..... *The Attack of the Robots from Nebula 5*, A.K.A. *El ataque de los robots de Nebulosa 5*
FanCine Málaga — Festival de Cine Fantástico/Short Film Nomination for Méliès d'Or ..... *The End*
Fanomenon — Leeds International Film Festival/Méliès d'Argent ..... *Heartless*
Fanomenon — Leeds International Film Festival/Short Film Nomination for Méliès d'Or ..... *Pathos*
Imagine: Amsterdam Fantastic Film Festival/Méliès d'Argent ..... *Transmission*, A.K.A. *Adás*
Imagine: Amsterdam Fantastic Film Festival/Short Film Nomination for Méliès d'Or ..... *Pivot*
Lund International Fantastic Film Festival/Méliès d'Argent ..... *Red, White & Blue*
Lund International Fantastic Film Festival/Short Film Nomination for Méliès d'Or ..... *Out of a Forest*
Neuchâtel International Fantastic Film Festival/Méliès d'Argent ..... *Strigoi*
Neuchâtel International Fantastic Film Festival/Short Film Nomination for Méliès d'Or ..... *Try a Little Tenderness*
Carlos J. Plaza and Alfonso C. Lopez (San Sebastián Horror & Fantasy Film Festival/Short Film Nomination for Méliès d'Or ..... *Barbee Butcher*
Scienceplusfiction/Méliès d'Argent ..... *The Children*
Scienceplusfiction/Short Film Nomination for Méliès d'Or ..... *Virtual Dating*
Sitges Festival Internacional de Cinema de Catalunya/Méliès d'Argent ..... *The Eclipse*
Sitges Festival Internacional de Cinema de Catalunya/Short Film Nomination for Méliès d'Or ..... *One of Those Days*
Strasbourg European Fantastic Film Festival/Méliès d'Argent ..... *Buried*
Strasbourg European Fantastic Film Festival/Short Film Nomination for Méliès d'Or ..... *Mr. Foley*
Utopiales — Festival International de Science-Fiction de Nantes/Short Film Nomination for Méliès d'Or ..... *Maquetas*

2009

Méliès d'Or/Best European Fantastic Feature Film ..... *Martyrs*
Méliès d'Or/Best European Fantastic Short Film ..... *Cold and Dry*, A.K.A. *Tørt og kjølig*
Brussels International Fantastic Film Festival/Méliès d'Argent ..... *Sauna*
Espoo Ciné International Film Festival/Méliès d'Argent ..... *Moon*
Espoo Ciné International Film Festival/Short Film Nomination for Méliès d'Or ..... *Die Schneider Krankheit*
FanCine Málaga — Festival de Cine Fantástico/Short Film Nomination for Méliès d'Or ..... *Dans leur Peau*
Fanomenon — Leeds International Film Festival/Méliès d'Argent ..... *Mum and Dad*
Fanomenon — Leeds International Film Festival/Short Film Nomination for Méliès d'Or ..... *Short Cut*, A.K.A. *Coupé Court*
Fantafestival, Rome/Méliès d'Argent ..... *Butterfly Zone, Butterfly zone — Il senso della farfalla*

Fantasporto — Oporto International Film Festival/Méliès d'Argent ..... *Absurdistan*
Fantasporto — Oporto International Film Festival/Short Film Nomination for Méliès d'Or ..... *Mamá*
Imagine: Amsterdam Fantastic Film Festival/Méliès d'Argent ..... *Before the Fall*, A.K.A. *Tres Dìas*
Imagine: Amsterdam Fantastic Film Festival/Short Film Nomination for Méliès d'Or ..... *Cold and Dry*, A.K.A. *Tørt og kjølig*
Lund International Fantastic Film Festival/Méliès d'Argent ..... *A Town Called Panic*, A.K.A. *Panique au village*
Lund International Fantastic Film Festival/Short Film Nomination for Méliès d'Or ..... *Because There Are Things You Never Forget*, A.K.A. *Porque hay cosas que nunca se olvidan*
Neuchâtel International Fantastic Film Festival/Méliès d'Argent ..... *Left Bank*, A.K.A. *Linkeroever*
Neuchâtel International Fantastic Film Festival/Short Film Nomination for Méliès d'Or ..... *Tile M for Murder*, A.K.A. *Lägg M för Mord*
Ravenna Nightmare Film Festival/Short Film Nomination for Méliès d'Or ..... *Las Horas Muertas*
Carlos J. Plaza and Alfonso C. Lopez (San Sebastián Horror & Fantasy Film Festival/Short Film Nomination for Méliès d'Or ..... *Cotton Candy*
Scienceplusfiction/Short Film Nomination for Méliès d'Or ..... *Kingz*
Sitges Festival Internacional de Cinema de Catalunya/Méliès d'Argent ..... *Martyrs*
Sitges Festival Internacional de Cinema de Catalunya/Short Film Nomination for Méliès d'Or ..... *Afterville*
Utopiales — Festival International de Science-Fiction de Nantes/Short Film Nomination for Méliès d'Or ..... *This Way Up*

2008

Méliès d'Or/Best European Fantastic Feature Film ..... *Let the Right One In*, A.K.A. *Låt den rätte komma in*
Méliès d'Or/Best European Fantastic Short Film ..... *Of Cats & Women*
Brussels International Fantastic Film Festival/Méliès d'Argent ..... *Frontière(s)*
Brussels International Fantastic Film Festival/Short Film Nomination for Méliès d'Or ..... *Of Cats & Women*
Dead by Dawn Horror Film Festival/Short Film Nomination for Méliès d'Or ..... *Bitten*
Espoo Ciné International Film Festival/Méliès d'Argent ..... *The Substitute*, A.K.A. *Vikaren*
Espoo Ciné International Film Festival/Short Film Nomination for Méliès d'Or ..... *Curse of the Remote Island*, A.K.A. *Kaukosaaren Kirous*

FanCine Málaga — Festival de Cine Fantástico/Short Film Nomination for Méliès d'Or ..... *Avant Petalos Grillados*
Fanomenon — Leeds International Film Festival/Méliès d'Argent ..... *The Orphanage*, A.K.A. *El Orfanato*
Fanomenon — Leeds International Film Festival/Short Film Nomination for Méliès d'Or ..... *Machine*, A.K.A. *Máquina*
Fantafestival, Rome/Méliès d'Argent ..... *The Girl by the Lake*, A.K.A. *La Ragazza del Lago*
Fantasporto — Oporto International Film Festival/Méliès d'Argent ..... *Fermat's Room*, A.K.A. *La Habitación de Fermat*
Fantasporto — Oporto International Film Festival/Short Film Nomination for Méliès d'Or ..... *Ark*, A.K.A. *Arka*
Imagine: Amsterdam Fantastic Film Festival/Méliès d'Argent ..... *King of the Hill*, A.K.A. *El Rey de la Montaña*
Imagine: Amsterdam Fantastic Film Festival/Short Film Nomination for Méliès d'Or ..... *De Overkant*
Lund International Fantastic Film Festival/Méliès d'Argent ..... *Left*, A.K.A. *Links*
Lund International Fantastic Film Festival/Short Film Nomination for Méliès d'Or ..... *Raymond*
Neuchâtel International Fantastic Film Festival/Méliès d'Argent ..... *Let the Right One In*, A.K.A. *Låt den rätte komma in*
Neuchâtel International Fantastic Film Festival/Short Film Nomination for Méliès d'Or ..... *Scary*, A.K.A. *Schrik*
Ravenna Nightmare Film Festival/Short Film Nomination for Méliès d'Or ..... *La Dama en el Umbral*
Carlos J. Plaza and Alfonso C. Lopez (San Sebastián Horror & Fantasy Film Festival/Short Film Nomination for Méliès d'Or ..... *The Pearce Sisters*
Scienceplusfiction/Short Film Nomination for Méliès d'Or ..... *Absence*
Sitges Festival Internacional de Cinema de Catalunya/Méliès d'Argent ..... *Inside*, A.K.A. *À L'intérieur*
Sitges Festival Internacional de Cinema de Catalunya/Short Film Nomination for Méliès d'Or ..... *The Big Garage*, A.K.A. *Die Grosse Werkstatt*
Utopiales — Festival International de Science-Fiction de Nantes/Short Film Nomination for Méliès d'Or ..... *DVD*

2007

Méliès d'Or/Best European Fantastic Feature Film ..... *Princess*
Méliès d'Or/Best European Fantastic Short Film ..... *Sniffer*
Brussels International Fantastic Film

Festival/Méliès d'Argent ..... *Dead in Three Days*, A.K.A. *In 3 Tagen Bist Du Tot*
Brussels International Fantastic Film Festival/Short Film Nomination for Méliès d'Or ..... *Droomtijd*
Cinénygma Luxembourg International Film Festival/Méliès d'Argent ..... *Grimm Love*, A.K.A. *Rohtenburg*
Cinénygma Luxembourg International Film Festival/Short Film Nomination for Méliès d'Or ..... *The Faeries of Blackheath Woods*
Dead by Dawn Horror Film Festival/Short Film Nomination for Méliès d'Or ..... *It Came from the West*
Espoo Ciné International Film Festival/Méliès d'Argent ..... *How To Get Rid of the Others*, A.K.A. *Hvordan vi slipper af med de andre*
Espoo Ciné International Film Festival/Short Film Nomination for Méliès d'Or ..... *The Blaxorcist*
Fanomenon — Leeds International Film Festival/Méliès d'Argent ..... *Isolation*
Fanomenon — Leeds International Film Festival/Short Film Nomination for Méliès d'Or ..... *Home Video*
Fantafestival, Rome/Méliès d'Argent ..... *Hell's Fever*
Fantasporto — Oporto International Film Festival/Méliès d'Argent ..... *Renaissance*
Fantasporto — Oporto International Film Festival/Short Film Nomination for Méliès d'Or ..... *Finkle's Odyssey*
Imagine: Amsterdam Fantastic Film Festival/Méliès d'Argent ..... *Them*, A.K.A. *Ils*
Imagine: Amsterdam Fantastic Film Festival/Short Film Nomination for Méliès d'Or ..... *Maestro*
Lund International Fantastic Film Festival/Méliès d'Argent ..... *A Quiet Love*, A.K.A. *Die Blaue Grenze*
Lund International Fantastic Film Festival/Short Film Nomination for Méliès d'Or ..... *Mebana*
Neuchâtel International Fantastic Film Festival/Méliès d'Argent ..... *Ugly Swans*, A.K.A. *Gadkie Lebedi*
Neuchâtel International Fantastic Film Festival/Short Film Nomination for Méliès d'Or ..... *Silence Is Golden*
Ravenna Nightmare Film Festival/Short Film Nomination for Méliès d'Or ..... *Plastic*
Carlos J. Plaza and Alfonso C. Lopez (San Sebastián Horror & Fantasy Film Festival/Short Film Nomination for Méliès d'Or ..... *Delivery*
Scienceplusfiction/Short Film Nomination for Méliès d'Or ..... *Final Journey*
Sitges Festival Internacional de Cinema de Catalunya/Méliès d'Argent ..... *Princess*
Sitges Festival Internacional de Cinema de Catalunya/Short Film Nomination for Méliès d'Or ..... *Doodle*
Utopiales — Festival International de Science-Fiction de Nantes/Short Film Nomination for Méliès d'Or ..... *Sniffer*

2006

Méliès d'Or/Best European Fantastic Feature Film ..... *Adam's Apples*, A.K.A. *Adams æbler*
Méliès d'Or/Best European Fantastic Short Film ..... *Starfly*
Brussels International Fantastic Film Festival/Méliès d'Argent ..... *Adam's Apples*, A.K.A. *Adams æbler*
Brussels International Fantastic Film Festival/Short Film Nomination for Méliès d'Or ..... *Doll 639*
Cinénygma Luxembourg International Film Festival/Méliès d'Argent ..... *Next Door*, A.K.A. *Naboer*
Cinénygma Luxembourg International Film Festival/Short Film Nomination for Méliès d'Or ..... *Starfly*
Dead by Dawn Horror Film Festival/Short Film Nomination for Méliès d'Or ..... *Alicia's Eyes*, A.K.A. *Los Ojos de Alicia*
Espoo Ciné International Film Festival/Méliès d'Argent ..... *Strings*
Espoo Ciné International Film Festival/Short Film Nomination for Méliès d'Or ..... *The Hidden Face*, A.K.A. *Het verborgen gezicht*
FanCine Málaga — Festival de Cine Fantástico/Short Film Nomination for Méliès d'Or ..... *Avatar*
Fanomenon — Leeds International Film Festival/Méliès d'Argent ..... *Hotel*
Fanomenon — Leeds International Film Festival/Short Film Nomination for Méliès d'Or ..... *Monsters*
Fantafestival, Rome/Méliès d'Argent ..... *H.P. Lovecraft: The Terror Within*, A.K.A. *Il Mistero di Lovecraft*
Fantasporto — Oporto International Film Festival/Méliès d'Argent ..... *Animal*
Fantasporto — Oporto International Film Festival/Short Film Nomination for Méliès d'Or ..... *The Legend of the Scarecrow*, A.K.A. *La Leyenda del Espantapajaros*
Imagine: Amsterdam Fantastic Film Festival/Méliès d'Argent ..... *Storm*
Imagine: Amsterdam Fantastic Film Festival/Short Film Nomination for Méliès d'Or ..... *El Ciclo*
Lund International Fantastic Film Festival/Méliès d'Argent ..... *The Descent*
Lund International Fantastic Film Festival/Short Film Nomination for Méliès d'Or ..... *The Old Pro*, A.K.A. *Der Beste*
Neuchâtel International Fantastic Film Festival/Méliès d'Argent ..... *The Bothersome Man*, A.K.A. *Den brysomme mannen*
Neuchâtel International Fantastic Film Festival/

Short Film Nomination for Méliès d'Or ..... *Dilemma*
Ravenna Nightmare Film Festival/Short Film Nomination for Méliès d'Or ..... *The Ten Steps*
Carlos J. Plaza and Alfonso C. Lopez (San Sebastián Horror & Fantasy Film Festival/Short Film Nomination for Méliès d'Or ..... *Rare Exports Inc.*
Scienceplusfiction/Short Film Nomination for Méliès d'Or ..... *Terra Incognita*
Sitges Festival Internacional de Cinema de Catalunya/Méliès d'Argent ..... *Trouble*
Sitges Festival Internacional de Cinema de Catalunya/Short Film Nomination for Méliès d'Or ..... *City Paradise*
Utopiales — Festival International de Science-Fiction de Nantes/Short Film Nomination for Méliès d'Or ..... *Murielle moi non plus*

2005/2004

Méliès d'Or/Best European Fantastic Feature Film ..... *Code 46*
Méliès d'Or/Best European Fantastic Short Film ..... *The Last Minute*, A.K.A. *La dernière minute*
Brussels International Fantastic Film Festival/Méliès d'Argent ..... *Hypnos*, A.K.A. *Hipnos*
Brussels International Fantastic Film Festival/Short Film Nomination for Méliès d'Or ..... *Schijn van de Maan*
Cinénygma Luxembourg International Film Festival/Short Film Nomination for Méliès d'Or ..... *The Next One*, A.K.A. *El Siguiente*
Espoo Ciné International Film Festival/Méliès d'Argent ..... *The Last Horror Movie*
Espoo Ciné International Film Festival/Short Film Nomination for Méliès d'Or ..... *Cinemare*
FanCine Málaga — Festival de Cine Fantástico/Short Film Nomination for Méliès d'Or *U43*
Fantafestival, Rome/Méliès d'Argent ..... *Evilenko*
Fantafestival, Rome/Short Film Nomination for Méliès d'Or ..... *Belmondo*
Fantasporto — Oporto International Film Festival/Méliès d'Argent ..... *Les Revenants*
Fantasporto — Oporto International Film Festival/Short Film Nomination for Méliès d'Or ..... *The Last Minute*, A.K.A. *La dernière minute*
Imagine: Amsterdam Fantastic Film Festival/Méliès d'Argent ..... *Calvaire*
Lund International Fantastic Film Festival/Méliès d'Argent ..... *Tempus Fugit*
Lund International Fantastic Film Festival/Short Film Nomination for Méliès d'Or ..... *Daddy's Boy*
Neuchâtel International Fantastic Film Festival/Méliès d'Argent ..... *The Machinist*
Neuchâtel International Fantastic Film Festival/Short Film Nomination for Méliès d'Or ..... *7:35 de la Mañana*
Ravenna Nightmare Film Festival/Short Film Nomination for Méliès d'Or ..... *The Carpenter and His Clumsy Wife*
Carlos J. Plaza and Alfonso C. Lopez (San Sebastián Horror & Fantasy Film Festival/Short Film Nomination for Méliès d'Or ..... *Tea Break*
Sitges Festival Internacional de Cinema de Catalunya/Méliès d'Argent ..... *Code 46*
Sitges Festival Internacional de Cinema de Catalunya/Short Film Nomination for Méliès d'Or ..... *El Soñador*
Utopiales — Festival International de Science-Fiction de Nantes/Short Film Nomination for Méliès d'Or ..... *Personne n'est parfait*

2003

Méliès d'Or/Best European Fantastic Feature Film ..... *The Green Butchers*, A.K.A. *De Gröna Slaktarna*
Méliès d'Or/Best European Fantastic Short Film ..... *The Spook House*, A.K.A. *El tren de la Bruja*
Brussels International Fantastic Film Festival/Méliès d'Argent ..... *The Green Butchers*, A.K.A. *De Gröna Slaktarna*
Brussels International Fantastic Film Festival/Short Film Nomination for Méliès d'Or ..... *Day 26*, A.K.A. *Tag 26*
Cinénygma Luxembourg International Film Festival/Méliès d'Argent ..... *Tears of Kali*
Cinénygma Luxembourg International Film Festival/Short Film Nomination for Méliès d'Or ..... *Nosferatu Tango*
Dead by Dawn Horror Film Festival/Short Film Nomination for Méliès d'Or ..... *R.I.P.*
Espoo Ciné International Film Festival/Méliès d'Argent ..... *Deathwatch*
Espoo Ciné International Film Festival/Short Film Nomination for Méliès d'Or ..... *Kala*, A.K.A. *Fish*
Fantafestival, Rome/Méliès d'Argent ..... *FearDotCom*
Fantafestival, Rome/Short Film Nomination for Méliès d'Or ..... *Space Off*
Fantasporto — Oporto International Film Festival/Méliès d'Argent ..... *Killing Words*, A.K.A. *Palabras Encadenadas*
Fantasporto — Oporto International Film Festival/Short Film Nomination for Méliès d'Or ..... *I'll See You in My Dreams*
Imagine: Amsterdam Fantastic Film Festival/Méliès d'Argent ..... *My Little Eye*
Imagine: Amsterdam Fantastic Film Festival/Short Film Nomination for Méliès d'Or ..... *Roadkill*
Lund International Fantastic Film Festival/Méliès d'Argent ..... *Beyond Re-Animator*
Lund International Fantastic Film Festival/Short Film Nomination for Méliès d'Or ..... *My Bearded Mother*, A.K.A. *Min Skäggiga Mamma*

Neuchâtel International Fantastic Film Festival/Short Film Nomination for Méliès d'Or ..... *Loups*
Sitges Festival Internacional de Cinema de Catalunya/Méliès d'Argent ..... *Switchblade Romance*, A.K.A. *Haute Tension*
Sitges Festival Internacional de Cinema de Catalunya/Short Film Nomination for Méliès d'Or ..... *The Spook House*, A.K.A. *El tren de la Bruja*
Utopiales — Festival International de Science-Fiction de Nantes/Short Film Nomination for Méliès d'Or ..... *Culpiix*

2002

Méliès d'Or/Best European Fantastic Feature Film ..... *Fausto 5.0*
Méliès d'Or/Best European Fantastic Short Film ..... *Oh My God?!*
Brussels International Fantastic Film Festival/Méliès d'Argent ..... *Dead End*
Brussels International Fantastic Film Festival/Short Film Nomination for Méliès d'Or ..... *Copy Shop*
Cinénygma Luxembourg International Film Festival/Méliès d'Argent ..... *Dog Soldiers*
Cinénygma Luxembourg International Film Festival/Short Film Nomination for Méliès d'Or ..... *Oh My God?!*
Dead by Dawn Horror Film Festival/Short Film Nomination for Méliès d'Or ..... *Comptine*
Espoo Ciné International Film Festival/Méliès d'Argent ..... *Fausto 5.0*
Espoo Ciné International Film Festival/Short Film Nomination for Méliès d'Or ..... *...ya no puedo caminar*
Fantafestival, Rome/Méliès d'Argent ..... *Stranded*, A.K.A. *Stranded — Náufragos*
Fantasporto — Oporto International Film Festival/Méliès d'Argent ..... *28 Days Later*
Fantasporto — Oporto International Film Festival/Short Film Nomination for Méliès d'Or ..... *Venus Velvet*
Imagine: Amsterdam Fantastic Film Festival/Méliès d'Argent ..... *The Devil's Backbone*, A.K.A. *Espinazo del diablo*
Imagine: Amsterdam Fantastic Film Festival/Short Film Nomination for Méliès d'Or ..... *The Rise and Fall of the Legendary Anglobilly Feverson*
Lund International Fantastic Film Festival/Méliès d'Argent ..... *Doctor Sleep*, A.K.A. *Hypnotic*
Lund International Fantastic Film Festival/Short Film Nomination for Méliès d'Or ..... *Forbidden Eyes*, A.K.A. *Verboden Ogen*
Neuchâtel International Fantastic Film Festival/Short Film Nomination for Méliès d'Or ..... *Joshua*
Sitges Festival Internacional de Cinema de Catalunya/Méliès d'Argent ..... *Second Name*, A.K.A. *El segundo nombre*
Sitges Festival Internacional de Cinema de Catalunya/Short Film Nomination for Méliès d'Or ..... *Cry for Bobo*

2001

Méliès d'Or/Best European Fantastic Feature Film ..... *Thomas in Love*, A.K.A. *Thomas est amoureux*
Brussels International Fantastic Film Festival/Méliès d'Argent ..... *The Art of Dying*, A.K.A. *El Arte de Morir*
Cinénygma Luxembourg International Film Festival/Méliès d'Argent ..... *The Unknown*, A.K.A. *Det Okända*
Espoo Ciné International Film Festival/Méliès d'Argent ..... *Thomas in Love*, A.K.A. *Thomas est amoureux*
Fantafestival, Rome/Méliès d'Argent ..... *Marsal*
Fantasporto — Oporto International Film Festival/Méliès d'Argent ..... *Vidocq*
Imagine: Amsterdam Fantastic Film Festival/Méliès d'Argent ..... *The Heart of the Warrior*, A.K.A. *El Corazón del guerrero*
Sitges Festival Internacional de Cinema de Catalunya/Méliès d'Argent ..... *Brotherhood of the Wolf*, A.K.A. *Le Pacte des Loups*

2000

Méliès d'Or/Best European Fantastic Feature Film ..... *Possessed*, A.K.A. *Besat*
Brussels International Fantastic Film Festival/Méliès d'Argent ..... *Possessed*, A.K.A. *Besat*
Cinénygma Luxembourg International Film Festival/Méliès d'Argent ..... *Lighthouse*
Espoo Ciné International Film Festival/Méliès d'Argent ..... *Tuvalu*
Fantafestival, Rome/Méliès d'Argent ..... *Angel of the Night*, A.K.A. *Nattens engel*
Fantasporto — Oporto International Film Festival/Méliès d'Argent ..... *The Ugliest Woman in the World*, A.K.A. *La mujer más fea del mundo*
Sitges Festival Internacional de Cinema de Catalunya/Méliès d'Argent ..... *Promenons — Nous dans les Bois*

1999

Méliès d'Or/Best European Fantastic Feature Film ..... *The Nameless*, A.K.A. *Los sin nombre*
Brussels International Fantastic Film Festival/Méliès d'Argent ..... *The Wisdom of Crocodiles*
Espoo Ciné International Film Festival/Méliès d'Argent ..... *Goodbye 20th Century*, A.K.A. *Zbogum na dvadesetiot vek*
Fantafestival, Rome/Méliès d'Argent *99.9*
Fantasporto — Oporto International Film Festival/Méliès d'Argent ..... *The Acid House*

Sitges Festival Internacional de Cinema de Catalunya/Méliès d'Argent ..... *The Nameless*, A.K.A. *Los sin nombre*

1998

Méliès d'Or/Best European Fantastic Feature Film ..... *Photographing Fairies*
Brussels International Fantastic Film Festival/Méliès d'Argent ..... *Lawn Dogs*
Fantafestival, Rome/Méliès d'Argent ..... *The Thousand Miracles of the Universe*, A.K.A. *Les mille merveilles de l'univers*
Fantasporto — Oporto International Film Festival/Méliès d'Argent ..... *Photographing Fairies*
Sitges Festival Internacional de Cinema de Catalunya/Méliès d'Argent ..... *The Hole*, A.K.A. *Dong*

1997

Méliès d'Or/Best European Fantastic Feature Film ..... *Tren de sombras*, A.K.A. *Train of Shadows*
Brussels International Fantastic Film Festival/Méliès d'Argent ..... *Thesis*, A.K.A. *Tesis*
Fantafestival, Rome/Méliès d'Argent ..... *Chasing the Kidney Stone*, A.K.A. *Jakten på nyresteinen*
Fantasporto — Oporto International Film Festival/Méliès d'Argent ..... *Darklands*
Sitges Festival Internacional de Cinema de Catalunya/Méliès d'Argent ..... *Tren de sombras*, A.K.A. *Train of Shadows*

1996

Méliès d'Or/Best European Fantastic Feature Film ..... *The Day of the Beast*, A.K.A. *El dia de la bestia*
Brussels International Fantastic Film Festival/Méliès d'Argent ..... *The Day of the Beast*, A.K.A. *El dia de la bestia*
Fantasporto — Oporto International Film Festival/Méliès d'Argent ..... *Taxandria*
Sitges Festival Internacional de Cinema de Catalunya/Méliès d'Argent ..... *Sólo se muere dos veces*

Mile High Horror Film Festival

2010

Best Feature Film ..... *Rammbock* (dir: Marvin Kren)
Audience Award for Best Feature Film ..... *True Nature* (dir: Patrick Steele)
Best Short Film ..... *Love Me Tender* (dir: Matthew Morgenthaler)
Audience Award for Best Short Film ..... *The Familiar* (dir: Kody Zimmermann)
Best Shock Factor ..... *La Petite Mort* (dir: Jan Gallasch)
Mile High Gore Award ..... *Axed* (dir: Joshua Long)
Best Animation ..... *White Room* (dir: Chris Chitaroni)

Montevideo Fantástico

Their first edition, in 2006, was noncompetitive. Festival official Alejandro Yamgotchian confirms that this listing of winners is complete.

5th — 2010

Best Film ..... *Strigoi* (dir: Faye Jackson)
Best Latin American Film ..... *TL-2: La felicidad es una leyenda urbana* (dir: Tetsuo Lumière)
Best Director ..... Cory McAbee (*Stingray Sam*)
Best Actor ..... Catalin Paraschiv (*Strigoi*)
Best Actress ..... Roxana Guttmann (*Strigoi*)
Best Cinematography ..... Christian Rivera (*La pantera negra*)
Best Music/Original Score ..... Bill Nayer Show (*Stingray Sam*)
Audience Choice Award, Best Film ..... *The Life and Death of a Porno Gang* (dir: Mladen Djordjevic)
Audience Choice Award, Best Latin American Film ..... *Beyond the Grave* (dir: Davi de Oliveira Pinheiro)
Best Short Film ..... *Intercambio* (dir: Antonello Novellino, Antonio Quintanilla)
Best Latin American Short Film ..... *Gato* (dir: Joel Caetano)
Best Uruguayan Short Film ..... *Radiación* (dir: Adrián Barrera)
Best Director ..... Guzmán Vila (*Plutón*)
Best Screenplay (tie) ..... *La-Menta* (sc/dir: Víctor Vidangossy) and *Nación no identificada* (sc/dir: Manuel Facal)
Best Actor (tie) ..... Eduardo Soto Laris and Miguel Ángel Oñate (*Últimos pasajeros*)
Audience Choice Award, Best Short Film ..... *En la cripta* (dir: Willy Burrut)
Audience Choice Award, Best Latin American Short Film ..... *En la cripta* (dir: Willy Burrut)
Audience Choice Award, Best Uruguayan Short Film ..... *Los Revoltosos — Episodio 2: Cafest* (dir: Felipe Buchelli, Franco Mangone, Felipe Sosa)

4th — 2009

Best Film ..... *Altar* (dir: Rico María Ilarde)
Best Latin American Film ..... *No Moriré Sola* (dir: Adrián García Bogliano)
Special Mention ..... *Morgue Story: Blood, Blowfish and Comics* (dir: Paulo Biscaia Filho)
Special Mention ..... *Muñeco Viviente V* (dir: Maximiliano Contenti)

Special Mention ..... *Sonámbulos* (dir: Christian Aylwin)
Audience Choice Award, Best Film ..... *La Balada de Vlad Tepes* (dir: Guzmán Vila)
Audience Choice Award, Best Latin American Film ..... *La Balada de Vlad Tepes* (dir: Guzmán Vila)
Best Short Film ..... *Dedicado a Nadie* (dir: Andrés Borghi)
Best Latin American Short Film ..... *Dedicado a Nadie* (dir: Andrés Borghi)
Best Uruguayan Short Film ..... *Tren Fantasma* (dir: Darío Núñez)
Special Mention, Best Director, Short Film ..... *Magritte Moment* (dir: Ian Fischer)
Special Mention, Best Screenplay, Short Film ..... *Side Effect* (dir: Liz Adams)
Special Mention, Best Animated Short Film ..... *La Ferra: Ciudad Dormida* (dir: Arturo Quezada Torres)
Special Mention, Best Production, Short Film ..... *Los Señalados de Dios* (dir: Juma Fodde)
Audience Choice Award, Best Short Film ..... *Manual Práctico del Amigo Imaginario* (dir: Ciro Altabás)
Audience Choice Award, Best Latin American Short Film ..... *La Ferra: Ciudad Dormida* (dir: Arturo Quezada Torres)
Audience Choice Award, Best Uruguayan Short Film ..... *Entre las Vías* (dir: Antonella Tambasco)

3rd — 2008

Best Film ..... *The Man from Earth* (dir: Richard Schenkman)
Best Latin American Film ..... *Filmatrón* (dir: Pablo Parés)
Special Mention ..... *Dark Remains* (dir: Brian Avenet-Bradley)
Special Mention ..... *Song of the Dead* (dir: Chip Gubera)
Special Mention ..... *The Day of the Dead* (dir: Ricardo Islas)
Audience Choice Award ..... *The Man from Earth* (dir: Richard Schenkman)
Best Short Film ..... *Barbara Broadcast* (dirs: Jean Julien-Collette and Olivier Tollet)
Special Mention ..... *Made in Japan* (dir: Ciro Altabás)
Special Mention ..... *Poza Cisza* (dir: Piotr Ryczko)
Special Mention ..... *Rojo en el Bosque Sangriento* (dir: Tetsuo Lumière)
Special Mention ..... *Soy una Manzana* (dir: DJ Peluca)
Best Uruguayan Short Film ..... *Attack of the Disco Zombies* (dir: Darío Núñez)
Audience Choice Award, Best Short Film ..... *El Concurso de Manchas* (dir: Juan Manuel Bertozzi)
Audience Choice Award, Best Uruguayan Short Film ..... *28* (dir: Pablo Moreira)

2nd — 2007

Best Film ..... *The Last Horror Movie* (dir: Julian Richards)
Special Mention ..... *A Tale of Two Sisters* (dir: Kim Ji-woon)
Special Mention, Best Actress ..... Kate Greenhouse (*The Dark Hours*)
Special Mention, Best Actor ..... Kevin Howarth (*The Last Horror Movie*)
Special Mention, Best Director ..... Tetsuo Lumière (*TL-1: Mi Reino por un Platillo Volador*)
Audience Choice Award, Best Film ..... *Lockout* (dir: Ricardo Islas)
Best Short Film ..... *Extra, Extra* (dir: Diego Melo)
Best Uruguayan Short Film ..... *Extra, Extra* (dir: Diego Melo)
Special Mention ..... *Broch-Man* (dir: Alejandro Starópoli)
Special Mention ..... *Escarnio* (dir: Raúl Cerezo)
Special Mention ..... *Megazorg Z* (dir: Pablo Praino)
Audience Choice Award, Best Short Film ..... *Ella o Yo* (dir: Sebastián Franco)
Audience Choice Award, Best Uruguayan Short Film ..... *Extra, Extra* (dir: Diego Melo)

Morbido Film Fest

A.K.A. MORBIDO Festival Internacional de Cine Fantastico y de Terror. In 2010 their two winning directors received Golden Sugar Skull trophies, and each of the ten official selections got a Silver Sugar Skull trophy. In 2009 the winners received a Silver Sugar Skull trophy. In 2008 it was the Funeral Urn Trophy.

2010

Golden Sugar Skull (Audience Award) ..... *El Sanatorio* (dir: Miguel Gomez)
Golden Sugar Skull (Tribute Award) ..... Rene Cardona III (director)
Silver Sugar Skull ..... *Angel Caido* (dir: Arturo Anaya)
Silver Sugar Skull ..... *Conozca la cabeza de Juan Perez*, A.K.A. *Meet the Head of Juan Perez* (dir: Emilio Portes)
Silver Sugar Skull ..... *Depositarios*, A.K.A. *Depositories* (dir: Rodrigo Ordonañez)
Silver Sugar Skull ..... *La pantera negra*, A.K.A. *The Black Panther* (dir: Iyari Wertta)
Silver Sugar Skull ..... *Somos lo que hay*, A.K.A. *We Are What We Are* (dir: Jorge Michel Grau)
Silver Sugar Skull ..... *Viernes de animas* (dir: Raul P. Gamez)
Silver Sugar Skull ..... *Sudor frio* (dir: Adrian Garcia Bogliano)
Silver Sugar Skull ..... *In 3 tagen bist du tot*, A.K.A. *Dead in 3 Days* (dir: Andreas Prochaska)

Silver Sugar Skull ..... *Los cronocrímenes*, A.K.A. *Timecrimes* (dir: Nacho Vigalondo)
Silver Sugar Skull ..... *Atrocious* (prods: David Sanz, Jessica Villegas)

2009

Golden Sugar Skull (Tribute Award) ..... Abel Salazar (producer, RIP)
Silver Sugar Skull ..... *Masacre esta noche*, A.K.A. *Watch 'em Die* (dir: Adrian Garcia Bogliano)
Silver Sugar Skull ..... *Auf Bösem Boden*, A.K.A. *On Evil Grounds* (dir: Peter Koller)
Silver Sugar Skull ..... *Plano Detalle* (dir: Sergio Blasco)
Silver Sugar Skull ..... *Kilometro 31*, A.K.A. *KM 31* (dir: Rigoberto Castañeda)

2008

Funeral Urn (Tribute Award) ..... Fernando Mendez (director, RIP)
Funeral Urn ..... *Keiko en peligro* (dir: Rene Cardona III)
Funeral Urn ..... *Cañitas* (dir: Julio Cesar Estrada)
Funeral Urn ..... *Tears of Kali* (prod: Tim Luna)

MOTELx — Lisbon International Horror Film Festival

2010

Best Portuguese Horror Short Film ..... *Bats in the Belfrey* (dir: João Alves)
Special Mention ..... *Nocturna* (dir: Francisco Carvalho)

2009

Best Portuguese Horror Short Film ..... *Sangue Frio* (dir: Patrick Mendes)
Special Mention ..... *Papá Wrestling* (dir: Fernando Alle)

Nebula Award

Nebula Awards honor works released the previous year (i.e., the 2009 awards are presented in 2010, etc.). The Nebulas are primarily a literary award, first presented in 1965. Their recognition of films and scripts has been spotty. Their Best Script Nebula Award did not appear until 2000. In 2009 it was replaced by the Ray Bradbury Award for Outstanding Dramatic Presentation. Until then, the Ray Bradbury Award was only presented occasionally, to honor writers with an impressive body of work. Some say the Ray Bradbury Award is technically not a Nebula, but even so, it's presented at the Nebula Awards ceremony, and follows the Nebula rules and procedures for nomination and voting.

Below is a complete list of these dramatic awards' winners. It does not include Nebula's many non-dramatic categories. By "sc" I mean screenplay.

2009, Ray Bradbury Award ..... *District 9* (Neill Blomkamp, Terri Tatchell)
2008, Best Script ..... *WALL-E* (sc: Andrew Stanton, Jim Reardon; original story: Andrew Stanton, Pete Docter)
2008, Ray Bradbury Award ..... Joss Whedon
2007, Best Script ..... *Pan's Labyrinth* (Guillermo del Toro)
2006, Best Script ..... *Howl's Moving Castle* (Hayao Miyazaki, Cindy Davis Hewitt, Donald H. Hewitt)
2005, Best Script ..... *Serenity* (Joss Whedon)
2004, Best Script ..... *The Lord of the Rings: The Return of the King* (Fran Walsh, Philippa Boyens, Peter Jackson; based on *The Lord of the Rings* by J.R.R. Tolkien)
2003, Best Script ..... *The Lord of the Rings: The Two Towers* (Fran Walsh, Philippa Boyens, Stephen Sinclair, Peter Jackson; based on *The Lord of the Rings* by J.R.R. Tolkien)
2002, Best Script ..... *The Lord of the Rings: The Fellowship of the Ring* (Fran Walsh, Philippa Boyens, Peter Jackson; based on *The Lord of the Rings* by J.R.R. Tolkien)
2001, Best Script ..... *Crouching Tiger, Hidden Dragon* (James Schamus, Kuo Jung Tsai, Hui-Ling Wang; from the book by Du Lu Wang)
2000, Best Script ..... *Galaxy Quest* (Robert Gordon, David Howard)
2000, Ray Bradbury Award ..... Yuri Rasovsky, Harlan Ellison (*2000X—Tales of the Next Millennia*)
1999, Best Script ..... *The Sixth Sense* (M. Night Shyamalan)
1998, Ray Bradbury Award ..... J. Michael Straczynski (*Babylon 5*)
1991, Ray Bradbury Award ..... James Cameron (*Terminator 2: Judgment Day*)
1977, Special Award ..... *Star Wars*
1975, Best Dramatic Writing ..... Mel Brooks, Gene Wilder (*Young Frankenstein*)
1974, Best Dramatic Presentation ..... *Sleeper* (Woody Allen)
1973, Best Dramatic Presentation ..... *Soylent Green* (Stanley R. Greenberg for sc; based on the novel *Make Room! Make Room!!* by Harry Harrison)

Neuchâtel International Fantastic Film Festival

Farida Khali, from their press office, emails me: "This year [2010] is our 10th anniversary edition. The festival is born in 2000 and didn't exist before. There was no edition at all in 2001."

2010

H.R. Giger Award Narcisse for the Best Feature Film ..... *Enter the Void* (Gaspar Noé)
TSR Audience Award ..... *Black Death* (Chris Smith)
Denis-de-Rougemont Youth Award ..... *Strayed* (Akan Satayev)
Méliès d'Argent for the Best European Feature Film ..... *Strigoi* (Faye Jackson)
Mad Movies Award for the Maddest Film ..... *Dream Home* (Pang Ho-Cheung)
Special mention of the Jury ..... *Dream Home* (Pang Ho-Cheung)
Best Asian Movie Award ..... *Wig* (Renpei Tsukamoto)
Titra Film Award ..... *Valhalla Rising* (Nicolas Winding Refn)
H.R. Giger Award Narcisse for the Best Swiss Short ..... *Danny Boy* (Marek Skrobecki)
Taurus Studio Award ..... *Danny Boy* (Marek Skrobecki)
Taurus Studio for Innovation Award ..... *Ich bin's. Helmut* (Nicolas Steiner)
Nomination for the Méliès d'Or for the Best European Short Film ..... *Try a Little Tenderness* (Benjamin Teske)

2009

H.R. Giger Award Narcisse for the Best Feature Film ..... *Fish Story* (Yoshihiro Nakamura)
Denis-de-Rougemont Youth Award ..... *Fish Story* (Yoshihiro Nakamura)
Special Mention of the Jury ..... *Infestation* (Kyle Rankin)
TSR Audience Award ..... *Connected* (Benny Chan)
Méliès d'Argent for the Best European Feature Film ..... *Left Bank* (Pieter Van Hees)
Mad Movies Award for le film le plus Mad ..... *Left Bank* (Pieter Van Hees)
Best Asian Movie Award ..... *The Handsome Suit* (Tsutomu Hanabusa)
Titra Film Award ..... *Antichrist* (Lars Von Trier)
H.R. Giger Award Narcisse for the Best Swiss Short ..... *Le Petit Dragon* (Bruno Collet)
Taurus Studio Award ..... *Le Petit Dragon* (Bruno Collet)
Taurus Studio for Innovation Award ..... *Déjà* (Antonin Schopfer)
Nomination for the Méliès d'Or for the Best European Short Film ..... *Tile M for Murder* (Magnus Holmgren)

2008

H.R. Giger Award Narcisse for the Best Feature Film ..... *Sleep Dealer* (Alex Rivera)
Special Mention of the Jury ..... *Tokyo!* (Bong Joon-ho, Leos Carax, Michel Gondry)
Titra Film Award ..... *Tokyo!* (Bong Joon-ho, Leos Carax, Michel Gondry)
TSR Audience Award ..... *CJ7* (Stephen Chow)
Méliès d'Argent for the Best European Feature Film ..... *Let the Right One In* (Tomas Alfredson)
Special mention of the Jury ..... *Let the Right One In* (Tomas Alfredson)
Denis-de-Rougemont Youth Award ..... *Let the Right One In* (Tomas Alfredson)
Mad Movies Award for the Best Asian Movie ..... *Om Shanti Om* (Farha Khan)
H.R. Giger Award Narcisse for the Best Swiss Short ..... *Vincent le Magnifique* (Pascal Forney)
H.R. Award Narcisse for the Best Art Video, Actual Fears ..... *The Counterfeiters* (Katia Bassanini)
Nomination for the Méliès d'Or for the Best European Short Film ..... *Scary* (Martijn Hullegie)

2007

H.R. Giger Award Narcisse for the Best Feature Film ..... *You, the Living* (Roy Andersson)
Titra Film Award ..... *You, the Living* (Roy Andersson)
Special Mention of the Jury ..... *The Ugly Swans* (Konstantin Lopushansky)
Méliès d'Argent for the Best European Feature Film ..... *The Ugly Swans* (Konstantin Lopushansky)
TSR Audience Award ..... *Black Sheep* (Jonathan King)
Mad Movies Award for the Best Asian Movie ..... *Don* (Farhan Aklıtar)
Denis-de-Rougemont Youth Award ..... *La Antena* (Esteban Sapir)
H.R. Giger Award Narcisse for the Best Swiss Short ..... *City Wasp* (Stephan Wicki, Steven Tod)
Nomination for the Méliès d'Or for the Best European Short Film ..... *Silence Is Golden* (Chris Sheperd)

2006

H.R. Giger Award Narcisse for the Best Feature Film ..... *The Bothersome Man* (Jens Lien)
Méliès d'Or for the Best European Feature Film ..... *The Bothersome Man* (Jens Lien)
TSR Audience Award ..... *Adam's Apples* (Anders Thomas Jensen)
Denis-de-Rougemont Youth Award ..... *Adam's Apples* (Anders Thomas Jensen)
Mad Movies Award for the Best Asian Movie ..... *Saat po long* (Wilson Yip)
H.R. Giger Award Narcisse for the Best Swiss Short ..... *Une Nuit Blanche* (Maja Gehrig)
Nomination for the Méliès d'Or for the Best

European Short Film ..... *Dilemma* (Boris Paval Conen)

2005

H.R. Giger Award Narcisse for the Best Feature Film ..... *Innocence* (Lucile Hadzihalilovic)
Denis-de-Rougemont Youth Award ..... *Innocence* (Lucile Hadzihalilovic)
TSR Audience Award ..... *Zeburaman* (Miike Takashi)
Mad Movies Award for the Best Asian Movie ..... *Zeburaman* (Miike Takashi)
Méliès d'Or for the Best European Feature Film ..... *Code 46* (Michael Winterbottom)
H.R. Giger Award Narcisse for the Best Swiss Short ..... *Terra Incognita* (Peter Volkart)

2004

H.R. Giger Award Narcisse for the Best Fantastic Feature Film ..... *The Machinist* (Brad Anderson)
Méliès d'Argent for the Best Fantastic Feature Film ..... *The Machinist* (Brad Anderson)
TSR Audience Award ..... *Tokyo Godfathers* (Satoshi Kon, Shôgo Furuya)
Mad Movies Award for the Best Asian Movie ..... *Tokyo Godfathers* (Satoshi Kon, Shôgo Furuya)
Denis-de-Rougemont Youth Award ..... *The Taste of Tea* (Katsuhito Ishii)
SSA/Suissimage Prize for the Best Swiss Short Feature ..... *Belmondo* (Annette Carle)
Nomination for the Méliès d'Or for Best European Short Film ..... *7:35 de la Manana* (Nacho Vigalondo)

2003

H.R. Giger Award Narcisse for the Best Feature Film ..... *28 Days Later* (Danny Boyle)
Special Mention of the Jury ..... *Gozu* (Takashi Miike)
Mad Movies Award for the Best Asian Movie ..... *Gozu* (Takashi Miike)
TSR Audience Award ..... *The Invisible* (Joel Bergvall, Simon Sandquist)
Denis-de-Rougemont Youth Award ..... *New Blood* (Pou-soi Cheang)
H.R. Giger Award Narcisse for the Best Swiss Short ..... *Loups* (Hugo Veludo)
Special Mention of the SSA/Suissimage Jury ..... *La Clé d'Argent* (Victor Jaquier)

2002

H.R. Giger Award Narcisse for the Best Feature Film ..... *The Yin Yang Master* (Takita Yojiro)
Jury's Omnicom Prize ..... *Ichi the Killer* (Miike Takashi)
TSR Audience Award ..... *Don't Ask, Don't Tell* (Doug Miles)

H.R. Giger Award Narcisse for the Best Swiss Short ..... *Joshua* (Andreas Müller)

2000

H.R. Giger Award Narcisse for the Best Feature Film ..... *Gemini* (Shinya Tsukamoto)
Special Mention of the Jury ..... *Blood* (Charly Cantor)
H.R. Giger Award Narcisse for the Best Swiss Short ..... *Time With Nyenne* (Olivier Béguin)

New York City Horror Film Festival

2010

Best Feature ..... *Yellowbrickroad* (Andy Mitton, Jesse Holland)
Best Director ..... Stevan Mena (*Bereavement*)
Best Short ..... *Ninjas* (Dennison Ramalho)
Best Actor ..... James Nesbitt (*Outcast*)
Best Actress ..... Emilie Dequenne (*The Pack*, A.K.A. *La meute*)
Best Cinematography ..... Marco Cappetta (*Bereavement*)
Best FX ..... Jenn Rose (*Kiss the Abyss*)
Best Screenplay ..... Franck Richard (*The Pack*, A.K.A. *La meute*)
Audience Choice ..... *The Living Want Me Dead* (Bill Palmer)
Wizard World Award ..... *Written By* (Karni Baghdikian)
Lifetime Achievement Award ..... Mr. Robert Englund
Best Screenplay (unproduced) ..... *The Call of the Jersey Devil* (Aurelio Voltaire)
Special Mention (unproduced screenplay) ..... *Hoax* (Matt Allen, Scott Park)
Special Mention (unproduced screenplay) ..... *When Darkness Falls* (Arturo Portillo)
Special Mention (unproduced screenplay) ..... *Killer Granny* (Eric Lee, Kevin Armento, Taylor Jackson)

2009

Best Feature ..... *The Revenant*
Best Director ..... D. Kerry Prior (*The Revenant*)
Best Short ..... Eric Scherbarth (*Sinkhole*)
Best Actor (tie) ..... David Anders and Chris Wylde (*The Revenant*)
Best Actress ..... Ellia English (*Cornered*)
Best Cinematography ..... Pier Luigi Santi (*The Shadow Within*)
Best Special Effects ..... *Sweatshop*
Best Screenplay ..... Andreas Schaap (*Must Love Death*)
Audience Choice ..... *The Revenant*
Best Screenplay (unproduced) ..... *Gargoyle* (Vincent Ho and Stan Shaw)

2008

Best Feature ..... *Bad Biology* (dir: Frank Henenlotter)
Best Director ..... Jennifer Chambers Lynch (*Surveillance*)
Best Short ..... *Altar* (dir: Nathan Bezner)
Best Actor ..... Dameon Clarke (*How to be a Serial Killer*)
Best Actress ..... Ryan Simpkins (*Surveillance*)
Best Cinematography ..... Stephanie Martin (*The Objective*)
Best Special Effects ..... Gabriel Bartalos (*Bad Biology*)
Best Screenplay ..... *Timecrimes*, A.K.A. *Los cronocrímenes* (Nacho Vigalondo)
Audience Choice Award (feature) ..... *Timecrimes*, A.K.A. *Los cronocrímenes* (Nacho Vigalondo)
Audience Choice Award (short) ..... *Treevenge* (Jason Eisener)
Lifetime Achievement ..... Frank Henenlotter
Best Screenplay (unproduced) ..... *Remake* (Jason Contino)

2007

Best Feature ..... *Botched* (dir: Kit Ryan)
Best Short ..... *Criticized* (dir: Richard Gale)
Best Cinematography ..... *Nobody*
Best Actor ..... Stephen Dorff (*Botched*)
Best Actress ..... Masha Wattanapanich (*Alone*)
Best Special Effects ..... *Seed*
Best Screenplay ..... *Death of a Ghost Hunter*
Audience Choice ..... *Dara* (dir: Timothy Tjahjanto, Kimo Stamboel)
Lifetime Achievement ..... Herschell Gordon Lewis
Best Comic Book ..... *Johnny Gruesome* (writer: Gregory Lamberson)
Best Screenplay (unproduced) ..... *Dose* (James T. Nelson)
2nd Place Screenplay (unproduced) ..... *The Cow* (The Brothers Cleveland)
3rd Place Screenplay (unproduced) ..... *Y* (B.C. Furtney)
Honorable Mention Screenplay (unproduced) ..... *The Horrifying Ordeal of Pilar Mallard* (B.C. Furtney)

2006

Best Feature ..... *Fingerprints*
Best Short ..... *Happy Birthday to You*
Best Screenplay ..... *Last Rites of the Dead*
Best Cinematography ..... *The Marsh*
Best Special Effects ..... *The Marsh*
Best Actor ..... Robert "Opal" Oppel (*Rapturious*)
Best Actress ..... Gina Ramsden (*Last Rites of the Dead*)
Audience Choice Award ..... *Eddie Loves You*
Lifetime Achievement ..... Mick Garris
Excellence in Acting ..... Tony Todd

2005

Best Feature ..... *The Dark Hours* (dir: Paul Fox)
Best Short ..... *Zombie Movie* (dir: Ben Stenbeck)
Best Actor ..... Jason Campbell (*Nightmare*)
Best Actress ..... Nicole Roderick (*Nightmare*)
Best Screenplay ..... *Headspace*
Best Cinematography ..... William Miller (*Headspace*)
Best Makeup Effects ..... Leonard MacDonald (*Neighborhood Watch*)
Audience Choice ..... *Road Kill* (dir: Mark Mardini)
Lifetime Achievement ..... Roger Corman

2004

Best Feature ..... *The Last Horror Movie* (dir: Julian Richards)
Best Short ..... *Herbie* (dir: Drew Barnhardt)
Best Actor ..... Kevin Howarth (*The Last Horror Movie*)
Best Cinematography ..... *London Voodoo*
Best Special Effects ..... *Cube Zero*
Best Screenplay ..... *The Ghouls*
Audience Choice ..... *Unwelcome* (dir: Gentry Smith)
Lifetime Achievement ..... Tobe Hooper

2003

Best Feature ..... *Malevolence* (dir: Stevan Mena)
Best Short ..... *Scream for Me* (dir: Christopher Alan Broadstone)
Best Actor ..... Kristina Copeland (*Savage Island*)
Best Cinematography ..... Richard Siegel (*Flesh for the Beast*)
Best Makeup Effects ..... G&S Effects (*Flesh for the Beast*)
Audience Choice ..... *Strange Things Happen at Sundown* (dir: Marc Fratto)
Lifetime Achievement ..... Tom Savini

2002

Best Feature ..... *Lucky* (Steve Cuden)
Best Short ..... *The Human Beeing*
Best Actor ..... Dana J. Ryan (*Den*)
Best Cinematography ..... Timothy Naylor (*Horror*)
Lifetime Achievement ..... George A. Romero

A Night of Horror International Film Festival

Their Independent Spirit Award should not be confused with the Independent Spirit Award that is presented by the Los Angeles–based Film Independent (formerly the Independent Feature Project/West).

2010

Best Film ..... *The Revenant* (dir: Kerry Prior)
Special Judges' Mention ..... *Heart of Karl* (dir: Steven Kostanski)
Best Lovecraft Short Film ..... *Frank Dancoolo: Paranormal Drug Dealer* (dir: Andrew Jones)
Best Animated Short Film ..... *The Screaming Skull* (dir: Ashley Thorpe)
Best Australian Short Film ..... *A+Positive* (dir: Chris Bamford, Serge Ou)
Best Short Film ..... *2:22* (dir: Steven Shea)
Audience Choice Award, Australian Short Showcase (tie) ..... *The Clothes* (dir: Toby Morris) and *Mr. Pin* (dir: Andrew Daley)
Best Music Video ..... Living Lâche—*It Was So Mad* (dir: Lucas Zach)
Best Special Effects ..... *The Dark Lurking* (dir: Gregory Connors)
Best Director ..... Kerry Prior (*The Revenant*)
Best Female Performance ..... Caroline Marohasy (*The Horseman*)
Best Male Performance ..... Peter Marshall (*The Horseman*)
Best Australian Director ..... Steven Kastrissios (*The Horseman*)
Best Australian Film ..... *The Horseman* (dir: Steven Kastrissios)
Independent Spirit Award, Feature Film ..... *House of Flesh Mannequins* (dir: Domiziano Cristopharo)
Independent Spirit Award, Short Film ..... *The Dead Wastes* (dir: Wade K. Savage)
Feature Screenplay, 1st Place (unproduced) ..... *Curse of the Swampies* (Steve Carter, Antoinette Rydyr, Paul Elliott)
Feature Screenplay, 2nd Place (unproduced) ..... *#14* (Solomon Grundy)
Feature Screenplay, 3rd Place (unproduced) ..... *Macau Twilight* (Tony Shyu)
Short Screenplay, 1st Place (unproduced) ..... *Gabriel-Ernest* (Valentine Stockdale)
Short Screenplay, 2nd Place (unproduced) ..... *Stranger* (Bryn Tilly)
Short Screenplay, 3rd Place (unproduced) ..... *Rabbit* (Paul Robson)

2009

Best Film ..... *Splinter*
Best Foreign Language Film ..... *No Morire Sola*, A.K.A. *I'll Never Die Alone*
Best Australian Film ..... *I Know How Many Runs You Scored Last Summer*
Best Director ..... Adrián García Bogliano (*I'll Never Die Alone*)
Best Australian Director ..... Ursula Dabrowsky (*Family Demons*)
Best Female Performance ..... Olga Fedori (*Mum and Dad*)
Best Male Performance ..... Shea Whigham (*Splinter*)
Best Special Effects, Feature Film ..... *Splinter*
Best Special Effects, Short Film ..... *Treevenge*
Best Short Film ..... *Una Storia Di Lupi*, A.K.A. *A Wolf's Tale*
Best Short Animation Film ..... *The Facts in the Case of Mr. Hollow*
Best Lovecraft Film ..... *AM 1200*
Best Short Australian Film ..... *A Break in the Monotony*
Best Music Video ..... *More Control* (by The Heist and the Accomplice; dir Steve Daniels)
Directors' Choice, Best Feature ..... *Reel Zombies*
Directors' Choice, Best Short ..... *Allure*
Independent Spirit Award, Feature Film ..... *Finale*
Independent Spirit Award, Short Film ..... *The Red Hours*
Independent Spirit Award, Australian Film ..... *Taber Corn*
Feature Screenplay, 1st Place (unproduced) ..... *Terminal* (Paul Campion, Elisabeth Pinto)
Feature Screenplay, 2nd Place (unproduced) ..... *Children of the Night* (Harry Basil)
Feature Screenplay, 3rd Place (unproduced) ..... *Footage* (Duncan Samarasinghe)
Short Screenplay, 1st Place (unproduced) ..... *Brother Moose's Broken Shorts* (A. J. Mitchler)
Short Screenplay, 2nd Place (unproduced) ..... *Fragments of Normal* (Gwyn Duffy)
Short Screenplay, 3rd Place (unproduced) ..... *Mr. Roach* (Franck Zuanic)

2008

Best Film ..... *Brain Dead*
Best Foreign Language Film ..... *La Antena*
Best Short Film ..... *Pumpkin Hell*
Best Australian Film ..... *When Sally Met Frank*
Best Lovecraft Film ..... *The Call of Cthulhu*
Best Animation Film ..... *Egg Ghost*
Best Music Video ..... *Torture Device* (by Dawn of Ashes)
Best Director ..... Paco Limon (*Doctor Infierno*)
Best Performance ..... Sammi Davis (*The Double Born*)
Best Scream Queen ..... Tess McVicker (*Brain Dead*)
Best Special Make-Up Effects ..... *Brain Dead*
Best Visual Effects ..... *Eel Girl*
Directors' Choice Award, Best Feature ..... *Murder Loves Killers Too*
Directors' Choice Award, Best Short ..... *Kirksdale*

2007

Best Score ..... Milan Rusko, *Nazdravicko!*
Best Scream Queen ..... Kaja Trøa (*The New Life*)
Best Special Effects ..... Stuart Rowsell (*The Ancient Rite of Corey McGillis*)
Best Performance ..... Emma Caulfield (*Hollow*)
Best Director ..... Paul Campion (*Night of the Hell Hamsters*)

Best Zombie Film ..... *Love is a Shotgun*
Best Lovecraft Film ..... *From Beyond*
Best Animation ..... *The Tell Tale Heart*
Best Film ..... *Happy Birthday to You*
Best of Fest ..... *The Ancient Rite of Corey McGillis*

A Nightmare To Remember

A.K.A. A Nightmare to Remember San Francisco Horror Film Festival. Presents Coffin Award.

2010

1st Place ..... *Death in Charge* (Devi Snively)
2nd Place ..... *Callous Sentiment* (Vincent Grashaw)
3rd Place ..... *Horror of our Love* (Dave Reda)

2009

1st Place ..... *Now That You're Dead* (Patrick Rea, Senoreality Pictures)
2nd Place ..... *Spilt Milk* (Kevin MacDonald)
3rd Place ..... *Vadata* (Manuel Lebelt)

2008

1st Place ..... *#19* (Tommy Merry)
2nd Place ..... *The Cleaner* (Michelle Fatale)
3rd Place ..... *Reversal* (Rock Shaink, Jr.)

Oklahoma Horror Film Festival & Convention

2010

Grand Jury, Best Feature ..... *The Prometheus Project*
Grand Jury, Best Short ..... *Off Season*
Best Director of a Feature ..... Sean Tretta (*The Prometheus Project*)
Best Director of a Short ..... Devi Snively (*Death in Charge*)
Best Actress in a Feature ..... Marianne Porter (*True Nature*)
Best Actor in a Feature ..... Scott Anthony Leet (*The Prometheus Project*)
Best Supporting Actor in a Feature ..... Carlos Larkin (*George's Intervention*)
Best Supporting Actress in a Feature ..... Patti Tindall (*The Prometheus Project*)
Best Actress in a Short ..... Zoe Daelman Chlanda (*By Her Hand, She Draws You Down*)
Best Actor in a Short ..... Jerry Murdock (*By Her Hand, She Draws You Down*)
Best Unproduced Screenplay ..... Joe Randazzo (*Ripper*)
Best Unproduced Oklahoma Screenplay ..... Catherine Johnson (*The Handler*)
Best Produced Feature Screenplay ..... Sean Tretta (*The Prometheus Project*)
Best Produced Short Screenplay ..... Chris Keaton (*Devil's Toy*)
Best Foreign Feature ..... *El Monstro del Mar!*
Best Foreign Short ..... *Remote*
Audience Choice ..... Tate Steinsiek (*The Devoured*)
Best Animated Film ..... *The Terrible Thing of Alpha 9*
Best Horror Comedy ..... *Rise of the Appliances*
Best Oklahoma Film ..... *Flowers for Norma*
Best Special Effects ..... *The Taken*
Best Cinematography ..... *The Sacred*
Best Editing ..... *The Taken*
Best Sound ..... *Cockpit: The Rule of Engagement*
Best Soundtrack/Score ..... *El Monstro del Mar!*

Paranoia Horror Film Festival

2010

Best Feature Film *D4*
Best Short Film ..... *Let Them Eat*
Best Music Video ..... *Combichrist — Sent to Destroy*
Best Trailer ..... *The Drawing*
Best Screenplay (unproduced) ..... *The Drowning* (Emily Platt)

2009

Best Feature Film ..... *The Beacon* (dir: Michael Stokes)
Best Short Film ..... *Criticized* (dir: Richard Gale)
Best Actor ..... Armand Assante (*Soul's Midnight*)
Best Actress ..... Teri Polo (*The Beacon*)
Best Music Video ..... *The Beauty* (dir: Luca Vecchi)
Best Special Effects ..... *Lucifer*
Best Trailer ..... *Blood Bunny* (dir: Molly Madfis)
Best Screenplay (unproduced) ..... *Devil's Playground* (Ryan Gilmore)

Phoenix Fear Film Festival

Website has winners for 2006 and 2008, but none for 2007 or 2009. However, their MySpace page says 2010 was their *third* event; their website says 2008 was their *second*. This means that 2007 and 2009 are not missing; there's just nothing to report. But this festival does not necessarily run every other year. Their website promises that their *fourth* event will be in 2011.

2010

Best Feature ..... *Shellter* (dir: Dan Donley)
Best Short ..... *Blockhead* (dir: John Francis Conway III)
Audience Favorite ..... *Roman's Bride* (dir: Michael Paul)
Best Ensemble ..... *Trippin'*
Best Editing ..... *Sinkhole*

Best Cinematography ..... *Dead Creek*
Short We Most Want to See as a Feature ..... *Neon Killer*
Best Use of an Electric Toothbrush ..... *Ouija Board*

2008

Best Feature ..... *Sick Girl* (dir: Eben McGarr)
Best Short ..... *Cheerbleeders* (dir: Peter Podgursky)
Audience Favorite ..... *Genital Genocide* (dir: Doug Gehl)

2006

Best Feature ..... *Caregiver*
Best Short ..... *Flesh-Eating Ghouls from Outer Space*
Audience Favorite ..... *Malediction*

Puchon International Fantastic Film Festival

Presents the Puchon Choice Award.

2010

Best of Puchon ..... *Bedevilled* (dir: Jang Cheol Su, A.K.A. Jang Cheol-so)
Best Director ..... Gareth Edwards (*Monsters*)
Best Actor ..... Richie Jen (*Fire of Conscience*)
Best Actress ..... Seo Yeong Hee (*Bedevilled*)
Prugio Citizen's Choice ..... *Gintama: The Movie* A.K.A. *Gin Tama* (dir: Takamatsu Shinji)
Jury's Choice ..... *Confessions* (dir: Nakashima Tetsuya)
Best Short Film ..... *Play* (dir: David Kaplan)
Jury's Choice for Short Film ..... *St. Christophorus: Roadkill* (dir: Gregor Erler)
Best Korean Short Film ..... *Rail* (dir: Myung Bae Young)
Citizen's Choice for Short Film ..... *Melt Down* (dir: David Green)
European Fantastic Film Festival Federation Asian Award ..... *Bestseller* (dir: Lee Jeong Ho)
Netpac Award ..... *Permanent Nobara* (dir: Yoshida Daihachi)
Fujifilm Eterna Award ..... *Bedevilled* (dir: Jang Cheol Su, A.K.A. Jang Cheol-so)

2009

Best of Puchon ..... *The Forbidden Door* (dir: Joko Anwar)
Best Director ..... Dante Lam (*The Beast Stalker*)
Best Actress ..... Shareefa Daanish (*Macabre*)
Best Actor ..... Stephen McHattie (*Pontypool*)
Special Mention, Actor ..... Nick Cheung (*The Beast Stalker*)
Prugio Citizen's Choice ..... *The Neighbor Zombie* (dir: Oh Young Doo, Ryu Hoon, Hong Young Guen, Jang Yoon Jung)
Jury's Choice ..... *My Neighbor Zombie* (dir: Oh Young Doo, Ryu Hoon, Hong Young Guen, Jang Yoon Jung)
Best Short Film ..... *The Horribly Slow Murderer with the Extremely Inefficient Weapon* (dir: Richard Gale)
Special Mention, Short Film ..... *Dust Kid* (dir: Jung Yu Mi)
Jury's Choice for Short Film ..... *Dance Macabre* (dir: Pedro Pires)
Citizen's Choice for Short Film ..... *The Horribly Slow Murderer with the Extremely Inefficient Weapon* (dir: Richard Gale)
Best Korean Short Film ..... *Dust Kid* (dir: Jung Yu Mi)
Fujifilm Eterna Award ..... *Turn It Up to 11* (dir: Baek Seung Hwa)
Netpac Award ..... *8000 Miles* (dir: Irie Yu)
Netpac Special Mention ..... *Halfway* (dir: Kitakawa Enriko)
Netpac Special Mention ..... Mitsushima Hikari (*Love Exposure, Pride*)
Netpac Special Mention ..... Ando Sakura (*Ain't No Tomorrow, Love Exposure*)
European Fantastic Film Festival Federation Asian Award ..... *Chocolate* (dir: Prachya Pinkaew)

2008

Best of Puchon ..... *The Chaser* (dir: Na Hong Jin)
Best Director ..... Tomas Alfredson (*Let the Right One In*)
Best Actress ..... Seo Yeong Hee (*The Chaser*)
Best Actor ..... Ekin Cheng, Shawn Yue (*Rule Number One*)
Prugio Citizen's Choice ..... *Let the Right One In* (dir: Tomas Alfredson)
Jury's Choice ..... *Fear(s) of the Dark* (various directors)
European Fantastic Film Festival Federation Asian Award ..... *The Chaser* (dir: Na Hong Jin)
Special Mention ..... *Hansel and Gretel* (dir: Yim Phil Sung)
Special Mention ..... *Tokyo Gore Police* (dir: Yoshihiro Nishimura)
Best Short Film ..... *The Facts in the Case of Mister Hollow* (dir: Rodrigo Gudino)
Jury's Choice for Short Film ..... *Schausteins Final Film* (dir: Christian Klandt)
Citizen's Choice for Short Film ..... *A Coffee Vending Machine and Its Sword* (dir: Chang Hyung Yun)
Best Korean Short Film ..... *A Coffee Vending Machine and Its Sword* (dir: Chang Hyung Yun)

2007

Best of Puchon ..... *13 13* (dir: Chookiet Sakveerakul)
Best Director ..... Martin Weisz (*Grimm Love*)
Best Actress ..... Charlene Choi (*Diary*)

Best Actor ..... Thomas Kretschmann and Thomas Huber (*Grimm Love*)
Prugio Citizen's Choice ..... *The Matsugane Potshot Affair* (dir: Yamashita Nobuhiro)
Jury's Choice ..... *Special* (dir: Haberman & Passmore)
European Fantastic Film Festival Federation Asian Award ..... *13 13* (dir: Chookiet Sakveerakul)
Special Mention ..... *Victor and the Machine* (Carlos Talamanca)
Best Short Film ..... *Juanito Under the Orange Tree* (dir: Yohann Gloaguen)
Jury's Choice for Short Film ..... *Sweat* (dir: Na Hong Jin)
Citizen's Choice for Short Film ..... *The Eyes of Edward James* (dir: Rodrigo Gudino)
Best Korean Short Film ..... *The Villains* (dir: Chang Hoon)

2006

Best of Puchon ..... *Adam's Apples* (dir: Anders Thomas Jensen)
Best Director ..... *Storm* (dir: Måns Mårlind, Björn Stein)
Best Actress ..... Kazue Fukiishi (*Noriko's Dinner Table*)
Best Actor ..... Ulrich Thomsen and Mads Mikkelsen (*Adam's Apples*)
Prugio Citizen's Choice ..... *Noriko's Dinner Table* (dir: Sion Sono)
Kid's Special Choice ..... *Tori & Rabi* (dir: Choi Jae Jin)
European Fantastic Film Festival Federation Asian Award ..... *The Maid* (dir: Kelvin Tong)
Special Mention ..... *D-Day* (dir: Kim Eun Kyung)
Grand Prize for Short Film ..... *It's in the Air* (dir: Yohann Gloaguen)
Jury's Choice for Short Film ..... *Cutting Edge* (dir: Gregory Morin)
Citizen's Choice for Short Film ..... *Lock Smith* (dir: Park Jae-hong)

2005

Best of Puchon ..... *The Dark Hours* (dir: Paul Fox)
Best Director ..... Joaquin Oristrell (*Unconscious*)
Best Actress (tied) ..... Orsi Tóth (*Johanna*) and Kate Greenhouse (*The Dark Hours*)
Best Actor ..... Phan Rajanarangsee, Supakorn Srisawat, Somjai Sukjai, Banphot Weerarat (*Rahtree Returns*)
Prugio Citizen's Choice ..... *Hari Om* (dir: Bharatbala Ganapathy)
Jury's Choice ..... *Nuit noire* (dir: Olivier Smolders)
Grand Prize for Short Film ..... *Ryan* (dir: Chris Landreth)
Jury's Choice for Short Film ..... *The Ten Steps* (dir: Brendan Muldowney)
Citizen's Choice for Short Film ..... *Alice and I* (dir: Micha Wald)

2004

Best of Puchon ..... *Arahan* (dir: Ryoo Seung-wan)
Best Director ..... Leonardo Di Cesare (*Good Life Delivery*)
Best Actress ..... Nat Wattanapat (*Suicide Me*)
Best Actor ..... Benoît Delépine, Gustave de Kervern (*Aaltra*)
Prugio Citizen's Choice ..... *Arahan* (dir: Ryoo Seung-wan)
Jury's Choice ..... *The Taste of Tea* (dir: Katsuhito Ishii)
Grand Prize for Short Film ..... *Goodbye, Cruel World* (dir: Vito Rocco)
Jury's Choice for Short Film ..... *My Parents* (dir: Neele Leana Vollmar)
Citizen's Choice for Short Film ..... *My Parents* (dir: Neele Leana Vollmar)
European Fantastic Film Festival Federation (EFFFF) Asian Award ..... *Virumandi* (dir: Kamal Hassan)
EFFFF Special Mention ..... *Ghost in the Shell 2: Innocence* (dir: Mamoru Oshii)

2003

Best of Puchon ..... *Save the Green Planet!* (dir: Jang Jun-hwan)
Best Director ..... Greg Pak (*Robot Stories*)
Best Actress ..... Wai Ching Ho (*Robot Stories*)
Best Actor ..... Beak Yoon-Sik (*Save the Green Planet!*)
Citizen's Choice ..... *Save the Green Planet!* (dir: Jang Jun-hwan)
Jury's Choice ..... *They're Watching Us* (dir: Norberto Lopez)
Grand Prize for Short Film ..... *DEF* (dir: Ian Clark)
PRUGIO Award–Jury's Choice for Short Film ..... *United We Stand* (dir: Hans Petter Moland)
Citizen's Choice for Short Film ..... *DEF* (dir: Ian Clark)

2002

Best of Puchon ..... *Getting My Brother Laid* (dir: Sven Taddicken)
Best Director ..... Sven Taddicken (*Getting My Brother Laid*)
Best Actress ..... Christiane Hörbiger (*The Praying Mantis*)
Best Actor ..... Roman Knizka (*Getting My Brother Laid*)
Citizen's Choice ..... *Bet on My Disco* (dir: Kim Dong-won)
Jury's Choice ..... *Dark Water* (dir: Hideo Nakata)
Grand Prize for Short Film ..... *Salad Days* (dir: Gustavo Salmerón)
Kookmin Credit Card Award–Jury's Choice for Short Film ..... *The Pitch* (dir: Nash Edgerton)
Citizen's Choice for Short Film ..... *Salad Days* (dir: Gustavo Salmerón)

2001

Best of Puchon ..... *The Price of Milk* (dir: Harry Sinclair)
Best Director ..... Hideyuki Hirayama (*Turn*)
Best Actress ..... Kang Haejung (*The Butterfly*)
Best Actor ..... Boris Aljinovic (*Three Chinamen with a Double Bass*)
Jury's Choice ..... *Tears of the Black Tiger* (dir: Wisit Sasanatieng)
Grand Prize for Short Film ..... *The Tale of the Rat that Wrote* (dir: Billy O'Brien)
Kodak Award–Jury's Choice for Short Film ..... *Copy Shop* (dir: Virgil Widrich)
Citizen's Choice for Short Film ..... *Rejected* (dir: Don Hertzfeldt)

2000

Best of Puchon ..... *The Ugliest Woman in the World* (dir: Miguel Bardem)
Best Director ..... Masahiro Shinoda (*Owl's Castle*)
Best Actress ..... Sara Dogg Asgeirsdottir (*Witchcraft*)
Best Actor ..... Pascal Greggory (*Why Get Married the Day the World Ends?*)
Jury's Choice ..... *The Nameless* A.K.A. *Los sin nombre* (dir: Jaume Balagueró)
Grand Prize for Short Film ..... *The Periwig-Maker* (dir: Steffen Schäffler)
Jury's Choice for Short Film ..... *La Comtesse de Castiglione* (dir: David Lodge)
Citizen's Choice for Short Film ..... *Black XXX-Mas* (dir: Pieter Van Hees)
Special Prize ..... the late Choi Moo-ryong (actor), A.K.A. Mu-ryong Choi

1999

Best of Puchon ..... *Siam Sunset* (dir: John Polson)
Jury's Choice ..... *Cube* (dir: Vincenzo Natali)
Citizen's Choice ..... *Between Your Legs* (dir: Manuel Gomez Pereira)
Netizen's Choice ..... *The Blair Witch Project* (Daniel Myrick, Eduardo Sanchez)
Grand Prize for Short Film ..... *2+1 Human Mistake* (dir: Christian Boisliveau)
Unitel Award–Grand Prize for Short Film ..... *The Periwig-Maker* (dir: Steffen Schäffler)
Jury's Choice for Short Film ..... *You Are the Hero in This Film* (dir: Pascal Rocteur)
Citizen's Choice for Short Film ..... *One Day a Man Bought a House* (dir: Pjotr Sapegin)

1998

Best of Puchon ..... *Samurai Fiction* (dir: Hiroyuki Nakano)
Jury's Choice ..... *Arcane Sorcerer* (dir: Pupi Avati)
Citizen's Choice ..... *The Unfish* (dir: Robert Dornhelm)
Netizen's Choice ..... *Alexander Senki* (dir: Kanemori Yoshinori)

1997

Best of Puchon ..... *Kitchen* (dir: Yim Ho)
Jury's Choice ..... *Freeway* (dir: Matthew Bright)
Citizen's Choice ..... *The Ugly* (dir: Scott Reynolds)
Netizen's Choice ..... *The Contact* (dir: Jang Yoonhyun)

Ravenna Nightmare Film Festival

2010

Best Feature ..... *Godspeed* (Robert Saitzyk)
Special Mention ..... *Red White & Blue* (Simon Rumley)

2009

Best Feature ..... *The Human Centipede (First Sequence)* (Tom Six)
Special Mention ..... *The Life and Death of a Porno Gang* (Mladen Djordjevic)

2008

Best Feature ..... *Frontière(s)* (Xavier Gens)
Special Mention ..... *Eden Lake* (James Watkins)
Special Mention ..... *The Disappeared* (Johnny Kevorkian)
Best Short ..... *Las horas muertas* (Haritz Zubillaga)

2007

Best Feature ..... *The Ugly Swans* (Kostantin Lopushansky)
Special Mention ..... *The Diabolikal Super-Kriminal* (Ss-Sunda)
Best Short ..... *La dama en el Umbral* (Jorge Dayas)

2006

Best Feature ..... *Them*, A.K.A. *Ils* (David Moreau, Xavier Palud)
Special Mention ..... *Frostbiten* (Anders Banke)
Special Mention ..... *The Woods* (Lucky McKee)
Best Short ..... *Virus* (Jerker Josefsson)
Short Special Mention ..... *Plastic* (Mark Davis)

2005

Best Feature ..... *Satan's Little Helper* (Jeff Lieberman)
Special Mention ..... *The Lost* (Chris Sivertson)
Best Short ..... *The Ten Steps* (Brendan Muldowney)

2004

Best Feature ..... *Tears of Kali* (Andreas Marschall)
Special Mention ..... *May* (Lucky McKee)
Special Mention ..... *Willard* (Glen Morgan)

Best Short ..... *Inside Out* (Oliver Knott)
Short Special Mention ..... *The Carpenter and His Clumsy Wife* (Peter Foott)

2003

Best Feature ..... *T.T. Syndrome* (Dejan Zecevic)
Special Mention ..... *Alter Ego* (Shimizu Takashi, Shibata Issey)
Special Mention ..... *Bloody Mallory* (Julien Magnat)

Razor Reel Fantastic Film Festival

Patrick Van Hauwaert tells me: "The Razor Reel Fantastic Film Festival has only one award to be given and that is the plain and most simple of all awards, the Audience award."

2010 ..... *The Loved Ones*
2009 ..... *[Rec] 2*
2008 ..... *A L'Interieur*

Reaper Award

A.K.A. the Grim Reaper Award, or the Grimmy Award. Not a film festival, but a "horror on home video" award. Judges pick the nominees, and the fans (or anyone else) vote for the winners online. Run by *Home Media Magazine* and DreadCentral.com.

2010

Best of Show ..... *Never Sleep Again: The Elm Street Legacy* (1428 Films and CAV Distributing)
Best Direct-to-Video ..... *Never Sleep Again: The Elm Street Legacy* (1428 Films and CAV Distributing)
Best Packaging ..... *Friday the 13th: Part VII—The New Blood* (deluxe edition) (Paramount Home Entertainment)
Best Boxed Set or TV Show Collection ..... *True Blood: The Complete Second Season* (HBO Home Entertainment)
Best Re-Release ..... *Friday the 13th: Part VII—The New Blood* (deluxe edition) (Paramount Home Entertainment)
Best Blu-ray ..... *True Blood: The Complete Second Season* (HBO Home Entertainment)
Best Indie or Foreign Title ..... *Grace* (Anchor Bay Entertainment)
Best Theatrical ..... *Trick 'R Treat* (Warner Home Video)
Most Anticipated Theatrical ..... *A Nightmare on Elm Street* (2010) (Warner Home Video)
Most Anticipated Nontheatrical ..... *30 Days of Night: Dark Days* (Sony Pictures Home Entertainment)
Most Anticipated Catalog Release ..... *Alien Anthology Blu-ray* (20th Century–Fox Home Entertainment)
Lifetime Achievement Grimmy ..... Tom Holland

2009

Best in Show ..... *Hellraiser Box Set* (Anchor Bay Entertainment)
Best Direct-to-Video ..... *Alien Raiders* (Warner Home Video)
Best Packaging ..... *Hellraiser Box Set* (Anchor Bay Entertainment)
Best Boxed Set or TV Series ..... *Dexter: The Complete Third Season* (Paramount Home Entertainment/CBS/Showtime)
Best Re-Release ..... *Friday the 13th: Deluxe Editions (Parts 1–6)* (Paramount Home Entertainment)
Best Blu-ray ..... *Ghostbusters* (Sony Pictures Home Entertainment)
Best Indie/Foreign (with domestic release) ..... *[REC]* (Sony Pictures Home Entertainment)
Best Re-Mastering ..... *Hellraiser* (Anchor Bay Entertainment)
Best Theatrical ..... *The Last House on the Left* (2009) (Universal Studios Home Entertainment)
Best Zombie ..... *Quarantine* (Sony Pictures Home Entertainment)
Best Slasher ..... *The Last House on the Left* (1972) (20th Century–Fox Home Entertainment/MGM)
Best Ghost Story ..... *The Haunting in Connecticut* (Lionsgate)
Best Vampire/Werewolf ..... *Underworld: Rise of the Lycans* (Sony Pictures Home Entertainment)
Lifetime Achievement ..... Michael Felsher (Red Shirt Pictures)

Rhode Island International Horror Film Festival

Executive Director/CEO George T. Marshall informs me that the RIIHFF's First Place award is a "runner up" to their Grand (A.K.A. Best) prize.

2010

Best Feature (tie) ..... *True Nature* (dir: Patrick Steele) and *Zombie Dearest* (dir: David Kemker)
First Place, Feature ..... *Mørke Sjeler*, A.K.A. *Dark Souls* (dir: César Ducasse, Mathieu Peteul)
Best Short (tie) ..... *The Happiness Salesman* (dir: Krishnendu Majumdar) and *Natural Selection* (dir: Brett Foraker)
First Place, Short (tie) ..... *The Continuing and Lamentable Saga of The Suicide Brothers* (dir:

Arran Brownlee, Corran Brownlee) and *Meth* (dir: Michael Maney)
Directorial Discovery ..... *Red Balloon* (dir: Damien Mace, Alexis Wajsbrot)
Best New England ..... *Lizbeth: A Victorian Nightmare* (dir: Ric Rebello)
Best Makeup FX ..... *Tell Him Next Year* (dir: David Margolis)
Best Animation ..... *The Tell-Tale Heart, Animated Horror Short* (dir: Michael Swertfager)

2009

Best Picture (tie) ..... *Dawning* (dir: Gregg Holtgrewe) and *Circuit* (dir: Andrew Landauro)
Best Short (tie) ..... *Lazarus Taxon* (dir: Denis Rovira) and *The Taxidermist* (dir: Bert & Bertie)
Best Documentary ..... *Nightmares in Red, White and Blue* (dir: Andrew Monument)
Directorial Discovery ..... *Happy Face* (dir: Franklin P. Laviola)
Best New England ..... *Crooked Lane* (dir: Chase Bailey)
Best Makeup FX ..... *Werewolf Trouble* (dir: Charlie Anderson)

2008

Best Picture (tie) ..... *Sea of Dust* (dir: Scott Bunt) and *Epitaph* (dir: the Jung Brothers)
Best Short ..... *AM1200* (dir: David Prior)
Best Documentary ..... *Spine Tingler! The William Castle Story* (dir: Jeffrey Schwarz)
Directorial Discovery ..... *Conjurer* (dir: Clint Hutchison)
Best Student Film ..... *Kirksdale* (dir: Ryan Spindell)
Best New England ..... *The Curse of Micah Rood* (dir: Alec Asten)
Best Makeup FX ..... *Eel Girl* (dir: Paul Campion)

2007

Best Picture ..... *Brain Dead* (dir: Kevin S. Tenney)
Best Short ..... *The Demonology of Desire* (dir: Rodrigo Gudiño)
Best New Director ..... Richard Terrasi (*Am I Evil*)
Best New England ..... *The Terror Factor* (dir: Garry Medeiros)
Best Makeup FX ..... *Penance* (dir: Fred Vogel)

2006

Best Picture ..... *The Slaughter* (dir: Jay Lee)
Best Short ..... *Grace* (dir: Paul Solet)
Best New Director ..... Scott Goldberg (*The Day They Came Back* and *All I Want for Christmas*)
Best New England ..... *Die You Zombie Bastards* (dir: Caleb Emerson)
Best Genre Cross Over ..... *Seepage!*, A.K.A. *Creature from the Hillybilly Lagoon* (dir: Richard Griffin)
Best Makeup FX ..... *Bone Sickness* (dir: Brian Paulin)
Audience Award ..... *Camp Blood: The Musical* (Tanner Barklow, Jefferson Craig, Thomas Hughes)

2005

Best Picture ..... *Dark Remains* (Brian Avenet-Bradley)
Best Short ..... *Means to an End* (Paul Solet, Jake Hamilton)
Best Animated ..... *Tell Tale Heart*
Best Director ..... Jason Hack (*Day X*)
Best Effects ..... *We All Fall Down*
Horror Excellence Award ..... *Cruel World*
Vanguard Award ..... Fred Vogel (*August Underground*)
Vanguard Award ..... Paul Etheredge-Outzts (*Hellbent*)

2004

Best Feature ..... *Dead and Breakfast* (dir: Matthew Leutwyler)
Best Director ..... Julian Richards (*The Last Horror Movie*)
Best Short (tie) ..... *The Crypt Club* (dir: Miguel Gallego) and *There's Something Out There* (dir: Brian Pulido)
Best Visual Effects ..... *Cube Zero* (dir: Ernie Barbarash)
Best Genre Crossover (tie) ..... *Freak Out* (dir: Christian James) and *Graveyard Alive* (dir: Elza Kephart)
Viola M. Marshall Audience Choice Award ..... *The Strange Killers* (dir: Shunsuke Yamamoto)

2003

Best Feature ..... *Ghost of the Needle* (dir: Brian Avenet-Bradley)
Best Short (tie) ..... *Filthy* (dir: Karliss & Lalino) and *William Wilson* (dir: Nicholas Davis)
Best Special Effects ..... *Headhunter* (Matthew Morgan)
Best Director ..... *Blood of the Beast* (Georg Koszulinski)

2002

Best Picture ..... *Tomorrow by Midnight* (dir: Rolfe Kanefsky)
Best Short (tie) ..... *Timmy's Wish* (dir: Patrick Cannon) and *Off* (dir: Tyler Polhemus)

Rondo Hatton Classic Horror Award

A.K.A., the Rondo. Not a film festival, but an online award presented by fans (or whoever cares to vote online). Honors works released in the previous year (e.g., the 2009 awards honor 2009 works, and are voted on/presented in 2010).

2009 (announced in 2010, etc.)

Best Film ..... *District 9*
Best TV Presentation ..... *Doctor Who: End of Time*
Best Classic DVD ..... *An American Werewolf in London* (Full Moon Edition)
Best Classic Horror Collection ..... *William Castle Collection*
Best Classic TV Collection ..... *Alfred Hitchcock Presents* (Season Four)
Best Restoration ..... *Faust* (1926), *Restoration by Murnau Foundation*
Best DVD Extra ..... *An American Werewolf in London: "Beware the Moon"* documentary
Best DVD Commentary ..... Director Fred Dekker: *Night of the Creeps*
Best Independent Film or Documentary ..... *American Scary* (John Hudgens, Sandy Clark)
Best Book ..... *Bela Lugosi and Boris Karloff: The Expanded Story of a Haunting Collaboration*, by Gregory William Mank
Best Magazine ..... *Rue Morgue*
Best Article ..... "Bad Moon Rising," by Jovanka Vuckovic and Jason Lapeyre (with Bruce McVicar), *Rue Morgue* #93
Best Cover ..... *Monsters from the Vault* #26, by Daniel Horne
Best Website ..... *Dread Central*
Best Blog ..... The Drunken Severed Head
Best Convention ..... Monster Bash
Best Fan Event ..... Tribute to Forrest J Ackerman, Hollywood, organized by Joe Moe
Favorite Horror Host ..... Count Gore De Vol
Best Horror Audio Site ..... Rue Morgue Radio
Best CD ..... *Star Trek II: Wrath of Khan* (James Horner; Film Score Monthly/Retrograde)
Best Horror Comic Book ..... *Batman: Gotham After Midnight*, by Steve Niles and Kelley Jones
Best Toy, Model or Collectible ..... Twilight Zone Talking Tina (BifBangPow!)
Count Alucard's Controversy of the Year ..... "No, but I can burn one for you." Studios offer some classics on DVD-Rs only.
Film Most in Need of DVD Release or Restoration ..... *Island of Lost Souls* (1932)
Writer of the Year ..... Gregory William Mank
Artist of the Year ..... Gary Pullin
Linda Miller Award for Fan Artist of the Year ..... Robert A. Scott
DVD Reviewer of the Year ..... Kim Newman
Monster Kid of the Year ..... Eliot Brodsky
Monster Kid Hall of Fame (inductees) ..... Bill Lemon, Ray Meyers, Dennis Druktenis, Sammy Terry, Bill Warren, Frederick S. Clarke

2008

Best Film ..... *The Dark Knight*
Best TV Presentation ..... *Doctor Who: Silence in the Library*
Best Classic DVD ..... *Psycho* (Special Edition)
Best Classic Horror Collection ..... Ray Harryhausen Collectible DVD Set
Best Classic TV Collection ..... *The Munsters: The Complete Series*
Best Restoration ..... *Vampyr* (1932, Carl Dreyer; Criterion Edition)
Best DVD Extra ..... *Night of the Living Dead*: "One for the Fire" documentary
Best DVD Commentary ..... *The Mummy* (1932): Rick Baker, Scott Essman, Bob Burns, Steve Haberman, Brent Armstrong
Best Independent Film ..... *Spine-Tingler: The William Castle Story* (dir: Jeffrey Schwarz)
Best Book ..... *The Twilight Zone*, by Martin Grams
Best Magazine ..... *Rue Morgue*
Best Article ..... "Coffin Joe Resurrected," by Scott Gabbey and Jovanka Vuckovic, *Rue Morgue* #85
Best Cover ..... *Rue Morgue* #83, by Basil Gogos
Best Website ..... Trailers from Hell
Best Blog ..... Video Watchblog
Best Convention ..... Wonderfest
Best Fan Event ..... World Zombie Day
Favorite Horror Host (active) ..... Svengoolie (Rich Koz)
Best Horror Audio Site ..... Rue Morgue Radio
Best CD ..... *The Blob* (Monstrous Movie Music)
Best Horror Comic Book ..... *Hellboy: In the Chapel of Moloch*, by Mike Mignola
Best Toy, Model or Collectible ..... "Hitchcock's *The Birds*" Barbie
Count Alucard's Controversy of the Year ..... Lost or found? Fan says he found *London After Midnight*.
Film Most in Need of DVD Release or Restoration ..... *Island of Lost Souls* (1932)
Writer of the Year ..... Tim Lucas
Artist of the Year ..... Basil Gogos
DVD Reviewer of the Year ..... Glenn Erickson (The DVD Savant)
Vasaria Public Service Award ..... Cameron McCasland and Chiller Cinema for Nashville Traffic Safety and Go-Green Campaign
Monster Kid of the Year ..... Joe Moe
Monster Kid Hall of Fame (inductees) ..... Calvin T. Beck, Jim and Marian Clatterbaugh, Paul Naschy, Lux Interior, Ken Kelly, Bob Wilkins

2007

Best Movie ..... *Rob Zombie's Halloween*
Best TV Presentation ..... The BBC's *Doctor Who*: "Blink"
Best Classic DVD ..... *Nosferatu: The Ultimate Edition*

Best Classic DVD Collection ..... *Universal Horror Classic Movie Archive*
Best Restoration ..... *Nosferatu: The Ultimate Edition*
Best DVD Extra ..... Bonus disc on *Halloween: The Happy Haunting of America*
Best DVD Commentary ..... Malcolm McDowell: *A Clockwork Orange*
Best Independent Production ..... *Vampira: The Movie*
Best Book ..... *Mario Bava: All the Colors of the Dark*, by Tim Lucas
Best Magazine ..... *Rue Morgue*
Best Article ..... "Adult Fairy Tales & Frustrated Love Stories: The Cinematic Legacy of Terence Fisher," by Neal Barrow, *Little Shoppe of Horrors* #19
Best Cover ..... *Scary Monsters Magazine* #64, by Terry Beatty
Best Website or Blog ..... Trailersfromhell.com
Best Convention ..... Monster Bash
Best Fan Event ..... Monroeville Mall Zombie Walk
Best Horror Host (active) ..... Penny Dreadful
Best Horror Audio Site or Podcast ..... Cult Radio a Go-Go
Best CD ..... *Mysterious Island* soundtrack
Best Horror Comic Book ..... *Buffy the Vampire Slayer*, Season 8, by Joss Whedon.
Best Toy, Model or Collectible ..... Universal Monster action figures, by Toy Island
Count Alucard's Controversy of the Year ..... "Do I have to buy that one too?" Fans object when new releases are packaged with films they already have.
DVD Company of the Year ..... Anchor Bay
Monster Kid of the Year ..... Michael Schlesinger
Monster Kid Hall of Fame ..... Cortlandt Hull and Dennis Vincent, Bernie Wrightson, Archie Goodwin, Ed "Big Daddy" Roth, Ghoulardi, Ben Chapman.

2006

Best Film ..... *Pan's Labyrinth*
Best TV Presentation ..... *Doctor Who*: "The Girl in the Fireplace"
Best Classic DVD ..... *Gojira/Godzilla*
Best Classic TV DVD ..... *The Addams Family*
Best Restoration ..... *75th Anniversary Dracula*
Best DVD Extra ..... Universal Horror documentary with *Dracula* and *Frankenstein* DVDs
Best DVD Commentary ..... *The Wicker Man*: Christopher Lee, Ed Woodward, Robin Hardy, Mark Kermode
Best Independent Film ..... *The Sci-Fi Boys*
Best Book ..... *Famous Monster Movie Art of Basil Gogos*, by Kerry Gammill and J. David Spurlock
Best Magazine ..... *Video Watchdog*

Best Article ..... "Dracula & Frankenstein: 75 Years of Fear," by Bob Statzer, *Scary Monsters* #60
Best Cover ..... *Monsters from the Vault* #21, by Joe Schovitz
Best Website ..... Video Watchblog
Best Convention ..... Monster Bash
Fan Event ..... Forrest J Ackerman Celebrates 90th Birthday
Best CD ..... *Zacherley: Interment for Two*
Best Horror Comic ..... *Universal Monsters Cavalcade of Horror*
Best Model or Collectible ..... Universal Monsters Headknockers (NECA)
Count Alucard's Controversy of the Year ..... "Nowhere to browse." Closing of Tower, loss of genre magazines, threatens hobby.
Best DVD Company ..... Casa Negra
Classic Most Needed on DVD ..... *Island of Lost Souls*
Writer of the Year ..... Tim Lucas
Artist of the Year ..... Frank Dietz
Monster Kid of the Year ..... Raymond Castile
Monster Kid Hall of Fame (inductees) ..... Paul Blaisdell, Jackie Blaisdell, Joe Dante, Don Glut, Jack Davis, Frank Frazetta, German Robles

2005

Best Film ..... *King Kong*
Best TV Presentation ..... *I'm King Kong: Exploits of Merian C. Cooper*
Best Classic DVD ..... *The King Kong Collection* (1933)
Best Restoration ..... *King Kong* (1933)
Best DVD Extra ..... *King Kong* (1933): Lost Spider Scene Recreated
Best DVD Commentary ..... Joe Dante, Bill Warren, Bob Burns: *War of the Worlds* (1953)
Best Independent Film ..... *Monster Kid Home Movies*
Best Book ..... *The Lost One: A Life of Peter Lorre*, by Stephen D. Youngkin
Best Magazine ..... *Video Watchdog*
Best Article ..... *Our Skull Island Odyssey*, by Bob Burns as told to Tom Weaver, *Starlog* #343
Best Cover ..... *Monster Bash* #4, by Lorraine Bush
Best Website ..... Dr. Gangrene's Chiller Cinema
Best Convention ..... Monster Bash
Best Fan Event ..... Dan Roebuck's Spook Show
Best CD ..... *The Thing from Another World*, Film Score Monthly
Best Horror Comic ..... *The Black Forest* # 2
Best Model or Collectible ..... Hawthorne Collection's Universal Monster Village
Count Alucard's Controversy of the Year ..... Co-star Boris Karloff's name missing from *Bela Lugosi Collection*
Best DVD Company ..... Warner Bros

Classic Most Needed on DVD ..... *Island of Lost Souls*
Writer of the Year ..... Tom Weaver
Monster Kid of the Year ..... Joe Busam
Monster Kid Hall of Fame (inductees) ..... Basil Gogos, James Bama, Roger Corman, Bobby "Boris" Pickett, Gary and Sue Svehla, Dick Klemensen

2004

Best Film ..... *Shaun of the Dead*
Best TV Presentation ..... *Bravo's 100 Scariest Movie Moments*
Best Classic DVD Released ..... *Creature from the Black Lagoon*, Legacy Collection
Best Restoration ..... *Dr. Jekyll and Mr. Hyde* (1932)
Best DVD Extra ..... Universal Monsters Legacy Collection busts
Best Independent Film ..... *Flip!*
Best Book ..... *An Animated Life*
Best Magazine ..... *Video Watchdog*
Best Article ..... "Donnie Dunagan Interview," by Tom Weaver, *Video Watchdog* #112
Best Cover ..... *Chiller* #21, by Daniel Horne
Best Website ..... Count Gore De Vol
Best Convention ..... Chiller
Best Fan Event ..... Godzilla gets star on Hollywood Walk of Fame
Best CD ..... *Dawn of the Dead* (Romero; incidental music)
Best Horror Comic ..... *The Black Forest*
Best Model or Collectible ..... *Trilogy of Terror*'s Zuni Fetish Doll
Count Alucard's Controversy of the Year ..... *Van Helsing* (the film)
Best DVD Company ..... Universal
Classic Most Needed on DVD ..... *King Kong*
Writer of the Year ..... Tom Weaver
Monster Kid of the Year ..... Larry Blamire
Monster Kid Hall of Fame (inductees) ..... William K. Everson, Rick Baker, Alex Gordon, Richard Gordon, Ray Harryhausen, Ray Bradbury

2003

Best Film ..... *Lord of the Rings: Return of the King*
Best TV Presentation ..... *The Twilight Zone* episode with Billy Mumy: "It's Still a Good Life"
Best Classic DVD Release ..... *20,000 Leagues Under the Sea*
Best Restoration ..... *The Ghoul*
Best DVD Extra ..... Michael F. Blake commentaries: *Lon Chaney Collection*
Best Book ..... *Monster Kid Memories*, by Bob Burns as told to Tom Weaver
Best Magazine ..... *Video Watchdog*
Best Article ..... "Horror Film Crisis of 1932, Parts 1 and 2," by Gary Don Rhodes, *Monsters from the Vault* #16, 17
Best Cover ..... *Creature and Friends*, by Vincent DiFate, Monster-Mania Convention Program
Best Website ..... Astounding B-Monster
Best Convention ..... Monster Bash
Best Fan Event ..... World 3-D Film Expo
Best CD ..... *Day the Earth Stood Still*
Best Toy, Figure or Model ..... 12-inch *Creature from the Black Lagoon*, by Sideshow
Count Alucard's Controversy of the Year ..... Fox Movie Channel drops Charlie Chan
Best DVD Company ..... MGM
Classic Most Needed on DVD ..... *The Black Cat*
Writer of the Year ..... Tom Weaver
Monster Kid of the Year ..... Arnold Kunert
Monster Kid Hall of Fame (inductees) ..... Forrest J Ackerman, James Warren, Zacherley, Vampira, Bob Burns and Kathy Burns

2002

Best Genre Film ..... *Lord of the Rings: The Two Towers*
Best TV Presentation ..... *Buffy, The Vampire Slayer*
Best DVD ..... *Curse of the Demon/Night of the Demon*
Best Restoration (tie) ..... *London After Midnight* and *Metropolis*
Best Book ..... *Heaven and Hell to Play With: The Filming of Night of the Hunter*, by Preston Neal Jones
Best Article ..... "Kay Linaker," by Tom Weaver, *Video Watchdog* #90
Best Magazine ..... *Video Watchdog*
Best Convention ..... Monster Bash
Best Horror Board ..... Monster Kid Online Magazine
Best Fan Event ..... Bob Burns Halloween: Recreation of *The Thing*
Count Alucard's Controversy of the Year ..... Forry vs. Ferry
Comeback of the Year ..... Forrest J Ackerman
Classic Most in Need of Release ..... *King Kong*
Writer of the Year ..... Tom Weaver

Sacramento Horror Film Festival

2010

Best of Festival Feature Film Award ..... *Rogue River* (dir: Jourdan McClure)
Best Director, Feature Film ..... Ezequiel and Juan Riedinger (*On a Dark & Stormy Night*)
Best of Festival Short Film Award ..... *Within* (dir: Chelsea Mead)
Best Director, Short Film ..... Micah Gallo (*Wick*)
Best Cinematography, Feature Film ..... Maxwell Stein
Best Cinematography, Short Film ..... *Wick*

Best Editing, Feature Film ..... *Maxwell Stein*
Best Editing, Short Film *2095*
Best Visual FX, Feature Film ..... *Maxwell Stein*
Best Visual FX, Short Film ..... *Zombies and Cigarettes*
Audience Choice Award, Feature Film ..... *Rogue River* (dir: Jourdan McClure)
Audience Choice Award, Short Film ..... *Devil's Creek* (dir: Mohit Ramchandani)
Film Challenge Winner, Audience Choice ..... *5250* (dir: Stephanie Hyden)
Film Challenge Winner, Judges' Choice ..... *Mask of Evil* (dir: Jeffrey C. Vanacore)

2009

Best of Festival Feature Film Award ..... *Cryptic*
Best of Festival Short Film Award ..... *Dead Exit*
Best Direction Feature Film Award ..... Danny Kuchuck and John Weiner (*Cryptic*)
Best Direction Short Film Award ..... Turner Van Ryn (*The Hell Patrol*)
Best Actor Feature Film Award ..... Julie Carlson (*Cryptic*)
Best Actor Short Film Award ..... Marina Benedict (*Death in Charge*)
Best FX Feature Award ..... *Blood Night: The Legend of Mary Hatchet*
Best FX Short Award ..... *Aqua ad lavandum — in brevi*
2009 Film Challenge Award (Judges Choice) ..... *Zombies: A Love Story* (Gary Nyland)
2009 Film Challenge Award (Audience Choice) ..... *Zombies: A Love Story*

2008

Best of Festival Feature ..... *Bonnie & Clyde vs. Dracula*
Best of Festival Short ..... *Excision*
Best Editing *AM1200*
Best Cinematography *AM1200*
Best Script *AM1200*
Best Direction ..... *Downsized*
Most Originality ..... *Prombies*
Best Art Direction ..... *The Sleuth Incident*
Filmmaker Challenge, Judges Choice ..... *The Rising Dead*
Filmmaker Challenge, Audience Choice (tie) ..... *Mainstream Massacre* and *Old Macdonald's Farm*

2007

Best Feature ..... *Beneath the Surface*
Best Short ..... *Summer Job*
Audience Gross Out Award ..... *Neighborhood Watch*

Salty Horror Film Festival

In addition to their main awards, they have a Demon Chaser challenge. Contestants complete a film that has salt in it, within 36 hours, and is 6 minutes and 66 seconds (i.e., 7 minutes, 6 seconds) long. In 2010, six films were entered in the Demon Chaser challenge.

2010

Best Film (over 50k) ..... *The Maze*
Best Film (under 50k) ..... *Aaah! Zombies!*
Best Short Film (over 50k) ..... *Paranormal Drug Dealer*
Best Short Film (under 50k) ..... *A Taste of Love*
Best Actress ..... *El Monstro Del Mar*
Best Actor ..... *Aaah! Zombies!*
Best Directing ..... *Aaah! Zombies!*
Best Writing ..... *Aaah! Zombies!*
Best Screenplay, Short Film (unproduced) ..... *Revenge Smells Like Peppermint*
Best Cinematography ..... *The Maze*
Best Sound ..... *Evil Things*
Best Score ..... *Werewolf Fever*
Best Effects ..... *El Monstro Del Mar*
Best Make-Up ..... *Aaah! Zombies!*
Best Editing ..... *Evil Things*
Best Kill ..... *El Monstro Del Mar*
Audience Favorite Film ..... *Ground Zero*
Audience Favorite Short Film ..... *Horror of Our Love*
Demon Chaser Challenge, Demon Award ..... *Amendment*
Demon Chaser Challenge, Best Film ..... *The Thing from the Cellar*
Demon Chaser Challenge, Best Acting ..... *Exhibit A*
Demon Chaser Challenge, Best Scream Queen ..... *The Thing from the Cellar*
Demon Chaser Challenge, Best Directing ..... *Amendment*
Demon Chaser Challenge, Best Writing ..... *Baby*
Demon Chaser Challenge, Best Cinematography ..... *Amendment*
Demon Chaser Challenge, Best Kill ..... *Amendment*
Demon Chaser Challenge, Best Make-Up/Effects ..... *Amendment*
Demon Chaser Challenge, Audience Choice ..... *The Thing from the Cellar*

San Sebastián Horror and Fantasy Film Festival

Prior to 1994 the festival was noncompetitive. Its head of production, Alfonso C. López, tells me: "The awards go to the director of the film, except for the cash of the best feature." In that category, "the audience votes for the winning film. Trophy plus € 6,000 (Euros) go to the distributor holding the Spanish distribution rights for the winning Feature Film. Should the winning Feature Film not have a Spanish distributor, the prize will go to the company which registered the movie, be this its production company or the company responsible for its international distribution." In 2010 their Youth Jury was composed of 150 young people.

21th — 2010

Best Short Film, International Jury Award ..... *Maquetas* (Carlos Vermut)
Méliès d'Or Short Film Nomination ..... *Hatch* (Damian McCarthy)
Best Short Film, Youth Jury Award ..... *Pixels* (Patrick Jean)
Audience Award for Best Feature Film ..... *Black Death* (Chris Smith)
Audience Award for Best Short Film ..... *Pixels* (Patrick Jean)
Audience Award for Best Spanish Short Film ..... *Brutal Relax* (Rafa Dengrá, Adrián Cardona, David Muñoz)
Audience Award for Best Animated Film ..... *Boogie, el aceitoso* (Gustavo Cova)
Special Audience Award for Becoming a Symbol of the Freedom of Speech Without Being Screened ..... *A Serbian Film*, A.K.A. *Srpski film* (Srdjan Spasojević)

20th — 2009

Audience Award for Best Feature Film ..... *Lesbian Vampire Killers* (dir: Phil Claydon)
Audience Award for Best Short Film ..... *Arbeit für Alle* (dir: Thomas Oberlies, Matthias Vogel)
Best Short Film, Jury Award ..... *Barbee Butcher* (dir: Sophie Lagües)
Best Short Film, Youth Jury Award ..... *Miracle Fish* (dir: Luke Doolan)
Audience Award for Best Spanish Short Film ..... *Amona Putz!* (dir: Telmo Esnal)
Méliès d'Or Short Film Nomination ..... *Barbee Butcher* (dir: Sophie Lagües)

19th — 2008

Audience Award for Best Feature Film ..... *Déjame entrar*, A.K.A. *Let the Right One In*, A.K.A. *Lat den rätte komma in* (dir: Tomas Alfredson)
Audience Award for Best Short Film ..... *Spider* (dir: Nash Edgerton)
Best Short Film, Jury Award ..... *Next Floor* (dir: Denis Villeneuve)
Best Short Film, Youth Jury Award ..... *Spider* (dir: Nash Edgerton)
Audience Award for Best Spanish Short Film ..... *Porque hay cosas que nunca se olvidan* (dir: Lucas Figueroa)
Méliès d'Or Short Film Nomination ..... *Cotton Candy* (dir: Aritz Moreno)

18th — 2007

Audience Award for Best Feature Film ..... *How to Get Rid of the Others / Hvordan vi slipper af med de andre* (dir: Anders Rønnow Klarlund)
Audience Award for Best Short Film ..... *Même les pigeons vont au paradis* (dir: Samuel Tourneux)
Best Short Film, Jury Award ..... *The Pearce Sisters* (dir: Luis Cook)
Best Short Film, Youth Jury Award ..... *In the Wall* (dir: Mike Williamsom)
Audience Award for Best Spanish Short Film ..... *El ataque de los Kriters asesinos* (dir: Samuel Ortí Martí "Sam")
Méliès d'Or Short Film Nomination ..... *The Pearce Sisters* (dir: Luis Cook)

17th — 2006

Audience Award for Best Feature Film ..... *Renaissance* (dir: Christian Volckman)
Audience Award for Best Short Film ..... *Still Life* (dir: Jon Knautz)
Best Short Film, Jury Award ..... *Delivery* (dir: Till Nowak)
Best Short Film, Youth Jury Award ..... *La chute de l'ange* (dir: Geoffroy Barbet Massin)
Audience Award for Best Spanish Short Film ..... *Y que cumplas muchos más* (dir: David Alcalde)
Méliès d'Or Short Film Nomination ..... *Delivery* (dir: Till Nowak)

16th — 2005

Audience Award for Best Feature Film ..... *Survive Style 5+* (dir: Gen Sekiguchi)
Audience Award for Best Short Film ..... *Rare Exports Inc.* (dir: Jalmari Helander)
Best Short Film, Jury Award ..... *Rare Exports Inc.* (dir: Jalmari Helander)
Best Spanish Short Film ..... *La leyenda del espantapájaros* (dir: Marco Besas)
Méliès d'Or Short Film Nomination ..... *Rare Exports Inc.* (dir: Jalmari Helander)

15th — 2004

Audience Award for Best Feature Film ..... *Saw* (dir: James Wan)
Audience Award for Best Short Film ..... *Ward 13* (dir: Peter Cornwell)
Best Short Film, Jury Award (tie) ..... *The Final Solution (Intolerance III)* (dir: Phil Mulloy) and *Ward 13* (dir: Peter Cornwell)
Best Spanish Short Film ..... *El tren de la bruja* (dir: Koldo Serra)
Méliès d'Or Short Film Nomination ..... *Tea Break* (dir: Sam Walker)

14th — 2003

Audience Award for Best Feature Film ..... *Dead End* (dir: Jean-Baptiste Andréa, Fabrice Canepa)

Audience Award for Best Short Film ..... *Sang froid* (dir: Pierre-Louis Levacher)
Best Short Film, Jury Award ..... *The Separation* (dir: Robert Morgan)

13th — 2002

Audience Award for Best Feature Film ..... *Dog Soldiers* (dir: Neil Marshall)
Audience Award for Best Short Film ..... *Der Schlangemann* (dir: Björn Renberg, Andreas Hansson)
Best Short Film, Jury Award ..... *Duck Children* (dir: Sam Walker, Bob Bludon)
Best Actress ..... Leslie Bais (*Heart of the World*)
Best Actor ..... Bryan Clark (*Pearl Harbor II: Pearlmageddon*)

12th — 2001

Audience Award for Best Feature Film ..... *Battle Royale* (dir: Kinji Fukasaku)
Audience Award for Best Short Film ..... *Staplerfahrer Klaus* (dir: Jörg Wagner, Stefan Prehn)
Best Short Film, Jury Award ..... *Staplerfahrer Klaus* (dir: Jörg Wagner, Stefan Prehn)
Best Actress ..... Laura Inclán (*El hombre ubicuo*)
Best Actor ..... Kenneth Branagh (*Schneider's 2nd Stage*)

11th — 2000

Audience Award for Best Short Film ..... *George Lucas in Love* (dir: Joe Nussbaum)
Best Short Film, Jury Award ..... *The Periwig-maker* (dir: Steffen Schäffler)
Best Actress ..... Marta Bekaustegui (*7337*)
Best Actor ..... Martin Hynes (*George Lucas in Love*)

10th — 1999

Audience Award for Best Short Film ..... *Les beaux-pères* (dir: Guillaume Tunzini)
Best Short Film, Jury Award ..... *Fetch* (dir: Lynn-Maree Danzey)
Best Actress ..... Andrea Vagn Jensen (*Mothers in Arms*)
Best Actor ..... Manuel Gancedo (*Viet-ñam*)

9th — 1998

Audience Award for Best Short Film ..... *Génesis* (dir: Nacho Cerdà)
Best Short Film, Jury Award ..... *The Man Who Couldn't Open Doors* (dir: Paul Arden)

8th — 1997

Audience Award for Best Short Film ..... *Flatworld* (dir: Daniel Greaves)
Best Short Film, Jury Award ..... *Bryllupsnatten* (dir: Mads Tobias Olsen)

7th — 1996

Audience Award for Best Short Film ..... *A Close Shave* (dir: Nick Park)
Best Short Film, Jury Award (tie) ..... *The Chicken from Outer Space* (dir: John R. Dilworth) and *The Prodigal Son* (dir: Chris W. Mitchell)

6th — 1995

Audience Award for Best Short Film ..... *Surprise!* (dir: Veit Helmer)
Best Short Film, Jury Award ..... *Some Folks Call It a Sling Blade* (dir: George Hickenlooper)

5th — 1994

Audience Award for Best Short Film ..... *Gastropotens II. Mutación tóxica* (dir: Pablo Llorens)
Best Short Film, Jury Award ..... *Evilio vuelve. El purificador* (dir: Santiago Segura)

FIXION-SARS

Festival de Cine Fantástico y de Terror de Santiago. Founded 2007. They apparently presented no awards in 2007 and held no event in 2009, but were back for 2010. Its New Blood Award is for a debut director. In 2010 both the jury and audience participated in choosing this award's winners. Formerly: SARS, or Santiago Rojo Sangre.

2010

Best Feature, Jury Award ..... *The Life and Death of a Porno Gang*
Best Director, Jury Award ..... Mladen Djordjevic (*The Life and Death of a Porno Gang*)
Best Screenplay, Jury Award ..... Mladen Djordjevic (*The Life and Death of a Porno Gang*)
Best Actor, Jury Award ..... Ramón Llao (*Humanimal*)
Best Actress, Jury Award ..... Jenny Cavallo (*Humanimal*)
Special Mention, Jury Award ..... *PIG* (for special effects makeup and cinematography)
Special Mention, Jury Award ..... *The Sea Monster!* (for soundtrack)
Best Short, Chilian, Jury Award ..... *The Law of Ice* (Ignacio Rodriguez, Sebastian Pose)
Best Short, Latin American, Jury Award ..... *Deus Irae* (Pedro Cristiani)
Best Short, International, Jury Award ..... *All Users Guide for the Imaginary Friend (Abridged)* (Cyrus Altabás)
Best Feature, Audience Award ..... *Humanimal* (Francesc Morales)
Best Short, Chilian, Audience Award ..... *Clara* (Alvaro Pruneda)

Best Short, Latin American, Audience Award ..... *Deus Irae* (Pedro Cristiani)
Best Short, International, Audience Award ..... *All Users Guide for the Imaginary Friend (Abridged)* (Cyrus Altabás)
New Blood Award, Feature ..... Stuart Simpson (*The Sea Monster!*)
New Blood Award, Short ..... Pedro Cristiani (*Deus Irae*)

2008

Best Feature, Jury Award ..... *No Moriré Sola*
Best Director, Jury Award ..... Adrián García Bogliano (*No Moriré Sola*)
Best Actor, Jury Award ..... Felipe Braun (*Oscuro/Iluminado*)
Best Actress, Jury Award ..... Gimena Blesa, Marisol Tur, Andrea Duarte, and Magdalena de Santos (*No Moriré Sola*)
Best Screenplay, Jury Award ..... *The Man from Earth* (Jerome Bixby, posthumous award)
Best Short, Chilian, Jury Award ...... *Valdemar* (dir: Rodrigo Hidalgo)
Best Short, Latin American, Jury Award ..... *Attack of the Disco Zombies* (dir: Darío Núñez)
Best Short, International, Jury Award ..... *Anónimos* (dir: Cristián Pozo)
Best Feature, Audience Award ..... *Jerome Bixby's The Man From Earth* (dir: Richard Schenkman)
Best Short, Chilian, Audience Award ...... *Strogonoff* (dir: Esteban Rojas)
Best Short, Latin American, Audience Award ..... *Mati* (dir: Diego Melo)
Best Short, International, Audience Award ..... *Made in Japan* (dir: Ciro Altabás)
New Blood Award, Feature ..... Rodrigo Aragão (*Mud Zombies*)
New Blood Award, Chilian ..... Esteban Rojas (*Strogonoff*)
New Blood Award, Latin American ..... Carlos Gananian (*Akai*)
Special Mention, Feature ..... *Mud Zombies*
Special Mention, Feature ..... *On Evil Grounds*

Saturn Award

Presented by the Academy of Science Fiction, Fantasy & Horror Films (ASFFHF). Many horror film awards claim to be "the Oscar of horror," but that distinction rightfully belongs to the Saturn. Like the Oscar, the Los Angeles based Saturn is supported by the studios, which provide Academy members with free screenings of upcoming studio releases. I suspect this is why so many ASFFHF screenings are of non-genre films, and why award categories have mushroomed over the years. Rather than focus on indie films (as do many horror film festivals and awards), the Saturn seems to have morphed into an arm of studio marketing.

The Saturn's dates can be confusing. Most festivals consider any film that's submitted before the entry deadline. A 2009 winning film may have been finished or distributed in 2009 or 2004. But Saturn, like Oscar, only considers films that were commercially released the *previous* year. So all 2009 winners were released in 2008. (Well, mostly. The IMDb indicates that *Cloverfield* was released in January 2008, yet apparently it was still eligible for the 2008 Saturn consideration for 2007 releases.) Still more confusing, Saturn's website lists one set of winners under 2006 (the year of the films' releases) on one webpage, and the same set of films under 2007 (the year the films were honored) on another webpage. Perhaps to mitigate any confusion, the Saturn creates consistency by numbering its award years (e.g., the 23rd Saturn Awards).

36th — 2009 (presented in 2010, etc.)

Best Science Fiction Film ..... *Avatar*
Best Fantasy Film ..... *Watchmen*
Best Horror Film ..... *Drag Me to Hell*
Best Action/Adventure/Thriller Film ..... *Inglourious Basterds*
Best Actor ..... Sam Worthington (*Avatar*)
Best Actress ..... Zoe Saldana (*Avatar*)
Best Supporting Actor ..... Stephen Lang (*Avatar*)
Best Supporting Actress ..... Sigourney Weaver (*Avatar*)
Best Performance by a Younger Actor ..... Saoirse Ronan (*The Lovely Bones*)
Best Director ..... James Cameron (*Avatar*)
Best Writer ..... James Cameron (*Avatar*)
Best Music ..... James Horner (*Avatar*)
Best Costume ..... Michael Wilkinson (*Watchmen*)
Best Make-Up ..... Barney Burman, Mindy Hall, Joel Harlow (*Star Trek*)
Best Production Design ..... Rick Carter, Robert Stromberg (*Avatar*)
Best Special Effects ..... Joe Letteri, Stephen Rosenbaum, Richard Baneham, Andrew R. Jones (*Avatar*)
Best International Film ..... *District 9*
Best Animation Film ..... *Monsters vs. Aliens*
Best Television Series ..... *Lost*
Best Syndicated/Cable Television Series ..... *Breaking Bad*
Best Presentation on Television ..... *Torchwood: Children of Earth*
Best Actor on Television ..... Josh Holloway (*Lost*)
Best Actress on Television ..... Anna Torv (*Fringe*)

Best Supporting Actor on Television ..... Aaron Paul (*Breaking Bad*)
Best Supporting Actress on Television ..... Julie Benz (*Dexter*)
Guest Starring Role on Television ..... Leonard Nimoy (*Fringe*)
Best DVD Release ..... *Nothing But the Truth*
Best DVD Television Release ..... *Lost* (The Complete Fifth Season)
Best DVD Special Edition ..... *Watchman: The Ultimate Cut*
Best DVD Collection ..... *Star Trek Original Motion Picture Collection*
Best Local Stage Production, Fantasy/Musical ..... *Mary Poppins* (Ahmanson Theatre)
Best Local Stage Production, Play/Dramatic Musical ..... *Parade* (Mark Taper Forum)
Best Local Stage Production, Small Theatre ..... *Fellowship: The Musical* (Falcon Theatre)
Visionary Award ..... James Cameron
George Pal Memorial Award ..... Roberto Orci & Alex Kurtzman
Producers Showcase Award ..... Lauren Shuler Donner
Life Career Award ..... Irvin Kershner

35th — 2008

Best Science Fiction Film ..... *Iron Man*
Best Horror Film ..... *Hellboy II: The Golden Army*
Best Fantasy Film ..... *The Curious Case of Benjamin Button*
Best Action/Adventure/Thriller Film ..... *The Dark Knight*
Best Animated Film ..... *Wall-E*
Best International Film ..... *Let the Right One In*
Best Actor ..... Robert Downey, Jr. (*Iron Man*)
Best Actress ..... Angelina Jolie (*Changeling*)
Best Supporting Actor ..... Heath Ledger (*The Dark Knight*)
Best Supporting Actress ..... Tilda Swinton (*The Curious Case of Benjamin Button*)
Best Performance by a Younger Actor ..... Jaden Christopher Smith (*The Day the Earth Stood Still*)
Best Director ..... Jon Favreau (*Iron Man*)
Best Writer ..... Christopher Nolan and Jonathan Nolan (*The Dark Knight*)
Best Music ..... Hans Zimmer and James Newton Howard (*The Dark Knight*)
Best Costume ..... Mary Zophres (*Indiana Jones & the Kingdom of the Crystal Skull*)
Best Make-Up ..... Greg Cannom (*The Curious Case of Benjamin Button*)
Best Special Effects ..... Nick Davis, Chris Corbould, Timothy Webber and Paul J. Franklin (*The Dark Knight*)
Best Television Series ..... *Lost*
Best Syndicated/Cable Television Series ..... *Battlestar Galactica*

Best Presentation on Television ..... *The Librarian: The Curse of the Judas Chalice*
Best Actor on Television ..... Edward James Olmos (*Battlestar Galactica*)
Best Actress on Television ..... Mary McDonnell (*Battlestar Galactica*)
Best Supporting Actor on Television ..... Adrian Pasdar (*Heroes*)
Best Supporting Actress on Television ..... Jennifer Carpenter (*Dexter*)
Guest Starring Role on Television ..... Jimmy Smits (*Dexter*)
Best DVD Release ..... *Jack Brooks: Monster Slayer*
Best DVD Special Edition Release ..... *Stephen King's The Mist* (2 disc Special Edition)
Best DVD Classic Film Release ..... *Psycho* (Universal Legacy Series)
Best DVD Collection ..... *The Godfather: The Coppola Restoration*
Best Series on DVD ..... *Moonlight*
Best Retro Series on DVD ..... *The Invaders*
Life Career Award ..... Lance Henriksen
Lifetime Achievement Award ..... Leonard Nimoy
Visionary Award ..... Jeffrey Katzenberg

34th — 2007

Best Science Fiction Film ..... *Cloverfield*
Best Horror Film ..... *Sweeney Todd: The Demon Barber of Fleet Street*
Best Fantasy Film ..... *Enchanted*
Best Action/Adventure/Thriller Film *300*
Best Animated Film ..... *Ratatouille*
Best International Film ..... *Eastern Promises*
Best Actor ..... Will Smith (*I Am Legend*)
Best Actress ..... Amy Adams (*Enchanted*)
Best Supporting Actor ..... Javier Bardem (*No Country for Old Men*)
Best Supporting Actress ..... Marcia Gay Harden (*The Mist*)
Best Performance by a Younger Actor ..... Freddie Highmore (*August Rush*)
Best Director ..... Zack Snyder (*300*)
Best Writer ..... Brad Bird (*Ratatouille*)
Best Music ..... Alan Menken (*Enchanted*)
Best Costumes ..... Colleen Atwood (*Sweeney Todd*)
Best Make-Up ..... Ve Neill and Martin Samuel (*Pirates of the Caribbean: At World's End*)
Best Special Effects ..... *Transformers*
Best DVD Release ..... *The Cabinet of Dr. Caligari* (Remix)
Best DVD Special Edition ..... *Blade Runner* (5 Disc Ultimate Edition)
Best DVD Classic Film ..... *The Monster Squad*
Best DVD Collection ..... *Mario Bava* (Box Sets 1 & 2)
Best Television Series on DVD ..... *Heroes* (Season 1)
Best Network Television Series ..... *Lost*
Best Syndicated / Cable Television Series ..... *Dexter*

Best Presentation on Television ..... *Family Guy: Blue Harvest*
Best Actor on Television ..... Matthew Fox (*Lost*)
Best Actress on Television ..... Jennifer Love Hewitt (*Ghost Whisperer*)
Best Supporting Actor on Television ..... Michael Emerson (*Lost*)
Best Supporting Actress on Television (tie) ..... Summer Glau (*Terminator: The Sarah Connor Chronicles*) and Elizabeth Mitchell (*Lost*)
Best Retro Television Series Release on DVD ..... *Twin Peaks (Definitive Gold Box Edition)*
Filmmakers Showcase Award ..... Matt Reeves (*Cloverfield*)
Life Career Award ..... Robert Halmi, Sr. and Robert Halmi, Jr.
George Pal Memorial Award ..... Guillermo del Toro
Special Achievement Award ..... Tim & Donna Lucas
Service Award ..... Fred Barton

Best Supporting Actor on Television ..... Masi Oka (*Heroes*)
Best Supporting Actress on Television ..... Hayden Panettiere (*Heroes*)
Best DVD Release ..... *The Sci Fi Boys*
Best DVD Special Edition Release ..... *Superman II (The Richard Donner Cut)*
Best DVD Classic Film Release ..... *Gojira*, A.K.A. *Godzilla*
Best DVD Collection ..... *James Bond Ultimate Edition (Collections 1–4)*
Best DVD Television Release ..... *Masters of Horror*
Best DVD Retro Television Release ..... *Adventures of Superman (The Complete Six Seasons)*
Rising Star Award ..... Matt Dallas (*Kyle XY*)
Filmmakers Showcase Award ..... James Gunn (director, *Slither*)
Service Award ..... Kerry O'Quinn (former publisher, *Starlog* magazine)
Special Recognition Award ..... *Alien Xmas* (written by Stephen Chiodo and Jim Strain)

33rd—2006

Best Science Fiction Film ..... *Children of Men*
Best Horror Film ..... *The Descent*
Best Fantasy Film ..... *Superman Returns*
Best Action/Adventure/Thriller Film ..... *Casino Royale*
Best Animated Film ..... *Cars*
Best International Film ..... *Pan's Labyrinth*
Best Actor ..... Brandon Routh (*Superman Returns*)
Best Actress ..... Natalie Portman (*V For Vendetta*)
Best Supporting Actor ..... Ben Affleck (*Hollywoodland*)
Best Supporting Actress ..... Famke Janssen (*X-Men: The Last Stand*)
Best Performance by a Younger Actor ..... Ivana Baquero (*Pan's Labyrinth*)
Best Direction ..... Bryan Singer (*Superman Returns*)
Best Writing ..... Michael Dougherty and Dan Harris (*Superman Returns*)
Best Music ..... John Ottman (*Superman Returns*)
Best Make-Up ..... Todd Masters and Dan Rebert (*Slither*)
Best Costume ..... Yee Chung-Man (*Curse of the Golden Flower*)
Best Special Effects ..... John Knoll, Hal Hickel, Charles Gibson and Allen Hal (*Pirates of the Caribbean: Dead Man's Chest*)
Best Network Television Series ..... *Heroes*
Best Syndicated/Cable Television Series ..... *Battlestar Galactica*
Best Single Television Presentation ..... *The Librarian: Return to King Solomon's Mines*
Best Actor on Television ..... Michael C. Hall (*Dexter*)
Best Actress on Television ..... Jennifer Love Hewitt (*Ghost Whisperer*)

32nd—2005

Best Science Fiction Film ..... *Star Wars: Episode III—Revenge of the Sith*
Best Horror Film ..... *The Exorcism of Emily Rose*
Best Fantasy Film ..... *Batman Begins*
Best Action/Adventure/Thriller Film ..... *Sin City*
Best Animated Film ..... *The Corpse Bride*
Best Actor ..... Christian Bale (*Batman Begins*)
Best Actress ..... Naomi Watts (*King Kong*)
Best Supporting Actor ..... Mickey Rourke (*Sin City*)
Best Supporting Actress ..... Summer Glau (*Serenity*)
Best Performance by a Younger Actor ..... Dakota Fanning (*War of the Worlds*)
Best Direction ..... Peter Jackson (*King Kong*)
Best Writing ..... Christopher Nolan and David S. Goyer (*Batman Begins*)
Best Music ..... John Williams (*Star Wars: Episode III—Revenge of the Sith*)
Best Make-Up ..... Howard Berger, Nikki Gooley and Greg Nicotero (*The Chronicles of Narnia: The Lion, The Witch and the Wardrobe*)
Best Costume ..... Isis Mussenden (*The Chronicles of Narnia: The Lion, the Witch and the Wardrobe*)
Best Special Effects ..... Joe Letteri, Richard Taylor, Christian Rivers and Brian Van't Hul (*King Kong*)
Best Network Television Series ..... *Lost*
Best Syndicated/Cable Television Series ..... *Battlestar Galactica*
Best Single Television Presentation (tie) ..... *Masters of Horror* and *The Triangle*
Best Actor on Television ..... Matthew Fox (*Lost*)
Best Actress on Television ..... Kristen Bell (*Veronica Mars*)
Best Supporting Actor on Television ..... James Callis (*Battlestar Galactica*)

Best Supporting Actress on Television ..... Katee Sackhoff (*Battlestar Galactica*)
Best DVD Release ..... *Ray Harryhausen: The Early Years Collection*
Best DVD Special Edition Release ..... *Sin City: Recut, Extended, Unrated*
Best DVD Classic Film Release ..... *The Wizard of Oz*
Best DVD Collection ..... *Bela Lugosi Collection*
Best DVD Television Release ..... *Lost (Season 1)*
Best DVD Retro Television Release ..... *The Greatest American Hero*

31st—2004

Best Science Fiction Film ..... *Eternal Sunshine of the Spotless Mind*
Best Horror Film ..... *Shaun of the Dead*
Best Fantasy Film ..... *Spider-Man 2*
Best Action/Adventure/Thriller Film ..... *Kill Bill: Vol. 2*
Best Animated Film ..... *The Incredibles*
Best Actor ..... Tobey Maguire (*Spider-Man 2*)
Best Actress ..... Blanchard Ryan (*Open Water*)
Best Supporting Actor ..... David Carradine (*Kill Bill: Vol. 2*)
Best Supporting Actress ..... Daryl Hannah (*Kill Bill: Vol. 2*)
Best Performance by a Younger Actor ..... Emmy Rossum (*Phantom of the Opera*)
Best Direction ..... Sam Raimi (*Spider-Man 2*)
Best Writing ..... Alvin Sargent (*Spider-Man 2*)
Best Music ..... Alan Silvestri (*Van Helsing*)
Best Make-Up ..... Jake Garber, Matt Rose and Mike Elizalde (*Hellboy*)
Best Costume ..... Kevin Conran (*Sky Captain & the World of Tomorrow*)
Best Special Effects ..... John Dykstra, Scott Stokdyk, Anthony LaMolinara and John Frazier (*Spider-Man 2*)
Best Network Television Series ..... *Lost*
Best Syndicated/Cable Television Series ..... *Stargate SG-1*
Best Single Television Presentation ..... *Farscape: Peacekeeper Wars*
Best Actor on Television ..... Ben Browder (*Farscape: Peacekeeper Wars*)
Best Actress on Television ..... Claudia Black (*Farscape: Peacekeeper Wars*)
Best Supporting Actor on Television ..... Terry O'Quinn (*Lost*)
Best Supporting Actress on Television ..... Amanda Tapping (*Stargate SG-1*)
Best DVD Release ..... *Starship Troopers 2: Hero of the Federation*
Best DVD Special Edition Release ..... *Lord of the Rings: The Return of the King*
Best DVD Classic Film Release ..... *Dawn of the Dead (Ultimate Edition)*
Best DVD Collection ..... *Star Wars Trilogy*
Best DVD Television Release ..... *Smallville (Season 2 & 3)*
Best DVD Retro Television Release ..... *Star Trek (The Original Series)*

30th—2003

Best Science Fiction Film ..... *X2: X-Men United*
Best Horror Film ..... *28 Days Later*
Best Fantasy Film ..... *Lord of the Rings: The Return of the King*
Best Action/Adventure/Thriller Film ..... *Kill Bill: Vol. 1*
Best Actor ..... Elijah Wood (*Lord of the Rings: The Return of the King*)
Best Actress ..... Uma Thurman (*Kill Bill: Vol. 1*)
Best Supporting Actor ..... Sean Astin (*Lord of the Rings: The Return of the King*)
Best Supporting Actress ..... Ellen Degeneres (*Finding Nemo*)
Best Performance by a Younger Actor ..... Jeremy Sumpter (*Peter Pan*)
Best Direction ..... Peter Jackson (*Lord of the Rings: The Return of the King*)
Best Writing ..... Fran Walsh, Philippa Boyens, and Peter Jackson (*Lord of the Rings: The Return of the King*)
Best Music ..... Howard Shore (*Lord of the Rings: The Return of the King*)
Best Make-Up ..... Richard Taylor and Peter King (*Lord of the Rings: The Return of the King*)
Best Costume ..... Penny Rose (*Lord of the Rings: The Return of the King*)
Best Special Effects ..... Jim Rygiel, Joe Letteri, Randall William Cook and Alex Funke (*Lord of the Rings: The Return of the King*)
Best Network Television Series (tie) ..... *Angel* and *CSI: Crime Scene Investigation*
Best Syndicated/Cable Television Series ..... *Stargate SG-1*
Best Single Television Presentation ..... *Battlestar Galactica* (the mini-series)
Best Actor on Television ..... David Boreanaz (*Angel*)
Best Actress on Television ..... Amber Tamblyn (*Joan of Arcadia*)
Best Supporting Actor on Television ..... James Marsters (*Angel & Buffy the Vampire Slayer*)
Best Supporting Actress on Television ..... Amy Acker (*Angel*)
Best DVD Release ..... *Bionicle–Mask of Light*
Best DVD Special Edition Release ..... *The Lord of the Rings: The Two Towers (Extended)*
Best DVD Classic Film Release ..... *The Adventures of Robin Hood*
Best DVD Collection ..... *The Adventures of Indiana Jones*
Best DVD Television Release ..... *The Complete Firefly*

29th — 2002

Best Science Fiction Film ..... *Minority Report*
Best Horror Film ..... *The Ring*
Best Fantasy Film ..... *Lord of the Rings: The Two Towers*
Best Action/Adventure/Thriller Film ..... *Road to Perdition*
Best Actor ..... Robin Williams (*One Hour Photo*)
Best Actress ..... Naomi Watts (*The Ring*)
Best Supporting Actor ..... Andy Serkis (*Lord of the Rings: The Two Towers*)
Best Supporting Actress ..... Samantha Morton (*Minority Report*)
Best Performance by a Younger Actor ..... Tyler Hoechlin (*Road to Perdition*)
Best Direction ..... Steven Spielberg (*Minority Report*)
Best Writing ..... Scott Frank and Jon Cohen (*Minority Report*)
Best Music ..... Danny Elfman (*Spider-Man*)
Best Make-Up ..... Peter Owen and Peter King (*The Lord of the Rings: The Two Towers*)
Best Costume ..... Trisha Biggar, Ngila Dickson and Richard Taylor (*The Lord of the Rings: The Two Towers*)
Best Special Effects ..... Rob Coleman, Pablo Helman, John Knoll and Ben Snow (*Star Wars: Episode II: Attack of the Clones*)
Best Network Television Series ..... *Alias*
Best Syndicated/Cable Television Series ..... *Farscape*
Best Single Television Presentation ..... *Steven Spielberg Presents Taken*
Best Actor on Television ..... David Boreanaz (*Angel*)
Best Actress on Television ..... Jennifer Garner (*Alias*)
Best Supporting Actor on Television ..... Victor Garber (*Alias*)
Best Supporting Actress on Television ..... Alyson Hannigan (*Buffy The Vampire Slayer*)
Best DVD Release ..... *Dog Soldiers*
Best DVD Special Edition Release ..... *The Lord of the Rings: The Fellowship of the Ring (Extended)*
Best DVD Classic Film Release ..... *E.T. The Extra-Terrestrial*
Best DVD Television Release ..... *Star Trek: The Next Generation (Seasons 1–7)*

28th — 2001

Best Science Fiction Film ..... *A.I. Artificial Intelligence*
Best Horror Film ..... *The Others*
Best Fantasy Film ..... *Lord of the Rings: The Fellowship of the Rings*
Best Action/Adventure/Thriller Film ..... *Memento*
Best Actor ..... Tom Cruise (*Vanilla Sky*)
Best Actress ..... Nicole Kidman (*The Others*)
Best Supporting Actor ..... Ian McKellen (*Lord of the Rings: The Fellowship of the Rings*)
Best Supporting Actress ..... Fionnula Flanagan (*The Others*)
Best Performance by a Younger Actor ..... Haley Joel Osment (*A.I. Artificial Intellegence*)
Best Direction ..... Peter Jackson (*Lord of the Rings: The Fellowship of the Rings*)
Best Writing ..... Steven Spielberg (*A.I. Artificial Intelligence*)
Best Music ..... John Williams (*A.I. Artificial Intelligence*)
Best Make-Up ..... Greg Cannom and Wesley Wofford (*Hannibal*)
Best Costume ..... Judianna Makovsky (*Harry Potter and the Sorcerer's Stone*)
Best Special Effects ..... Dennis Muren, Scott Farrar, Stan Winston and Michael Lantieri (*A.I. Artificial Intelligence*)
Best Network Television Series ..... *Buffy the Vampire Slayer*
Best Syndicated/Cable Television Series ..... *Farscape*
Best Single Television Presentation ..... *Jack and the Beanstalk: The Real Story*
Best Actor on Television ..... Ben Browder (*Farscape*)
Best Actress on Television ..... Yancy Butler (*Witchblade*)
Best Supporting Actor on Television ..... Michael Rosenbaum (*Smallville*)
Best Supporting Actress on Television ..... Jolene Blalock (*Enterprise*)
Best DVD Release ..... *Ginger Snaps*
Best DVD Special Edition Release ..... *Shrek*

27th — 2000

Best Science Fiction Film ..... *X-Men*
Best Horror Film ..... *Final Destination*
Best Fantasy Film ..... *Frequency*
Best Action/Adventure/Thriller Film ..... *Crouching Tiger, Hidden Dragon*
Best Actor ..... Hugh Jackman (*X-Men*)
Best Actress ..... Tea Leoni (*Family Man*)
Best Supporting Actor ..... Willem Dafoe (*Shadow of the Vampire*)
Best Supporting Actress ..... Rebecca Romijn-Stamos (*X-Men*)
Best Performance by a Younger Actor ..... Devon Sawa (*Final Destination*)
Best Direction ..... Bryan Singer (*X-Men*)
Best Writing ..... David Hayter (*X-Men*)
Best Music ..... James Horner (*How the Grinch Stole Christmas*)
Best Make-Up ..... Rick Baker and Gail Ryan (*How the Grinch Stole Christmas*)
Best Costume ..... Louise Mingenbach (*X-Men*)
Best Special Effects ..... Scott E. Anderson, Craig Hayes, Scott Stokdyk and Stan Parks (*Hollow Man*)
Best Home Video Release ..... *Princess Mononoke*

Best Network Television Series ..... *Buffy the Vampire Slayer*
Best Syndicated/Cable Television Series ..... *Farscape*
Best Single Television Presentation ..... *Fail Safe*
Best Actor on Television ..... Robert Patrick (*The X-Files*)
Best Actress on Television ..... Jessica Alba (*Dark Angel*)
Best Supporting Actor on Television ..... James Marsters (*Buffy the Vampire Slayer*)
Best Supporting Actress on Television ..... Jeri Ryan (*Star Trek Voyager*)

26th — 1999

Best Science Fiction Film ..... *The Matrix*
Best Horror Film ..... *The Sixth Sense*
Best Fantasy Film ..... *Being John Malkovich*
Best Action/Adventure/Thriller Film ..... *The Green Mile*
Best Actor ..... Tim Allen (*Galaxy Quest*)
Best Actress ..... Christina Ricci (*Sleepy Hollow*)
Best Supporting Actor ..... Michael Clarke Duncan (*The Green Mile*)
Best Supporting Actress ..... Patricia Clarkson (*The Green Mile*)
Best Performance by a Younger Actor ..... Haley Joel Osment (*The Sixth Sense*)
Best Direction ..... Andy and Larry Wachowski (*The Matrix*)
Best Writing ..... Charlie Kaufman (*Being John Malkovich*)
Best Music ..... Danny Elfman (*Sleepy Hollow*)
Best Make-Up ..... Nick Dudman and Aileen Seaton (*The Mummy*)
Best Costume ..... Trisha Biggar (*Star Wars: Episode One — The Phantom Menace*)
Best Special Effects ..... Rob Coleman, John Knoll, Dennis Muren and Scott Squires (*Star Wars: Episode One — The Phantom Menace*)
Best Home Video Release ..... *Free Enterprise*
Best Network Television Series ..... *Now and Again*
Best Syndicated/Cable Television Series ..... *Stargate SG-1*
Best Single Television Presentation ..... *Storm of the Century*
Best Actor on Television ..... David Boreanaz (*Angel*)
Best Actress on Television ..... Margaret Colin (*Now and Again*)
Best Supporting Actor on Television ..... Dennis Haysbert (*Now and Again*)
Best Supporting Actress on Television ..... Justina Vail (*7 Days*)

25th — 1998

Best Science Fiction Film (tie) ..... *Armageddon*; *Dark City*
Best Horror Film ..... *Apt Pupil*
Best Fantasy Film ..... *The Truman Show*
Best Action/Adventure/Thriller Film ..... *Saving Private Ryan*
Best Actor ..... James Woods (*John Carpenter's Vampires*)
Best Actress ..... Drew Barrymore (*EverAfter*)
Best Supporting Actor ..... Ian McKellen (*Apt Pupil*)
Best Supporting Actress ..... Joan Allen (*Pleasantville*)
Best Performance by a Younger Actor ..... Tobey Maguire (*Pleasantville*)
Best Direction ..... Michael Bay (*Armageddon*)
Best Writing ..... Andrew Niccol (*The Truman Show*)
Best Music ..... John Carpenter (*John Carpenter's Vampires*)
Best Make-Up ..... Robert Kurtzman, Greg Nicotero and Howard Berger (*John Carpenter's Vampires*)
Best Costume ..... Jenny Beavan (*EverAfter*)
Best Special Effects ..... Volker Engel, Patrick Tatopolous, Karen Goulekas and Clay Pinney (*Godzilla*)
Best Home Video Release ..... *From Dusk Till Dawn 2: Texas Blood Money*
Best Network Television Series ..... *The X-Files*
Best Syndicated/Cable Television Series ..... *Babylon 5*
Best Single Television Presentation ..... no winner
Best Actor on Television ..... Richard Dean Anderson (*Stargate SG-1*)
Best Actress on Television ..... Sarah Michelle Gellar (*Buffy The Vampire Slayer*)

24th — 1997

Best Science Fiction Film ..... *Men in Black*
Best Horror Film ..... *The Devil's Advocate*
Best Fantasy Film ..... *Austin Powers*
Best Action/Adventure/Thriller Film ..... *L.A. Confidential*
Best Actor ..... Pierce Brosnan (*Tomorrow Never Dies*)
Best Actress ..... Jodie Foster (*Contact*)
Best Supporting Actor ..... Vincent D'Onofrio (*Men in Black*)
Best Supporting Actress ..... Gloria Stuart (*Titanic*)
Best Performance by a Younger Actor ..... Jena Malone (*Contact*)
Best Direction ..... John Woo (*Face/Off*)
Best Writing ..... Mike Werb and Michael Colleary (*Face/Off*)
Best Music ..... Danny Elfman (*Men in Black*)
Best Make-Up ..... Rick Lazzarini and Gordon Smith (*Mimic*)
Best Costume ..... Ellen Mirojnick (*Starship Troopers*)
Best Special Effects ..... Phil Tippett, Scott E. Anderson, Alec Gillis, Tom Woodruff, Jr. and John Richardson (*Starship Troopers*)

Best Home Video Release ..... *Cats Don't Dance*
Best Network Television Series ..... *Buffy the Vampire Slayer*
Best Syndicated/Cable Television Series ..... *The Outer Limits*
Best Single Television Presentation ..... *The Shining*
Best Actor on Television ..... Steven Weber (*The Shining*)
Best Actress on Television ..... Kate Mulgrew (*Star Trek: Voyager*)

23rd—1996

Best Science Fiction Film ..... *Independence Day*
Best Horror Film ..... *Scream*
Best Fantasy Film ..... *Dragonheart*
Best Action/Adventure/Thriller Film ..... *Fargo*
Best Actor ..... Eddie Murphy (*The Nutty Professor*)
Best Actress ..... Neve Campbell (*Scream*)
Best Supporting Actor ..... Brent Spiner (*Star Trek: First Contact*)
Best Supporting Actress ..... Alice Krige (*Star Trek: First Contact*)
Best Performance by a Younger Actor ..... Lucas Black (*Sling Blade*)
Best Direction ..... Roland Emmerich (*Independence Day*)
Best Writing ..... Kevin Williamson (*Scream*)
Best Music ..... Danny Elfman (*Mars Attacks*)
Best Make-Up ..... Rick Baker and David Leroy Anderson (*The Nutty Professor*)
Best Costume ..... Deborah Everton (*Star Trek: First Contact*)
Best Special Effects ..... Volker Engel, Clay Pinney, Douglas Smith and Joe Viskocil (*Independence Day*)
Best Home Video Release ..... *The Arrival*
Best Network Television Series ..... *The X-Files*
Best Syndicated/Cable Television Series ..... *The Outer Limits*
Best Single Television Presentation ..... *Dr. Who*
Best Actor on Television ..... Kyle Chandler (*Early Edition*)
Best Actress on Television ..... Gillian Anderson (*The X-Files*)

22nd—1995

Best Science Fiction Film ..... *12 Monkeys*
Best Horror Film ..... *From Dusk 'Til Dawn*
Best Fantasy Film ..... *Babe*
Best Action/Adventure/Thriller Film ..... *The Usual Suspects*
Best Actor ..... George Clooney (*From Dusk Till Dawn*)
Best Actress ..... Angela Bassett (*Strange Days*)
Best Supporting Actor ..... Brad Pitt (*12 Monkeys*)
Best Supporting Actress ..... Bonnie Hunt (*Jumanji*)
Best Performance by a Younger Actor ..... Christina Ricci (*Casper*)
Best Direction ..... Kathryn Bigelow (*Strange Days*)
Best Writing ..... Andrew Kevin Walker (*Se7en*)
Best Music ..... John Ottman (*The Usual Suspects*)
Best Make-Up ..... Jean Black and Rob Bottin (*Se7en*)
Best Costume ..... Julie Weiss (*12 Monkeys*)
Best Special Effects ..... Stan Parks, ILM and ADI (*Jumanji*)
Best Television Series ..... *The Outer Limits*
Best Single Television Presentation ..... *Alien Nation: Dark Horizon*

21st—1994

Best Science Fiction Film ..... *Stargate*
Best Horror Film ..... *Interview With The Vampire*
Best Fantasy Film ..... *Forrest Gump*
Best Action/Adventure/Thriller Film ..... *Pulp Fiction*
Best Actor ..... Martin Landau (*Ed Wood*)
Best Actress (tie) ..... Sandra Bullock (*Speed*); Jamie Lee Curtis (*True Lies*)
Best Supporting Actor ..... Gary Sinise (*Forrest Gump*)
Best Supporting Actress ..... Mia Sara (*Timecop*)
Best Performance by a Younger Actor ..... Kirsten Dunst (*Interview with The Vampire*)
Best Direction ..... James Cameron (*True Lies*)
Best Writing ..... Jim Harrison and Wesley Strick (*Wolf*)
Best Music ..... Howard Shore (*Ed Wood*)
Best Make-Up ..... Rick Baker and Ve Neill (*Interview with the Vampire*)
Best Costume ..... Sandy Powell (*Interview with the Vampire*)
Best Special Effects ..... John Bruno and Digital Domain (*True Lies*)
Best Television Series ..... *The X-Files*
Best Single Television Presentation ..... *Alien Nation: Millennium*

20th—1993

Best Science Fiction Film ..... *Jurassic Park*
Best Horror Film ..... *Army of Darkness*
Best Fantasy Film ..... *Nightmare Before Christmas*
Best Actor ..... Robert Downey, Jr. (*Hearts and Souls*)
Best Actress ..... Andie MacDowell (*Groundhog Day*)
Best Supporting Actor ..... Lance Henriksen (*Hard Target*)
Best Supporting Actress ..... Amanda Plummer (*Needful Things*)
Best Performance by a Younger Actor ..... Elijah Wood (*The Good Son*)
Best Direction ..... Steven Spielberg (*Jurassic Park*)
Best Writing ..... Michael Crichton and David Koepp (*Jurassic Park*)
Best Music ..... Danny Elfman (*The Nightmare Before Christmas*)

Best Make-Up ..... Kevin C. Haney (*Addams Family Values*)
Best Costume ..... Mary Vogt (*Hocus Pocus*)
Best Special Effects ..... Dennis Muren, Stan Winston, Phil Tippett and Michael Lantieri (*Jurassic Park*)
Best Television Series ..... *Lois & Clark: The New Adventures of Superman*

19th — 1992

Best Science Fiction Film ..... *Star Trek 6: The Undiscovered Country*
Best Horror Film ..... *Bram Stoker's Dracula*
Best Fantasy Film ..... *Aladdin*
Best Actor ..... Gary Oldman (*Bram Stoker's Dracula*)
Best Actress ..... Virginia Madsen (*Candyman*)
Best Supporting Actor ..... Robin Williams (*Aladdin*)
Best Supporting Actress ..... Isabella Rossellini (*Death Becomes Her*)
Best Performance by a Younger Actor ..... Scott Weinger (*Aladdin*)
Best Direction ..... Francis Ford Coppola (*Bram Stoker's Dracula*)
Best Writing ..... James V. Hart (*Bram Stoker's Dracula*)
Best Music ..... Angelo Badalamenti (*Twin Peaks: Fire Walk With Me*)
Best Make-Up ..... Stan Winston and Ve Neill (*Batman Returns*)
Best Costume ..... Eiko Ishioka (*Bram Stoker's Dracula*)
Best Special Effects ..... Ken Ralston, ILM, Tom Woodruff, Jr. and Alec Gillis (*Death Becomes Her*)
Best Television Series ..... *The Simpsons*

18th — 1991

Best Science Fiction Film ..... *Terminator 2: Judgment Day*
Best Horror Film ..... *Silence of the Lambs*
Best Fantasy Film ..... *Edward Scissorhands*
Best Actor ..... Anthony Hopkins (*Silence of the Lambs*)
Best Actress ..... Linda Hamilton (*Terminator 2: Judgment Day*)
Best Supporting Actor ..... William Sadler (*Bill and Ted's Bogus Journey*)
Best Supporting Actress ..... Mercedes Ruehl (*The Fisher King*)
Best Performance by a Younger Actor ..... Edward Furlong (*Terminator 2: Judgment Day*)
Best Direction ..... James Cameron (*Terminator 2: Judgment Day*)
Best Writing ..... Ted Tally (*The Silence of the Lambs*)
Best Music ..... Loek Dikker (*Body Parts*)
Best Make-Up ..... Carl Fullerton and Neal Martz (*The Silence of the Lambs*)

Best Costume ..... Marilyn Vance Straker (*The Rocketeer*)
Best Special Effects ..... Stan Winston, ILM, Fantasy II and 4 Ward Productions (*Terminator 2: Judgment Day*)
Best Television Series ..... *Dark Shadows*

17th — 1989/90

Best Science Fiction Film ..... *Total Recall*
Best Horror Film ..... *Arachnophobia*
Best Fantasy Film ..... *Ghost*
Best Actor ..... Jeff Daniels (*Arachnophobia*)
Best Actress ..... Demi Moore (*Ghost*)
Best Supporting Actor ..... Thomas F. Wilson (*Back to the Future II*)
Best Supporting Actress ..... Whoopi Goldberg (*Ghost*)
Best Performance by a Younger Actor ..... Adan Jodorowsky (*Santa Sangre*)
Best Direction ..... James Cameron (*The Abyss*)
Best Writing ..... William Peter Blatty (*The Exorcist III*)
Best Music ..... Alan Silvestri (*Back to the Future III*)
Best Make-Up ..... John Caglione, Jr., Doug Drexler and Cheri Minns (*Dick Tracy*)
Best Costume ..... Erica Edell Phillips (*Total Recall*)
Best Special Effects ..... Ken Ralston and ILM (*Back to the Future II*)
Best Television Series ..... *Star Trek: The Next Generation*

16th — 1988

Best Science Fiction Film ..... *Alien Nation*
Best Horror Film ..... *Beetlejuice*
Best Fantasy Film ..... *Who Framed Roger Rabbit*
Best Actor ..... Tom Hanks (*Big*)
Best Actress ..... Catherine Hicks (*Child's Play*)
Best Supporting Actor ..... Robert Loggia (*Big*)
Best Supporting Actress ..... Sylvia Sidney (*Beetlejuice*)
Best Performance by a Younger Actor ..... Fred Savage (*Vice Versa*)
Best Direction ..... Robert Zemeckis (*Who Framed Roger Rabbit*)
Best Writing ..... Gary Ross and Anne Spielberg (*Big*)
Best Music ..... Christopher Young (*Hellbound: Hellraiser 2*)
Best Make-Up ..... Ve Neill, Steve LaPorte and Robert Short (*Beetlejuice*)
Best Costume ..... Barbara Lane (*Willow*)
Best Special Effects ..... George Gibbs, ILM, Ken Ralston and Richard Williams (*Who Framed Roger Rabbit*)
Best Television Series ..... *Star Trek: The Next Generation*

15th — 1987

Best Science Fiction Film ..... *Robocop*
Best Horror Film ..... *The Lost Boys*
Best Fantasy Film ..... *The Princess Bride*
Best Actor ..... Jack Nicholson (*The Witches of Eastwick*)
Best Actress ..... Jessica Tandy (*Batteries Not Included*)
Best Supporting Actor ..... Richard Dawson (*The Running Man*)
Best Supporting Actress ..... Anne Ramsey (*Throw Momma from the Train*)
Best Performance by a Younger Actor ..... Kirk Cameron (*Like Father, Like Son*)
Best Direction ..... Paul Verhoeven (*Robocop*)
Best Writing ..... Michael Miner and Edward Neumier (*Robocop*)
Best Music ..... Alan Silvestri (*Predator*)
Best Make-Up ..... Rob Bottin and Stephen Dupuis (*Robocop*)
Best Costume ..... Phyliss Dalton (*The Princess Bride*)
Best Special Effects ..... Peter Kuran, Phil Tippett, Rob Bottin and Rocco Gioffre (*Robocop*)

14th — 1986

Best Science Fiction Film ..... *Aliens*
Best Horror Film ..... *The Fly*
Best Fantasy Film ..... *The Boy Who Could Fly*
Best Actor ..... Jeff Goldblum (*The Fly*)
Best Actress ..... Sigourney Weaver (*Aliens*)
Best Supporting Actor ..... Bill Paxton (*Aliens*)
Best Supporting Actress ..... Jeanette Goldstein (*Aliens*)
Best Performance by a Younger Actor ..... Carrie Henn (*Aliens*)
Best Direction ..... James Cameron (*Aliens*)
Best Writing ..... James Cameron (*Aliens*)
Best Music ..... Alan Menken (*The Little Shop of Horrors*)
Best Make-Up ..... Chris Walas (*The Fly*)
Best Costume ..... Robert Fletcher (*Star Trek IV: The Voyage Home*)
Best Special Effects ..... Stan Winston and L.A. Effects Group (*Aliens*)

13th — 1985

Best Science Fiction Film ..... *Back to the Future*
Best Horror Film ..... *Fright Night*
Best Fantasy Film ..... *Ladyhawke*
Best Actor ..... Michael J. Fox (*Back to the Future*)
Best Actress ..... Coral Browne (*Dreamchild*)
Best Supporting Actor ..... Roddy McDowall (*Fright Night*)
Best Supporting Actress ..... Anne Ramsey (*The Goonies*)
Best Performance by a Younger Actor ..... Barret Oliver (*D.A.R.Y.L.*)
Best Direction ..... Ron Howard (*Cocoon*)
Best Writing ..... Tom Holland (*Fright Night*)
Best Music ..... Bruce Broughton (*Young Sherlock Holmes*)
Best Make-Up ..... Tom Savini (*Day of the Dead*)
Best Costume ..... Nana Cecchi (*Ladyhawke*)
Best Special Effects ..... Kevin Pike (*Back to the Future*)

12th — 1984

Best Science Fiction Film ..... *The Terminator*
Best Horror Film ..... *Gremlins*
Best Fantasy Film ..... *Ghostbusters*
Best Actor ..... Jeff Bridges (*Starman*)
Best Actress ..... Daryl Hannah (*Splash*)
Best Supporting Actor ..... Tracey Walter (*Repo Man*)
Best Supporting Actress ..... Polly Holliday (*Gremlins*)
Best Performance by a Younger Actor ..... Noah Hathaway (*The Neverending Story*)
Best Direction ..... Joe Dante (*Gremlins*)
Best Writing ..... James Cameron and Gale Anne Hurd (*The Terminator*)
Best Music ..... Jerry Goldsmith (*Gremlins*)
Best Make-Up ..... Stan Winston (*The Terminator*)
Best Costume ..... Bob Ringwood (*Dune*)
Best Special Effects ..... Chris Walas (*Gremlins*)

11th — 1983

Best Science Fiction Film ..... *Return of the Jedi*
Best Horror Film ..... *The Dead Zone*
Best Fantasy Film ..... *Something Wicked This Way Comes*
Best Actor ..... Mark Hamill (*Return of the Jedi*)
Best Actress ..... Louise Fletcher (*Brainstorm*)
Best Supporting Actor ..... John Lithgow (*Twilight Zone: The Movie*)
Best Supporting Actress ..... Candy Clark (*Blue Thunder*)
Best Direction ..... John Badham (*Wargames*)
Best Writing ..... Ray Bradbury (*Something Wicked This Way Comes*)
Best Music ..... James Horner (*Brainstorm*)
Best Make-Up ..... Phil Tippett and Stuart Freeborn (*Return of the Jedi*)
Best Costume ..... Aggie Guerard Rodgers and Nilo Rodis-Jamero (*Return of the Jedi*)
Best Special Effects ..... Richard Edlund, Dennis Muren and Ken Ralston (*Return of the Jedi*)

10th — 1982

Best Science Fiction Film ..... *E.T. The Extra-Terrestrial*
Best Horror Film ..... *Poltergeist*
Best Fantasy Film ..... *The Dark Crystal*
Best Actor ..... William Shatner (*Star Trek II: The Wrath of Khan*)

Best Actress ..... Sandahl Bergman (*Conan the Barbarian*)
Best Supporting Actor ..... Richard Lynch (*The Sword and the Sorcerer*)
Best Supporting Actress ..... Zelda Rubinstein (*Poltergeist*)
Best Direction ..... Nicholas Meyer (*Star Trek II: The Wrath of Khan*)
Best Writing ..... Melissa Matheson (*E.T. The Extra-Terrestrial*)
Best Music ..... John Williams (*E.T. The Extra-Terrestrial*)
Best Make-Up ..... Dorothy Pearl (*Poltergeist*)
Best Costume ..... Eloise Jenssen and Rosanna Norton (*Tron*)
Best Special Effects ..... Carlo Rambaldi and Dennis Muren (*E.T. The Extra-Terrestrial*)

9th — 1981

Best Science Fiction Film ..... *Superman 2*
Best Horror Film ..... *An American Werewolf in London*
Best Fantasy Film ..... *Raiders of the Lost Ark*
Best Actor ..... Harrison Ford (*Raiders of the Lost Ark*)
Best Actress ..... Karen Allen (*Raiders of the Lost Ark*)
Best Supporting Actor ..... Burgess Meredith (*Clash of the Titans*)
Best Supporting Actress ..... Frances Sternhagen (*Outland*)
Best Direction ..... Steven Spielberg (*Raiders of the Lost Ark*)
Best Writing ..... Lawrence Kasdan (*Raiders of the Lost Ark*)
Best Music ..... John Williams (*Raiders of the Lost Ark*)
Best Make-Up ..... Rick Baker (*An American Werewolf in London*)
Best Costume ..... Bob Ringwood (*Excalibur*)
Best Special Effects ..... Richard Edlund (*Raiders of the Lost Ark*)

8th — 1980

Best Science Fiction Film ..... *The Empire Strikes Back*
Best Horror Film ..... *The Howling*
Best Fantasy Film ..... *Somewhere in Time*
Best Actor ..... Mark Hamill (*The Empire Strikes Back*)
Best Actress ..... Angie Dickinson (*Dressed to Kill*)
Best Supporting Actor ..... Scatman Crothers (*The Shining*)
Best Supporting Actress ..... Eve Brent Ashe (*Fade to Black*)
Best Direction ..... Irvin Kershner (*The Empire Strikes Back*)
Best Writing ..... William Peter Blatty (*Twinkle Twinkle Killer Kane*)
Best Music ..... John Barry (*Somewhere in Time*)
Best Make-Up (tie) ..... Dick Smith (*Altered States*) and (*Scanners*)
Best Costume ..... Jean-Pierre Dorleac (*Somewhere in Time*)
Best Special Effects ..... Brian Johnson and Richard Edlund (*The Empire Strikes Back*)

7th — 1979

Best Science Fiction Film ..... *Alien*
Best Horror Film ..... *Dracula*
Best Fantasy Film ..... *The Muppet Movie*
Best Actor ..... George Hamilton (*Love at First Bite*)
Best Actress ..... Mary Steenburgen (*Time After Time*)
Best Supporting Actor ..... Arte Johnson (*Love at First Bite*)
Best Supporting Actress ..... Veronica Cartwright (*Alien*)
Best Direction ..... Ridley Scott (*Alien*)
Best Writing ..... Nicholas Meyer (*Time After Time*)
Best Music ..... Miklos Rózsa (*Time After Time*)
Best Make-Up ..... William Tuttle (*Love at First Bite*)
Best Costume ..... Jean-Pierre Dorleac (*Buck Rogers in the 25th Century*)
Best Special Effects ..... Douglas Trumbull, John Dykstra and Richard Yuricich (*Star Trek: The Motion Picture*)

6th — 1978

Best Science Fiction Film ..... *Superman: The Movie*
Best Horror Film ..... *The Wicker Man*
Best Fantasy Film ..... *Heaven Can Wait*
Best Actor ..... Warren Beatty (*Heaven Can Wait*)
Best Actress ..... Margot Kidder (*Superman: The Movie*)
Best Supporting Actor ..... Burgess Meredith (*Magic*)
Best Supporting Actress ..... Dyan Cannon (*Heaven Can Wait*)
Best Direction ..... Philip Kaufman (*Invasion of the Body Snatchers*)
Best Writing ..... Elaine May and Warren Beatty (*Heaven Can Wait*)
Best Music ..... John Williams (*Superman: The Movie*)
Best Make-Up ..... William Tuttle and Rick Baker (*The Fury*)
Best Costume ..... Theoni V. Aldredge (*The Eyes of Laura Mars*)
Best Special Effects ..... Colin Chilvers (*Superman: The Movie*)

5th—1977

Best Science Fiction Film ..... *Star Wars*
Best Horror Film ..... *The Little Girl Who Lives Down the Lane*
Best Fantasy Film ..... *Oh, God!*
Best Actor ..... George Burns (*Oh, God!*)
Best Actress ..... Jodie Foster (*The Little Girl Who Lives Down the Lane*)
Best Supporting Actor ..... Alec Guinness (*Star Wars*)
Best Supporting Actress ..... Susan Tyrrell (*Bad*)
Best Direction (tie) ..... George Lucas (*Star Wars*), Steven Spielberg (*Close Encounters of the Third Kind*)
Best Writing ..... George Lucas (*Star Wars*)
Best Music (tie) ..... John Williams (*Star Wars*) and (*Close Encounters of the Third Kind*)
Best Make-Up ..... Rick Baker and Stuart Freeborn (*Star Wars*)
Best Costume ..... John Mollo (*Star Wars*)
Best Special Effects ..... John Dykstra and John Stears (*Star Wars*)

4th—1976

Best Science Fiction Film ..... *Logan's Run*
Best Horror Film ..... *Burnt Offerings*
Best Fantasy Film ..... *The Holes*
Best Actor ..... David Bowie (*The Man Who Fell to Earth*)
Best Actress ..... Blythe Danner (*Futureworld*)
Best Supporting Actor ..... Jay Robinson (*Train Ride to Hollywood*)
Best Supporting Actress ..... Bette Davis (*Burnt Offerings*)
Best Direction ..... Dan Curtis (*Burnt Offerings*)
Best Writing ..... Jimmy Sangster (Career Winner)
Best Music ..... David Raksin (Career Winner)
Best Make-Up ..... William Tuttle (*Logan's Run*)
Best Costume ..... Bill Thomas (*Logan's Run*)
Best Special Effects ..... L.B. Abbott (Career Winner)

3rd—1974/75

Best Science Fiction Film ..... *Rollerball*
Best Horror Film ..... *Young Frankenstein*
Best Fantasy Film ..... *Doc Savage*
Best Actor (tie) ..... James Caan (*Rollerball*), Don Johnson (*A Boy and His Dog*)
Best Actress ..... Katharine Ross (*The Stepford Wives*)
Best Supporting Actor ..... Marty Feldman (*Young Frankenstein*)
Best Supporting Actress ..... Ida Lupino (*The Devil's Rain*)
Best Direction ..... Mel Brooks (*Young Frankenstein*)
Best Writing ..... Ib J. Melchior and Harlan Ellison (Career Winner)
Best Music ..... Miklos Rózsa (Career Winner)
Best Make-Up ..... William Tuttle (*Young Frankenstein*)
Best Special Effects ..... Douglas Knapp, Bill Taylor, John Carpenter and Dan O'Bannon (*Dark Star*)

2nd—1973

Best Science Fiction Film ..... *Soylent Green*
Best Horror Film ..... *The Exorcist*
Best Fantasy Film ..... *The Golden Voyage of Sinbad*
Best Music ..... Bernard Herrmann (Career Winner)
Best Make-Up ..... Dick Smith (*The Exorcist*)
Best Special Effects ..... Marcel Vercoutere (*The Exorcist*)

1st—1972

Best Science Fiction Film ..... *Slaughterhouse Five*
Best Horror Film ..... *Blacula*

Other Recipients Without Regard to Year

The Academy's **George Pal Memorial Award** has been presented to C. Dean Anderson, John Badham, Charles Band, Ray Bradbury, John Carpenter, Larry Cohen, David Cronenberg, Dean Devlin, Don Fanzo, William Friedkin, Kathleen Kennedy, Frank Marshall, Nicholas Meyer, Sam Raimi, Gene Roddenberry, Gloria Swanson, Douglas Trumbull, Douglas Z. Wick, Stan Winston, Fay Wray.

The Academy's **President's Memorial Award** has been presented to Woody Allen, Jack Arnold, *Batman* (1989), Dustin Lance Black, Marshall Brickman, James Cameron, Roger Corman, Steven E. De Souza, Richard Donner, Carrie Fisher, William Friedkin, *Gods and Monsters*, Gale Anne Hurd, Elsa Lanchester, *The Purple Rose of Cairo*, Robert Shaye, David Shepard, Bryan Singer, Steven Spielberg, Joseph Stefano, Billy Bob Thornton, *Time Bandits*, Robert Wise, *The Wizard of Speed and Time*.

The Academy's **Life Career Award** has been presented to Dario Argento, Samuel Z. Arkoff, Whit Bissell, Marshall Brickman, Albert R. Broccoli, James Coburn, Sean Connery, Roger Corman, Wes Craven, Dino De Laurentiis, Robert Englund, Richard Fleischer, Harrison Ford, John Frankenheimer, Brian Grazer, Ray Harryhausen, Hurd Hatfield, Alfred Hitchcock, Nathan Juran, James Karen, Sid & Marty Krofft, Carl Laemmle, Jr., Fritz Lang, Christopher Lee, Leonard Nimoy, Edward R. Pressman, Vincent

Price, Gene Roddenberry, Kurt Russell, William Shatner, Joel Silver, Joseph Stefano, Dick Van Dyke, Jeffrey Walker, Ray Walston.

"**Selective Television Saturn Awards**" have been presented to George Takei and Patrick Stewart (*Star Trek*); Robert Culp and Linda Hamilton (*The Greatest American Hero*); Lorne Greene and Dirk Benedict (*Battlestar Galactica*).

Science+Fiction

Urania d'Argento means Silver Urania. The festival's Giovanni Barbo confirms to me that this is a complete list of their winners.

2010

Asteroide Award ..... *Transfer*
Special Mention ..... *Norwegian Ninja*
Méliès d'Argent ..... *Rare Exports: A Christmas Tale*
Special Mention ..... *Technotise*
Méliès d'Or Short Film Nomination ..... *Daddy's Girl*
Special Mention ..... *Teleportation*
Nocturno Nuove Visioni Award ..... *Rammbock*

2009

Asteroide Award ..... *First Squad: The Moment of Truth* (dir: Yoshiharu Ashino)
Méliès d'Argent ..... *The Children* (dir: Tom Shankland)
Urania d'Argento ..... Roger Corman and Christopher Lee

2008

Asteroide Award ..... *Tres Días* (dir: F. Javier Gutiérrez)
Urania d'Argento ..... Ray Harryhausen

2007

Asteroide Award ..... *Los cronocrímenes*, A.K.A. Timecrimes (dir: Nacho Vigalondo)
Urania d'Argento ..... Joe Dante

2006

Asteroide Award ..... *Manga* (dir: Peter Khazizov)
Urania d'Argento ..... Terry Gilliam and Enki Bilal

2005

Asteroide Award ..... *Puzzlehead* (dir: James Bai)
Urania d'Argento ..... Lamberto Bava

2004

Asteroide Award ..... *Able Edwards* (dir: Graham Robertson)
Urania d'Argento ..... Jimmy Sangster

2003

Urania d'Argento ..... Dario Argento

2002

Urania d'Argento ..... Pupi Avati

Science Fiction + Fantasy Short Film Festival

2010

Grand Prize ..... *The Control Master*
Second Place ..... *Alma*
Third Place ..... *Charlie Thistle*
Audience Favorite ..... *Charlie Thistle*
Douglas Trumbull Award for Best Special Effects ..... *Hangar No. 5*

2009

Grand Prize ..... *Fade* (dir: Vincent Taylor)
Second Place ..... *Outsource* (dir: Daniel Trezise)
Third Place ..... *Notes from the Acrid Plain with Burton Hoary, Vol. 7* (dir: Jonathan Ashley)
Audience Favorite ..... *Hirsute* (dir: A.J. Bond)
Douglas Trumbull Award for Best Special Effects ..... *Outsource*

2008

Grand Prize ..... *Forecast* (dir: Erik Courtney)
Second Place ..... *Four Corners* (dir: Douglas Mueller)
Third Place ..... *Escape! From Robot Island* (dir: Timothy Thompson)
Audience Favorite ..... *Operation: Fish* (dir: Jeff Riley)
Douglas Trumbull Award for Best Special Effects ..... *E:D:E:N*

2007

Grand Prize ..... *Transgressions* (dir: Valerie Weiss)
Second Place ..... *The Un-Gone* (dir: Simon Bovey)
Third Place ..... *13 Ways to Die at Home* (dir: Lee Lanier)
Audience Favorite ..... *Maklar, Anyone?* (dir: Phil Guzzo)
Douglas Trumbull Award for Best Special Effects ..... *13 Ways to Die at Home*

2006

Grand Prize ..... *They're Made Out of Meat* (dir: Stephen O'Regan)
Second Place ..... *Red Planet Blues* (dir: David H. Brooks)
Third Place ..... *Microgravity* (dir: David Sanders)
Honorable Mention ..... *Cost of Living* (dir: Jonathan Joffe)
Honorable Mention ..... *Circus of Infinity* (dir: Sue Corcoran)

Honorable Mention ..... *Heartbeat* (dir: Omri Bar-Levy)
Audience Favorite ..... *Cost of Living* (dir: Jonathan Joffe)
Douglas Trumbull Award for Best Special Effects ..... *Microgravity*

Sci-Fi–London Film Festival

A.K.A. the London International Festival of Science Fiction and Fantastic Film.

2010

Best Short Film ..... *Mr Green*
Audience Award, Best Short Film ..... *Schizofredric*

2009

Best Short Film ..... *Well Founded Concerns*
Audience Award, Best Short Film ..... *The Day the Robots Woke Up*

2008

Best Short Film ..... *Ascension*
Audience Award, Best Short Film ..... *Final Journey*

2007

Best Short Film ..... *The Angel*
Audience Award, Best Short Film ..... *Coming to Town*

2006

Best Feature Film ..... *Subject Two*
Best Short Film ..... *X*
Audience Award, Best Short Film ..... *Plastic*

2005

Best Feature Film ..... *Primer*
Best Short Film ..... *La vie d'un chien*
Audience Award, Best Short Film ..... *Netherbeast of Berm-Tech Industries*

2004

Best Feature Film ..... *Robot Stories*
Best Short Film ..... *Chaingangs*
Audience Award, Best Short Film ..... *Annie & Boo*

2003

Best Feature Film ..... *Ever Since the World Ended*
Best Short Film ..... *The Town of the One-Handed People*
Audience Award, Best Short Film ..... *The Cat With Hands*

2002

Best Feature Film ..... *Avalon*
Best Short Film ..... *Inferno*

Scream Award

2010

The Ultimate Scream ..... *Inception*
Most Anticipated Movie ..... *Green Lantern*
Best Science Fiction Movie ..... *Inception*
Best Fantasy Movie ..... *The Twilight Saga: Eclipse*
Best Horror Movie ..... *Zombieland*
Best TV Show ..... *True Blood*
Best Director ..... James Cameron (*Avatar*)
Best Scream-Play ..... *Shutter Island* (Laeta Kalogridis)
Best Fantasy Actress ..... Kristen Stewart (*The Twilight Saga: Eclipse*)
Best Fantasy Actor ..... Robert Pattinson (*The Twilight Saga: Eclipse*)
Best Science Fiction Actress ..... Scarlett Johansson (*Iron Man 2*)
Best Science Fiction Actor ..... Leonardo DiCaprio (*Inception*)
Best Horror Actress ..... Anna Paquin (*True Blood*)
Best Horror Actor ..... Alexander Skarsgård (*True Blood*)
Best Villain ..... Mickey Rourke (*Iron Man 2*)
Best Superhero ..... Robert Downey, Jr. (*Iron Man 2*)
Best Supporting Actor ..... Joseph Gordon-Levitt (*Inception*)
Best Supporting Actress ..... Anne Hathaway (*Alice in Wonderland*)
Best Breakout Performance, Female ..... Chloë Moretz (*Kick-Ass*)
Best Breakout Performance, Male ..... Tom Hardy (*Inception*)
Best Cameo ..... Bill Murray (*Zombieland*)
Best Ensemble ..... *Zombieland*
Fight Scene of the Year ..... anti-gravity hotel fight (*Inception*)
Holy Sh*t Scene of the Year ..... head twisted 180 degrees during sex (*True Blood*)
Most Memorable Mutilation ..... the human centipede, first sequence (*The Human Centipede*)
3-D Top Three ..... *Avatar*
Best F/X ..... *Avatar*
Best Television Performance ..... Matthew Fox (*Lost*)
Best Comic Book or Graphic Novel ..... (*The Walking Dead*)
Best Comic Book Writer ..... Geoff Johns
Best Comic Book Artist ..... Frank Quitley (*Batman and Robin: Batman*)
Best Comic Book Movie ..... *Kick-Ass*

2009

The Ultimate Scream ..... *Star Trek*
Best Horror Movie ..... *Drag Me to Hell*
Best Science Fiction Movie ..... *Star Trek*
Best Fantasy Movie ..... *Twilight*
Best TV Show ..... *True Blood*
Best Horror Actress ..... Anna Paquin (*True Blood*)
Best Horror Actor ..... Stephen Moyer (*True Blood*)

Best Fantasy Actress ..... Kristen Stewart (*Twilight*)
Best Fantasy Actor ..... Robert Pattinson (*Twilight*)
Best Science Fiction Actress ..... Megan Fox (*Transformers: Revenge of the Fallen*)
Best Science Fiction Actor ..... Chris Pine (*Star Trek*)
Best Supporting Actress ..... Jennifer Carpenter (*Dexter*)
Best Supporting Actor ..... Ryan Reynolds (*X-Men Origins: Wolverine*)
Breakout Performance, Female ..... Isabel Lucas (*Transformers: Revenge of the Fallen*)
Breakout Performance, Male ..... Taylor Lautner (*Twilight*)
Best Cameo ..... Winona Ryder (*Star Trek*)
Best Ensemble ..... *Harry Potter and the Half Blood Prince*
Best Director ..... J. J. Abrams (*Star Trek*)
Best Foreign Movie ..... *Let the Right One In*
Best Sequel ..... *Transformers: Revenge of the Fallen*
Best F/X ..... *Transformers: Revenge of the Fallen*
Scream Song of the Year ..... "New Divide" by Linkin Park (*Transformers: Revenge of the Fallen*)
Best Comic Book Artist ..... Steve McNiven (*Wolverine: Old Man Logan*)
Best Villain ..... Alexander Skarsgård (*True Blood*)
Best Superhero ..... Hugh Jackman (*X-Men Origins: Wolverine*)
Best Scream-Play ..... *Drag Me to Hell*
Most Memorable Mutilation ..... the pendulum trap (*Saw V*)
Fight Scene of the Year ..... Kirk vs. Spock (*Star Trek*)
Holy Sh!t Scene of the Year ..... the death eaters attack London (*Harry Potter and the Half-Blood Prince*)
Best Comic Book ..... *Green Lantern*
Best Comic Book Writer ..... Geoff Johns
Best Comic Book Movie ..... *Watchmen*

2008

Best Fantasy Movie ..... *Hellboy 2: The Golden Army*
Best Fantasy Actor ..... Heath Ledger (*The Dark Knight*)
Best Fantasy Actress ..... Angelina Jolie (*Wanted*)
Best Comic Book ..... *Y: The Last Man*
Best Villain ..... Heath Ledger (*The Dark Knight*)
Most Memorable Mutilation ..... penis bitten off by vagina with teeth (*Teeth*)
Best Horror Actor ..... Johnny Depp (*Sweeney Todd: The Demon Barber of Fleet Street*)
Best TV Show ..... *Dexter*
Best Horror Actress ..... Liv Tyler (*The Strangers*)
Best Supporting Actor ..... Gary Oldman (*The Dark Knight*)
Best Science Fiction Movie ..... *Iron Man*
Best Superhero ..... Christian Bale (*The Dark Knight*)
Best Science Fiction Actress ..... Milla Jovovich (*Resident Evil: Extinction*)
Best Science Fiction Actor ..... Robert Downey, Jr. (*Iron Man*)
Breakout Performance ..... WALL-E (*WALL-E*)
Best Director ..... Christopher Nolan (*The Dark Knight*)
Best Sequel ..... *The Dark Knight*
Best F/X ..... *The Dark Knight*
Best Remake ..... *Halloween*
Best Line ..... "I believe whatever doesn't kill you makes you stranger." (*The Dark Knight*)
Best Comic Book Artist ..... Gabriel Ba (*The Umbrella Academy: Apocalypse Suite*)
Best Comic Book Writer ..... Grant Morrison
Best Comic Book Movie ..... *The Dark Knight*
The Ultimate Scream ..... *The Dark Knight*
Best Scream-Play ..... *The Dark Knight*
Best Scream-to-Comic-Adaptation ..... *Buffy the Vampire Slayer* (season eight)
The Holy Sh!t Scene of the Year ..... big rig flips over (The Dark Knight)

2007

The Ultimate Scream *300*
Best Horror Movie ..... *28 Weeks Later*
Best Fantasy Movie ..... *Pan's Labyrinth*
Best Science Fiction Movie ..... *Transformers*
Best TV Show ..... *Heroes*
Best Sequel ..... *Harry Potter and the Order of the Phoenix*
Best Superhero ..... Tobey Maguire (*Spider-Man 3*)
Best Comic-to-Screen Adaptation *300*
Scream Queen ..... Kate Beckinsale (*Vacancy*)
Scream King ..... Shia LaBeouf (*Disturbia*)
Most Vile Villain ..... Ralph Fiennes (*Harry Potter and the Order of the Phoenix*)
Most Memorable Mutilation ..... dismembered in car crash (*Grindhouse*)
Breakout Performance ..... Hayden Panettiere (*Heroes*)
"Jump-From-Your-Seat" Scene of the Year ..... final battle, Megatron vs. Optimus Prime (*Transformers*)

2006

The Ultimate Scream ..... *Batman Begins*
Best Horror Movie ..... *The Devil's Rejects*
Best Fantasy Movie ..... *Pirates of the Caribbean: Dead Man's Chest*
Best Science Fiction Movie ..... *V for Vendetta*
Best TV Show ..... *Battlestar Galactica*
Best Sequel ..... *Pirates of the Caribbean: Dead Man's Chest*
Best Remake ..... *King Kong*
Best Superhero ..... Brandon Routh (*Superman Returns*)
Best Comic-to-Screen Adaptation ..... *X-Men: The Last Stand*

Most Memorable Mutilation ..... the eye removal (*Hostel*)
Most Heroic Performance ..... Johnny Depp (*Pirates of the Caribbean: Dead Man's Chest*)
Scream Queen ..... Kate Beckinsale (*Underworld: Evolution*)
Most Vile Villain ..... Leslie Easterbrook, Sid Haig, Bill Moseley, Sheri Moon Zombie as the Firefly Family (*The Devil's Rejects*)
Breakout Performance ..... Jennifer Carpenter (*The Exorcism of Emily Rose*)
The "Holy Sh!t"/"Jump-From-Your-Seat" Award ..... the eye removal (*Hostel*)
Best Rack on the Rack ..... *Vampirella*

Screamfest L.A.

2010

Best Picture ..... *Caged*
Best Director ..... Chris Smith (*Black Death*)
Best Short ..... *The Legend of Beaver Dam*
Best Actor ..... Sean Bean (*Black Death*)
Best Actress ..... Zoe Felix (*Caged*, A.K.A. *Captifs*)
Best Cinematography ..... Sebastian Edschmid (*Black Death*)
Best Editing ..... Olivier Gajan (*The Pack*)
Best Special Effects ..... *The Pack*
Best Makeup ..... *Needle*
Best Musical Score ..... Christian Henson (*Black Death*)
Best Screenplay (unproduced) ..... *Controlled* (Craig Cambria)

2009

Best Picture ..... *The Human Centipede*
Best Director ..... Javier Gutierrez (*Before the Fall*)
Best Actor ..... Victor Clavijo (*Before the Fall*)
Best Actress ..... Jocelin Donahue (*The House of the Devil*)
Best Cinematography ..... Miguel A. Mora (*Before the Fall*)
Best Editing ..... Nacho Ruiz Capillas (*Before the Fall*)
Best Special Effects ..... Paul Staples (*The Revenant*)
Best Makeup ..... Jason Collins, Amy Mills, Chris Mills (*The Revenant*)
Best Musical Score ..... Jeff Grace (*The House of the Devil*)
Best Short ..... *Prelude to Hell* (Harry Doright)
Best Student Short ..... *Else* (dir: Thibault Emin)
Best Screenplay (unproduced) ..... *Hate Night* (VJ Boyd, Justin Boyd)

2008

Best Picture ..... *Splinter*
Best Directing ..... Toby Wilkins (*Splinter*)
Best Actor ..... Leonardo Sbaraglia (*El Rey De La Montana*)
Best Actress ..... María Valverde (*El Rey De La Montana*)
Best Cinematography ..... José David Montero (*El Rey De La Montana*)
Best Editing ..... David Michael Maurer (*Splinter*)
Best Special Effects ..... Quantum Creation FX
Best Makeup ..... Ozzy Alvarez (*Splinter*)
Best Musical Score ..... Elia Cmiral (*Splinter*)
Best Short ..... K. Akeseh Tsakpo (*Detour*)
Best Student Short ..... James Darling (*Citizen*)
Honorable Mention ..... *Dance of the Dead*
Audience Choice Award ..... *Trick 'R Treat*
Audience Choice for Best Documentary ..... *Spine Tingler! The William Castle Story*
Boost Mobile's Best of the Next in Horror Award ..... Tate Steinsiek (*Clown*)
Best Screenplay (unproduced) ..... *Haunted High* (MV Gerhard, Matt Verboys)

2007

Best Picture ..... *Alone*
Best Directing ..... Banjong Pisanthanakun, Parkpoom Wongpoom (*Alone*)
Best Actor ..... Everon Jackson Hooi (*Dead End*)
Best Actress ..... Katie Featherston (*Paranormal Activity*)
Best Cinematography ..... Niramon Ross (*Alone*)
Best Editing ..... Vijja Kojew, Thammarat Sumetsupachok (*Alone*)
Best Special Effects ..... Gab Facchinei, Justin Dix (*Storm Warning*)
Best Makeup ..... Jacques-Olivier Molon (*Inside*)
Best Musical Score ..... Jamie Blanks (*Storm Warning*)
Honorable Mention ..... *Paranormal Activity*
Audience Choice Award ..... *Wasting Away*
Boost Mobile's Best of the Next in Horror Award ..... *Stem* (dir: Iqbal Ahmed)
Best Short Film ..... *In the Wall* (dir: Mike Williamson)
Best Student Short ..... *Ange* (dir: Nikolas List)
Best Screenplay (unproduced) ..... *The Palace* (Adam Aresty, Jon D.A.)

2006

Best Film ..... *Isolation*
Best Director ..... Billy O'Brien (*Isolation*)
Best Actor ..... Marc Senter (*The Lost*)
Best Actress ..... Essie Davis (*Isolation*)
Best Cinematography ..... *The Marsh*
Best Editing ..... *The Beach Party at the Threshold of Hell*
Best Special Effects ..... *Frostbitten*
Best Makeup ..... *Frostbitten*
Best Musical Score ..... *Frostbitten*
Best Short ..... *Happy Birthday to You*
Achievement Award ..... Clive Barker

Honorable Mention ..... *The Beach Party at the Threshold of Hell*
Honorable Mention ..... *The Tripper*
Best Screenplay (unproduced) ..... *Childish Things* (Alex Greenfield)

2005

Best Picture ..... *Cookers* (prod: Jeff Ritchie)
Best Director ..... Dan Mintz (*Cookers*)
Best Actor ..... Brad Hunt (*Cookers*)
Best Actress ..... Cyia Batten (*Cookers*)
Best Cinematography ..... Christopher Duddy (*The Cabinet of Dr. Caligari*)
Best Editing ..... F. Javier Gutierrez (*Brasil*)
Best Special Effects ..... David Lee Fisher, Josiah Holmes Howison, Barbara K. Hintz (*The Cabinet of Dr. Caligari*)
Best Makeup ..... Kyla Rose Tremblay (*Severed—Forest of the Dead*)
Best Musical Score ..... Jesse Lucas (*Sigaw*, A.K.A. *The Echo*)
Best Horror Short ..... *Staring at the Sun* (dir: Toby Wilkins)
Best Animated Horror Short ..... *Little Dead Girl* (dir: Lee Lanier)
Best Comedy Horror Short ..... *Zombie Movie* (prod: Michael J. Asquith, dir: Ben Stenbeck)
Best Student Horror ..... *Dead West* (dir: Eli Sasich)
Audience Choice Award ..... *The Cabinet of Dr. Caligari* (Remix)
Career Achievement Award ..... Sean S. Cunningham
Best Screenplay (unproduced) ..... *Nightfall* (Paul J. Da Silva)

2004

Best Picture ..... *The Invisible* (prod: Joakim Hansson)
Best Director ..... Mikael Håfström (*The Invisible*)
Best Actor ..... Gustaf Skarsgård (*The Invisible*)
Best Actress ..... Tuva Novotny (*The Invisible*)
Best Cinematography ..... Joel Bergvall, Simon Sandquist (*The Invisible*)
Best Editing ..... Joel Bergvall, Darek Hodor (*The Invisible*)
Best Special Effects ..... Aaron Weintraub, Dennis Berardi, Jeff Skochko (*Cube Zero*)
Best Makeup ..... A. Scott Hamilton, Maya Kulenovic (*Cube Zero*)
Best Musical Score ..... Anders Ehlin (*Drowning Ghost*)
Best Horror Documentary ..... *H.H. Holmes: America's First Serial Killer* (John Borowski)
Best Horror Short ..... *El Ciclo* (Víctor García)
Best Student Horror Short ..... *The Taking* (Matt Eskandari)
Best Animated Horror Short ..... *Day Off the Dead* (Lee Lanier, Jeffery Dates)
Best Screenplay (unproduced) ..... *The Domain* (Michael Raymond)
Best Short Screenplay (unproduced) ..... *Lock Up* (Jennifer Martin)

2003

Best Picture ..... *A Tale of Two Sisters* (Oh Kimin, Oh Jung-Wan)
Best Director ..... Kim Jee-Woon (*A Tale of Two Sisters*)
Best Actor ..... Juan Pablo Ogalde (*Sangre Eterna*)
Best Actress ..... Lim Soo-Jung (*A Tale of Two Sisters*)
Best Cinematography ..... Lee Mogae (*A Tale of Two Sisters*)
Best Editing ..... Lee Kyun-Mi, Kim Jin-Hee (*A Tale of Two Sisters*)
Best Special Effects ..... *Ghost System*
Best Makeup ..... Sebastian Carvajal (*Sangre Eterna*)
Best Musical Score ..... *Ghost System*
Best Horror Short ..... *Ice Cold* (dir: Frederick D'Amours)
Best Horror Comedy Short ..... *R.I.P.* (Jan Doense)
Best Animated Short ..... *Deadtime Stories* (Michael Dougherty)
Best Student Film ..... *3 A.M.* (dir: Stewart Hopewell)
Best Screenplay (unproduced) ..... *Desolate* (Francisco Castro)
Best Short Screenplay (unproduced) ..... *Souls* (James Stevens-Arce)

2002

Best Picture ..... *Kolobos*
Best Director ..... Todd Ocvirk, Daniel Liatowitsch (*Kolobos*)
Best Actor ..... Rick Otto (*R.S.V.P.*)
Best Actress ..... Marianne Hayden (*Ghostwatcher*)
Best Cinematography ..... Thom Stukas, Christian Grosselfinger (*R.S.V.P.*)
Best Special Effects ..... John Carl Buechler (*Miner's Massacre*, A.K.A. *Curse of the Forty-Niner*)
Best Makeup ..... Jason Collins, Elizabeth Villamarin (*Kolobos*)
Best Foreign Film ..... *Ju-on: The Grudge* (dir: Takashi Shimizu)
Best Documentary ..... *ISRP Investigates: The Ghosts of Belgrave Hall* (Daena Smoller, Larry Montz)
Best Horror Short ..... *Repossessed* (dir: John Coven)
Best Horror Comedy Short ..... *The Bad Father* (dir: Robert Benson)
Best Animation ..... *Puphedz* (Jurgen Heimann)
Best Student Film ..... *Off* (dir: Tyler Polhemus)
Best Horror Feature Screenplay (unproduced) ..... *Bloodlines* (Jamie Deise)

Best Horror Short Screenplay (unproduced) ..... *Reset* (Andrew Hunt, Christina Hall)
Best Horror Comedy Screenplay (unproduced) ..... *Ravenna* (William Sheck)

2001

Best Picture *Y2K*
Most Creative ..... *Earth Day*
Best Director ..... Jeff Rector (*Fatal Kiss*)
Best Actor ..... Jeff Rector (*Fatal Kiss*)
Best Actress ..... Jennifer De Martino (*The Appointment*)
Best Cinematography ..... *Deep in the Woods*
Best Editing ..... *Cradle of Fear*
Best Special Effects ..... *Cradle of Fear*
Best Makeup ..... *Night of the Headsman*
Best Foreign Film ..... *Blood: The Last Vampire*
Best Animation ..... *Blood: The Last Vampire*
Audience Choice Award ..... *Night of the Headsman*
Scariest Student Short ..... *The Appointment*
Best Feature Screenplay (unproduced) ..... *Vampire's Hell* (Jordan Wendkos)
Best Short Screenplay (unproduced) ..... *The Bloated Beetle* (Haren Dent)
Screenplay Honorable Mention (unproduced) ..... *Shadows of Life* (Gary Lumpp)
Screenplay Honorable Mention (unproduced) ..... *Abductions* (Paul Van Camp)

ShockerFest

Shockerfest did not reply to my emails, nor does its website list its 2009 winners. I pieced together the below 2009 list from the IMDb (which doesn't list the Horror category winner) and *Blood Night*'s website (which touts its Horror category win, but says nothing else of Shockerfest). I assume that the below 2009 winners list remains incomplete. For 2003, Shockerfest listed *Robot Stories* as a winner in both its Science Fiction and Fantasy categories.

2010

Best Picture, Feature (Horror) ..... *Rage*
Honorable Mention, Feature (Horror) ..... *Dawning*
Honorable Mention, Feature (Horror) ..... *Golden Earrings*
Honorable Mention, Feature (Horror) ..... *George's Intervention*
Best Picture, Short (Horror) ..... *Devil's Creek*
Honorable Mention, Short (Horror) ..... *Caprice*
Honorable Mention, Short (Horror) ..... *Inside of a Lamb*
Best Picture, Mini-Short (Horror) ..... *Visiting Ellie*
Honorable Mention, Mini-Short (Horror) ..... *The Necronomicon*
Honorable Mention, Mini-Short (Horror) ..... *Playtime*
Honorable Mention, Mini-Short (Horror) ..... *Enter the Dark*
Honorable Mention, Mini-Short (Horror) ..... *Clemency*
Best Picture, Feature (Science Fiction) ..... *H1N1: Virus X*
Honorable Mention, Feature (Science Fiction) ..... *Destination Outer Space*
Honorable Mention, Feature (Science Fiction) ..... *Grey Skies*
Honorable Mention, Feature (Science Fiction) ..... *Lunopolis*
Best Picture, Mini-Short (Science Fiction) ..... *Assimilation*
Honorable Mention, Mini-Short (Science Fiction) ..... *Frank Dancoolo: Paranormal Drug Dealer*
Honorable Mention, Mini-Short (Science Fiction) ..... *Cockpit: The Rule of Engagement*
Honorable Mention, Mini-Short (Science Fiction) ..... *Unearthed*
Best Picture, Feature (Fantasy) ..... *My Bloody Wedding*
Best Picture, Mini-Short (Fantasy) ..... *Pisces Arise*
Honorable Mention, Mini-Short (Fantasy) ..... *Toothnapped*
Honorable Mention, Mini-Short (Fantasy) ..... *Demiurge Emesis*
Audience Choice Award, Feature ..... *Golden Earrings*
Audience Choice Award, Short or Mini-Short ..... *Simone*
Directors' Choice Award, Short ..... *Frank Dancoolo: Paranormal Drug Dealer*
Directors' Choice Award, Mini-Short ..... *The Necronomicon*

2009

Best Picture, Feature (Horror) ..... *Blood Night: The Legend of Mary Hatchet*
Best Picture, Short (Science Fiction) ..... *Mindbender*
Best Picture, Short (Fantasy) ..... *Firemount*
B-Movie Award ..... *Grave Mistakes*
Showbiz Software Award (best use of CGI effects) ..... *Firemount*

2008

Best Picture, Feature (Horror) ..... *Paper Dolls*
Honorable Mention, Feature (Horror) ..... *The Shadow Within*
Honorable Mention, Feature (Horror) ..... *The Assessment*
Best Picture, Short (Horror) *AM1200*
Honorable Mention, Short (Horror) ..... *The Consumed*
Best Picture, Mini-Short (Horror) ..... *Excision*
Honorable Mention, Mini-Short (Horror) ..... *Peekers*

Honorable Mention, Mini-Short (Horror) ..... *Penny Dreadful*
Honorable Mention, Mini-Short (Horror) ..... *Kirksdale*
Best Actor (Horror) ..... Keith Blaser (*The Assessment*)
Honorable Mention, Actor (Horror) ..... Eric Lange (*AM1200*)
Best Actress (Horror) ..... Tessa Ferrer (*Excision*)
Honorable Mention, Actress (Horror) ..... Kristin Mellian (*Without Within*)
Honorable Mention, Actress (Horror) ..... Victoria Engelmayer (*Hanah's Gift*)
Best Picture, Feature (Science Fiction) ..... *Alien Raiders*
Honorable Mention, Feature (Science Fiction) ..... *Plaguers*
Honorable Mention, Feature (Science Fiction) ..... *Cave Women on Mars*
Best Picture, Mini-Short/Short (Science Fiction) ..... *Superhuman*
Honorable Mention, Mini-Short/Short (Science Fiction) ..... *God's Marble*
Honorable Mention, Mini-Short/Short (Science Fiction) ..... *Well Founded Concerns*
Best Actor (Science Fiction) ..... Steve Railsback (*Plaguers*)
Honorable Mention, Actor (Science Fiction) ..... Carlos Bernard (*Alien Raiders*)
Best Actress (Science Fiction) ..... Courtney Ford (*Alien Raiders*)
Honorable Mention, Actress (Science Fiction) ..... Alexis Zibolis (*Plaguers*)
Best Picture, Feature (Fantady) ..... *Yesterday Was a Lie*
Honorable Mention, Feature (Fantasy) ..... *Nobody*
Honorable Mention, Feature (Fantasy) ..... *Carnivorous*
Best Picture, Mini Short (Fantasy) ..... *Believe*
Honorable Mention, Mini Short (Fantasy) ..... *Mirror, Mirror*
Honorable Mention, Mini Short (Fantasy) ..... *Epicac*
Best Actor (Fantasy) ..... Costas Mandylor (*Nobody*)
Honorable Mention, Actor (Fantasy) ..... Ed O'Ross (*Nobody*)
Honorable Mention, Actor (Fantasy) ..... Ryan Schaufler (*Carnivorous*)
Best Actress (Fantasy) ..... Kipleigh Brown (*Yesterday Was a Lie*)
Honorable Mention, Actress (Fantasy) ..... Leah Rose (*Carnivorous*)
Rising Star Award ..... Victoria Englemayer (*Hanah's Gift*)
Honorable Mention, Rising Star ..... Molly Chiffer (*Mirror, Mirror*)
Honorable Mention, Rising Star ..... Laurence Belcher (*The Shadow Within*)
Director's Choice ..... *Without, Within*
Audience Choice Award ..... *Hanah's Gift*
Contribution to the Arts Award ..... Vernon Wells
Larry Stanley B-Movie Award ..... *Plaguers*
Fujifilm Award ..... *Excision*
Gorilla Software Awards ..... *Yesterday Was a Lie* and *The Consumed*

2007

Best Picture, Feature (Horror) ..... *Book of Lore*
Honorable Mention, Feature (Horror) ..... *Portal*
Honorable Mention, Feature (Horror) ..... *Days of Darkness*
Best Picture, Short (Horror) ..... *Zombie Love*
Honorable Mention, Short (Horror) ..... *Tree*
Honorable Mention, Short (Horror) ..... *Lily*
Best Picture, Mini-Short (Horror) ..... *A.W.O.L.*
Honorable Mention, Mini-Short (Horror) ..... *Seekers*
Honorable Mention, Mini-Short (Horror) ..... *The Dollhouse*
Best Actor (Horror) ..... David Morse (*A.W.O.L.*)
Honorable Mention, Actor (Horror) ..... Thomas Calabro (*Chill*)
Honorable Mention, Actor (Horror) ..... Peter Facinelli (*Lily*)
Best Actress (Horror) ..... Robin Hathaway (*Chains*)
Honorable Mention, Actress (Horror) ..... Axelle Grelet (*Killing Ariel*)
Best Picture — Feature (Science Fiction) ..... *It Came from Another World*
Honorable Mention, Feature (Science Fiction) ..... *Decaying Orbit*
Best Picture, Short (Science Fiction) ..... *Deployment Strategy*
Honorable Mention, Short (Science Fiction) ..... *Gunmen*
Best Picture, Mini-Short (Science Fiction) ..... *Eight Thirty Two*
Honorable Mention, Mini-Short (Science Fiction) ..... *A Thousand Words*
Honorable Mention, Mini-Short (Science Fiction) ..... *Genesis Antipode*
Best Actor (SF/Fantasy) ..... John Soares (*Gauntlet of Sorrow*)
Honorable Mention, Actor (SF/Fantasy) ..... Andy Allen (*Decaying Orbit*)
Best Actress (SF/Fantasy) ..... Åsa Wallander (*Decaying Orbit*)
Best Picture, Short (Fantasy) ..... *Vanished Acres*
Honorable Mention, Short (Fantasy) ..... *Gauntlet of Sorrow*
Best Picture, Mini-Short (Fantasy) ..... *Folklore*
Honorable Mention, Mini-Short (Fantasy) ..... *Lucifer*
Honorable Mention, Mini-Short (Fantasy) ..... *Tyrants of Nazca*
Rising Star Award ..... Christina Barlas (*The Dollhouse*)
Fujifilm Award ..... *God of Vampires*

AVID Editing Award ..... *Folklore*
Gorilla Software Awards ..... *Chains* and *Gauntlet of Sorrow*
Production Pro Budgeting Awards ..... *Tree* and *Lily* and *Cecila Rose*
Digital Hotcakes Awards ..... *Gunmen* and *Vanished Acres*
Creative Cow Awards ..... *Consciousness* and *Noesis* and *Genesis Antipode* and *Jamie Hit Single* and *Diabolical Tales 2*
Director's Choice ..... *God of Vampires*
Larry Stanley B-Movie Award ..... *Brain Dead*

2006

Best Picture, Feature (Horror) ..... *Seance*
Honorable Mention, Feature (Horror) ..... *The Monster of Phantom Lake*
Best Picture, Mini-Short (Horror) ..... *Room to Breathe*
Honorable Mention, Mini-Short (Horror) ..... *Suffer the Little Children*
Honorable Mention, Mini-Short (Horror) ..... *The Resurrectionist*
Best Actor (Horror) ..... Scott Graham (*Oculus*)
Honorable Mention, Actor (Horror) ..... Adam Montgomery (*Suffer the Little Children*)
Best Actress (Horror) ..... Tiffany Shepis (*Nightmare Man*)
Honorable Mention, Actress (Horror) ..... Amy Jean Page (*The Librarian*)
Best Picture—Feature (Science Fiction) ..... *The Time Travelers*
Best Picture, Short/Mini-Short (Science Fiction) ..... *Assumption*
Honorable Mention, Short/Mini-Short (Science Fiction) ..... *Say That You Love Me*
Best Actor (SF/Fantasy) ..... James Denton (*Assumption*)
Honorable Mention, Actor (SF/Fantasy) ..... Robert Wagner
Honorable Mention, Actor (SF/Fantasy) ..... Ron Roggé (*Berserker*)
Best Actress (SF/Fantasy) ..... Tarika Brandt (*Microgravity*)
Honorable Mention, Actress (SF/Fantasy) ..... Lori Singer (*Little Victim*)
Honorable Mention, Actress (SF/Fantasy) ..... Joy Ramsey
Best Bicture, Short/Mini-Short (Fantasy) ..... *Unfinished Business*
Honorable Mention, Short/Mini-Short (Fantasy) ..... *Berserker*
Honorable Mention, Short/Mini-Short (Fantasy) ..... *Little Victim*
Rising Star Award ..... Adam Montgomery (*Suffer the Little Children*)
Honorable Mention, Rising Star ..... Camile Jones (*Sucker*)
Best Score ..... Holly Amber Church (*Berserker*)
Fujifilm Award ..... Susan Bell (*The Resurrectionist* and *The Boarder*)
AVID Editing Award ..... *Diabolical Tales: Part I*
Gorilla Software Awards ..... Cheryl McIntire (of McIntire Casting); *Paradise Road* (Rosie Ramirez); and Johannson High School Film Department
Production Pro Budgeting Awards ..... *The Monster of Phantom Lake*; *Suffer the Little Children*; *Paradise Road*; and Johannson High School Film Department
Director's Choice ..... *The Monster of Phantom Lake*
Special Contribution ..... Ron Adams (for artistic contributions)

2005

Best Picture, Feature (Horror) ..... *Graves End*
Honorable Mention, Feature (Horror) ..... *Nightmare*
Honorable Mention, Feature (Horror) ..... *X, Y*
Honorable Mention, Feature (Horror) ..... *Hospitality*
Best Picture, Short (Horror) ..... *A Feast of Souls*
Honorable Mention, Short (Horror) ..... *The Girlfriend*
Best Picture, Mini-Short (Horror) ..... *Road Kill*
Honorable Mention, Mini-Short (Horror) ..... *The Tall Tale Heart*
Honorable Mention, Mini-Short (Horror) ..... *My Skin*
Best Actor, Feature (Horror) ..... Steven Williams (*Graves End*)
Best Actor, Short (Horror) ..... Jacob Medjuck (*The Tall Tale Heart*)
Best Actress, Feature (Horror) ..... Melissa Murphy (*X, Y*)
Best Actress, Short (Horror) ..... Ra Sylver (*A Feast of Souls*)
Best Score (Horror) ..... *Nightmare*
Best Picture, Feature (Science Fiction) ..... *Experiment*
Honorable Mention, Feature (Science Fiction) ..... *Outerworld*
Honorable Mention, Feature (Science Fiction) ..... *After the Apocalypse*
Honorable Mention, Feature (Science Fiction) ..... *Screech of the Decapitated*
Best Picture, Mini-Short/Short (Science Fiction) ..... *Cost of Living*
Honorable Mention, Mini-Short/Short (Science Fiction) ..... *Apartment 206*
Honorable Mention, Mini-Short/Short (Science Fiction) ..... *We All Fall Down*
Best Actor (Science Fiction) ..... William B. Davis (*Cost of Living*)
Honorable Mention, Actor (Science Fiction) ..... Andrew Krivanek (*Cost of Living*)
Honorable Mention, Actor (Science Fiction) ..... Troy Bishop (*Apartment 206*)

Best Actress (Science Fiction) ..... Nicki Hersh (*Apartment 206*)
Honorable Mention, Actress (Science Fiction) ..... Jacqueline Bowman (*After the Apocalypse*)
Best Picture, Mini-Short/Short (Fantasy) ..... *Enter the Dragonfly*
Honorable Mention, Mini-Short/Short (Fantasy) ..... *Rainbow's End*
Best Actor (Fantasy) ..... Mark Povinelli (*Rainbow's End*)
Honorable Mention, Actor, (Fantasy) ..... Kyle Hamon (*Enter the Dragonfly*)
Best Picture (Animation) ..... *Joyride*
Honorable Mention (Animation) ..... *Pest*
Honorable Mention (Animation) ..... *Zoom Suit*
Honorable Mention (Animation) ..... *Little Dead Girl*
Rising Star Award ..... Bailey Slattery (*Delirium and the Dollman*)
Honorable Mention, Rising Star ..... Kyle Hamon (*Enter the Dragonfly*)
Honorable Mention, Rising Star ..... Hilary Wagner (*Predator*)
Fujifilm Award ..... *Delirium and the Dollman*
Digital Hotcakes Award ..... MJC Productions
Gorilla Software Awards ..... *Confederate Zombie Massacre* and *Predator* and MJC Productions
Director's Choice ..... William Herrell
Lifetime Achievement Award ..... Ann Robinson
Technical Contribution Award ..... Steve Wozniak
Contribution to the Arts Award ..... Melanee Wyatt

2004

Best Picture, Feature (Horror) ..... *Sonata*
Honorable Mention, Feature (Horror) ..... *Haunted Boat*
Honorable Mention, Feature (Horror) ..... *The Last Horror Movie*
Best Picture, Short (Horror) ..... *The Last Stop Café*
Honorable Mention, Short (Horror) ..... *Filthy*
Honorable Mention, Short (Horror) ..... *Kin*
Best Picture, Mini-Short (Horror) ..... *Conversations*
Honorable Mention, Mini-Short (Horror) ..... *Latchkey*
Honorable Mention, Mini-Short (Horror) ..... *Crypt Club*
Best Actor (Horror) ..... Curtis Armstrong (*Conversations*)
Honorable Mention (Horror) ..... Andrew Michaelson (*Latchkey*)
Best Actress (Horror) ..... Margot Kidder (*Death 4 Told*)
Honorable Mention (Horror) ..... Jane Evans (*Latchkey*)
Best Score (Horror) ..... *Wrecker*
Best Picture, Feature (Science Fiction) ..... *Spectres*
Honorable Mention, Feature (Science Fiction) ..... *Borrowing Time*
Honorable Mention, Feature (Science Fiction) ..... *Moonlight by the Sea*
Best Picture, Mini-Short/Short (Science Fiction) ..... *A Can of Paint*
Honorable Mention, Mini-Short/Short (Science Fiction) ..... *Fall of a Saga*
Honorable Mention, Mini-Short/Short (Science Fiction) ..... *Phoenix*
Best Actor (Science Fiction) ..... Bruce Collier (*Fall of a Saga*)
Honorable Mention, Actor (Science Fiction) ..... Aaron Robson (*A Can of Paint*)
Best Actress (Science Fiction) ..... Marina Sirtis (*Spectres*)
Honorable Mention, Actress (Science Fiction) ..... Susannah Anderson (*Borrowing Time*)
Best Score (Science Fiction) ..... *Gone*
Honorable Mention (Science Fiction) ..... *Time and Again*
Best Picture, Feature (Fantasy) ..... *Tales from Beyond*
Best Picture, Mini-Short/Short (Fantasy) ..... *My Beautiful Wickedness*
Honorable Mention, Mini-Short/Short (Fantasy) ..... *Neila*
Honorable Mention, Mini-Short/Short (Fantasy) ..... *Tea Time*
Best Actor (Fantasy) ..... Wyatt Denny (*My Beautiful Wickedness*)
Honorable Mention, Actor (Fantasy) ..... Jonathan Mangum (*Tea Time*)
Best Actress (Fantasy) ..... Seiko Higuma (*Neila*)
Honorable Mention, Actress (Fantasy) ..... Maria Fernanda Calandrelo (*Armadillo*)
Best Score (Fantasy) ..... *Tea Time*
Best Screenplay (Fantasy) (unproduced) ..... Michael Raymond (*The Domain*)
Best Picture (Animation) ..... *Rockfish*
Honorable Mention (Animation) ..... *The Black Violin*
Honorable Mention (Animation) ..... *Flyaway*
Honorable Mention (Animation) ..... *Willis Sillim's Tall Tales*
Director's Choice ..... Mark Redfield
Special Achievement Award ..... *The Black Violin*
Lifetime Technical Achievement Award ..... Ricardo "Rick" Gonzales

2003

Best Picture, Feature (Horror) ..... *Savage Island*
Honorable Mention, Feature (Horror) ..... *Director's Cut*
Honorable Mention, Feature (Horror) ..... *Dr. Jekyll and Mr. Hyde*
Honorable Mention, Feature (Horror) ..... *No Return*
Honorable Mention, Feature (Horror) ..... *Searching for Haizmann*
Best Picture, Short (Horror) ..... *The Visage*

Best Picture, Mini-Short (Horror) ..... *Toci: A Mexica Tale*
Honorable Mention, Mini-Short (Horror) ..... *Confessions*
Honorable Mention, Mini-Short (Horror) ..... *Little Ricky*
Honorable Mention, Mini-Short (Horror) ..... *Nightsweats: The Collector*
Best Actor (Horror) ..... Mark Redfield (*Dr. Jekyll and Mr. Hyde*)
Honorable Mention, Actor (Horror) ..... Darien Weiss (*Little Ricky*)
Best Actress (Horror) ..... Elena Torrez (*Dr. Jekyll and Mr. Hyde*)
Honorable Mention, Actress (Horror) ..... Stephanie Colet (*No Return*)
Best Director (Horror) ..... Tom Sylla (*No Return*)
Honorable Mention, Director (Horror) ..... Jeffrey Lando (*Savage Island*)
Honorable Mention, Director (Horror) ..... Mark Redfield (*Dr. Jekyll and Mr. Hyde*)
Best Picture, Feature (Science Fiction) ..... *Robot Stories*
Honorable Mention, Feature (Science Fiction) ..... *Corner of Your Eye*
Best Picture, Short (Science Fiction) ..... *Embryo*
Honorable Mention, Short (Science Fiction) ..... *Rosewood Avenue*
Honorable Mention, Short (Science Fiction) ..... *Hyte*
Best Picture, Mini-Short (Science Fiction) ..... *Time Copy*
Honorable Mention, Mini-Short (Science Fiction) ..... *Circle*
Honorable Mention, Mini-Short (Science Fiction) ..... *In/Out*
Best Actor (Science Fiction) ..... Sab Shimono (*Robot Stories*)
Honorable Mention, Actor (Science Fiction) ..... Greg Pak (*Robot Stories*)
Best Actress (Science Fiction) ..... Tamlyn Tomita (*Robot Stories*)
Honorable Mention, Actress (Science Fiction) ..... Wai Ching Ho (*Robot Stories*)
Best Director (Science Fiction) ..... Greg Pak (*Robot Stories*)
Honorable Mention, Director (Science Fiction) ..... Mario Coello (*Rosewood Avenue*)
Honorable Mention, Director (Science Fiction) ..... Mike Goedecke (*Embryo*)
Best Picture, Feature (Fantasy) ..... *Gory Gory Hallelujah*
Honorable Mention, Feature (Fantasy) ..... *Frazetta: Painting with Fire*
Best Picture, Short (Fantasy) ..... *Tao of the Meteor Serpent*
Best Picture, Mini-Short (Fantasy) ..... *String of the Kite*
Honorable Mention, Mini-Short (Fantasy) ..... *Bluefish*
Honorable Mention, Mini-Short (Fantasy) ..... *Hope*
Honorable Mention, Mini-Short (Fantasy) ..... *Professional Courtesy*
Best Actor (Fantasy) ..... John Schuck (*String of the Kite*)
Honorable Mention, Actor (Fantasy) ..... Henry Czerny (*Johnston ... Johnston*)
Best Actress (Fantasy) ..... Kathy Trageser (*Hope*)
Best Director (Fantasy) ..... Michael Fallavollita (*String of the Kite*)
Honorable Mention, Director (Fantasy) ..... Mark Price (*Professional Courtesy*)
Honorable Mention, Director (Fantasy) ..... Danishka Esterhazy (*Endings*)
Best Score, Feature (Fantasy) ..... (*Robot Stories*)
Honorable Mention, Score (Fantasy) ..... *Tao of the Meteor Serpent*
Best Score, Short Film (Fantasy) ..... *String of the Kite*
Honorable Mention, Score, Short Film (Fantasy) ..... *Trippin'*
Best Screenplay (Fantasy) (unproduced) ..... Jeremy Rubin and Gary M. Lumpp (*Sk8r 666*)
Honorable Mention, Screenplay (Fantasy) (unproduced) ..... Michael Kazlo (*Bloodlust*)
Rising Star ..... Kevin DeSimone
Director's Choice ..... Brinke Stevens

Shockfest

2010

Shocker Award ..... *Anti-Samaritan Hotline*
Best Shockingly Scary Short ..... *Tombstone Brides*
Best Shockingly Silly Short ..... *April*
Best Documentary Short ..... *Domace je najbolje*
Best Director ..... Alex Ferarri (*Red Princess Blues*)
Best Writer ..... Federico D'Alessandro, Christopher Ryan Yeazel (*Recollection*)
Best Cinematographer ..... Daniel Ainsworth (*Recollection*)
Best Editor ..... Coral D'Alessandro (*Recollection*)
Best Visual Effects ..... *Tombstone Brides*
Best Music Video ..... "Kill for You" (Dawn Cobalt)
Best Actor ..... Jeremy Jackson (*Tombstone Brides*)
Best Actress ..... Rachel Grant (*Red Princess Blues*)
Monster Character Award ..... Aimee-Lynn Chadwick (*A Killer App*)
Sexiest Shockfest Sweetheart ..... Jackie Nico ("Kill for You")
Best Fight Sequence ..... *Red Princess Blues*
Audience Award ..... *A Killer App*
Best Haunted Experience Design Award ..... Shane Womboldt, Sean Enns
Miss Shockfest ..... Erendira Ibarra

2009

Shocker Award for Overall Excellence ..... *Loma Lynda: The Red Door*
Best Shockingly Scary Short ..... *Stink Meat*
Best Shockingly Silly Short ..... *The Ballad of Angel Face*
Best Cinematography ..... Michael Alba (*Liminal*)
Best Writer ..... Spence Griffith (*The Family Recipes*)
Best Director ..... Michael Regalbuto (*The Embalmer*)
Best Actor ..... David Fine (*Loma Lynda: The Red Door*)
Best Actress ..... Estefania Iglesias (*Loma Lynda: The Red Door*)
Best Music Video ..... *Booty Sex*
Audience Choice Award ..... *Booty Sex*
Best Haunted House Design ..... *The Hall!*
Miss Shockfest ..... Jeri Lynn Thompson

2008

Shocker Award for Overall Excellence ..... *Excision*
Best Feature ..... *Blood on the Highway*
Best Short ..... *Soylent Red*
Miss Shockfest ..... Claudia Yvonne

2007

Miss Shockfest ..... Leticia Prado

Shriekfest

A.K.A. Shriekfest Horror/SciFi Film Festival & Screenplay Competition. Presents the Shriekfest Tombstone trophy. Its Pretty Scary Award (no longer extant) was sponsored and chosen by Pretty-Scary.net.

2010

Best Horror Feature Film ..... *Ashes*
Best Sci-Fi Feature Film ..... *Transfer*
Best Super Short Film ..... *Rise of the Appliances*
Best Short Film ..... *Serum 1831*
Best Under 18 Film ..... *On the Other Line*
Audience Choice ..... *Grey Skies*
Best Webisode ..... *Shady Texas*
Best Original Song ..... *Rekindled*
Best Feature Screenplay (unproduced) ..... *Dead Crows*
Best Under 18 Screenplay (unproduced) ..... *Ain't No Wolves 'Round Here*
Best Short Screenplay (unproduced) ..... *Carbon Dating*

2009

Best Horror Feature Film ..... *Dark House* (dir: Darin Scott)
Best Fantasy Feature Film ..... *Spike* (dir: Robert Beaucage)
Best Horror Short Film ..... *Death in Charge* (dir: Devi Snively)
Best Sci-Fi Short Film ..... *Enigma* (dir: The Shumway Brothers)
Best Super Short Film ..... *Rift* (dir: Andrew Huang)
Pretty Scary Award ..... *Death in Charge* (dir: Devi Snively)
Best Acting Performance ..... Dameon Clarke (*How to Be a Serial Killer*)
Audience Choice Award ..... *Lo* (dir: Travis Betz)
Best Under 18 Film/Screenplay ..... *Lock (ed) In* (dir: Lea McMahan; script: Peter Jones, McKenzie Cupp, Molly Morgan, Katie Herbst, Ali Gianutsos, Jean Jamison)
Best Horror Feature Screenplay (unproduced) ..... *Dead After Tomorrow* (written by Benjamin Pollack)
Best Sci-Fi Feature Screenplay (unproduced) ..... *Upgrade* (written by Louis Rosenberg)
Best Short Screenplay (unproduced) ..... *Seekers* (written by L.C. Cruell)

2008

Best Horror Feature Film ..... *Bane* (dir: James Eaves)
Best Thriller Feature Film ..... *Alien Raiders* (dir: Ben Rock)
Best Short Film ..... *Kirksdale* (dir: Ryan Spindell)
Best Super Short Film ..... *Eel Girl* (dir: Paul Campion)
Pretty Scary Award ..... *Side Effect* (dir: Liz Adams)
Best Acting Performance ..... Rhoda Jordan (*Rule of Three*)
Audience Choice Award ..... *The Open Door* (dir: Doc Duhame)
Best Under 18 Film ..... *The Perfect Victim* (dir: Eric Badger)
Best Under 18 Screenplay (unproduced) ..... *Big Kids Play Manslaughter* (Kelsey Bollig)
Best Horror Feature Screenplay (unproduced) ..... *The Great American Nightmare* (Tom Manning)
Best Sci-Fi Feature Screenplay (unproduced) ..... *Scavengers* (Diana Kemp-Jones)
Best Fantasy Feature Screenplay (unproduced) ..... *The Hercynian Ocrhid* (Melisa Ford)
Best Short Screenplay (unproduced) ..... *Making the List* (Jesse Kyle Reisman)

2007

Best Feature Film ..... *The Chair* (dir: Brett Sullivan)
Best Super Short Film ..... *No Sanctuary* (dir: Dan Lovallo)
Best Short Film ..... *A.W.O.L.* (dir: Jack Swanstrom)
Pretty Scary Award ..... *The Cellar Door* (dir: Matt Zettell)
Best Cinematography ..... *Death's Requiem* (DP: Carl Robertson; dir: Marc Furmie)

Audience Choice Award ..... *The Cellar Door* (dir: Matt Zettell)
Best Acting Performance ..... James DuMont (*The Cellar Door*)
Best Special Effects in a Feature Film ..... *Atom Nine Adventures* (dir: Christopher Farley)
Best Special Effects in a Short Film ..... *Postcards from the Future* (dir: Alan Chan)
Best Key Art Award ..... *Zombie Love*
2nd Place Key Art Award ..... *House of Fears*
Best under 18 Film ..... *Vanilla County* (dir: Nick Diramio)
Best under 18 Screenplay (unproduced) ..... *Empire of Wonders* (David Siudzinski)
Best Feature Screenplay (unproduced) ..... *The Lost Girl* (Michael Mongillo)
2nd Place Feature Screenplay (unproduced) ..... *Horror World* (Rolfe Kanefsky)
Best Short Screenplay (unproduced) ..... *Safe Passage* (Michael Raymond)

2006

Best Horror Feature Film ..... *The Other Side* (dir: Gregg Bishop)
2nd Place Horror Feature Film ..... *Unrest* (dir: Jason Todd Ipson)
Best Super Short Film ..... *Itsy Bitsy* (dir: David May)
2nd Place Super Short Film ..... *The Boarder* (dir: Susan Bell)
Best Horror Short Film ..... *Penny Dreadful* [the Short] (dir: Bryan Norton)
2nd Place Horror Short Film ..... *Avatar* (dir: Lluís Quílez)
Best Cinematography ..... *Penny Dreadful* [the feature] (dir: Richard Brandes)
Best Special Effects ..... *Itsy Bitsy* (dir: David May)
Best Makeup Effects ..... *Night of the Dead: Leben Tod* (dir: Eric Forsberg)
Best Acting Performance ..... Amy Beth Sherman (*Desperation*)
Audience Choice Award ..... *Bad Reputation* (dir: Jimmy Hemphill)
Best Under 18 Film ..... *Repossessed* (dir: Dustin Murphy)
Best Feature Screenplay (unproduced) ..... *The Next Plane* (Christopher Moro)
2nd Place Feature Screenplay (unproduced) ..... *Reincarnate* (Carl Melchior)
3rd Place Feature Screenplay (unproduced) ..... *I, Detective* (Dean Alioto)
Best Short Screenplay (unproduced) ..... *Adrian of Death* (Terence Brody)
2nd Place Short Screenplay ..... *The Last Request* (Joe Randazzo)

2005

Best Horror Feature Film ..... *Dark Remains* (dir: Brian Avenet-Bradley)
Best Sci-Fi Feature Film ..... *Experiment* (dir: Daniel Turner)
Best Thriller Feature Film ..... *Razor Eaters* (dir: Shannon Young)
Best Horror Short Film ..... *We All Fall Down* (Jake Kennedy)
Best Sci-Fi Short Film ..... *Apartment 206* (dir: Gregory Zymet)
Best Thriller Short Film ..... *1309* (dir: Christian Davis)
Best Super Short Film ..... *Into the Maelstrom* (dir: Peter Sullivan)
Best Under 18 Film ..... *Sinners* (dir: Michael DeVeau)
Best Director ..... Hurt McDermott (*Nightingale in a Music Box*)
Best Actor ..... Richard Cawthorne (*Razor Eaters*)
Best Actress ..... April Adamson (*Descent*)
Best Ensemble Cast ..... *Sharkskin 6*
Best Editing in a Feature Film ..... *The Passing*
Best Editing in a Short Film ..... *The Absence of Emily*
Best Cinematography ..... *WithIn*, A.K.A. *The Cavern*
Best Makeup/Special FX ..... *Guardian of the Realm*
Best Music ..... *Sharkskin 6*
Fan Favorite ..... *WithIn*, A.K.A. *The Cavern* (dir: Olatunde Osunsanmi)
Special Mention Award ..... Olatunde Osunsanmi (first time feature director, *WithIn*)
Best Feature Screenplay (unproduced) ..... *The Bond of Saint Marcel* (Jennifer Quintenz)
2nd Place Feature Screenplay (unproduced) ..... *Utterson* (Nathan Hill & Nick Levy)
Best Short Screenplay (unproduced) ..... *Details* (Thomas Hill)

2004

Best Horror Feature Film ..... *Dead and Breakfast* (dir: Matthew Leutwyler)
Best Sci-Fi Feature Film ..... *Tales from Beyond* (dir: Josh Austin, Nate Barlow, Eric Manning, Russell Scott)
Best Horror Short Film ..... *Roadside Attractions* (dir: CJ Roy)
2nd Place Horror Short Film ..... *A Visit from the Sergeant Major with Unintended Consequences* (dir: Don Hannah)
3rd Place Horror Short Film ..... *Husk* (dir: Brett Simmons)
Best Sci-Fi Short Film ..... *A Can of Paint* (Winston Engle)
2nd Place Sci-Fi Short Film ..... *Perfect Sec-Illusion* (dir: Jeremy Pollack)
Best Super Short Film ..... *The G.I.* (dir: Mike Nelson)
2nd Place Super Short Film ..... *Sawbones* (dir: Brad Palmer)
Fan Favorite ..... *Roadside Attractions* (dir: CJ Roy)

Best Under 18 Film ..... *Semi-Colon* (dir: Matt Porter, with Drew Lewis)
Fan Favorite ..... *Roadside Attractions* (dir: CJ Roy)
Special Award ..... James Kassier (*Deja Vu Deception*)
Best Under 18 Screenplay (unproduced) ..... *Safe in the House* (Katherine Morton)
Best Horror Feature Screenplay (unproduced) ..... *Retard* (Christopher Alan Broadstone, John Franklin)
2nd Place Horror Feature Screenplay (unproduced) ..... *Scary Larry* (Hamilton Underwood)
Best Sci-Fi Feature Screenplay (unproduced) ..... *First Born* (Michael C. McPherson)
Best Short Screenplay (unproduced) ..... *Still Life* (Charles Johnston)
2nd Place Short Screenplay (unproduced) ..... *Outside the Lines* (John Sullivan)

2003

Best Film in the Feature Category ..... *Lucky* (dir: Steve Cuden)
2nd Place in the Feature Category ..... *Next Victim* (dir: Timothy Gates, Jeff Solano, Michael Chamberlain)
Best Film in the Short Horror Category ..... *Black Gulch* (dir: Michael Strode)
2nd Place in the Short Horror Category ..... *My Skin* (dir: Christopher Alan Broadstone)
3rd Place in the Short Horror Category ..... *On Edge* (dir: Frazer Lee)
Best Film in the Sci-Fi Category ..... *Transfer* (dir: John Turbyne)
2nd Place in the Sci-Fi Category ..... *Robot Rumpus* (dir: Jason Dunn)
Best Film in the Super Short Category ..... *Paper or Plastic?* (dir: Blake Horobin)
2nd Place in the Super Short Category ..... *Final Appointment* (dir: Michelle Deal)
Fan Favorite ..... *Lucky* (dir: Steve Cuden)
Best Screenplay in the Feature Category ..... *Bathory* (James D. Clayton)
2nd Place Screenplay in the Feature Category ..... *Gomorrah* (Phil Penningroth)
3rd Place Screenplay in the Feature Category ..... *Ark* (Alan Chan)
4th Place Screenplay in the Feature Category ..... *The Shepherd* (Ryan Golembeske, Ezra Werb)
Best Feature Screenplay in the Under 18 Category ..... *My Boyfriend's Back* (Stephanie Wood)
Best Screenplay in the Short Category ..... *Dead Sober* (Stephan A. Foley)
2nd Place Screenplay in the Short Category ..... *Eyewitness* (Gary Davidson)

2002

Best Film in the Feature Category ..... *Terror Tract* (dir: Clint Hutchison, Lance W. Dreeson)
2nd Place in the Feature Category ..... *Dr. Jekyll and Mr. Hyde* (dir: Mark Redfield)
Best Film in the Short Category ..... *Blood on the Backlot* (dir: Michelle Deal)
2nd Place in Short Category ..... *Human* (dir: CJ Roy)
Best Comedy Horror ..... *Burning Passion* (dir: Brian Belefant)
Best Special FX in the Feature Category ..... *Despiser* (dir: Philip Cook)
Best Special FX in the Short Category ..... *Samuel* (dir: Jody Fedele)
Fan Favorite ..... *Hell's Highway* (dir: S. Lee Taylor)
Shriekfest Award ..... Mark Redfield
Best Feature Screenplay (unproduced) ..... *Cruel Logic* (Brian Godawa)
Best Short Screenplay (unproduced) ..... *Lost Night* (Michael Trentacosti)
2nd Place Screenplay (unproduced) ..... *Thy Neighbor's Wife* (Michael C. McPherson)
3rd Place Screenplay (unproduced) ..... *Mastering Chauncey* (Lawrence Monaco)
4th Place Screenplay (unproduced) ..... *Happy Jack* (Eric Frost Barnes)

2001

Youngest Director ..... *The Monster Killers* (Nicholas Robert Bryan)
Best Film in the Thriller Category ..... *Siren* (Steve Morris)
Best Film in the Feature Category ..... *The Wind* (Michael Mongillo)
Best Film in the Short Category ..... *When Zombies Attack* (Chad Waters, Matt Rose)
Scariest Film ..... *Memorial Day* (Marcos Gabriel, Chris Alender)
Best Makeup/Special FX for a Feature ..... *Things II* (Mike Bowler, Steve Jarvis, Dennis Devine)
Best Makeup for a Short ..... *When Zombies Attack* (Chad Waters, Matt Rose)
Best Special FX for a Short ..... *Y2K: Shutdown Detected* (Slava Siederman, John Gonzales, Trent Shumway)
Most Unique ..... *Stop It, You're Killing Me* (Kenny Yakkel)
Fan Favorite for Saturday Night ..... *Y2K: Shutdown Detected* (Slava Siederman, John Gonzales, Trent Shumway)
Fan Favorite for Sunday Night ..... *Memorial Day* (Marcos Gabriel and Chris Alender)
Best Screenplay (unproduced) ..... *Karma* (Jacqueline McKinley)

SITGES: Festival Internacional de Cinema Fantàstic de Catalunya

Its website lists no awards for its first three award years: 1968, 1969, 1970. From 1968 to

1972 Sitges was called the Semana Internacional de cine Fantástico y de Terror. From 1973 to 1982 it was Festival Internacional de Cinema Fantàstic i de Terror. From 1983 to 1996: Festival Internacional de Cinema Fantàstic de Sitges. It assumed its current name in 1997. Its awards' names have likewise changed over the years.

43rd—2010

Oficial Fantàstic Competició Sitges 43, Best Motion Picture ..... *Rare Exports: A Christmas Tale* (Jalmari Helander)
Oficial Fantàstic Competició Sitges 43, Special Jury Award ..... *We Are the Night* (Dennis Gansel)
Oficial Fantàstic Competició Sitges 43, Best Director ..... Jalmari Helander (*Rare Exports: A Christmas Tale*)
Oficial Fantàstic Competició Sitges 43, Best Actor ..... Patrick Fabian (*The Last Exorcism*)
Oficial Fantàstic Competició Sitges 43, Best Actress ..... Josie Ho (*Dream Home*)
Oficial Fantàstic Competició Sitges 43, Best Script ..... Nicolás Goldbart (*Fase 7*)
Oficial Fantàstic Competició Sitges 43, Best Production Design ..... Yuji Hayashida (*Thirteen Assassins*)
Oficial Fantàstic Competició Sitges 43, Best Make Up FX ..... Vitaya Deerattakul and Andrew Lin (*Dream Home*)
Oficial Fantàstic Competició Sitges 43, Best Special Effects ..... Gareth Edwards (*Monsters*)
Oficial Fantàstic Competició Sitges 43, Best Original Soundtrack ..... Seppuku Paradigm and Alex & Willie Cortes (*Nuits rouges du bourreau de jade*, A.K.A. *Red Nights*)
Oficial Fantàstic Competició Sitges 43, Best Cinematography ..... Mika Orasmaa (*Rare Exports: A Christmas Tale*)
Oficial Fantàstic Competició Sitges 43, Best Short Film ..... *The Legend of Beaver Dam* (Jérôme Sable)
Oficial Fantàstic Competició Sitges 43, Special Mention ..... *Vicenta* (Sam Millor)
Oficial Fantàstic Competició Panorama, Best Motion Picture ..... *Tucker & Dale vs. Evil* (Eli Craig)
Oficial Fantàstic Competició Panorama, Best Short Film ..... *The Familiar* (Kody Zimmermann)
Carnet Jove Jury, Best Motion Picture, Fantàstic ..... *Rubber* (Quentin Dupieux)
Carnet Jove Jury, Best Motion Picture, Midnight X-Treme ..... *Mutant Girls Squad* (Noboru Iguchi, Yoshihiro Nishimura, Tak Sakaguchi)
Noves Visions, SEAT, Best Motion Picture ..... *Simon Werner a disparu*, A.K.A. *Lights Out* (Fabrice Gobert)
Noves Visions, SEAT, Special Mention ..... *Sound of Noise* (Ola Simonsson, Johannes Stjarne Nilsson)
Noves Visions, SEAT, Special Mention ..... *5150, Rue des Ormes*, A.K.A. *5150 Elm's Way* (Éric Tessier)
Noves Visions, SEAT, Non-Fiction Motion Picture Diploma ..... *Vampires* (Vincent Lannoo)
Noves Visions, SEAT, Discovery Motion Picture Diploma ..... *Tony* (Gerard Johnson)
Casa Àsia ..... Best Motion Picture ..... *Cold Fish* (Sion Sono)
Nova Autoria SGAE Award, Best Director ..... Sílvia Subirós (*La edad del sol*)
Nova Autoria SGAE Award, Best Screenplay ..... Jaime Serrano (*La Lona*)
Nova Autoria SGAE Award, Best Original Score ..... Gonçal Perales Roy (*The Smiley*)
Anima't, Gertie Award, Best Animated Film ..... *Jackboots on Whitehall* (Edward McHenry, Rory McHenry)
Anima't, Gertie Award, Best Animated Short Film ..... *Une nouvelle vie!*, A.K.A. *A New Life!* (Fred Joyeux)
Anima't, Gertie Award, Best Animated Feature for Kids ..... *The Ugly Duckling* (Garri Bardin)
Audience Award el Periódico de Catalunya, Best Motion Picture ..... *Thirteen Assassins* (Takashi Miike)
Méliès d'Argent for Best European Motion Picture ..... *Rubber* (Quentin Dupieux)
Méliès d'Argent, Special Mention ..... *Rare Exports: A Christmas Tale* (Jalmari Helander)
Méliès d'Argent for Best European Short Film ..... *Les bessones del carrer de Ponent* (Marc Riba, Anna Solanas)
Méliès d'Or for Best European Motion Picture ..... *Buried* (Rodrigo Cortés)
Méliès d'Or for Best European Short Film ..... *El ataque de los robots de nebulosa-5* (Chema García Ibarra)
Jose Luis Guarner Critic Award ..... *Uncle Boonmee Who Can Recall His Past Lives* (Apichatpong Weerasethakul)
Citizen Kane Award to an Up-and-Coming Director ..... Quentin Dupieux (*Rubber*)
Brigadoon Paul Naschy Award, Best short film ..... *St. Christophorus Roadkill* (Gregor Erler)

42nd—2009

Oficial Fantàstic, Best Motion Picture ..... *Moon* (Duncan Jones)
Oficial Fantàstic, Special Jury Award ..... *Enter the Void* (Gaspar Noé)
Oficial Fantàstic, Best Director ..... Brillante Mendoza (*Kinatay*)
Oficial Fantàstic, Best Actor ..... Sam Rockwell (*Moon*)

Oficial Fantàstic, Best Actress (tie) ..... Elena Anaya (*Hierro*) and Kim Ok-bin (*Thirst*)
Oficial Fantàstic, Best Script ..... Nathan Parker, based on the original story of Duncan Jones (*Moon*)
Oficial Fantàstic, Best Cinematography ..... Benoit Debie (*Enter the Void*)
Oficial Fantàstic, Best Original Soundtrack ..... Teresa Barrozo (*Kinatay*)
Oficial Fantàstic, Best Special Effects ..... C.O.R.E. Digital Pictures, Mac Guff, BUF (*Splice*)
Oficial Fantàstic, Best Make Up FX ..... Kaatje Van Damme (*Mr. Nobody*)
Oficial Fantàstic, Best Production Design ..... Tony Noble (*Moon*)
Oficial Fantàstic, Best Short Film ..... *One of Those Days* (Hattie Dalton)
Oficial Fantàstic, Special Mention ..... *The Boy Who Wouldn't Kill* (Linus de Paoli)
Carnet Jove Jury, Best Motion Picture, Fantàstic (tie) ..... *Dogtooth*, A.K.A. *Canino* (Yorgos Lanthimos) and *Les derniers jours du monde* (Arnaud Larrieu, Jean-Marie Larrieu)
Carnet Jove Jury, Best Motion Picture, Midnight X-Treme ..... *Wasting Away* (Matthew Kohnen)
Noves Visions SEAT, Best Motion Picture ..... *Deliver Us from Evil* (Ole Bornedal)
Noves Visions SEAT, Special Mention ..... *Van Diemen's Land* (Jonathan auf der Heide)
Noves Visions SEAT, Non-Fiction Motion Picture Diploma ..... *Best Worst Movie* (Michael Paul Stephenson)
Noves Visions SEAT, Discovery Motion Picture Diploma ..... *Amer* (Hélène Cattet and Bruno Forzani)
Premio Nova Autoria SGAE Award, Best Director ..... *Swingers* (Javier Rodríguez Espinosa)
Premio Nova Autoria SGAE Award, Best Screenplay ..... *44987373-V* (Robert Ors Griera)
Premio Nova Autoria SGAE Award, Best Original Score ..... *The Last Drag* (Gonçal Perales Roy)
Premio Nova Autoria SGAE Award, Special Mention for the global quality of the piece ..... *Pin up* (Tania Verduzco)
Orient Express/Casa Àsia, Best Motion Picture ..... *IP Man* (Yip Wai-shun)
Anima't, Gertie Award, Best Animated Film ..... *Summer Wars* (Mamoru Hosoda)
Anima't, Gertie Award, Best Animated Short Film ..... *Le petit dragon* (Bruno Collet)
Anima't, Gertie Award, Best Animated Feature Film for Kids ..... *Panique au village* (Stéphane Aubier and Vincent Patar)
Méliès d'Argent for Best European Motion Picture ..... *The Eclipse* (Conor McPherson)
Méliès d'Argent for Best European Short Film ..... *One of Those Days* (Hattie Dalton)
Méliès d'Or for Best European Motion Picture ..... *Martyrs* (Pascal Laugier)
Méliès d'Or for Best European Short Film ..... *Cold and Dry* (Kristoffer Joner, Bjørn Arne Odden)
Audience Award el Periódico de Catalunya, Best Motion Picture ..... *Zombieland* (Ruben Fleischer)
Jose Luis Guarner Critic Award ..... *Les derniers jours du monde* (Arnaud Larrieu, Jean-Marie Larrieu)
Citizen Kane Award to an Up-and-Coming Director ..... *Dogtooth* A.K.A. *Canino* (Yorgos Lanthimos)
Brigadoon Paul Naschy Award, Best Short Film ..... *Torbellino de hostias* (Adrián Cardona)
Ben & Jerry's Award ..... *[REC] 2* (Jaume Balagueró, Paco Plaza)

41st— 2008

Oficial Fantàstic, Best Motion Picture ..... *Surveillance* (Jennifer Lynch)
Oficial Fantàstic, Special Jury Award ..... *Eden Lake* (James Watkins)
Oficial Fantàstic, Best Director ..... Kim Jee-woon (*The Good, the Bad, the Weird*)
Oficial Fantàstic, Best Actor ..... Brian Cox (*Red*)
Oficial Fantàstic, Best Actress ..... Semra Turan (*Fighter*)
Oficial Fantàstic, Best Script ..... Alexis Alexiou (*Tale 52*)
Oficial Fantàstic, Best Cinematography ..... Angus Hudson (*The Broken*)
Oficial Fantàstic, Best Production Design ..... Tulé Peak (*Blindness*)
Oficial Fantàstic, Best Make Up FX ..... Benoît Lestang, Adrien Morot (*Martyrs*)
Oficial Fantàstic, Best Special Effects ..... Jung Do-Ahn (*The Good, the Bad, the Weird*)
Oficial Fantàstic, Best Original Soundtrack ..... Kenji Kawai (*The Sky Crawlers*)
Oficial Fantàstic, Best Short Film ..... *Next Floor* (Denis Villeneuve)
Oficial Fantàstic, Jury Special Mention to the Short Film ..... *Centigrade* (Collin Cunningham)
Carnet Jove Jury, Best Motion Picture, Fantàstic (tie) ..... *The Sky Crawlers* (Mamoru Oshii) and *Vinyan* (Fabrice du Welz)
Carnet Jove Jury, Best Motion Picture, Midnight X-Treme ..... *Encarnaçaô do Demônio* (José Mojica Marins)
Noves Visions SEAT, Best Motion Picture ..... *Los Bastardos* (Amat Escalante)
Noves Visions SEAT, Special Mention ..... *God's Puzzle* (Takashi Miike)
Noves Visions SEAT, Non Fiction Motion Picture Diploma ..... *Religulous* (Larry Charles)
Noves Visions SEAT, Discovery Motion Picture Diploma ..... *Ramírez* (Albert Arizza)
Premio Nova Autoria SGAE, Best Director ..... Dögg Mósesdóttir (*Eyja*)

Premio Nova Autoria SGAE, Best Screenplay ..... Dea Pompa (*Restaurando a Héctor*)
Premio Nova Autoria SGAE, Best Original Score ..... Hilmar Örn Hilmarsson and Örn Eldjàrn (*Eyja*)
Orient Express/Casa Àsia, Best Motion Picture ..... *The Chaser* (Na Hong-jin)
Anima't, Gertie Award, Best Animated Film ..... *From Inside* (John Bergin)
Anima't, Gertie Award, Best Animated Short Film ..... *The Facts in the Case of Mr. Hollow* (Rodrigo Gudiño & Vincent Marcone)
Brigadoon Paul Naschy, Best Short Film ..... *La Victoria de Félix* (Jordi Pastor, Albert Miró)
Méliès d'Argent for Best European Motion Picture ..... *Martyrs* (Pascal Laugier)
Méliès d'Argent for Best European Short Film ..... *Afterville* (Fabio Guaglione & Fabio Resinaro)
Méliès d'Or for Best European Motion Picture ..... *Let the Right One In* (Tomas Alfredson)
Méliès d'Or for Best European Short Film ..... *Of Cats & Women* (Jonas Govaerts)
Audience Award el Periódico de Catalunya, Best Motion Picture ..... *Blindness* (Fernando Meirelles)
Jose Luis Guarner Critic Award ..... *The Sky Crawlers* (Mamoru Oshii)
Citizen Kane Award to an Up-and-Coming Director ..... *Home Movie* (Christopher Denham)

40th — 2007

Oficial Fantàstic, Best Motion Picture ..... *The Fall* (Tarsem Singh)
Oficial Fantàstic, Best Director ..... Jaume Balaguero, Paco Plaza *[fflREC]*
Oficial Fantàstic, Best Actress ..... Manuela Velasco *[fflREC]*
Oficial Fantàstic, Best Actor ..... Sam Rockwell (*Joshua, El Hijo del Mal*)
Oficial Fantàstic, Best Script ..... Chung Seo-Kyung, Park Chan-Wook (*I'm a Cyborg but That's OK*)
Oficial Fantàstic, Best Cinematography ..... Toyomichi Kurita (*Sukiyaki Western Django*)
Oficial Fantàstic, Best Production Design ..... Takashi Sasaki (*Sukiyaki Western Django*)
Oficial Fantàstic, Best Make Up FX ..... *À L'Intérieur*
Oficial Fantàstic, Best Special Effects ..... *Mushishi*
Oficial Fantàstic, Best Original Soundtrack ..... Kuniaki Haishima (*Mushishi*)
Oficial Fantàstic, Best Short Film ..... *Saliva* (Esmir Filho)
Carnet Jove Jury, Best Motion Picture, Fantàstic ..... *À L'Intérieur* (Julien Maury, Alexandre Bustillo)
Carnet Jove Jury, Best Motion Picture, Midnight X-Treme ..... *Jack Brooks: Monster Slayer* (Jon Knautz)
Noves Visions SEAT Jury, Best Motion Picture ..... *Zoo* (Robinson Devor)
Noves Visions SEAT Jury, Special Mention ..... *It Is Fine. Everything Is Fine!* (Crispin Hellion Glover & David Brothers)
Nova Autoria SGAE Award, Best Director ..... *Lizania* (Marta Palacín, Elisabet Sort)
Nova Autoria SGAE Award, Best Screenplay ..... *OP. 1207-x* (Julião Luciana)
Nova Autoria SGAE Award, Best Original Score ..... *Vestido Nuevo* (Roger Padilla)
Orient Express–Casa Àsia, Best Motion Picture ..... *Dororo* (Akihiko Shiota)
Orient Express–Casa Àsia, Special Mention ..... *Mad Detective* (Johnnie To, Ka-Fai Wai)
Anima't, Gertie Award, Best Animated Film ..... *Aachi & Ssipak* (Joe Bum-jin)
Anima't, Gertie Award, Special Mention ..... *Tekkonkinkreet* (Michael Arias)
Anima't, Gertie Award, Best Animated Short Film ..... *The Pearce Sisters* (Luis Cook)
Brigadoon Paul Naschy, Best Short Film ..... *Brico Killer* (Adrián Cardona)
Méliès d'Argent for Best European Motion Picture ..... *À L'Intérieur* (Julien Maury, Alexandre Bustillo)
Méliès d'Argent Special Mention ..... *[fflREC]* (Jaume Balaguero, Paco Plaza)
Méliès d'Argent for Best European Short Film ..... *Die Grosse Werkstatt (The Big Garage)* (Uwe Nagel)
Audience Award El Periódico de Catalunya, Best Motion Picture ..... *[fflREC]* (Jaume Balaguero, Paco Plaza)
Jose Luis Guarner Critic Award ..... *[fflREC]* (Jaume Balaguero, Paco Plaza)
Jose Luis Guarner Critic Award, Special Mention ..... George Ratliff (*Joshua, El Hijo del Mal*)
Citizen Kane Award to an Up-and-Coming Director ..... Julien Maury, Alexandre Bustillo (*À L'Intérieur*)

39th — 2006

Oficial Fantàstic, Best Short Film (tie) ..... *A For(r)est in the Des(s)ert* (Luiso Berdejo) and *Handyman* (Simon Rumley)
Oficial Fantàstic, Best Production Design ..... Are Sjaastad (*The Bothersome Man*)
Oficial Fantàstic, Best Make Up FX ..... Jang Jin (*Time*)
Oficial Fantàstic, Best Special Effects — Premio Infinia ..... Jang Heui-cheol (*The Host*)
Oficial Fantàstic, Best Original Soundtrack ..... East (*Tzameti (13)*)
Oficial Fantàstic, Best Cinematography ..... Jonathan Sela (*Grimm Love*)

Oficial Fantàstic, Best Script ..... Sam Hamm (*Homecoming (Masters of Horror)*)
Oficial Fantàstic, Best Actress ..... Sandra Hüller (*Requiem*)
Oficial Fantàstic, Best Actor (tie) ..... Thomas Kretschmann and Thomas Huber (*Grimm Love*)
Oficial Fantàstic, Best Director ..... Martin Weisz (*Grimm Love*)
Oficial Fantàstic, Special Jury Award ..... *Homecoming (Masters of Horror)* (Joe Dante)
Oficial Fantàstic, Best Motion Picture ..... *Requiem* (Hans-Christian Schmid)
Carnet Jove Jury, Fantàstic ..... *Exiled* (Johnnie To)
Carnet Jove Jury, Special Mention ..... *Cigarette Burns (Masters of Horror)* (John Carpenter)
Carnet Jove Jury, Midnight X-Treme ..... *What Is It?* (Crispin Glover)
Carnet Jove Jury, Special Mention ..... *Behind the Mask: The Rise of Leslie Vernon* (Scott Glosserman)
Noves Visions ..... *Edmond* (Stuart Gordon)
Noves Visions, Special Mention ..... *The Living and the Dead* (Simon Rumley)
Nova Autoria Award, Best Direction ..... Jorge Tur Moltó (*De Funcion*)
Nova Autoria Award, Best Script ..... David Jiménez, Rubén Molina, Albert Solà, Joseph Lluís Marín (*Bowman*)
Nova Autoria Award, Best Original Music ..... Roger Padilla (*No Quiero la Noche*)
Orient Express–Casa Àsia ..... *The Host* (Bong Joon-ho)
Animat, Premi Gertie, Best Animated Film ..... *The Girl Who Leapt Through Time* (Mamoru Hosoda)
Animat, Premi Gertie, Best Animated Short Film ..... *Dreams and Desires: Family Ties* (Joanna Quinn)
Animat, Premi Gertie, Special Mention ..... *The Book of the Dead* (Kihachiro Kawamoto)
Brigadoon Best Short Film ..... *Tight* (Sergio Vizcaíno)
Méliès d'Argent for Best European Motion Picture ..... *Princess* (Anders Morgenthaler)
Méliès d'Argent for Best European Short Film ..... *Doodle* (Sam Rogers)
Audience Award for Best Motion Picture ..... *La Ciencia del Sueno* (Michel Gondry)
Jose Luis Guarner Critic Award ..... *Requiem* (Hans-Christian Schmid)
Citizen Kane Award to an Up-and-Coming Director ..... Rian Johnson (*Brick*)

38th — 2005

Oficial Fantàstic, Best Short Film ..... *Respire* (Wi Ding Ho)
Oficial Fantàstic, Best Art Direction ..... Dave McKean (*Mirrormask*)
Oficial Fantàstic, Best Make Up FX ..... Michele Davidson Bell (*Mirrormask*)
Oficial Fantàstic, Best Special Effects ..... Thomas Mulack (*The Piano Tuner of Earthquakes*)
Oficial Fantàstic, Best Original Soundtrack ..... Dalpalan and Jang Yeong-gyu (*A Bittersweet Life*)
Oficial Fantàstic, Best Cinematography ..... Keung Kwok Man (*Seven Swords*)
Oficial Fantàstic, Best Script ..... Brian Nelson (*Hard Candy*)
Oficial Fantàstic, Best Actress ..... Lee Yeong-ae (*Sympathy for Lady Vengeance*)
Oficial Fantàstic, Best Actor ..... Lee Kang-sheng (*El Sabor de la Sandia*, A.K.A. *The Wayward Cloud*)
Oficial Fantàstic, Best Director ..... Johnnie To (*Election*)
Oficial Fantàstic, Special Jury Award ..... *El Sabor de la Sandia*, A.K.A. *The Wayward Cloud* (Tsai Ming-liang)
Oficial Fantàstic, Best Motion Picture ..... *Hard Candy* (David Slade)
Carnet Jove Jury, Fantastic ..... *Election* (Johnnie To)
Carnet Jove Jury, Midnight X-Treme ..... *The Dark Hours* (Paul Fox)
Carnet Jove Jury, Special Mention ..... *The Wild Blue Yonder* (Werner Herzog)
Noves Visions ..... *The Girl from Monday* (Hal Hartley)
Noves Visions, Special Mention ..... *Grizzly Man* (Werner Herzog)
Orient Express–Casa Àsia ..... *Antarctic Journal* (Yim Phil-sung)
Animat, Gertie Award, Best Animated Film ..... *The District* (Áron Gauder)
Animat, Gertie Award, Best Animated Short Film ..... *Cirkus* (Thomas Pors)
Brigadoon, Best Short Film ..... *Graveless* (Christian Ray)
Méliès d'Argent for Best European Motion Picture ..... *Trouble* (Harry Cleven)
Short Film nominee for Méliès d'Argent ..... *City Paradise* (Gäelle Denis)
Audience Award, Best Motion Picture ..... *Hard Candy* (David Slade)
Nova Autoria Award, Best Director ..... *La última Polaroid* (Mar Coll)
Nova Autoria Award, Best Script ..... *Sin Piedras* (Quim Fuster, Pau Iriarte)
Nova Autoria Award, Best Soundtrack ..... *14 apóstoles* (Oier Sarasúa)
Jose Luis Guarner Critic Award ..... *El Sabor de la Sandia*, A.K.A., *The Wayward Cloud* (Tsai Ming-liang)
Citizen Kane Award to an Up-and-Coming Director ..... *La Moustache* (Emmanuel Carrère)
Special Mention ..... *Zulo* (Carlos Martín Ferrera)

37th — 2004
Award "Maria Honorífica"

Best Film ..... *OldBoy* (dir: Park Chan-wook)
Best Director ..... Johnnie To (*Breaking News*)
Best Actor ..... Christian Bale (*The Machinist*)
Best Actress ..... Mónica López (*El habitante incierto*)
Best Cinematography ..... Xavi Giménez (*The Machinist*)
Best Script ..... Frank Cottrell Boyce (*Code 46*)
Best Original Soundtrack ..... Joshua Hyams, Mark Revel, "The Free Association" (*Code 46*)
Best FX ..... *Izo* (dir: Takashi Miike)
Best Make Up FX ..... *Three ... Extremes* (dir: Takashi Miike, Fruit Chan, Park Chan-wook)
Best Art Direction ..... Javier Alvariño, Daniel Izar (*The Birthday*)
Best Short Film ..... *The Ten Steps* (dir: Brendan Muldowney)
Gertie Award Best Animation Film ..... *Steamboy* (dir: Katsuhiro Otomo)
Orient Express–Casa Asia Award ..... *Innocence: Ghost in the Shell 2* (dir: Mamoru Oshii)
Gertie Award, Best Animation Short Film ..... *Le Régulateur* (dir: Philippe Grammaticopoulos)
Best European Fantasy Film ..... *Code 46* (dir: Michael Winterbottom)
Best European Short Film ..... *El soñador* (dir: Oskar Santos)
Citizen Kane Award for Best New Director ..... Anders Rønnow Klarlund (*Strings*)
Nova Autoria Award, Best Music ..... Francisco García (*Vidas en Flamenco*)
Nova Autoria Award, Best Script ..... *La ruta natural*
Nova Autoria Award Millor Best Director ..... Alba Mora, Anna SanMartí (*Memories Without Remember*)
Time Machine Honorary Award ..... John Landis, Paul Naschy, Joel Schumacher
Honorary Award "La General" ..... Andrew Lloyd Webber
Brigadoon Award Best Short Film ..... *Amazing Unmasked vs. El Eoctor Calavera Maligna* (dir: Dani Moreno)

36th — 2003
Award "Maria Honorífica"

Best Film ..... *Zatoichi* (dir: Takeshi Kitano)
Best Director ..... Alexandre Aja (*Haute Tension*)
Best Actor ..... Robert Downey, Jr. (*The Singing Detective*)
Best Actress ..... Cécile de France (*Haute Tension*)
Best Cinematography ..... Decha Seementa (*The Tesseract*)
Best Script ..... Michael Haneke (*Le Temps du Loup*)
Best Original Soundtrack ..... Keitchi Suzuki (*Zatoichi*)
Best Make-Up ..... Giannetto De Rossi (*Haute Tension*)
Best Visual Effects ..... *Gozu* (dir: Takashi Miike)
Best Art Direction ..... Scott Gallagher (*The Texas Chainsaw Massacre*)
Best Short Film ..... *El tren de la bruja* (dir: Koldo Serra)
Anima't Award Best Animation Short Film ..... *Mantis* (dir: Jordi Moragues)
Orient Express–Casa Àsia Award ..... *Ong-bak* (dir: Prachya Pinkaew)
Orient Express–Casa Àsia Award Special Mention ..... *Tokyo Godfathers* (dir: Satoshi Kon)
Audience Award (tie) ..... *Zatoichi* (dir: Takeshi Kitano) and *Kill Bill vol. 1* (dir: Quentin Tarantino)
Audience Award Best Feature Animation Film ..... *Tokyo Godfathers* (dir: Satoshi Kon)
Audience Award Best Animation Short Film ..... *Harvie Krumpet* (dir: Adam Elliot)
Audience Award Best Film New Visions ..... *Ascension* (dir: Karim Hussain)
Audience Award Best Film New Visions, Special Mention ..... *All Tomorrow's Parties* (dir: Yu Lik Wai)
Citizen Kane Award for Best New Director ..... Lee Soo-yuon (*The Uninvited*)
Best European Fantasy Film ..... *Haute Tension* (dir: Alexandre Aja)
Best European Fantasy Short Film Award ..... *El tren de la bruja* (dir: Koldo Serra)
Critic's Award "Jose Luis Guarner" ..... *Le temps du loup* (dir: Michael Haneke)
Critic's Award "Jose Luis Guarner" Special Mention ..... *Twenty-Nine Palms* (dir: Bruno Dumont)
Time Machine Honorary Award ..... Stan Winston, Stuart Gordon, Brian Yuzna, Tobe Hooper, Takashi Miike
Maria honorifica ..... Narciso Ibáñez Serrador

35th — 2002
Award "Maria Honorífica"

Best Film ..... *Dracula: Pages from a Virgin's Diary* (dir: Guy Maddin)
Best Director ..... David Cronenberg (*Spider*)
Best Actor ..... Jeremy Northam (*Cypher*)
Best Actress ..... Angela Bettis (*May*)
Best Cinematography ..... Decha Srimantra (*The Eye*)
Best Script ..... Lucky McKee (*May*)
Best Original Soundtrack ..... Sonic Youth (*Demonlover*)
Best Make-Up ..... Robert Kurtzman, Greg Nicotero, Howard Berger (*Cabin Fever*)
Best Visual Effects ..... Richard R. Hoover (*Reign of Fire*, A.K.A. *El imperio del fuego*)
Best Short Film ..... *La chambre jaune* (dir: Hélène Cattet, Bruno Forzani)

Best Animation Short Films ..... *La mort de Tau* (dir: Jérôme Boulbès)
Orient Express Award (tie) ..... *Araburu tamashii-tachi*, A.K.A. *Agitator* (dir: Takashi Miike) and *Na Bdun–Nam-Ja*, A.K.A. *Bad Guy* (dir: Kim Ki-duk)
Audience Award Best Animation Film ..... *Mercano el marciano* (dir: Juan Antin)
Audience Award Best Animation Short Film ..... *Last Rumba in Rochdale* (dir: John Chorlton)
Best Film, Gran Angular ..... *Cravan vs. Cravan* (dir: Isaki Lacuesta)
Citizen Kane Award for Best New Director ..... Isaki Lacuesta (*Cravan vs. Cravan*)
Best European Fantasy Film ..... *El segundo nombre* (dir: Paco Plaza)
Best European Fantasy Short Film Award ..... *Cry for Bobo* (dir: David Cairns)
Critic's Award "Jose Luis Guarner" ..... *Demonlover* (dir: Olivier Assayas)
Time Machine Honorary Award ..... David Cronenberg, Guillermo del Toro
Honorary Award "La General" ..... Dino de Laurentiis

34th — 2001
Award "Maria Honorífica"

Best Film ..... *Vidocq* (dir: Pitof)
Best Director ..... Brad Anderson (*Session 9*)
Best Actor ..... Eduard Fernández (*Fausto 5.0*)
Best Actress ..... Yuki Amami (*Inugami*)
Best Cinematography ..... Grzegorz Kedzierski (*Avalon*)
Best Script ..... Richard Kelly (*Donnie Darko*)
Best Original Soundtrack ..... Bruno Coulais (*Vidocq*)
Best Make-Up ..... *Vidocq*
Millors Efectes Visuals ..... Pitof (*Vidocq*)
Best Short Film (tie) ..... *In Absentia* (dir: Quay Brothers) and *Brasil* (dir: Francisco Javier Gutiérrez)
Orient Express Award ..... *Millenium Actress* (dir: Satoshi Kon)
Best Animation Short Films ..... *Le Processus* (dir: Xavier de l'Hermuziere & Philippe Grammaticopoulos)
Audience Award Best Animation Short Film ..... *Strange Invaders* (dir: Cordell Barker)
Best Film Gran Angular ..... *The Curse of the Jade Scorpion*, A.K.A. *La maldición del escorpión de jade* (dir: Woody Allen)
Citizen Kane Award for Best New Director ..... Pitof (*Vidocq*)
Time Machine Honorary Award ..... Peter Greenaway
Best European Fantasy Film ..... *Le pacte des loups*, A.K.A. *El pacto de los lobos* (dir: Christophe Gans)
Critic's Award "Jose Luis Guarner" ..... *Kairo* (dir: Kiyoshi Kurosawa)

33rd — 2000
Award "Maria Honorífica"

Best Film ..... *Ed Gein* (dir: Chuck Parello)
Best Director ..... Geoffrey Wright (*Cherry Falls*)
Best Actor ..... Steve Railsback (*Ed Gein*)
Best Actress ..... Ryoko Hirosue (*Himitsu*)
Best Cinematography ..... Gyula Pados (*Hotel Splendide*)
Best Script ..... Hiroshi Saitô (*Himitsu*)
Best Original Soundtrack ..... Chu Ishikawa (*Soseiji*)
Best FX ..... *Faust* (SMG Effects, Screaming Mad George, Poli Cantero)
Best Short Film ..... *Coup de lune* (dir: Yann Piquer)
Best Animation Short Films ..... *Ring of Fire* (dir: Andreas Hykade)
Audience Award ..... *For the Birds* (dir: Ralph Eggleston)
Gran Angular Award, Best Actor ..... Willem Dafoe (*Shadow of the Vampire*)
Gran Angular Award, Best Actress ..... Mercedes Sampietro (*Women*)
Gran Angular Award, Millor película y Director ..... Tim Robbins (*Cradle Will Rock*)
Honorary Award "La General" ..... Tony Curtis
Citizen Kane Award for Best New Director ..... Terence Gross (*Hotel Splendide*)
Nova Autoria Award ..... David Gallart (*La Escapada*)
Best European Fantasy Film ..... *Promenons-nous dans les bois* (dir: Lionel Delplanque)
Critic's Award ..... *Memento* (dir: Christopher Nolan)

32nd — 1999
Award "Maria Honorífica"

Best Film ..... *Ringu*, A.K.A. *The Ring* (dir: Hideo Nakata)
Best Director ..... Ben Hopkins (*Simon Magus*)
Best Actor ..... Noah Taylor (*Simon Magus*)
Best Actress ..... Emma Vilarasau (*Los Sin Nombre*)
Best Cinematography (tie) ..... Yujiro Yajima (*Samurai Fiction*) and Xavi Giménez (*Los Sin Nombre*)
Best Script ..... François Ozon (*Les Amants Criminels*)
Best Original Soundtrack ..... Tomoyasu Hotei (*Samurai Fiction*)
Best FX ..... Hajime Matsumoto (*Ringu*, A.K.A. *The Ring*)
Best Short Film ..... *The Cyclop of the Sea* (dir: Philippe Jullien)
Best Animation Short Films ..... *Huset pa kampen* (dir: Pjotr Sapegin)
Audience Award ..... *Smoke City* (dir: Eduard Martin, Mario Terraves, Victor Fernandez, Albert Uria)
Gran Angular Award ..... *Les Enfants du marais* (dir: Jean Becker)

Time Machine Honorary Award ..... Dario Argento
Meliès d'Or ..... *Los sin nombre* (dir: Jaume Balagueró)
Best European Fantasy Film ..... *Los sin nombre* (dir: Jaume Balagueró)
Critic's Award ..... *Mones com la Becky* (dir: Joaquim Jordà, Núria Villazán)

31st — 1998
Award "Maria Honorífica"

Best Film ..... *Cube* (dir: Vincenzo Natali)
Best Director ..... Michael Di Jiacomo (*Animals*)
Best Actor ..... Jared Harris (*Trance*)
Best Actress ..... Évelyne Dandry
Best Cinematography ..... Luca Bigazzi (*Totò che visse due volte*)
Best script (tie) ..... Vincenzo Natali, André Bijelic, Graeme Manson (*Cube*), and Gaspar Noé (*Seul Contre Tous*)
Best Original Soundtrack ..... Jerry Goldsmith
Best FX ..... Stefen Fangmeier (*Small Soldiers*)
Best Short Film (tie) ..... *Genesis* (dir: Nacho Cerdà) and *More Sex and Violence* (dir: Bill Plympton)
Best Animation Short Films ..... *Un jour* (dir: Marie Paccou)
Gran Angular Award ..... *Lluvia en los zapatos* (dir: Maria Ripoll)
Time Machine Honorary Award ..... Roger Corman
Best European Fantasy Film ..... *Dong*, A.K.A. *The Hole* (dir: Tsai Ming-liang)
Critic's Award ..... *L'arbre de les cireres* (dir: Marc Recha)

30th — 1997
Award "Maria Honorífica"

Best Film ..... *Gattaca* (dir: Andrew Niccol)
Best Director ..... Scott Reynolds (*The Ugly*)
Best Actor ..... Sam Rockwell (*Lawn Dogs*)
Best Actress ..... Reese Witherspoon (*Freeway*)
Best Cinematography ..... Javier Aguirresarobe (*99.9*)
Best Script ..... Naomi Wallace (*Lawn Dogs*)
Best Original Soundtrack ..... Michael Nyman (*Gattaca*)
Best FX ..... *Spawn* (Industrial Light and Magic)
Best Short Film ..... *How Wings Are Attached to the Backs of Angels* (dir: Craig Welch)
Best Animation Short Film ..... *A.D.N.* (dir: Giorgio Valenti)
Gran Angular Award ..... *Knockin' on Heaven's Door* (dir: Thomas Jahn)
Time Machine Honorary Award ..... Douglas Trumbull
Best European Fantasy Film ..... *Tren de Sombras* (dir: José Luís Guerín)
Critic's Award ..... *Tren de Sombras* (dir: José Luís Guerín)

29th — 1996
Award "Maria Honorífica"

Best Film ..... *The Pillow Book* (dir: Peter Greenaway)
Best Director ..... Mohsen Makhmalbaf (*Gabbeh*)
Best Actor ..... James Woods (*Killer: A Journal of Murder*)
Best Actress ..... Melinda Clarke (*La lengua asesina*)
Best Cinematography ..... Sacha Vierny (*The Pillow Book*)
Best Script ..... Elio Quiroga (*Fotos*)
Best Original Soundtrack ..... Christopher Young (*Head Above Water*)
Best FX ..... Richard Taylor (*The Frighteners*)
Best Short Film ..... *Abductees* (dir: Paul Vester)
Best animation Short Film (tie) ..... *Bird in a Window* (dir: Igor Kovalyov) and *Quest* (dir: Tyron Montgomery)
Time Machine Honorary Award ..... Quentin Tarantino
Best European Fantasy Film ..... Esteban Ibarretxe (*Sólo se muere dos veces*)
Critic's Award ..... Mohsen Makhmalbaf (*Gabbeh*)
Special Prize of the Jury ..... Elio Quiroga (*Fotos*)

28th — 1995
Award "Maria Honorífica"

Best Film ..... *Citizen X* (dir: Chris Gerolmo)
Best director (tie) ..... Chris Gerolmo (*Citizen X*) and Michael Almereyda (*Nadja*)
Best Actor ..... Stephen Rea (*Citizen X*)
Best Actress ..... Bridget Fonda (*Rough Magic*)
Best Cinematography ..... Nick Knowland (*Institute Benjamenta*)
Best Script ..... Eliseo Subiela (*No te mueras sin decirme adónde vas*)
Best Original Soundtrack ..... Nick Bicat (*The Passion of Darkly Noon*)
Best FX ..... Steve Johnson, Richard Edlund (*Species*)
Best Short Film ..... *How to Make Love to a Woman* (dir: Bill Plympton)
Special Mention ..... *Ubu* (dir: Manuel Gómez)
Time Machine Honorary Award ..... Ray Harryhausen
Critic's Award ..... *O Convento* (dir: Manoel de Oliveira)

27th — 1994
Award "Maria Honorífica"

Best Film ..... *71 Fragmente einer Chronologie des Zufalls* (dir: Michael Haneke)
Best Director ..... Scott McGehee, David Siegel (*Suture*)
Best Actor ..... Saturnino Garcia (*Justino*)
Best Actress ..... Jane Horrocks (*Deadly Advice*)
Best Cinematography ..... Emmanuel Lubezki (*Ambar*)

Best Script ..... Michael Haneke (*71 Fragmente einer Chronologie des Zufalls*)
Best Original Soundtrack ..... Santiago Ojeda (*Ambar*)
Best FX ..... Ken Ralston, Greg Cannom (*The Mask*)
Best Short Film ..... *Alicia* (dir: Jaume Balagueró)
Time Machine Honorary Award ..... Saul Bass
Critic's Award ..... Michael Haneke (*71 Fragmente einer Chronologie des Zufalls*)

26th—1993
Award "Maria Honorífica"

Best Film ..... *Orlando* (dir: Sally Potter)
Best Director ..... Dave Borthwick (*The Secret Adventures of Tom Thumb*)
Best Actor ..... Federico Luppi (*Cronos*)
Best Actress ..... Jennifer Ward-Lealand (*Desperate Remedies*)
Best Cinematography ..... Sacha Vierny (*The Baby of Mâcon*)
Best Script ..... Guillero del Toro (*Cronos*)
Best Original Soundtrack ..... Carl Vine (*Bedevil*)
Best FX ..... Cineflex Workshop (*The Wicked City*)
Best Short Film ..... Arturo Gámez (dir: Miguel Navarro)
Time Machine Honorary Award ..... Don Bluth
Critic's Award ..... *El acto en cuestión* (dir: Alejandro Agresti)

25th—1992
Award "Maria Honorífica"

Best Film ..... *C'est arrivé près de chez vous* (dir: Rémy Belvaux, André Bonzel, Benoît Poelvoorde)
Best Director ..... Quentin Tarantino (*Reservoir Dogs*)
Best Actor ..... Benoît Poelvoorde (*C'est arrivé près de chez vous*)
Best Actress ..... Joey Wang (*A Chinese Ghost Story III*)
Best Cinematography ..... Ramón Suarez (*L'Oeil qui ment*)
Best Script ..... *Reservoir Dogs* (dir: Quentin Tarantino)
Best Original Soundtrack ..... Jorge Arriagada (*L'Oeil qui ment*)
Best FX ..... Richard Taylor, Bob McCarron (*Braindead*)
Best Short Film ..... *Jadoube* (dir: Antonio Morales)
Special Mention ..... *Tetsuo II—The Body Hammer* (Shinya Tsukamoto)
Time Machine Honorary Award ..... Sam Raimi

24th—1991
Award "Maria Honorífica"

Best Film ..... *Europa* (Lars Von Trier)
Best Director ..... Jean-Pierre Jeunet, Marc Caro (*Delicatessen*)
Best Actor ..... Dominique Pinon (*Delicatessen*)
Best Actress ..... Juliet Stevenson (*Truly, Madly, Deeply*)
Best Cinematography ..... Henning Bendtsen, Jean-Paul Meurisse, Edward Klosinski (*Europa*)
Best Script ..... Samir, Martin Witz (*Immer & Ewig*)
Best Original Soundtrack ..... Carlos D'Alessio (*Delicatessen*)
Best FX ..... *The Borrower*
Best Short Film ..... *Push Comes to Shove* (dir: Bill Plympton)
Critic's Award ..... Jean-Pierre Jeunet, Marc Caro (*Delicatessen*)

23rd—1990
Award "Maria Honorífica"

Best Film ..... *Henry: Portrait of a Serial Killer* (dir: John McNaughton)
Best director (tie) ..... Sam Raimi (*Darkman*) and John McNaughton (*Henry: Portrait of a Serial Killer*)
Best Actor ..... Jeff Goldblum (*Mister Frost*)
Best Actress ..... Lindsay Duncan (*The Reflecting Skin*)
Best Cinematography ..... Dick Pope (*The Reflecting Skin*)
Best Script ..... Jean-Claude Carrière, Peter Fleischmann (*Es ist nicht leicht ein Gott zu sein*)
Best Original Soundtrack ..... Jürgen Fritz (*Es ist nicht leicht ein Gott zu sein*)
Best FX ..... *Darkman* (dir: Sam Raimi)
Best Short Film ..... *For God's Sake* (dir: Enric Folch)
Critic's Award ..... *Henry: Portrait of a Serial Killer* (dir: John McNaughton)

22nd—1989
Award "Maria Honorífica"

Best Film ..... *Heart of Midnight* (dir: Matthew Chapman)
Best Director ..... Peter Greenaway (*The Cook, the Thief, His Wife and Her Lover*)
Best actor (tie) ..... Michael Gambon (*The Cook, the Thief, His Wife and Her Lover*) and Nicolas Cage (*Vampire's Kiss*)
Best Actress ..... Rosanna Arquette (*Black Rainbow*)
Best Cinematography ..... Sacha Vierny (*The Cook, the Thief, His Wife and Her Lover*)
Best Script ..... Mike Hodges (*Black Rainbow*)
Best Original Soundtrack ..... Michael Nyman (*The Cook, The Thief, His Wife and Her Lover*)
Best FX ..... *Miracle Mile* (dir: Steve De Jarnatt)
Best Short Film ..... *Kitchen Sink* (dir: Alison Maclean)
Critic's Award ..... *La banyera* (dir: Jesús Garay)

21st—1988
Award "Maria Honorífica"

Best Film ..... *The Navigator*, A.K.A. *Navigator, una odisea en el tiempo* (dir: Vincent Ward)
Best Director ..... George A. Romero (*Monkey Shines*)
Best Actor ..... Grigoriy Gladiy (*Otstupnik*)
Best Actress ..... Kate McNeil (*Monkey Shines*)
Millor fotografia ..... Yuri Yelkhov (*Otstupnik*)
Best Script (tie) ..... Hugh Leonard (*Da*) and George A. Romero (*Monkey Shines*)
Best Music ..... Nicholas Pike (*Critters 2: The Main Course*)
Best Original Soundtrack ..... Joao Paes (*Os Canibais*)
Best FX ..... *A Nightmare on Elm Street 4: The Dream Master*
Best Short Film ..... *Le Diner des bustes*

20th—1987
Award "Maria Honorífica"

Best Film ..... *Hol Volt, Hol Nem Volt*, A.K.A. *A Hungarian Fairy Tale* (dir: Gyula Gazdag)
Best Director ..... Paul Verhoeven (*Robocop*)
Best Actor ..... Michael Nouri (*The Hidden*)
Best Actress ..... Jill Schoelen (*The Stepfather*)
Best Script ..... Martin Suter, Daniel Schmid (*Jenatsch*)
Best Cinematography ..... Morten Bruus (*Mandem i Manem*)
Best Original Soundtrack ..... Maurice Jarre (*Julia and Julia*)
Best FX ..... *A Chinese Ghost Story*
Best Short Film ..... *Crash* (dir: John Stewart)
Critic's Award ..... Jack Sholder (*The Hidden*)

19th—1986

Best Film ..... *Blue Velvet*, A.K.A. *Terciopelo Azul* (dir: David Lynch)
Best Director ..... Sergei Parajanov, Dodo Abashidze (*The Legend of Suram Fortress*)
Best Actress ..... Caroline Williams (*The Texas Chainsaw Massacre II*)
Best Actor ..... Juanjo Puigcorvé (*Més enllà de la passió*)
Best Cinematography ..... Frederick Elmes (*Blue Velvet*)
Best FX ..... John Naulin, Anthony Doublin (*From Beyond*)
Best Short Film ..... *Street of Crocodiles* (Quay Brothers)
Critic's Award ..... *From Beyond* (dir: Stuart Gordon)

18th—1985

Best Film ..... *Re-animator* (dir: Stuart Gordon)
Best Director ..... Shuji Terayama (*Saraba Hakobune*)
Best Actress ..... Lori Cardille (*Day of the Dead*)
Best Actor ..... John Walcutt (*Return*)
Best Script ..... Heiner Stadler (*King Kongs Faust*)
Best Cinematography ..... Tatsuo Suzuki (*Saraba Hakobune*)
Best FX ..... John Dykstra (*Lifeforce*)
Best Short Film ..... *Wings of the Dead* (dir: Nicolas Bruce, Michael Coulson)
Critic's Award ..... *Saraba Hakobune* (dir: Shuji Tereyama)

17th—1984

Best Film ..... *The Company of Wolves* (dir: Neil Jordan)
Best Director ..... Carl Schenkel (*Abwarts*)
Best Actress ..... Amy Madigan (*Streets of Fire*)
Best Actor ..... Joe Morton (*The Brother from Another Planet*)
Best Script ..... John Sayles (*The Brother from Another Planet*)
Best Cinematography ..... Tom Cowan (*One Night Stand*)
Best FX ..... Christopher Tucker (*The Company of Wolves*)
Best Short Film ..... *Christ* (dir: Ramon García, Josep Maria Torras)
Critic's Award ..... *The Company of Wolves* (dir: Neil Jordan)
Special Mention ..... *Abwarts* (dir: Carl Schenkel)

16th—1983

Best Feature Film ..... *Le Dernier Combat* (Luc Besson)
Best Director ..... Luc Besson (*Le Dernier Combat*)
Best Actor ..... Vincent Price, Christopher Lee, Peter Cushing, John Carradine (*House of the Long Shadows*)
Best Actress ..... Elizabeth Ward (*Alone in the Dark*)
Best Cinematography ..... Jacques Steyn (*Feuer und Schwert— Die Legende von Tristan and Isolde*)
Best FX ..... Bob McCarron (*The Return of Captain Invincible*)
Best Short Film ..... *Sombras trágicas* (dir: Raúl Román)
Critic's Award ..... *The Lost Tribe* (dir: John Laing)
Special Mention ..... *Pura Sangre* (dir: Luis Ospina)

15th—1982

Best Feature Film Director ..... Tony Williams (*Next of Kin*)
Best Short Film Director ..... *Muha* (dir: Vladimir Jutrisa)
Best Script ..... Jean-Claude Romer, Jean-Pierre Mocky, Patrick Granier, Scott Baker, Suzi Baker (*Litan*)
Best Actor ..... Richard Chamberlain (*The Last Wave*)

Best Actress ..... Annie McEnroe (*Battletruck*)
Best Cinematography ..... Thomas F. Denove (*The Last Horror Film*)
Best FX ..... Tom Sullivan (*Evil Dead*)
Critic's Award ..... *Evil Dead* (dir: Sam Raimi)

14th — 1981

Best Feature Film Director ..... Walerian Borowczyk (*Docteur Jekyll et Miss Osborne*)
Best Short Film Director ..... Lubomir Benes
Best Script ..... David Ambrose (*The Survivor*)
Best Actor ..... Mircea Bogdan (*Povestea Dragostei*)
Best Actress ..... Linda Haynes (*Human Experiments*)
Best Cinematography ..... Jochen Richter (*Geburt Der Hexe*)
Best FX ..... *Hell Night*
Critic's Award ..... *The Survivor* (dir: David Hemmings)

13th — 1980

Best Feature Film Director ..... Veljko Bulajic (*Legenda O Caru Scepanu Malom*)
Best Short Film Director ..... Josko Marusic (*Riblje Oko*)
Best Script ..... Everett de Roche (*Harlequin*)
Best Actor ..... Nicholas Worth (*Don't Answer the Phone*)
Best Actress ..... Cyd Hayman (*The Godsend*)
Best Cinematography ..... Gary Hansen (*Harlequin*)
Best FX ..... Wang Shin-Li (*Sacrificio Nocturno*)
Critic's Award ..... *Harlequin* (dir: Simon Wincer)

12th — 1979

Best Director ..... Juraj Herz (*Panna a netvor*)
Best Script ..... Barry Pearson, Ed Hunt (*Plague*)
Best Actor ..... Gerhad Olschewki (*Der morder*)
Best Actress ..... Lisa Pelikan (*Jennifer*)
Best Cinematography ..... Peter Jessop (*The Comeback*)
Best FX ..... *Thirst* (Conrad Rothmann)
Best Short Film Director ..... Guido Manuli (*Fantabiblical*)
Critic's Award ..... *Plague* (dir: Ed Hunt)

11th — 1978

Best Feature Film Director ..... Richard Franklin (*Patrick*)
Best Short Film Director ..... Gerard Collín (*La Nichee*)
Best Script ..... Francesco Barbieri, Lamberto Bava, Paolo Brigenti, Dardano Sacchetti (*Shock*)
Best Actor ..... John Hargreaves (*Long Weekend*)
Best Actress ..... Camille Keaton (*Day of the Woman*)
Best Cinematography ..... Jaroslav Kucera (*Adela no ha cenado todavía*)
Best FX ..... Dan Genis (*Las abejas*)
Critic's Award ..... *Long Weekend* (dir: Colin Eggleston)

10th — 1977

Best Feature Film Director ..... Dan Curtis (*Burnt Offerings*)
Best Short Film Director ..... M. Bogdan Zizic (*Putovanje*)
Best Actor ..... Burgess Meredith (*The Sentinel* and *Burnt Offerings*)
Best Actress ..... Karen Black (*Burnt Offerings*)
Best Script ..... David Cronenberg (*Rabid*)
Best Cinematography ..... Phillippe Theaudiere (*Les Week Ends Malefiques du Compte Zaroff*)
Best FX ..... Al Griswold (*Rabid*)
Critic's Award ..... *The Hills Have Eyes* (dir: Wes Craven)

9th — 1976

Best Director ..... Dario Argento (*Profondo Rosso*)
Best Script ..... William Fruet (*Death Weekend*)
Best Actor ..... Peter Cushing (*The Ghoul*)
Best Actress ..... Brenda Vaccaro (*Death Weekend*)
Best Cinematography ..... Jean-Jacques Mathy (*Le nosferat ou les eaux glacées de calcul égoiste*)
Best Production ..... *Death Weekend*
Best FX ..... Phil Cory (*Bug*)
Best Short Film Director ..... Vanca Kljakovic (*Hotelska Sova*)

8th — 1975

Best Feature Film Director ..... David Cronenberg (*The Parasite Murders*, A.K.A. *Shivers*)
Best Short Film Director ..... Tomás Muñoz (*Valdemar*)
Best Actor ..... Paul Naschy (*La maldición de la bestia*)
Best Actress ..... Lana Turner (*Persecution*)
Best Cinematography ..... Peter Hurst (*Ghost Story*)
Best FX ..... Li Khek (*Devil Crows*)
Best Script ..... Alan Ormsby (*Dead of Night*)
Critic's Award ..... *Ghost Story* (dir: Stephen Weeks)

7th — 1974

Best Feature Film Director ..... Robert Fuest (*Dr. Phibes Rises Again*)
Best Short Film Director ..... Marçal Moliné (*Ta ta boom boom*)
Best FX ..... Luciano Byrd, Antonio Balandín (*No profanar el sueño de los muertos*)
Best Cinematography ..... Denis Gingras (*The Possession of Virginia*)
Best Script ..... Igaal Niddam, Yves Navarre (*Le troisieme cri*)
Best Actress ..... Cristina Galbó (*No profanar el sueño de los muertos*)
Best Actor ..... Mark Burns (*The House of the Living Dead*)

6th—1973

Best Feature Film Director ..... Juan Luis Buñuel (*Au Rendez-vous de la Mort Joyeuse*)
Best Short Film ..... *La Cabina* (dir: Bruno Bozzetto)
Best Actress ..... Andrea Martin (*Cannibal Girls*)
Best Actor ..... Eugene Levy (*Cannibal Girls*)
Best FX ..... Oldrich Bosak (*Divka na kosteti*)
Best Script ..... *Malpertuis* (Jean Ferry)

5th—1972

Best Feature Film Director ..... Robert Mulligan (*The Other*)
Best Short Film Director ..... *System* (dir: Janusz Majewski)
Best Feature Film ..... *Spalovac mrtvol*, A.K.A. *The Cremator*, A.K.A. *El incinerador de cadáveres* (dir: Juraj Herz)
Best Actress ..... Geraldine Chaplin (*Zero Population Growth*)
Best Actor ..... Rudolf Hrusinsky (*Spalovac mrtvol*, A.K.A. *The Cremator*, A.K.A. *El incinerador de cadáveres*)
Critic's Award Best Script ..... Eugenio Martín (*Pánico en el Transiberiano*)

4th—1971
Palmarés

Best Feature Film Director (tie) ..... Janusz Majewski (*Lokis*) and Michael Skaife (*Necrophagus*)
Best Short Film Director ..... Anthony Scott (*One of the Missing*)
Best Actress ..... Yun Yeo-Jung (*Fire Woman*)
Best Actor ..... Vincent Price (*The Abominable Dr. Phibes*)
Best FX ..... *Antefatto*
Special Mention ..... Paul Naschy

South African HORRORFEST Film Festival

Festival director Paul Blom tells me that no awards were presented in 2005, their first year.

2010

Best Feature ..... *Kaalo*
Audience Choice ..... *Phantom of the Opera* (soundtrack by The Makabra Ensemble)
Best Female Lead ..... Kristina Klebe (*Zone of the Dead*)
Best Male Lead ..... Ken Foree (*Zone of the Dead*)
Best Screenplay ..... Adam Mason, Simon Boyes (*Blood River*)
Best Cinematography ..... Pushpank Gawade (*Kaalo*)
Best Special FX Make-Up ..... *Walking Distance*

Hall of Fame Inductee ..... Joe Spinell (*Maniac*)
Best South African Short Film ..... *Regression*
Runner-Up, South African Short Film ..... *Kult Without a Name*
Audience Choice, South African Short Film ..... Terminatryx "Virus" music video and its short film version *Marked*
Best Female Lead, South African Short Film ..... Vandiet Marx (*Siel Spieël*)
Best Male Lead, South African Short Film ..... Brendan Murray (*Day Zero*)
Best Make-Up FX, South African Short Film ..... Clinton Smith & Cosmesis (Terminatryx, "Virus" and *Marked*)
Best International Short Film ..... *The Twin Sisters of Sunset Street*, A.K.A. *Les bessones del carrer de Ponent*
Runner-Up, International Short Film ..... *Deriva*
Audience Choice, International Short Film ..... *Opstandelsen*
Best Cinematography, International Short Film ..... *Day Before* (Tania Lambert)
Best Screenplay, International Short Film ..... *The Eyes of Edward James* (Rodrigo Gudiño)
Best Female Lead, International Short Film ..... Sonia Caselli (*Betania*)
Best Male Lead, International Short Film ..... Neil Patrick Harris (*Dracula's Daughters vs. the Space Brains*)
Best Scare, International Short Film ..... *Stay*

2009

Best Picture, Feature Film ..... *Strigoi* (dir: Faye Jackson)
Best Director, Feature Film ..... Juraj Herz (*T.M.A.—The Missing Address*)
Indie Spirit Award, Feature Film ..... *Colin* (dir: Marc Price)
Best Male Actor, Feature Film ..... Alastair Kirton (*Colin*)
Best Female Actor, Feature Film ..... Daisy Aitkens (*Colin*)
Best Female Supporting Role, Feature Film ..... Maria Olsen (*Die-ner*)
Best Male Supporting Role, Feature Film ..... Bill Moseley (*Blood Night: The Legend of Mary Hatchet*)
Best Ensemble Cast, Feature Film ..... *The Human Centipede* (Dieter Laser, Ashley C. Williams, Ashlynn Yennie, Akihiro Kitamura, Andreas Leupold)
Best Cinematography, Feature Film ..... Jirí Macháne (*T.M.A.—The Missing Address*)
Best Post Production, Feature Film ..... *Pandorum*
Best Make-Up FX, Feature Film ..... *Zombieland*
Best Documentary, Feature Film ..... *Beware the Moon* (dir: Paul Davis)
Best Opening Title Sequence, Feature Film ..... *I Know How Many Runs You Scored Last Summer*

Best South African Short Film ..... *Izingwe* (dir: Gideon Van Eeden)
Runner-Up, South African Short Film ..... *Emma-O* (dir: Ronnie Belcher, Dr-Benway)
Best Experimental South African Short Film ..... *Project Morningstar* (dir: Grant Wheeler)
Something Wicked Best South African Short Screenplay Award ..... *Emma-O* (Ronnie Belcher, Dr-Benway)
Best Cinematography, South African Short Film ..... *Izingwe* (Marnus Tredoux)
Best Post-Production, South African Short Film ..... *Die Stilte* (Leon Visser)
Best Production Design, South African Short Film ..... *Vegas & Charlie* (Tinneke Nel)
Best Make-Up FX, South African Short Film ..... Clinton Smith & Daleen Badenhorst (*Siek+Sat* music video)
Best Visual FX, South African Short Film ..... *The Screen Behind the Mirror*
Best International Short Film ..... *Séance* (dir: Robin Kasparik)
Best Comedy International Short Film ..... *Treevenge* (dir: Jason Eisener)
Best Experimental International Short Film ..... *Shrove Tuesday* (dir: Lee Andrew Matthews)
Best Ensemble Cast, International Short Film ..... *The Deaf Game* (Camille Figuereo, Joan Mompart, Diane Stolojan, Gérald Morales, Alban Casterman)
Best Screenplay, International Short Film ..... *Abraham's Boys* (Matt Duffer, Dorothy Street, based on a short story by Joe Hill)
Best Cinematography, International Short Film ..... *Zombies & Cigarettes* (Ana Pozo)
Best Post-Production, International Short Film ..... *Beyond Twilight* (dir: Javier Yanez Sanz)
Best Production Design, International Short Film ..... *Tropezones* (dir: David Macian, Eduardo Molinari)
Best Make-Up FX, International Short Film ..... *Langliena* (Emanuele De Luca)
Best Visual FX, International Short Film ..... *Beyond Twilight* (Javier Yanez Sanz)

2008

Best Picture, Feature Film ..... *Maldito Bastardo!* (dir: Javi Camino)
Best Lead Actor, Feature Film ..... Juanilo Esteban (*Maldito Bastardo!*)
Best Lead Actress, Feature Film ..... Tracy Coogan (*Zombie Honeymoon*)
Best Supporting Actor, Feature Film ..... Lance Henriksen (*Dark Reel*)
Best Special FX, Feature Film ..... Melanie Tooker (*Dark Reel*)
Best Soundtrack, Feature Film ..... Kurnalcool (*Bumba Atomika*)
Worst Picture, Feature Film ..... *Things*

Best Poster Design, Feature Film ..... *Maldito Bastardo!*
Best South African Short Film ..... *Donker Herfs* (dir: Donnie Conradie)
Runner-Up, South African Short Film ..... *Muti* (dir: Marthinus Lamprecht)
Runner-Up, South African Short Film ..... *Cain* (dir: Howard Fyvie)
Best Experimental/Innovative South African Short Film ..... *Making a Man* (dir: Garreth Fradgley)
Best Ensemble Cast, South African Short Film ..... *Seethe*
Best Sound Design, South African Short Film ..... *Making a Man*
Best Screenplay, South African Short Film ..... *Muti*
Best Cinematography, South African Short Film ..... *Eviscerate*
Best Title Sequence, South African Short Film ..... *Eviscerate*
Best Make-Up, South African Short Film ..... *Cain*
Best Visual FX, South African Short Film ..... *Cain*
Best Genre Homage, South African Short Film ..... *On the Verge of Blood*
Best Trailer, South African Short Film ..... *The Lambda Child*
Best International Short Film ..... *Vadata* (dir: Manuel Lebelt)
Best Animated International Short Film ..... *The Facts in the Case of Mister Hollow* (dir: Rodrigo Gudino, Vincent Marcone)
Best International Music Video ..... *Isis* (band: Holy Tears; dir: Dominic Hailstone)
Best Cinematography, International Short Film ..... *By Appointment Only*
Best Post-Production, International Short Film ..... *Dead Bones*
Best Homage/Spoof, International Short Film ..... *The Auburn Hills Breakdown* (dir: Geoff Redknap)
Best Special FX, International Short Film ..... *Snip*
Best Male/Female Ensemble Leads, International Short Film ..... Jaime Andrews & Joe Bob Briggs (*Wretched*)
Best Adaptation, International Short Film ..... *Foet*

2007

Best South African Short Film ..... *The Mamtsotsi Bird* (dir: Jo Horn)
Best South African Digital FX ..... *The Mamtsotsi Bird*
Best South African Music Video ..... *Terug Van Die Dood* (band: Insek; dir: Vos)
Best South African Soundtrack ..... *Terug Van Die Dood* by Insek
Best South African Cinematography ..... *Valentine*
Best South African Ensemble Cast ..... *Crawl*

Best South African Editing ..... *Crawl*
Best South African Trailer ..... *Duiwel Vleis* (dir: Richard Muller)
Best International Short Film ..... *Cannibal Flesh Riot!* (dir: Gris Grimly)
Best International Soundtrack ..... Hola Ghost for *Cannibal Flesh Riot!*
Best International Male Leads ..... David Backus & Vince Buckley (*Cannibal Flesh Riot!*)
Best International Female Lead ..... Laura Domínguez (*Happy Birthday to You* A.K.A. *Y que cumplas muchos mas*)
Best International Cinematography ..... *Happy Birthday to You* A.K.A. *Y que cumplas muchos mass*
Best International Editing ..... *We All Fall Down*
Best International Screenplay ..... *Naufrage*, A.K.A. *Shipwrecked*
Best International Special FX ..... *Naufrage*, A.K.A. *Shipwrecked*

2006

Best South African Short Film ..... *Scarecrow Bones* (dir: Josie Minty)
Best International Short Film ..... *The Eel* (dir: Dominic Hailstone)

Spacey Award

Presented by Canada's cable TV Space Channel. Space employees voted for the Space Choice Awards. Viewers voted for the Viewers Choice Awards. Alas, the Space Channel tells me that they "no longer have the Spaceys."

2007

Best Movie, Space Choice Award ..... *Pan's Labyrinth*
Best Comic Book Adaptation, Space Choice Award ..... *Superman Returns*
Best Horror, Space Choice Award ..... *Saw 3*
Best Villain, Space Choice Award ..... Lex Luthor (*Superman Returns*)
Best Animated Movie, Space Choice Award ..... *Happy Feet*
Best Action Sequence, Space Choice Award ..... construction site chase (*Casino Royale*, 2006)
Best Heroic Performance, Space Choice Award ..... Clark "Superman" Kent (*Superman Returns*)
Favorite Character You Love to Hate, Viewers Choice Award ..... Lex Luthor (*Smallville*)
Favorite TV Character, Viewers Choice Award ..... Rodney McKay (*Stargate Atlantis*)
Favorite Kick-Ass Character, Viewers Choice Award ..... James Bond (*Casino Royale*, 2006)
Favorite Classic TV Show, Viewers Choice Award ..... *Star Trek*
Favorite TV Show, Viewers Choice Award ..... *Stargate Atlantis*
Favorite Movie, Viewers Choice Award ..... *Pirates of the Caribbean: Dead Man's Chest*
Favorite Video Game, Viewers Choice Award ..... *The Legend of Zelda: The Twilight Princess*

2006

Best Non-Human Performer, Space Choice Award ..... King Kong (*King Kong*)
Best Movie Villain, Space Choice Award ..... Ian McDiarmid (*Star Wars III: Revenge of the Sith*)
Best Movie Hero, Space Choice Award ..... Christian Bale (*Batman: Batman Begins*)
Best Horror Movie, Space Choice Award ..... *Land of the Dead*
Best Animated Movie, Space Choice Award ..... *Wallace and Gromit: Curse of the Were-Rabbit*
Best Comic Adaptation Movie, Space Choice Award ..... *Sin City*
Best Sci-Fi/Fantasy Movie, Space Choice Award ..... *King Kong*
Favorite Movie, Viewers Choice Award ..... *Serenity*
Favorite TV Show, Viewers Choice Award ..... *Battlestar Galactica*
Favorite TV Ensemble Cast, Viewers Choice Award ..... *SG-1 Season 9*
Favorite New TV Character, Viewers Choice Award ..... Lt.-Col. Mitchell (*Stargate SG-1*)
Favorite Video Game, Viewers Choice Award ..... *Resident Evil 4* (Capcom)
Favorite Action Sequence, Viewers Choice Award ..... Anakin/Kenobi light saber fight (*Star Wars Episode III: Revenge of the Sith*)
Favorite FX, Viewers Choice Award ..... *Star Wars Episode III: Revenge of the Sith*

2005

Best Action Sequence, Space Choice Award ..... subway fight sequence (*Spider-Man 2*)
Best Comic Book Adaptation Movie, Space Choice Award ..... *Spider-Man 2*
Best Horror Movie, Space Choice Award ..... *Shaun of the Dead*
Best Movie F/X, Space Choice Award ..... *Sky Captain and the World of Tomorrow*
Best Animated Movie, Space Choice Award ..... *The Incredibles*
Best Science Fiction/Fantasy Movie, Space Choice Award ..... *Sky Captain and the World of Tomorrow*
Special Achievement Award, Space Choice Award ..... George Romero
Lifetime Achievement Award, Space Choice Award ..... Stan Lee
Favorite TV Character, Male, Viewers Choice Award ..... General Jonathan "Jack" O'Neill (*Stargate SG-1*)
Favorite TV Character, Female, Viewers Choice Award ..... T'Pol (*Star Trek: Enterprise*)
Favorite Movie Villain, Viewers Choice Award ..... Doc Ock (*Spider-Man 2*)

Favorite Canadian TV Series, Viewers Choice Award ..... *Stargate SG-1*
Favorite TV Series, Viewers Choice Award ..... *Star Trek: Enterprise*
Favorite Movie Hero, Viewers Choice Award ..... Spider-Man (*Spider-Man 2*)
Favorite Video Game, Viewers Choice Award ..... *Halo 2*
Favorite Limited TV Series, Viewers Choice Award ..... *Battlestar Galactica*
Favorite Movie, Viewers Choice Award ..... *Harry Potter and the Prisoner of Azkaban*

2004

Best Action Sequence, Space Choice Award ..... freeway chase (*The Matrix Reloaded*)
Best Comic Book Adaptation Movie, Space Choice Award ..... *X2: X-Men United*
Best Horror/Suspense Movie, Space Choice Award ..... *28 Days Later*
Best Science Fiction/Fantasy Movie, Space Choice Award ..... *The Lord of the Rings: The Return of the King*
Best Visual SFX, Space Choice Award ..... *The Lord of the Rings: The Return of the King*
Best Animated Movie, Space Choice Award ..... *Finding Nemo*
Special Achievement Award, Space Choice Award ..... Peter Jackson
Lifetime Achievement Award, Space Choice Award ..... Ray Harryhausen
Favorite TV Character, Male, Viewers Choice Award ..... Spike (*Angel*)
Favorite TV Character, Female, Viewers Choice Award ..... T'Pol (*Star Trek: Enterprise*)
Favorite Movie Villain, Sci-Fi/Fantasy, Viewers Choice Award ..... Agent Smith (*The Matrix Reloaded* and *The Matrix Revolutions*)
Favorite Canadian TV Series, Viewers Choice Award ..... *Stargate SG-1*
Favorite TV Series, Viewers Choice Award ..... *Angel*
Favorite Movie Hero, Viewers Choice Award ..... Jack Sparrow (*Pirates of the Caribbean: The Curse of the Black Pearl*)
Favorite Video Game, Viewers Choice Award ..... *Star Wars: Knights of the Old Republic*
Favorite Movie Villain, Horror, Viewers Choice Award ..... Death (*Final Destination 2*)

2003

Best Science Fiction/Fantasy Movie, Space Choice Award ..... *The Lord of the Rings: The Two Towers*
Best Horror/Suspense Movie, Space Choice Award ..... *The Ring*
Best Animated Movie, Space Choice Award ..... *Spirited Away*
Best Visual SFX, Space Choice Award ..... *Star Wars Episode II: Attack of the Clones*
Best Action Sequence, Space Choice Award ..... Battle of Helm's Deep (*The Lord of the Rings: The Two Towers*)
Lifetime Achievement Award, Space Choice Award ..... William Shatner
Special Achievement Award, Space Choice Award ..... Vulcan, Alberta [ed: Vulcan is a city in Alberta)
Favorite TV Series, Viewers Choice Award ..... *Buffy the Vampire Slayer*
Favorite Canadian TV Series, Viewers Choice Award ..... *Stargate SG-1*
Favorite Movie Villain, Viewers Choice Award ..... Dr. Evil (*Austin Powers in Goldmember*)
Favorite TV Hottie, Viewers Choice Award ..... T'Pol (*Star Trek: Enterprise*)
Favorite Movie Hero, Viewers Choice Award ..... Aragorn (*The Lord of the Rings: The Two Towers*)
Favorite Creature Character, Viewers Choice Award ..... Gollum (*The Lord of the Rings: The Two Towers*)

Spooky Movie

A.K.A. Spooky Movie: The Washington D.C. International Horror Film Festival. They apparently present no film awards, but their screenplay contest presents the DarkHart Screenplay Award (sponsored by DarkHart Press).

2010

Best Feature Screenplay (unproduced) ..... *Cult Flick* (Brian Hauser)
Feature Screenplay, Runner-Up (unproduced) ..... *The Jersey Devil* (Aurelio Voltaire)
Feature Screenplay, Runner-Up (unproduced) ..... *Killer Granny* (Kevin Armento)
Feature Screenplay, Runner-Up (unproduced) ..... *Cockpit* (Jesse Griffith)
Best Short Screenplay (unproduced) ..... *United We Survive* (Isaac Loftus)
Short Screenplay, Runner-Up (unproduced) ..... *Trunk or Treat* (Ron Podell)
Short Screenplay, Runner-Up (unproduced) ..... *The Curfew* (Brian Hauser)

2009

1st Place, Feature Screenplay (unproduced) ..... *Rose Marie's Egg* (Sophia Vassilakidis)
2nd Place, Feature Screenplay (unproduced) ..... *Horror Comic* (Stephen Hoover)
1st Place, Short Screenplay (unproduced) ..... *He Knows* (Stuart A. Creque)
2nd Place, Short Screenplay (unproduced) ..... *Room Service* (Michael William Hogan)

Tabloid Witch Award

In its first year (2004) the award was called the Hollywood Investigator Halloween Horror Film Award. From 2004–2006, Best Film and Honorable Mention were presented to the film's director. Beginning in 2007, Best Film and Honorable Mention were shared by the director and writer. In 2011, it was just the director.

2010

Best Horror Feature Film ..... Jose Zambrano Cassella, Sharon Reed (*The Sacred*)
Best Feature Film Screenplay ..... Steve Hudgins (*Hell Is Full*)
Best Dramatic Horror Short Film ..... Devi Snively (*Death in Charge*)
Best Comedic Horror Short Film ..... Trevor Carroll, Max Mosher (*The Haunted Restaurant*)
Best Avant-Garde Horror Short Film ..... Lee Andrew Matthews (*Shrove Tuesday*)
Best Actress ..... Marina Benedict (*Death in Charge*)
Best Actor ..... Manolo Solo (*El tren de la bruja*)
Best Supporting Actress ..... Lauren Brown (*The Sacred*)
Best Supporting Actor ..... John Kyle (*The Sacred*)
Best Cinematography ..... Peter Frederick Davies (*Shrove Tuesday*)
Best Sound ..... Nacho Royo (*El tren de la bruja*)
Best Visual Effects ..... Dutch Dallas (*Shrove Tuesday*)
Best Make-Up Effects ..... Rabbid EFX (*Deus Irae*)
Best Music Soundtrack ..... Peter Rutland (*Shrove Tuesday*)
Honorable Mention ..... Tim Aldridge, Julia Camara (*Scream Machine*)
Honorable Mention ..... Koldo Serra, Nacho Vigalondo (*El tren de la bruja*)
Honorable Mention ..... Pedro Cristiani (*Deus Irae*)
Honorable Mention ..... Davide Melini (*The Sweet Hand of the White Rose*)
Honorable Mention ..... Rafael DeLeon, Jr. (*Waffle*)

2009

Best Horror Feature Film ..... Hanelle M. Culpepper, Rebecca Sonnenshine (*Within*)
Best Dramatic Horror Short Film ..... Damian McCarthy (*He Dies at the End*)
Best Comedic Horror Short Film ..... Raymond Castile (*The Blind Date of Coffin Joe*)
Best Animated Horror Short Film ..... Jorge Morais Valle (*The Painter of Skies*)
Best Avant-Garde Horror Short Film ..... Rory Leydier, Deborah Bento (*Bad Friday*)
Best Actress ..... Claire Lindsay (*Don't Call Me Zombie*)
Best Actor ..... Raymond Castile (*The Blind Date of Coffin Joe*)
Best Supporting Actress ..... Colleen Boag (*Bled White*)
Best Supporting Actor ..... Brent Sexton (*Within*)
Best Child Actress ..... Mia Ford (*Within*)
Best Cinematography ..... Cat Deakins (*Body of Work*)
Best Sound ..... Simon White, Adam Bowden (*Bloody Daisies*)
Best Make-Up Effects ..... Simon Ratziel (*El hombre de la bolsa*)
Best Music Soundtrack ..... D.C. McAuliffe (*Bled White*)
Honorable Mention ..... Jose Carlos Gomez (*Bled White*)
Honorable Mention ..... Alex Bram, Shayla Beesley (*Body of Work*)
Honorable Mention ..... Patrick Clement (*The Eternal Pitfall of Prokofiev*)
Honorable Mention ..... Pedro Cristiani, Guille Gatti (*El hombre de la bolsa*)

2008

Best Horror Feature Film ..... Balaji K. Kumar, Eric Massey (*9 Lives of Mara*)
Best Dramatic Horror Short Film ..... Manuel Lebelt (*Vadata*)
Best Comedic Horror Short Film ..... Peter Podgursky (*Cheerbleeders*)
Best Animated Horror Short Film ..... Joe Fontano (*The Butterfly Hole*)
Best Avant-Garde Horror Short Film ..... Damon Packard (*Chemtrails: An Investigative Report*)
Best Horror Music Video ..... Shannon Lark (*Brains*)
Best Actress ..... Georgia Chris (*100 Tears*)
Best Actor ..... Chad Donella (*9 Lives of Mara*)
Best Supporting Actress ..... Raine Brown (*100 Tears*)
Best Supporting Actor ..... Troy Gentile (*9 Lives of Mara*)
Best Cinematography ..... Joseph Rubinstein (*9 Lives of Mara*)
Best Sound ..... Manuel Lebelt (*Vadata*)
Best Visual Effects ..... Matt Holland (*Eel Girl*)
Best Make-Up Effects ..... Marcus Koch (*100 Tears*)
Best Music Soundtrack ..... Ganesh Kumar (*9 Lives of Mara*)
Honorable Mention ..... Marcus Koch, Joe Davison (*100 Tears*)
Honorable Mention ..... Jose Zambrano Cassella (*Mina*)
Honorable Mention ..... Paul Campion (*Eel Girl*)
Honorable Mention ..... Nick Thiel, C.J. Johnson (*Creepers*)

2007

Best Horror Feature Film ..... Daniel de la Vega, Demián Rugna (*Death Knows Your Name*)

Best Dramatic Horror Short Film ..... Miguel Gallego (*The Crypt Club*)
Best Comedic Horror Short Film ..... Erasmo Romero III (*Skin Deep*)
Best Animated Horror Short Film ..... Jim Minton, Michael Arnzen (*The Scab*)
Best Actress ..... Casey Halter (*Fast Forward*)
Best Actor ..... James Rollyson (*Skin Deep*)
Best Supporting Actress ..... Nancy Sinclair (*By Appointment Only*)
Best Supporting Actor ..... Kevin Schiele (*Death Knows Your Name*)
Best Cinematography ..... Ben Robinson, Jono Smith (*Night of the Hell Hamsters*)
Best Sound ..... Jimmy Crispin (*Death Knows Your Name*)
Best Visual Effects ..... James Teague (*Dead Noon*)
Best Make-Up Effects ..... Simon Ratziel (*Death Knows Your Name*)
Best Music Soundtrack ..... Joseph Y. Kamiya (*Skin Deep*)
Honorable Mention ..... Andrew Wiest, Matthew Taggart, Keith Suta (*Dead Noon*)
Honorable Mention ..... Paul Campion, Hadyn Green, Mike Roseingrave (*Night of the Hell Hamsters*)
Honorable Mention ..... John Faust (*By Appointment Only*)
Honorable Mention ..... Nicholas Humphries (*The One That Got Away*)
Honorable Mention ..... CJ Johnson (*The Signal*)
Honorable Mention ..... Jason Holler, Terry Fisher (*Fast Forward*)
Honorable Mention ..... Mike Doyle (*The Strain*)
Honorable Mention ..... Shawna Baca (*3:52*)
Honorable Mention ..... Paul Solet (*Grace*)
Honorable Mention ..... Yfke van Berckelaer (*Zombie Love*)

2006

Best Horror Feature Film ..... Rolfe Kanefsky (*Nightmare Man*)
Best Horror Short Film ..... Mike Flanagan (*Oculus*)
Best Actress ..... Blythe Metz (*Nightmare Man*)
Best Actor ..... Scott Graham (*Oculus*)
Best Supporting Actress ..... Tiffany Shepis (*Nightmare Man*)
Best Supporting Actor ..... Jerry Lloyd (*Strange Aeons*)
Best Cinematography ..... Juan Rodriguez (*Moloch*)
Best Sound ..... Mike Flanagan (*Oculus*)
Best Music Soundtrack ..... Christopher Farrell (*Nightmare Man*)
Honorable Mention ..... Bill Whirity (*Zombie Island*)
Honorable Mention ..... Kenny Selko (*Alone*)
Honorable Mention ..... Aldo E. Serrano (*Moloch*)

Honorable Mention ..... Eric Morgret (*Strange Aeons*)
Honorable Mention ..... Paul Carty (*The Kooky Kastle*)

2005

Best Horror Feature Film ..... Rich Mauro, Anthony Savini (*Mole*)
Best Horror Short Film ..... Robert Sexton (*Legion: The Word Made Flesh*)
Best Actress ..... Sam Tsao (*Mole*)
Best Actor ..... Tony Simmons (*Human No More*)
Best Supporting Actress ..... Sabrina Bertaccini (*Legion: The Word Made Flesh*)
Best Supporting Actor ..... James Cox (*Mole*)
Best Visuals ..... Bobby Eras, Marshall Plante (*Legion: The Word Made Flesh*)
Best Sound ..... Christopher Alan Broadstone (*Human No More*)
Honorable Mention ..... Jennifer Soemantri (*Hollow*)
Honorable Mention ..... Jamie Renee Williams (*Slinky Milk*)
Honorable Mention ..... Michael Fiore (*Cadaverous*)
Honorable Mention ..... Sam Zalutsky (*SuperStore*)
Honorable Mention ..... Christopher Alan Broadstone (*Human No More*)
Audience Favorite ..... *SuperStore*

2004

Best Horror Feature Film ..... Michael D. Sellers (*Vlad*)
Best Horror Micro-Budget Feature Film ..... Steven Stevens, Jr. (*Skinwalker: Curse of the Shaman*)
Best Horror Short Film ..... Rick Lavon (*Stiffs by Sid*)
Best Horror Music Video ..... Paul Hough (*You Make Me Feel So Dead*)
Honorable Mention ..... Paul Carty (*Jeremy's Wake-Up Call*)

Terror Film Festival

Presents the Claw Award. Claw is also the name of the festival's founder and director.

2010

Best Feature Film ..... *Recreator*
Audience Favorite ..... *Hypochondriac*
Best Director ..... Neil Meschino (*Mold!*)
Best Screenplay ..... *Recreator* (Gregory Orr)
Best Director of Photography (tie) ..... Bart Mastronardi (*Vindication*) and Bart Mastronardi (*By Her Hand, She Draws You Down*)
Best Horror Short Film ..... *Daniel*
Best Fantasy Short Film ..... *Jacob and Death*
Best Science Fiction Short Film ..... *Attackazoids, Deploy!!*

Best Thriller Short Film ..... *Unit 30*
Best Drama Short Film ..... *Midwestern Summer: Controlled Pain*
Best Actor (tie) ..... Keith Fraser (*Vindication*) and Jerry Murdock (*By Her Hand, She Draws You Down*)
Best Actress ..... Zoe Daelman Chlanda (*By Her Hand, She Draws You Down*)
Best Supporting Actor ..... Alan Rowe Kelly (*Vindication*)
Best Supporting Actress ..... Tenley Bank (*Jacob and Death*)
Best Cinematography ..... *Jackpot!*
Best Editing ..... *Vindication*
Best Sound Design ..... *Gitchy*
Best Special Effects ..... *The Black Cat*
Best Original Music Score ..... *By Her Hand, She Draws You Down*
Best Original Music Theme Song ..... *Walk Away*
Honorable Mention, Special Effects ..... *A Study in Red*
Honorable Mention, Actor ..... Danny Elfman (*DemiUrge Emesis*)
Honorable Mention, Special Effects ..... *DemiUrge Emesis*
Honorable Mention, Director ..... Jeff Bellantine (*Foreclosed*)
Honorable Mention, Producer ..... Mara Lesemann, Jeff Bellantine (*Foreclosed*)
Honorable Mention, Actor ..... Conor Timmis (*H.P. Lovecraft's The Silver Key*)
Honorable Mention, Screenplay ..... *Torment*
Feature Screenplay, 1st Place (unproduced) ..... *Ripper* (Joe Randazzo)
Feature Screenplay, 2nd Place (unproduced) ..... *The Devil's Deed* (Joshua Echevarria)
Feature Screenplay, 3rd Place (unproduced) ..... *Wherever There Is Gold, Hell Is Nearby* (Jonathan Weichsel)
Short Screenplay, 1st Place (unproduced) ..... *Predation* (Karl White)
Short Screenplay, 2nd Place (unproduced) ..... *Mr. Phang and the Blood Princess* (Derek Prusak)
Short Screenplay, 3rd Place (unproduced) ..... *Trunk or Treat* (Ron Podell)
Honorable Mention in Screenwriting (unproduced) ..... *American Macabre* (Brett Creane, Jason Dugre)
Honorable Mention in Screenwriting (unproduced) ..... *Devil* (Michael Wasielewski, Warren Brigham)
Honorable Mention in Screenwriting (unproduced) ..... *The Fool of Muncaster* (Dawn McElligott)

2009

Best Feature Film ..... *Evil Angel*
Audience Favorite ..... *Scare Zone*
Best Director ..... Mike Turner (*Dead Creek*)
Best Screenplay ..... *Cold October* (Andrew Gilbert, Mikel J. Wisler)
Best Horror Short Film ..... *The Institute of Séance*
Best Fantasy Short Film ..... *X-Mess Detritus*
Best Science Fiction Short Film ..... *Two Miles Below the Surface of the Earth*
Best Thriller Short Film ..... *Let Me Go*
Best Drama Short Film ..... *The Curse of Micah Rood*
Best Actor ..... Alan Rowe Kelly (*A Far Cry from Home*)
Best Actress ..... Arian Waring Ash (*Scare Zone*)
Best Supporting Actor ..... John Savage (*From a Place of Darkness*)
Best Supporting Actress ..... Marie Westbrook (*Evil Angel*)
Best Director of Photography ..... Chris Freilich (*Downriver*)
Best Cinematography ..... *Marcella and Sofia*
Best Editing ..... *Scare Zone*
Best Sound Design ..... *Wade*
Best Special Effects ..... *A Far Cry from Home*
Best Original Music Score ..... John Frizzell (*Evil Angel*)
Best Original Music Theme ..... Mark Nutter (*The Baby Shredder Song*)
Notable Distinction ..... *The Rocking Horse* (drama, short film)
Notable Distinction ..... Keith Pillow (actor, *The Rocking Horse*)
Feature Screenplay, 1st Place (unproduced) ..... *Brood 19* (David Altman)
Feature Screenplay, 2nd Place (unproduced) ..... *Stand Up and Die* (Dominic Pereira, Demetri Panayotopoulos)
Feature Screenplay, 3rd Place (unproduced) ..... *Dead Winter Run* (Jake Hart, Mike Brown, Raven Solomon)
Short Screenplay, 1st Place (unproduced) ..... *Fourth Floor Seige* (John Riddlebaugh)
Short Screenplay, 2nd Place (unproduced) ..... *Love's a Drag* (Kirk Bierbauer)
Short Screenplay, 3rd Place (unproduced) ..... *Investment* (Rick Tobin)
Notable Distinction for a Screenplay (unproduced) ..... *Couchsurfing* (Jenny Krumrine)
Notable Distinction for a Screenplay (unproduced) ..... *Shadow People* (Fernando Ortiz)
Notable Distinction for a Screenplay (unproduced) ..... *Shadow War* (Jerome A. Dolan)

2008

Best Feature Film ..... *Alien Raiders* (dir: Ben Rock; prod: Daniel Myrick, John Shiban, Steve Ecclesine, Tony Krantz)
Best Director ..... Tony Swansey (*Squeal*)
Best Screenplay ..... *Excision* (Richard Bates, Jr.)
Best Director of Photography ..... Mathew Rudenberg (*Basement Jack*)

Audience Favorite ..... *Swamp Devil* (dir: David Winning; prod: Irene Litinsky, Ric Nish)
Best Horror Short Film ..... *The Procedure* (dir: Sergio Pinheiro; prod: Sergio Pinheiro)
Best Fantasy Short Film ..... *Transrexia* (dir: Aurelio Voltaire; prod: Aurelio Voltaire)
Best Science Fiction Short Film ..... *Attackazoids!* (dir: Brian Lonano; prod: Erin Horsey)
Best Thriller Short Film ..... *Nothing Face* (dir: Mitch Csanadi; prod: Dan Maher)
Best Drama Short Film ..... *All for Love* (dir: Ron E. Harris; prod: Jared Johnson, Ron E. Harris)
Best Actor ..... Eric Peter-Kaiser (*Basement Jack*)
Best Actress ..... Mary Ann Biewener (*Absent*)
Best Supporting Actor ..... Bruce Dern (*Swamp Devil*)
Best Supporting Actress ..... Lynn Lowry (*Basement Jack*)
Best Cinematography ..... Mathew Rudenberg (*Basement Jack*)
Best Editing ..... *Squeal* (Dennis Doornbos, Joe Burke)
Best Sound Design ..... *Gomeda* (Jan Peridar)
Best Special Effects ..... *The 9th Circle* (Damien Leone)
Best Original Music Score ..... *Basement Jack* (Alan Howarth)
Best Original Music Theme ..... *Gomeda* (Semih Tareen)
Feature Screenplay, 1st Place (unproduced) ..... *Cadaver* (Steven Arvanites)
Feature Screenplay, 2nd Place (unproduced) ..... *Truckers vs. Bikers* (Aaron Granlund, Sean Huet)
Feature Screenplay, 3rd Place (unproduced) ..... *Vermin* (Bo Ransdell)
Short Screenplay, 1st Place (unproduced) ..... *Enemy Combatant* (Ron Albury)
Short Screenplay, 2nd Place (unproduced) ..... *New Year's Eve* (Rick Tobin)
Short Screenplay, 3rd Place (unproduced) ..... *The Words and the Bees* (Ron Podell)

2007

Best Feature Film ..... *Side Sho* (dir: Mike D'Anna; prod: Paula Fox)
Best Director ..... John Faust (*By Appointment Only*)
Best Screenplay ..... *The Wish* (Christian Jude Grillo)
Best Horror Short Film ..... *Red Harvest* (dir: Dylan Griffith; prod: Dylan Griffith)
Best Fantasy Short Film ..... *Regret* (dir: Craig Sudac; prod: Craig Sudac)
Best Science Fiction Short Film ..... *Electrical Skeletal!* (dir: Brian Lonano; prod: Erin Horsey, Brian Lonano)
Best Thriller Short Film ..... *Bacchus* (dir/prod: Laurent Fabre)
Best Drama Short Film ..... *Arena* (dir: Michael Wallace; prod: Michael Wallace)
Best Actor ..... Leo Rossi (*Diamond Zero*)
Best Actress in a Thriller film ..... Nancy Sinclair (*By Appointment Only*)
Best Actress in a Horror film ..... Christina Barlas (*The Dollhouse*)
Best Director of Photography ..... Chris LaPointe (*Primevil*)
Best Cinematography ..... *One Soul* (Tim Naylor)
Best Editing ..... *Til Night* (Matt Boatright-Simon)
Best Sound Design ..... *Dead Tired* (Ernie Rockelman)
Best Special Effects ..... *The Unholy Sideshow* (Matt Broomfield)
Best Music Score ..... *Side Sho* (Leonard Wolf)
Feature Screenplay, 1st Place (unproduced) ..... *My Immortal* (Lee Rudnicki)
Feature Screenplay, 2nd Place (unproduced) ..... *Sentenced* (Colin Costello, Ken Nared)
Feature Screenplay, 3rd Place (unproduced) ..... *Where the Dead Go* (Mark Kratter)
Short Screenplay, 1st Place (unproduced) ..... *Livin' in a 'V' World* (Jennifer Bogush)
Short Screenplay, 2nd Place (unproduced) ..... *Interrogation* (Rick Tobin)
Short Screenplay, 3rd Place (unproduced) ..... *Bloodletter* (Jennifer M. Oaks)

2006

Best Feature Film ..... *The Murder Game* (dir: Robert Harari)
Best Director ..... Kenneth Selko (*Alone*)
Best Screenplay ..... *Under Surveillance* (David Campfield)
Best Horror Short Film ..... *The Descendent* (dir: Robert Glickert)
Best Fantasy Short Film ..... *The Faeries of Blackheath Woods* (dir: Ciaran Foy)
Best Science Fiction Short Film ..... *Project: Adam* (dir: Jacob Buchheit)
Best Thriller Short Film ..... *Alone* (dir: Kenneth Selko)
Best Actor ..... Logan Brown (*Steves*)
Best Actress ..... Betsy Palmer (*Penny Dreadful*)
Best Cinematography ..... *The Faeries of Blackheath Woods* (Patrick Jordan)
Best Editing ..... *The Mamtsotsi Bird* (Walter Green)
Best Special Effects ..... *The Faeries of Blackheath Woods* (Ciaran Foy)
Best Music Score ..... *Alone* (Jasper Randall)

Thriller Award

Presented by the International Thriller Writers, which primarily comprises and serves thriller novelists and short story writers. They used to present a Thriller Award for Best Screenplay (below), but no longer.

2007 ..... *The Good Shepherd* (Eric Roth)
2006 ..... *Cache (Hidden)* (Michael Haneke)

Thriller! Chiller!

All awards are called Groovy Awards, unless it says otherwise. Recipients of the Storey Award (named in honor of the late journalist and community activist Drew Storey) are honored for their body of work, and their contribution to promoting and connecting Michigan artists. Festival director Anthony E. Griffin informs me: "We took 2009 off, but sent films from our '08 season to Muskegon Film Festival's Scarefest in October 2009 instead. There were no awards that year." Muskegon was a mainstream festival, now defunct.

2010

Best Feature ..... *True Nature* (dir: Patrick Steele)
Best Short ..... *The Familiar* (dir: Kody Zimmermann)
Best Thrill ..... *On Air* (dir: Carsten Vauth, Marco J. Riedl)
Best Chill ..... *S&Man* (dir: J.T. Petty)
Best FX ..... *Forge* (dir: Jason Windsor)
Jury Award ..... *The Empty Space in Between* (dir: Maria Tornberg)
Director's Choice Award ..... *Clean Break* (dir: Ryan Lieske)
Audience Choice Award ..... *GR30K* (dir: Daniel F. Falicki)
Boomstick! Award! (for best Michigan genre film) ..... *GR30K* (dir: Daniel E. Falicki)
Storey Award ..... Erin Wilson

2008

Best Feature ..... *VLOG*
Best Short ..... *Kirksdale*
Best Thrill ..... *Alien Raiders*
Best Chill ..... *Excision*
Best FX ..... *Kirksdale*
Best One-Liner ..... *Vito Power*

2007

Best Feature ..... *The Shadow Within*
Best Short ..... *Rose*
Best Thrill ..... *Nobody*
Best Chill ..... *Of Darkness*
Best FX ..... *Razor Sharp*
Best Student Film ..... *Recently Deceased*
Best One-Liner ..... *Brain Dead*

2006

Best Feature ..... *Zombie Honeymoon*
Best Short ..... *The Listening Dead*
Best Thrill ..... *The Slaughter*
Best Chill ..... *The Lost*
Best FX ..... *The Quick and the Undead*

Toronto After Dark Film Festival

2010

Audience Award, Best Feature Film, Gold ..... *The Last Exorcism*
Audience Award, Best Feature Film, Silver ..... *The Human Centipede*
Audience Award, Best Feature Film, Bronze ..... *I Spit on Your Grave*
Vision Award, Best Independent Feature Film, Gold ..... *Heartless*
Vision Award, Best Independent Feature Film, Silver ..... *The Last Lovecraft*
Vision Award, Best Independent Feature Film, Bronze ..... *All About Evil*
Audience Award, Best Canadian Short Film, Gold ..... *Junko's Shamisen*
Audience Award, Best Canadian Short Film, Silver ..... *King Chicken*
Audience Award, Best Canadian Short Film, Bronze (tie) ..... *Fireman!* and *Game Night*
Audience Award, Best International Short Film, Gold ..... *Off Season*
Audience Award, Best International Short Film, Silver ..... *Pumzi*
Audience Award, Best International Short Film, Bronze ..... *Deus Irae*
Fans' Choice Award, Best Horror Film ..... *The Last Exorcism*
Fans' Choice Award, Best Sci-Fi Film ..... *Cargo*
Fans' Choice Award, Best Action Film ..... *Centurion*
Fans' Choice Award, Best Comedy Film ..... *High School*
Fans' Choice Award, Best Director ..... Steven R. Monroe (*I Spit On Your Grave*)
Fans' Choice Award, Best Screenplay ..... *The Last Exorcism* (Huck Botko, Andrew Gurland)
Fans' Choice Award, Best Leading Actor ..... Patrick Fabian (*The Last Exorcism*)
Fans' Choice Award, Best Leading Actress ..... Sarah Butler (*I Spit On Your Grave*)
Fans' Choice Award, Best Ensemble Cast (tie) ..... *Doghouse* and *High School*
Fans' Choice Award, Best Special Effects ..... *Cargo* and *RoboGeisha*
Fans' Choice Award, Best Make-Up ..... *Doghouse*
Fans' Choice Award, Best Soundtrack ..... *High School*

Fans' Choice Award, Best Fight ..... *Alien vs. Ninja*
Fans' Choice Award, Best Kills ..... *I Spit On Your Grave*
Fans' Choice Award, Scariest Film ..... *The Last Exorcism*
Fans' Choice Award, Most Original Film ..... *Rubber*
Fans' Choice Award, Most Disturbing Film ..... *I Spit On Your Grave*
Fans' Choice Award, Best Trailer ..... *RoboGeisha*
Fans' Choice Award, Best Festival Bumper ..... *5 Years Young*

2009

Audience Award, Best Feature Film, Gold ..... *Dead Snow*
Audience Award, Best Feature Film, Silver ..... *Trick 'R Treat*
Audience Award, Best Feature Film, Bronze ..... *Black Dynamite*
Vision Award, Best Independent Feature Film, Gold ..... *Strigoi*
Vision Award, Best Independent Feature Film, Silver ..... *The Revenant*
Vision Award, Best Independent Feature Film, Bronze ..... *Grace*
Audience Award, Best Canadian Short Film, Gold ..... *Captain Coulier (Space Explorer)*
Audience Award, Best Canadian Short Film, Silver ..... *Blackheads*
Audience Award, Best Canadian Short Film, Bronze ..... *Danse Macabre*
Audience Award, Best International Short Film, Gold ..... *The Users Guide to Imaginary Friends (Abridged)*
Audience Award, Best International Short Film, Silver ..... *The Horribly Slow Murderer With the Extremely Inefficient Weapon*
Audience Award, Best International Short Film, Bronze ..... *King of Power 4 Billion %*

2008

Audience Award, Best Feature Film, Gold ..... *Let the Right One In*
Audience Award, Best Feature Film, Silver ..... *Repo! The Genetic Opera*
Audience Award, Best Feature Film, Bronze ..... *4bia* A.K.A. *Phobia*
Vision Award, Best Independent Feature Film, Gold ..... *I Sell the Dead*
Vision Award, Best Independent Feature Film, Silver ..... *Home Movie*
Vision Award, Best Independent Feature Film, Bronze ..... *South of Heaven*
Audience Award, Best Canadian Short Film, Gold ..... *Treevenge*
Audience Award, Best Canadian Short Film, Silver ..... *The Facts in the Case of Mister Hollow*
Audience Award, Best Canadian Short Film, Bronze ..... *The Flower*
Audience Award, Best International Short Film, Gold ..... *I Live in the Woods*
Audience Award, Best International Short Film, Silver ..... *Kingz*
Audience Award, Best International Short Film, Bronze ..... *Martians Go Home: The Revenge of Sara Clockwork*

2007

Audience Choice Award, Best Feature Film, Gold ..... *Alone*
Audience Choice Award, Best Feature Film, Silver ..... *Murder Party*
Audience Choice Award, Best Feature Film, Bronze ..... *Wolfhound*
Audience Choice Award, Best International Short Film, Gold ..... *It Came From the West*
Audience Choice Award, Best International Short Film, Silver ..... *Operation Fish*
Audience Choice Award, Best International Short Film, Bronze ..... *Dear Beautiful*
Audience Choice Award, Best International Short Film, Gold ..... *Terror on the 3918*
Audience Choice Award, Best International Short Film, Silver ..... *Latchkey's Lament*
Audience Choice Award, Best International Short Film, Bronze ..... *Zombie Jesus*
Toronto After Dark Spirit Award, Best Independent Feature Film, Gold ..... *Mulberry Street*
Toronto After Dark Spirit Award, Best Independent Feature Film, Silver ..... *Blood Car*
Toronto After Dark Spirit Award, Best Independent Feature Film, Bronze ..... *Automaton Transfusion*
Toronto After Dark Spirit Award, Best International Short Film, Gold ..... *Ambassadors Day*
Toronto After Dark Spirit Award, Best International Short Film, Silver ..... *Hairlady*
Toronto After Dark Spirit Award, Best International Short Film, Bronze ..... *The Drift*
Toronto After Dark Spirit Award, Best Canadian Short Film, Gold ..... *Terror on the 3918*
Toronto After Dark Spirit Award, Best Canadian Short Film, Silver ..... *Key Lime Pie*
Toronto After Dark Spirit Award, Best Canadian Short Film, Bronze ..... *The Tragic Story of Nling*

Toronto International Film Festival

This mainstream/indie film festival has a horror program called Midnight Madness. "These weird and wonderful films from misfit directors are for those audiences who appreciate the wild side of cinema; featuring thrillers, chillers and outlandish capers to drive you into frenzy." The festival's online archives go back to 1978, but 2009 appears to be the founding year of the Midnight Madness Award, apparently sponsored by Cadillac.

2010, Cadillac People's Choice Midnight Madness Award ..... *Stake Land* (dir: Jim Mickle)
2009, Cadillac People's Choice Midnight Madness Award ..... *The Loved Ones* (dir: Sean Byrne)

Underground Horror Filmfest

Different from, but affiliated with, the Underground Horror Fest. Both in Tulsa, Oklahoma.

2010

Best Scream Queen ..... Anjanette Clewis
Outstanding Performance ..... Bryan Haber (*DJ Blackskull*)
Best Oklahoma Movie ..... *Bloodstained Romance* (dir/writer: Travis M. Miller)
Best Story/Theme ..... *The Path of Torment* (dir/writer: Gary C. Warren)
Best of Show ..... *Incest Death Squad* (dir/writer: Cory J. Udler)
Best Movie To Smoke To ..... *Nixon and Hogan Smoke Christmas* (dir/writer: Kevin Strange)
Best Monster ..... *Sewer Chewer* (dir/writer: James Hawley)

Vampire Film Festival

Festival director Asif Ahmed emails me that the VFF was founded in 2003. I don't know the presentation years for the below "Previous Winners" and Ahmed can provide me with nothing beyond what's here.

2010

Outstanding Vampire Feature ..... *Daylight Fades* (dir: Brad Ellis)
Outstanding Vampire Short ..... *The Familiar* (dir: Kody Zimmermann)
Outstanding Foreign Vampire Short ..... *La reina vampira* (dir: Paulo J. Maia)
Outstanding Award for Writing ..... Lisa Hunter (*You Are So Undead*)
Best Performance by a Vampire ..... Mera Summers (*Vicky*)
Outstanding Mythic Horror Film ..... *Mørke sjeler*, A.K.A. *Dark Souls* (dir: Cesar Ducasse, Mathieu Peteul)
Bloodiest Film ..... *Statt Coven*

2009

Outstanding Vampire Feature ..... *The Revenant* (dir: Kerry Prior)

Outstanding International Vampire Film ..... *D'Entre Les Morts* (dir: Alain Basso)
Outstanding Vampire Short ..... *Initiation* (dir: Stéphane Beaudoin)
Audience Award ..... *Shadowland* (dir: Wyatt Weed)
Best Gothic Film ..... *The Music of Erich Zahn* (dir: Jared Skolnick)
Best Mythic Film ..... *Shrove Tuesday* (dir: Lee Matthews)
Best Anime ..... *CannibAlien* (dir: David Kame Tsai)
Acting Award, Best Vampire Portrayal ..... Estes Tarver (*Mr. Moonlight*)

Previous Winners

Outstanding Vampire Feature ..... *Demon Under Glass*
Outstanding Vampire Short ..... *Midnight Sun*
Best Vampire Portrayal ..... Jason Carter as Simon Molinar (*Demon Under Glass*)
Audience Award ..... *The Evil Basement of Count Worlock*
Special Award, Outstanding Art Direction ..... Mina Seward

Viscera Award

Every year, one Viscera Award is presented to a short horror film that is created entirely by women, in front of and behind the camera. Viscera had its first theatrical screening in 2010, during which every selection from its three previous years were eligible for non–Viscera Awards. To win the latter, it's enough for a film to have a woman in a key role (writer, director, or producer), rather than being created entirely by women.

2010

Viscera Award ..... Ginnetta Corelli (*Mary Jane Go Round*)
Best Direction ..... *Side Effect* (Liz Adams)
Best Cinematography ..... *Wretched* (Jessica Gallant)
Best Storyline ..... *Beautiful as You Are* (dir: Doug Mallette, prod: Mary Katherine Sisco)
Audience Choice ..... *Side Effect* (Liz Adams)

2009

Viscera Award ..... *The Date* (Jennifer Gigantino, Natasia Schibinger)

2008

Viscera Award ..... *Out of Print* (Reyna Young)

Weekend of Fear

A.K.A. Weekend of Fear: Internationales Filmfestival für Horror, Thriller, Science Fiction & Obskure Film.

2010

Golden Glibb, Best Film (Audience) ..... *George's Intervention* (dir: J.T. Seaton)
Small Golden Glibb, Best Short Film (Audience) ..... *Pixels* (dir: Patrick Jean)

2009

Golden Glibb, Best Film (Audience) ..... *Making of Teeny-Stuten 7* (dir: Daniel Hyan)
Small Golden Glibb, Best Short Film (Audience) ..... *The Horribly Slow Murderer with the Extremely Inefficient Weapon* (dir: Richard Gale)

2008

Golden Glibb, Best Film (Audience) ..... *Babysitter Wanted* (dir: Jonas Barnes, Michael Manasseri)
Small Golden Glibb, Best Short Film (Audience) ..... *Fireproof Agent* (dir: Daniel Flügger)

2007

Golden Glibb, Best Film (Jury) ..... *The Living and the Dead* (dir: Simon Rumley)
Silver Glibb, 2nd Best Film (Jury) ..... *Rooms for Tourists* (dir: Adrián Garcia Bogliano)
Green Glibb, Best Actress (Jury) ..... Angelique Hennessy (*Bad Reputation*)
Green Glibb, Best Actor (Jury) ..... Leo Bill (*The Living and the Dead*)
Special Award (Jury) ..... *DVD* (dir: Ciro Altabás)
Small Golden Glibb, Best Short Film (Jury) ..... *Delivery* (dir: Till Nowak)
Golden Glibb, Best Film (Audience) ..... *To Kako* (dir: Yorgos Noussias)
Small Golden Glibb, Best Short Film (Audience) ..... *DVD* (dir: Ciro Altabds)

2006

Golden Glibb, Best Film (Jury) ..... *Nuit Noire* (dir: Olivier Smolders)
Golden Glibb, Best Film (Audience) ..... *Brutal Inca$$o* (dir: Jonas Kvist Jensen)
Special Golden Glibb, Best Film (Publikum-Sonderpreis) ..... *Bagman* (dir: Anouk Whissell, Francois Simard, Jonathan Prévost)
Silver Glibb, 2nd Best Film (Jury) ..... *Necromancer* (dir: Piyapan Choopetch)
Green Glibb, Best Actor (Jury) ..... Chatchai Plengpanich (*Necromancer*)
Green Glibb, Best Actress (Jury) ..... Asia Argento (*The Heart Is Deceitful Above All Things*)
Special Glibb (Jury) ..... Melanie & Daniel Ittenbach (*Familienradgeber*)

2005

Golden Glibb, Best European Film (Jury) ..... *EMR* (dir: James Erskine, Danny McCullough)
Golden Glibb, Best International Film (Jury) ..... *Casshern* (dir: Kazuaki Kiriya)
Golden Glibb, Best Film (Audience) ..... *P* (dir: Paul Spurrier)
Green Glibb, 2nd Best Film (Jury) ..... *P* (dir: Paul Spurrier)
Silver Glibb, Best Actor (Jury) ..... Paul Naschy (*Rojo Sangre*)
Silver Glibb, Best Actress (Jury) ..... Paige Richards (*Bettie Page: Dark Angel*)
Special Glibb, Best Party Movies (Festival) ..... *Cannibal World* (dir: Vincent Dawn, A.K.A. Bruno Mattei)
Special Glibb, Best Party Movies (Festival) ..... *Land of Death* (dir: Martin Miller, A.K.A. Bruno Mattei)

2004

Red Glibb, Best Film (Audience) ..... *Una de zombis* (dir: Miguel Ángel Lamata)
Red Glibb, Best Film (Jury) ..... *Dead & Breakfast* (dir: Matthew Leutwyler)
Special Glibb (Festival) ..... Timo Rose, for his achievement for German Independent cinema.

2003

Golden Glibb, Best Film (Jury) ..... *Lucky* (dir: Steve Cuden)
Golden Glibb, Best Film (Audience) ..... *Mucha Sangre* (dir: Pepe de las Heras)
Silver Glibb, 2nd Best Film (Jury) ..... *Ice from the Sun* (dir: Eric Stanze)

Winnipeg Horror Cinema

Short films only. In 2010 they presented an Audience Award, but next year they plan to expand their award categories.

2010 ..... Natalee Dacquisto (*Vinnie's Tale*)

Winnipeg Short Film Massacre

Canadian horror short films. Their website only lists "winners" for each year, without specifying any award categories. Now defunct, 2009 was their final year, so this is a complete list. Kevin Bacon, who won in 2007 and 2009, now manages the Winnipeg Horror Cinema film festival.

2009

Fireman (Adam Brooks)
Outer Space (Dylan Gyles, Evan Petkau)
Extension in Use (Kevin Bacon)

2008
Heart of Karl (Steven Kostanski)
Kevin and Owen Kill a Vampire (Dylan Gyles)
Holy Shit 2 (Will O'Donnell)

2007
Insanophenia (Steven Kostanski)
H.I.Z. (Matthew Kennedy, Conor Sweeney)
Foot of the Bed (Kevin Bacon)

2006
Fantasy Beyond (Steven Kostanski)
Ena Lake Blues (Matthew Kennedy, Conor Sweeney)
Addiction Is Murder (Adam Brooks)

2005
Slaughter Bed (Mike Maryniuk)
Rasguno (Matthew Kennedy, Conor Sweeney)
All Things Which Splatter (Alex Ferron)

2004
Clay Girl (Victoria Prince)
Museal (James Craig, Krisjanis Katkins-Gorsiline)
Dial M for Monster (Kevin Nikkel)

Wonder Award

When they say "Horror, Fantasy, or Science Film," I assume they mean "Horror, Fantasy, or Science *Fiction* Film."

2010
Best Horror, Fantasy, or Science Film ..... *Avatar*
Best Direction ..... James Cameron (*Avatar*)
Best Screenplay (tie) ..... Neill Blomkamp, Terri Tatchell (*District 9*) and Pete Docter, Bob Peterson; story by Docter, Peterson, Thomas McCarthy (*Up*)
Best Performance by an Actress in a Leading Role ..... Saoirse Ronan (*The Lovely Bones*)
Best Performance by an Actor in a Leading Role (tie) ..... Robert Downey, Jr. (*Sherlock Holmes*) and Sam Rockwell (*Moon*)
Best Performance by an Actress in a Supporting Role ..... Vera Farmiga (*Orphan*)
Best Performance by an Actor in a Supporting Role ..... Jackie Earle Haley (*Watchmen*)
Best Special Effects ..... *Avatar*
Best Makeup ..... *My Bloody Valentine*
Best Production Design ..... Henry Selick (*Coraline*)
Best Cinematography ..... Mauro Fiore (*Avatar*)
Best Editing ..... James Cameron, John Refoua, Stephen E. Rivkin (*Avatar*)
Best Music ..... Michael Giacchino (*Star Trek*)
Edgar G. Ulmer Award ..... *Moon*

2009
Best Picture (tie) ..... *Let the Right One In* and *The Dark Knight*
Best Director ..... Christopher Nolan (*The Dark Knight*)
Best Screenplay ..... Jonathan & Christopher Nolan (*The Dark Knight*)
Best Performance by an Actress in a Leading Role (tie) ..... Cate Blanchett (*The Curious Case of Benjamin Button*) and Lina Leandersson (*Let the Right One In*)
Best Performance by an Actor in a Leading Role ..... Robert Downey, Jr. (*Iron Man*)
Best Performance by an Actress in a Supporting Role (tie) ..... Tilda Swinton (*The Curious Case of Benjamin Button*) and Judi Dench (*Quantum of Solace*)
Best Performance by an Actor in a Supporting Role ..... Heath Ledger (*The Dark Knight*)
Best Special Effects ..... *Hellboy 2: The Golden Army*
Best Makeup ..... *The Curious Case of Benjamin Button*
Best Production Design ..... Stephen Scott (*Hellboy 2: The Golden Army*)
Best Cinematography ..... Wally Pfister (*The Dark Knight*)
Best Editing ..... Lee Smith (*The Dark Knight*)
Best Music ..... Thomas Newman (*WALL-E*)
Edgar G. Ulmer Award ..... *Diary of the Dead*

Yubari International Fantastic Film Festival

Yubari's English language website pages consistently and repeatedly refer to this festival's July Prize, but Wikipedia refers to it as a Jury Prize. Since some of Yubari's pages list the "Members of July" I assume they mean Jury. The below winners are mostly from the Yubari site, but it doesn't list winners for 2002–03 and 2007–10. For those years, I refer to Wikipedia, which claims to list this festival's "major awards." Wikipedia reports that this festival was canceled in 2007, yet the Yubari site lists official selections for that year. However, Yubari may have selected its films, then canceled before the screening. The Minami Toshiko Award is a "Critics Award."

2009
Fantastic Off-Theater Competition, Grand Prize ..... *SR: Saitama's Rapper*, A.K.A. *SR: Saitama no rappā* (dir: Yū Irie)
Fantastic Off-Theater Competition, Special Jury Prize ..... *Big Gun*, A.K.A. *Dai kenjū* (dir: Ōhata Hajime)

Fantastic Off-Theater Competition, Governor's Award ..... *Night Games*, A.K.A. *Yoru no geemu* (dir: Choi Uian)

2008

Fantastic Off-Theater Competition, Grand Prize ..... *A Woman Who Is Beating the Earth*, A.K.A. *Daichi o tataku onna* (dir: Tsuki Inoue)
Fantastic Off-Theater Competition, Special Jury Prize ..... *Coming with My Brother*, A.K.A. *One-chan, otōto to iku* (dir: Kouta Yoshida)
Fantastic Off-Theater Competition, Governor's Award ..... *Seikilos and I*, A.K.A. *Seikilos-san to Watashi* (dir: Kenji Itoso, Hiroshi Kamebuchi)

2006

Young Fantastic Competition, Yubari Grand Prize ..... *Blood Rain* (dir: Kim Dae-Seung)
Young Fantastic Competition, Special Jury Prize ..... *Never Belongs to Me* (dir: Nam Ki-Woong)
Young Fantastic Competition, Minami Toshiko Award ..... *Citizen Dog* (dir: Wisit Sasanatieng)
Fantastic Off-Theater Competition, Grand Prize ..... *Nama-natsu* (dir: Keisuke Yoshida)
Fantastic Off-Theater Competition, Special Jury Prize ..... *Hakko* (dir: Madoka Kumagai)

2005

Young Fantastic Competition, Grand Prize ..... *My Mother, The Mermaid* (dir: Park Heung-Shik)
Young Fantastic Competition, Special Jury Prize ..... *Innocence* (dir: Lucile Hadzihalilovic)
Young Fantastic Competition, Minami Toshiko Award ..... *The Neighbor No. Thirteen* (dir: Yasuo Inoue)
Fantastic Off-Theater Competition, Grand Prize ..... *Mariko's 30 Pirates* (dir: Tetsuya Mariko)
Fantastic Off-Theater Competition, Special Jury Prize ..... *Be the World for Her* (dir: Daisuke Hosaka)

2004

Young Fantastic Competition, Grand Prize ..... *Mokpo the Harbor* (dir: Kim Ji-hoon)
Young Fantastic Competition, Special Jury Prize ..... *Robot Stories* (dir: Greg Pak)
Young Fantastic Competition, Minami Toshiko Award ..... *Better Than Sex* (dir: Chao Pin Su, Lee Feng Bor)
Fantastic Off-Theater Competition, Grand Prize ..... *The Far East Apartment* (dir: Tetsuya Mariko)
Fantastic Off-Theater Competition, Special Jury Prize ..... *Utsu-musume sayuri* (dir: Takashi Kimura)

2003

Grand Prize ..... *Battlefield Baseball*, A.K.A. *Jigoku Kōshien* (dir: Yūdai Yamaguchi)
Fantastic Off-Theater Competition, Grand Prize ..... *Bijo-can* (dir: Masaya Kakei)
Fantastic Off-Theater Competition, Special Jury Prize ..... *Ski Jumping Pairs* (dir: Riichiro Mashima)

2002

Grand Prize ..... *My Sassy Girl* (dir: Kwak Jae-yong)
Fantastic Off-Theater Competition, Grand Prize ..... *Run! Yamazaki! Run!* (dir: Naoko Johnori)
Fantastic Off-Theater Competition, Special Jury Prize ..... *Nuts* (dir: Yoko Chukira, Tomokazu, Shu Kageyama)

2001

Young Fantastic Competition, Grand Prize ..... *New Year's Day* (dir: Suri Krishnamma)
Young Fantastic Competition, Special Jury Prize ..... *Animals* (dir: Michael Di Giacomo)
Young Fantastic Competition, Minami Toshiko Award ..... *Siam Sunset* (dir: John Polson)
Fantastic Off-Theater Competition, Grand Prize ..... *Tokyo A Go Go* (dir: Ryuichi Honda)
Fantastic Off-Theater Competition, Special Jury Prize ..... *L'Ilya* (dir: Tomoya Sato)
Fantastic Video Festival, Grand Prize ..... *Pop & Me*
Fantastic Video Festival, Special Jury Prize ..... *Deuce Bigalow*
Yubari Citizens Award ..... *Crazy in Alabama*

2000

Young Fantastic Competition, Grand Prize ..... *Across a Gold Prairie* (dir: Isshin Inudo)
Young Fantastic Competition, Special Jury Prize ..... *Pups* (dir: Ash Baron-Cohen)
Young Fantastic Competition, Minami Toshiko Award ..... *Jin-Roh* (dir: Hiroyuki Okiura)
Fantastic Off-Theater Competition, Grand Prize ..... *Hazy Life* (dir: Atsuhiro Yamashita)
Fantastic Off-Theater Competition, Special Jury Prize ..... *Let's Go Strawberry Girl* (dir: Shinobu Kuribayashi)
Fantastic Video Festival, Grand Prize ..... *Harsh Realm* (dir: Daniel Sackheim)
Fantastic Video Festival, Special Jury Prize ..... *Michael Angel* (dir: William Gove)
Yubari Citizens Award ..... *Michael Angel* (dir: William Gove)

1999

Young Fantastic Competition, Grand Prize ..... *Bandits* (dir: Katja Von Garnier)
Young Fantastic Competition, Special Jury Prize ..... *Moonlight Whispers* (dir: Akihiko Shiota)
Young Fantastic Competition, Minami Toshiko Award ..... *Moonlight Whispers* (dir: Akihiko Shiota)
Fantastic Off-Theater Competition, Grand Prize ..... *Tel-Club* (dir: Kenji Murakami)

Fantastic Off-Theater Competition, Special Jury Prize ..... *Kaidohryoku/Real* (dir: Katsushi Bowda)
Fantastic Video Festival, Grand Prize ..... *Lewis & Clarke & George* (dir: Rod McCall)
Fantastic Video Festival, Special Jury Prize ..... *Eight Heads in a Duffel Bag* (dir: Tom Schulman)
Yubari Citizens Award ..... *Man, a Natural Girl* (dir: Takashi Miike)

1998

Young Fantastic Competition, Grand Prize ..... *Bernie* (dir: Albert Dupontel)
Young Fantastic Competition, Jean-Hugues Anglade Award ..... *Detective Riko* (dir: Satoshi Isaka)
Young Fantastic Competition, Adventure Film Prize ..... *The Ground* (dir: Atsushi Muroga)
Young Fantastic Competition, Minami Toshiko Award ..... *Illtown* (dir: Nick Gomez)
Fantastic Off-Theater Competition, Grand Prize ..... *Midnight Three* (dir: Yasushi Koshizaka)
Fantastic Off-Theater Competition, Special Jury Prize ..... *Variations for Movements* (dir: Yoshinao Sato)
Fantastic Off-Theater Competition, Encouragement Prize ..... *Kurushime Girl* (dir: Noboru Iguchi)
Fantastic Video Festival, Grand Prize ..... *God of Gamblers 3: The Early Stage* (dir: Barry Wong)
Fantastic Video Festival, Jury Prize ..... *Steel* (dir: Kenneth Johnson)
Yubari Citizens Award ..... *God of Gamblers 3: The Early Stage* (dir: Barry Wong)

1997

Young Fantastic Competition, Grand Prize ..... *Closing Time* (dir: Masahiro Kobayashi)
Young Fantastic Competition, Special Jury Prize ..... *Little Sister* (dir: Robert Jan Westdijk)
Young Fantastic Competition, Minami Toshiko Award ..... *Drive* (dir: Steve Wang)
Fantastic Off-Theater Competition, Grand Prize ..... *Party* (dir: Mayumi Uchiumi)
Fantastic Off-Theater Competition, Jury Prize ..... *L & D* (dir: Hideki Kimura)
Fantastic Video Festival, Grand Prize ..... *Joe's Apartment* (dir: John Payson)
Fantastic Video Festival, Jury Prize ..... *Lexx the Dark Zone Stories* (dir: Paul Donovan, Ron Oliver, Rainer Matsutani)
Yubari Citizens Award ..... *Joe's Apartment* (dir: John Payson)

1996

Young Fantastic Competition, Grand Prize ..... *Accumulator 1* (dir: Jan Sverak)
Young Fantastic Competition, Special Jury Prize ..... *Manneken Pis* (dir: Frank Van Passel)
Young Fantastic Competition, Minami Toshiko Award ..... *Secret Waltz* (dir: Akira Nobi)
Fantastic Off-Theater Competition, Grand Prize ..... *Brain Holiday* (dir: Hineki Mito)
Fantastic Off-Theater Competition, Jury Prize ..... *Blood Red Girls* (dir: Daisuke Yamanouchi)
Fantastic Off-Theater Competition, Encouragement Prize ..... *Rest Room* (dir: Muneyoshi Murakami)
Fantastic Off-Theater Competition, Encouragement Prize ..... *To Be or Not to Be* (dir: Tomoko Matsunashi)
Fantastic Video Festival, Grand Prize ..... *Princess Caraboo* (dir: Michael Austin)
Fantastic Video Festival, Jury Prize ..... *Alien Nation: Body and Soul* (dir: Kenneth Johnson)
Yubari Citizens Award ..... *Fluke* (dir: Carlo Carlei)

1995

Young Fantastic Competition, Grand Prize ..... *Tombes du Ciel* (dir: Philippe Lioret)
Young Fantastic Competition, Special Jury Prize ..... *The Secret Adventures of Tom Thumb* (dir: Dave Borthwick)
Young Fantastic Competition, Minami Toshiko Award ..... *Wizard of Darkness* (dir: Shimako Sato)
Fantastic Off-Theater Competition, Grand Prize ..... *The Incredible Haniwa-Man* (dir: Shin Yasuhara)
Fantastic Off-Theater Competition, Jury Prize ..... *Anatomia Extinction* (dir: Yoshihiro Nishimura)
Fantastic Off-Theater Competition, Special Jury Prize ..... *A Room Without Wind* (dir: Ryuta Miyake)
Fantastic Video Festival, Foreign Film Grand Prize ..... *The Scout* (dir: Michael Ritchie)
Fantastic Video Festival, Japanese Film Grand Prize ..... *Promise of August* (dir: Katsuhito Ishii)
Yubari Citizens Award ..... *The Cowboy Way* (dir: Gregg Champion)

1994

Young Fantastic Competition, Grand Prize ..... *Killing Zoe* (dir: Roger Roberts Avary)
Young Fantastic Competition, Special Jury Prize ..... *C'est Arrive Pres de Chez Vous* (dir: Rémy Belvaux, André Bonzel, Benoît Poelvoorde)
Young Fantastic Competition, Minami Toshiko Award (Critics Award) ..... *Carne* (dir: Gaspar Noe)
Young Fantastic Competition, Most Entertaining Award ..... *El Mariachi* (dir: Robert Rodriguez)
Fantastic Off-Theater Competition, Grand Prize ..... *Family Time* (dir: Ryota Kawaguchi)
Fantastic Off-Theater Competition, Jury Prize ..... *My Favorite Skyline* (dir: Shin Yasuhara)
Fantastic Off-Theater Competition, Jury Prize ..... *Vending Machine and a Girl* (dir: Kiyohide Otani)

Fantastic Video Festival, Foreign Film Grand Prize ..... *Body Snatchers* (dir: Abel Ferrara)
Fantastic Video Festival, Japanese Film Grand Prize ..... *Knockin' on Hell's Door* (dir: Toshiyuki Mizutani)
Yubari Citizens Award ..... *The Right Facing Left* (dir: Kenji Tominaga)

1993

Young Fantastic Competition, Grand Prize ..... *Children of Nature* (dir: Fridrik Thor Fridriksson)
Young Fantastic Competition, Special Jury Prize ..... *Winds of God* (dir: Yoko Narahashi)
Young Fantastic Competition, Critics Award ..... *Reservoir Dogs* (dir: Quentin Tarantino)
Fantastic Off-Theater Competition, Grand Prize ..... *Trash* (dir: Naoki Kubo)
Fantastic Off-Theater Competition, Jury Prize ..... *My Daddy Long Legs* (dir: Shin Yasuhara)
Fantastic Video Festival, Foreign Film Grand Prize ..... *Leaving Normal* (dir: Edward Zwick)
Fantastic Video Festival, Japanese Film Grand Prize ..... *Maohgai*, A.K.A. *Sadistic City* (dir: Ryuichi Hiroki)

1992

Young Fantastic Competition, Grand Prize ..... *The Swordsman in Double-Flag Town* (dir: He Ping)
Young Fantastic Competition, Special Jury Prize ..... *A Demon in My View* (dir: Petra Haffter)
Young Fantastic Competition, Critics Award ..... *Tetsuo II: The Body Hammer* (dir: Shinya Tsukamoto)
Fantastic Off-Theater Competition, Grand Prize ..... *Diamonds Moon* (dir: Akira Nobi)
Fantastic Off-Theater Competition, Jury Prize ..... *Kappas* (dir: Katsuya Ohsawa)
Fantastic Video Festival, Grand Prize ..... *Teen Agent* (dir: William Dear)
Fantastic Video Festival, Jury Prize ..... *Teen Agent* (dir: William Dear)

1991

Young Fantastic Competition, Grand Prize ..... *Miracle in Valby* (dir: Ake Sandgren)
Young Fantastic Competition, Special Jury Prize ..... *Windwalker* (dir: Kieth Merrill)
Young Fantastic Competition, Critics Award ..... *Miller's Crossing* (dir: Joel Coen)
Fantastic Off-Theater Competition, Grand Prize ..... *Death Express* (dir: Hiroyuki Terada)
Fantastic Off-Theater Competition, Jury Prize ..... *Rice Game* (dir: Hideaki Kobayashi)
Fantastic Video Festival, Grand Prize ..... *Stranger in the Night Fright* (dir: Shuichi Nagasaki)

1990

Young Fantastic Competition, Grand Prize ..... *Pathfinder* (dir: Nils Gaup)
Young Fantastic Competition, Special Prize ..... *Spirits of the Air, Gremlins of the Clouds* (dir: Alex Proyas)
Fantastic Off-Theater Competition, Grand Prize ..... *Takesita Performance Higei Mito-Komon* (dir: Sinya Takesita)
Fantastic Off-Theater Competition, Special Prize ..... *Gig* (dir: Kosuke Ienaga)
Toroma Prize ..... *Meilin Adventure* (dir: Satoshi Imai)
Fantastic Video Festival, Grand Prize ..... *Twin Peaks* (dir: David Lynch)
Yubari Citizen Prize ..... *The Shadow of the Raven* (dir: Hrafn Gunnlaugsson)

Zompire: The Undead Film Festival

Canceled for 2010, but plans to return in 2011.

2009

Best of Festival, Audience Award ..... *The Revenant*
Best Feature, Jury Award ..... *The Revenant*
Best Director, Jury Award ..... *The Revenant*
Best Feature, Audience Award ..... *Morgue Story: Blood, Blowfish and Comics*
Best Short, Audience Award ..... *The Horribly Slow Murderer with the Extremely Inefficient Weapon*

2008

Best of Festival Award (short) ..... *ZombieWestern: It Came from the West* (dir: Tor Fruergaard)
Best of Festival Award (short) ..... *Prombies!* (dir: Frederick Snyder)
Audience Award (short) ..... *Zombie Jesus!* (dir: Steve Miller)
Audience Award (feature) ..... *Wasting Away* (dir: Matthew Kohnen)
Best of Festival Award (feature) .... *Wasting Away* (dir: Matthew Kohnen)

2007

Best of Festival Award (short) ..... *By Appointment Only* (dir: John Faust)
Best of Festival Award (short) ..... *The Lycanthrope* (dir: Lucas Peltonen)
Audience Award (short) ... *Zombie Love* (dir: Yfke Van Berckelaer)

NOTES

Preface

1. The Trieste International Science Fiction Film Festival first screened in 1963. SITGES: Festival Internacional de Cinema Fantàstic de Catalunya first screened in 1968. Not *horror specific* enough for you? The Academy of Science Fiction, Fantasy & Horror Films presented its first Best Horror Film Saturn Award in 1972 (to *Blacula*).

2. An orphaned webpage is no longer linked from other pages on the website. It can only be found by knowing or guessing its url, or through a web search hit.

1: How to Run a Film Festival on Pennies a Day!

1. There's another Screamfest in Florida. It's more of a convention than a film festival, and is unaffiliated with Belofsky's Screamfest L.A.

2. After announcing the Tabloid Witch Award winners one year, a disappointed filmmaker sent me the following MySpace message: "*Hello, I understand that my movie* [the losing film] *is only enjoyed by 50% of the population (judging that the reviews are split down the middle). But, even many of the reviewers who didn't enjoy it, thought the acting was exceptional for a micro-budget production. Having seen the trailer for* [the winning film] *and seeing* [the winning actor's] *'performance' (yes you can tell talent from a trailer), how is it possible he beat* [the losing actor]*? Aren't you located in Hollywood? Even if you didn't like the movie, not recognizing his performance is mind boggling, especially given who you chose as Best Actor.*" Actually, I thought this rejected film was sordid, vile, ugly, and mean-spirited. Its actor was, at best...not so good. I don't get many such emails. I suspect I'd get many more were I to charge an entry fee. This filmmaker was disappointed, but it's doubtful that he felt ripped off.

3. Loscon and WHC charge admission to the convention, but no additional fees to attend the screenings. The Miles Memorial Playhouse charged admission to the 2010 Tabloid Witch screenings, but all the money went to the playhouse; the Tabloid Witch took no cut.

4. Unique no more. In 2010, Elisabeth Fies founded BleedFest, a Los Angeles festival likewise devoted to horror films by women. Lark and Martinuzzi have assisted in promoting BleedFest, but are unaffiliated with it.

5. Just how competitive are some top festivals? The filmmaker who traveled to Sundance told me that Sundance picked seventeen dramatic features that year from among thousands of entries. He griped to me about how "phony" Sundance was for rejecting his work. He was *so* certain his film deserved to be among the chosen few. He was stunned the judges at Sundance didn't agree.

6. The Tabloid Witch is primarily an *award*, not a *festival*. Awards normally honor works that have already been released. While Sundance requires premiere screening rights, Oscar wouldn't consider a feature film *unless* it's been previously screened. When I founded the Tabloid Witch, I was expecting to get a lot more commercially released DVDs. I was surprised that most entries were still seeking a distributor. I was perceived as a *festival* with an award, rather than an *award* that happens to screen winners.

7. When I reject a film that was well received at other festivals, it's usually because of a poor story. I think some festivals are overly impressed by slick production values. I've seen way more award-winning films that look great but tell dull or derivative stories, than visa versa.

8. My italics. I hear this *a lot* from filmmakers—about having spent all their money on their film, with nothing left for promotion. It's a recurring theme in this book, so keep it in mind.

9. http://sacredmovie.blogspot.com/2010/06/without-box-helpful-or-harmful.html. June 23, 2010. Reprinted with Ms. Reed's permission.

10. http://jneilschulman.rationalreview.com/2010/03/more-quotations-from-easychairman-neil. March 13, 2010. Reprinted with Mr. Schulman's permission.

11. While Screamfest L.A. is the top horror film festival in Los Angeles County, it's no small thing to be number two. Shriekfest still outranks (in no particular order) BleedFest, Carnival of Darkness, Paranoia Fest, Shockfest, Viscera, and the Tabloid Witch Awards.

12. http://darkcarnivalfilmfest.com/popupex.html.

13. "On With or Withoutabox?: A look at how the festival tool Withoutabox has changed the way festival directors and filmmakers handle submissions," by Jen Swanson, *The Independent*, November 10, 2008. http://independent-magazine.org/08/11/or-withoutabox.

14. Ibid.

15. Comment posted by Anonymous. December 31, 2008. http://independent-magazine.org/08/11/or-withoutabox.

16. Comment posted by (a presumably different) Anonymous. November 17, 2008. http://independent-magazine.org/08/11/or-withoutabox.

17. Comment posted by (yet another) Anonymous. November 12, 2008. http://independent-magazine.org/08/11/or-withoutabox.

18. Jeni Thornley. http://independent-magazine.org/08/11/or-withoutabox. Thornley repeats a common complaint among indie filmmakers: spending all their money on shooting the film, with no money left for marketing. See footnote 8.

19. "Cyberclinic: Why won't they let me delete my Facebook page?" by Rhodri Marsden, *The Independent*, February 13, 2008. http://www.independent.co.uk/life-style/gadgets-and-tech/features/cyberclinic-why-wont-they-let-me-delete-my-facebook-page-781472.html.

2: How to Make an Award Winning Horror Film!

1. I'm not the only festival director to occasionally ignore deadlines. Bryan Wolford of Drunken Zombie says, "If we know the quality of a filmmaker's work, we're more than willing to bend deadlines to take a look at it." Apart from *ignoring* deadlines for *special cases*, film festivals and script contests sometimes *extend* deadlines for *everyone*. I suspect this is usually done because not enough entry fees were collected.

2. Sure, I thought they were good films. I wouldn't have screened *The Ancient Law* were I embarrassed to be seen in it. I can't say that for every film I've been in. Even so, actors need never worry about competing against me in my own festival. (I'm sure George Clooney is breathing a sigh of relief.)

3. If a past Tabloid Witch winner emails me about their current project, I post the information on the Tabloid Witch's blog. Many festivals try to promote their past winners' latest achievements.

Doing so validates the festival's critical judgment, and encourages other filmmakers to enter.

4. Hollywood abounds with networking socials. Their biggest drawback, usually, is that the job seekers far outnumber the job offerers. Sometimes, *only* job seekers attend. In 2008, I attended a "writers pitch session" sponsored by Film Independent. There was no fee to attend — it was free to members — so it was not a scam. (Many "for profit" pitch sessions are suspected, by writers, of being scams.) Unfortunately, only writers came. No producers, agents, managers, or development executives. Writers ended up pitching their projects to each other. The second biggest drawback with Hollywood networking socials is that they often resemble singles bar/meat markets. People lie about themselves, try to catch the other person's lies ("Is he *really* friends with an agent at ICM?"), and keep glancing past each other to see if there's someone better in the room to meet.

5. Based on the book *Going to Pieces: The Rise and Fall of the Slasher Film, 1978–1986*, by Adam Rockoff (Jefferson, NC: McFarland, 2002).

6. Some of the documentary's interview subjects include Wes Craven, Sean S. Cunningham, Armand Mastroianni, Betsy Palmer, Felissa Rose, Rob Zombie, and Tom Savini.

7. There's an old *Mary Tyler Moore Show* episode wherein news anchor Ted Baxter loses his abilities after losing his confidence. Until Mary discovers that there are myriad organizations just looking for celebrities to accept their awards, because of the publicity generated for the organization. The celebrity need only guarantee in advance that he'll show up to accept the award. Whereupon Ted gleefully accepts a new award every week, reinvigorating his ego. Compare that to *Welcome Home, Roxy Carmichael* (1990), wherein Roxy was too famous to return to her home town to accept her award. For a real life example, in 2010 filmmaker Jean-Luc Godard refused to travel to the U.S. even to accept an Honorary Oscar.

8. "The De-Pressing Truth About DVDs," by James Grimmelmann, May 13, 2008. http://www.concurringopinions.com/archives/2008/05/the_depressing.html

3: Working the Film Festival!

1. Don't be jealous. Your festival can screen there too, or at most any other Hollywood studio, provided you pay the rental fee. Shockfest now also screens at Raleigh.

2. Despite his literary/bourgeois lifestyle, Ben Pleasants is an unabashed anarchist. The late Charles Bukowski dubbed Pleasants "the Beverly Hills anarchist." This was during their many interviews and conversations, culminating in Pleasants's book, *Visceral Bukowski: Inside the Sniper Landscape of L.A. Writers* (Northville, MI: Sun Dog Press, 2004).

3. "Best Tombs With a View: Cinespia at Hollywood Forever Cemetery," by Gendy Alimurung, *L.A. Weekly.* http://www.cinespia.org/_press/laweekly_102008.pdf.

4. *Hammocking* is an old TV programming concept. It means to schedule a new or weaker show between two popular shows. According to theory, viewers of the first popular show will sit through the weaker/new show as they wait for the second popular show to begin. Thus the two popular shows build an audience for the weaker/new show. They support the weaker/new show, as though on a hammock suspended between them.

5. If you watch C-SPAN 2's *Book TV* for any length of time, you'll eventually discern which authors are seasoned public speakers, and which are newbies. The newbies read woodenly, and answer questions accurately. Authors who are seasoned pros *speak* rather than *read* to the audience, and don't so much answer questions as relate colorful stories and funny anecdotes.

6. See *Hollywood Mistress* (aka *Mistress*; 1992) for a hilarious satire about some of the men who invest in independent films, and their reasons for doing so. I've assisted a few indie filmmakers in trying to find investors for their projects, mostly around Los Angeles, and I can attest that there's much truth in *Hollywood Mistress*'s "satire."

7. This is also why actors are generally more supportive of each other than are writers. If a writer finds a buyer for his screenplay, he'll keep the details a secret. He has other scripts to sell. Conversely, actors often refer other actors to producers or directors. This makes sense because, due to typecasting, actors rarely compete with *most* other actors. A beautiful, twentysomething actress knows she has nothing to lose, and much to gain, by referring her balding, thirtysomething actor friend. They'll never be up for the same part, and if she refers him today, he may refer her tomorrow. Writers *commiserate* with other writers (misery loves company), but they're less inclined, than are actors, to share information. I speak mainly from my experiences, but I assume it works as a general rule.

8. A *sync license* means that the composer (or whoever owns the music) keeps the rights to the music, but grants the filmmaker the right to *synchronize* that music to that one film. Sync licenses vary in scope (e.g., exclusive or nonexclusive; festival rights, or DVD only, or all media; North American or worldwide; five years or in perpetuity, etc.). If a filmmaker wants to distribute that music *apart* from the film (i.e., not synchronized to the film), such as on a soundtrack album, that will require additional types of licenses.

9. According to Filmins.com: "Insurance for Errors & Omissions (E&O) is a pre-requisite for establishing a distribution network for your production. Errors & Omissions insurance is not limited to movie producers. In fact, radio and television producers [and, I assume, film festivals] are also eligible for liability coverage. What Errors & Omissions insurance does is indemnify producers from lawsuits that may arise from the content of a production, including lawsuits alleging (a) infringement of copyright, (b) libel or slander, (c) invasion of privacy, (d) plagiarism or unauthorized copying of ideas, (e) defamation or degrading of products (trade libel), and (f) infringement on title, slogan, or trademark." For details, see: http://www.filmins.com/programs/errors-omissions-insurance.htm.

INDEX

Numbers in ***bold italics*** indicate pages with photographs.

07 136
1 (2009) 131, 147
2+1 Human Mistake (aka *2 + 1 erreur humaine*) 194
2:22 174, 190
3 a.m. (2003 short film; dir: Hopewell) 218
3 Chinesen mit dem Kontrabass see *Three Chinamen with a Double Bass*
3:52 55, 242
3 Stories About Evil 135
4 Ward Productions 210
4bia (aka *See prang*, aka *Phobia*) 143, 246
Le 5 ème règne (novel) 164
5 Years Young 246
7 Days see *Seven Days* (1998–2001 TV series)
7:35 in the Morning (aka *7h35 in the Morning* and *7:35 de la mañana*) 175, 182, 188
7th Orbit Award 126–27
8 Films to Die For After Dark Horrorfest 93
8 Heads in a Duffel Bag (aka *Eight Heads in a Duffel Bag*) 127, 251
The 8th Plague 161
8th Wonderland 142, 143, 172
9 Lives of Mara 163, 168, 241
The 9th Circle 244
11 Minutes Ago 172
XII 172
12 Monkeys (aka *Twelve Monkeys*) 209
12:01 (1993) 128, 166
12h01—prisonnier du temps see *12:01* (1993)
13 Assassins (aka *Thirteen Assassins*, aka *Jûsan-nin no shikaku*) 227
13 Beloved (aka *13: Game of Death*, aka *13 13*?) 127, 144, 192
13: Game of Death see *13 Beloved*
13 game sayawng see *13 Beloved*
13 Hrs 166
13 Seconds 160
13 Tzameti (aka *Tzameti (13)*) 229
13 Ways to Die at Home 214
14 apóstoles 230
20 Secondes 144
20th Century Fox Home Entertainment 195
25-Hour Horror Feast 116
28 (dir: Moreira) 185
28 Days Later 138, 139, 141, 149, 183, 188, 206, 240
28 giorni dopo see *28 Days Later*

28 Hours Later (film festival) 118, 119
28 Weeks Later 216
30 Days of Night: Dark Days 195
"30 Seconds to Mars" 138
"33" (*Battlestar Galactica* TV episode) 169
36 (2006 short film) 173
36 pasos 129
71 Fragments of a Chronology of Chance (aka *71 Fragmente einer Chronologie des Zufalls*) 233, 234
99.9 183, 233
100 Tears 47, 161, 241
"200" (*Stargate SG-1* TV episode) 133
300 204, 216
A 639. baba see *Doll No. 639*
893 Pike Street 160
1309 225
13 13 see *13 Beloved*
1428 Films 195
1888 143
1982s 178
2000X—Tales of the Next Millennia 186
2001: A Space Odyssey 170
2009: Lost Memories 164
2010 170
2058 172
2095 200
4321 Films 14
5150 Elm's Way see *5150, Rue des Ormes*
5150, Rue des Ormes 134, 163, 227
5250 200
7337 150, 202
8000 Miles (aka *SR: Saitama no rappâ*) 192
20,000 Leagues Under the Sea (1954?) 199
44987373-V 228

À l'arraché (1995 short film) 166
À l'intérieur see *Inside* (2007)
À mère et marées 143
À Vif 142
A+Positive 123, 190
Aaah! Zombies! see *Wasting Away* (2007)
Aachi & Ssipak 144, 156, 229
Aakeson, Kim Fupz 148
Aaltra (2004) 193
Aaron, Paul 128
Abades, Reyes 146
Abbott, L.B. 213
Abductees (1996 short film) 233
Abduction (dir: Campbell) 161
Abductions (unproduced script) 219

Las abejas see *The Bees* (1978)
Abertoir Horror Festival vii, 32–***33***, ***44***, 53–55, 63, ***67–69***, 74, ***76***, 78, 92, 117, 121–22, 191
Aberystwyth Arts Centre 117
Able (2008 feature?) 174
Able Edwards 214
Abominable (2006) 156
The Abominable Dr. Phibes 237
Abra Cadaver 171
Abraço do Vento 149
Abraham's Boys 238
Abrams, J.J. 216
Abramson, Jeff 30
Abril, Victoria 148
Absence (short film; 2007?) 180
The Absence of Emily 225
Absent (2008 short film; dir: Mento) 244
Absolution (2009 short film) 124
Absurdistan 26, 147, 180
Abwärts 154, 235
The Abyss (1989) 210
Acacia (2003) 149
Academy Award see Oscar
Academy of Science Fiction, Fantasy & Horror Films 3, 5, 103, 114, 203, 253n1
Acción mutante 141
Accumulator 1 (1994) 128, 166, 251
The Acid House 150, 151, 183
Acker, Amy 206
Ackerman, Forrest J. 138, 197, 198, 199
Acolytes 155, 177
Acrofobia 137
Across a Gold Prairie (aka *Kinpatsu no sougen*) 250
The Act in Question (1993, aka *El acto en cuestión*) 234
The Action Hero's Guide to Saving Lives 132, 135, 157
El acto en cuestión see *The Act in Question* (1993)
The Actress (2005 feature) 178
Adams, Amy 204
Adams, Corey 122
Adams, John Joseph 11
Adams, Liz 185, 224, 247
Adams, Ron 221
Adams æbler see *Adam's Apples*
Adam's Apples (2005) 127, 141, 148, 171, 181, 187, 193
Adamson, April 225
Adás see *Transmission*
The Addams Family (1964–66 TV series) 198

257

The Addams Family (1991 film) 141
Addams Family Values 210
The Adder's Bite 142
Addiction Is Murder 249
Adéla jeste nevecerela (aka *Adela no ha cenado todavía?*) 236
ADI *see* Amalgamated Dynamics
"Adicolor Green" 173
Adidas—"*Adicolor Green*" 173
Adjani, Isabelle 154
Adlon, Percy 128
A.D.N. (1997 animated short film) 233
Adrian of Death 225
Adrift in Tokyo 143
AdventureCon Horror Film Festival 103
The Adventures of Eon Delevan/The Making of the Adventures of Eon Delevan 157
The Adventures of Indiana Jones (DVD Collection) 206
The Adventures of Robin Hood (1938 film?) 206
Adventures of Superman (1952–58 TV series) 205
"Adult Fairy Tales & Frustrated Love Stories: The Cinematic Legacy of Terence Fisher" (article) 198
The Aerial (aka *La antena*) 127, 144, 187, 190
The Affidavit 159
Affleck, Ben 205
AFM *see* American Film Market
After Dark Films 103
After Dark Horrorfest: 8 Films to Die For 103
After Dolly 178
After the Apocalypse (2004 feature) 221, 222
Afterville 180, 229
AFTRA *see* American Federation of Television and Radio Artists
Agent Smith (*Matrix* character) 240
Agitator see Araburu tamashii-tachi (2001)
Agnieszka 157
Agresti, Alejandro 234
Aguirresarobe, Javier 153, 233
Ahlberg, Mac 153
Ahmad, Mian Adnan 142
Ahmanson Theatre 204
Ahmed, Asif viii, 117, 247
Ahmed, Barbar 161
Ahmed, Iqbal 217
A.I. Artificial Intellegence 207
Ai qing ling yao see Better Than Sex (2002)
Ainsworth, Daniel 223
Ain't No Tomorrow (2009, aka *Oretachi ni asu wa naissu*) 192
Ain't No Wolves 'Round Here 224
Air Doll 142
Aire (2005) 58
Aitkens, Daisy 237
Aja, Alexandre 231
Akai (2006 short film) 173, 203
Akasia see Acacia (2003)
Akhtar, Farhan 187
Akiko 136
Akira (1988) 171
Akron Screams 103–4
Akumulátor 1 see Accumulator 1 (1994)
Aladdin (1992) 210
Alamo Drafthouse Cinema 101, 109
Alaoui, Morjana 138

Alapont, David 158
Alarm Call (music video) 165
Alastruey, Karlos 158
Alba, Jessica 208
Alba, Michael 224
Alberny, Nicolas 142, 143
Albornoz, Jaime viii, 98
Albury, Ron 244
Alcalde, David 123, 201
Aldredge, Theoni V. 212
Aldridge, Tim 241
Alender, Chris 226
Alex, Vampire Slayer 130, 145
Alexander (dir: Dengrá) 159
Alexander, Chris v
Alexander, Vanessa 150
Alexander Senki see Reign: The Conqueror (1997)
Alexiou, Alexis 228
Alfred Hitchcock Presents (Season Four) 197
Alfredson, Tomas 126, 143, 163, 170, 187, 192, 201, 229
Ali, Christophe 160
Alianza Latinoamericana de Festivales de Cine Fantástico 102
Alias (2001–06 TV series) 207
Alice and I (2004 short film, aka *Alice et moi*) 193
Alice in Wonderland (2010) 215
Alice Jacobs Is Dead 131, 132, 135, 162, 174
Alicia (1994 short film; dir: Balagueró) 234
Alicia's Eyes see Los ojos de Alicia
Alicja Wonderland 158
Alien (1979) 5, 126, 170, 212
Alien Anthology Blu-ray (DVD set) 195
Alien Apocalypse 164
Alien Factor 2: The Alien Rampage see Alien Rampage
Alien Nation (1988) 210
Alien Nation: Body and Soul 251
Alien Nation: Dark Horizon 209
Alien Nation: Millennium 209
Alien Raiders 161, 168, 172, 195, 220, 224, 243, 245
Alien Rampage 160
Alien: Resurrection 139
Alien Rose 173
Alien vs. Ninja (2010) 246
Alien Xmas 205
Aliens 126, 170, 211
Alimurung, Gendy 254n3
Alioto, Dean 225
Aljinovic, Boris 194
All About Evil 245
All for Love (2008 short film; dir: Harris) 244
"All Good Things..." (*Star Trek: The Next Generation* TV series) 169
All I Want for Christmas (2006 short film) 196
All Nite Scream-O-Rama 104
All Things Which Splatter 249
All Tomorrow's Parties (2003 feature, aka *Mingri tianya*) 231
All Users Guide for the Imaginary Friend (Abridged) see *Manual práctico del amigo imaginário (abreviado)*
Allard, Louis 142
Alle, Fernando 168, 186
Allen, Andy 220
Allen, Joan 208

Allen, Karen 212
Allen, Matt 172, 188
Allen, Tim 208
Allen, Woody 170, 186, 213, 232
Allison, John 97
Allure (2009 short film) 190
Alma (2009 short film; dir: Blaas) 146, 155
Alma (year?) 214
A Alma do Negócio (aka *The Soul of Business*) 176
Almereyda, Michael 166, 233
Almodóvar, Pedro 153
Alone (length?; year?) 162
Alone (short film; year?) 157
Alone (2005 short film; dir: Selko) 9, 110, 242, 244
Alone (2007 feature; dir: Banjong & Parkpoom) 156, 189, 217, 246
Alone in the Dark (1982 feature) 141, 235
Alonso, Maria Inez 146
Al's Beef 132, 135, 136
Altabás, Ciro 121, 132, 185, 202, 203, 248
Altamont Now 122
Altar (2007 feature; dir: Ilarde) 184
Altar (2008 short film; dir: Bezner) 189
Alter Ego (2002, aka *Mô hitori iru*; dir: Issei) 195
Altered States (1980) 212
Altman, David 243
Álvarez, Fede (aka Federico Álvarez) 129, 133
Alvarez, Ozzy 138, 217
Alvariño, Javier 231
Alvart, Christian 175
Alves, João 186
Am I Evil 196
Amado, Norberto López 149
Amalgamated Dynamics (aka ADI) 209
Amami, Y ki 232
Les amants criminels see *Criminal Lovers*
Amaral, Vivi vii, 32, 38, 42–43, 45, 47, 50, 53, 64, 67, 70, 79–80, 93, 96
Amazing Unmasked vs. El Eoctor Calavera Maligna 231
Amazon.com 29, 72, 79, 94
Ámbar (1994) 233, 234
Ambassadors Day 246
Amberg Horror Fest 99
Ambrose, David 236
AMD K6 165
Ameli, Jonathan 160
Amenabar, Alejandro 128
Amendment (2010 short film) 200
Amer 166, 179, 228
American Federation of Television and Radio Artists 89
American Film Market 19, 77
American Macabre 243
American Psycho 139
American Scary 197
An American Werewolf in London (1981) 197, 212; *see also Beware the Moon*
An American Werewolf in Paris 165
Amicus Mortis 137
Amona Putz! see *The Inflatable Grandma*
Amores perros 150
Amsterdam Fantastic Film Festival *see* Imagine: Amsterdam Fantastic Film Festival

AM1200 (2008 short film) 122, 131, 168, 190, 196, 200, 219, 220
Anakin (*Star Wars* character) 239
The Analyst's Goodbye 136
Anatomia Extinction (aka *Genkai jinkô keisû*) 251
Anatomy (dir: Pandolfi) 167
Anaya, Arturo 185
Anaya, Elena 147, 228
Anchor Bay Entertainment 195, 198
The Ancient Law (2008 short film) 56, 254n2
The Ancient Rite of Corey McGillis 190, 191
Anders, Allison 150
Anders, David 188
Anderson, Brad 188, 232
Anderson, C. Dean 213
Anderson, Charlie 196
Anderson, David Leroy 209
Anderson, Gillian 209
Anderson, Joel 131
Anderson, Lindsay 154
Anderson, Paul 127
Anderson, Richard Dean 208
Anderson, Scott E. 207, 208
Anderson, Susannah 222
Andersson, Roy 147, 187
Andô, Masahiro 146
Andô, Sakura 192
André, Michael 178
Andréa, Jean-Baptiste 127, 201
Andrejew, Piotr 154
Andrews, Gary 160
Andrews, Jaime 238
Andrews, Shaun 159
Andy Warhol's Bad see *Bad* (1977)
Anesthesia (2006 short film) 172
Anganuzzi, Jimena 146
Ange (2006 short film) 217
Angel (1999–2004 TV series) 137, 206, 207, 208, 240
The Angel (2007 short film; dir: Hough) 144, 215
Angel caido (2010) 185
Angel de fuego 152
Angel of the Night (1998, aka *Nattens engel*) 183
Angela 128
Angelier, François 165
Angels and Fire 162
Anguish (1987) 128
Animal (2005; dir: Bosch) 148, 181
Animal Farm (1999) 150
Animal Kingdom (2010) 47
Um animal menor 132, 146
Animals see *Animals with the Tollkeeper* (1998)
Animals with the Tollkeeper (1998 feature; aka *Animals*) 233, 250
Animated American 132, 135
An Animated Life (book) 199
O Anjo da Guarda (1999) 151
Anjos no Meio da Praça 146
Annie & Boo 215
Annie Award 104
Annila, Antti-Jussi 127, 163
Anónimos 203
Another Flush 160
Another Hole in the Head: Two Weeks of Horror, Sci-Fi and Fantasy vii, 104
Ansara, Alice 177
Ansin, Greg 123
Antarctic Journal (2005, aka *Namgeukilgi*) 230
The Ante (2006) 143
Antefatto (1970/71?) 237
La antena see *The Aerial*
Anti-Samaritan Hotline 223
Antibodies (aka *Antikörper*) 175
Antichrist (2009 feature) 187
Antikörper see *Antibodies* (2005)
Antin, Juan 232
Antunez, Noelia 129
Anwar, Joko 192
Apartment 206 136, 221, 222, 225
Aphex Twin (band) 165
Apollo 11 news coverage 170
The Apostate (1987, aka *Otstupnik*) 235
Appel, Craig 113
The Appointment (short film; dir: Clinton Gleason) 219
Après rasage 154
April (short film; year?) 223
Apt Pupil 208
Aqua ad lavandum — in brevi 134, 200
Aqueles Olhos 132
Aquellos ojos brujos 129
Arabian, Vatche 158
Araburu tamashii-tachi (2001, aka *Agitator*) 232
Arachnophobia 210
Aragami 127
Aragão, Rodrigo 129, 203
Aragorn (character) 240
Arahan 145, 193
Araújo, Artur Serra 148
Arbeit für Alle see *Full Employment*
L'arbre de les cireres see *The Cherry Tree* (1998)
Arcane Sorcerer (aka *L'arcano incantatore*) 127, 194
Arden, Paul 202
La ardilla roja 166
Arena (short film; dir: Wallace) 244
Aresty, Adam 217
Argent content (2000, short film; aka *Easy Money*) 175
Argento, Asia 178, 248
Argento, Dario 100, 149, 171, 213, 214, 233, 236
Arias, Michael 144, 229
Arija, Jaume García 148
Arizona Underground Film Festival vii, 49, 104, 122
Ariztical Entertainment 11
Arizza, Albert 228
The Ark (2007 Polish short film) 148, 180
Ark (unproduced script) 226
Arka see *The Ark* (2007)
Arkoff, Samuel Z. 213
Armadillo (2004 short film; dir: Vidal) 222
Armageddon (1998) 208
Armento, Kevin 188, 240
Armero, Álvaro Fernández 127
Armstrong, Brent 197
Armstrong, Curtis 222
Armstrong, Jake 131, 133
Army of Darkness 128, 140, 152, 209
Arnfred, Morten 150
Arnold, Andrea 147
Arnold, Jack 170, 213
Arnold, Tracy 153
Arnzen, Michael 242
Aronofsky, Darren 147
Arquette, Patricia 137
Arquette, Rosanna 148, 153, 234
Arrebato see *Rapture* (1980)
Arriaga, Guillermo 150
Arriagada, Jorge 234
The Arrival (1996) 209
Arsenault, Mathieu 122, 142
The Art of Dying (2000, aka *El arte de morir*) 127, 183
El arte de morir see *The Art of Dying*
Arthur, Colin 147
Arturo Gámez 234
Arvanites, Steven 244
ASCAP 91
Ascension (2002 feature; dir: Hussain) 231
Ascension (short film; year?) 215
Ásgeirsdóttir, Sara Dögg 194
Ash, Arian Waring 243
Ashe, Eve Brent see Eve Brent
Ashes (2010 feature; dir: Matar) 171, 224
Ashes to Ashes (unproduced script) 172
Ashino, Yoshiharu 147, 214
Ashley, Jonathan Arthur 214
Ashtoberfest Horror Film Festival 104
Asleep in the Deep 169
Asquith, Michael J. 218
Assante, Armand 191
Assayas, Olivier 232
The Assessment see *Headhunter: The Assessment Weekend*
Assimilation (short film) 219
Assumption (2006 short film; dir: Keller) 173, 221
Asten, Alec 196
Asterión 129
Asteroide Award 100, 214
Astin, Sean 206
Astounding B-Monster (website) 199
L'astronaute 143
Astropia 147
Astuko's Legend 142
Asylum (2005) 141
At Night (2002 short film; aka *Dans la nuit*) 175
At World's End 142
El ataque de los Kriters asesinos 201
El ataque de los robots de nebulosa-5 see *The Attack of the Robots from Nebula 5*
Ataque de pánico! (2009 short film) 129, 133
Atkins, Tom 138, 162
Atlanta Horror Fest 104, 106, 122, 130
Atlanta Horror Film Festival 104, 122–23, 130
Atom Nine Adventures 225
Atraksion 149
Atrocious 186
Attack of the Disco Zombies 185, 203
The Attack of the Robots from Nebula 5 (aka *El ataque de los robots de nebulosa-5*) 179, 227
Attackazoids! (2008 short film) 123, 244
Attackazoids, Deploy!! (2009 short film) 242
Atwood, Colleen 204
Au rendez-vous de la mort joyeuse see *Expulsion of the Devil* (1973)
Aube nébuleuse see *Nebulous Dawn*
Aubert, Robin 148
Aubier, Stéphane 155, 228
The Auburn Hills Breakdown 162, 175, 238

Index

Audition (1999; dir: Miike) 150
Auf bösem Boden (aka *On Evil Grounds*) 129, 186, 203
auf der Heide, Jonathan 228
August Rush 204
August Underground (2001) 196
August Underground's Penance (2007, aka *Penance*) 196
Aurora: Cuarta Muestra de cine de Horror 100
Ausentes 148
Austin, Daniel 159
Austin, Josh 225
Austin, Michael 251
Austin Powers in Goldmember 240
Austin Powers: International Man of Mystery (aka *Austin Powers*) 208
Auto da Fe (2007 short film) 172
Automaton Transfusion 246
Aux frontières du réel 166; also see *The X-Files*
Avalon (2001 feature) 215, 232
Avant pétalos grillados 180
Avary, Roger Roberts 251
Avatar (short film; year?) 181
Avatar (2005 short film; dir: Quílez) 225
Avatar (2009 feature) 132, 203, 215, 249
Avati, Pupi 127, 194, 214
Avella, Joe 121
Avenet-Bradley, Brian 185, 196, 225
Avenged Sevenfold 138
Avenging Angel (short film) 160
A.W.O.L. (2006 short film) 172, 220, 224
Ax Wound 14
Axed (2010 short film; dir: Long) 126, 184
Ayassi 149
Ayats, Eva 168
Aylwin, Christian 185
Ayotte, Pierre 143
Ayson, Steve 135
Azione mutante see *Acción mutante*

B Movie Celebration 104, 123–24
B-Movie Film Festival 104, 124
B-Movie Madness 111
B-Movies, Underground & Trash Film Festival see BUT
B-Side Entertainment 30
Ba, Gabriel 216
Babe 209
Baby (2010 short film) 200
The Baby of Mâcon 234
The Baby Shredder Song 243
Babylon 2084 158, 176
Babylon 5 (1994–98 TV series) 169, 186, 208
Babysitter Wanted 248
Baca, Shawna 55, 242
Bacchus (short film; dir: Fabre) 244
Bacchus Award 106
Bach, Laura 162
Back in the Woods (2010 French short film) 158
Back to the Future 170, 211
Back to the Future Part II 210
Backus, David 239
Bacon, Kevin (not the famous actor) viii, 98, 248, 249
Bad (1977, aka *Andy Warhol's Bad*) 213
Bad Behaviour (2010) 176, 177
Bad Biology 189
Bad Dreams (2006 short film) 163, 173

The Bad Father 218
Bad Friday 55, 241
Bad Guy (2001, aka *Nabbeun namja*; aka *Na Bdun-Nam-Ja?*) 232
Bad Habits (2009 feature) 177
Bad Land 123
Bad Lieutenant 102, 152
"Bad Moon Rising" (article) 197
Bad Reputation 93, 163, 225, 248
Bad Taste (1987) 141
Badalamenti, Angelo 139, 140, 210
Badenhorst, Daleen 238
Badger, Eric 224
Badham, John 211, 213
Baek, Seung-hwa 192
Baek, Yun-shik (aka Yoon-Sik Beak) 193
Baghdikian, Karni 188
Bagman (2004 short film, aka *Le bagman — Profession: Meurtrier*) 248
Le bagman — Profession: Meurtrier see *Bagman* (2004)
Bai, James 125, 214
Bai fa mo nu zhuan see *The Bride with White Hair*
Bailey, Chase 196
Bailey, Gareth "Gaz" vii, 32–**33**, **44**, 47, 50, 53–55, 63, 67, 74, 77–81, 88, 92, 117
Bailey-Bond, Prano 158
Baillet, Jean-Luc 159
Bais, Leslie 202
Le baiser see *The Kiss* (2005)
Baker, Dylan 138
Baker, George 115
Baker, Louise 115
Baker, Rick 137, 197, 199, 207, 209, 212, 213
Baker, Roy W. 141
Baker, Scott 235
Baker, Shay 124
Baker, Suzi 235
Bakjwi see *Thirst* (2009)
Le bal du minotaure see *Minotaure's Ball*
La balada de Vlad Tepes 185
Balagueró, Jaume 127, 141, 143, 144, 147, 148, 150, 163, 164, 165, 170, 176, 194, 228, 229, 233, 234
Balandín, Antonio 236
Bale, Christian 139, 205, 216, 231, 239
The Ballad of Angel Face 224
Ballegeer, Yves 96
Balme, Timothy 92
Baltera, Pablo 129
Bama, James 199
Bamford, Chris 123, 190
Band, Charles 213
Band, Richard 168
Bandits (1997 feature; dir: Von Garnier) 250
Banderas, Antonio 140
The Band's Visit 147, 148
Bane (2009 feature) 224
Banjong, Pisanthanakun 143, 145, 164, 217
Bank, Dylan 156
Bank, Tenley 243
Banke, Anders 148, 194
The Banquet (2006) 144
La banyera 128, 153, 234
Baquero, Ivana 205
Bar-Levy, Omri 215
Barbara Broadcast 185
Barbarash, Ernie 196
Barbeau, Adrienne 131, 139

Barbee Butcher 179, 201
Barbie doll 197
Barbieri, Francesco 236
Barbo, Giovanni viii, 100, 214
Bardem, Miguel 150, 194
Bardin, Garri 227
Barges, Henri 128
Barker, Clive 137, 153, 171, 217
Barker, Cordell 232
Barklow, Tanner 196
Barlas, Christina 220, 244
Barlow, Nate 225
Barnes, Eric Frost 226
Barnes, Jonas 248
Barnes, Michael 159
Barnett, Kristi 126
Barnhardt, Drew 168, 176, 189
Baron-Cohen, Ash 250
Barr, Nathan 139
Barrander, Johan 103
Barreiro, Francisco 166
Barrera, Adrián 184
Barrett, Sam 177
Barrett, Simon 155
Barrow, Neal 198
Barrozo, Teresa 228
Barry, John 212
Barrymore, Drew 140, 208
BARS see Buenos Aires Rojo Sangre
Bartakiáda 153
Bartalos, Gabriel 189
Bartas, Sharunas 152
Bartholomew's Song 173
Barthonieu, Roman 150
Barton, Fred 205
À bas l'éternité 153
Basement Jack (2009 feature) 243, 244
Basement Jaxx (music band) 164
Basil, Harry 190
The Basket Case (short film) 146
Bass, Saul 234
Bassanini, Katia 187
Bassett, Angela 209
Bassett, Michael J. 145, 147
Basso, Alain 158, 247
Los bastardos 228
Bates, Robert, Jr. 122, 155, 243
Bates, Tyler 138
Bateman, Colin 151
Bathory (unproduced script) 226
Bathtub to Happiness 135
Batman II
Batman (1989) 213
Batman Begins 205, 216, 239
Batman and Robin: Batman (comic book) 215
Batman: Dead End (fan film) 157
Batman: Gotham After Midnight (comic book) 197
Batman Returns 210
Bats in the Belfrey (2010 short film) 186
Batten, Cyia 218
Batteries Not Included (aka *batteries not included*) 211
Battle Chess 130
Battle of the Bone 161
Battle Royale (2000, aka *Batoru rowaiaru*) 202
Battlefield Baseball (aka *Jigoku Kōshien*) 250
Battlestar Galactica (mini-series) 206
Battlestar Galactica (1978–79 TV series) 214
Battlestar Galactica (2004–09 TV

series) 132, 133, 204, 205, 206, 216, 239, 240
Battletruck (1982, aka *Warlords of the 21st Century*) 236
Bava, Lamberto 100, 141, 214, 236
Bava, Mario 139, 198, 204, 236
Baxter, Jessica 167
Baxter, Ted (character) 254n7
Bay, Michael 208
Bayer, Benjamin 134
Bayona, Juan Antonio 147, 163
Bazán, Géraldine 167
Be-seu-teu-sel-leo see *Bestseller* (2010)
Be the World for Her (aka *Sekai wa kanojo no tame ni aru*) 250
Be with Me (2005) 148
The Beach Party at the Threshold of Hell 217, 218
The Beacon (2009) 191
Beak, Yoon-Sik see Yun-shik Baek
Bean, Sean 217
Bear, Robert 93
Beast and the Harlot (music video) 138
Beast of Burden (2009 short film) 130
The Beast Stalker (aka *Ching yan*) 192
Beatty, David 150
Beatty, Terry 198
Beatty, Warren 212
Beaucage, Robert 224
Beaudoin, Stéphane 176, 247
The Beautiful and Damned (2010 feature; dir: Wolstencroft) 177
Beautiful as You Are 247
The Beauty (music video) 191
Beauty and the Beast (1981, aka *Panna a netvor*) 154, 236
Les beaux-pères see *Fathers in Law* (1998)
Beavan, Jenny 208
Because There Are Things You Never Forget (aka *Porque hay cosas que nunca se olvidan*) 123, 132, 146, 157, 175, 180, 201
Bechard, Shera 155
Beck, Calvin T. 197
Becker, Jean 232
Becker, Josh 164
Beckinsale, Kate 216, 217
Bedevil (1993) 234
Bedevilled (2010, aka *Kim Bok-nam salinsageonui jeonmal*) 155, 166, 192
Bedfellows (2008 short film; dir: Daywalt) 137, 167
The Bees (1978 feature, aka *Las abejas*) 236
Beesley-Brown, Andrea vii, 41, 50, 53, 67, 70, 73
Beesley, Shayla 241
Beetlejuice (aka *Beetle Juice*) 126, 210
Before Dawn (2005 short film) 144
Before the Fall (2008, aka *Tres días*) 170, 180, 214, 217
Beg, Scream and Shout! 95
Beggs, Amanda 158
Béguin, Olivier 188
Behind the Mask: The Rise of Leslie Vernon 145, 230
Being John Malkovich 208
Bekaustegui, Marta 202
Bekmambetov, Timur 127
Bela Lugosi and Boris Karloff: The Expanded Story of a Haunting Collaboration (book) 197
Bela Lugosi Collection (DVD) 198, 206
Belcebú 129

Belcher, Laurence 220
Belcher, Ronnie 238
Belefant, Brian 226
Beliën, Dirk 17
Believe (short film; year?) 220
Bell, Barbara 162
Bell, Kristen 156, 205
Bell, Michele Davidson 230
Bell, Susan 221, 225
Bell, Sv 143
Bell, Tobin 137, 138
Bellantine, Jeff 243
Bellucci, Monica 139
Belmondo 182, 188
Belofsky, Rachel 6, 58, 115, 253n1
Beltrán, Josemi 103
Belvaux, Rémy 234, 251
Ben & Jerry's Award 228
Benages, Gallard 102
Benages, Toni 102
Benard, Carlos 161
Bendito Machine 175
Bendtsen, Henning 234
Beneath the Cogon see *Sa Ilalim ng cogon*
Beneath the Frost Line 160
Beneath the Surface (2007 feature; dir: Reigle) 200
Benedict, Dirk 214
Benedict, Marina 174, 200, 241
Benes, Lubomir 154, 236
Benscoter, Wes 142
Benson, Robert 218
Bento, Deborah 55, 241
Benton, Robert 170
Benullo, David 148
Benway, Dr. **70**, 238
Benz, Julie 137, 203
Berardi, Dennis 218
Berdahl, Robert O. 171
Berdejo, Luiso 229
Bereavement (2010 feature) 188
Berger, Howard 138, 205, 208, 231
Berger, Katherine viii, 96
Bergin, John 143, 229
Bergman, Sandahl 212
Bergvall, Joel 188, 218
Berlin Film International Festival 22
Bernard, Carlos 220
Bernardo, Nuria Leon 168
Bernauer, Andreas 99
Bernie (1996 feature) 251
Bernie's Doll 156
Berrokal, Issac (aka Issac Berrocal) 133
Berry, Abel 125
Berryman, Michael 137
Bernstien, Les 150
Berserker (2005 short film; dir: Eckberg) 221
Bert & Bertie 196
Bertaccini, Sabrina 242
Berthomieu, Romain 165
Bertozzi, Juan Manuel 185
Bertram, Dean 95
Bérubé, Simon 143
Besas, Marco 148, 201
Besat see *Possessed* (1999)
Beshir, George 178
Besson, Luc 128, 154, 235
Les bessones del carrer de Ponent (aka *The Twin Sisters of Sunset Street*) 227, 237
Best Buy 93
Best Worst Move 143, 228
Der Beste (2005 short film, aka *The Old Pro*) 159, 175, 181

Bestseller (2010 feature, aka *Be-seu-teu-sel-leo*) 192
Bet on My Disco 193
Betancourt, Juan Manuel 144, 147
Betania (2010 short film) 237
Better Housekeeping 150
Better Than Sex (2002 feature, aka *B.T.S. (Better Than Sex)*, aka *Ai qing ling yao*) 250
Bettie Page: Dark Angel 248
Bettis, Angela 121, 138, 231
Between Your Legs (1999 feature, aka *Entre las piernas*; dir: Pereira) 194
Betz, Travis 224
Beware the Moon: Remembering "An American Werewolf in London" (2009) 197, 237
Beyond Re-Animator 175, 182
Beyond the Door II (1977, aka *Shock*, aka *Schock*) 236
Beyond the Grave (2010) 122, 184
Beyond Twilight (short film; dir: Sanz) 238
Bezner, Nathan 189
Bharat, Ganapathy (aka Bharat Bala) 193
Bhukya, Mamatha 147
Bi-mong see *Dream* (2008) 127
Bias Peak 4 (computer program) 45
Bias Sound Soap (computer program) 45
Bicât, Nick 233
Bicho (Brazilian short film) 146
Bielinsky, Fabián 150
Bienvenue à gattaca see *Gattaca*
Bierbauer, Kirk 243
Biewener, Mary Ann 244
Bif 163
BifBangPow! 197
BIFFF see Brussels International Fantastic Film Festival
Big (1988) 210
Big Bear Horror Film Festival vii, 6, 12; sponsorship rates 27–28; **43**, 51–**52**, 57–58, 66, 73, 81, 88, 91, 93, 104–5, 124–25
The Big Empty 145
Big Fish in Middlesex 124
Big Foot 124
The Big Garage (aka *Die grosse Werkstatt*) 180, 229
Big Gay Horror Fan Film Festival vii, 105
Big Gun (aka, *Dai kenj*) 249
Big Kids Play Manslaughter 224
Bigazzi, Luca 233
Bigelow, Kathryn 128, 209
Biggar, Trisha 207, 208
Bijelic, André 233
Bijitā Q see *Visitor Q*
Bijocan (aka *Bijo-can*) 250
Bikini Bloodbath Carwash 122
Bikini Girls on Ice 162
Bikur Ha-Tizmoret see *The Band's Visit*
Bilal, Enki 214
Bill, Leo 156, 248
Bill & Ted's Bogus Journey 210
Bill Cothron Best Emerging Filmmaker Award 123
Bind (2009 short film; dir: Forrest) 171
Binding Silence 169
Bionicle: Mask of Light 206
Bird, Antonia 141
Bird, Brad 169, 204

Index

Bird in a Window 233
Birdday 136
The Birds (1963) 197
"Birthday" (episode in *Tokyo Noir*) 148
The Birthday (2004 feature; dir: Mira) 231
Bishop, Gregg 225
Bishop, Troy 221
Bismuth, Pierre 125
Bissell, Whit 213
Bitch (short film; dir: Read) 159
The Bitch Is Back 152
The Bite see *La morsure* (2009)
Bitten (short film; 2007?) 180
A Bittersweet Life 144, 145, 230
Bittner, Andy 160
Bixby, Jerome 203
Bizien, Jean-Luc 164
Bjerre, David 160
Björk (singer) 165
Blaas, Rodrigo 146, 155
Black (2009) 143
Black, Claudia 132, 133, 206
Black, Dustin Lance 213
Black, Jean 209
Black, Karen 137, 139, 148, 149, 236
Black, Lucas 209
The Black Cat (1934) 199
The Black Cat (2010) 130, 243
Black Coffee (year?) 178
Black Death 187, 201, 217
Black Dynamite 246
The Black Forest (comic book) 198, 199
Black Gulch 226
The Black Panther see *La pantera negra* (2010)
Black Rainbow (1989) 153, 234
Black Sheep (2006; dir: King) 127, 163, 164, 187
Black Swamp International Film Festival 105
Black Tulip Award 170–71
The Black Violin (animation) 222
The Black Waters of Echo's Pond 161
Black Widow (2001, aka *The Praying Mantis* and *Die Gottesanbeterin*) 193
Black XXX-Mas 194
Blackheads 246
Blackmore, Jessica **89**
Blacula (1972) 213, 253n1
Blade 139
Blade II 139
Blade Runner 126, 170, 204
Blades of Blood 141
Blair, Linda 172
The Blair Witch Project 7, 49–50, 139, 194
Blaisdell, Jackie 198
Blaisdell, Paul 198
Blake, Michael F. 199
Blake, Rachael 149
Blake, Robert 139
Blalock, Jolene 207
Blamire, Larry 199
Blanc, Cheveux 143
Blanchett, Cate 249
Blanks, Jamie 217
Blarghaaahrgarg 168
Blasco, Sergio 78, 186
Blaser, Keith 220
Blatty, William Peter 210, 212
Die blaue Grenze (2005, aka *A Quiet Love*) 148, 156, 175, 181
The Blaxorcist 181

Bled Fest 105
Bled White 241
BleedFest vii, 6, 47, 57, **62**, **85**, 105, 113, 117, 253n4, 253n11
Bleedy Award 105
Blesa, Gimena 203
The Blind Date of Coffin Joe 241
The Blind Swordsman: Zatoichi (2003, aka *Zatôichi*) 231
Blindness (2008 feature; dir: Meirelles) 228, 229
"Blink" (*Doctor Who* TV episode) 133, 169, 197
Blinkers (dir: Major) 160
The Bloated Beetle 219
The Blob (1958) 105
The Blob (CD) 197
BlobFest 105
Blockbuster 93
Blockhead (2010 short film; dir: Conway) 191
Blogger.com 33
Blom, Paul viii, 102, 237
Blomkamp, Neill 186, 249
Blondes in the Jungle 177
Blood (2000 feature; dir: Cantor) 188
Blood and Roses (1960) 50
Blood Bath Film Festival vii, 105, 109, 113, 116, 125
Blood Bath 2: The Film Festival 105, 125
Blood, Boobs & Beast 123, 124, 157
Blood Bunny (trailer) 191
Blood Car 123, 246
Blood Feast (1963) 45
Blood Night: The Legend of Mary Hatchet (aka *Blood Night*) 200, 219, 237
Blood of the Beast 196
Blood on the Backlot 226
Blood on the Highway 123, 146, 162, 176, 224
Blood Rain 250
Blood Red Girls 251
Blood River (2009) 237
The Blood Shed 134
Blood Simple 154
Blood Tea and Red String 145, 156
Blood: The Last Vampire (2000 animated short film) 219
Blood Ties (TV series) 133
Blood Trails 134
Bloodbath at the House of Death 128
Bloodletter (unproduced script) 244
Bloodlines (unproduced script) 218
Bloodlust (unproduced script) 223; later produced in 2004
Bloodspit 167
Bloodstained Romance 247
Bloody Christmas (2003 short film) 164
Bloody Daisies 241
Bloody Harvest Film Festival vii, 105
Bloody Mallory 195
Bloody Sunday 150
Bloody Valentine Film Festival vii, 105
Bloom, Matt 158
Bludon, Bob 202
"Blue Harvest" (*Family Guy* TV episode) 205
Blue Notes 177, 178
Blue Thunder (1983) 211
Blue Velvet (aka *Terciopelo azul*) 235
Blueberry see *Renegade* (2004)
Bluefish 223

Blumenstein, David 178
Bluth, Don 234
BMI 91
Bo chi tung wah see *Connected* (2008)
Boag, Colleen 241
Boam, Jeffrey 170
The Boarder (2005 short film) 173, 221, 225
Boatright-Simon, Matt 244
Bob Wilkins Award for Best Horror Host 124
Bobby Yeah 131
Bodies, Rest & Motion 152
Body of Work (2009 short film; dir: Bram) 6, 161, 241
Body Parts (1991) 141, 210
Body Snatchers (1993 feature) 252
Body Troopers (aka *Chasing the Kidneystone* and *Jakten på nyresteinen*) 184
Boesen, Tobias Gundorff 174
Bogdan, Mircea 236
Bogliano, Adrián García 58, 129, 130, 185, 186, 190, 203, 248
Bogliano, Ramiro 129
Bogush, Jennifer 244
Bohemibot 172
Bohlinger, Don 150
Boingboing.net 32
Boisliveau, Christian 194
Bold, Brandyn 158
Bollig, Kelsey 224
The Bolt Who Screwed Christmas 135
Bon Appetit (2005 short film) 124, 136
Bond, A.J. 214
Bond, David 97
Bond, James (character) 40, 205, 239
The Bond of Saint Marcel 225
Bondi Tsunami 178
Bone Eater 123
Bone Sickness 196
Bonet, José Antonio 159
Boneville, Daniel 162
Bong, Joon-ho 127, 148, 187, 230
Bonilauri, Nicolas 160
Bonilla, George 162
Bonnie & Clyde vs. Dracula 122, 162, 200
Bonzel, André 234, 251
Boogie, el aceitoso (aka *Boogie*) 201
The Book Dealers 135
Book of Lore 220
Book of Shadows: Blair Witch 2 139
The Book of the Dead (2005, aka *Shisha no sho*) 230
The Book of Tomorrow 132
Book TV (TV show) 254n5
Booty Sex (music video) 224
Bordage, Pierre 99
Bordas, Arnaud 146
Boreanaz, David 206, 207, 208
Borges, Victor-Hugo 146
Borghi, Andrés 185
Borkowski, Marc 147
Born, Adolf 154
Bornedal, Ole 128, 141, 146, 158, 228
Borowczyk, Walerian 236
Borowski, John 218
Borowski, Rasmus 159, 175
The Borrower (1991) 234
Borrowing Time (2004 feature) 124, 222
Borthwick, Dave 152, 234, 251
Bosák, Oldrich 237
Bosch, Roselyne (aka Rose Bosch) 148
El bosque animado see *The Living Forest*

Boston Fantastic Film Festival 105, 125
Boston Independent Film Festival *see* Independent Film Festival of Boston
Boston LGBT Film Festival 106
Boston Science Fiction Film Festival vii, 105–6, 125
Boston Underground Film Festival 106
Boston Terror'thon vii, 106, 116, 125
Boswell, Simon 140
Botched (2007 feature; dir: Ryan) 189
Both 124
The Bothersome Man 148, 163, 164, 171, 181, 187, 229
Botko, Huck 245
Botnik! 157
Bottin, Rob 209, 211
Bottles (2010 short film) 135
Bouchard, Simon 144
Bouchon, Pierre 166
Boulbès, Jérôme 232
Bound (1996; dir: Wachowski) 151
Bousman, Darren Lynn 143
Bout d'essai 152
Bovey, Simon 214
The Bow see *Hwal*
Bowda, Katsushi 251
Bowden, Adam 241
Bowen, AJ 155
Bowie, David 213
Bowler, Mike 226
Bowman (2006 short film) 230
Bowman, Jacqueline 222
A Boy and His Dog (1975) 170, 213
The Boy Who Could Fly 211
The Boy Who Wouldn't Kill 228
Boyce, Frank Cottrell 231
Boyd, Justin 217
Boyd, VJ 217
Boyens, Philippa 169, 186, 206
Boyes, Simon 134, 237
Boyle, Danny 141, 149, 152, 188
Boynton, Alex 156
Bozzetto, Bruno 237
Bracket, Leigh 170
Bradbury, Ray 8, 172, 199, 211, 213; *also see* Ray Bradbury Award
Bradley, Brian Avenet 160
Bradley, Doug 149, 168
Braga, Brannon 169
Brain Dead (2007) 124, 157, 172, 176, 190, 196, 221, 245
Brain Holiday 251
Brain Suckers (short film) see *Chucladores de Cerebros*
Braindead (1992, aka *Dead Alive*) 92, 140, 152, 171, 234
Brains (2007 music video) 14, 241
Brainstorm (1983) 211
Bram, Alex vii, 6, 9–*10*, 31, 39–40, 49, 53, 58, 67, 83, 87, 106, 241
Bram Stoker Award 5, 106, 125–26
Bram Stoker International Film Festival 117, 126
Bram Stoker's Dracula (1992) 50, 140, 210
Branagh, Kenneth 202
Brand Upon the Brain! 127
Brandes, Richard 225
Brandt, Tarika 221
Brandt, Vitor 132
Branney, Sean 168
Brasil see *Brazil* (2002)
The Brattle Theatre 105
Braun, Felipe 203
Bravo's 100 Scariest Movie Moments 199

Brazeau, Shawn 124
Brazil (2002 short film, aka *Brasil*) 218, 232
Brdecka, Jirí 154
A Break in the Monotony 123, 132, 190
Breakfast with the Colonel 160
Breaking Bad 203, 204
Breaking News (2004 feature, aka *Dai si gin*; dir: To) 231
Breaking Nikki 146
Breaking the Code 157
Breath (2007 South Korean feature) 147
Breathers: A Zombie's Lament (novel) 10–*11*
Breathless (2009; dir: Yang) 142, 155
Breck, Jonathan 139
Brent, Eve (aka Eve Brent Ashe) 212
Bress, Eric 127
Bressane, Júlio 151
Bretin, Denis 164
Brian Sipe Special Effects 162
Briceño, Luis 158
Brick 230
Brickle, Justin 177
Brickman, Marshall 170, 213
Brico Killer 230
Bride of Chucky 139, 165
Bride of Re-Animator 140
The Bride with White Hair (1993, aka *Bai fa mo nu zhuan*) 166
Bridges, Jeff 211
Brigadoon Award 230–31
Brigadoon Paul Naschy Award 227–29
Brigenti, Paolo 236
Briggs, Joe Bob 238
Brigham, Warren 243
Bright, Matthew 194
Bring It Up 174
Briski, Norman 146
Britannia Hospital 154
British Fantasy Award 117, 118, 126
British Fantasy Society 117
British Horror Film Festival vii, 117, 126
British Independent Film Festival 117
Broadstone, Christopher Alan viii, 41, 45, 167, 189, 226, 242
Broadway Media Centre (in Nottingham, UK) 119
Broccoli, Albert R. 213
Broch-Man 185
Brodsky, Eliot 197
Brody, Terence 225
Brog, Cesar Leonardo Delgado 129
Broken (2006 feature; dir: Boyes & Mason) 134
The Broken (2008 feature; dir Ellis) 228
Broken (year?) 156
Bronzit, Konstantin 175
Brood 19 243
Brooks, Adam (Canadian short film director) 248, 249
Brooks, Adam Edward (American director, born 1969) 134
Brooks, David H. 214
Brooks, Mel 170, 186, 213
Broomfield, Matt 244
Broomstick! Award! 245
Brosnan, Pierce 208
The Brother from Another Planet 235
Brother Moose's Broken Shorts (unproduced script) 190
Brotherhood of the Wolf (aka *Le pacte des loups*) 139, 183, 232

Brothers, David 229
The Brothers Cleveland 189
Brother's Keeper (2008 Dutch short film) 136
Broughton, Bruce 211
Browder, Ben 206, 207
Brown, Kipleigh 220
Brown, Lauren **89**, 241
Brown, Logan 244
Brown, Mike 243
Brown, Raine 134, 241
Brown, Scott **43**, **52**
Brown Jenkin Award 168–69
Browne, Coral 211
Browne, S.G. viii, 10–*11*
Brownfield, Anna 178
Brownlee, Arran 196
Brownlee, Corran 196
Brownrigg, Anthony 126
Bruce, Nicolas 235
Bruckheimer, Jerry 36
Bruckner, David 144
Bruno, John 209
Brussels International Fantastic Film Festival vii, 96, 126, 179–84
Brutal Incasso (aka *Brutal Inca$$o*) 248
Brutal Relax 168, 201
Bruus, Morten 235
Bryan, Nicholas Robert 226
Bryan Singer and Dean Devlin Present The Triangle see *The Triangle* (2005)
Bryllupsnatten (1997 short film; *The Wedding Night*) 176, 202
Den brysomme mannen see *The Bothersome Man*
Brzhestovsky, Sergei 153
B.T.S. (Better Than Sex) see *Better Than Sex* (2002)
Bubba Ho-Tep 126, 138, 148
Bucci, Alberto viii
Buchelli, Felipe 184
Buchheit, Jacob 244
Buck Rogers in the 25th Century (1979) 212
Buckley, Vince 239
Budbringeren 151
Buechler, John Carl 218
Buenos Aires Rojo Sangre vii, 95, 128–30
BUF (special effects house) 228
Buffalo Screams Horror Film Festival 106, 130
Buffy the Vampire Slayer (1997–2003 TV series) 137, 169, 198, 199, 206, 207, 208, 209, 216, 240
Bug (1975 feature) 236
Bug (2002 feature) 149
De Bug (2007 Dutch short film) 136
Bugcrush 145
Bukowski, Charles 254n2
Bulajic, Veljko 236
Büld, Wolfgang 159
Bullet Ballet 176
A Bullet in the Arse 178, 179
Bulletface 123
Bullock, Sandra 209
Bullock, Tim 135
Bulshinjiok see *Possessed* (2010)
Bumba atomika 238
Bunt, Scott 196
Buñuel, Juan Luis (son of Luis Buñuel) 237
Buñuel, Luis 77
Buñuel, Rafael 77

Buppah Rahtree Phase 2: Rahtree Returns see *Rahtree Returns*
Burgess, Anthony 170
Burial Party 163
Buric, Zlatko 144
Buried (2003 short film) 135
Buried (2010) 157, 179, 227
Buried Alive Horror Film Festival 104, 106, 122, 130
Burke, Charlotte 153
Burke, Joe 244
Burke, Michele 139
Burke, Robin 160
Burlesque 177
Burman, Barney 203
Burn City 177
Burning Passion (1999 short film; dir: Belefant) 226
Burns, Bob 197, 198, 199
Burns, George 213
Burns, Kathy 199
Burns, Marilyn 172
Burns, Mark 236
Burns, Scott Z. *see* Christian Lajarescu
Burnt Offerings 213, 236
Burrut, Willy 184
Burstyn, Ellen 139
Burton, Tim 139, 170
Busam, Joe 199
Buscemi, Steve 147
Bush, Dan 144
Bush, Lorraine 198
Bustillo, Alexandre 229
BUT: B-Movies, Underground & Trash Film Festival vii, 101, 131
The Butcher (2007 short film) 172
The Butcher of Binbrook (1971, aka *Necrophagus*) 237
Butler, Sarah 245
Butler, Yancy 207
The Butterfly (2001 feature, aka *Nabi*) 194
The Butterfly Effect 127
The Butterfly Hole 241
Butterfly Zone (aka *Butterfly zone — Il senso della farfalla*) 179
Buttgereit, Joerg 92
Buxton, Felix 164
By Appointment Only (2007 short film) 136, 238, 242, 244, 252
By Her Hand, She Draws You Down 191, 242, 243
Byrd, Luciano 236
Byrne, Gabriel 153
Byrne, Sean 174, 247

C-SPAN 2 (network) 254n5
CAA 19
Caan, James 213
Cabin Fever (2002) 139, 231
La cabina (1973 short film) 237
Cabine of the Dead 129
The Cabinet of Dr. Caligari (Remix) (2005) 204, 218
Cabuleros (2007 short film) 146
Caché (Hidden) (aka *Caché*) 245
Cadaver (unproduced script) 244
Cadaver Girls 14
Cadaverous 242
Cadima, Ryan 162
Caetano, Joel 93, 132, 184
Caffrey, David 151
Cage, Nicolas 234
Caged (2010 feature, aka *Captifs*) 217

Caglione, John, Jr. 210
Cain (2008 short film; dir: Fyvie) 238
Cairns, David 232
Calabro, Thomas 220
Calandrelo, Maria Fernanda 222
Calandrini, Franco 100
Caldeira, Oswaldo 150
Calgary Underground Film Festival 97
California International Animation Film Festival 106, 115
The Call of Cthulhu (2005 short film) 136, 159, 169, 190
The Call of C'Thulu (2010 short film) 168
The Call of the Jersey Devil 188
Callis, James 205
Callous Sentiment 166, 191
Calvaire see *Calvary* (2004)
Calvary (2004, aka *The Ordeal* and *Calvaire*; dir: Du Welz) 164, 171, 182
Cam 2 Cam 161
Camara, Julia 241
Camardella, Juan (aka Juan Carlos Camardella) 129
Camargo, Alêxandre 131, 146
Camargo, Marcos 131
Cambria, Craig 217
Cameron, James 170, 186, 203, 204, 209, 210, 211, 213, 215, 249
Cameron, Jessica 124
Cameron, Kirk 211
Cameron, Ray 128
Camerota, Remo 178
Camino, Javi 123, 238
Camp Blood: The Musical 196
Campbell, Ben 161
Campbell, Bruce 138, 140, 148
Campbell, Jason Scott 189
Campbell, Neve 140, 209
Campbell, Ramsey 168
Campfield, Dave (aka David) 134, 244
Campillo, Robin 148, 149
Campion, Anna 152
Campion, Gregg 251
Campion, Paul 123, 134, 168, 190, 196, 224, 241, 242
Campos, Antonio 144
A Can of Paint 157, 159, 222, 225
Candon, Sean 158
Candyman 140, 210
Candyman (film series) 88
Canepa, Fabrice 127, 201
Caniche (1983) 154
Canino see *Dogtooth*
Cañitas 186
Cannes Film Festival 2, 8, 15, 22, 32, 35, 58, 65, 92
Cannibal Flesh Riot 123, 239
Cannibal Girls 237
Cannibal Grave Yard 173
Cannibal Suburbia (2008 feature) 177
Cannibal World (2003 feature, aka *Mondo cannibale*) 248
CannibAlien 247
Canning, Célia 165
Cannom, Greg 140, 204, 207, 234
Cannon, Dyan 212
Cannon, Patrick 160, 196
Cantero, Poli 232
Cantor, Charly 188
Capcom 239
Cape Fear Independent Film Festival 106
Capillas, Nacho Ruiz 217
Cappetta, Marco 188

Caprice (2010 short film; dir: Bennett) 219
Caprino, Carl 130
Captain Coulier (Space Explorer) 246
Caramagna, Romina 129
Carancho 155
Carax, Leos 187
Carbon Dating 224
Cardille, Lori 235
Cardona, Adrián 168, 201, 228, 229
Cardona, Andrea **52**
Cardona, René, III **52**, 185, 186
Cardoso, Ivan 151
Caregiver (2007 feature; dir: Devine) 192
The Caretaker 123
Cargo (2009 feature?; dir: Engler & Etter?) 245
Cargo 200 (aka *Gruz 200*) 155
Carl, Jim viii, 112–13
Carle, Annette 188
Carlei, Carlo 251
Carlson, Julie 200
Carmilla Hyde 177
Carmo, Dalila 151
Carmody, Matt 161
Carnage Film Festival 106
Carne (1991 short film; dir: Noé) 251
Carne de tu carne 154
Carney, Jason vii, 41, 50, 53, 67, 70, 73, 111
Carney, Jeff 167
Carnior 142
Carnival of Darkness vii, 6, **10**, 24, 31, 39–40, 58, 67, 83, 87–**88**, 106, 131, 253n11
Carnivorous (2007; dir: Maxwell) 220
Caro, Marc 153, 234
Carolina Theatre 51, 112–13
Caron, Donald 145
Carpenter, Jennifer 204, 216, 217
Carpenter, John 139, 152, 168, 208, 213, 230
Carpenter, Karen 90
The Carpenter and His Clumsy Wife 182, 195
Carr, Demetria J. 114
Carr, John 160
Carradine, David 206
Carradine, John 154, 235
Carré, Héctor 151
Carrell, Allyn 167
Carreras, David 127
Carrère, Emmanuel 230
Carrie (1976) 126
Carrière, Jean-Claude 234
Carrington, Tom viii
Carroll, Trevor 241
Carrossine, Camila 131, 146
Carrot (short film; year?) 177
Cars 205
La carte (2009 French short film) 147
Carter, Helena Bonham 151
Carter, Jason 247
Carter, Rick 203
Carter, Sam 130
Carter, Steve 190
Cartwright, Veronica 212
Carty, Paul 93, 242
Carvajal, Sebastian 218
Carvalho, Francisco 186
Carver 161
Le cas estrange du Dr. Jekyll et de Miss Osbourne see *The Strange Case of Dr. Jekyll and Miss Osbourne*

Index

Casa, Sandra 177
La casa see *The Evil Dead*
La Casa Brown 133
Casa da luz vermelha 146
Casa Negra (DVD company) 198
La casa nera see *The People Under the Stairs*
Casa 0101 Theater 109
Casabé, Laura (aka María Laura Casabé) 129
Casal, Alfons 129
Caselli, Sonia 237
Cash Flow (short film; dir: Andrews) 159
Casimiro, Vinícius 132
Casino Royale (2006) 205, 239
Casper (1995) 209
Cassavetes, Nick 151
Cassella, Jose Zambrano 241
Casshern 248
Castañeda, Rigoberto 186
Castaway on the Moon (2009) 141, 142
Castells, Maria viii, 103
Casterman, Alban 238
Castile, Ray (aka Raymond) viii, 62, 198, 241
Castilla, Marco 151
Castillo, Tommy *11*
Castle, William 50, 121, 124, 196, 197, 217
Castle Freak 140
Castro, Francisco 218
The Cat with Hands 150, 215
Cat's Cradle (1992 short film) 152
Cats Don't Dance 209
Cattet, Hélène 166, 228, 231
Cattet, Hélène 149
Caulfield, Emma 190
CAV Distributing 195
Cavallo, Jenny 202
Cave Women on Mars 220
The Cavern (2005 feature, aka *WithIN*) 225
Cawood, Trevor 155
Cawthorne, Richard 225
CBS 195
CC Entertainment 99
Ceaser and Otto's Summer Camp Massacre 162
Cecchi, Nanà 211
Cecila Rose 221
Cegavske, Christiane 145
Celda 211 see *Cell 211* (2009)
Celenza, Richard T., Jr. 158
The Cell (2000) 139
Cell 211 (2009) 126
The Cellar Door (2007 feature) 224, 225
Celludroid Sci-Fi, Anime, Fantasy Film Festival 102
Celluloid Screams: Sheffield Horror Film Festival vii, 28, 34, 38, 53, 70, 80, 91, 117–18, 131
Cemetery Man 140, 141, 151, 166, 171
Cencoroll 143
Centigrade 135, 228
Central Valley Horror Club 14
Centurion (2010 feature?) 245
Cerdà, Nacho 202, 233
Cerezo, Raúl 185
C'est arrivé près de chez vous see *Man Bites Dog* (1992)
Chadwick, Aimee-Lynn 223
Chaingangs 215
Chains (2006 feature; dir: France) 220, 221

Chainsaw Award see Fangoria Chainsaw Award
Chainsaw Cheerleaders 122
Chainsaw Mafia (film collective & festival) 13–15, 106, 117
The Chair (2007 feature) 224
Chamber of Chills 110
Chamberlain, Michael 226
Chamberlain, Richard 235
The Chambermaid see *Lovesick: Sick Love*
Chambre jaune 231
Chamish, Leanna 8
Champagne, Andre 160
Chan, Alan 225, 226
Chan, Benny 187
Chan, Charlie (character) 199
Chan, Fruit 231
Chandler, Kyle 209
Chaney, Lon 199
Chang, Hoon 193
Chang, Hyung-Yun 192
Chang, Lisa 145
Chang, Yoon-Hyun (aka Jang Yoon-hyun) 194
Change of Life 11
Changeling (2008) 204
Chaplin, Geraldine 237
Chapman, Ben 198
Chapman, Matthew 234
Chappelle, Joe 141
Character (1997) 151
Charles, Larry 228
Charlie Thistle 214
Charlotte, Sol vii, 102–3
The Chaser (2008, aka *Chugyeogja*) 127, 147, 192, 229
Chasing Sleep (2000) 164, 175
Chasing the Kidneystone see *Body Troopers*
Chason, Gary 122
Cheang, Pou-soi 188
Cheerbleeders 192, 241
Chemtrails: An Investigative Report 55, 241
Chen, Kaigé 148
Cheng, Ekin 192
Cheonhajangsa madonna see *Like a Virgin* (2006)
Cherry Falls 139, 232
The Cherry Tree (1998, aka *L'arbre de les cireres*) 233
Chers Parents 143
Cheung, Nick 192
Chi ha paura delle streghe see *The Witches* (1990; dir: Roeg)
Chianello, Lavinia 146
Chicago Horror Film Festival 106
Chicken Ass 2 167
The Chicken from Outer Space 202
Los chicos desaparecen 146
Un chien andalou 40
Le chien qui rit (novel) 166
Chiffer, Molly 220
Childish Things (unproduced script) 218
The Children (2008) 142, 158, 179, 214
"Children of Earth" (*Torchwood* TV episode) 203
Children of Men 205
Children of Nature (aka *Börn náttúrunnar*) 252
Children of the Corn 128
Children of the Night (unproduced script) 190

Child's Play (1988) 210
Chill (2007; dir: Rodnunsky) 158, 220
Chiller (convention) 199
Chiller (magazine) 199
Chiller Cinema 197
Chiller Drive-In 124
Chiller Eyegore Award 106, 108, 137
Chiller Theatre Convention 107
Chiller TV 108, 110
Chillón, Javier 133
Chilvers, Colin 212
A Chinese Ghost Story (1987, aka *Sien nui yau wan*) 235
A Chinese Ghost Story III (1991, aka *Sien lui yau wan III: Do do do*) 234
Chiodo, Stephen 205
Chitaroni, Chris 184
Chlanda, Zoe Daelman 191, 243
Cho, Dong-oh 127
Chocolate (2008 feature; dir: Prachya) 192
Choi, Charlene 192
Choi, Jae-jin 193
Choi, Jin-ho 142
Choi, Min-sik 145
Choi, Moo-ryong (aka Mu-ryong Choi) 194
Cholodenko, Lisa 151
Chookiat, Sakveerakul see Chookiet Sakveerakul
Chookiet, Sakveerakul (aka Chukiat or Chookiat) 192
Choopetch, Piyapan 248
Chopper Chicks in Zombietown see *Chrome Hearts*
Chorlton, John 232
Chow, Christopher C. F. 159
Chow, Stephen 171, 187
Choyonghan kajok 151
Chris, Georgia 241
Christ (1984 short film) 235
Christie, Agatha 5
Christie, Julie 154
Christopher, Boyd 119
Christopher Roth 131
Chroma Chameleon 135
Chrome Hearts 153
The Chronicles of Narnia: The Lion, The Witch and the Wardrobe (2005) 205
Chronopolis 154
Chrysler building 90
Chucladores de Cerebros 168
Chugyeogja see *The Chaser* (2008)
Chukiat, Sakveerakul see Chookiet, Sakveerakul
Chukira, Yoko 250
Chung, Seo-Kyung see Jeong, Seo-Gyeong
Chupacabre Surprise Award 166
Church, Holly Amber 217
La chute de l'ange (short film; dir: Massin) 201
El ciclo (2003 short film; dir: García) 181, 218
La ciencia del sueño see *The Science of Sleep* (2006)
"Cigarette Burns" (*Masters of Horror* TV episode) 230
Cigarette Girl 122
Cincinnati Horror Film Festival 107
Cinefamily Halloween Horror Film Fest 107
Cinefantastique (magazine) 117
Cinefantastique Online 117

Index

Cinefantasy International Film Festival vii, 32, 34, 38, 64, 67, 70, 79–80, 93, 96, 131–32
Cineflex Workshop 234
Cinema Edge Award 107
Cinemagic (magazine) 124
Cinemare 182
Cinénygma Luxembourg International Film Festival 181–83
Cinespia 78, 107, 254*n*3
Cinesploitation 14
CineVegas (film festival) 23
Circle (short film; year?) 223
Circuit (2009 feature; dir: Landauro) 196
Circus of Infinity 214
Circus of Terror 107
Cirino, Chuck 123
Cirkus (2004 animated short film; dir: Pors) 230
La cité des monstres see *Freaked* (1993)
Citizen (2007 short film; dir: Darling) 217
Citizen Dog 145, 250
Citizen Kane 85
Citizen Kane Award 227–32
Citizen X (1995 TV movie) 233
The City Eats Its Weak 129
City of Violence 144
"The City on the Edge of Forever" (*Star Trek* TV episode) 170
City Paradise 182, 230
City Wasp 187
Civic Theatre 103
CJ7 187
Clague, Tim 161
Clara (short film; dir: Pruneda) 202
Clark, Bryan 202
Clark, Candy 211
Clark, Ian 193
Clark, Sandy 197
Clark, Zach 122, 177
Clarke, Arthur C. 170
Clarke, Dameon 189, 224
Clarke, Frederick S. 197
Clarke, Mindy 140
Clarkson, Patricia 208
Clash of the Titans (1981) 212
Classic Horror Film Boards 114
Clatterbaugh, Jim 197
Clatterbaugh, Marian 197
Claveria, G.R. viii, *22*, 115
Clavijo, Víctor 217
Claw (festival director) viii, 28, 36, 42, 49, 52–53, 66, 79, 115, 242
Claw Award 93, 116, 242
Clay, Barney 148
Clay, Thomas 177
Clay Girl 249
Claydon, Phil 201
Clayton, James D. 226
La clé d'argent (2003 short film) 188
Clean Break (2010 short film; dir: Lieske) 245
Clean Carousel 142
Clean, Shaven 152
The Cleaner (2007 short film; dir: Fatale) 191
Clemency 124, 131, 157, 219
Clemens, Paul 133
Clement, Patrick 241
Cleven, Harry 145, 150, 164, 230
Clewis, Anjanette 247
Click (short film) 166

Clifford, Rhiannon vii, 166
Clingman, Wayne 111
A Clockwork Orange (1971 film) 170, 198
The Clone Returns Home 142
Clooney, George 140, 209, 254*n*2
Close Encounters of the Third Kind 126, 213
A Close Shave see *Wallace and Gromit in A Close Shave* (1995)
Close Your Eyes (2002, aka *Doctor Sleep*, aka *Hypnotic*) 175, 183
Closing Time (1996 feature; dir: Kobayashi) 251
The Clothes 190
Cloud Zero 108
Cloverfield 203, 204, 205
Clown (2005 short film; dir: Hirsch) 178
Clown (2008 short film; dir: Steinsiek) 217
Il club dei mostri see *Monster Club*
Cmiral, Elia 217
Cobalt, Dawn 223
The Cobbler's Daughter 173
Coburn, James 213
Cochrane, Rory 144
Cockerill, Jacqueline vii, 117
Cockpit (unproduced script) 240
Cockpit: The Rule of Engagement 171, 191, 219
Cocoon (1985) 211
Coda (2008 short film; dir: Camargo) 131
Code 13 143
Code 46 182, 188, 231
Coello, Mario R. 223
Coen, Joel 154, 252
A Coffee Vending Machine and Its Sword (short film) 192
Coffin Award 113, 191
Coffin Joe 146; also see *The Blind Date of Coffin Joe*
"Coffin Joe Resurrected" (article) 197
Cofradia 78
Cogne Fou (Canadian short film) 145
Cohen, Daniel vii, 99
Cohen, Jon 207
Cohen, Larry 213
Cohen, Lynn 123
El cojonudo 129
Cold and Dry (aka *Tørt og kjølig*) 158, 179, 180, 228
Cold Fish (2010) 155, 227
Cold October 243
Cold Storage (2009) 134
Cold Sweat see *Sudor frío* (2010)
Coleman, Rob 207, 208
Colet, Stephanie 223
Colin (2008) 92, 129, 237
Colin, Margaret 208
Coll, Mar 230
Colleary, Michael 208
La collection de Judicaël 164
Collet, Bruno 146, 187, 228
Collet-Serra, Jaume 126
Collette, Toni 139
Collier, Bruce 222
Collin, Gérard 236
Collins, Jason 217, 218
Colonial Theater 105
Colour Blind (2004 short film; dir: Breitenmoser ?) 136
Colour Blind (2007 short film; dir: Tyrell) 158
Colour from the Dark 168

The Colour of Magic 146
Colton, David viii, 114
Combichrist (band) 191
Combs, Jeffrey 71, 140, 141, 172
Come Get Some More 123
Come to Daddy (music video) 165
The Comeback (1978 feature; dir: Walker) 236
Comic-Con International Independent Film Festival 107, 132
Comics Scene (magazine) 124
Coming Home (short film; dir: Falardeau) 133
"The Coming of Shadows" (*Babylon 5* TV series) 169
Coming to Town (short film; 2006?) 172, 215
Coming with My Brother (aka *One-chan, ot to to iku*) 250
Comme un air see *It's in the Air*
Au commencement (music video) 165
The Commune: A New Cult Classic *62*, 123, 126
In compagnia dei lupi see *The Company of Wolves*
The Company of Wolves 141, 154, 235
A Complex Villainelle 176
Comptine (2003) 183
Comstock, Tony 178
El Comte Yácula 129
La comtesse de Castiglione 194
Con Nooga 107
Conan the Barbarian (1982) 212
Conceptual 159
El Concurso de Manchas 185
Condon, Bill 126
Condon, Kristen 177
Conen, Boris Paval 137, 188
Confederate Zombie Massacre! 136, 174, 222
Confessions (short film; year?) 223
Confessions (2010, aka *Kokuhaku*) 192
Conjurer (2008 feature) 196
The Conjurer (length, year?) 162
Connected (2008 feature, aka *Bo chi tung wah*; dir: Chan) 187
Connery, Sean 213
Connors, Gregory 190
Conozca la cabeza de Juan Pérez see *Meet the Head of Juan Pérez*
Conradie, Donnie 238
Conran, Kevin 206
Consciousness (year?) 221
Constantine (2005) 149
Constellation Award vii, 97, 132–33
The Consumed 219, 220
Contact (1997 feature; dir: Zemeckis) 169, 208
The Contact (1997 feature, aka *Cheobsok*; dir: Chang) 194
Contagion (2010 feature) 131
The Container 129
Contenti, Maximiliano 184
Contino, Jason 189
The Continuing and Lamentable Saga of the Suicide Brothers 195
Contre, Patrick 166
Contreras, Marcos 146
Contretemps (2006 short film; dir: Baillet) 159
The Control Master 142, 214
Controlled (unproduced script) 217
The Convent (1995 feature, aka *O Convento*; dir: De Oliveira) 233

The Convent (2000 feature; dir: Mendez) 139
O Convento see *The Convent* (1995)
Conversations (2004 short film; dir: Rock) 222
"Conversations with Dead People" (*Buffy the Vampire Slayer* TV episode) 169
Conway, John Francis, III 191
Coogan, Tracy 238
Cook, Luis 201, 229
Cook, Philip J. 226
Cook, Randall William 206
The Cook, the Thief, His Wife and Her Lover 234
Cooke, Chris 119
Cookers 218
Cooper, Alice 137
Cooper, Merian C. 198
Cooper, Robert C. 133
Copeland, Kristina 189
Copia A 129
Coppola, Francis Ford 204, 210
Copy Shop 183, 194
Coraline 249
El corazón del guerrero see *Heart of the Warrior*
Corbould, Chris 204
Corcoran, Sue 214
C.O.R.E. Digital Pictures 228
Corelli, Ginnetta 247
Cormack, Danielle 150
Corman, Roger 15, 100, 109, 137, 138, 171, 189, 199, 213, 214, 233
Corman Award 109
Corner of Your Eye 223
Cornerboys 157
Cornered (2009 feature; dir: Maze) 188
Cornwell, Peter 135, 201
"Coronation" (*Profiler* TV episode) 165
The Corpse Bride 205
Correl, John, Jr. 167
Corridori, Giovanni 131
Corridori, Stefano 131
Cortes, Alex 227
Cortés, Rodrigo 157, 227
Cortes, Willie 227
Cory, Phil 236
Coscarelli, Don 126, 139, 148
Cosmesis 237
Cost of Living (2005 short film; dir: Joffe) 136, 156, 214, 215, 221
Costa, José Fonseca e 147
Costanzo, Julian Vincent 177
Costas, Jerod 125
Costello, Colin 244
Cotton Candy (2008 short film) 180, 201
Cottonmouth 134
Couchsurfing 243
Coulais, Bruno 232
Coulombe, Michael vii, 6, 12, 32, 35, *43*, 47, 51–52, 57–58, 66, 70, 75, 81, 91, 104
Coulson, Michael 235
Count Alucard's Controversy of the Year 197–99
Count Gore De Vol 197, 199
The Counterfeiters (dir: Katia Bassanini) 187
Coup de lune (2003 short film) 232
Coupé court see *Short Cut*
Un Court Sans Titre 142
Courtney, Erik 132, 214
Courtois, Miguel 145

Cova, Gustavo 201
Coven, John 218
The Cow (unproduced script) 189
Cowan, Tom 235
The Cowboy Way 251
Cowie, Norman 178
Cox, Alex 150
Cox, Brian 147, 228
Cox, Courteney 139
Cox, James 242
Cradle of Fear (British short film) 219
Cradle Will Rock 232
Craig, Alex 122
Craig, Eli 141, 145, 227
Craig, James 249
Craig, Jefferson 196
Craigslist.org 33
Cramez, Jorge 150
Crampi, Mad 129
Crash (1987 short film; dir: Stewart) 235
Crash Test (2004) 159
Cravan vs. Cravan 232
Craven, Wes 128, 140, 141, 152, 165, 171, 213, 236, 254n6
Crawl (South African film; year?) 238, 239
Crawler (2009) 143
Crazy in Alabama 250
Crazy in the Night 177
Creane, Brett 243
CreateSpace 94
Creation Entertainment 108–9
Creation's Weekend of Horrors see Fangoria's Weekend of Horrors
Creative Artists Agency see CAA
Creature and Friends (convention program) 199
Creature from the Black Lagoon (figurine/model) 199
Creature from the Black Lagoon (film, 1954) 199
Creature from the Hillbilly Lagoon (2005, aka *Seepage!*) 196
Créatures célestes see *Heavenly Creatures*
Creepers (2008 short film; dir: Thiel) 241
Creepy (music video) 122
Creepy Crawly (short film) 160
Creepy Susie and 13 Other Tragic Tales for Troubled Children 87
The Cremator (1969, aka *El incinerador de cadáveres*, aka *Spalovac mrtvol*) 237
La crème 155
Cremonese, Diego 129
Creque, Stuart A. 240
Cresswell, Kat 167
Creus, Tomás 146
Crichton, Michael 128, 169, 209
Crijns, Lodewijk 137
The Criminal (1999) 150
Criminal Lovers (1999, aka *Les amants criminels*) 232
En la cripta (short film) 184
Crispin, Jimmy 242
Cristiani, Pedro 131, 132, 155, 202, 203, 241
Cristóbal, Manuel 123
Cristopharo, Domiziano 190
Criterion 197
Criticized 134, 135, 144, 172, 189, 191
Critters 2 (aka *Critters 2: The Main Course*) 235

Cronenberg, David 97, 128, 154, 171, 213, 231, 232, 236
Los cronocrímenes see *Timecrimes*
Cronos 128, 152, 234
Crooked Lane 196
Crossing Borders (2006) 148
Crosstalk (short film) 160
Crotch Rot 167
Crothers, Scatman 212
Crouching Tiger, Hidden Dragon 169, 186, 207
The Crow 140
The Crow: City of Angels 140
Crowell, Webster 124
Cruel Logic (unproduced script) 226; later produced in 2007
Cruel World (2005 feature) 196
Cruell, L.C. 224
Cruise, Jerami 161
Cruise, Tom 207
The Crusaders #357—Experiment in Evil! 157
Cruseturner, Wayne 170
Cry for Bobo 183, 232
Cryer, Loyd 116
Crying Fist 145
Crying Freeman (1995) 176
The Crypt Club 159, 167, 196, 222, 242
The Crypt Club Productions 93
Cryptic (2009 feature) 200
Crypticon (in Minnesota) 107
Crypticon Horror Convention (in Washington state) 107
Cryptshow Festival vii, 102, 133
Csanadi, Mitch 167, 244
CSI 25
CSI: Crime Scene Investigation 206
Cthulhu (2007; dir: Gildark) 168
Cube 102, 127, 150, 151, 165, 194, 233
Cube 2: Hypercube 149
Cube Zero 189, 196, 218
Cuden, Steve 189, 226, 248
Cuerda, José Luis 153
Cuesta, Michael 149
Cujo 153
Culp, Bret 149
Culp, Robert 214
Culpepper, Hanelle viii, 93, 241
CûLPiiX 183
Cult Flick 240
Cult Radio a Go-Go 198
Cummings, Axelle see Axelle Grelet
Cunningham, Beth 104
Cunningham, Chris 165
Cunningham, Collin 228
Cunningham, Sean S. 218, 254n6
Cupid's Arrow (1997) 161
Cupp, McKenzie 224
The Curfew 240
The Curious Case of Benjamin Button 204, 249
Currie, Andrew 163
The Curse (dir: Harvey) 159
The Curse of Dr. Mongoo 161
The Curse of El Charro 173
The Curse of Micah Rood 162, 196, 243
Curse of the Dead (1976, aka *The House of the Living Dead*) 236
Curse of the Demon (1957, aka *Night of the Demon*) 199
Curse of the Flesh 162
Curse of the Forty-Niner (aka *Miner's Massacre*) 218
Curse of the Golden Flower 205

Index

The Curse of the Jade Scorpion (aka *La maldición del escorpión de jade*) 232
Curse of the Remote Island (aka *Kaukosaaren kirous*) 180
Curse of the Swampies 190
Curtis, Dan 213, 236
Curtis, Jamie Lee 139, 140, 209
Curtis, Tony 232
Cushing, Peter 140, 154, 235, 236
CutThroat Films 14
Cutting Edge (2005 short film, aka *Dernier cri*) 193
Cutting Room (2008; dir: Ammons) 167
The Cyclop of the Sea (aka *Le cyclope de la mer*) 232
Cypher 127, 149, 231
Cyphers, Charles 171
Cyrus — Mind of a Serial Killer 122, 131
Cyxork 7 (2006) 124
Czerny, Henry 223
Czule miejsca 154

D 136
D-Day (2006 feature; dir: Kim) 193
D4 191
Da (1988) 235
DA, Jon (aka Jon D.A.) 217
Daanish, Shareefa 192
Dabrowsky, Ursula 190
Dacquisto, Natalee 248
Daddy (aka D.A.D.D.Y.) 157, 158
Daddy's Boy (2004 short film) 175, 182
Daddy's Girl (year?) 214
Dafoe, Willem 150, 207, 232
Dagon 168
Dahan, Yannick 141, 146, 163
Daho, Étienne 165
Dai kenji see *Big Gun*
Daichi o tataku onna see *A Woman Who Is Beating the Earth*
D'Alessandro, Coral 223
D'Alessandro, Federico 223
D'Alessio, Carlos 234
Daley, Andrew 190
Dallas, Dutch 241
Dallas, Matt 205
Dalle, Béatrice 138
Dalpalan (aka Dalparan, aka Dal Palan) 230
Dalparan see Dalpalan
Dalton, Hattie 228
Dalton, Phyliss 211
Daly, Garen vii, 105, 125
La dama en el umbral 180, 194
Dame algo 151
Damn Bastard! see *Maldito Bastardo!*
Damn Your Eyes 130
Damoiseaux, Lars 161
Damon, Jerel 172
Damon and Hunter: Doing It Together 178
D'Amours, Frédéric (aka Frederick) 218
Dan Roebuck's Spook Show 198
Dance Macabre see *Danse macabre* (2009)
Dance of the Dead (2008) 217
Dancey, Elias 162
Dandry, Évelyne 233
The Dandy Doctrine (A Delightful Illusion) 177
Daneliya, Georgi 153
Danger. Zombies. Run. 162
Dani California (music video) 138

Daniel (2010 short film; dir: Furcajg) 242
Daniels, Jeff 152, 210
Daniels, Ken vii, 28, 32, 42, 47, 51, 66–67, 70, 73, 79, 93, 109
Daniels, Marc 170
Daniels, Steve 190
Daniloff, David viii, 97
D'Anna, Micheal (aka Mike) 244
Danner, Blythe 213
Dannied, Danniel 153
Danny Boy (2010 animated short film; dir: Skrobecki) 187
Dano, Paul Franklin 149
Dans la nuit see *At Night*
Dans la tête 146
Dans leur peau 163, 179
Dans ton sommeil 126
Danse macabre (2009 short film; dir: Pires) 133, 134, 142, 192, 246
Danse Macabre International Horror Film Festival 97
Dante, Joe 100, 128, 139, 198, 211, 214, 230
Danzey, Lynn-Maree 202
Dara (2007 short film) 172, 189
Daredevil: The Teaser 160
Darie, Frédéric 152
Dark Angel (2000–02 TV series) 208
Dark Bridges Film Festival 97
Dark Carnival Film Festival 29–31, 108, 133–34
The Dark Ceremony 103
Dark City (1998) 126, 127, 139, 171, 208
The Dark Crystal 211
Dark Eyes (2001) 160
The Dark Half 140
Dark Heaven 160
Dark Horse (2009 short film) 177
Dark Horse & The Zimmer Gang 177
The Dark Hours (2005) 134, 145, 173, 185, 189, 193, 230
Dark House 71, 224
The Dark Knight 126, 197, 204, 216, 249
The Dark Lurking 190
Dark Moon Rising 105
Dark Night (2006; dir: Grant) 159
Dark Reel 122, 134, 238
Dark Remains 185, 196, 225
Dark Revelations Film Festival see Duistere Openbaringen Film Festival
Dark Shadows (1991 TV series) 210
The Dark Side of the Moon (1987, aka *Manden i månen*) 235
Dark Souls (2010, aka *Mørke sjeler*) 131, 177, 195, 247
Dark Star (1974) 213
Dark Visions (dir: Highly) 160
Dark Water (2002; dir: Nakata) 127, 164, 193
Dark Woods Con 108
DarkHart Press 115, 240
DarkHart Screenplay Award 115, 240
Darklands 151, 184
Darklovestory 177
Darkman (1990) 234
Darling, James 217
Darnstädt, Christoph 150
D.A.R.Y.L. 211
Da Silva, Carlos 151
Da Silva, Paul J. 218
The Date see *Stævnemødet* (1998)
The Date (short film; year?) 247

Date of the Dead (aka 2006's *A Date with the Dead?*) 162
A Date with the Dead (2006 short film; dir: Smith) 144
Dates, Jeffrey 218
Davey-Fitzpatrick, Seamus 138
Davidson, Gary 226
Davidson, Michael 109
Davidson, Stacy 125
Davidtz, Embeth 140
Davies, Peter Frederick 241
Davies, Russell T. 126, 169
Davis 130
Davis, Andy 160
Davis, Bette 213
Davis, Brian Philip 159
Davis, Christian 225
Davis, Essie 217
Davis, Jack 198
Davis, Jason R. (Chicago Horror Film Festival) 106
Davis, Jason R. (Indy Horror Film Festival) vii, 111
Davis, Mark 194
Davis, Mitch 97
Davis, Nicholas 196
Davis, Nick 204
Davis, Paul 237
Davis, Sammi 190
Davis, William B. 221
Davison, Joe 241
Dawn, Vincent see Bruno Mattei
Dawn of Ashes (band) 190
Dawn of the Dead (CD, year?) 199
Dawn of the Dead (1978) 41, 206
Dawning (2009 feature; dir: Holtgrewe) 196
Dawning (feature; year?) 219
Dawson, Richard 211
Day, Patrick Kevin 172
Day Before (short film) 237
The Day of the Beast (1995, aka *El día de la bestia*) 128, 139, 165, 184
Day of the Dead (1985) 211, 235
The Day of the Dead (2007 feature, aka *El día de los muertos*; dir: Islas) 185
Day of the Woman see *I Spit on Your Grave* (1978)
Day Off the Dead (2004 short film) 218
The Day the Earth Stood Still (CD, year?) 199
The Day the Earth Stood Still (1951) 125
The Day the Earth Stood Still (2008) 204
The Day the Robots Woke Up 215
The Day They Came Back 163, 196
Day 26 see *Tag 26*
Day X (2005) 196
Day Zero (South African short film) 237
Dayas, Jorge 194
Daylight Fades 247
Days of Darkness (2007) 220
Days Without Light see *Días sin luz* (1995)
The Daytrippers 151
Daywalt, Drew 10, 131, 137, 167
Ddongpari see *Breathless* (2009; dir: Yang)
Deacon, Dominic 177
Dead After Tomorrow 224
Dead Alive see *Braindead* (1992)
Dead & Breakfast (2004) 92, 196, 225, 248

Dead Bones 238
Dead by Dawn: Scotland's International Horror Film Festival vii, 118, 121, 134–35, 180–83
Dead Channels Film Festival 13, 101, 108, 135
Dead Creek (2008 short film; dir: Turner) 157, 192, 243
Dead Crows 172, 224
Dead End (2003 feature; dir: Andrea & Canepa) 127, 183, 201
Dead End (2006 feature, aka *Dood eind*; dir: van den Eshof) 217
Dead Exit (short film) 200
Dead Hooker in a Trunk 85, 131
Dead in 3 Days (aka *In 3 Tagen bist du tot*) 127, 181, 185
Dead Man (novel) 164
The Dead Matter 123
Dead Meat (2004) 130
Dead Meat: O Banquete dos Zumbis see *Dead Meat* (2004)
Dead Moon Rising 93, 163
Dead Noon 13, 93, 167, 242
Dead of Night see *Deathdream* (1974)
Dead of Night (unproduced script) 172
Dead Ringers (1988) 153
Dead Scared see *The Hazing*
Dead Snow 123, 124, 158, 246
Dead Sober (unproduced script) 226
Dead Sucks 162
Dead Tired (2007 short film) 244
The Dead Wastes 190
Dead West (2005 short film) 218
Dead Winter Run 243
Dead Wood 124
The Dead Zone (1983) 211
Deadgirl (2008, aka *Dead Girl*) 137, 155, 177
Deadland (2009) 176
Deadlands (film series) 93
Deadlands: The Rising 163
Deadlands 2: Trapped 162
Deadly Advice 233
Deadly Tantrum 173
Deadtime Stories (animated short film) 218
Deadwood Park 161
The Deaf Game (short film) 238
Deakins, Cat 241
Deal, Michelle 226
De Almeida, Bruno 147
DeAngelis, Mario viii, 114
Dear, William 252
Dear Beautiful 246
Death (*Final Destination* character) 240
Death Becomes Her 210
Death Express (dir: Terada) 252
Death 4 Told 222
Death in Charge 135, 157, 174, 176, 191, 200, 224, 241
Death Kappa 128
Death Knows Your Name 158, 241, 242
Death Note 127
Death of a Ghost Hunter 189
Death of the Reel 122
Death Row Diet 123, 135
Death Waltz (2010) 131
Death Weekend 236
Deathdream (1974, aka *Dead of Night*) 236
Death's Requiem 224
Deathwatch (2002 feature) 182

Debie, Benoît 228
De Caro, Sebastián 130, 131
De Carvalho, Ruy 148
Decaying Orbit 220
Decker, Jerry 160
Dedicado a nadie 185
Dee, Eddie 116
Deep in the Woods (2000 feature, aka *Promenons-nous dans les bois*) 183, 219, 232
Deep One Award 168
Deep Red (1975, aka *Profondo rosso*) 236
Deep Red International Festival of Fantastic Film vii, 6, 58, 108
Deerattakul, Vitaya 227
DEF (2003 short film) 193
De Felipe, Fernando 149
Defenceless: A Blood Symphony 178
Defense of the Realm 153
De France, Cécile 138, 231
Degeneres, Ellen 206
Deise, Jamie 218
Déjà 187
Deja Vu Deception 226
De Jager, Danny 137
Déjame entrar see *Let the Right One In*
De Jarnatt, Steve 234
De Kervern, Gustave 193
Dekker, Fred 128, 197
De La Cruz, Ángel 150
Delacruz, Vincent 52
De La Fuente, Daniel Izar (aka Daniel Izar) 231
De La Iglesia, Álex 128, 141, 165
Delaney 133
De Largie, Vanessa 177
De Las Heras, Pepe 248
De Laurentiis, Dino 213, 232
De La Vega, Daniel 158, 241
DeLeon, Rafael, Jr. 241
Delépine, Benoît 193
De L'Hermuzière, Xavier 232
Délicatessen 153, 234
Delirium and the Dollman 222
Deliver Us from Evil (2009 Danish) 146, 228
Delivery (2005 short film; dir: Nowak) 181, 201, 248
Delivery (2006 feature; dir: Cassella) 161
The Delivery (2008 short film; dir: DeCuir) 135
Dellamorte Dellamore see *Cemetery Man*
Dellinger, Terry 134
Del Monte, Peter 128, 153
Delorme, Jason 160
Delpeut, Peter 152
Delplanque, Lionel 165, 232
Delta (2008 Hungarian feature) 147
Delta Award (aka Delta Film Award) 158–61
Del Toro, Guillermo 128, 139, 148, 149, 152, 164, 169, 171, 186, 205, 232, 234
De Luca, Emanuele 238
Delvaux, André 152
Demagogue 161
De Martino, Jennifer (or Jennifer DeMartino?) 219
The Demise 136
DemiUrge Emesis 122, 123, 131, 134, 219, 243
Demme, Jonathan 171
Demon Chaser challenge 114, 200

A Demon in My View (aka *Der Mann nebenan*) 252
Demon Is on the Island (aka *Le démon dans l'île*) 154
Demon Under Glass 247
Dèmoni see *Demons* (1985)
Demonlover 231, 232
The Demonology of Desire 130, 196
Demons (1985) 141
Demonsamongus 177, 178
Den 189
Dench, Judi 249
Dengrá, Rafa 159, 168, 201
Denham, Christopher 229
De Niro, Robert 23
Denis, Gaëlle 230
Denis, Mathieu L. 143
Denis-de-Rougemont Youth Award 187–88
Denise Calls Up 152
Denove, Thomas F. (aka Tom de Nove?) 236
Dent, Haren 219
The Dentist (1996) 165, 176
Le dentiste see *The Dentist* (1996)
Denton, James 221
D'entre les morts 247
De Oliveira, Manoel 148, 233
De Oliveira Pinheiro, Davi 122, 184
De Paoli, Linus 228
Deployment Strategy 220
Depositarios (2010, aka *Depositories*) 185
Depositories see *Depositarios*
Depp, Johnny 139, 216, 217
Dequenne, Émilie 188
Déraciné (2007) 142
Derailed (2010 short film) 168
De Rijk, Sandesh 137
Deriva 131, 237
Dern, Bruce 244
Le dernier combat (1983) 128, 154, 235
Le dernier rêve see *The Last Dream* (2001)
La dernière minute see *The Last Minute* (2001 feature)
La dernière minute (2004 short film, aka *The Last Minute*; dir: Salis) 140, 149, 182
Les derniers jours du monde 228
De Roche, Everett 236
De Rossi, Giannetto 131, 231
De Santos, Magdalena 203
Desaliñada see *Salad Days* (2001)
The Descendant (short film; year?) 172
The Descendent (2006 short film; dir: Glickert) 244
Descent (2004 short film) 225
The Descent (2005 feature) 145, 175, 181, 205
Desert Dogs (unproduced script) 130
Dési, András 171
DeSimone, Kevin 223
Desjardins, Benoît 144
Desmichelle, Hugues 154
Desolate (unproduced script) 218
De Souza, Steven E. 213
Despain & Vainwad 178
Desperate Remedies (1993) 234
Desperation (2006 feature; dir: Clark) 225
Despins, Claude 143
Despiser 226
Después de Recién 130
Destination Moon (1950) 169

Destination: Outer Space 219
Destroyer see *Shadow of Death* (1988)
De Sylva, Jean-François 125
Details (unproduced script) 225
Detained (2004 short film) 159
Detective Riko (1998 feature, aka *Onna keiji Riko*) 251
Detour (2008 short film; dir: Tsakpo) 217
Détour mortel 2 see *Wrong Turn 2: Dead End*
Deuce Bigalow (aka *Deuce Bigalow: Male Gigolo*) 250
Deus ex machina (1994 short film) 166
Deus Irae 131, 132, 155, 174, 202, 203, 241, 245
Deux soeurs see *A Tale of Two Sisters*
Dever, William 104
Devereaux, Maurice 134, 144
De Vestele, Kristof 96
Devil (unproduced script) 243
Devil, Kevin 110
Devil Crows (aka *Ya mo*) 236
The Devil Dared Me To 135
Devil Girl 124
The Devil's Advocate (1997) 139, 208
The Devil's Backbone (aka *El espinazo del diablo*) 164, 171, 183
The Devil's Chair 156
Devil's Creek 124, 131, 171, 200, 219
The Devil's Deed 243
Devil's Gateway 177
Devil's Grove 162
The Devil's Music 158
Devil's Playground (2010) 126
Devil's Playground (unproduced script) 191
The Devil's Rain 213
The Devil's Rejects 138, 145, 216, 217
The Devil's Toy 123, 191
Devilwood 173
Devine, Aidan 173
Devine, Dennis 226
Devlin, Dean 205, 213
De Vol, Gore see Count Gore De Vol
Devor, Robinson 144, 229
De Vore, Brian 137
De Vore, Jeffrey 137
The Devoured 191
Dexter (TV series) 195, 204, 205, 216
El día de la bestia see *The Day of the Beast* (1995)
El día de los muertos see *The Day of the Dead* (2007)
Diabolical Tales: Part I 174, 221
Diabolical Tales: Part II 221
The Diabolikal Super-Kriminal 194
Dial "A" for Alphaman 173
Dial M for Monster 249
Diamond Zero 244
Diamonds Moon 252
Diani, Gabriel 124
Diary (2006 feature, aka *Mon seung*) 192
The Diary of Anne Frank of the Dead 136
Diary of the Dead (2007) 163, 249
Días sin luz (1995 short film; aka *Days Without Light*) 176
Díaz, R. Patricio vii
DiCaprio, Leonardo 215
Di Cesare, Leonardo 193
Dicht hinter der Tür 154
Dick, Philip K. 170

Dick Tracy (1990) 210
Dickinson, Angie 212
Dickson, Ngila 207
Diderot, Vincent 131
Die-ner 237
Die You Zombie Bastards! 196
Dieter, Dieter 50
Dietz, Frank 198
DiFate, Vincent 199
Dig Comics 132
Di Giovanni, Adrian 124
Digital Domain 209
Di Jiacomo, Michael 233, 250
Dikker, Loek 210
Dilemma (2005 Dutch short film; dir: Conen) 137, 182, 188
Dilworth, John R. 202
D-I-M, Deus in Machina 136, 172
Dimensions, Part 1 172
Le dîner des bustes 235
Dinter, Matthias 145
Diramio, Nick 225
Director's Cut (2003 feature; dir: Stacey) 222
Dirt Dauber 168
Dirth (short film) 166
The Disappeared (2008 feature; dir: Kevorkian) 194
The Discarnates 128
Disconnected (year?, short film) 163
Dissimulation 167
The Distance Between (short film; dir: Hickinbotham) 179
The District (2004, aka *Nyócker!*) 230
District 9 186, 197, 203, 249
Disturbia 216
División Bahia 129
Divka na kosteti see *The Girl on the Broomstick* (1972)
Divorcing Jack 151
Dix (2008 French short film?, aka *Ten*?) 163
Dix, Justin 217
DJ Blackskull 247
Djordjevic, Mladen 128, 141, 145, 184, 194, 202
Do san 3: Chi siu nin do san see *God of Gamblers 3: The Early Stage* (1997)
DOA Blood Bath Entertainment 125
Dobbs, Lem 126, 139
Doc Savage: The Man of Bronze (1975, aka *Doc Savage*) 213
Doc Ock (character) 239
Docter, Pete 169, 186, 249
Dr. Crosier 160
"The Doctor Dances" (*Doctor Who* TV episode) 169
Dr. Evil (*Austin Powers* character) 240
Dr. Gangrene's Chiller Cinema (website) 198
Dr. Giggles 140
Dr. Hell see *Doctor Infierno*
Dr. Horrible's Sing-Along Blog 169
Doctor Infierno (aka *Dr. Hell*) 129, 190
Dr. Jekyll and Mr. Hyde (1932) 199
Dr. Jekyll & Mr. Hyde (2002; dir: Redfield) 160, 222, 223, 226
The Dr. Jekyll & Mr. Hyde Rock 'n Roll Musical 160
Dr. Phibes Rises Again 236
Doctor "S" Battles the Sex Crazed Reefer Zombies: The Movie 122, 135, 176
Doctor Sleep see *Close Your Eyes* (2002)

Dr. Strangelove or: How I Learned to Stop Worrying and Love the Bomb 170
Doctor Who 11, 90, 126, 132, 133, 169, 197, 198, 209
Doctorow, Cory 63
Dodge, Joseph 163
Doense, Jan 218
Dog Days (2001 feature; dir: Seidl) 150
Dog Soldiers 127, 139, 183, 202, 207
Doghouse (2009 feature?) 245
The Dogs of Chinatown 162
Dogtooth (aka *Kynodontas*, aka *Canino*) 228
Dohler, Don 169
Dokter Vogel 137
Dolan, Jerome A. 243
Dolen, Kelly 177
Dolera, Leticia 155
Dolev, Gili 160
Dolina 147
Doll No. 639 (aka *A 639. baba*) 171, 181
The Dollhouse (2007 short film; dir: DeGaetani) 220, 244
Domace je najbolje 223
The Domain (unproduced script) 218, 222
Dome (unproduced script) 172
Dominator 160
Domingues, Léonardo 146
Domínguez, Laura 239
Domino (1998 short film) 161
Don (2006 feature; dir: Akhtar) 187
Donahue, Heather 139
Donahue, Jocelin 217
Donck, Matthieu 146
Donella, Chad 241
À donf 150
Dong see *The Hole* (1998)
Donker Herfs (short film) 238
Donkey Punch 155
Donley, Dan 191
Donnadieu, Bernard-Pierre 153
Donnell, Bryan 178
Donnelly, Sean 144
Donner, Lauren Shuler 204
Donner, Richard 170, 205, 213
Donnie Darko 164, 171, 175, 232
"Donnie Dunagan Interview" (article) 199
D'Onofrio, Vincent 139, 208
Donovan, Paul 251
Don't Answer the Phone (1980) 236
Don't Ask Don't Tell 188
Don't Call Me Zombie 241
Don't Die Without Telling Me Where You're Going (aka *No te mueras sin decirme adónde vas*) 233
Don't Look in the Attic 159
Don't Look in the Basement (1973) 45
Donzelot, Philippe 166
Dood eind see *Dead End* (2006)
Doodle (short film) 181, 230
Doolan, Luke 201
Doolittle, Aaron 130
Doomsday County 161
The Door (2009) 126, 163, 179
Doornbos, Dennis 244
Doorways Magazine 108
Doorways Unhinged Horror Film Festival 108
Dorff, Stephen 189
Doright, Harry 136, 217
The Dork of the Rings 174
Dorléac, Jean-Pierre 212

Dornhelm, Robert 194
Dororo 229
Dorra, Max 165
Dose (unproduced script) 189
Dossiê Rê Bordosa 146
"Le dossier secret" 166; *also see The X-Files*
Double (short film) 162
The Double Born 190
Doublin, Anthony 235
Doubrava, Jaroslav 154
Dougherty, Michael 205, 218
Dourif, Brad 139, 141
Dowell, Kenneth 162
Down Terrace 155
Downey, Robert, Jr. 132, 204, 209, 215, 231, 249
Downriver (2007 short film; dir: Greenberg) 243
Downsized (2008 short film?) 200
Downtown Independent (theater) 15
Doyle, Mike 242
Dracula (1931) 198
Dracula (1979) 212
"Dracula & Frankenstein: 75 Years of Fear" (article) 198
Dracula: Pages from a Virgin's Diary 231
Dracula's Daughters vs. the Space Brains 237
Drag Me to Hell 138, 203, 215, 216
Dragon (2006 animated short film) 136
Dragon*Con Independent Short Film Festival vii, 31, 36, 38, 51, 70, 79, 89–90, 93, 108, 135–36
Dragonheart 209
Drake, David 8
The Drawing (trailer) 191
DreadCentral.com 113, 137, 195, 197
Dreadful, Penny 198
Dream (2008) 127
Dream Home (2010, aka *Wai dor lei ah yut ho*) 142, 187, 227
Dreamcast 165
Dreamchild (1985) 153, 211
Dreams and Desires: Family Ties 230
Dreamscape (1984; dir: Ruben) 128
Dreamscape (2009; dir: Fox) 158
Dreamtime see *Droomtijd* (2006 short film)
Dreamtime's Over (2009 feature; aka *Prey*) 177
Dreamworks 19
Dreesen, Lance W. 127, 226
Dressed to Kill (1980) 212
Drexler, Doug 210
Dreyer, Carl 197
Dribbling Fate 151
The Drift (2007 short film) 246
Drive (1997 feature; dir: Wang) 251
Drive-In Horrorshow 123
Driven (1996) 88
Droomtijd (2006 short film, aka *Dreamtime*) 129, 181
The Drowning (unproduced script) 191
Drowning Ghost (aka *Strandvaskaren*) 218
Druktenis, Dennis 197
The Drunken Severed Head (blog) 197
Drunken Zombie Film Festival vii, 6, 57, 108, 254n1
Drury, David 153
Druyan, Ann 169
Dry Corpse Award 96, 131
Duarte, Andrea 203

Dubois, Bastien 141
Ducasse, César 131, 195, 247
Duchamp Award 111
Duck Children 202
Duddy, Christopher 218
Dudman, Nick 208
Duffer, Matt 238
Duffy, Gwyn 190
Dugre, Jason 243
Dugüel, Anne 166
Duhame, Doc 224
Duigan, John 127
Duistere Openbaringen Film Festival vii, 101, 136–37
Duiwel Vleis 239
Dumont, Bruno 231
DuMont, James 225
Dunagan, Donnie 199
Duncan, Lindsay 234
Duncan, Michael Clarke 208
Dune (1984) 211
Dunn, Jason 226
Dunst, Kirsten 140, 209
Dunstan, John 130
Dunwich 168
Dupe (2005 short film; dir: Waitt) 175
Duperey, Anny 154
Dupieux, Quentin 227
Duplicity (2005, aka *Trouble*; dir: Cleven) 145, 164, 182, 230
Dupont, David 159
Dupontel, Albert 251
Dupuis, Stephen 211
Du Potet, Caroline 126
Du Potet, Éric 126
Durand 165
Dussol, Philippe 175
Dust Kid 192
Dutcher, Richard 122, 158
Du Welz, Fabrice 158, 164, 171, 228
Duzel, Ivan 178
DVD (2006 short film) 132, 180, 248
The DVD Savant 197
Dyer, Danny 126
Dykstra, John 206, 212, 213, 235

Eagle, David 169
Early Edition (1996–2000 TV series) 209
Earnshaw, Tony 118
Earth Day (2001 short film) 219
Earth Song (music video) 166
Earthling (2010) 131
Easeman, Laurence 158
East (music band; aka EAST Troublemakers) 229
East Is East 150
East of Euclid 124
Easterbrook, Leslie 138, 217
Eastern Promises (2007) 204
Easy Living (short film; dir: Kasparian & Tremblay) 144
Easy Money see *Argent content* (2000)
Eat Me: The Musical 162
Eaves, James 224
Eccles, Caroline 158
Ecclesine, Steve 243
L' Écervelé 144
Echevarria, Joshua 243
L'Echine du diable see *The Devil's Backbone*
The Echo (2004, aka *Sigaw*; dir: Laranas) 127, 218
Echo (2007 short film; dir: Gozlan) 164

Echo (year?) 167, 179
Eclipse see *The Twilight Saga: Eclipse*
The Eclipse (2009; dir: Conor McPherson) 179, 228
Eclosion see *They Nest* (2000)
L'Écran Fantastique Award 142–45
L'Ecureuil rouge see *La ardilla roja*
Ed Gein (2000, aka *In the Light of the Moon*) 232
Ed Wood 209
La edad del sol (dir: Subirós) 227
Eddie Loves You 159, 189
Eden (dir: Maloney) 160
E:D:E:N (2004 short film; dir: Guaglione & Resinaro) 159, 214
Eden Lake 147, 194, 228
Edgar G. Ulmer Award 249
Edgerton, Joel 177
Edgerton, Nash 133, 134, 193, 201
The Edison Death Machine 163, 174
Edlund, Richard 211, 212, 233
Edmond 144, 230
Edschmid, Sebastian 217
Edward Scissorhands 170, 210
Edwards, Gareth 192, 227
Edwards-Behi, Nia 44
The Eel (short film; year?) 239
Eel Girl 123, 134, 168, 190, 196, 224, 241
Eerie Horror Film Festival vii, 28, 34, 39, 65, 72–73, 75–76, 79–80, 91, 108
Effulgence 168
Egg Ghost 190
Eggers, Robert 130
Eggink, Dorien vii, 131
Eggleston, Colin 236
Eggleston, Ralph 232
Eggs see *Oeufs* (1994)
Ehlin, Anders 218
Ei 153
Eight Heads in a Duffel Bag see *8 Heads in a Duffel Bag*
Eight Thirty Two 220
Einsturzende Neubauten (music band) 165
Eisenberg, Jesse 138
Eisener, Jason 133, 144, 189, 238
Eisenstadt, Josh 122, 134
Eiss, Jennifer 158
Eko Eko Azarak: Wizard of Darkness (1995, aka *Eko eko azaraku*, aka *Wizard of Darkness*) 251
ELA in Love at First Byte 129
Eldjàrn, Örn 229
Election (2005 feature, aka *Hak se wui*) 230
Electric Fence 156
Electrical Skeletal! 244
Elejalde, Karra 152
The Element of Crime 153
The Elemental 121
The Elementary School 152
Elfman, Danny 139, 140, 150, 207, 208, 209, 243
ELI (2007 short film) 172
Elizalde, Mike 138, 206
Elkayem, Ellroy 165, 176
Elkins, Brian 123
Elkins, Robert 162
Ella o yo (2005 short film; dir: Franco) 185
Elle voit des nains partout! 154
Ellektra (2004) 124

Elliot, Adam 170, 231
Elliot, Kate 149
Elliott, Mick 178
Elliott, Paul 190
Elliott, Stephan 127, 128
Ellis, Brad 247
Ellison, Harlan 170, 186, 213
Elmes, Frederick 151, 235
The Elusive Man 135
Ellwood, Katie (aka Bertie) *see* Bert & Bertie
Else 217
Elwood, Tony 134
The Embalmer (2009 short film) 224
Embargo (2010) 147
Embodiment of Evil (2008, aka *Encarnaçaô do Demônio*) 143, 228
Embryo see Untitled: 003-Embryo (2002 short film)
Emerging Past 161
Emerson, Caleb 196
Emerson, Michael 205
Emery, Chris 98
Emin, Thibault 217
Emma-O 238
Emmerich, Roland 209
Emmy Award 1, 56
Empire of Wonders 225
The Empire Strikes Back see Star Wars, Episode V: The Empire Strikes Back
"The Empty Child" (*Doctor Who* TV episode) 169
The Empty Mirror 151
The Empty Space in Between 245
EMR 248
Ena Lake Blues 249
Encarnaçaô do Demônio see Embodiment of Evil (2008)
Enchanted (2007) 204
Enchanted Island 158
L'enchanteur (1995 short film) 151
Encounter at Black Ridge 160
Encyclopedia Horrifica **11**
The End (short film; year?) 179
The End (2005 Dutch short film) 137
End of the Line (2007 feature; dir: Devereaux) 134, 144, 156
"End of Time" (*Doctor Who* TV episode) 197
Endings (2003 short film) 223
Enemy Combatant (unproduced script) 244
Les enfants du Marais 232
Engel, Volker 208, 209
Engelhardt, Matthias viii, **40**, 45–**46**, 50–51, 60–61, 73–77, 92, 99
Engelmayer, Victoria 220
England, Yan 144
Engle, Liam 158
Engle, Winston 225
English, Corri 173
English, Ellia 188
Englund, Robert 188, 213
Enigma (2009) 135, 224
Ennis, Jacob 162
Enns, Sean 223
Enter the Dark 133, 219
Enter the Dragonfly 136, 222
Enter the Sandbox 176
Enter the Void 187, 227, 228
Enterprise see Star Trek: Enterprise
Entre las Vías 185
D'entre les morts 158
Epicac (short film) 172, 220

Epidermique 165
Epitaph (2007 feature, aka *Gidam*; dir: the Jeong Brothers) 196
Epperson, Tom 152
Epstein, Barak 123, 176
Eras, Bobby 242
Eraser Children 177
Erler, Gregor 123, 192
Erickson, Glenn 197
errors & omissions insurance 255n9
Erskine, James 248
Es ist nicht leicht ein Gott zu sein 153, 234
Escalante, Amat 228
La escapada (2000 short film) 232
Escape! From Robot Island 214
Escape from the Planet of the Tapes 178
The Escapist 147
Escarnio 185
Les escarpins sauvages see The Wild Heels
Eskalofrío see Shiver (2008)
Eskandari, Matt 218
Eskimo Hill 160
Esmeralda Video 178
Esnal, Telmo 201
Espenson, Jane 169
El espinazo del diablo see The Devil's Backbone
Espinosa, Javier Rodríguez 228
Espinoza, Ernesto Díaz 155
Espoo Ciné International Film Festival 98, 179–83
Essman, Scott 160, 197
Esteban, Juanilo 238
Estefania, Iglesias (aka in reverse order: Iglesias, Estefania) 224
Esterhazy, Danishka 223
Estrada, Julio Cesar 186
E.T.: The Extra-Terrestrial 207, 211, 212
Eternal Blood (aka *Sangre eterna*) 218
The Eternal Pitfall of Prokofiev 241
Eternal Sunshine of the Spotless Mind 125, 206
Etheredge, Paul (aka Paul Etheredge-Outzts) 196
Étoile 153
L'étranger (2006 short film) 144
Europa (1991) 152, 234
European Fantastic Film Festivals Federation 96, 101, 109, 141, 179
Evacuación 129
Evans, Jane 222
Evans, Marc 164, 171
Even Pigeons Go to Heaven (aka *Même les pigeons vont au paradis*) 201
Event Horizon 127
Ever After: A Cinderella Story see EverAfter
Ever Since the World Ended 215
EverAfter (1998, aka *Ever After: A Cinderella Story*) 208
Everett, Rupert 151
Everson, William K. 199
Everton, Deborah 209
Everything Burns (music video) 122
Everything Will Be OK 144, 156
Everything's Eventual 171
Evil see To kako (2005)
Evil Angel 122, 131, 158, 161, 243
The Evil Basement of Count Worlock 247
The Evil Dead 141, 236
Evil Keg 123

Evil Things 200
Evilenko 141, 182
Evilio vuelve (El purificador) 202
Eviscerate (short film) 238
Evrenol, Can 168
Evry, Max 160
Ex Drummer 143, 155
Excalibur (1981) 212
Excalibur (music video) 165
Excision (2008 short film) 122, 155, 174, 200, 219, 220, 224, 243, 245
The Executioner (2009) 142
Exiled (2006 feature) 144, 230
Existenz 171
Exofest 97
The Exorcism of Emily Rose 205, 217
The Exorcist 126, 213
The Exorcist III 210
Experience Music Project, Science Fiction Museum 114
Das Experiment (2001) 150
Experiment (2005) 159, 173, 221, 225
Exposure (2010; dir: *Messenger*) 171
Expulsion of the Devil (1973, aka *Au rendez-vous de la mort joyeuse*) 237
Exquisite Corpse (2004) 178
Exte: Hair Extentions 144, 156
Extension in Use (Canadian short film) 248
Extra, Extra (short film) 185
La extravagante y poco práctica venganza de la momia 129
Extreme Nature of Bats 122, 134
Exhibit A (2010 short film) 200
Exhuming Mr. Rice 150
The Eye (2002, aka *Gin gwai*) 231
Eye of the Beholder (1999) 127
Eyeborgs 172
Eyegore Award 106, 108, 110, 137, 167
Eyegore Horror Award 108, 137
Eyepole 174
Eyes Beyond 123, 130, 174
The Eyes of Edward James 193, 237
Eyes of Laura Mars 212
Eyewitness (unproduced script) 226
Eyja 228, 229
Ezequiel (aka Ezequiel Martinez Jr.) 199

Fabian, Patrick 227, 245
Fabre, Laurent 244
Facal, Manuel 184
Facchinei, Gab 217
Face Machine 172
Face/Off 176, 208
Facebook.com 32–33, 254n19
Faceless (short film; year?) 173
Facinelli, Peter 220
The Facts in the Case of Mister Hollow 133, 143, 156, 190, 192, 229, 238, 246
Fade (2008 short film; dir: Taylor) 214
Fade to Black (1980) 212
The Faeries of Blackheath Woods 181, 244
Fagnoli, Marco 130
Fahy, Kate 156
Fail Safe (2000) 208
Fair Use (copyright exemption) 90–91
Fairfield Community Arts Center-Theater 107
Fait d'hiver see Gridlock
Falardeau, Éric 133
Falcon Theatre 204
Falicki, Daniel E. 245

The Fall (feature; year?) 175
The Fall (2006 feature; dir: Singh) 229
Fall of a Saga 222
Fallavollita, Michael 223
Fallen Angels (2006; dir: Thomas) 158
Falzone, Dan 134
The Familiar (2009 short film) 126, 130, 176, 184, 227, 245, 247
Familienradgeber (2006 feature, aka *Family Saga*) 248
Familjen Jacobssons öden och äventyr 176
Family Demons 162, 190
Family Guy (TV series) 205
The Family Man (2000) 207
The Family Recipes 224
Family Saga see *Familienradgeber* (2006)
Family Time (1993 short film) 251
Famous Monster Movie Art of Basil Gogos (book) 198
fan films 90, 103, 107, 109, 115, 157, 162
Fancher, Hampton 170
FanCine Málaga — Festival de Cine Fantástico 179–82
FanGirltastic.com 15, 113
Fangmeier, Stefen 233
Fangoria (magazine) 3, 14, 88, 108, 124, 137; Weekend of Fear 99; *see also* Fangoria Chainsaw Award
Fangoria Chainsaw Award vii, 3, 108, 137–41
Fangoria's Weekend of Horrors (aka Creation's Weekend of Horrors) vii, 108–9, 117, 137
Fangs for the Memories (short film) 163
Fanning, Dakota 205
Fanomenon — Leeds International Film Festival 118, 179–81
Fanta Festival vii, 100, 141, 179–84
Fantabiblical 236
Fantasia International Film Festival 97, 101, 141–45
Fantasme (2009 short film; dir Grondin) 142
Fantaspoa: Internacional de Cinema Fantástico de Porto Alegre vii, 13, 26, 27, 34, 96, 97, 145–46
Fantasporto 101–2, 146–54, 180–84
Fantastic Fest 101, 109, 154–56
Fantastic Films Weekend 118
Fantastisk Filmfestival 103
Fantasy see *Fantasme* (2009 short film; dir Grondin)
Fantasy Beyond 249
Fantasy Film Fest 99
Fantasy II 210
FantasyCon 117, 118
Fanzo, Don 213
A Far Cry from Home (year?) 243
The Far East Apartment 250
Far Out 156
Fard 158
Farewell to the Ark (1984, aka *Saraba hakobune*) 235
Fargo (1996) 209
Fargo Fantastic Film Festival vii, 109, 156–57
Fargo Theatre 109, 157
Farley, Christopher 225
Farmer, Donald 122
Farmhouse 172
Farmiga, Vera 249
Farrar, Scott 207
Farrell, Christopher 242

Farris, Lindsay 176
Farscape (1999–2003 TV series) 207, 208
Farscape: The Peacekeeper Wars (2004) 206
Fast Forward (2007 short film; dir: Holler) 242
Fâsuto sukuwaddo see *First Squad* (2009)
Fatal Kiss (2002 short film) 219
Fatale, Michelle 191
Fatherland (1994 TV movie) 166
Father's Day (short film; dir: S. Fritz) 174
Father's Day (2011 feature) 93
Fathers in Law (1998, aka *Les beaux-pères*) 202
Faust (1926) 197
Faust (1994; dir: Svankmajer) 152
Faust (2000, aka *Faust: Love of the Damned*; dir: Yuzna) 232
Faust, John 242, 244, 252
Fausto 5.0 127, 149, 164, 183, 232
Favreau, Jon 204
Fawcett, Marlowe 148
Fear Fiesta 109
Fear the Reaper (unproduced script) 134
Fear X 149
FeardotCom 139, 182
FearFest 109
Fearless Tales Genre Fest 109, 157
Fearnet.com 107
Fears for Queers GLBT Film Festival 105, 109
Fear(s) of the Dark (2007 feature, aka *Peur(s) du noir*) 192
A Feast of Souls 221
Feast 2 155
Feathers (dir: Rogers) 159
Featherston, Katie 217
Fecteau, Simon Olivier 142
Fedele, Jody 226
Fedori, Olga 146, 190
Feijó, Abi 153
Feldman, Corey 137
Feldman, Marty 213
Félix, Zoé 217
Fell (2010 feature film) 125
Fell, Chris 118
Fellowship: The Musical (stage production) 204
Felsher, Michael 195
Feng, Xiaogang 144
Feo Award 15
FeoAmante.com 15, 94
Ferarri, Alex 223
Fermat's Room see *La habitación de Fermat*
Fernández, Eduard 149, 232
Fernandez, Julio 149
Fernandez, Victor 232
Ferns, Michael 158
Ferozz: The Wild Red Riding Hood see *Molina's Ferozz*
La Ferra: Ciudad Dormida (animated short film) 185
Ferrara, Abel 252
Ferreira, António 147
Ferrer, Tessa 220
Ferrera, Carlos Martín 230
Ferrin, Chad 122
Ferron, Alex 249
Ferry, Jean 237

Festival Européen du Film Fantastique de Strasbourg vii, 99, 157–58, 179
Festival Internacional de Cinema Fantàstic de Sitges 227
Festival Internacional de Cinema Fantàstic i de Terror 227
Festival International du Film Fantastique de Gérardmer vii, 99, 163–66
Festival of Fantastic Films 118, 158–61
Festival of Fear 109
Fest21.com 24, 34, 70–71
Fetch (1998 short film; dir: Danzey) 202
Feuer und Schwert — Die Legende von Tristan und Isolde see *Tristan and Isolde* (1982)
La fiancée aux cheveux blancs see *The Bride with White Hair*
La fiancée de chucky see *Bride of Chucky*
Fido (2006) 163
Fiedel, Brad 141
Fields, Peter Allan 169
Fiennes, Ralph 139, 216
Fies, Brenda **62**, 105
Fies, Elisabeth vii, 6, **62**, 105, 123, 126, 253n4
The Fifth (2007 short film) 134, 136, 144, 156
The Fifth Province 151
Fighter (2007 feature; dir: Arthy) 228
Figuereo, Camille 238
Figueroa, Lucas M. 123, 132, 201
Filho, Esmir 229
Filho, Kleber Mendonça 146
Filho, Paulo Biscaia 184
Filion, Robert W. 123
Filippi, Francesco 158
Film Independent 5, 34, 189, 254n4
Film Score Monthly 197, 198
Filmatrón 129, 185
Film4 FrightFest 118
Filmhouse Cinema (in Edinburgh, UK) 118
Filmins.com 255n9
FilmProposals.com 34
Filthy (2003 short film; dir: Karliss & Lalino) 196, 222
La fin de notre amour 149
Final Appointment 226
Final Cut Pro 45
Final Destination (film series) 50
Final Destination 207
Final Destination 2 240
Final Girl 14
Final Journey (short film; year?) 181, 215
Final Sale 136
The Final Solution (Intolerance III) see *Intolerance III: The Final Solution*
Finale (2009 feature; dir: Elfers) 190
Fincher, David 151
Finding Nemo 206, 240
Fine, David 224
Fingerprints (2006 feature; dir: Basil) 189
Finkle's Odyssey 148, 181
Fiore, Mauro 249
Fiore, Michael 242
Fire, Richard 153
Fire of Conscience 192
Fire Woman (1970, aka *Hwanyeo*) 237
Fireball (2009) 143
Firecracker (2005) 148
Firefly (2002–03 TV series) 206
Firefly (2005 feature; dir: Marcy?) 156, 172

Fireman! (Canadian short film; year?) 245, 248
Firemount 219
Fireproof Agent 248
Fireside Foundation 106, 115
First Born (unproduced script) 226
First Light (2002 short film; dir: Galant) 160
First Squad (2009, aka *First Squad: The Moment of Truth*, aka *Fâsuto sukuwaddo*) 147, 214
The First Vampire (short film) 172
Fischer, Ian 185
Fish (2002 short film, aka *Kala*) 182
Fish Story 155, 187
Fish Tank 147
Fishel, David 178
Fisher, Carrie 213
Fisher, David Lee 218
Fisher, Ted 179
Fisher, Terence 198
Fisher, Terry 242
Fisher, Tom 150
The Fisher King 210
Fisheye (1980, aka *Riblje oko*) 236
Fistful of Brains 167
Fitzpatrick, Nina 151
Five Thousand Years 172
FIXION-SARS: Festival de Cine Fantástico y de Terror de Santiago viii, 98, 202–3
Flanagan, Fionnula 207
Flanagan, Mike 134, 159, 242
FlashForward (TV series) 132
Flatlife (2004 short film) 145
Flatworld 202
Fleck, João vii, 26–27, 96, 97
Fleischer, Richard 213
Fleischer, Ruben 228
Fleischmann, Peter 153, 234
Flesh-Eating Ghouls from Outer Space 192
Flesh for the Beast 189
Flesh of My Flesh (2009 short film) 174
Fletcher, Bruce 108
Fletcher, Louise 211
Fletcher, Robert 211
FLICKERS: Rhode Island International Horror Film Festival vii, 72, 114, 195–96
Flip! (2004 short film; dir: Demarais) 199
The Flower (2007 animated short film; dir: Hayward & Dubrovsky) 246
Flowers for Norma 191
Flügger, Daniel 248
Fluke (1995 feature) 251
Flush! (short film; dir: Grenier) 144
Flutter (short film; dir: Shia) 144
The Fly (1986) 211
Flyaway (animated short film) 124, 222
Flyer (dir: Yusof) 159
Flying Saucer Exodus 162
Flying Saucer Rock'n'Roll 151
Fodde, Juma 185
Foet (short film; year?) 238
The Fog (2005) 138
Folch, Enric 152, 171, 175, 234
Foley, Stephan A. 226
Folino, Christopher 178
Folklore (2007 short film) 220, 221
Follia see *Asylum* (2005)
Fonda, Bridget 233
Fong yuk see *Exiled* (2006) 144
Fontaine, Mathieu 145

Fontano, Joe 241
Food Bank of NW Pennsylvania 108
The Fool of Muncaster 243
Foot of the Bed 249
Footage (unproduced script) 190
Foott, Peter 195
Foque, Christoph vii, 96
For God's Sake (1990 short film) 234
For the Birds (2000 short film; dir: Eggleston) 232
Foraker, Brett 195
The Forbidden Door (aka *Pintu terlarang*) 192
Forbidden Eyes (2002, aka *Verboden ogen*) 175, 183
The Forbidden Quest 152
Ford, Courtney 220
Ford, Harrison 212, 213
Ford, Melisa 224
Ford, Mia 241
Ford, Phil 169
Forecast (2007 short film; dir: Courtney) 132, 214
Foreclosed (2010 short film; dir Bellantine) 243
Foree, Ken 172, 237
Forever (1997, UK) see *Photographing Fairies*
Forge 245
Forged 136
The Forgotten (1973) see *Don't Look in the Basement*
Forgotten Silver 151
Forklift Driver Klaus: The First Day on the Job (aka *Staplerfahrer Klaus—Der erste Arbeitstag*) 202
Forney, Pascal 187
Forrest Gump 79, 209
For(r)est in the Des(s)ert 229
Forsberg, Eric 225
Forsythe, William 138
Fortin, Guillaume 144
Forzani, Bruno 149, 166, 228, 231
Foster, Jodie 140, 208, 213
Foster, Matthew M. vii, 31, 36, 38–39, 41–43, 47, 51, 70, 79, 89–90, 93, 108, 135
Fotos (1996 feature) 233
Foulkes, Mirrah 133
Four Corners (2005 short film; dir Mueller) 214
A Four Course Meal 167
Fournier, Alain 143
Fourth Floor Seige 243
Fowler, Pauline 139
Fox, Daniel J. 158
Fox, Matthew 205, 215
Fox, Megan 216
Fox, Michael J. 211
Fox, Paul 134, 173, 189, 193, 230, 244
Fox Movie Channel 199
Foy, Ciaran 244
Frachon, James L. 164
Fracture (2004) 149
FracturedAtlas.org 17
Fradgley, Garreth 238
Fragile (2005, aka *Frágiles*; dir: Balaguero) 164
Fragments of Normal (unproduced script) 190
Frailty 126, 139
Françaix, Pascal 165
Francese, Bernardo 130
Franco, Sebastián 185

Un franco, 14 pesetas see *Crossing Borders* (2006)
Frank, Scott 207
Frank DanCoolo: Paranormal Drug Dealer 135, 168, 190, 200, 219
Frankenheimer, John 213
Franklin, John 226
Franklin, Paul J. 204
Franklin, Richard 236
Frankenberry cereal 48
Frankenstein (book) 90
Frankenstein (1930s film series) 48
Frankenstein (1931) 198
Frankenstein (2004 TV movie) 39
Frankenstein and Me 151
Frankenstein 90 154
The Frankenstein Syndrome (aka *The Prometheus Project*) 134, 162, 191
Frankenstein Unlimited 142
Franzen, Till 148, 175
Fraser, Keith 243
Fratto, Marc 189
Fratzscher, Peter 176
Frauds 128
Fräulein Gertie see *Señorita Gertie*
Frayed (2007 feature) 172
Frazetta, Frank 198
Frazetta: Painting with Fire 160, 223
Frazier, John 206
Freak (1999, aka *The Last Roadstop*) 161
Freak Out (2004) 159, 196
Freak Show Horror Film Festival vii, 83, 109, 161–62
Freaked (1993) 166
Freaky Award 109, 161
Freaky Friday the #13 167
Fred 166
Freddy vs. Jason 139
Freddy's Dead: The Final Nightmare 141
The Free Association (music band) 231
Free Enterprise (1998) 208
Free Tibet (2005) 58
Freeborn, Stuart 211, 213
Freeway (1996 feature; dir: Bright) 194, 233
Freeze Frame 125
Freilich, Chris 243
The French Doors 135
Frequency (2000) 207
Fresnadillo, Juan Carlos 149
Frías, Martin 129
Frid, Jonathan 8
Friday the 13th (film series) 161
Friday the 13th (2009) 138
Friday the 13th: Deluxe Editions (Parts 1–6) 195
Friday the 13th: Part VII—The New Blood 195
The Fridays of Eternity 154
Fridriksson, Fridrik Thor 252
Friedkin, William 213
Friend, Timothy 122
Fright Flick 167
Fright Night (1985) 154, 211
Fright Night Film Fest vii, 28, 32, 42, 51, 66, 73, 79, 83, 93, 109, 162–63
The Frighteners (1996 feature) 140, 233
FrightFest vii, 118
Frightmares Film Festival vii, 109, 166
Fringe (TV series) 203, 204
Fritz, James 174
Fritz, Jürgen 234
Fritz Niedsone Is the New Black 178
Frizzell, John 243

Index

From a Place of Darkness 243
From Beyond (1986 feature) 235
From Beyond (2006 animated short film) 136, 191
From Dusk Till Dawn 140, 171, 209
From Dusk Till Dawn 2: Texas Blood Money 208
From Inside 143, 229
Frontière(s) (2007) 127, 180, 194
Frost, Nick 138
Frostbitten (aka *Frostbiten*) 148, 194, 217
A Frozen Flower 147
Fruergaard, Tor 252
Fruet, William 236
Fuchs, Jurriaan 136
Fudoh: The New Generation 151
Fuego eterno 153
Fuest, Robert 236
Fukasaku, Kinji 202
Fukiishi, Kazue 193
Fulci, Lucio 140
Full Employment 155, 158, 201
Full Metal Alchemist 145
Full Moon (DVD distributor) 197
Fuller, Amanda **25**
Fuller, Andrew 168
Fullerton, Carl 210
Fun on Earth 132, 162
De función see *The Last Performance* (2006)
La Funcionaria Asesina 122
Funeral Urn Trophy 185–86
Funke, Alex 206
Funky Forest: The First Contact 145
Funny Games (1997) 151
Funny Games (2007) 86
Fuori di testa see *Bad Taste* (1987)
Furlong, Edward 210
Furmie, Marc 224
The Furred Man 171
Furtney, B.C. 189
Furuya, Shôgo 188
The Fury (1978) 212
Fuse Chainsaw Award (aka Fangoria/Fuse Chainsaw Award) 138
Fuse Channel 137
Fusion 21 (2002 short film) 160
Fuster, Quim 230
Future Life (magazine) 124
Futureworld 213
The Futurist (2005 short film) 173
Fyren (2010 short film) 168
Fyvie, Howard 238

G&S Effects 189
Gabai, Sasson 147
Gabbeh 233
Gabbey, Scott 197
Gabriel, Marcos 226
Gabriel, Peter 166
Gabriel-Ernest 190
Gabriel's Word 160
Gadkie lebedi see *Ugly Swans* (2006)
Gaiman, Neil 169, 171
Galant, Alexander 160
Galaxina 128
Galaxy Quest 127, 169, 171, 186, 208
Galbó, Cristina 236
Galceran, Jordi 149
Gale, Bob 170
Gale, Richard 133, 134, 143, 144, 189, 191, 192, 248
Galinsky, Robert Lewis 177
Gallagher, Scott 231

Gallant, Jessica 57, 247
Gallart, David 232
Gallasch, Jan 184
Gallego, Miguel 159, 167, 196, 242
Gallo, Micah 199
Gambon, Michael 234
Game Night (Canadian short film; year?) 245
Gamers (2006) 178
Gamez, Raul P. (aka Perez Gamez Raul) 185
Gammill, Kerry 114, 198
Gananian, Carlos G. 203
Gancedo, Manuel 202
Gans, Christophe 176, 232
Gansel, Dennis 227
Garay, Jesús 128, 153, 234
Garber, Jake 206
Garber, Victor 207
Garci, Armando 159
García, Francisco 231
García, Lawrence 172
García, Ramon 235
García, Saturnino 233
García, Víctor 218
Garden of Earthly Delights 177
Gardner, Chris 146
Gardner, Tony 140
Garetano, Christopher P. 134
Garfin, Corinne 164
Gargoyle (unproduced script) 188
Garland, Alex 139
Garner, Jennifer 207
Garris, Mick 173, 189
The Garth Method 178
Gasparilla Film Festival 109, 110
Gastropotens II. Mutación tóxica 202
Gates, Timothy 226
The Gates of Hell (2008 feature; dir: Dolen) 177
The Gathering (2003; dir: Gilbert) 164
Gatlin Pictures 106
Gato 132, 184
Gattaca 165, 233
Gatti, Guille 241
Gaudcr, Áron 230
Gaudino, Giuseppe M. 151
Gauntlet of Sorrow 220, 221
Gaup, Nils 252
Gauthier, Philippe 165
Gavreau, Martin (aka Martin Waltz) 158
Gawade, Pushpank 237
Gay Zombie 125, 172
Gazdag, Gyula 235
Geburt der Hexe 236
Gee, Joshua **11**
Gégauff, Paul 154
Gehl, Doug 192
Gehrig, Maja 187
Gehron, Rich 106
Geirnaert, Jonas 145
Gekijouban Gintama: Shin'yaku benizakura hen see *Gintama: The Movie* (2010)
Gekkô no sasayaki see *Moonlight Whispers* (1999)
Gélinas, Francis 142
Gellar, Sarah Michelle 208
Geller, Stephen 170
Gemini (1999 feature, aka *Sôseiji*) 188, 232
Gen Art (film festival) 30
Gendel, Morgan 169

Génesis (1998 short film; dir: Cerdà) 202, 233
Genesis Antipode 173, 220, 221
Genis, Dan 236
Genital Genocide 192
Genius Party Beyond 143
Genocchio, Samuel 178
Gens, Xavier 127, 194
Gentile, Troy 241
Gentry, Jacob 144
George, Peter 170
George Lucas in Love 202
George Pal Memorial Award 204–5, 213
George's Intervention 191, 219, 248
Geoul sokeuro see *Into the Mirror*
Gérardmer Fantastic Film Festival *see* Festival International du Film Fantastique de Gérardmer
Gerhard, MV 217
Gerolmo, Chris 233
Gerron, Don 174
Gertie Award 227–31
Get Off My Porch 162
Get Rich Quick (2004) 178
Getting My Brother Laid see *My Brother the Vampire*
Ghost (1990) 210
Ghost Busted 173
Ghost Dog: The Way of the Samurai 90
Ghost Droppings 14
Ghost from the Machine see *Phasma Ex Machina*
Ghost in the Shell 151, 165
Ghost in the Shell 2: Innocence 193, 231
Ghost of the Needle 160, 196
Ghost Rock 157
Ghost Story (1974, aka *Madhouse Mansion*) 236
Ghost System (2002, aka *Gosuto shisutemu*) 218
Ghost Town (1988) 153
Ghost Whisperer (2005–10 TV series) 205
Ghost World (2001 film) 90
Ghostbusters 126, 195, 211
Ghosts of Cité Soleil 144
GhostWatcher 218
The Ghoul (1933) 199
The Ghoul (1975) 236
Ghoulardi 198
The Ghouls (2003 feature?) 189
The G.I. 225
Giacchino, Michael 249
Giamatti, Paul 148
Gianutsos, Ali 224
Gibault, Alexandre 142
Gibbs, George 210
Gibson, Charles 205
Gibson, Michael Ferris 160
Gidam see *Epitaph* (2007)
Gielen, Ryan 30
The Gift (2000; dir: Raimi) 127
The Gift (dir: Hannafey) 161
Gig (dir: Ienaga) 252
Gigantino, Jennifer 247
Giger Award *see* H.R. Giger Award
Giguère, Denis-Steve 145
Gil, Ariadna 148
Gilbert, Andrew 243
Gilbert, Brian 164
Gilbert, Lewis 128
Gildark, Daniel (aka Dan) 168
Giler, David 170

Gill, Kayla 124
Gillespie, Jeremy 98
Gillette, John vii, 28, 32, 35, 42, 49, 66, 75, 77, 82, 89, 113
Gilliam, Terry 171, 214
Gillis, Alec 208, 210
Gillmore, Geoffrey 21
Gilmore, Ryan 171, 191
Giménez, Xavi 231, 232
Gimme Skelter 163
Gin Tama see *Gintama: The Movie* (2010)
Gingell, Christabel 159
Gingell, Zoe 159
Ginger Snaps 139, 207
Ginger Snaps 2: Unleashed 138
Gingold, Mike vii, 137
Gingras, Denis 236
Gintama: The Movie (2010, aka *Gekijouban Gintama: Shin'yaku benizakura hen*) 192
Gioffre, Rocco 211
Giordano, Domiziana 153
Giordano, Mario 150
Giorgi, Consuela 159
The Girl by the Lake 180
The Girl from Monday 230
"The Girl in the Fireplace" (*Doctor Who* TV episode) 133, 169, 198
The Girl Next Door 156
The Girl on the Broomstick (1972, aka *Divka na kosteti*) 237
The Girl Who Leapt Through Time (aka *Toki o kakeru shōjo*) 230
The Girlfriend (2005 short film) 221
Giroux, Pascal 150
Gitchy 243
Gladiy, Grigoriy (aka Gregory Hlady) 235
Gladwell, David 154
Glass (short film; dir: Duzel) 178
Glastonbury Horror Festival 118
Glau, Summer 205
Glendening, Jonathan 166
Glickert, Robert 244
Glitch (2003 animated short film) 160, 172
Gloaguen, Yohann 193
The Globe Theatre 96
Glosserman, Scott 145, 230
Glover, Crispin Hellion 229, 230
Glut, Don 198
GNR (music band) 149
Go-Green Campaign 197
Gobert, Fabrice 227
The God 175
God of Gamblers 3: The Early Stage (1997, aka *Do san 3: Chi siu nin do san*) 251
God of Vampires 162, 220, 221
God Thinks You're a Loser 122
Godard, Jean-Luc 254n7
Godawa, Brian 226
Goddard, Drew 169
The Godfather (1972 film) 204
Godfrey, Lucas 104
Godron, Sébastien 143
Gods and Monsters 126, 213
God's Marble 220
God's Puzzle (aka *Kamisama no pazuru*) 228
The Godsend (1980) 236
Godspeed (2009 feature; dir: Saitzyk) 194
Godzilla (character) 199

Godzilla (1954, aka *Gojira*) 198, 205
Godzilla (1998) 208
Godzilla: Final Wars (2004) 145
Goedecke, Mike 223
Gogos, Basil 197, 198, 199
Going Nuts see *Gritos en el pasillo*
Going to Pieces: The Rise and Fall of the Slasher Film (2002 book) 254n5
Going to Pieces: The Rise and Fall of the Slasher Film (2006 film) 58
Gojira see *Godzilla* (1954)
Goldbart, Nicolás 227
Goldberg, Scott 163, 196
Goldberg, Whoopi 210
Goldblum, Jeff 140, 211, 234
Golden Cob Award 123
Golden Earrings (2010) 219
Golden Glibb Award 99, 248
Golden Méliès see Méliès d'Or
Golden Octopus Award 99, 158
Golden Raven Award 126–28
Golden Scythe Award 166
Golden Slumber 155
Golden Sugar Skull Award *52*, 101, 185–86
Golden Tooth Award 100
The Golden Voyage of Sinbad 213
Goldenberg, Michael 169
Goldman, Jane 169
Goldman, William 170
Goldsmith, Jerry 211, 233
Goldstein, Jeanette 211
Golembeske, Ryan 226
Goligher, Tristan 160
Gollum 169, 240
Gomeda 244
Gómez, Felipe 148
Gomez, Jose Carlos 241
Goméz, Macarena 147
Gómez, Manuel 150, 233
Gomez, Miguel Alejandro 185
Gomez, Nick 251
Gomorrah (unproduced script) 226
Gondry, Michel 125, 187, 230
Gone (2004 short film; dir: Petersen) 222
Gonzales, John 226
Gonzales, Ricardo "Rick" 222
Gonzalez, Marcos 132
Good Life Delivery 193
The Good Shepherd (2006) 245
The Good Son (1993) 209
The Good, the Bad, the Weird 228
Goodbye, Cruel World (2003 short film) 193
Goodbye, 20th Century (aka *Zbogum na dvadesetiot vek*) 183
Goode, Andrew 175
Goodwin, Archie 198
Google.com 2, 7, 34–35, 63
Gooley, Nikki 205
The Goonies 211
Gorak, Chris 144
Gordon, Alex 199
Gordon, Jesse 132
Gordon, Richard 199
Gordon, Robert 169, 186
Gordon, Seth 144
Gordon, Stuart 127, 134, 140, 141, 230, 231, 235
Gordon-Levitt, Joseph 215
Gorenight 99
Gorgonas 130
Gorman, Jonathan 122

Gort Award 106, 125
Gory Gory Hallelujah 223
Gossett, Denise viii, 6–7, 24, 43–*44*, 50–51, 57–58, 67, 71, 74, 78, 92–93, 115, 121
Gosti iz galaksije 154
Gothic (1986) 153
Die Gottesanbeterin see *Black Widow* (2001)
Gottlieb, Michael 153
Goulekas, Karen 208
Gourmet (2007 short film) 172
Govaerts, Jonas 229
Gove, William 250
Goyer, David 126, 139, 205
Gozlan, Yann 164
Gozu 127, 188, 231
GR30k 245
Gråbøl, Sofie 150
Grace, Helen 92
Grace, Jeff 217
Grace (2006 short film; dir: Solet) 72, 163, 196, 242
Grace (2009 feature; dir: Solet) 72, 195, 246
Gracie, Marc 177
Graham, Jeff Dylan 125
Graham, Scott 221, 242
Grammaticopoulos, Philippe 231, 232
Grammy Award 1, 56
Grams, Martin 197
Granberry, Michael 169
Grand Center Intersection for Life and Arts 116
The Grandfather Paradox 125, 173
Grandinetti, Dario 149
Granier, Patrick 235
Granier-Deferre, Christopher *67*
Granlund, Aaron 244
Granny & Death 175
Grant, Daniel 159
Grant, Julian 150
Grant, Rachel 223
Graphic Sexual Horror 162
Grashaw, Vincent 191
Gratte-Papier 144
Grau, Jorge Michel 142, 155, 185
Grave Mistakes 219
Grave Reality (Florida short film) 161
Graveless 230
Graves End 221
Graveyard Alive 196
Graveyard Shift (radio show) 109
The Graveyard Show 14
GravitonCreations.com 9
Grazer, Brian 213
The Great American Nightmare 224
Great Lakes Independent Film Festival 11
The Great Vincent see *Vincent, le magnifique*
Great Yokai War 145
The Greatest American Hero (1981–83 TV series) 206, 214
The Greatest Story of All Time 136
Greaves, Daniel 130, 202
Greeb, Gabriela 165
Greek, Janet 169
Green, Adam 144
Green, David 192
Green, Hadyn 242
Green, Walter 244
The Green Butchers (aka *De grønne*

slagtere, aka *De gröna slaktarna*) 127, 149, 171, 182
Green Glibb Award 248
The Green Goblin's Last Stand 157
Green Lantern 215, 216
The Green Mile 208
Green Vinyl 146
Greenaway, Peter 232, 233, 234
Greenberg, Stanley R. 186
Greene, Lorne 214
Greenfield, Alex 218
Greengrass, Paul 150
Greenhouse, Kate 145, 185, 193
The Greens 142
Greenwood, Bruce 132
Greggory, Pascal 194
Grelet, Axelle (aka Axelle Cummings) 220
Gremlins 211
Gremm, Wolf 154
Grenier, Jef 144
Grey Skies 219, 224
Gridlock (2002 short film; aka *Fait d'hiver*) 175
Grieco, David 141
Grieco, Gabriel 129
Grieco, Jim 172
Griera, Robert Ors 228
Griffin, Anthony E. viii, 116, 245
Griffin, Richard 196
Griffith, Dylan 244
Griffith, Jesse 240
Griffith, Spence 224
Grillo, Christian Jude 244
Grim (2004 short film) 178
Grim Reaper Award 110, 113, 195
Grimly, Gris 123, 239
Grimm Love (aka *Rohtenburg*) 181, 192, 193, 229
Grimm Up North vii, 118, 166
Grimmelmann, James 62, 254n8
Grimmfest *see* Grimm Up North
Grimmy Award 110, 113, 195
Grimshaw, Ellen 176
Grimshaw, Mike (aka Michael) 175
Grindhouse (2007) 216
Grindhouse Film Festival 109
Griscelda 129
Griswold, Al 236
Grité una noche 130
Gritos en el pasillo 123
Grizzly Man 230
Groen, Jeroen 136
De gröna slaktarna see *The Green Butchers*
Grondin, Izabel 14, 142
De grønne slagtere see *The Green Butchers*
Groovy Award 245
Gross, Eldar 137
Gross, Jose 104
Gross, Terence 232
Gross Movie Reviews (book) 110
Gross Out Contest 10–11, 73–74
Die grosse Werkstatt see *The Big Garage*
Grosselfinger, Christian 218
The Ground 251
Ground Zero (2010 feature?) 200
Groundhog Day 209
Groves, Andrew 178
Gruber, J. Mackye 127
The Grudge (2004) 138
Grundy, Solomon 190
Guaglione, Fabio 159, 229

The Guardian (2007 short film; dir: Marshall) 163
Guardian of the Realm 162, 225
Guarner, Jose Luis *see* Jose Luis Guarner Critic Award
Gubera, Chip 129, 185
Gudiño, Rodrigo 130, 133, 143, 192, 193, 196, 229, 237, 238
Gudmundsson, Gunnar 147
Guerín, José Luís 233
Guff, Mac 228
Guía, Paula 130
Guignol 122
Guillon, Yvon 166
Guinness, Alec 213
Gumbs, Joseph 172
Gun Town (2009) 162
Gunmen (2007 short film) 220, 221
Gunn, James 205
Gunnlaugsson, Hrafn 252
Gunther Toody's Happy Time Fun Show 162
Guðmundsdóttir, Björk *see* Björk
Gurland, Andrew 245
Gurudata, Andrew vii
Gusman, Martina 155
Gustafsson, Allan 175
Gustafsson, Anders 176
Gutiérrez, F. Javier (aka Francisco Javier Gutiérrez) 170, 214, 217, 218, 232
Guttman, Roxana 128, 184
Guy's Guide to Zombies 159
Guzman, Joseph 122
Guzzo, Phil 214
Gwoemul see *The Host*
Gyles, Dylan 248, 249
Gyllenhaal, Maggie 149
The Gynecologist 162

Ha, Jung-Woo 148
Ha, Yoo 147
Haaga, Trent 162, 177
Haapsalu Horror & Fantasy Film Festival vii, 98, 166–67
Haber, Bryan 247
Haberle, Oldrich 153
Haberman, Hal 193
Haberman, Steve 197
La habitaciónde Fermat 147, 180
Habitaciones para turistas 130
El habitante incierto see *The Uninvited Guest*
La hacienda del terror 167
Hack, Jason 196
Hadida, Samuel 147
Hadzihalilovic, Lucile 188, 250
Haffter, Petra 252
Håfström, Mikael 218
Hagan, Dave 112
The Hagstone Demon 130
Haig, Sid 137, 138, 139, 217
Hailstone, Dominic 238, 239
Hair Extentions see *Exte: Hair Extentions*
Hairlady 246
The Hairy Fairy 159
Haishima, Kuniaki 229
Hajaig, Hadi 160
Hajime, Ôhata 249
Hakko (aka *Hakko — fermentation*) 250
Hal, Allen 205
Halálkeringö see *Death Waltz* (2010)
Haley, Jackie Earle 249

Half Life (dir: Jacobs) 159
Half Spirit: Voice of the Spider 128
Halfway (2009 feature, aka *Harufuwei*; dir: Kitakawa) 192
Halfway (dir: Holt) 159
Hall, Charles 173
Hall, Christina 219
Hall, Michael C. 205
Hall, Mindy 203
The Hall! (year?) 224
Halligan, Simeon 118, 167
Halloween (2007, aka *Rob Zombie's Halloween*) 197, 216
Halloween: The Curse of Michael Myers 140
Halloween: The Happy Haunting of America 198
Halloween: H20 139
Halloween Horror Film Fest 107
Halloween Horror Nights — Rob Zombie Film Competition 110
Halloween Horror Nights Scary Film Competition 108, 110, 137, 167
Halloween Horror Picture Show 109, 110
Halloween Monster Movie Challenge vii, 33, 42, 50–51, 76, 80, 118
Halloweenapalooza 110
Hallucinations in Croissant Sauce 160
Halmi, Robert, Jr. 205
Halmi, Robert, Sr. 205
Halo 2 (video game) 240
Halter, Casey 242
Hamer, Bent 147
Hamill, Mark 211, 212
Hamilton, A. Scott 218
Hamilton, George 212
Hamilton, Jake 196
Hamilton, Linda 210, 214
Hamm, Sam 230
Hammer Film Festival 99
Hammer films 117, 126
hammocking (1 V programming strategy) 254n4
Hammond, Stephen 158
Hamon, Kyle 222
The Hamster Cage 156
Han, Jae-rim 144
Hanabusa, Tsutomu 187
Hanah's Gift 220
Handfield, Mathieu 133
The Handler (unproduced script) 191
The Handsome Suit (aka *Hansamu sûtsu*) 187
The Handyman (2006 short film; dir: Rumley) 135, 229
Haneke, Michael 151, 231, 233, 234, 245
Haney, Kevin C. 210
Hangar No. 5 214
Hanks, Tom 210
Hanley, Brent 126, 139
Hannah, Daryl 206, 211
Hannah, Don 225
Hannibal (2001) 139, 207
Hannigan, Alyson 207
Hansamu sûtsu see *The Handsome Suit*
Hansel & Gretel (2007, aka *Henjel gwa Geuretel*) 147, 192
Hansen, Gary 236
Hansen, Gunnar 137
Hansen, John 159
Hanson, Andrew 172
Hansson, Andreas 202

Hansson, Joakim 218
Happiness (1998) 102, 151
Happiness of the Katakuris (2001) 164
The Happiness Salesman 195
Happy Birthday to You (2006 short film; dir Alcalde; aka *Y que cumplas muchos más*) 123, 189, 191, 201, 217, 239
Happy Face 196
Happy Feet 239
Happy Jack (unproduced script) 226
Happyjack-McKenzie, Kris 142
Haraguchi, Tomoo 128
Harari, Robert 244
Harbinger (2007 short film) 172
Harbon, Rudy 173
Hard Candy 230
Hard Target 209
Harden, John 160
Harden, Marcia Gay 204
Harders, Katie vii, 109
Hardiman, Neasa 160
Hardware 128, 153
Hardy, Robin 198
Hardy, Tom 215
Hargreaves, John 236
Hari Om 193
Hark, Tsui 147
Harlequin (1980) 236
Harlow, Joel 203
Harman, Toni 175
Harmon, Robert 141
Harper, Graeme 169
Harres, Pedro 146
Harris, Dan 205
Harris, Jared 233
Harris, Neil Patrick 237
Harris, Ron E. 244
Harrison, Andrew 159, 160
Harrison, Harry 186
Harrison, Jim 209
Harry Doright's Prelude to Hell 136, 217
Harry Potter and the Half-Blood Prince 216
Harry Potter and the Order of the Phoenix 133, 216
Harry Potter and the Prisoner of Azkaban 240
Harry Potter and the Sorcerer's Stone 207
Harryhausen, Ray 126, 171, 197, 199, 206, 213, 214, 233, 240
Harry's Joint 160
Harsh Realm (1999–2000 TV miniseries) 250
Hart, Jake 243
Hart, James V. 140, 169, 210
Hart (2009 short film) 176
Hartley, Adele vii, 118, 121, 134
Hartley, Hal 230
Hartz, Thomas 99
Harvest Moon 135
Harvey, Brett 159
Harvie Krumpet 231
Haskin, Byron 169
Hassan, Kamal 193
Hassan, Omar 160
Hatch (2009 short film; dir: McCarthy) 201
Hatchet 144, 156
Hate Night 217
Hatfield, Hurd 213
Hathaway, Anne 215
Hathaway, Noah 211
Hathaway, Robin 220

Haugegaard, Casper 166
HAuNTcon Amateur Horror Film Festival 110, 167
Haunted (1995 feature) 128
Haunted Attraction National Tradeshow & Convention 110
Haunted Boat 222
Haunted High (unproduced script) 217
Haunted Newport Horror Film Festival 110
Haunted Planet 172
The Haunted Report 14
The Haunted Restaurant 241
The Haunting (1999) 139
The Haunting in Connecticut 195
The Haunting of North 3rd Street 167
Hauser, Brian R. 168, 240
Hauser, Murilo 132
Hausschmid, Susanne 178
Haute tension see *High Tension* (2003)
Hawes, James 169
Hawkins, J.D. 167, 168
Hawkinson, James 147
Hawley, James 247
Hawthorne Collection's Universal Monster Village 198
Hayashi, Tamio 155
Hayashida, Yuji 227
Hayden, Marianne 218
Hayes, Craig 207
Hayman, Cyd 236
Haynes, Linda 236
Haynes, Todd 153
Haysbert, Dennis 208
Hayter, David 207
Hazel's Hips 136
The Hazing (year?, aka *Dead Scared*?) 163
Hazy Life (aka *Donten seikatsu*) 250
HBO Home Entertainment 195
He, Ping 252
He Dies at the End 158, 241
He Knows 240
Head Above Water (1996 feature; dir: Wilson) 233
Headey, Lena 132
Headhunter (dir: Morgan) 196
Headhunter: The Assessment Weekend (aka *The Assessment*) 219, 220
Headspace (2005 feature; dir: van den Houten) 189
Heal (2010 short film; dir: Ahmad) 142
The Heart Is a Hidden Camera 122
The Heart Is Deceitful Above All Things 248
Heart of Karl 190, 249
Heart of Midnight 234
Heart of the Warrior (aka *El corazón del guerrero*) 150, 171, 183
The Heart of the World (2000 short film) 202
Heartbeat (dir: Bar-Levy) 215
Heartless (2009) 146, 179, 245
Hearts and Souls (1993) 209
Heaven and Hell to Play With: The Filming of Night of the Hunter (book) 199
Heaven Can Wait (1978) 212
Heavenly Creatures 166
Hector Corp. 135
He'd Never Do That (2009, aka *Él nunca lo haría*) 146
Hedman, Maria 175
Heggelman, Ruwan 136

Heimann, Jurgen 218
Hein, Michael J. viii, 88, 113
Heinlein, Robert A. 169
The Heist and the Accomplice (music band) 190
Hel on Ice 124
Helander, Jalmari 121, 201, 227
Helix (2006 short film) 136
Hell Is Full 241
Hell Night (1981) 236
The Hell Patrol 200
Hellbent (2004) 196
Hellbound: Hellraiser II 210
Hellboy 138, 206
Hellboy: In the Chapel of Moloch (comic book) 197
Hellboy II: The Golden Army 138, 204, 216, 249
Hellbride 158
Hellebust, Kristin 124
Hellraiser 126, 153, 195
Hellraiser: Bloodline 141
Hellraiser: Deader—Winter's Lament 162, 167
Hellraiser Box Set (DVD set) 195
Hells (2008) 143
Hell's Fever 181
Hell's Half Mile Film & Music Festival vii, 110
Hell's Highway (dir: Taylor) 160, 226
Helman, Pablo 207
Helmer, Veit 147, 150, 175, 202
Hemker, Todd 122
Hemmings, David 236
Hemphill, Jimmy 225
Henderson, Kirk 159
Hendrix, Duke 167
Henenlotter, Frank 130, 189
Henn, Carrie 211
Hennessy, Angelique 248
Henriksen, Lance 141, 156, 171, 204, 209, 238
Henrique, Fernando 96
Henry: Portrait of a Serial Killer 128, 153, 234
Henson, Brian 164
Henson, Christian 217
Henson, Jim see Jim Henson's Creature Shop
Herbie! (2004 short film) 168, 173, 189
Herbst, Katie 224
The Hercynian Orchid 224
La herencia Valdemar 146
Herman, Mark 150
Herman: Am I Proud 177
Herman, the Legal Labrador 178
Hero (dir: Carnior) 142
Heroes (2006–10 TV series) 204, 205, 216
Heroic Performance Award 114
Herpes Boy 132
Herrán, Adriana 154
Herrell, William 222
Herrmann, Bernard 213
Herschell Gordon Lewis: The Godfather of Gore 130
Hersh, Nicola (aka Nicki Hersh) 222
Hertzfeldt, Don 142, 144, 155, 194
Herz, Juraj 147, 154, 237
Herz, Michael 153
Herzog, Werner 145, 230
A hetedik kör see *The Seventh Circle* (2009)
Hewitt, Cindy Davis 186

Hewitt, Donald H. 186
Hewitt, Jennifer Love 205
Hewitt, Jon 177
Heyerdahl, Christopher 169
H.H. Holmes: America's First Serial Killer 218
Hickel, Hal 205
Hickenlooper, George 202
Hickinbotham, Andrew 179
Hicks, Catherine 210
Hicks, Scott 151
Hidalgo, Rodrigo 203
The Hidden (1987) 153, 235
The Hidden Face (aka *Het verborgen gezicht*) 181
The Hidden Life of the Burrowing Owl 132, 143
Hierro 147, 228
Higgins, Caitlin 178
Higgins, Pat 158
High Art 151
High School (2010 feature?) 245
High Tension (2003, aka *Haute tension*, aka *Switchblade Romance*) 138, 183, 231
Higher Plane 177
Highfill, Lisa 104
Highly, Enric Folch 159
Highly, Jackson Sharp 160
Highmore, Freddie 204
Highway 61 128
Higuma, Seiko 222
Hilhorst, Alexander 172
Hill, George Roy 170
Hill, Joe 238
Hill, Nathan 225
Hill, Robin 155
Hill, Thomas 225
Hill, Walter 170
Hill Holiday (ad agency) 165
Hillcoat, John 165
The Hills Have Eyes (1977) 236
The Hills Have Eyes (2006) 138
Hilmarsson, Hilmar Örn 229
Himitsu (1999 feature; dir: Takita) 232
Hintz, Barbara K. 218
Hipnos (2004 feature, aka *Hypnos*; dir: Carreras) 127, 182
Hirayama, Hideyuki 194
Hiroki, Ryuichi 252
Hirosue, Ryôko 232
Hirsch, Karl T. 178
Hirsute 132, 214
A História de Lia 131
Historias del desencanto 148
Historietas Assombradas (para Crianças Mal Criadas) 146
Hitchcock, Alfred 39, 49, 197, 213
The Hitcher (1986) 141
H.I.Z. 249
Hlady, Gregory *see* Gladiy, Grigoriy
Ho, Josie 227
Ho, Vincent 188
Ho, Wai Ching 193, 223
Ho, Wi Ding 230
Hoax (unproduced script) 172, 188
Hobbs, Rebecca 151
Hocus Pocus (1993) 210
Hodder, Kane 156, 162
Hodges, Mike 153, 234
Hodgson, Bradford 123
Hodor, Darek 218
Hoechlin, Tyler 207
Hoerauf, Faye 167

Hogan, Michael 132
Hogan, Michael William 240
Hogan, Sean 161
Hogfather 146
Hol volt, hol nem volt see *A Hungarian Fairy Tale*
Hola Ghost (music band) 239
Hold Your Fire 142
Holden, Gina 137
Holder, Christine 167
The Hole (1998 feature, aka *Dong*; dir: Tsai) 184, 233
The Holes (feature, 1976?) 213
Holgi 150
Holguin, Robert 103
Holiday, Hill *see* Hill Holiday
Holiday of Horrors 111
The Holiday Plan (2002) 175
Hollaar, Wolfgang 137
Holland, Jesse 188
Holland, Matt 241
Holland, Tom 154, 195, 211
Holler, Jason 242
Holliday, Polly 211
Hollow (2004 short film; dir: Soemantri) 242
Hollow (2007 short film; dir: Bickel) 190
Hollow, Johnny 133
Hollow Man (2000) 207
Holloway, Josh 203
Hollywood Award 110
Hollywood Forever Cemetery 78, 107
Hollywood Horror Film Festival 110
Hollywood Investigator (website) 6–9, 12, 13–15, 45, 54, 59–60, 86, 93
Hollywood Investigator Halloween Horror Film Award 7–9
Hollywood Mistress see *Mistress* (1992)
Hollywood Skin 14
Hollywood Walk of Fame 199
Hollywood Witches (novel) 7
HollywoodInvestigator.com *see Hollywood Investigator*
Hollywoodland 205
Holm, Ian 153
Holman, Theodor 147
Holmes, H.H. 218
Holmes, Mark 160
Holmes, Sherlock 40
Holmgren, Magnus 187
Holt, Karl 159
Holtgrewe, Gregg 196
Holtzer, Consuelo 99
Holy Shit 2 249
Holy Tears (music band) 238
Hom, Ray 35
El hombre de la bolsa 132
El hombre ubicuo 202
Home (dir: Filippi) 158
Home Delivery (short film) 148
Home Media Magazine 113, 195
Home Movie (2008 feature; dir: Denham) 229, 246
Home Video (short film; 2005?) 181
"Homecoming" (*Masters of Horror* TV episode) 230
Honda, Ryûichi 250
H1N1: Virus X see *Virus X*
Honeycutt, Heidi *see* Martinuzzi, Heidi
Hong, Young-Guen 192
Honogurai mizu no soko kara see *Dark Water* (2002)
Honour (short film) 178

Hoogendoorn, Peter 137
Hooi, Everon Jackson 217
Hookman, Esther 119
Hooper, Tobe 137, 173, 189, 231
Hoover, Richard R. 231
Hoover, Stephen 240
Hope (2002 short film; dir: Brinkman) 223
Hopewell, Stewart 218
Hopkins, Anthony 139, 140, 210
Hopkins, Ben 150, 232
Hopkins, Stephen 153
Hora 131
Las horas muertas 180, 194
Hörbiger, Christiane 193
The Horde (2009) 141, 146, 163
La horde see *The Horde* (2009)
Horizonica 136
Horn, Jo 238
Horne, Daniel 197, 199
Horner, James 197, 203, 207, 211
Horns and Halos 178
Horobin, Blake 226
A Horrible Way to Die 155
The Horribly Slow Murderer with the Extremely Inefficient Weapon 133, 135, 143, 156, 174, 192, 246, 248, 252
Horrid 167
Horrific Film Fest 110, 167
The Horrifying Ordeal of Pilar Mallard 189
Horrocks, Jane 233
Horror (2002 feature; dir: Tomaselli) 189
Horror Comic 240
Horror Dance 17, 110, 167–68
Horror Express (1972, aka *Pánico en el Transiberiano*) 237
Horror Fans 173
Horror Fest UK 118
Horror Festacular 102
Horror Fiesta Film Festival 101
"Horror Film Crisis of 1932" (article) 199
Horror Gathering Film Festival 110
Horror of Our Love (aka *Horror of Our Love: A Short Film*) 174, 191, 200
Horror Realm 110–11
Horror Society Film Festival 105, 111
Horror UK 118, 119
Horror World 225
Horror Writers Association 5, 106
Horrorfind Weekend Film Festival 111
Horrorfind.com 6, 111
Horrors of War (2006) 163
Horrorthon 100
Horrorvision: Spanish Horror Trash Film Festival vii, 102–3, 168
The Horseman (2008) 47, 49, 146, 177, 190
Horsey, Erin 244
Horwitz, Alex 162, 174
Hosaka, Daisuke 250
Hose, Zillah 96
Hoshi, Mamoru 164
Hoskins, Dan 153
Hosoda, Mamoru 228, 230
Hospitality (2005 feature; dir: Ducret) 221
Hoss-Desmarais, Emanuel 142
Hosszú alkony see *Long Twilight*
Host (short film) 167
The Host 127, 148, 229, 230
Hostel (2005 feature) 46, 217
Hotei, Tomoyasu 232

Hotel (2004 feature; dir: Hausner) 181
Hotel (2007 short film; dir: Blouin) 144
Hotel Splendide (2000) 232
Hotelska sova 236
Hottarake no shima — Haruka to maho no kagami see *Oblivion Island*
Hough, Paul 144, 242
House of Fears 225
House of Flesh Mannequins 190
House of Horrors (1946) 114
House of Horrors: The Movie (2009) 130
House of 1000 Corpses 138, 139, 149
House of the Dead 139
The House of the Devil 217
The House of the Living Dead see *Curse of the Dead* (1976)
House of the Long Shadows 154, 235
The House of Usher Does Not Fall (novel) 165
House of Wolves 172
Houser, Gretchen 104
Housset, Morgane 174
How the Grinch Stole Christmas (2000) 207
How to Be a Serial Killer 189, 224
How to Get Rid of Others (aka *Hvordan vi slipper af med de andre*) 147, 155, 181, 201
How to Make Love to a Woman (1995 animated short film) 233
How Wings Are Attached to the Backs of Angels 233
Howard, Andrew 128
Howard, David 169, 186
Howard, James Newton 204
Howard, Ron 211
Howarth, Alan 244
Howarth, Kevin 130, 185, 189
Howatt-Jackman, Elizabeth 177
Howell, Gareth 119
Howie Award 111, 168
Howison, Josiah Holmes 218
The Howling 212
Howl's Moving Castle 186
Howson, Frank 177, 178
H.P. Lovecraft Award 111
H.P. Lovecraft Film Festival & CthulhuCon vii, 111, 117, 168–69
The H.P. Lovecraft Historical Society 168, 169
H.P. Lovecraft: The Terror Within (aka *Il mistero di Lovecraft*) 181
H.P. Lovecraft's The Other Gods 167
H.P. Lovecraft's The Silver Key 243
H.R. Giger Award 187–88
Hrusínský, Rudolf 237
Huang, Andrew 224
Huber, Thomas 193, 230
Hubris: A Short Film 35
Hudgens, John 197
Hudgins, Steve 241
Hudson, Angus 228
Huet, Sean 244
Huey, Yap Jen 167
Huff, Tanya 133
Hughes, Enda 151
Hughes, Gavin *11*
Hughes, Liz 152
Hughes, Thomas 196
Hugo Award 111, 169–70
Huguet, J.P. 154
Hull, Cortlandt 198
Hullegie, Martijn 158, 187
Hüller, Sandra 230

Human (2003 short film; dir: Roy) 226
The Human Beeing 189
The Human Centipede 155, 194, 215, 217, 237, 245
Human Experiments (1980 feature; dir: Goodell) 236
"Human Nature/The Family of Blood" (*Doctor Who* TV episode) 133
Human No More 41, 44–45, 242
Humanimal (2010) 202
Humbertclaude, Anthony vii, 99
Humphrey, Jimmy 162
Humphreys, Matthew 159
Humphries, Nicholas 242
Huneman Brown Eagle for Mrs. Brummetts Garden 162
A Hungarian Fairy Tale (aka *Hol volt, hol nem volt*) 235
Hunt, Andrew 219
Hunt, Bonnie 209
Hunt, Brad 218
Hunt, Ed 236
Hunter, Lisa 247
Hurd, Gale Anne 211, 213
Hurst, Peter 236
Hurt, John 149
Hurwitz, Sam 160
Huset på Kampen see *One Day a Man Bought a House*
Husk (2005 short film; dir: Simmons) 225
Hussain, Karim 231
Hutchison, Clint 196, 226
Hvordan vi slipper af med de andre see *How to Get Rid of Others*
Hwal 148
Hwang, Jeong-min 155
Hwang, Jo-yun 149
Hyams, Joshua 231
Hyams, Peter 170
Hyan, Daniel 248
Hychondriac 134
Hyden, Stephanie 200
Hyers, Jon 167
Hykade, Andreas 144, 232
Hyn huet ching nin see *New Blood* (2002)
Hynes, Martin 227
Hypnos (dir: Bryan Turell) 161
Hypnos see *Hipnos* (2004 feature)
Hypnose see *Stir of Echoes* (1999)
Hypnotic see *Close Your Eyes* (2002)
Hypochondriac (year?) 242
Hyte 223

I Am Legend (2007 feature) 133, 204
I Am Peter Cushing 160
I Am So Proud of You 155
I Can See You 123
I, Detective 225
I Don't Sleep I Dream 162
I Know How Many Runs You Scored Last Summer 190, 237
I Live in the Woods 131, 246
I Love Sarah Jane 143, 156
I Must Destroy You 173
I-Newswire.com 34
I Sell the Dead 145, 246
I Spit on Your Grave (1978, aka *Day of the Woman*) 236
I Spit on Your Grave (2010) 245, 246
I Stand Alone (1998, aka *Seul contre tous*) 233
I Still Know What You Did Last Summer 139

I Think We're Alone Now 144
I, Zombie: The Chronicles of Pain 161
Ibáñez, Gabe 129, 144, 146
Ibarra, Chema García 227
Ibarra, Erendira 223
Ibarretxe, Esteban 233
Ice Cold (2005 short film) 218
Ice Cream Social (Loscon event) 11
Ice from the Sun 248
Ich bin's. Helmut (aka *It's Me. Helmut*) 187
Ichi the Killer (aka *Koroshiya 1*) 188
ICM 254n4
Idiots & Angels 129, 143, 147
Iedereen Die Iets Betekent 136
Ienaga, Kosuke 252
If I Could Only… 159
If I Had a Hammer 156, 173
If Looks Could Kill (1991 feature, aka *Teen Agent*) 252
IFP 22
Iglésias, Carlos 148
Iglesias, Estefania see Estefania, Iglesias
Iguchi, Noboru 130, 227, 251
Ilarde, Rico María 130, 184
Iliadis, Dennis 127
I'll Never Die Alone see *No moriré sola* (2008)
I'll See You in My Dreams (2003 short film) 149, 182
Illtown 251
L'illusion (dir: Greeb) 165
ILM see Industrial Light & Magic
Ils see *Them* (2006)
I'm a Cyborg, But That's OK 147, 229
I'm Gonna Do It Until the Day I Die 122
I'm King Kong: Exploits of Merian C. Cooper (TV special) 198
Image Animation 151
"Imagine" (song) 90
Imagine: Amsterdam Fantastic Film Festival vii, 101, 170–71, 179–83
Imagine Time Capsule Award 170
Imai, Satoshi 252
IMDb 29, 32, 35, 59, 66, 121, 137, 141, 146, 203, 219
The Immaculate Conception of Little Dizzle 142
Immer & ewig 234
Immortal (novel, aka *Immortalis*) 164
Immortalis see *Immortal* (novel)
El imperio del fuego see *Reign of Fire*
Impolex 177
In Absentia (2000 short film; dir: Quay Brothers) 232
In Blood 178
In Bright Darkness 168
In Dreams (1999) 127
In Memorium 173
In/Out (short film) 223
In the Dark (dir: Goligher) 160
In the Mouth of Madness 152
In the Wall 156, 201, 217
In Their Skin see *Dans leur peau*
In Their Sleep see *Dans ton sommeil*
In 3 Tagen bist du tot see *Dead in 3 Days*
Inanna Award 105
Iñárritu, Alejandro González 150
Inception 215
Incest Death Squad 247
Inciarte, Juan 151
El incinerador de cadáveres see *The Cremator* (1969)

Inclán, Laura 202
The Incredible Haniwa-Man 251
The Incredible Shrinking Man 170
The Incredibles 169, 206, 239
The Incredibly Strange People Show 160
Independence Day (1996) 209
The Independent (British newspaper) 33, 254n19
Independent Feature Project/West *see* Film Independent (new name); *see also* IFP
Independent Film Festival of Boston 30
Independent Spirit Award 5, 34, 63, 189
Indiana Jones and the Kingdom of the Crystal Skull 204
Indiana Jones and the Last Crusade 126, 170
Indiana Jones and the Mummies Skull 162
Indie Horror Film Festival (Canadian fest) 97, 111
Indochine 166
Industrial Light & Magic (aka ILM) 133, 209, 210, 233
Indy Horror Film Festival (U.S. fest) vii, 97, 111, 171
Ineo gongju see My Mother the Mermaid
Inferiority Complex 154
Infernal Affairs 125
Inferno (2002 short film; dir: Kousoulides) 215
Infestation (2009 feature; dir: Rankin) 187
The Inflatable Grandma (aka *Amona Putz!*) 201
Ingalls, Rob 171
Inglourious Basterds 203
Ingram, Steve 152
Ingression 167
The Inherited 167
Initiation (short film; dir: Beaudoin) 176, 247
"The Inner Light" (*Star Trek: The Next Generation* TV series) 169
Innocence (2004 feature; dir: Hadzihalilovic) 188, 250
Innocence: Ghost in the Shell 2 see Ghost in the Shell 2: Innocence
Inoue, Tsuki 250
Inoue, Yasuo 250
Insanity (2005; dir: Celenza) 158
Insanophenia 249
L' insaziabile see Ravenous
Insecticidal 173
Insek (music band) 238
Inside (dir: Papamichael) 163
Inside (2005 short film; dir: Davis) 159
Inside (2007, aka *À l'intérieur*; dir: Bustillo & Maury) 138, 180, 195, 217, 229
Inside of a Lamb (short film) 219
Inside Out (2003 short film; dir: Knott) 175, 195
The Insomniac see L'insomniaque (2009)
L'insomniaque (2009 short film) 158
Insomnies see Chasing Sleep (2000)
Institute Benjamenta, or This Dream That One Calls Human Life 152, 233
The Institute of Séance 243
Intact see Intacto
Intacto 149
Intercambio (2010 short film) 184
Interment for Two (CD) 198

International Animated Film Society 104
International Fantastic Film Festival of Porto Alegre *see* Fantaspoa
International Horror and Sci-Fi Film Festival vii, 41, 67, 111, 113, 171–73
International Surrealist Film Festival vii, 111
International Thriller Writers 116, 244
International Vampire Film Festival 117
Internet Movie Database *see* IMDb
Interpretation 135
Interrogation (unproduced script) 244
Interview (2007 feature) 147
Interview (2011 short film) 129
Interview with the Vampire (1994, aka *Interview with the Vampire: The Vampire Chronicles*) 140, 209
Into the Maelstrom 225
Into the Mirror 164
Into the Shadows (2009 documentary) 177
Intolerance III: The Final Solution (aka *The Final Solution (Intolerance III)*) 201
Inudô, Isshin 250
Inugami 232
The Invaders (1967–68 TV series) 204
Invasion of the Body Snatchers (1978) 212
Inversus 136
Investment 243
The Invisible (2002 feature, aka *Den osynlige*) 188, 218
IP Man 142, 143, 228
IP Man 2 142, 155
Ipson, Jason Todd 225
Iriarte, Pau 230
Irie, Y 192, 249
Irish Film Institute 100
Iron Doors 167
Iron Man (2008) 132, 204, 216, 249
Iron Man 2 215
Irons, Jeremy 153
Irwin, Gary E. 123, 134, 162, 168
Isaac, James 143
Isabella (2006 Chinese feature) 148
Isaka, Kotaro 155
Isaka, Satoshi 251
Iser, Andrew 178
Ishii, Katsuhito 127, 145, 188, 193, 251
Ishii, Yuya 141
Ishikawa, Chu 232
Ishimine, Hajime 145
Ishioka, Eiko 210
Ishioka, Masato 150
Isis (music video) 238
Iskanov, Andrey 167
Island of Lost Souls (1932) 197, 198, 199
Islas, Ricardo 185
The Isle (2000) 127, 150
Isolation (2005; dir: O'Brien) 156, 164, 181, 217
ISRP Investigates: Ghosts of Belgrave Hall 218
It Came from Another World (2007) 220
It Came From Lake Michigan (film festival) 111–12, 173–74
It Came from the West (aka *ZombieWestern: It Came from the West*) 181, 246, 252
It Is Fine. Everything Is Fine! 229
It Was so Mad (music video) 190
Itoso, Kenji 250

It's in the Air (2006 short film, aka *Comme un air*) 193
It's Me. Helmut see Ich bin's. Helmut
It's My Birthday 14, 56
It's My Party and I'll Die If I Want To 134, 167
"It's Still a Good Life" (*The Twilight Zone* TV episode) 199
Itsy Bitsy 172, 225
Ittenbach, Daniel 248
Ittenbach, Melanie 248
Ittenbach, Olaf 92
Ivory Bastards Against Extinction 124
Izar, Daniel *see* Daniel Izar de la Fuente
Izbavitelj 154
Izingwe 238
Izo 231

Jabre, Elias 164
Jacelone, Pete 123
Jack 142
Jack and the Beanstalk: The Real Story (aka *Jack et le haricot magique*) 164, 207
Jack Be Nimble 152
Jack Brooks: Monster Slayer 146, 155, 204, 229
Jack et le haricot magique see Jack and the Beanstalk: The Real Story
Jack Ketchum's The Girl Next Door see The Girl Next Door
Jack Pierce: The Man Behind the Monsters 160
Jack Pierce Lifetime Achievement Award 137
Jack the Reaper 172
Jackboots on Whitehall 227
Jackman, Hugh 207, 216
Jackpot! (2010 short film; Ducret) 243
Jackson, Alix and Luke C. 178
Jackson, D.A. 177
Jackson, Faye 122, 128, 131, 184, 187, 237
Jackson, Jeremy 223
Jackson, Michael (singer) 166
Jackson, Peter 59, 92, 126, 140, 141, 151, 152, 166, 169, 171, 186, 205, 206, 207, 240
Jackson, Taylor 188
Jacob and Death 242, 243
Jacobs, Emma Julia 130
Jacobs, Luke 159
Jacobs, Nova 161
Jacobs, Roy 136
Jacobs, Tom 136
Jadoube 234
Jahn, Thomas 233
J'ai échoué 166
Jakob and the Angels 136
Jakten på nyresteinen see Body Troopers
James, Caradog W. 159
James, Christian 159, 196
James, Terry 153
James Bond Ultimate Edition (DVD) 205
Jamie Hit Single 221
Jameson, Jodie 156
Jamison, Jean 224
Janaud, Jules 175
Jang, Cheol-so *see* Jang, Chul-soo
Jang, Cheol-su *see* Jang, Chul-soo
Jang, Chul-soo (aka Cheol-so, aka Chul-soo) 155, 166, 192
Jang, Heui-cheol 229
Jang, Hun 143

Index

Jang, Jin 229
Jang, Jin-young 149
Jang, Joon-hwan (aka Jun-hwan Jang) 127, 193
Jang, Jun-hwan *see* Jang, Joon-hwan
Jang, Yeong-gyu 230
Jang, Yoonhyun *see* Chang, Yoon-Hyun
Jang, Yoon-jung 192
Janghwa, Hongryeon see *A Tale of Two Sisters*
Janisch, Attila 161
Janssen, Famke 205
Jaquier, Victor 188
Jarre, Maurice 235
Jarvis, Steve 226
Jasper 110, 137, 167
Jaws (1975 film) 49
Jean, Patrick 201, 248
Jean, Vadim 146
Jeepers Creepers 139
Jen, Richie 192
Jenatsch 235
Jennifer (1978 feature; dir: Mack) 236
Jensen, Anders Thomas 127, 148, 149, 171, 187, 193
Jensen, Andrea Vagn 202
Jensen, Jonas Kvist 248
Jenssen, Eloise 212
Jeong, Beom-sik (aka Bum-sik Jung?) *see* Jung Brothers
Jeong, Seo-Gyeong (aka Chung, Seo-Kyung) 229
Jeong, Sik (aka Sik Jung?) *see* Jung Brothers
Jeong Brothers *see* Jung Brothers
Jeremy's Wake-Up Call 242
The Jersey Devil (unproduced script) 240
Jesabelle 160
Jespers, Emmanual 161
Jessop, Peter 236
Jessua, Alain 154
Jeunet, Jean-Pierre 153, 234
Ji, Seong-won (aka Sung-won Ji) 155
Ji, Sung-won *see* Ji, Seong-won
Jiang Hu: Between Love and Glory see *The Bride with White Hair*
Jigoku Kôshien see *Battlefield Baseball*
Jihad Joe II 144
Jim Henson's Creature Shop 150
Jiménez, David 230
Jin-Roh: The Wolf Brigade (aka *Jin-Roh*, aka *Jin-Rô*) 150, 151, 250
Jiphaengja see *The Executioner* (2009)
Jo, Beom-jin (aka Joe, Bum-jin, aka Joe, Bum-in) 144, 229
Joan of Arcadia (2003–05 TV series) 206
Jodorowsky, Adan 210
Joe, Bum-jin *see* Jo, Beom-jin
Joe's Apartment 251
Joffe, Jonathan 214, 215
Johanna (2005) 148, 193
Johannson High School Film Department 221
Johansson, Scarlett 215
John Carpenter's Vampires see *Vampires* (1998)
Johnny Gruesome (comic book) 189
Johnori, Naoko 250
Johns, Geoff 215, 216
Johnson, Arte 212
Johnson, Brian 212
Johnson, Catherine 191
Johnson, CJ 86, 241, 242

Johnson, Curt 144
Johnson, Don 213
Johnson, Gerard 227
Johnson, Jared 244
Johnson, John vii, 109, 166
Johnson, Kenneth 251
Johnson, Rian 230
Johnson, Ron 123
Johnson, Steve 139, 233
Johnston, Charles 226
Johnston... Johnston (1995 short film) 223
Jolie, Angelina 82, 87, 204, 216
Joner, Kristoffer 158, 228
Jones, Andrew R. 203
Jones, Andrew W. 168, 190
Jones, Bryn 160
Jones, Camile 221
Jones, Doug 138
Jones, Duncan 158, 163, 169, 227, 228
Jones, Kelley 197
Jones, Kelly vii, 33, 35, 42, 50–51, 76, 80, 118
Jones, L.Q. 170
Jones, Marc Wyn 159
Jones, Peter 224
Jones, Preston Neal 199
Jonkajtys, Grzegorz 148
Jonker, Sophie 136
Jonsson, Emil 129
Joong-cheon see *The Restless*
Jordà, Joaquim 233
Jordan, Gregor 150
Jordan, Neil 127, 154, 235
Jordan, Patrick 244
Jordan, Rhoda 224
Jose Luis Guarner Critic Award 227–232
Josefsson, Jerker 194
Joshua (feature; year?) 163
Joshua (2002 short film; dir: Müller) 183, 188
Joshua (2007 feature, aka *Joshua: El hijo del mal*; dir: Ratliff) 229
Un jour (2001 short film; dir: Paccou) 233
Le jour de la bête see *The Day of the Beast* (1995)
A Journey (1972 short film, aka *Putovanje*) 236
Journey to Mars (2005 animated short film, aka *Viaje a Marte*) 146
Jovovich, Milla 216
Joyeux, Fred 227
Joyride (animation) 222
Jozwiak, Jenn 98
Juanito Under the Orange Tree 193
Judet-Weinshel, Gabriel 122
Julia and Julia (1987, aka *Giulia e Giulia*) 235
Julien-Collette, Jean 185
Julietta (2001) 150
Jullien, Philippe 232
Jumanji (1995) 209
O Jumento Santo e a Cidade que Acabou Antes de Começar 146
Jump Rope with Gutz! 123
Jumping Jack (2008 short film) 177
Jung, Do-ahn 228
Jung, Yu-mi 192
Jung Brothers (aka Jeong Brothers) 196
Junko's Shamisen 245
Ju-on (2002, aka *Ju-on: The Grudge*) 218
Jupiter Love 178
Juran, Nathan 213

Jurassic Park (1993 film) 140, 169, 209
Jurassic Park (music video) 166
Justino (aka *Justino, un asesino de la tercera edad*) 233
Jutrisa, Vladimir 235
J'veux qu'on m'aime 166
Jysch, Arne 159, 175

Kaalo 237
Kabler, David 123
Kagamiko 122, 142
Kageyama, Shu 250
Kaidohryoku/Real 251
Kairo see *Pulse* (2001)
Kakei, Masaya 250
Kakurenbo: Hide and Seek (2005 short film) 145
Kala see *Fish*
Kalin, Tom 152
Kalogridis, Laeta 215
Kamazawa, Naoto 148
Kamebuchi, Hiroshi 250
Kamikaze 89 154
Kamiya, Joseph Y. 242
Kamler, Piotr 154
Kamogawa horumô 155
Kane, Brandon 174
Kane, Cassandra 162
Kanefsky, Rolfe 196, 225, 242
Kaneko, Shûsuke 127
Kanemori, Yoshinori 194
Kang, Hye-jeong (aka Kang Haejung) 194
Kaplan, David 192
Kappas 252
Kardenas, Sergio 122
Karen, James 213
Karliss, John 196
Karloff, Boris 53, 197, 198; *Kreating Karloff* 158
Karma (unproduced script) 226
Karmina 128
Karnabal (1985) 153
Karner, Nick 116
Kasdan, Lawrence 170, 212
Kasparian, Berge 144
Kasparík, Robin 134, 238
Kassier, James 226
Kastrissios, Steven 177, 190
Kat Cresswell Memorial Scream Queen Award 167
De Kat, De Kast en De Krijsende Vrouw 136
Katabuchi, Sunao 141
Katakuri-ke no kôfuku see *Happiness of the Katakuris*
Katie Bird 163
Katkins-Gorsiline, Krisjanis 249
Katrina, Al 130
Katz, Steven 126, 139
Katzenberg, Jeffrey 204
Kaufman, Charlie 125, 208
Kaufman, Lloyd 17, 153, 162, 171, 173
Kaufman, Pat 19
Kaufman, Philip 150, 170, 212
Kaukosaaren kirous see *Curse of the Remote Island*
Kavanagh, Ivan 177
Kawaguchi, Ryota 251
Kawai, Kenji 228
Kawajiri, Yoshiaki 127
Kawamoto, Kihachiro 230
Kay, Marysia 126
"Kay Linaker" (article) 199

Kazlo, Michael 223
Kazura see *Wig* (2010)
Kearns, Noel 158
Keaton, Camille 236
Keaton, Chris 191
Kedzierski, Grzegorz 232
Keeper of the Light see *Fyren* (2010)
Keiko en peligro 186
Keitel, Harvey 58, 152
Keller, Val 161
Kelly, Alan Rowe 134, 243
Kelly, Brett 130
Kelly, Damien 160
Kelly, Ken 197
Kelly, Mike N. 131
Kelly, Richard 164, 171, 175, 232
Kelly, Suzanne 172
Kemker, David 195
Kemp-Jones, Diana 224
Kendall, Nicholas 150
Kennedy, Jake 225
Kennedy, Kathleen 213
Kennedy, Matthew 249
Kenobi (*Star Wars* character) 239
Kent, Clark (character) 239
Kent, Jennifer 134
Kent, Larry 156
Kenyeres, Bálint 144
Kephart, Elza 196
Kermode, Mark 198
Kerrigan, Lodge 152
Kershner, Irvin 170, 204, 212
Ketchum, Jack 177
Keung, Kwok-Man 230
Kevin and Owen Kill a Vampire 249
Kevorkian, Johnny 194
Key Lime Pie 246
Khali, Farida viii, 103, 186
Khan, Farha 187
Khazizov, Peter 214
Khoo, Eric 148
Khoshnazar, Omid 144
Kick-Ass 215
Kickox, Anthony 128
Kidder, Margot 212, 222
Kidman, Nicole 139, 207
Kidnapped (2010) 155
Kier, Udo 139
Kiersch, Fritz 128
Kiil, Reinert 131
Kilar, Wojciech 139, 140
The Kill (music video) 138
Kill Bill: Vol. 1 206, 231
Kill Bill: Vol. 2 206
Kill for You (music video) 223
Kill Zone see *Saat po long* (2005)
Killer: A Journal of Murder 233
A Killer App 223
Killer Film Fest vii, 112, 174
Killer Granny 188, 240
Killer Tongue see *La lengua asesina*
Killing Ariel 220
Killing Words (2003, aka *Palabras encadenadas*) 149, 182
Killing Zoe 251
Kilómetro 31 see *KM 31: Kilómetro 31*
Kim, Dae-Seung 250
Kim, Dong-won 193
Kim, Eun-kyung 193
Kim, Jee-woon (aka Kim Ji-woon, aka Kim Ji-yong) 127, 144, 145, 149, 151, 164, 185, 218, 228
Kim, Ji-hun (aka Kim Ji-hoon) 250
Kim, Jin-Hee 218

Kim, Ji-woon see Kim, Jee-woon
Kim, Ji-yong see Kim, Jee-woon
Kim, Ki-duk 127, 147, 148, 150, 232
Kim, Moon-saeng 164
Kim, Ok-bin 228
Kim, Seong-ho see Kim, Sung-ho
Kim, Sung-ho (aka Seong-ho) 164
Kim Bok-nam salinsageonui jeonmal see *Bedevilled* (2010)
Kimura, Hideki 251
Kimura, Takashi 250
Kin (2004 short film?: dir: Backer?) 222
Kin-Dza-Dza 153
Kinatay 227, 228
King, Adrienne 172
King, Ed 100
King, John 178
King, Jonathan 127, 163, 164, 187
King, Peter 206, 207
King, Stephen 204
King Chicken 245
King Kong (1933) 198, 199
King Kong (2005) 198, 205, 216, 239
The King Kong Collection (DVD set) 198
King Kongs Faust 235
King of Kong 144
King of Power 4 Billion % 246
King of the Hill (2007 feature, aka *El rey de la montaña*) 170, 180, 217
King of the Zombies 8
King of Thorns 142
The Kingdom of Shadows 159
The Kingdom II 150
Kings for a Day 151
Kingsley, Ben 152
Kingz 180, 246
Kinhart, John Paul 123, 124
Kirby, Jon 160
Kiriya, Kazuaki 248
Kirk (2009 feature) 158
The Kirkie (2009 short film) 176
Kirksdale 123, 134, 172, 190, 196, 220, 224, 245
Kiros, Chris 162
Kirst, Brian vii, 105
Kirton, Alastair 237
The Kiss (2005, aka *Le baiser*, dir: Le Lay) 164
Kiss the Abyss 122, 161, 188
Kitakawa, Eriko 192
Kitamura, Akihiro 237
Kitamura, Ryûhei 127, 141, 143, 145, 163
Kitano, Takeshi 231
Kitchen (1997 feature, aka *Wo ai chu fang*; dir: Yim) 194
Kitchen Sink (1989 short film) 153, 234
Klandt, Christian 192
Klarlund, Anders Rønnow 127, 147, 201, 231
Klebe, Kristina 237
Klemensen, Dick 199
Kljakovic, Vanca 236
Kloetzer, Guillermo 130, 145
Klosinski, Edward 234
Klutinis, Barbara 122
KM 31: Kilómetro 31 186
Knapp, Douglas 213
Knautz, Jon 201, 229
KNB EFX 138, 139, 140
Kneen, Kris 178
Knek, D. Li (aka Knek, Li) 236
Knicker Knockers 167
Knight, Daniel 144
Knight, Monica 162

Knight of the Headsman see *Night of the Headsman*
KnightQuest 157
Knizka, Roman 193
Knockin' on Heaven's Door (1997 feature) 233
Knockin' on Hell's Door 252
Knoll, John 205, 207, 208
The Knot (aka *Liten Knute*; dir: Steinsbo) 158
Knott, Oliver 175, 195
Knowland, Nicholas D. (aka Nic or Nick) 233
Knoxville Horror Film Fest 112, 174
Kobayashi, Hideaki 252
Kobayashi, Masahiro 251
Koch, Marcus 241
Kodak Film Award 19
Kodie 125
Koepp, David 165, 169, 209
Koester, Anne viii, 18–19, 116
Koestinger, Pablo Guisa viii, 6, *47*, 52, 58, 64, 78, 81, 101
Kohnen, Matthew 228, 252
Kojew, Vijja 217
Kokuhaku see *Confessions* (2010)
Kolbe, Winrich 169
Kolirin, Eran 148
Kolkovalis, Stsampani P. 160
Koller, Peter 129, 186
Kolobos 218
Kolodziejczyk, Kayah 136
Kon, Satoshi 148, 151, 188, 231, 232
Kontakt (short film; year?) 171
The Kooky Kastle 93, 242
Kopczynski, Jerzy 153
Koppe, Renko 136
Koppel, Andrés 149
Korea Manhwa Contents Agency 102
Kore-eda, Hirokazu 142
Koroshiya 1 see *Ichi the Killer*
Koshizaka, Yasushi 251
Koskenmakl, Katie 161
Kostanski, Steven 190, 249
Koszulinski, Georg 196
Kounen, Jan 175
Kouyoumdjian, Aram 122
The Kovak Box 175
Kovalyov, Igor 233
Köves, Krisztián Károly 131
Koz, Rich see Svengoolie
Kraftverk 3714 129
Kram 166
Krantz, Tony 243
Kratina, Al 145
Kratter, Mark 244
Krause, Robert 134
The Krays 153
Kreating Karloff 158
Kreh, Robert 167
Kren, Marvin 184
Kretschmann, Thomas 193, 230
Krige, Alice 140, 209
Krishnamma, Suri 250
Kristen, Jamie 58, 104
Krivanek, Andrew 221
Krofft, Marty 213
Krofft, Sid 213
Kroot, Jennifer 130
Krueger, Freddy 46
Krumrine, Jenny 243
Kubo, Naoki 252
Kubrick, Stanley 170
Kucera, Jaroslav 236

Kuchuck, Danny 200
Kuczynski, Anna 159
Kui, Jonathan S. 162, 167
Kuijpers, Pieter 148
Kuipers, Sander 136
Kuismin, Timo 98
Kulenovic, Maya 218
Kult Without a Name 237
Kumagai, Madoka 250
Kumar, Balaji K. 163, 168, 241
Kumar, Ganesh 241
Kunert, Arnold 199
Kung Fu Hustle 171
Kupfer, Jason 122
Kuppens, Eline 142
Kuran, Peter 211
Kuribayashi, Shinobu 250
Kurita, Toyomichi 229
Kuriyama, Chiaki 155
Kurnalcool (music band) 238
Kurosawa, Asuka 149
Kurosawa, Kiyoshi 232
Kurtzman, Alex 204
Kurtzman, Robert 208, 231
Kurushime Girl (1997, aka *Kurushime-san*) 251
Kwak, Jae-yong (aka Kwak Jae-young) 250
Kwong, Angie 178
Kyle XY (2006–09 TV series) 205
Kyvadlo, jáma a nadeje 154

L & D (dir: Kimura) 251
L.A. Confidential (1997) 208
L.A. Effects Group 211
L.A. Weekly (newspaper) 254n3
L.A. Zombie 177
LaBeouf, Shia 216
El laberinto del fauno see *Pan's Labyrinth*
Labohm, Mareille 136
Labrèche, Caroline 143
Labree, Emiel vii, 101, 136
La Bruce, Bruce (aka Bruce LaBruce) 177, 178
Lacuesta, Isaki 232
Lady Magdalene's 23
Lady Vengeance (2005, aka *Sympathy for Lady Vengeance*, aka *Chinjeolhan geumjassi*) 148, 230
Ladyhawke 211
Laemmle, Carl, Jr. 213
LaFave, Alan J. vii, 110
Laffargue, Pierre 143
Laffin, Cory 32
Lafia, John 166
LaFontaine, Pierre-Luc 142
Laganière, Simon 142
Lägg M för mord see *Tile M for Murder*
Lagües, Sophie 201
Laing, John 235
Lajarescu, Christian (aka Christian Lazarescu and/or Scott Z. Burns?) 161
Lake Mungo 80, 131
Lalino, Andy 196
Lam, Dante 192
Lam, Ringo 147
Lamata, Miguel Ángel 248
The Lambda Child 238
Lamberson, Gregory 106, 189
Lambert, Tania 237
Lambro, Matt 124
Lambs 142
La-Menta 184

LaMolinara, Anthony 206
La Monde, John 177
Lamprecht, Marthinus 238
Lanchester, Elsa 213
Land of Death (2003 feature, aka *Nella terra dei cannibali*) 248
Land of the Dead (2005) 138, 239
Landau, Martin 209
Landauro, Andrew 196
Landis, John 100, 231
Lando, Jeffrey Scott 223
Landreth, Chris 193
Landucci, Iru 129
Lane, Barbara 210
Lane-Young, Gil 118
Lanfranchi's Memorial Discotheque 177
Lang, Fritz 213
Lang, Stephen 203
Lange, Eric 220
Langenkamp, Heather 140, 162
Langliena 238
Lanier, Lee 161, 214, 218
Lanni, Jeremy Dylan 159
Lannoo, Vincent 126, 171, 227
Lanthimos, Giorgos (aka Yorgos Lanthimos) 228
Lantieri, Michael 207, 210
Lapeyre, Jason 197
LaPointe, Chris 244
LaPorte, Steve 210
Laranas, Yam 127
Larger Than Life (1998 short film) 176
Laris, Eduardo Soto 184
Lark, Shannon viii, 6, 13–15, 51, 57, 106, 117, 125, 241, 253n4; on the blood-stained carpet *14*
Larkin, Carlos 191
Larrieu, Arnaud 228
Larrieu, Jean-Marie 228
Larry in Relation to the Ground 179
Larry Stanley B-Movie Award 220–221
Lasaga, Manuel Ortega 168
Laser, Dieter 155, 237
Laspina, Lance 160
The Last Battle see *Le dernier combat* (1983)
The Last Blog on the Left 14
Last Call (2009 short film) 33, 56
Last Doorway Productions 113
The Last Drag 228
The Last Dream (2001 short film) 161
The Last Eve 124
The Last Exorcism 227, 245, 246
The Last 15 144
The Last Gateway 129
The Last Horror Film (1982) 236
The Last Horror Movie (2003) 130, 149, 160, 182, 185, 189, 196, 222
The Last House on the Left (1972) 195
The Last House on the Left (2009) 127, 195
The Last Lovecraft: Relic of Cthulhu 122, 245; see also *Relic of Cthulhu*
The Last Man (2000) 161
The Last Man in Brooklyn 173
The Last Man on Earth 8
The Last Minute (2001 feature, aka *La dernière minute*; dir: Norrington) 149
The Last Minute (2004 short film) see *La dernière minute*
Last Night (1998; dir: McKellar) 151
The Last Performance (2006, aka *De función*) 230
The Last Request (2006 short film) 225

Last Rites of the Dead see *Zombies Anonymous*
The Last Roadstop see *Freak* (1999)
Last Rumba in Rochdale 232
The Last Stop Café 222
The Last Wave (1977 feature) 235
LAsThePlace.com 137
Låt den rätte komma in see *Let the Right One In*
Latchkey (2004 short film; dir: Olson) 222
Latchkey's Lament 246
The Late Twentieth 160
Latin American Alliance of Fantastic Film Festivals see Alianza Latinoamericana de Festivales de Cine Fantástico
Lattuada, Jessica Villegas see Villegas, Jessica
Laugier, Pascal 138, 228, 229
laurel leaf logos **35**, 65, 93, 107
Laurence, Christian 143
Lauritson, Peter 169
Lautner, Taylor 216
Lauzon, Jean-Claude 152
Lavigne, Sylvain 143
Lavin, Andrew 130
Laviola, Franklin P. 196
Lavon, Rick 8, 242
The Law of Ice 202
Lawes, Thomas 161
Lawn Dogs 127, 184, 233
Lawrence, David 172
Lawrence, Elizabeth 122
Lawrence, Francis 149
Laxalde, Ignacio 130
Lazarescu, Christian see Lajarescu, Christian
Lázaro, Emilio Martínez 149
Lazarus Taxon 196
Lazer Ghosts 49
Lazzarini, Rick 208
Le Lay, Stefan 147, 164
Le Nezet, Fabrice 175
League, Tim 109
League of STEAM 157
Leandersson, Lina 138, 249
Leatherface 48
Leaving Normal 252
Lebelt, Manuel 77, 122, 191, 238, 241
Leboeuf, Laurence 142
Lechago, John 131
Ledger, Heath 204, 216, 249
Lee, Ang 169
Lee, Brandon 140
Lee, Christopher 100, 140, 154, 198, 213, 214, 235
Lee, Cinqué 122
Lee, Eric 188
Lee, Feng-bor 250
Lee, Frazer 160, 226
Lee, Hae-jun 141
Lee, Hyeon-mi (aka Kyun-Mi Lee) 218
Lee, Jay 159, 196
Lee, Jeong-ho 192
Lee, Jun-ik 141
Lee, Kyun-Mi see Lee, Hyeon-mi
Lee, Mo-gae (aka Mogae Lee) 218
Lee, Sheryl 139
Lee, Si-myung 164
Lee, Soo-yuon 231
Lee, Stan 239
Lee, Yeong-ae 230
Lee, Yong-ju 163

Leeds Anime Horror Film Festival 119
Leeds International Film Festival *see* Fanomenon
Leet, Scott Anthony 134, 191
Left (year?) 175
Left see Links (2008)
Left Bank 142, 180, 187
Left Films 92
Left for Dead 129
Left/Right 122
The Legacy (2010 short film) 132
Legacy Collection 199
The Legend of Beaver Dam 155, 217, 227
The Legend of Doom House (1974, aka *Malpertuis*) 237
Legend of Hell House 126
The Legend of Suram Fortress 235
The Legend of the Scarecrow (aka *La leyenda del espantapájaros*) 148, 181, 201
The Legend of Zelda: The Twilight Princess (video game) 239
Legenda o caru Scepanu Malom see The Man to Destroy
Legion: The Word Made Flesh 44–45, 242
Legrand, Benjamin 166
Leigh, Janet 137
Leman, Andrew 159, 168
Lemon, Bill 197
La lengua asesina 141, 151, 233
Lennon, John 90
Lenteveld 136
Léolo 152
Leonard, Hugh 235
Léonard, Steeve 143
Leone, Damien 244
Leong, Isabella 148
Leong, Po-chih 127, 165
Leoni, Téa 207
Lepola, Tommi **81**
Leprechaun 140
Leprechaun 2 140
Leray, Michel 164
Lesbian Vampire Killers see *Vampire Killers* (2009)
Lesbo-A-Go-Go 179
Lesemann, Mara 243
Lesson Faust see *Faust* (1994)
Lestang, Benoît 228
Let Me Go (short film; year?) 243
Let Sleeping Corpses Lie (1974, aka *No profanar el sueño de los muertos*) 236
Let the Right One In 126, 135, 138, 143, 155, 163, 170, 180, 187, 192, 201, 204, 216, 229, 246, 249
Let Them Eat (short film) 191
Leth, Asger 144
Leto, Jared 138
Let's Go Strawberry Girl 250
Letteri, Joe 203, 205, 206
Leupold, Andreas 237
Leutwyler, Matthew 196, 225, 248
Levin, Ryan A. 134, 144
Levitt, Cindy 115
Levitt, Michael 115
Levy, Eugene 237
Levy, Mariana 129
Levy, Nick 225
Lewin, Albert 169
Lewis, Brooke 123
Lewis, Drew 226
Lewis, Herschell Gordon 124, 130, 161, 189

Lewis & Clarke & George 251
Lexx: The Dark Zone Stories 251
Leydier, Rory 55, 241
La leyenda del espantapájaros see *The Legend of the Scarecrow*
L'histoire du corbac aux baskets 166
L' histoire du méchant dragon 142
L'homme, est-il bon? 150, 165
Li, Zhang 144
Liatowitsch, Daniel 218
The Librarian (2006 short film; dir: James) 221
The Librarian: Return to King Solomon's Mines 205
The Librarian: The Curse of the Judas Chalice 204
Lichtenstein, Mitchell 163
L.I.E. (2001) 149
Lieberman, Jeff 194
Lien, Jens 148, 163, 164, 171, 187
Lieske, Ryan 245
The Life and Death of a Porno Gang 128, 141, 145, 184, 194, 202
Lifeforce (1985) 235
Lifetime (TV network) 93
Liford, Clay 131, 167
The Light 157
Lighthouse (1999 feature) 183
Lights Out (2010 feature, aka *Simon Werner a disparu*; dir: Gobert) 227
Like a Virgin (2006) 144
Like Father Like Son 211
Lily (2007 short film; dir: Boneville) 162, 220, 221
L'Ilya (2001 documentary short film) 250
Lim, Jun-hyeong 149
Lim, Soo-jeong 149, 218
Lim, Soo-Jung see Lim, Soo-jeong
Lim, Su-jeong see Lim, Soo-jeong
Liminal (2008 short film; dir: Mills) 224
Limón, Paco 129, 190
Lin, Andrew 227
Linaker, Kay 199
Linda Miller Award 197
Linden, Shawn 168
Lindqvist, John Ajvide 138
Lindsay, Claire 241
Lindsey, Tim 114
A Língua das Coisas 132
Linkeroever see *Left Bank*
Links (2008, aka *Left*) 180
Lionsgate Entertainment (aka Lions Gate) 93, 103, 195
Lioret, Philippe 251
Lip Stick 125
Lipský, Oldrich 154
Lipstick Teeth 14
Lisbon International Horror Film Festival *see* MOTELx
List, Nikolas 217
The Listening Dead 148, 156, 162, 173, 245
Litan 235
Liten Knute see *The Knot*
Lithgow, John 211
Litinsky, Irene 244
Little Dead Girl (animated short film) 136, 218, 222
The Little Documentary That Couldn't 124
The Little Dragon (2009 short film, aka *Le petit dragon*) 146, 187, 228
The Little Girl Who Lives Down the Lane 213

A Little Night Fright 136
Little Ricky 223
Little Shop of Horrors (1986) 211
Little Shoppe of Horrors (magazine) 198
Little Sister see *Zusje* (1995)
The Little Theatre 116
Little Things (short film) 130
Little Victim 221
Live Freaky! Die Freaky! 145
Livin' in a "V" World 244
The Living and the Dead (2006 feature; dir: Rumley) 156, 230, 248
The Living Dead 2 (book) 11
The Living Forest (aka *El bosque animado*) 150, 153
Living Lâche (music band) 190
The Living Want Me Dead 188
Lizania 229
Lizbeth: A Victorian Nightmare 196
Lizier, Marc 136
Lizzie Borden Award 174
Llao, Ramón 202
Llorens, Pablo 202
Lloyd, Christopher 137
Lloyd, Jerry 242
La lluvia (2006 short film) 172
Lluvia en los zapatos see *Twice Upon a Yesterday*
Lo (2009 feature) 224
Loaded (1994; dir: Campion) 152
El Lobo see *Wolf* (2004)
Lock (ed) In 224
Lock Up (unproduced script) 218
Lockout (2006 feature; dir: Islas) 185
Lock-Smith (short film; dir: Park) 193
Lodge, David 194
Lodo (2009, aka *Mud*) 158
Lodovichetti, Andrea 158
Loduca, Joseph 140
Loft Cinema 104
Loftus, Isaac 240
Logan's Run (1976) 213
Loggia, Robert 210
Lois & Clark: The New Adventures of Superman 210
Lojo, Matías 129
Lokis 237
Loma Lynda: The Red Door 224
Lon Chaney Collection (DVD set) 199
La Lona (aka *The Boxing Ring*) 227
Lonano, Brian 123, 244
London After Midnight (1927) 197, 199
London FrightFest *see* FrightFest
London International Festival of Science Fiction and Fantastic Film *see* Sci-Fi-London Film Festival
London Voodoo 157, 159, 189
Long, Joshua 126, 184
Long, Tom 167
Long Pig (2008) 167
Long Pigs (2007) 172
Long Twilight 161
Long Weekend (1978 feature) 236
Looker 128
Lopes, Fernando 148
López, Alfonso C. viii, 103, 179–82, 200
Lopez, Josefina 109
López, Mónica 231
Lopez, Norberto 193
López, Sergi 148
López-Gallego, Gonzalo 170
Lopushansky, Konstantin 146, 187, 194
Lord of Illusions 140
The Lord of the Rings 11, 126, 186

The Lord of the Rings: The Fellowship of the Ring 169, 186, 207
The Lord of the Rings: The Return of the King 169, 186, 199, 206, 240
The Lord of the Rings: The Two Towers 169, 186, 199, 206, 207, 240
Lorelei 135
Loreti, Nicanor 128
Lorre, Peter 198
Los Angeles Film Festival 22, 75
Los Angeles Film School *10*, 83, **88**
Los Angeles Science Fantasy Society 9
Los Angeles Times 77
Loscon 9–15, 24, 36, 63, 66, 73–74, 76–77, 85, 90, 115, 253n3
Lost (2004–10 TV series) 203, 204, 205, 206, 215
The Lost (2006; dir: Sivertson) 146, 194, 217, 245
Lost: Black Earth 178
The Lost Boys (1987) 211
The Lost Girl (unproduced script) 225
Lost Highway 139, 140
Lost in Transit (1993, aka *Tombés du ciel*) 251
Lost Night (unproduced script) 226
The Lost One: A Life of Peter Lorre (book) 198
Lost Souls (2000) 45
The Lost Tribe (1983 feature) 235
Lou, Ye 150
Lou Perryman Audience Award 125
À louer (2001 short film) 164
Lougher, Al 160
Loughman, Mark 159
Le loup-garou de paris see *An American Werewolf in Paris*
Loups 183, 188
Lovallo, Dan 224
Love at First Bite (1979) 212
Love Exposure (2008 feature, aka *Ai no mukidashi*; dir: Sono) 142, 143, 192
Love Is a Shotgun 191
Love Is the Devil: Study for a Portrait of Francis Bacon 151
Love Me Tender (2010 short film) 184
Love Object (2003) 164
Love Tricycle 175
The Lovebirds (2007) 147
Lovecraft: Fear of the Unknown 157
The Loved Ones (2009) 174, 195, 247
The Lovely Bones 203, 249
Love's a Drag 243
Lovesick (year?) 178, 179
Lovesick: Sick Love (2004) 159
Löw, Victor 136
Lowe, Joanna 178
Lowenstein's a Terrorist 135
Lowry, Lynn 244
Lubezki, Emmanuel 233
Lucas, Donna 205
Lucas, George 170, 213
Lucas, Isabel 216
Lucas, Jesse 218
Lucas, Rachel 178
Lucas, Tim 197, 198, 205
Luciana, Julião 229
Lucifer (2007 short film?) 191, 220
Lucky (2004 feature; dir: Cuden) 189, 226, 248
Lugones, Alex 123
Lugosi, Bela 53, 197, 198, 206
Luke, Tony 160
Lullaby Crossing 136

Lumière, Tetsuo 184, 185
Lumley, Brian 168
Lumpp, Gary M. 219, 223
Luna, Bigas 128, 154
Luna, Tim 186
Luna e l'Altra 127
La luna negra 153
Lund International Fantastic Film Festival 103, 174–76, 179–83
La lunga strada della paura see *The Hitcher* (1986)
Lunopolis 171, 219
Luongo, Dominic 130
Lupino, Ida 213
Luppi, Federico 152, 234
Luthor, Lex (character) 239
Lux Interior 197
The Lycanthrope (short film) 172, 252
Lyn, Euros 169
Lynch, David 235, 252
Lynch, Jennifer Chambers 189, 228
Lynch, Joe 163
Lynch, Richard 212
Lyndon, Barré 169
Lyons, Michaele 172

M 130
M dot Strange 144
M. Foudamour, la lune promise 166
M-3: The Gemini Strain see *Plague* (1979)
Maas, Dick 170
Macabre (2009 feature, aka *Darah*) 192
Macabro: Festival de Horror en Cine y Video 140–1
Macau Twilight (unproduced feature script) 172, 190
MacDonald, Hettie 169
MacDonald, Kevin 191
MacDonald, Leonard 189
MacDowell, Andie 209
Macé, Damien 196
Mach, Jean 142, 143
Macháne, Jirí 237
Machine see *Máquina* (2006 short film; dir: Ibáñez)
The Machine Girl 146
The Machinist (2004) 182, 188, 231
Machotaildrop 122
Macian, David 238
Mack, Manuel 148
Mackenzie, David 141
MacLean, Adam 173
Maclean, Alison 153, 234
Macourek, Milos 154
Mad Detective (2007 feature) 229
Mad Movies Award 187–88
Madagascar, a Journey Diary (2010 animated short film) 141
Madagascar, carnet de voyage see *Madagascar, a Journey Diary*
Madagascar Skin 152
Madavi, Mansur (aka Mahdavi) 154
Maddin, Guy 127, 231
Made in Japan (2007 short film) 185, 203
Madfis, Molly 191
Madigan, Amy 235
Madison Horror Film Festival vii, 13, 112, 176
Madoff, Bernie 23
La madre muerta 152
Madrid, Miguel (aka Michael Skaife) 237

Madsen, Michael 39
Madsen, Virginia 140, 210
Maeda, Mahiro 143
Maelstrom International Fantastic Film Festival vii, 6, 42, 58, 66–67, 73–74, 107–8, 112, 176
Maestro (short film; 2005, dir: Tóth?) 181
Magee, Patrick 162
Mager, Jay 130
Magic (1978) 212
The Magic Umbrella 161
The Magician (1995 short film) 161
The Magician (2005 feature; dir: Ryan) 178
Magik and Rose 150
Magnat, Julien 195
Magritte Moment 185
Maguire, Tobey 206, 208, 216
Mahdavi, Mansur see Madavi, Mansur
Maher, Dan 244
Mahoney, Dennis 172
Mai Mai Miracle 141
Maia, Paulo J. 247
The Maid (2005 feature; dir: Tong) 193
Maimai Shinko to sennen no mahô see *Mai Mai Miracle*
Mainstream Massacre 200
La maison usher ne chutera pas see *The House of Usher Does Not Fall*
Majewski, Janusz 237
Major, Jake 160
Majumdar, Krishnendu 195
Mak, Tai Kit 152
The Makabra Ensemble 237
Make-A-Wish 108
Make Room! Make Room!! (novel) 186
Makhmalbaf, Mohsen 233
Making a Man (2008 short film) 238
Making of "Süsse Stuten 7" see *Making of Teeny-Stuten 7*
Making of Teeny-Stuten 7 (aka *Making of 'Süsse Stuten 7*) 248
Making the List 224
Maklar, Anyone? 172, 214
Makovsky, Judianna 207
Makrogiannis, Evan 125
El Mal de Schneider see *Die Schneider Krankheit*
La maldición de la bestia see *Night of the Howling Beast* (1975)
La maldición del escorpión de jade see *The Curse of the Jade Scorpion*
Maldito Bastardo! 123, 238
Maldito Sean 1º episodio 129
Malediction 192
Maléfique (2002) 164
Malevolence (2004 feature; dir: Mena) 189
Malherbe, Arnaud 163
Malis, Jossie 175
Mallette, Doug 247
Malling, Thomas Cappelen 155
Malone, Jena 208
Malone, William 76
Maloney, Tamara 160
Malpertuis see *The Legend of Doom House* (1974)
Mamá (2008 short film) 131, 132, 147, 180
Mamet, David 144
The Mamtsotsi Bird 238, 244
Man, a Natural Girl (aka *Tennen shôjo Man*) 251

Man Bites Dog (1992, aka *C'est arrivé près de chez vous*) 234, 251
The Man from Earth 129, 146, 172, 185, 203
Man Monkey 172
The Man to Destroy (aka *Legenda o caru Scepanu Malom*, aka *Covjek koga treba ubiti*) 236
Man vs. Woman (2006 short film) 173
The Man Who Collected Food 131, 171
The Man Who Couldn't Open Doors 202
The Man Who Fell to Earth (1976) 213
The Man with Rain in His Shoes see *Twice Upon a Yesterday*
Mañá, Laura 149
Manasseri, Michael 248
Mancini, Don 137
Manden i månen see *The Dark Side of the Moon* (1987)
Mandfredini, Harry 161
Mandrill 155
Mandy.com 33
Mandylor, Costas 220
Maney, Michael 196
Manfredi, Matt 149
Manga (2005) 214
Mangaravite, Bernardo 146
Mangone, Franco 184
Mangue Negro see *Mud Zombies*
Mangum, Jonathan 222
Maniac (1980) 237
Manjourides, Matt viii, 18–19, 35, 42, 49–50, 60, 79, 93
Mank, Gregory William 197
Manneken Pis 251
Mannequin (1987) 153
Manning, Delaney 133
Manning, Eric 225
Manning, Katy 177
Manning, Tom 224
Manoel de Oliveira Award 147
Man's Best Friend (1993; dir: Lafia) 166
Manson, Graeme 233
Mantelli, Fernando 131
Mantis (2002 short film; dir: Moragues) 231
Mantra (feature; year?) 162
Manual práctico del amigo imaginário (abreviado) (aka *All Users Guide for the Imaginary Friend (Abridged)*, aka *The Users Guide to Imaginary Friends (Abridged)*) 121, 132, 176, 185, 202, 203, 246
Manuel, Stephen 167
Manuli, Guido 236
Maohgai (aka *Sadistic City*) 252
Mapa-Múndi 146
Mapes, Justin 167
Maquetas 179, 201
Máquina (2006 short film; dir: Ibáñez) 129, 144, 146, 180
Marais, Jessica 126
Marcella and Sofia 243
Marck, Nick 169
Marcone, Vincent 133, 143, 229, 238
Marcotte, Serge 142
Mardini, Mark 189
Marebito 127
Margaret's Museum 151
Margolis, David 196
Mari, Veronica 146
El mariachi 251
Mariella, John 150
Mariko, Tetsuya 250

Mariko's 30 Pirates 250
Marín, Joseph Lluís 230
The Marina Experiment 177
Marinelli, John 161
Marini, Pablo 129
Marins, José Mojica 143, 150, 228; see also Coffin Joe
Marinucci, Phil 161
Mario Bava (DVD collection) 204
Mario Bava: All the Colors of the Dark (book) 198
Marius Borodine 142
Mark Macready and the Archangel Murders 158
Mark Taper Forum 204
Marka, Sebastian 129
Marked (short film) 237
Marks, Bill 130
Markwell, John 151
Mårlind, Måns 127, 171, 193
Marohasy, Caroline 190
Marquand, Richard 170
Marrale, Brent 142
Marriott Hotel 9, 66
Mars Attacks! 209
Marsal 183
Marschall, Andreas 194
Marsden, Rhodri 33, 254n19
The Marsh (2006 feature?) 189, 217
Marshall, Aaron 163
Marshall, Frank 213
Marshall, George T. vii, 30, 195
Marshall, Neil 127, 145, 175, 202
Marshall, Peter 146, 190
Marsters, James 206, 208
Martell, Lucas 158
Martens, Bernard 136
Martí, David 138
Martí, Miguel 127
Martí, Samuel "Sam" Ortí 201
Martians Go Home! The Revenge of Sara Clockwork (aka *Martians Go Home! La venganza de Sara Clockwork*) 246
Martin, Andrea 237
Martin, Duane L. 124
Martin, Eduard 232
Martín, Eugenio 237
Martin, Jennifer 218
Martin, Ross 6
Martin, Stephanie 189
Martin Luther King Jr. Auditorium 11
Martinez, Guillaume 144
Martinez, Rafael 123
Martinuzzi, Heidi (aka Heidi Honeycutt) viii, 6, 13, *15*, 51, 57, *84*, 105, 113, 117, 253n4
Martyrs (2008 feature) 138, 179, 180, 228, 229
Martz, Neal 210
Marusic, Josko 236
Marwencol 132, 142
Marx, Vandiet 237
Mary and Max 170
Mary Jane Go Round 247
Mary Poppins (stage production) 204
Mary Tyler Moore Show 254n7
Maryniuk, Mike 249
Mas, Hector 129
Masacre esta noche (aka *Watch 'Em Die*) 58, 129, 186
Masacre Marcial IVX 129
Mascara (1987) 153
Mashima, Riichiro 250
The Mask (1994) 234

Mask of Evil 200
Maslany, Tatiana 138
Mason, Adam 134, 167, 237
Masquerade Ball (Loscon event) 11, 73
Massacrator 143
Massacre, Tonight see *Masacre esta noche*
Massey, Eric 241
Massin, Geoffroy Barbet 201
Massoglia, Chris 124
Masson, Marie 99
Master of Macabre (short film fest) 112
Master of the Scream Contest 96
Mastering Chauncey 226
Masters, Todd 140, 205
Masters of Horror (TV series) 138, 205, 230
Masters of the Universe (1987) 153
Masterson, Fay 124
Masterson, Scott 114
Mastroianni, Armand 254n6
Mastronardi, Bart 125, 134, 242
Matador (1986) 153
Matheson, Melissa 212
Matheson, Richard 170
Mathieson, John 151
Mathieu, Victor 123
Mathy, Jean-Jacques 236
Mati 203
Matinee (1993 feature) 128
Matinee (short film) 177
The Matrix 208
The Matrix Reloaded 240
The Matrix Revolutions 240
The Matsugane Potshot Affair (aka *Matsugane ransha jiken*) 193
Matsumoto, Hajime 232
Matsumoto, Hitoshi 126
Matsunashi, Tomoko 251
Matsutani, Rainer 128, 165, 251
Mattei, Bruno (aka Vincent Dawn, aka Martin Miller) 248
Matthews, Lee Andrew 238, 241, 247
Matthews, Owen 160
Matushima, Kosuke 145
Mauméjean, Xavier 165
Maurer, David Michael 217
Maurette, Victoria 129
Mauro, Rich viii, 40, 242
Maury, Julien 229
Maverick Entertainment 93
Max the Hero 135
Maxie (1985) 128
Maxwell, Garth 152
Maxwell Medals 9–*10*
Maxwell Stein 199, 200
May (2002; dir: McKee) 121, 127, 138, 164, 194, 231
May, David 225
May, Elaine 212
May Hell Keep Her 123
Maya (2010 short film) 123
Mayhem Horror Festival 119
Mayhew, Peter 173
Mayrand, Vincent 166
Mayuzumi, Rintaro 152
The Maze (2010) 200
Mazomenos, Vasilis 150
Mazzarella, David 178
Mazzoni, Mathieu 158
McAbee, Cory 184
McAuliffe, D.C. 241
McCall, Rob 251
McCarron, Bob 234, 235
McCarter, Brooke 161

McCarthy, Colm 166
McCarthy, Damian 158, 201, 241
McCarthy, Michael 122
McCarthy, Thomas 249
McCarthy, Tom K. 166
McCasland, Cameron 197
McClelland, Joseph 104
McClory, Belinda 177
McClure, Jourdan 199, 200
McCormack, Gary 150
McCormack, Mary 144
McCormack, Pete 149
McCullough, Danny 248
McDermott, Hurt 225
McDiarmid, Ian 239
McDonald, Bruce 128
McDonnell, Mary 204
McDonough 158
McDowall, Roddy 211
McDowell, Malcolm 198
McElligott, Dawn 243
McEnroe, Annie 236
McEvoy, Tom 178
McGarr, Eben 192
McGehee, Scott 233
McGuigan, Paul 151
McGuiness, Kevin 124
McHattie, Stephen 192
McHenry, Edward 227
McHenry, Rory 227
McIntire Casting 221
McIntire, Cheryl 221
McIntosh, Caitlin 161
McIntosh, Neve 146, 155
McKay, Rodney (character) 239
McKean, Dave 171, 175, 230
McKee, Lucky 127, 164, 194, 231
McKellar, Don 151
McKellen, Ian 207, 208
McKidd, Kevin 150
McKinley, Jacqueline 226
McLellen, Ron 123
McLennan, Chris 113
McMahan, Lea 224
McMullen, Eddie 15, 33, 56, 94
McMullen, Ken 153
McNaughton, John 128, 153, 234
McNeil, Kate 235
McNiven, Steve 216
McPherson, Conor 228
McPherson, Michael C. 226
McQuaid, Glenn 145
McQueen, Alexander 165
McQueen, Mark 126
McQuilkin, Brian 123
McVicar, Bruce 197
McVicker, Tess 190
Mead, Chelsea 199
Mead, Morgan 162
Meade, Benjamin 122
Meagher, John 161
Means to an End (2005 short film; dir: Hamilton & Solet) 136, 196
The Measure of My Days 159
Meat Market (dir: Camerota) 178
Mebana 175, 181
Les mécaniques des ombres (novel) 166
Medeiros. Garry 196
Medem, Julio 166
Medjuck, Jacob 221
Medusa 134
Medvigy, Gábor 147
Meet the Head of Juan Pérez (aka *Conozca la cabeza de Juan Pérez*) 185

Mega Shark vs. Giant Octopus 123
Megazorg Z 185
Mehta, Soham 162
Meilin Adventure 252
Mein Bruder, der Vampir see *My Brother the Vampire*
Meine Heimatstadt 160
Meirelles, Fernando 229
Melbourne Underground Film Festival 95, 176-79
Melchior, Carl 225
Melchior, Ib Jørgen 213
Le mele di Adamo see *Adam's Apples*
Méliès Awards 96, 102, 141, 146-52, 174-75, **179-84**
Méliès d'Argent 96, 102, 126-28, 157, 170-71, 174-75, **179-84**, 187-88, 214, 227-30
Méliès d'Or 96, 121, 157-58, 174-75, **179-84**, 187-88, 227-29, 233
Melini, Davide 241
Mellian, Kristin 220
Mello, Rubens 131
Melo, Diego 129, 185, 203
La mélodie du malheur see *Happiness of the Katakuris*
The Melody of Woes see *Happiness of the Katakuris*
Meltdown (2009 short film, aka *Melt Down*: dir: Green) 192
Même les pigeons vont au paradis see *Even Pigeons Go to Heaven*
Memento 126, 207, 232
"Memento Mori" (*Stargate SG-1* TV episode) 133
Les mémoires de l'homme-éléphant 165
Memoirs of a Survivor 154
Memorial Day (1999 feature) 226
Memories of Matsuko 144
Memories Without Rememberer 231
Men in Black (1997) 208
Mena, Stevan 188, 189
"The Menagerie" (*Star Trek* TV episodes) 170
La menace vient de l'espace 129
Menaul, Christopher 166
Mendes, Patrick 186
Mendez, Fernando 186
Mendez, Natacha 129
Mendoza, Brillante 227
Mendoza, Gustavo Leonel 129
O menino que plantava invernos 146
Menken, Alan 204, 211
Merantau 155
Mercano, el marciano see *Mercano the Martian*
Mercano the Martian (aka *Mercano, el marciano*) 232
Meredith, Burgess 212, 236
Les mères noires (novel) 165
Merrill, Kieth 252
Merry, Tommy 191
Més enllà de la passió see *Pasión lejana*
Meschino, Neil 242
Messenger, Melinda 171
Messengers (2004 feature; dir: Farha) 173
Messerer, Phil 124
Meszaros, Evan 162
Meth (2010 short film, dir: Maney) 196
Metropolis (1927) 199
Metz, Blythe 242
Metzler, Chris 178
Meunier, Tim viii, 114
Meurisse, Jean-Paul 234

La meute see *The Pack* (2010)
Meyer, Nicholas 212, 213
Meyers, Ray 197
Meyjes, Menno 170
Meza-Valdes, Andres 134
Meza-Valdes, Diego 134
MGM 195, 199
Michael, Robi 159
Michael Angel (2000 feature) 250
Michael Morlock's Supernatural World 171
Michaelson, Andrew 222
Michaud, Maude **14**
Mickle, Jim 144, 247
Microgravity (2006 short film) 125, 173, 214, 215, 221
Microsoft 33
The Midas Touch (short film; dir: Folch) 152
Midnight Madness — Toronto International Film Festival 97, 246-47
Midnight Madness Award 247
The Midnight Meat Train 143, 163
Midnight Sun 247
Midnight Three 251
Midwestern Summer: Controlled Pain 243
Migliore, Andrew vii, 111, 117
Mignola, Mike 168
Miike, Takashi 127, 143, 145, 150, 151, 164, 175, 188, 227, 228, 231, 232, 251
Mijn Mooiste Creatuur 136
Mikels, Ted V. 172
Miki, Satoshi 143
Miki, Shinichiro 145
Mikkelsen, Mads 149, 193
Mil gritos tiene la noche see *Pieces* (1982)
Mile High Horror Film Festival vii-viii, 112, 184
Miles, Doug 188
Miles Memorial Playhouse **12**, 24, 253n3
Millán, Pablo 159
Millar, Gavin 153
Les mille merveilles de l'univers (aka *The Thousand Wonders of the Universe*) 176, 184
Millennium Actress (aka *Sennen joyû*) 232
Millennium Bug (1998 short film) 161
Miller, Bobby 130
Miller, Chris 123
Miller, Dick 124, 139
Miller, Linda see Linda Miller Award
Miller, Martin see Mattei, Bruno
Miller, Rebecca 128
Miller, Steve 252
Miller, Travis M. 247
Miller, Victor 88, 124
Miller, William M. 189
Miller's Crossing 252
Millor, Sam 227
Mills, Amy 217
Mills, Chris 217
Mills, Freddie Hutton 126
Mime Massacre 157
Mimic 208
Min, Byung-chun 148
Min skäggiga mamma see *My Bearded Mother*
Mina (2008 short film; dir: Cassella) 241
Minahan, Daniel 175
Minami Toshiko Award 249-51
Minas, Alan 132
Mind Game (2004) 145
Mindbender (short film; 2009?) 219
Mindfield (short film; dir: Andrews) 160

Index

Miner, Michael 211
Miner, Steve 128
Miner's Massacre see *Curse of the Forty-Niner*
Mingenbach, Louise 207
Minns, Cheri 210
Minority Report 207
Minotaure's Ball (aka *Le bal du minotaure*) 165
Minton, Jim 242
Minty, Josie 239
Mintz, Dan 218
Mira, Carles 153
Miracle Fish 201
Miracle in Valby (aka *Miraklet i Valby*) 252
Miracle Mile (1988) 234
Mirageman 156
Miraklet i Valby see *Miracle in Valby*
Miró, Albert 229
Mirojnick, Ellen 208
Mirror Mirror (2008 short film; dir: Champagne) 220
MirrorMask 171, 175, 230
Miss Misery 82
Missing (2007 short film; dir: Donck) 146
Missing Pages 173
Mission Creeps's (music band) 122
Mission Impossible (1960s TV series) 63
The Mist (2007, aka *Stephen King's The Mist*) 204
Mr. Foley 157, 158, 179
Mister Frost 234
Mr. Green (short film) 215
Mr. Moonlight 247
Mr. Nobody 228
Mr. Phang and the Blood Princess 243
Mr. Pin 190
Mr. Roach (unproduced script) 190
Il mistero di Lovecraft see *H.P. Lovecraft: The Terror Within*
Mistress (1992, aka *Hollywood Mistress*) 254n6
Mitchell, Chris W. 202
Mitchell, Eddy 154
Mitchell, Elizabeth 205
Mitchell, Lisa 95
Mitchell, Lt.-Col. (*Stargate SG-1* character) 239
Mitchler, A.J. 190
Mito, Hineki 251
Mitsushima, Hikari 141, 142, 192
Mitton, Andy 188
Miura, Tomokazu 143
Miyake, Ryuta 251
Miyazaki, Hayao 171, 186
Miyazaki, Masumi 144
Miyuki (2007) 93, 162
Mizar 125
Mizell, Matt 106
Mizell, Sarah 106
Mizushima, Seiji 145
Mizutani, Toshiyuki 252
MJC Productions 222
Mnemosyne Rising 135
Mô hitori iru see *Alter Ego* (2002)
Mocikat, Wolf 159
Mocky, Jean-Pierre 235
Model Man (2006 short film) 173
Modern Love Is Automatic 122, 177
Moe, Joe 197
Moffat, Steven 133, 169
Mogadon 7 (2003 short film) 172
Moi (2007 short film) 144

Moissakis, Stéphanie 146
Mokpo the Harbor (aka *Mokponeun hangguda*) 250
Moland, Hans Petter 193
Mold! 242
Mole (2001) 40, 44–45, 242
Molin, Tero **81**
Molina, Rubén 230
Molinari, Eduardo 238
Molina's Ferozz 129
Moliné, Marçal 236
Mollo, John 213
Moloch (2006 short film; dir: Serrano) 242
Molon, Jacques-Olivier 217
Moltó, Jorge Tur 230
Momani, Firas 142
Mompart, Joan 238
Monaco, Lawrence 226
Mondo cannibale see *Cannibal World* (2003)
Mondo Psycho 129
Mones com la Becky see *Monkeys Like Becky*
The Money Shot (2007; dir: Brownfield & Petrie) 178
Mongillo, Michael 225, 226
Monkey Shines: An Experiment in Fear 141, 153, 235
Monkey Shines: Esperimento nel terrore see *Monkey Shines: An Experiment in Fear*
Monkeys Like Becky (aka *Mones com la Becky*) 233
Monroe, Bob 149
Monroe, Steven R. 245
Monroeville Mall Zombie Walk 198
Monster Bash (convention) 197, 198, 199
Monster Bash (magazine) 198
Monster Club 141
Monster Cruise 124
Monster from Bikini Beach 123
Monster Job Hunter 136
Monster Kid Home Movies 198
Monster Kid Memories (book) 199
Monster Kid Online Magazine 199
The Monster Killers 226
Monster-Mania Con 112, 199
Monster Movie 158
The Monster Museum 103
Monster of 11.05 159
The Monster of Phantom Lake 221
Monster on My Mind 123
The Monster Squad 128, 204
Monsterpalooza 112
Monsters (2004 short film; dir: Morgan) 181
Monsters (2010 features; dir: Edwards) 192, 227
Monsters from the Vault (magazine) 197, 198, 199
Monsters vs. Aliens 203
El monstro del mar! 123, 130, 133, 134, 176, 191, 200
Monstrous Movie Music 197
Monteiro, João viii, 102
Montero, José David 217
Montevideo Fantástico viii, 119, 184–85
Montgomery, Adam 221
Montgomery, Tyron 233
Monty Python and the Holy Grail 126
Montz, Larry 218
Monument, Andrew 196
Monzón, Daniel 126, 171, 175

Moon (2009) 158, 163, 169, 175, 179, 227, 228, 249
Moonglow (2004 short film, aka *Schijn van de maan*) 182
Moonlight (2007–08 TV series) 204
Moonlight by the Sea 222
Moonlight Whispers (1999, aka *Sasayaki*, aka *Gekkô no sasayaki*) 250
Moon-Lite 162
Moore, Demi 210
Moore, Ronald D. 169
Mora, Alba 231
Mora, Miguel A. 217
Moragues, Jordi 231
Morales, Antonio 234
Morales, Francesc 202
Morales, Gérald 238
Morales, Guillem 146
The Morality Game 159
Moran, James 148
Moran, Tony 89, 163
Móray, Gábor 171
MORBIDO: Festival Internacional de Cine Fantastico y de Terror viii, 6, **47**, **52**, 58, 64, **75**, 78, 81, 101, 185–86
Mor(d) i mødregruppen see *Mothers in Arms* (1998)
Der Mörder 236
More Control (music video) 190
Moreau, David 171, 194
Moreira, Pablo 185
Moreno, Aritz 201
Moreno, Dani 231
Moreno, Lea (aka Lea Moreno Young) 173
Moretz, Chloë 215
Morgan, Glen 194
Morgan, Matthew 196
Morgan, Mitchell 160
Morgan, Molly 224
Morgan, Robert 131, 145, 150, 202
Morgana (2008 Dutch short film) 136
Morgenthaler, Anders 230
Morgenthaler, Matthew 184
Morgret, Eric vii, 6, 42–43, 49–51, 58, 66 67, 70, 73 74, 112, 242
Morgue, Paulo 168
Morgue Story (2009, aka *Morgue Story: Blood, Blowfish and Comics* and *Morgue Story: Sangue, Baiacu e Quadrinhos*) 129, 184, 252
Morgue Story: Blood, Blowfish and Comics see *Morgue Story* (2009)
Morgue Story: Sangue, Baiacu e Quadrinhos see *Morgue Story* (2009)
Morimoto, Koji 143
Morin, Grégory 193
Morita, Shuhei 145
Mørke sjeler see *Dark Souls* (2010)
Morlet, David 164
Morneau, Louis 128, 176
The Morning After (2006 short film; dir: Knight) 144
Moro, Christopher 225
Morot, Adrien 228
Morris, Steve 226
Morris, Toby 190
Morrison, Grant 216
Morrow, Scott 110
Morse, David 172, 220
Morse see *Let the Right One In*
La morsure (2009 short film, aka *The Bite*) 163

Index

La mort de Tau 232
Le Mort-Homme see *Dead Man* (novel)
Mortier, Koen 143
Mortified (2009) 143
Mortinho por Chegar a Casa 151
Morton, Joe 235
Morton, Katherine 226
Morton, Samantha 207
Moscou, Belgium 147
Moseley, Bill 123, 137, 138, 139, 217, 237
Mósesdóttir, Dögg 228
Mosher, Max 241
MOTELx — Festival Internacional de Cinema de Terror de Lisboa viii, 102, 186
Mother & Son (dir: Ahmed) 161
Mothers in Arms (1998, aka *Mor(d) i mødregruppen*) 202
Motor City Nightmares 112
Mottola, Greg 151
The Mouse That Soared 132
Mousoulis, Bill 177, 178
La moustache 230
Movie Monster Insurance 173
MovieBank 8
Moyer, Stephen 215
Mozos, Manuel 151
Mrad, Javier 155
Mrlja na savjesti 154
Mrs. Meitlemeihr 160
Ms. Monster 124
MTV Movie Awards 169
Mucci, Phil 148
Mucha sangre 248
Mucinho, Zé 146
Mucsi, Zóltan 147
Mud see *Lodo* (2009)
Mud Zombies 47, 129, 203
Mueck, Ron 151
Mueller, Douglas 214
Muha (1968 short film) 235
La mujer más fea del mundo see *The Ugliest Woman in the World*
Mulack, Thomas 230
Mulberry Street 144, 246
Muldowney, Brendan 134, 193, 194, 231
Mulgrew, Kate 209
Müller, Andreas 188
Muller, Richard 239
Mulligan, Carey 133
Mulligan, Robert 237
Mullins, Anthony 178
Mulloy, Phil 201
Mum & Dad (2008) 146, 179, 190
The Mummy (1932) 197
The Mummy (1999) 208
Mumy, Bill 199
Mundruczó, Kornél 147, 148
Muñeco viviente V 184
Muñoz, Armando D. 167
Muñoz, David 168, 201
Muñoz, Tomás 236
Munroe, Bob 150
Munster, Herman 48
The Munsters: The Complete Series 197
The Muppet Movie 212
Murakami, Kenji 250
Murakami, Muneyoshi 251
The Murder Game (2006 feature) 244
Murder Loves Killers Too 176, 190
Murder Party 129, 246
Murderabilia 161
Murdock, Jerry 134, 191, 243
Muren, Dennis 207, 208, 210, 211, 212

Murielle moi non plus 182
Murnau Foundation 197
Muro, Jim 128
Muroga, Atsushi 251
Murphy, Dominic 142
Murphy, Dustin 225
Murphy, Eddie 209
Murphy, Melissa 221
Murray, Bill 215
Murray, Brendan 237
Murray, Julian 139
Muschietti, Andres 131, 132, 147
Museal 249
Mushishi 229
The Music of Erich Zahn 247
The Musician and Death 154
Muskegon Film Festival 245
Mussenden, Isis 205
Must Love Death 143, 188
Mutant Girls Squad 227
Mutant Swingers from Mars 157
Mutantland 126
Mute Witness (1994) 165
Muti (short film) 238
Muto 156
Muyllaert, David 130
My Bearded Mother (aka *Min skäggiga mamma*) 175, 182
My Beautiful Wickedness 222
My Bloody Valentine (2009 feature) 249
My Bloody Wedding 162, 219
My Boyfriend's Back (unproduced script) 226
My Brother the Vampire (aka *Getting My Brother Laid* and *Mein Bruder, der Vampir*) 193
My Cousin's Keeper 122
My Daddy Long Legs 252
My Favorite Skyline 251
My Immortal 244
My Little Eye (2002) 164, 171, 182
My Love Lives in the Sewer 174
My Mother the Mermaid (aka *Ineo gongju*) 149, 250
My Parents (2004 short film, aka *Meine Eltern*) 193
My Sassy Girl (2001 feature, aka *Yeopgijeogin geunyeo*) 250
My Skin! 167, 221, 226
Myers, Blake 104, 123
Myers, Michael 46, 89
MyM Matilde y Malena 129
Myrick, Daniel 194, 243
MySpace.com 32–35, 59, 89, 93, 95, 253n2
The Mysterious Castle in the Carpathians 154
The Mysterious Geographic Explorations of Jasper Morello 136
Mysterious Island (CD) 198
Mystery Science Theater 3000 77
Mythic Journeys: The Bone Orchard 135
Myung, Bae Young 192

Na, Hong-jin 127, 147, 192, 193, 229
Na Bdun-Nam-Ja see *Bad Guy* (2001)
Na dnie szafy 153
Naai asok kap naangsaao phloenchit see *Suicide Me* (2003)
Nabbeun namja see *Bad Guy* (2001)
Naboer see *Next Door* (2005)
Nación no identificada 184
Nadie inquietó más 129
Nadja (1994 feature) 166, 233

Nagasaki, Shuichi 252
Nagel, Uwe 229
Nagle, Shane 177
Nájera, J. Oskura 133
Nakamura, Yoshihiro 187
Nakano, Hiroyuki 194
Nakashima, Tetsuya 143, 144, 192
Nakata, Hideo 127, 164, 193, 232
Nakazawa, Kazuto 143
Naked Horror 167
The Naked Monster 159
Nam, Ki-Woong 250
Nama-natsu 250
The Nameless (1999, aka *Los sin nombre*) 127, 141, 150, 165, 183, 184, 194, 232, 233
Narahashi, Yôko 252
Nared, Ken 244
Naschy, Paul 139, 151, 154, 171, 197, 231, 236, 237, 248; see also Brigadoon Paul Naschy Award
Nashawati, Joyce A. 163
Nashville Traffic Safety 197
Natali, Vincenzo 127, 148, 149, 150, 151, 165, 194, 233
National Enquirer 7
National Media Museum (in Bradford, UK) 118
Nattens engel see *Angel of the Night* (1998)
Nattevagten see *Nightwatch* (1994)
Natural City 148
Natural Cures for Common Ailments 159
Natural Selection (2010 short film; dir: Foraker) 195
Naturaleza muerta 129
Naufrage see *Shipwrecked*
Naulin, John 235
Navarre, Yves 236
Navarro, Miguel 234
Navarro, Tino 149
The Navigator: A Mediaeval Odyssey (aka *Navigator, una odisea en el tiempo*) 153, 235
Naylor, Timothy (aka Tim Naylor) 189, 244
Nazdravicko! 190
Near Dark (1987) 128
Nebula Award 5, 112, 186
Nebulous Dawn 160
NECA 198
Necrofilia (1985) 154
Necromancer (2005 feature, aka *Jom kha mung wej*) 248
The Necronomicon (2009 short film) 135, 219
Necronomicon: Book of Dead (1993) 152
Necrophagus see *The Butcher of Binbrook* (1971)
The Need (2006 short film) 173
Needful Things 209
Needle 126, 217
Neel, Michael 123
Neighbor 172
The Neighbor No. Thirteen 250
The Neighbor Zombie (2010 feature, aka *Yieutjib jombi*) 192
Neighborhood Watch (2005 feature; dir: Whifler) 189
Neighborhood Watch (year?) 200
Neila (short film) 222
Neill, Ryan 173
Neill, Ve 204, 209, 210
Nel, Tinneke 238

Index

Nella terra dei cannibali see *Land of Death* (2003)
Nelson, Brian 230
Nelson, James T. 189
Nelson, Matthew (aka Matt Nelson) 161
Nelson, Mike P. 225
Nelson, Yu Lik-wai see Yu, Lik-wai
Nemes, Laszlo 143
Neon Killer (short film) 192
Nesbitt, Evan A. 130
Nesbitt, James 188
Netflix 94
The Netherbeast of Berm-Tech Industries, Inc. 215
Neuchâtel International Fantastic Film Festival viii, 103, 179–83, 186–88
Neumier, Edward 211
Neun, Mike *81*, 99
Never Belongs to Me 156, 250
Never Sleep Again: The Elm Street Legacy 195
The NeverEnding Story (1984) 211
Neverlost 142
Nevermore Film Festival viii, 51, 112–13
Nevermore Horror, Gothic and Fantasy Film Festival 113
Nevitt, Robert vii, 28, 32, 38–39, 47, 53, 59, 70, 74, 80, 86, 88, 91, 117, 143
New Blood (2002 feature, aka *Hyn huet ching nin*) 188
New Blood Award 202–3
"New Divide" (song) 216
The New Life (2006 short film) 190
A New Life! see *Une nouvelle vie!* (2009)
New Nightmare see *Wes Craven's New Nightmare*
New Year's Day (2000 feature; dir: Krishnamma) 250
New Year's Eve (unproduced script) 244
New York City Horror Film Festival viii, 34, 88, 113, 188–89
Newby, Chris 152
Newell, Bethany 161
Newell, Jamie 124
Newman, David 170
Newman, Kim 197
Newman, Leslie 170
Newman, Matt 104
Newman, Thomas 249
Newport International Film Festival 117
Newsome, Ted 159
The Next (short film; year?) 174
Next Caller 171
Next Door (2005, aka *Naboer*) 171, 181
Next Floor 132, 133, 134, 147, 155, 201, 228
Next of Kin (1984 feature; dir: Williams) 235
The Next One see *El siguiente* (2004)
The Next Plane 225
Next Victim (2003 feature) 226
Nguyen, Kim 155
Nia (2006 short film) 173
Niccol, Andrew 165, 169, 208, 233
La nichée 236
Nichetti, Maurizio 127
Nicholson, Jack 211
Nicholson, Leo 161
Nickel, John-Paul 178
Nickel Children 157
Nico, Jackie 223
Nicotero, Greg 130, 138, 205, 208, 231

Niddam, Igaal 236
Niemi, Ilkka *81*
The Nigel Diaries 177
Night (2009 short film) 123
The Night Flier 139
Night Games (aka *Yoru no geemu*; dir: Uian) 250
A Night of Horror International Film Festival 13, 95, 189–91
Night of the Creeps 197
Night of the Dead: Leben Tod 225
Night of the Demon see *Curse of the Demon* (1957)
Night of the Headsman (short film; dir: Bohusz; aka *Knight of the Headsman?*) 219
Night of the Hell Hamsters 190, 242
Night of the Howling Beast (1975, aka *La maldición de la bestia*) 236
Night of the Hunter (1955) 199
Night of the Invisible Man 162
Night of the Living Dead (1968) 8, 197; see also *One for the Fire*
Night of the Living Dorks 145
Night of the Werewolf (1981) 154
Night Time see *Sieben Monde* (1998)
Night Train (1999; dir: Bernstien) 150
Night Watch (2004) 127
Nightbreed 153, 171
Nightfall (unproduced script) 218
Nightingale in a Music Box 225
Nightmare (2005 feature; dir: Bank) 156, 189, 221
Nightmare (short film; year?) 172
Nightmare at Bunnyman Bridge 162, 174
Nightmare at Number 92 174
The Nightmare Before Christmas 209
Nightmare Division, Tulsa International Film Festival 113
Nightmare Man (2006) 93, 163, 221, 242
Nightmare on Elm Street (1984) 126
A Nightmare on Elm Street (2010) 195
A Nightmare on Elm Street 3: Dream Warriors 153
A Nightmare on Elm Street 4: The Dream Master 235
A Nightmare on Elm Street 5: The Dream Child 153
A Nightmare to Remember San Francisco Horror Film Festival vii, 13, 28, 42, 66, 82, 89, 113, 191
Nightmares (1983) 128
Nightmares in Red, White and Blue 196
Nightsweats: The Collector 223
Nightwatch (1994) 128, 141
Niki Pretti Photography 14
Nikishow, Yevgeniy 147
Nikkel, Kevin 249
Niles, Steve 197
Nilsson, Johannes Stjärne 227
Nimoy, Leonard 204, 213
The Nine Lives of Tomas Katz 150
Nine Queens 150
Nineteen Eighty-Four (1984) 154
A Ninja Pays Half My Rent 146
Ninjas (2010 short film) 142, 188
Nintendo 165
The Ninth Configuration (aka *Twinkle Twinkle Killer Kane*) 212
The Ninth Gate 139
Nish, Ric 244
Nishimura, Yoshihiro 129, 143, 192, 227, 251

Nixon and Hogan Smoke Christmas 247
No Country for Old Men 204
No Exit (feature) 167
No. 14 (unproduced script) 190
No. 0014 (2005 short film) 137
"No More Good Days" (*FlashForward* TV episode) 132
No moriré sola (2008 feature, aka *I'll Never Die Alone*) 184, 190, 203
No. 19 (short film) 191
No One Is Innocent (music band) 165
No profanar el sueño de los muertos see *Let Sleeping Corpses Lie* (1974)
No quiero la noche 230
No Return (2003 feature) 222, 223
No Sanctuary (2005 short film) 173, 224
No te mueras sin decirme adónde vas see *Don't Die Without Telling Me Where You're Going*
No Through Road 177
No. 12 (2006 short film) 173
Nobi, Akira 251, 252
Noble, John 126
Noble, Tony 228
Nobody (2007; dir: Linden) 168, 172, 189, 220, 245
De noche van a tu cuarto 130
Nochnoy dozor see *Night Watch* (2004)
Nockles, Richard 148
Nocturna (2010 short film) 186
Nocturno Nuove Visioni Award 214
Nocturnos (2008 feature; dir: Medina, Ricciardi & Vitullo) 129
NoDance Film Festival 40
Noé, Gaspar 187, 227, 233, 251
Noesis (year?) 221
A Noite (1999 short film) 150
Nolan, Christopher 126, 204, 205, 216, 232, 249
Nolan, Jonathan 126, 204, 249
Au nom du fil 154
Nomenklatura (music video) 165
Noorbergen, Luc 154
Noriko's Dinner Table 193
Norrington, Stephen 149
North American Fantastic Festival Alliance 101
Northam, Jeremy 149, 231
Norton, Bryan 225
Norton, Rosanna 212
Norwegian Ninja 155, 214
Nos miran (aka *They're Watching Us*) 149, 193
Le nosferat ou les eaux glacées de calcul égoiste 236
Nosferatu: The Ultimate Edition (DVD) 197
Nosferatu Tango 182
Notes from the Acrid Plain with Burton Hoary, Volume 7 214
Nothing (2003) 148
Nothing But the Truth (2008 film; dir: Lurie) 204
Nothing Face 161, 167, 244
Nothing in the Dark 167
The Nothing Pill 172
Nouri, Michael 235
Noussias, Yorgos 248
Une nouvelle vie! (2009, animated short film, aka *A New Life!*) 227
Novak, Emil 106
Novak, Frank 150
Novellino, Antonello 184
Novo, Nancho 151

Novotny, Tuva 218
Now and Again (1999–2000 TV series) 208
Now That You're Dead 191
Now You See Me, Now You Don't 136
Nowak, Till 201
Nude Nuns with Big Guns 122
Une nuit blanche (2005 short film, aka *Somnambulist*) 187
Nuit noire (2005 feature; dir: Smolders) 193, 248
Les nuits rouges du bourreau de jade see *Red Nights*
Numb (2003) 160
Él nunca lo haría see *He'd Never Do That*
Nunca más asistas a este tipo de fiestas 128, 129
Núñez, Darío 185, 203
Núñez, Iván López 136
Nunez, Victor 151
Nur über meine Leiche see *Over My Dead Body* (1995)
Nursery Crimes 126
Nusch Award 111
Nussbaum, Joe 202
Nuts (year? length?) 250
Nutter, Mark 243
The Nutty Professor (1996) 209
Nyland, Garrett Paul (aka Gary Nyland) 200
Nyman, Michael 233, 234
Nympha (2007) 134

Oaks, Jennifer M. 244
The Oath (1996 short film) 151
O'Bannon, Dan 168, 170, 213
Obayashi, Nobuhiko 128
Oberlies, Thomas 155, 158, 201
Oberschule 158
Obispo, Pascal 165
The Object 156
The Objective 189
Oblivion Island 141
Oblong, Angus 87–**88**
The Oblongs 87
O'Brien, Billy 150, 156, 164, 194, 217
O'Brien, Michael 149
O'Brien, Riley 177
Obscure Horror 14
Ocean's Thirteen 23
Ochiai, Masayuki 164
Ochse, Weston 130
O'Connell, Jack 147
Oculus (2006 short film; aka *Oculus: Chapter 3—The Man with the Plan*) 134, 136, 159, 221, 242
Ocvirk, David Todd 218
Odagiri, Jô 143
Odden, Bjørn Arne 158, 228
Oddworld (video game) 165
O'Dea, Judith 172
O'Donnell, Damien 150
O'Donnell, Will 249
L'oeil qui ment 234
Oeufs (1994 short film) 166
Of Cats & Women 180, 229
Of Darkness 123, 134, 162, 168, 172, 245
Off (2001 short film; dir: Polhemus) 196, 218
Off Screen 148
Off Season (2009 short film) 130, 174, 191, 245
Offscreen (year?; aka *Off Screen*?) 156

Offspring (2009 feature; dir: van den Houten) 177
Ogalde, Juan Pablo 218
Ogura, Hisao 164
Oh, Jung-Wan 218
Oh, Ki-min (aka Kimin Oh) 218
Oh, Young-doo 192
Oh, God! (1977) 213
Oh My God?! (2001 short film; dir: Van Rompaey) 183
Oh My God! It's Harrod Blank! (2008 feature) 122
O'Hanlon, James 169
O'Hear, Michael 130
Ohira, Shinya 143
O'Horten 147
Ohsawa, Katsuya 252
Ojeda, Santiago 234
Los ojos de Alicia (aka *Alicia's Eyes*) 134, 181
Oka, Masi 205
Det okända see *The Unknown* (2000)
Okiura, Hiroyuki 150, 151, 250
Oklahoma Horror Film Festival & Convention 113
Okuyama, Kazuyoshi 152
Old Habits Die Hard 162
Old Macdonald's Farm 200
The Old Pro see *Der Beste* (2005)
Oldboy (2003, aka *Oldeuboi*) 148, 149, 231
Oldman, Gary 140, 210, 216
Oliver, Barret 211
Oliver, Ron 251
Ollé, Àlex 127, 149, 164
Olmos, Edward James 204
Olschewki, Gerhad 236
Olsen, Mads Tobias 176, 202
Olsen, Maria 237
Olson, Bryce Fridrik 123
Olsson, Robert P. 168
Om Shanti Om (2007 feature; dir: Khan) 187
Omega 35 157
The Omen (1976) 49, 126
The Omen (2006) 138
Ominous-events.com 34
On a Dark and Stormy Night 199
On Air (2010 short film; dir: Vauth & Riedl) 145
On Edge 135, 226
On Evil Grounds see *Auf bösem Boden*
On the Other Line 224
On the Verge of Blood 238
Oñate, Miguel Ángel 184
Once Were Warriors 152
Onda Curta Award 150
One Blood Planet 160
One D (animated short film) 175
One Day a Man Bought a House (aka *Huset på Kampen*) 194, 232
One False Move 152
One for the Fire (documentary) 197
One Hour Photo 139, 207
One Night Stand (1984 feature; dir: Duigan) 235
One Nite in Mongkok 145
One of the Missing (1969 short film) 237
One of Those Days (2008 short film; dir: Dalton) 179, 228
One Soul 244
The One That Got Away (2007 short film; dir: Humphries) 242

One-chan, otôto to iku see *Coming with My Brother*
O'Neill, Jonathan "Jack," General (character) 239
O'Neill, Miles 177
Ong-bak 125, 231
Onion (newspaper) 7
"Only Just Begun" (song) 90
Onmyoji see *The Yin Yang Master*
Onna keiji Riko see *Detective Riko* (1998)
O.P.1207-x 229
The Open Door 125, 224
Open Water 206
Operación Cannabis 129
Operation: Fish 136, 214, 246
Opium, Diary of a Madwoman see *Ópium: Egy elmebeteg nö naplója*
Ópium: Egy elmebeteg nö naplója 147
Oppel, Robert 189
Opstandelsen (2010) 166, 237
Opus 66 165
O'Quinn, Kerry 88, 124, 125, 205
O'Quinn, Terry 206
O'Quinn Award 88, 105, 124, 125
Orasmaa, Mika 227
Orci, Roberto 204
The Ordeal see *Calvary* (2004)
Ordinary Man (2005) 171
Ordonefiez, Rodrigo 185
O'Rear, Jim 123
O'Regan, Stephen 214
Oretachi ni asu wa naissu see *Ain't No Tomorrow* (2009)
El orfanato see *The Orphanage* (2007)
Organik (2004 short film; dir: Morlet) 164
Organization Arte Audiovisual Alternativo 101
Orient Express Award 147–49
Orient Express/Casa Àsia Award 227–32
Oristrell, Joaquín 193
Orkut.com 32
Orlando (1992) 234
Ormsby, Alan 236
Orocklou, Rena viii, 48, 51, 99
O'Ross, Ed 210
Orphan (2009) 126, 249
The Orphanage (2007) 147, 163, 180
L'orphelinat see *The Orphanage* (2007)
Orr, Alex 123
Orr, Gregory 242
Ortiz, Bryan 122, 176
Ortiz, Fernando 243
Ortiz, George L. 110
Ortiz, Isidro 149, 158, 164
Os anjos do meio da praça 131
Os Canibais 235
Oscar (Academy Award) 1, 9, 54, 56, 59, 203, 253n6, 254n7
Oscuro/Iluminado 203
Oshii, Mamoru 151, 165, 193, 228, 229, 231
Osment, Haley Joel 139, 207, 208
Ospina, Luis 235
O'Steen, Damon 176
Osterman, Matt 122
Osunsanmi, Olatunde 225
Den osynlige see *The Invisible* (2002)
Otani, Kiyohide 251
The Other (1972 feature) 237
The Other Half (2006; dir: Nockles & Fawcett) 148

The Other Side (2006 feature; dir: Bishop) 225
The Other Side of the Bed see *El otro lado de la cama*
Other Worlds (short film) 172
The Others (2001) 139, 207
Otomo, Katsuhiro 171, 231
El otro lado de la cama 149
Otstupnik see *The Apostate* (1987)
Ott, Jonas 131
Ottman, John 205, 209
Otto, Rick 218
O2 (2009 short film) 162
Ou, Serge 123, 190
Ouija Board (year?) 192
"Our Skull Island Odyssey" (article) 198
Ousdal, Mads 155
Out of a Forest 174, 179
Out of Print (2007 short film; dir: Young) 247
Outcast (2010) 166, 188
The Outcasts (1982) 154
The Outer Limits (1995–2002 TV series) 209
Outer Space (2009 short film) 248
Outerworld (feature) 221
Les Outils 142
Outland (1981) 212
Outside In (2006 short film) 173
Outside the Lines (unproduced script) 226
The Outsider (Lovecraft short story) 168
Outsource 136, 214
Ouvert 24/7 174
Over My Dead Body (1995, aka *Nur über meine Leiche*) 128, 165
De Overkant 136, 180
Ovo see *Oeufs* (1994)
Owen, Peter 207
Owen, Rena 152
Owensby, Earl 124
Owl's Castle (1999, aka *Owl's Castle* and *Fukuro no shiro*) 194
Ozon, François 232

P (2005 feature) 248
Paccou, Marie 233
Pacino, Al 139
The Pack (2010 feature, aka *La meute*; dir: Richard) 188, 217
The Pack (year?) 166
Pack of Pain 157
Packard, Damon 55, 241
Paco and the Magic Book 143
Le Pacte des loups see *Brotherhood of the Wolf*
El pacto de los lobos see *Brotherhood of the Wolf*
Padilla, Roger 229, 230
Pados, Gyula 232
Padrissa, Carles 149, 164
Paes, João 235
Page, Amy Jean 221
Paim, André 130
The Painter of Skies (aka *O Pintor de Ceos*) 241
Paiva, William 146
Pak, Greg 130, 175, 193, 223, 250
Pak, Hueng-Shik see Park, Heung-shik
Pakis, Gregory 178
Pal, George see George Pal Memorial Award
Palabras encadenadas see *Killing Words*
The Palace (unproduced script) 217

Palacín, Marta 229
Palacios, Víctor 133
Palan, Dal see Dalpalan
Palazzo Massacre 124
Palcy, Euzhan 128
Palermo Shooting 147
Pálfi, György 148
Palillo, Ron 162
Palinkas, Megan 177
The Palladium (in Worcester, MA) 114
palm leaves see laurel leaf logos
Palmer, Betsy 244, 254n6
Palmer, Bill 188
Palmer, Jeffrey Blake 168
Palomar, Raul 177
Palud, Xavier 171, 194
Pâmanento Nobara see *Permanent Nobara* (2010)
Panayotopoulos, Demetri 243
Pandolfi, Vincenzo 167
Pandorum 237
Panettiere, Hayden 205, 216
Pang, Danny 148
Pang, Ho Cheung 148, 187
Pang, Oxide 148
Panic Attack! see *Ataque de pánico!* (2009 short film)
Pánico en el Transiberiano see *Horror Express* (1972)
Panique au village see *A Town Called Panic*
Panna a netvor see *Beauty and the Beast* (1981)
Panorama: Seeking Voïvod 143
Pan's Labyrinth (aka *El laberinto del fauno*) 133, 148, 169, 186, 198, 205, 216, 239
Panter, Eric 104
La pantera negra (2010, aka *The Black Panther*) 184, 185
Papá Wrestling 168, 174, 186
Papamichael, Phedon 163
Paper Dolls (2007) 162, 219
Paper or Plastic? (short film; dir: Horobin) 226
Paper Shepherd 135
Paperhouse 128, 153
Papic, Krsto 154
Papier Hier 136
Papillons noirs 143
Paprika (2006) 148
Paquette, Benjamin 159
Paquin, Anna 215
Para-Normal 136, 172
Parade (stage production) 204
Paradigm, Seppuku 227
Paradise Road (year?) 221
Paraffin 158
Paramount 19
Paramount Home Entertainment 195
Paranoia Horror Film Festival 13, 113, 191, 253n11
Paranormal Activity 19, 50, 80, 217
Paranormal Drug Dealer see *Frank DanCoolo: Paranormal Drug Dealer*
Paraschiv, Catalin 184
The Parasite Murders see *They Came from Within* (1975)
Parasitic (2010) 161
Parasomnia 76
Parello, Chuck 232
Parés, Pablo 129, 185
Parigi, Robert 164
Parisot, Dean 127, 169, 171

Park, Chan-wook 126, 143, 147, 148, 149, 229, 231
Park, Heung-shik (aka Park Heung-Sik, aka Pak Hueng-Shik) 149, 250
Park, Jae-hong 193
Park, Jin-hie 143
Park, Ki-hyeong 149
Park, Linkin 216
Park, Nick 202
Park, Scott 172, 188
Parker, Christine 167
Parker, Jackie 124
Parker, Nathan 169, 228
Parkinson, Andrew 161
Parkpoom, Wongpoom 143, 145, 164, 217
Parks, Stan 207, 209
Parle, Michael 177
Party (1997 short film; dir: Uchiumi or Utusmi?) 251
Pasdar, Adrian 204
Pasión lejana (1986, aka *Més enllà de la passió*) 235
The Passing (2011 feature; sic) 173, 225
The Passion of Darkly Noon 151–52, 233
Passion to the Max 173
Passmore, Greg 122
Passmore, Jeremy 193
Pastor, Jordi 229
Patar, Vincent 155, 228
The Path of Torment 247
Pathfinder (1987, aka *Ofelas*) 252
Pathos (2009 short film; dir: Cabella, Ercole, Prati) 179
Patrick (1978 feature; dir: Franklin) 236
Patrick, Robert 208
Patterson, Casey 115
Patti, John Patrick 177
Pattinson, Robert 215, 216
A Paucity of Flying Dreams 128
Paul, Aaron 204
Paul, Michael 191
Paulin, Brian 196
Pavlicic, Pavao 154
Paween, Purikitpanya 143
Pawns of Paradise 124
Paxton, Bill 139, 211
Payne, Alexander 148
PayPal 17
Payson, John 251
Pazt, Michael 130
Peak, Tulé 228
Pearce, Oliver 167
The Pearce Sisters 180, 201, 229
Pearl, Dorothy J. 212
Pearl Harbor II: Pearlmageddon 202
Pearson, Barry 236
Pebler, Luke 125
Pedersen, Aaron 177
Pee Shy 136
Peekers 123, 134, 219
Pegg, Simon 125, 138
Pehme, Morgan 156
Peirse, Sarah 150
Pejo, Robert-Adrian 178
Peli, Oren 19
Pelikan, Lisa 236
Pelletier, Gabriel 128
Pelt 124
Peltonen, Lucas 252
Peluca, DJ 185
Penning, Tjebbo 151, 152
Penningroth, Phil 226
Penny (2005 short film) 178

Penny Dreadful (short film; year?) 220
Penny Dreadful (2005 short film; dir: Norton) 173, 225, 244
Penny Dreadful (2006 feature; dir: Brandes) 225
Penny Dreadful (TV horror hostess) *see* Dreadful, Penny
Penpusher see Gratte-Papier
The People Under the Stairs 128, 141
Peoples, David 170
Perdita Durango 141
Pereira, Dominic 243
Perez, Vincent 39
Perfect Blue (1997; dir: Kon) 151
Perfect Sec-illusion 225
Perfect Strangers (2003; dir: Preston) 149
The Perfect Victim 224
Peridar, Jan 244
Peri'l (2006 short film) 167
The Periwig-Maker 150, 194, 202
Perkins, Emily 138
Perlman, Ron 138
Permanent Nobara (2010, aka *Pâmanento Nobara*) 192
Perrier, Max 143
Persecution (1975) 236
Personne (music video) 165
Personne n'est parfait 182
Pervula 167
Pessoa, Regina 150
Pest (animation) 222
Peter-Kaiser, Eric 244
Peter Pan (2003) 206
Peterson, Bob 249
Peterson, Dale 122
Peterson, Rich vii, 112
Peteul, Mathieu 131, 195, 247
Le Petit Dragon see The Little Dragon
La Petite Mort (2010 short film; dir: Gallasch) 184
Petkau, Evan 248
Petke, Adam 122
Petrie, Lance 178
Petty, J.T. 245
Peur(s) du noir see Fear(s) of the Dark (2007)
Pevney, Joseph 170
Pfister, Wally 249
Phantasm (1979) 125
Phantasm III 140
The Phantom of the Opera (1925) 237
The Phantom of the Opera (2004) 206
Phase 7 (2011, aka *Fase 7*) 220
Phasma Ex Machina 122
Phillips, Erica Edell 210
Phobia (2008) *see 4bia*
Phoenix (short film; dir: Bordelon?) 222
Phoenix Fear Film Festival 113, 191–92
Phoenix Film Festival 111
Phoenix International Horror and Sci-Fi Film Festival 113
The Phoenix Lights (feature) 173
Photographing Fairies 151, 165, 184
The Piano Tuner of Earthquakes 230
Piccirilli, Michael 177
Piccoli fuochi 128
Pichel, Irving 169
Pickett, Bobby "Boris" 199
Pickman's Muse 168
Picnic at Hanging Rock 79
The Picture of Dorian Gray (1945) 169
Pieces (1982) 80
Piedrahita, Luis 147

The Pier Theatre (in Bournemouth, UK) 117
Piestrak, Marek 167
Pig (2010) 128, 167, 202
Pig Hunt 143
Pig Tale 172
Pigeon: Impossible 158
Pigott-Smith, Tim 150
Pike, David vii, 49, 104
Pike, Kevin 211
Pike, Nicholas 235
Pilegaard, Pil (aka Jens Pilgaard) 159, 160
Pillow, Keith 243
The Pillow Book 233
Pin Up (2009 short film) 228
Pinarelo, Jorge 129
Pine, Chris 216
Pinheiro, Sergio 244
Pinkett, Jada 140
Pinney, Clay 208, 209
Pintaldi, Adriano 100
Pinto, Elisabeth 190
O Pintor de Ceos see The Painter of Skies
Pintu terlarang see The Forbidden Door
Piquer, Yann 232
Pirates of the Caribbean: At World's End 204
Pirates of the Caribbean: Dead Man's Chest 205, 216, 217, 239
Pirates of the Caribbean: The Curse of the Black Pearl 240
Pires, Pedro 133
Pisces, Arise! 219
Piscis 129
The Pit and the Pendulum (Canadian animated short film) 173
The Pit and the Pendulum (1991 feature) 141
The Pitch (2001 short film; dir: Edgerton) 193
Pitof 150, 232
Pitstra, Alex 137
Pitt, Brad 209
Pittsburgh Horror Film Festival 113
Pivot (short film; year?) 179
Pixar Animation Studios 133
Pixels (2010 short film; dir: Jean) 201, 248
The Place Promised in Our Early Days 145
Plague (1979, aka *M-3: The Gemini Strain*) 236
Plaguers 220
Plagues and Pleasures on the Salton Sea 178
The Planet (2006; dir: Stirton) 158
Plano Detalle 186
Plantation (unproduced script) 171
Plante, Marshall 242
Plastic (short film) 215
Plastic (short film; dir: Davis) 181, 194
Platt, Emily 191
Play (2010 short film; dir: Kaplan) 192
Playing Truant 160
Playstation 165
Playtime (short film; year?) 219
Plaza, Carlos J. viii, 103, 179–82
Plaza, Paco 88, 143, 144, 147, 148, 163, 170, 228, 229, 232
Plea for Peace (film festival) 13
Pleasants, Ben 77, 254n2
Pleasantville (1998) 208

The Pledge (documentary) 135
Plengpanich, Chatchai 248
Plof 166
Plummer, Amanda 209
Plutón 184
Plympton, Bill 129, 143, 147, 148, 151, 233, 234
Podell, Ron 174, 240, 243, 244
Podgursky, Peter 192, 241
Poelvoorde, Benoît 234, 251
The Pointsman see De wisselwachter
Poiraud, Didier 152
Poiraud, Thierry 152
Poison (1991) 153
Polhemus, Tyler 196, 218
Pollack, Benjamin 224
Pollack, Jeremy 225
Polo, Teri 191
Polikar, Claude Samard 131
Polson, John 150, 250
Poltera, Frances 159
Poltergeist (1982) 211, 212
Polydeus 10, 131
Pompa, Dea 229
Poncela, Eusebio 154
Pongsuwan, Thanakorn 143
Pontypool 192
Poodle see Caniche
Poole, Mark 93
Pop & Me 250
Popatopolis 124, 131
Pope, Dick 234
Pope Leo Electrocutes an Elephant 159
Popescu, Stefan 96, 177
Popo 136
Poppe, Erik 150
Poppi, Christian 177
Pornstar Pets 178
Porque hay cosas que nunca se olvidan see Because There Are Things You Never Forget
Pors, Thomas 230
Portal (feature; 2009?) 220
Porter, Marianne 130, 191
Porter, Matt 226
Portes, Emilio 185
Portillo, Arturo 188
Portman, Natalie 133, 205
Portsmouth Scream 118, 119
Pose, Sebastian 202
Posey, Parker 39, 139
Possessed (1999, aka *Besat*) 127, 183
Possessed (2010, aka *Bulshinjiok*) 163
Possession (1981) 154
The Possession of Virginia see Satan's Sabbath (1972)
Postcards from the Future (2007 short film) 225
Potter, Sally 234
Povestea dragostei 236
Povinelli, Mark 222
Powder (1995) 166
Powell, Sandy 209
Poza Cisza 185
Pozo, Ana 238
Pozo, Cristián 203
PR.com 34
Prachya, Pinkaew 192, 231
Prado, Leticia 224
Praino, Pablo 185
Pratten, Robert 159
The Praying Mantis see Black Widow (2001)
Predation 243

Predator (1987 feature) 211
Predator (2005 short film) 222
Prehn, Stefan 202
Prelude to Hell see *Harry Doright's Prelude to Hell*
Prequel Apology Syndrome 157
The Presence (feature) 176
President's Day (2010) 174
President's Memorial Award 213
Pressman, Edward R. 213
Pretty-Scary 13–15, 105, 113, 117, 224
Pretty Scary Award 224
Pretty Scary Blood Bath Film Festival 105, 113
Prévost, Jonathan 248
Prey see *Dreamtime's Over* (2009)
Price, Jeffrey 170
Price, Marc 92, 129, 237
Price, Mark 223
The Price of Milk 194
Price, Robert 168
Price, Vincent 154, 213–14, 235, 237
The Price of Milk 150
The Price to Pay 135
Pride (2009 feature, aka *Puraido*; dir: Kaneko) 192
Pride & Prejudice with Zombies (book) 48
Primer 215
Primevil (2007 short film; dir: Turner) 244
Prince, Victoria 249
Princess (2006 feature; dir: Morgenthaler) 180, 181, 230
The Princess Bride 170, 211
Princess Caraboo 251
Princess Mononoke 207
Prior, David 122, 131, 168, 196
Prior, D. Kerry 125, 131, 155, 188, 190, 247
Private Eye (2009, aka *Geu-rim-ja sal-ín*) 155
Privett, Jonathan 150
Le Prix à payer see *The Price to Pay*
PRlog.com 34
PRnewswire.com 34
Probed 172
The Procedure 135, 244
Processo Andrómeda 154
Le processus 232
Prochaska, Andreas 127, 185
Prochorowski, Konstantin 150
The Prodigal Son (1995 short film; dir: Mitchell) 202
Professional Courtesy (2003 short film; dir: Price) 223
"Professional Human Toilet" (short story) 11
The Professor's Daughter 125
Profiler (TV series) 165
Profondo rosso see *Deep Red* (1975)
Project: Adam 244
Project Gamma 160
Project MorningStar 238
Prom Night (2008) 138
Prombies! 200, 252
Promenons-nous dans les bois see *Deep in the Woods* (2000)
The Promethean (short film) 173
The Prometheus Project see *The Frankenstein Syndrome*
The Promise (2005) 148
Promise of August 251
Pronath, James 167

The Prophecy (1995) 140
El propietario (2008) 146
Province of Twilight 157
Proyas, Alex 126, 127, 139, 171, 252
Pruett, David E. 29–31, 108
Prusak, Derek 243
PRweb.com 34
Psychiatric Channel 159
Psychic Experiment see *Walking Distance*
Psycho (1960) 5, 197, 204
Psycho Hillbilly Cabin Massacre 124, 125, 172
Psycho Killer Attack! 167
Psychotic Tendencies (DVD set) 40
Pu-239 161
Puchon International Fantastic Film Festival 102, 192–94
Puerto Rico Horror Film Fest 113
Pugh, Mark 177
Pujszo, Mariusz 151
Pulido, Brian 196
Pullin, Gary 197
Pulp Fiction (1994) 209
Pulp Fiction Art: Cheap Thrills and Painted Nightmares 136, 172
Pulp Science Fiction 174
Pulse (2001 feature, aka *Kairo*) 232
Pummell, Simon 152
Pumpkin Hell 190
Pumzi 245
Puphedz: The Tattle-Tale Heart 218
Puppet (animation film) 122, 136
Pups (1999 feature) 250
Pura sangre see *Pure Blood* (1982)
Pure Blood (1982, aka *Pura sangre*) 235
Pure Hearts (2006, aka *Rene hjerter*) 148
Purely Belter 150
Purgatory (2006 short film; dir: Chow) 159
The Purple Rose of Cairo 213
Push Comes to Shove 234
Pusher 3 144
Putovanje see *A Journey* (1972)
Puzo, Mario 170
Puzzlehead 125, 156, 214
Pyun, Albert 123, 128

La Qualité du silence (novel) 165
Quand on est amoureux c'est merveilleux see *A Wonderful Life* (1999)
Quantum Creation FX 217
Quantum of Solace 249
Quarantine (2008) 195
QuatreCon Film Festival 113
Quay, Stephen 152, 153, 232, 235
Quay, Timothy 152, 153, 232, 235
Les Quebecers contre les Zombies 2 142
Quest (1996 short film; dir: Montgomery) 233
The Quick and the Undead 245
The Quiet Family see *Choyonghan kajok*
A Quiet Love see *Die blaue Grenze*
Quigley, Linnea 140
Quiflez, Lluís 225
Quills 150
Quinn, Joanna 230
Quintanilla, Antonio 184
Quintenz, Jennifer 225
Quiroga, Elio 148, 233
Quiropterofobia 131
Quit 122
Quitley, Frank 215
Qureshi, Faisal A. 168

R-Squared Film Distribution Contest 112
Rabbid EFX 241
Rabbit (2005 short film; dir: Wrake) 144
Rabbit (unproduced script) 190
Rabid (1977 feature, aka *Rage*) 236
Das Rad see *Rocks*
Radclyffe, Curtis 151
Radenkovic, Pedja 134
Radiación (short film) 184
Radioactive Dreams 128
La ragazza del lago see *The Girl by the Lake*
Rage see *Rabid* (1977)
Rage (feature; year?) 171, 219
Rahtree Returns (aka *Buppah Rahtree Phase 2: Rahtree Returns*) 193
Raiders of the Lost Ark 126, 170, 212
Raimi, Sam 127, 128, 141, 152, 206, 213, 234, 236
Rail (short film; dir: Myung) 192
Railsback, Steve 220, 232
Rain (2001; dir: Jeffs) 150
The Rain (2001 short film; dir: Beatty) 150
Rain un Thunder (music video) 134
Rainbow's End (2005 short film; dir: Mancini) 222
Rajanarangsee, Phan 193
Raleigh, Justin 138
Raleigh Studios 44, 71, 72, 254n1
Ralston, Harry 161
Ralston, Ken 210, 211, 234
Ramalho, Dennison 188
Rambaldi, Carlo 212
Ramchandani, Mohit 200
Ramírez (2008 feature) 228
Ramirez, Rosie 221
Rammbock: Berlin Undead (aka *Rammbock*) 184, 214
Rampling, Charlotte 153
Rampo 152
Ramsden, Gina 189
Ramsey, Anne 211
Ramsey, Joy 221
Randall, Chris 116
Randall, Jasper 244
Randazzo, Joe 162, 171, 191, 225, 243
Rangressions 125
Rankin, Kyle 187
Ransdell, Bo 244
Rapture (1980) 154
Rapturious (2007) 189
Rare Exports: A Christmas Tale (2010 feature, aka *Rare Exports*) 121, 214, 227
Rare Exports Inc. (2003 short film) 182, 201
Raksin, David 213
Rasguno 249
Rasovsky, Yuri 186
The Raspberry Reich 178
The Rat see *Le Rat* (2001)
Le Rat (2001; dir: Ali & Bonilauri) 160
Ratatouille 204
Ratliff, George 229
Rats in the Wall 168
Rattus Pistofficus 136
Ratziel, Simon 241, 242
Raul, Perez Gamez see Gamez, Raul P.
Ravaglioli, Alberto vii, 100, 141
The Raven (short film) 129
Raven Gets a Life 136
Ravenna (unproduced script) 219

Ravenna Nightmare Film Festival viii, 100, 180–82, 194–95
Ravenous 141
Raver, Lorna 138
Ray, Christian 230
Ray Bradbury Award 112, 113, 186
Ray Bradbury's Chrysalis 172
Ray Harryhausen Collectible DVD Set 197
Ray Harryhausen: The Early Years Collection (DVD) 206
Raymond (2007 short film) 156, 175, 180
Raymond, Michael 218, 222, 225
Razor Blade Smile 165, 176
Razor Eaters 179, 225
Razor Reel Fantastic Film Festival viii, **25**–26, 32, 34, 47–48, 73, 80, 87–88, 93, 96, 195
Razor Sharp (year?) 162, 245
Razzano, Brian 167
Re-Animator 141, 235
Re-Cycle 148
Rea, Patrick 134, 162, 171, 191
Rea, Stephen 233
Read, Cristina 159
Ready Teddy 125
Reality Check (short film; 2006?) 173
Reaper Award 110, 113, 195
Reardon, Jim 169, 186
Rebello, Ricardo (aka Ric) 196
Rebert, Dan 205
Rebolledo, José Ángel 153
[Rec] 50, 127, 143, 144, 147, 148, 163, 170, 195, 229
[Rec] 2 88, 142, 195, 228
Recently Deceased 173, 245
Recha, Marc 233
Recio, Lorenzo 165
Recollection (2010 short film; dir: D'Alessandro) 223
Reconcilers 160
Recortadas 129, 131
Recreator 242
Rector, Jeff 219
Red (2010 feature) 228
Red (2010 short film) 124
Red, Axelle 124
Red Balloon (2010 short film, dir: Macé & Wajsbrot) 196
Red Dragon 139
Red Glibb Award 248
Red Harvest 244
Red Lines 160
Red Nights (2009, aka *Les Nuits rouges du bourreau de jade*) 227
Red Planet Blues 214
Red Princess Blues (2010 short film) 157, 223
The Red Hot Chili Peppers 138
The Red Hours 190
Red Shirt Pictures 195
Red Victoria 126
Red, White & Blue **25**, 141, 142, 174, 179, 194
Reda, Dave 191
Redfield, Mark 160, 222, 223, 226
Redknap, Geoff 238
Redrat, la rata retobada 130, 145
The Redsin Tower 161
"Redux" (*The X-Files* TV episode) 165
Reed, Sharon viii, 21–24, 241, 253n9
Reel Energy Entertainment 117
Reel Zombies 190
Reeves, Dale 178

Reeves, Matt 205
The Reflecting Skin 234
Reflections 135
Refn, Nicolas Winding 144, 147, 149, 187
Refoua, John 249
Regalbuto, Michael 224
Regression (2010 short film; dir: Belcher & Dorman) 237
Regret (short film; dir: Sudac) 244
Le Régulateur 231
Reign in Darkness 178
Reign of Fire (aka *El imperio del fuego*) 231
Reign: The Conqueror (1997 TV series, aka *Alexander Senki*) 194
La reina vampira 247
Reincarnate (unproduced script) 225
Reiner, Rob 170
Reininghaus, Daniel 123, 130, 174
Reisman, Jesse Kyle 224
Reiss, Addie 136
Rejected (2000 short film) 194
Rekindled 125, 224
Relic of Cthulhu 168; see also *The Last Lovecraft: Relic of Cthulhu*
Religulous 228
Remake (unproduced script) 189
Remembering Nigel 178
Remote (2010 short film; dir: Roussel) 191
Renaissance (2006 feature) 148, 181, 201
Renberg, Björn 202
Renders, Pierre-Paul 127, 164
Rene hjerter see *Pure Hearts*
Renegade (2004, aka *Blueberry*) 175
Renna, John 130
Repo Man (1984) 211
Repo! The Genetic Opera 123, 124, 143, 246
Repossessed (dir: Murphy) 225
Repossessed (2002 short film; dir: Coven) 218
Requiem (2001; dir: Morgan & Kirby) 160
Requiem (2006 feature; dir: Schmid) 230
Requiem for a Dream 139
Reservoir Dogs 234, 252
Reset (unproduced script) 219
Resident Evil (video game) 165
Resident Evil Code: Veronica (video game) 165
Resident Evil: Extinction 216
Resident Evil 4 (video game) 239
Resinaro, Fabio 159, 229
Respire (2005, aka *Hu xi*) 230
Rest Room (dir: Murakami) 251
Restaurando a Héctor 229
The Restless 127
The Resurrected (1992) 140
Resurrecting the Street Walker 92
The Resurrectionist (2005 short film; dir: Bell) 173, 221
Retard 226
Retro Hugo Award 111
Retroactive (1997) 128, 176
Retrograde 197
Retruc 130
Return (1986 feature; dir: Silver) 235
The Return of Captain Invincible 235
Return of the Jedi see *Star Wars, Episode VI: Return of the Jedi*
Return of the Living Dead III 140, 166, 171

The Return of the Milkman 131
Reumont, François 175
Revel, Mark 231
Revelation Nine 172
"Revelations" (*Battlestar Galactica* TV episode) 132
Revelation (2009 short film; dir: Graver) 162
La Révélation (2008 short film; dir: Diderot) 131
Revell, Graeme 140
The Revenant (2009; dir: Prior) 125, 131, 155, 188, 190, 217, 246, 247, 252
The Revenant (year?) 162
Les Revenants see *They Came Back* (2004 feature)
Revenge Smells Like Peppermint 200
Reverend Billy and the Church of Stop Shopping 178
Reversal (short film; dir: Shaink Jr.) 191
Los Revoltosos—Episodio 2: Cafest 184
Rex Havoc and the Ass-Kicker's of the Fantastic 157
El rey de la montaña see *King of the Hill* (2007)
Reynolds, Ryan 216
Reynolds, Scott 151, 194, 233
Rezazadeh, Amir 152
Rezende, Guilherme 132
Reznick, Graham 123
Rhode Island International Film Festival 30, 114
Rhode Island International Horror Film Festival see FLICKERS
Rhodes, Gary Don 199
Rhodes, Peter 167
Riba, Marc 227
Ribé, Montse 138
Ribeiro, José Miguel 149, 150, 166
Riblje oko see *Fisheye*
Ricci, Christina 141, 208, 209
Rice Game (dir: Kobayashi) 252
Richard, Franck 188
Richards, Julian 130, 149, 151, 160, 185, 189, 196
Richards, Paige 248
Richardson, John 208
Richter, Jochen 236
Riddlebaugh, John 243
Ridley, Philip 146, 151
Riedinger, Juan 199
Riedl, Marco J. 245
Rift (2009 short film; dir: Huang) 224
Riga International Fantasy Film Festival 100
Rigby Transmedia 95
Riggs, Ransom 125
Right at Your Door 144
The Right Facing Left 252
Riley, Jeff 214
The Ring (2002 film) 42, 139, 207, 240
Ring of Fire (2000 short film; dir: Hykade) 232
Ringu 127, 232
Ringwood, Bob 211, 212
Rintoul, Ian 161
Rio Fantastic Film Festival 96
RIOFAN see Rio Fantastic Film Festival
R.I.P. (2003 short film; dir: Doense) 182, 218
R.I.P., Rest in Pieces: A Portrait of Joe Coleman 178
Riparetti, Tony 123
Ripoll, María 233

Ripper (unproduced script) 162, 171, 191, 243
Ripple, Joe 111
Ripstein, Daniel Birman **52**
The Rise and Fall of the Legendary Anglobilly Feverson 183
Rise of the Appliances 191, 224
The Rising Dead 200
Ritam zlocina 154
Ritchie, Jeff 218
Ritchie, Michael 251
Rivera, Alex 187
Rivera, Christian 184
Rivera, Javier C. 134
Rivers, Christian 205
Rivkin, Stephen E. 249
Road Kill (2005 short film; dir: Mardini) 189, 221
Road Kill (2010 feature; aka *Road Train*) 177
Road to Oblivion 174
Road to Perdition 207
Road Train see *Road Kill* (2010)
Roadkill (2003 short film; dir: Annokkee) 182
Roadkill (student film; year?) 126
Roadside Attractions (2004 short film; dir: Roy) 225, 226
Rob Zombie Film Competition 110
Rob Zombie's Halloween see *Halloween* (2007)
Robb, Sean K. 130
Robbes, F. 154
Robbins, Tim 232
Robertson, Carl 224
Robertson, Graham 214
Robinson, Ann 222
Robinson, Ben 242
Robinson, Jay 213
Robles, German 198
Robocop (1987) 211, 235
RoboGeisha 130, 245, 246
Robot Rumpus 226
Robot Stories 125, 130, 175, 193, 215, 219, 223, 250
Robotech: Shadow Chronicles 173
Robots Are Blue 173
Robson, Aaron 222
Robson, Paul 190
Rocco, Vito 193
Rocher, Benjamin 141, 146, 163
Rochon, Debbie 123, 130
Rock, Ben 168, 224, 243
Rock and Shock Film Festival 114
Rockelman, Ernie 244
The Rocketeer 210
Rockfish 222
The Rocking Horse (2008 short film) 243
Rockoff, Adam 254n5
Rocks (2003 short film, aka *Das Rad*) 175
Rockwell, Sam 227, 229, 233, 249
Rocteur, Pascal 194
Roddenberry, Gene 170, 213, 214
Roderick, Nicole 156, 189
Rodgers, Aggie Guerard 211
Rodis-Jamero, Nilo 211
Rodnunsky, Serge 158
Rodriguez, Ignacio 202
Rodriguez, Juan 242
Rodriguez, Robert 171, 251
Rodríguez, Zoilo 113
Roebuck, Daniel 124, 198
Roecker, John 145
Roeg, Nicholas 141

Roffman, Adam 30
Rógairí 156
Rogers, Sam 159, 230
Roggé, Ron 221
Rogue Cinema 124
Rogue River (2010) 199, 200
Rohtenburg see *Grimm Love*
Roisin, François 175
Rojas, Esteban 203
Rojo en el Bosque Sangriento 185
Rojo Red 144, 147, 156
Rojo sangre (2004) 248
Rokoff, Marc 122
Rokotov, Sergey 147
Roll Out, Cowboy 122
Rollerball (1975) 213
Rollyson, James 242
Roman (2006) 156
Román, Raúl 235
Romance .38 132
Roman's Bride 191
Romer, Jean-Claude 235
Romero, Erasmo, III 242
Romero, George A. 140, 141, 153, 163, 189, 199, 235, 239
Romero, J. O. 168
Romero, Mapi 129
Romijn-Stamos, Rebecca (aka Rebecca Romijn) 207
Ronan, Saoirse 203, 249
Rondo Hatton Classic Horror Award viii, 114, 196–99
Rony, Philippe 153
Rooker, Michael 153
The Room (2007 short film) 134
Room Service (unproduced script) 240
Room to Breathe 173, 221
A Room Without Wind 251
Rooms for Tourists (aka *Habitaciones para turistas*) 248
Ropp, Greg vii, 28, 31–32, 39, 48–49, 53, 65–66, 72–73, 75–76, 79–80, 91–94, 108
Rose (short film; year?) 245
Rose, Andrew vii, 105
Rose, Bernard 128, 153
Rose, Charlie 83
Rose, Felissa 254n6
Rose, Graham 160
Rose, Jenn 188
Rose, Leah 220
Rose, Matt 138, 206, 226
Rose, Penny 206
Rose, Timo 92, 248
Rose Marie's Egg 240
Roseberry 7470 177
Rosebud Entertainment 99
Roseingrave, Mike 242
Rosemary's Baby 49
Rosenbaum, Michael 207
Rosenbaum, Stephen 203
Rosenberg, Louis 172, 224
Rosencrantz & Guildenstern Are Dead 153
Roses (unproduced script) 134
Rosewood Avenue 223
Rosfeld 135
Ross, Gary 210
Ross, Jeff vii, 104
Ross, Katharine 213
Ross, Niramon 217
Rossellini, Isabella 210
Rossi, Leo 244
Rossum, Emmy 206

Rotberg, Dana 152
Roth, Ed "Big Daddy" 198
Roth, Eli 137, 138
Roth, Eric 245
Roth, Matthew 171
Rothmann, Conrad 236
Rotolante, Ann 123
Rotztein, Sebastián 131
Rough Cut (2008; dir: Jang) 143
Rough Magic (1995 feature) 233
Round the Moons Between Earth and Sea 151
Rourke, Mickey 205, 215
Roush, Mike 143
Routh, Brandon 205, 216
Roux, Jean-Michel 176
Rovira, Denis 196
Rowan, Blair 123, 146
Rowe, Sue 150
Rowsell, Stuart 190
Roy, C.J. 225, 226
Roy, Gonçal Perales 227, 228
Roy, Jean-Marc E. 143
Roy, Niklas 150
Royall, Adam 177
Royo, Nacho 241
Rozon, Patrick 144
Rózsa, Miklós 212
R.S.V.P. (2002 feature) 218
R2 (distributor) 93
Rubber (short film) 159
Rubber (2010 feature) 142, 155, 227
Rubber (year?) 246
Ruben, Joseph 128
Rubin, Jeremy 223
Rubinchik, Valeri 128
Rubinstein, Joseph 241
Rubinstein, Zelda 212
Rudå, Morten 177
Rude, Dick 122
Rudenberg, Mathew 243, 244
Rudnicki, Lee 244
Rue Morgue (magazine) 197, 198
Rue Morgue Festival of Fear viii, 97, 109
Rue Morgue Radio 197
Rueda, Belén 147
Ruehl, Mercedes 210
Rugna, Demián 129, 241
Rule Number One (2008, aka *Dai yat gaai*; dir: Tong) 192
Rule of Three 143, 224
Rumley, Simon 142, 156, 174, 194, 229, 230, 248
The Run (2008 feature) 177
Run! Bitch Run! 122, 162
Run Monkey Run 161
Run! Yamazaki! Run! 250
Runeborg, Johannes 141
The Running Man 211
The Runt (2006 short film) 144
Rupe, Shade vii, 6, 58, 108
Ruppersberg, Sonja 102
Rusko, Milan 190
Ruspoli, Bart 126
Russell, Betsy 137
Russell, Chuck 153
Russell, George H. 167
Russell, Kurt 214
Russo, David 142
La ruta natural 231
Rutland, Peter 241
Ryan (2004 short film; dir: Landreth) 193

Ryan, Blanchard 206
Ryan, Dana J. 189
Ryan, Gail 207
Ryan, Jeri 208
Ryan, Kit 189
Ryan, Robby 156
Ryan, Scott 178
Rybakov, Vyacheslav 146
Ryczko, Piotr 185
Ryder, Winona 216
Rydyr, Antoinette 190
Rygiel, Jim 206
Rymer, Michael 169
Ryoo, Seung-wan 144, 145, 193
Ryu, Deok-hwan 144
Ryu, Hoon 192

S&Man 245
Sa Ilalim ng cogon 130
Saat po long (2005 feature, aka Kill Zone) 187
Saba, Ken 124
Sable, Jérôme 155, 227
El sabor de la sandía see The Wayward Cloud (2005)
Sabrina (music video) 165
Sabrosura, Violín y Perico 129
Sabuncu, Yasmin 178
Sacchetti, Dardano 236
Sachs, William 128
Sackheim, Daniel 250
Sackhoff, Katee 206
Sacramento Horror Film Festival viii, 114, 199–200
The Sacred (2009) 21, 23, **89**, 174, 191, 241
Sacrifi nocturn (aka Sacrificio nocturno) 236
The Sacrifice (animated short film) 135
Sacrificio nocturno see Sacrifi nocturn
Sadistic City see Maohgai
Sadler, William 210
Sadness (2010 short film) 130
Safe in the House 226
Safe Passage (unproduced script) 225
SAG see Screen Actors Guild
SAG Award see Screen Actors Guild Award
Sagan, Carl 169
La Sagesse des crocodiles see The Wisdom of Crocodiles
Saine, Henry 122
St. Christophorus: Roadkill 123, 192, 227
Saint Martyrs of the Damned 148
Saitô, Hiroshi 232
Saitzyk, Robert 194
Sakaguchi, Tak 227
Sakveerakul, Chukiat 127, 144
Salad Days (2001 short film, aka Desaliñada) 193
Salazar, Abel 186
Saldana, Zoe 132, 203
Salem "Amateur" Horror Film Festival 114
Salem Independent Horror Film Festival 114
The Salesman (2006 short film) 173
Salis, Nicolas 148, 149
Saliva (2007 short film; dir: Filho) 229
Salmerón, Gustavo 193
Salty Horror Film Festival viii, 114, 200
Saluveer, Sten-Kristian vii, 98
Salva, Mike 123, 135
Salva, Victor 166

Salvage (2009 UK) 146, 155
Salvation (2007; dir: Steel) 163
Salwen, Hal 152
Samarasinghe, Duncan 190
Samir 234
Sampietro, Mercedes 232
Samuel (short film; dir: Fedele) 226
Samuel, Martin 204
Samurai Fiction 194, 232
San Antonio Convention Center 110
San Diego Black Film Festival 23
San Roman, Inaki 123
San Sebastián Horror and Fantasy Film Festival viii, 103, 179–82, 200–2
El Sanatorio 185
Sánchez, Eduardo 194
Sánchez, Sergio G. 150
Sanders, David 125, 214
Sandgren, Ake 252
The Sandman (2001) 161
Sandquist, Simon 188, 218
Sang froid (short film; dir: Levacher) 202
Sangre Award for Best FX 168
Sangre eterna see Eternal Blood
Sangster, Jimmy 213, 214
Sangue Frio (short film) 186
SanMartí, Anna 231
Sans dessein 143
Sans titre (i.e., Without Title or Untitled) 142
Santa Monica Public Library 6, 11–12, 14, 24, 63, 74, 77, 85
Santa Sangre 210
Santamaria, Alejandro Montes 100
Santi, Pier Luigi 188
Santiago Martínez, cazador de ovnis y alienígenas 168
Santiago Rojo Sangre see FIXION-SARS
Santos 156
Santos, Oskar 231
Santucci, Chris 130
Sanz, David 186
Sanz, Hugo 134
Sanz, Javier Yanez 238
Sanz, Josefina 129
Sanz, Salvador 130
Saori 58
Sapegin, Pjotr 194, 232
Sapere, Pablo vii, 95
Sapir, Esteban 127, 144, 187
Sara, Mia 209
Saraba hakobune see Farewell to the Ark (1984)
Sarah Connor Chronicles (TV series) 132
Sarasúa, Oier 230
Sargent, Alvin 206
Sargent, Joseph 128
Sarmiento, Fernando 129
Sarrio, David 160
Sasaki, Takashi 229
Sasanatieng, Wisit 145, 194, 250
Sasayaki see Moonlight Whispers (1999)
Sasich, Eli 218
Satan Hates You 134
Satan's Little Helper 194
Satan's Sabbath (1972, aka The Possession of Virginia) 236
Satayev, Akan 187
Sato, Shimako 251
Sato, Shinsuke 141
Sato, Tomoya 250
Sato, Yoshinao 251

Saturn Award 3, 5, 56, 103, 114, 203–14, 253n1
Saul, Anno 163
Saul's Pupils 160
Sauna (2008) 127, 163, 179
Saura, Carlos 150
Sauvé, Claudine 144
Savage, Fred 210
Savage, John 243
Savage, Mark 178
Savage, Wade K. 190
Savage Hunt of King Stakh 128
Savage Island (2005 feature) 189, 222, 223
Savan, Ori 161
Save the Green Planet! 127, 193
Saving Private Ryan 208
Savini, Anthony 242
Savini, Tom 189, 211, 254n6
Savoure le rouge (music video) 166
Savy, Louis 119
Saw 127, 148, 164, 201
Saw (film series) 48–49, 137
Saw II 138
Saw III 239
Saw V 216
Sawa, Devon 207
Sawako Decides 141
Sawbones (short film; dir: Palmer) 225
Say That You Love Me... (2005 short film; dir: Yasuda) 173, 221
Sayles, John 166, 235
Sbaraglia, Leonardo 217
The Scab (short film) 242
Scab a Smoke 178
Scanners (1981) 154, 212
Scare Fest viii, 114, 121
The Scare: The Mansion of Terror Documentary (aka The Scare) 134
Scare Zone 161, 243
Scarecrow Bones 239
Scarefest (segment of the Muskegon Film Festival) 245
Scarfe, Alan 156
Scarlet Diva 178
Scarlet, Nelli 176
Scars (magazine) 14
Scary (2007 short film, aka Schrik) 158, 180, 221
Scary Brains Horror Film Festival 95
Scary Larry (unproduced script) 226
Scary Monsters Magazine 198
Scavengers (unproduced script) 224
Scenes from an Endless War 178
Schaap, Andreas 143, 188
Schäffler, Steffen 150, 194, 202
Schamus, James 169, 186
Schattenkind 173
Schaufler, Ryan 220
Schausteins Final Film (2008, aka Schausteins letzter Film) 192
Schausteins letzter Film see Schausteins Final Film (2008)
Schechter, David 147
Schenkel, Carl 154, 235
Schenkman, Richard 146, 185, 203
Scherbarth, Eric 188
Schibinger, Natasia 247
Schie, Stian A. 124
Schieffer, Elizabeth 110, 137, 167
Schiele, Kevin 242
Schijn van de maan see Moonglow
Schizofredric 172, 215
Der Schlangemann 202

Schleisiek, Christian 158
Schlesinger, Michael 198
Schlockfest 96
Schmid, Daniel 235
Schmid, Hans-Christian 230
Schnaas, Andreas 92
Die Schneider Krankheit 129, 133, 179
Schneider's 2nd Stage 202
Schnibbe, Margie 178
Schoelen, Jill 235
Schoft 136
Schönfeld, Floris 136
Schopfer, Antonin 187
Schovitz, Joe 198
Schpaaa 150
Schrader, Paul 147
Schram, Ingrid 177
Schrik see *Scary* (2007)
Schrodinger's Biro 158
Schrodinger's Cat 161
Schuck, John 223
Schulman, J. Neil viii, 23–24, 71, 74–75, 253n10
Schulman, Tom 127, 251
Schultz, Timothy vii, 112
Schulze, Douglas 160
Schumacher, Joel 231
Schwarz, Jeffrey 196, 197
Schwentke, Robert 149, 175
The Sci-Fi Boys 198, 205
Sci-Fi-London Film Festival (aka London International Festival of Science Fiction and Fantastic Film) viii, 119, 215
Sciamma, Alberto 141
La Science des rêves see *The Science of Sleep* (2006)
Science+Fiction (film festival; aka Scienceplusfiction) 100, 179–82, 214
Science Fiction and Fantasy Writers of America 5, 112
Science Fiction Museum 114
Science Fiction + Fantasy Short Film Festival 114, 214–15
Science Fiction Short Film Festival 114
The Science of Sleep (2006 feature, aka *La ciencia del sueño*, aka *La Science des rêves*) 230
Scienceplusfiction see Science+Fiction
Scorned 167
Scott, Anthony see Scott, Tony
Scott, Darin 224
Scott, Jerome 167
Scott, Ridley 170, 212
Scott, Robert A. 197
Scott, Russell 225
Scott, Stephen 249
Scott, Tony (aka Anthony Scott) 237
Scott Pilgrim vs. the World 174
The Scout (1994 feature) 251
Scoutman 150
Scrapbook (2000?) 162
Scream (1996) 140, 165, 209
Scream 2 139, 140
Scream 3 139
Scream Award 3, 114–15, 215–17
Scream for Me (2000 short film) 189
Scream Machine 241
Scream Queen Award 114
scream queens 46, 48–49, 123
Scream Queens (sponsor) 14
Scream the Night see *Grité una noche*
Screamfest (Florida convention) 8, 253n1
Screamfest L.A. (film festival) 2, 6–8, 15, 19–20, 34, 58, 75, 115, 217–19, 253n1, 253n11
Screamin' Athens Horror Film Festival viii, 48, 51, 99–100s
Screaming Mad George 232
The Screaming Skull (2008 short film) 190
Screech of the Decapitated 221
Screen Actors Guild 5, 89
Screen Actors Guild Award 5, 63
The Screen Behind the Mirror 238
Screen Jewels Productions 116
Scribble (2004 short film) 173
Scrimm, Angus 140, 162
Sculpture (2009) 123, 134
Scum (2010?) 167
The Sea Monster! 202, 203
Sea of Dust 162, 196
Seaman, Peter S. 170
Séance (2006 feature; dir: Smith) 221
Seance (2009 short film; dir: Kaspařík) 134, 238
Searching for Haizmann 222
The Season (2008 feature) 134
Seaton, Aileen 208
Seaton, J.T. 248
Sebastian's Voodoo 124
Second Name (aka *El segundo nombre*) 183, 232
Second Sight (1994) 128
The Secret Adventures of Tom Thumb 152, 234, 251
Secret Life of Sarah Sheldon 163
The Secret of Roan Inish 166
Secret Waltz 251
Secretary (2002) 149
La Secte sans nom see *The Nameless* (1999)
Sedazzari, Paolo 159
See Grace Fly 149
See prang see *4bia*
See the Dead 123
Seed (2007 feature; dir: Boll) 189
Seekers (short film) 220
Seekers (unproduced script) 224
Seeking Wellness: Suffering Through Four Movements 177
Seementa, Decha (aka Decha Srimantra) 231
Seepage! see *Creature from the Hillbilly Lagoon* (2005)
Seethe (short film) 238
Segal, Louis 159
Segan, Noah 137
El segundo nombre see *Second Name*
Segura, Santiago 202
Seib, Phillip viii, 51, 112
Seidl, Ulrich 150
Seikilos and I (aka *Seikilos-san to Watashi*) 250
Seikilos-san to Watashi see *Seikilos and I*
Seimetz, Amy 155
Sekai wa kanojo no tame ni aru see *Be the World for Her*
Sekiguchi, Gen 145, 201
Sekten 150
Sekula, Andrzej 149
Sela, Jonathan 229
Selby, Hubert, Jr. 149
Self-Inflicted 135
Selick, Henry 249
Selko, Kenny 9, 110, 242, 244
Sell Out! 142
The Seller (short film; dir: Humphreys) 159
Sellers, Michael D. 242
Semana de Cine Fantástico y de Terror see San Sebastián Horror and Fantasy Film Festival
Semana Internacional de cine Fantástico y de Terro 227
Semesterplaner see *The Holiday Plan*
Semi-Colon 226
Los Señalados de Dios 185
Sender, Max 131
Senior Moments 157
El señor Puppe 156
Senoreality Pictures 191
Señorita Gertie 146
Sent to Destroy (music video) 191
Sentenced (unproduced script) 244
Senter, Marc 146, 217
The Sentinel (1977 feature) 236
Seo, Yeong-hie (aka Seo Yeong-hee) 192
The Separation (2003 animated short film) 146, 202
Séquestrée (Canadian short film) 145
A Serbian Film (aka *Srpski film*) 141, 142, 201
Serenity (2005) 169, 186, 205, 239
Serial (unproduced script) 172
Series 7: The Contenders (2001 feature) 175
Serkis, Andy 207
Serling, Rod 170
Serra, Koldo 201, 231, 241
Serrador, Narciso Ibáñez 231
Serrano, Aldo E. 242
Serrano, David 149
Serrano, Jaime 227
Serrano, Julieta 153
Serum 1831 224
Servais, Raoul 149, 151, 152
Servicio a domicilio see *Home Delivery*
Session 9 232
Sete Vidas (2007 Brazilian short film) 146
Seul contre tous see *I Stand Alone* (1998)
Se7en 140, 151, 152, 209
Seven Corners 122
Seven Days (1998–2001 TV series, aka *7 Days*) 208
Seven Swords (2005 feature, aka *Qi jian*) 230
Seven Women for Satan (1976, aka *Les week-ends maléfiques du Comte Zaroff*) 236
The Seventh Circle (2009, aka *A hetedik kör*) 170
Severance 125, 148, 175
Severed (2005 feature, aka *Severed: Forest of the Dead*) 218
"Severed Dreams" (*Babylon 5* TV episode) 169
Severing the Soul 122
Sevilha, Fabiana 132
Seward, Mina 247
Sewer Chewer 247
Sex and Sensitivity 178
Sexton, Brent 241
Sexton, Robert 242
Sexykiller, morirás por ella 127, 147
Seymour, Thomas Edward 122
SF Documentary Festival 104
SF Independent Film Fest 104
SF IndieFest 104
Shadow Man (2004 short film) 148

Index

Shadow.net 135
Shadow of Death (1988) 128
Shadow of the Raven (aka *Í skugga hrafnsins*) 252
Shadow of the Vampire 126, 139, 150, 207, 232
Shadow People (unproduced script) 243
Shadow War (unproduced script) 243
The Shadow Within (2007 feature) 188, 219, 220, 245
Shadowland (2010) 161, 162, 247
Shadows (2010 short film) 57
Shadows in the Palace 143
Shadows of Life (unproduced script) 219
Shady Texas (webisode) 224
Shaink, Rock, Jr. 191
Shakhnazarov, Karen 147
Shallow Grave (1994) 152
Shallow Ground 135
Shankland, Tom 142, 158, 214
Sharkskin 6 (music video) 225
Sharkskin 6 (2005 feature) 225
Sharp, Chris 129
Shatner, William 211, 214, 240
Shatterbrain see *The Resurrecte* (1992)
Shaun of the Dead 125, 138, 199, 206, 239
Shaw, Stan 188
Shaye, Robert 213
She Wolf Rising 161
Shea, Steven 190
Sheck, William 219
Sheil, Steven 119
Sheller, William 165
Shelley, Mary 170
Shellter 134, 157, 162, 174, 191
Shepard, David 213
Shepard, Kristopher 161
Sheperd, Chris 187
Sheperd, David 172
The Shepherd (unproduced script) 226
Shepherd, Ross 159
Shepis, Tiffany 93, 134, 161, 221, 242
Sherlock Holmes (2009 feature) 249
Sherman, Amy Beth 225
Sherman, Jeffrey 172
Shh! It's Alive 162
Shi gan see *Time* (2006)
Shia, Howie 144
Shiban, John 243
Shibata, Issei (aka Shibata Issey) 195
Shields, Corey 167, 168
Shimizu, Takashi 127, 195, 218
Shimono, Sab 223
Shinboru see *Symbol* (2009)
Shine (1996; dir: Hicks) 151
The Shining (1980) 49, 212
The Shining (1997) 209
Shinkai, Makoto 145
Shinoda, Masahiro 194
Shiota, Akihiko 229, 250
Shipwrecked (aka *Naufrage*; year?) 239
Shiver (2008; dir: Ortiz) 158
Shivers see *They Came from Within* (1975)
Shock see *Beyond the Door II* (1977)
Shocker Award 223–24
Shockerfest 106, 115, 219–23
Shockfest Film Festival viii, **22**, 115, 223–24, 253n11, 254n1
The Shoe Collector 159
Sholder, Jack 128, 141, 153, 166, 235
Shoob, Michael 88

ShootingPeople.com 33
Shore, Howard 139, 206, 209
Short, Robert 210
Short Cut (short film, aka *Coupé court*; year?) 179
Short Lease 126, 158
ShortFilmCentral.com 34
The Shorty's Contest 105
Shosho 136
Show, Bill Nayer 184
The Show Must Go On 144
Showroom Cinema (in Sheffield, UK) 117
Showtime 195
Shrek 23, 207
Shrek Forever After 23
Shriekfest Horror/SciFi Film Festival & Screenplay Competition viii, 2, 6–8, 13, 15, 19, 24, 34, 43–**44**, 50, 57–58, 67, 71–75, 80, 92–93, 113, 115, 121, 224–26, 253n11; sponsorship rates 27–28; venue **72**
Shriekfest Tombstone Award 115, 224
The Shrine
Shrove Tuesday (2009 short film; dir: Matthews) 132, 238, 241, 247
Shumway, Jason (aka The Shumway Brothers) 224
Shumway, Matt (aka The Shumway Brothers) 224
Shumway, Trent 226
Shusett, Ronald 170
Shuster, Joe 170
Shutter (2004; dir: Wongpoom & Pisanthanakum) 164
Shutter Island 215
Shyamalan, M. Night 90, 126, 139, 186
Shyu, Tony 172, 190
Siam Sunset 150, 250
Sibley, Amber 139
Sick Girl 192
Side Effect (2008 short film; dir: Adams) 185, 224, 247
Side Sho 244
Sideshow 199
Sideways (2004) 148
Sidney, Sylvia 210
Sieben Monde (1998 feature; aka *Night Time*) 176
Siederman, Slava 226
Siege of Evil 167
Siegel, David 233
Siegel, Jerry 170
Siegel, Richard 189
Siegler, Ben 143
Siek+Sat (music video) 238
Siel Spieël (short film) 237
Sien lui yau wan III: Do do do see *A Chinese Ghost Story III*
Sien nui yau wan II yan gaan do 152
Sigaw see *The Echo* (2004)
Sigel, Newton Thomas 145
The Signal (2006 short film) 86, 242
The Signal (2007 U.S. feature) 144
El siguiente (2004 short film; aka *The Next One*) 182
Silberberg, David 122
Silence and Shadows see *Silêncio e Sombras*
"Silence in the Library" (*Doctor Who* TV episode) 133, 197
Silence Is Golden (short film; 2006?) 181, 187
Silence of Isbella 163

The Silence of the Lambs 140, 141, 171, 210
Silêncio e Sombras 132
Silent Hill (video game) 165
Silent Movie Theatre 107
Silicon 115
Silva, Vítor 154
Silver, Joel 214
Silver Glibb Award 248
Silver Méliès see Méliès d'Argent
Silver Raven Award 126–28
Silver Scream Award 109, 162; *also see* Sp!ts [sic] Silver Scream Award
Silver Sugar Skull Award 101, 185–86
Silver Tooth Award 100
Silver Urania Award see Urania d'Argento
Silvestri, Alan 206, 210, 211
Simard, François 248
Simeon 128
Simmons, Brett 225
Simmons, Tony 45, 242
Simón, Juan Piquer 80
Simon Lehembre 143
Simon Magus (1999 feature; dir: Hopkins) 232
Simon Werner a disparu see *Lights Out* (2010)
Simonac 143
Simone (short film; year?) 219
Simonetti, Claudio 149
Simonin, Nicolas 168
Simonsson, Ola 227
Simpkins, Ryan 189
Simpson, Geoffrey 153
Simpson, Julian 150
Simpson, Stuart 123, 130, 177, 178, 203
The Simpsons (1989- TV series) 210
Sims, Joseph Stephen 176, 177
Sin City 205, 206, 239
Los sin nombre see *The Nameless* (1999)
Sin piedras 230
Sin Shoes 177
Sinclair, Harry 149, 150, 151, 194
Sinclair, John Douglas 161
Sinclair, Nancy 242, 244
Sinclair, Stephen 169, 186
Singer, Bryan 205, 207, 213
Singer, Lori 221
Singh, Tarsem 229
The Singing Detective (2003) 231
Singleton, Brian 123
Siniestro (year?) 173
Sinise, Gary 209
Sinkhole (2009 short film) 188, 191
Sinners (dir: DeVeau) 215
Sipe, Brian see Brian Sipe Special Effects
Sipos, Thomas M. 115
Siren (2001, dir: Morris) 226
Siren (2010 feature; dir: Hull) **67**
The Siren (year?) 175
Sirens of the 23rd Century 130
Siritto, Elena 130
Sirtis, Marina 222
Sisco, Mary Katherine 247
Sisk, Melodie 177
Sisters (dir: Huey) 167
SITGES: Festival Internacional de Cinema Fantàstic de Catalunya viii, 103, 179–84, 226–37, 253n1
The Sitter (2006 short film) 172
Siudzinski, David 225
Sivertson, Chris 194
Six, Tom 155, 194

The Sixth Sense (1999) 126, 139, 186, 208
Sjaastad, Are 229
Skaife, Michael *see* Madrid, Miguel
Skarsgård, Alexander 215, 216
Skarsgård, Gustaf 218
Skarsgård, Stellan 155
Sk8r 666 (unproduced script) 223
Skeleton Crew (2009) **81**
Ski Jumping Pairs (2003 short film) 250
Skin Deep (2007 short film; dir: Romero III) 242
Skinner, John 112
Skinwalker: Curse of the Shaman 242
Skochko, Jeff 218
Skolnick, Jared 247
Skrobecki, Marek 187
Sky Blue (2003, aka *Wonderful Days*) 164
Sky Captain and the World of Tomorrow 206, 239
The Sky Crawlers (aka *Sukai kurora*) 228, 229
The Sky Has Fallen 161
Slade, David 230
Slamdance Film Festival 17–19
Slattery, Bailey 222
The Slaughter (2006) 159, 162, 173, 196, 245
Slaughter Bed 249
Slaughterhouse-Five 170, 213
The Slayer Bureaucrat see La Funcionaria Asesina
Sled (2010) 174
Sleep Dealer 187
Sleeper 170, 186
The Sleeping Deep 168
Sleepwalker (2000) 141
Sleepwalkers (1992) 140
Sleepy Hollow (1999) 139, 208
Sletaune, Pål 171
The Sleuth Incident 122, 161, 200
Slevin, Damien 123, 132, 160
Slices of Life (2010 feature) 134
Slime City Massacre 123
Sling Blade 209
Slinky Milk 40–41, 242
Slipoi, Damián 146
Slither (2006) 205
Sluizer, George 151, 153
Smacked Out Kisses 178
Small Soldiers 233
Small Things (2008 short film; dir: Bloom) 158
Smallville (2001–11 TV series) 206, 207, 239
SMG Effects 232
The Smiley 227
Smith, Agent (*Matrix* character) 240
Smith, Alison 145
Smith, Carter 145
Smith, Chris (Canadian) 144
Smith, Chris (aka Christopher Smith, b. 1970, UK) 175, 187, 201, 217
Smith, Christophe 166
Smith, Clinton 237, 238
Smith, Dick 212, 213
Smith, Douglas 209
Smith, Gentry 189
Smith, Gordon 208
Smith, Jaden Christopher 204
Smith, Jono 242
Smith, Julie K. 131
Smith, Justin 159
Smith, Lee 249
Smith, Michael Bailey (actor) 138
Smith, Patrick 122
Smith, Shawnee 137
Smith, Stuart 9
Smith, Will 133, 204
Smithee, Alan 141
Smits, Jimmy 204
Smits, Martijn 136
Smoke City 232
Smolders, Olivier 193, 248
Smoller, Daena 138
Smuts-Kennedy, Sarah 152
A Snake of June 149
Sneaky Pete's Sports Bar 116
Snider, Dee 8
Sniffer 156, 180, 181
Snip (short film; year?) 238
Snively, Devi 126, 135, 173–74, 176, 191, 224, 241
Het Snoepmonster 136
Snow, Ben 207
Snow Day, Bloody Snow Day 167
Snowmaniac 173
Snuff Massacre — Skeleton Crew see Skeleton Crew (2009)
Snyder, Frederick 252
Snyder, Tom 123
Snyder, Zack 204
Soares, John 220
Soavi, Michele 141, 166, 171
Society (1989) 128
Soderqvist, John 138
Soemantri, Jennifer 242
Soi Cowboy 177
The Soil's Soft Horizon 122
Solà, Albert 230
Solá, Miguel Ángel 149
Solanas, Anna 227
Solano, Jeff 226
Solet, Paul 72, 163, 196, 242
Solex 137
Solo, Manolo 241
Sólo se muere dos veces 151, 184, 233
Solomon, Raven 243
Solomon Kane 147
Solondz, Todd 151
Solum, Ola 128
Sombras indigus 235
Some Folks Call It a Sling Blade 202
"Some Must..." (*Sarah Connor Chronicles* TV episode) 132
Someone's Knocking at the Door 122
Something Beneath 178
Something Never Seen Before 175
Something Wicked This Way Comes 211
A Somewhat Gentle Man 155
Somewhere in Time 212
Sommers, Stephen 137
Somnambulist see *Une nuit blanche* (2005) 187
Somos lo que hay see *We Are What We Are*
El soñador (2004) 182, 231
Sonámbulos 185
Sonata (2004 feature) 222
Song of the Dead (2005 feature) 129, 185
Song, Kang-ho 144
Sonic Youth 231
Sonnenshine, Rebecca 241
Sono, Shion see Sono, Sion
Sono, Sion 142, 143, 144, 155, 193, 227
Sony Pictures Home Entertainment 195
Sopeña, Rodrigo 147
Sopsits, Árpád 170
Sorria 132
Sorry…I Love You (short film) 155
Sort, Elisabet 229
Sorum 149
Sosa, Evangelina 152
Sosa, Felipe 184
Sôseiji see *Gemini* (1999)
Soska, Jen and Sylvia 131
Sothcott, Jonathan 126
The Soul of Business see *A Alma do Negócio*
Souls (unproduced script) 218
Soul's Midnight 191
Sound of Noise 155, 227
South African HORRORFEST Film Festival viii, 13, **70**, 102, 237–39
South of Heaven 155, 246
Southern, Terry 170
Sovagovic, Fabijan 154
Soy una Manzana 185
Soylent Green (1973) 186, 213
Soylent Red 224
SP Terror — Festival Internacional de Cinema Fantástico 96
Sp!ts [sic] Silver Scream Award 170–71
Space Battleships Yamato: Resurrection 142
Space Channel 98, 239
Space Monster (short film; dir: Romero) 168
Space Off 182
Spaceboy 125
Spacey, Kevin 140
Spacey Award 97–98, 239–40
Spalovac mrtvol see *The Cremator* (1969)
Spandex Man 156
Spank 157
Sparrow, Jack (character) 240
Sparrow, Pater 131, 147
Spasojevi, Srdjan 141, 201
Spawn 140, 233
Speakman, Georgii 177
Special (2006 feature; dir: Haberman & Passmore) 193
Species 233
Spectre Film Festival 99
Spectres (2004 feature) 222
Speed (1994; dir: De Bont) 209
Speed Freak 124
The Spell (2006 short film) 159
Spencer, Andrew 160
Spider (2002 feature; dir: Cronenberg) 231
Spider (2007 short film) 133, 134, 201
Spider-Man (character) 240
Spider-Man (2002) 207
Spider-Man 2 (2004) 206, 239, 240
Spider-Man 3 (2007) 216
Spielberg, Anne 210
Spielberg, Steven 169, 170, 207, 209, 212, 213
Spike (*Angel* character) 240
Spike (2008 feature) 224
Spike TV 3, 115
Spilt Milk (short film; dir: MacDonald) 191
Spindell, Ryan 123, 134, 196, 224
Spine Tingler! The William Castle Story 196, 197, 217
Spinell, Joe 237
Spiner, Brent 209
Spiral 156
Spirit of Dragon*Con Award 135
Spirited Away (2001, aka *Sen to Chihiro no kamikakushi*) 171, 240

Spirits of the Air, Gremlins of the Clouds 252
Splash (1984) 211
Splice 228
Splinter (2008 feature) 138, 190, 217
Splintered (2010) 167
Spomberg, Marcelo 146
The Spook House see *El tren de la bruja* (2003)
Spooky Movie: The Washington D.C. International Horror Film Festival 115, 240
Spring Rhapsody (2005) 178
Springer, Jeff 178
Springer, Jon 130
Sproul-Cran, Robert 121
Spurlock, J. David 198
Spurrier, Paul 248
Squeal (2008 feature) 243, 244
Squires, Scott 208
SR: Saitama's Rapper (aka *SR: Saitama no rapp*) 249
Srbova, Tereza 67
Srimantra, Decha see Seementa, Decha
Srisawat, Supakorn 193
Srpski film see *A Serbian Film*
Ss-Sunda 194
SSA/Suissimage Prize 188
Stadler, Heiner 235
Stævnemødet (1998 short film; *The Date*) 176
Stagman 156
Stake Land 247
Stalker (1979) 154
Stamboel, Kimo 189
Stan & Vince 166
Stanbridge, Hanna 166
"Stand by Your Man" (song) 90
Stand Up and Die 243
Stanley, Jack Daniel 125, 162
Stanley, Larry see Larry Stanley B-Movie Award
Stanley, Richard 128, 153
Stanton, Andrew 169, 186
Stanze, Eric 161, 248
Staplerfahrer Klaus — Der erste Arbeitstag see *Forklift Driver Klaus: The First Day on the Job*
Staples, Paul 217
Stapleton, Frank 151
Star Trek (film series) 204
Star Trek (franchise) 5, 90, 214
Star Trek (1966–69 TV series) 170, 206, 214, 239
Star Trek (2009 feature) 132, 203, 215, 216, 249
Star Trek: The Motion Picture (1979) 212
Star Trek II: The Wrath of Khan (CD) 197
Star Trek II: The Wrath of Khan (1982) 211, 212
Star Trek IV: The Voyage Home 211
Star Trek VI: The Undiscovered Country 210
Star Trek: Enterprise (2001–05 TV series, aka *Enterprise*) 207, 239, 240
Star Trek: First Contact 209
Star Trek: The Next Generation (1987–94 TV series) 169, 207, 210, 214
Star Trek: Voyager (1995–2001 TV series) 208, 209
Star Wars, Episode I: The Phantom Menace 208

Star Wars, Episode II: Attack of the Clones 207, 240
Star Wars, Episode III: Revenge of the Sith 205, 239
Star Wars, Episode IV: A New Hope (aka *Star Wars*) 170, 186, 213
Star Wars, Episode V: The Empire Strikes Back 126, 170, 212
Star Wars, Episode VI: Return of the Jedi 170, 211
Star Wars: Knights of the Old Republic (video game) 240
Star Wars Trilogy (DVD) 206
Stardust (2007) 169
Starfish Hotel 156
Starfly 181
Stargate (franchise) 133
Stargate (1994) 209
Stargate Atlantis 239
Stargate: Continuum (2008) 132
Stargate SG-1 (1997–2007 TV series) 133, 206, 208, 239, 240
Staring at the Sun (2005 short film) 218
Stark, Christoph 150
Starlog (magazine) 88, 124, 198, 205
Starman (1984) 211
Starópoli, Alejandro 185
Starship Troopers 140, 208
Starship Troopers 2: Hero of the Federation 206
Statt Coven 247
Statzer, Bob 198
Stay (short film; year?) 237
Steam (music video) 166
Steamboy (aka *Suchîmubôi*) 231
Stearns, Jeff Chiba 143
Stears, John 213
Steel (1997 feature; dir: Johnson) 251
Steel, J.A. 163
Steele, Patrick 123, 160, 184, 195, 245
Steenburgen, Mary 212
Steensland, Mark 123, 134
Stefano, Joseph 213, 214
Stefanou, Peter 178
Stein, Björn 127, 171, 193
Steinberg, Michael 152
Steiner, Nicolas 187
Steinsbo, Jersti 158
Steinsiek, Tate 191, 217
Stelling, Jos 128, 153
Stem 217
Stenbeck, Ben 189, 218
Stenner, Chris 175
The Stepfather (1987) 235
The Stepford Wives (1975) 213
Stephen King's The Mist see *The Mist* (2007)
Stephens, Kyle 158
Stephenson, Michael Paul 143, 228
Stern, Tom 166
Sternhagen, Frances 212
Steven Spielberg Presents Taken see *Taken* (2002)
Stevens, Brinke 223
Stevens, Steven, Jr. 242
Stevens-Arce, James 218
Stevenson, Juliet 152, 234
Steves 244
Stewart, John 235
Stewart, Kristen 215, 216
Stewart, Patrick 214
Steyn, Jacques 235
Stiffs by Sid 8, 47, 242

Still Life (2005 short film; dir: Knautz) 201
Still Life (unproduced script) 226; later produced in 2005
Die Stilte 238
Stingray Sam 132, 184
Stink Meat 224
Stir of Echoes (1999) 165
Stirton, Mark 158
Stockdale, Valentine 190
Stojanovic, Uros 142
Stokdyk, Scott 206, 207
Stokes, Michael 191
Stolojan, Diane 238
Stolze, Pierre 165
Stomp! Shout! Scream! 157
Stop It, You're Killing Me 226
Stoppard, Tom 153
Storey, Drew 245
Storey Award 245
Una storia di lupi (2008, aka *A Wolf's Tale*) 190
Storm (2005 feature; dir: Mårlind & Stein) 127, 171, 181, 193
Storm of the Century (1999) 208
Storm Warning (2007) 217
Stout, Jon 172
Straczynski, J. Michael 169, 186
The Strain 242
Strain, Jim 205
Straiton, Jonathan 124
Straker, Marilyn Vance 210
Stranded (2001 feature, aka *Stranded (Náufragos)*) 183
Strange, Kevin 247
Strange Aeons 6, 242
The Strange Case of Dr. Jekyll and Miss Osbourne (1981, aka *Le Cas estrange du Dr. Jekyll et de Miss Osbourne*) 236
Strange Circus 144
Strange Days (1995) 209
Strange Invaders (2002 animated short film) 232
The Strange Killers (dir: Yamamoto) 196
Strange Things Happen at Sundown 189
Stranger (unproduced script) 190
Stranger in the Night Fright 252
The Strangers (2008 feature) 216
Strasbourg European Fantastic Film Festival see Festival Européen du Film Fantastique de Strasbourg
Strayed (2009) 187
Street, Dorothy 238
Street Angel (2009 short film) 157, 176
Street of Crocodiles 153, 235
Street Tales of Terror 168
Street Trash (1987) 128
Streets of Fire (1986) 235
Strick, Wesley 209
Strigoi 122, 128, 131, 176, 179, 184, 187, 237, 246
Strike (2009 Dutch short film) 136
Striker Bob 161
Striking Metal 135
String of the Kite 223
Strings (2004 feature; dir: Klarlund) 231
Strings (year?) 181
Strode, Michael 226
Strogonoff 203
Stromberg, Robert 203
Stuart, Gloria 137, 208
Stubø, Kirsti 147
Stuck (2007 feature; dir: Gordon) 127, 134

StudentFilmmakers.com 33
A Study in Red 243
Stukas, Thom 218
Sturgess, Jim 146
Su, Chao-Bin (aka Su, Chao Pin) 250
Su, Chao Pin *see* Su, Chao-Bin
Suarez, Alfonso S. 160
Suárez, Ramón F. 234
Sub-Films 103
Subiela, Eliseo 233
Subirós, Sílvia 227
Subject Two 215
The Substitute (2007, aka *Vikaren*; dir: Bornedal) 158, 180
Succubus: The Motion Picture 161
Sucesión 129
Suck 142
Sucker (2006 short film; dir: Steensland) 221
Sudac, Craig 244
Sudina, Marina *see* Zudina, Marina
Sudor frío (2010, aka *Cold Sweat*) 185
Suff Dead Oscar 96
Suffer the Little Children (2006) 221
Sugar Town (1999) 150
Sugawa, Eizo 128
Suh, Jung 150
Suicide Me (2003, aka *Naai asok kap naangsaao phloenchit*) 193
Suicídio Encomendado 148
Suityman 156
Sukiyaki Western Django 143, 229
Sukjai, Somjai 193
Sukuts, Augusts 100
Sullivan, Brett 224
Sullivan, John 226
Sullivan, Peter 225
Sullivan, Tom 236
Sumarwata, Alin 177
Sumetsupachok, Thammarat 217
Summer Job (2007 short film) 172, 200
Summer of Slaughter 111
Summer School 124
Summer Wars (aka *Samâ wôzu*) 142, 228
Summers, Mera 247
Sumner, Anthony G. 123, 134
Sumpter, Jeremy 206
Sunda, Ss *see* Ss-Sunda
Sundance Film Festival 2, 15, 17–22, 36, 59, 65, 73, 75, 108, 253n5, 253n6
Sunday, Art viii, 116
Sunday Punch 135
Sunny's Nights 172
Sunset 157
The Super 125
Super Freq 45
Super Seiserzauger 131
Superhuman (short film; dir: Taylor) 143, 144
Superhuman (short film; dir: ?) 220
Superman TV series *see Adventures of Superman*
Superman (1978, aka *Superman: The Movie*) 170, 212
Superman II (1980) 205, 212
Superman Returns (2006) 205, 216, 239
Supernatural (TV series) 132, 133
SuperStore 242
Surprise! (1996 short film; dir: Helmer) 202
Surveillance (2008 feature; dir: Lynch) 189, 228
Survive Style 5+ 145, 201

The Survivor (1981 feature; dir: Hemmings) 236
The Survivor (2007 short film; dir: Warrack) 159
Survivors (2009 short film; dir: Mehta) 162, 174
A Suspeita (2000 short film) 150
Susser, Spencer 143
Sussfeld, Jean-Claude 154
Suta, Keith 242
Suter, Martin 235
Suture (1993 feature) 233
Suzhou he see *Suzhou River*
Suzhou River 150
Suzuki, Keitchi 231
Suzuki, Masayuki 164
Suzuki, Tatsuo 235
Svankmajer, Jan 152, 153
Svehla, Gary and Sue 199
Svengoolie (aka Rich Koz) 197
Sverák, Jan 128, 152, 166, 251
Swamp Devil 244
Swansey, Tony 243
Swanson, Gloria 213
Swanson, Jen 30, 253n13
Swanstrom, Jack 224
Sweat (short film; dir: Na) 193
Sweatshop (2009) 125, 188
Sweeney, Conor 249
Sweeney Todd: The Demon Barber of Fleet Street (2007) 204, 216
Sweet, Gary 177
Sweet Angel Mine 151
The Sweet Hand of the White Rose 241
Sweet Karma 155
Swertfager, Michael 196
Swindled (2004) 148
Swingers (2009 short film) 228
Swinton, Tilda 204, 249
Switch VFX 124
Switchblade Romance see *High Tension* (2003)
Swoon 152
The Sword and the Sorcerer 212
Sword of the Stranger 146
The Swordsman in Double Flag Town (aka *Shuang-Qi-Zhen daoke*) 252
Sydney Underground Film Festival viii, 96
SyFy.com 110
Sylla, Tom 223
Sylver, Ra 179
Symbol (2009) 126, 142
Sympathy for Lady Vengeance see *Lady Vengeance* (2005)
sync license 255n8
Syndikas, Jean-Luc 177
System (1972 short TV movie) 237
Szász, János 147
Szulkin, Piotr 154

Ta-ta-boom-boom 236
Taan see *Turn* (2001)
Tabloid Witch Awards 2; official seal *9*; origins and history 5–13; 2010 screening *12*; 13–15, 19–20, 24, 29, 31, 33–34, 36–37, 46–47, 49–50, 53–57, 59–66, 71–74, 76–78, 82–83, 85–86, 89, *89*, 93, 115, 241–42, 253n2, 253n3, 253n6, 253n11, 254n3
Taber Corn 190
Taddicken, Sven 193
Tag 26 (aka *Day 26*) 182

Taggart, Matthew 242
The Taint (2010 feature) 134
Tajemství hradu v Karpatech see *The Mysterious Castle in the Carpathians*
Takahashi, Yoshiki 155
Takamatsu, Shinji 192
Takei, George 214
Taken (2002, aka *Steven Spielberg Presents Taken*) 207
The Taken (2009 feature; dir: Valentine) 162, 191
Takesita, Sinya 252
Takesita Performance Higei Mito-Komon 252
The Taking (2004 short film) 218
Takita, Yōjirō 188
Talamanca, Carlos 193
Talavera, Francesc 130
Tale 52 (aka *Istoria 52*) 228
The Tale of the Rat That Wrote 150, 194
A Tale of Two Sisters 127, 149, 164, 185, 218
TalentCircle.org 33
Tales from Beyond 222, 225
Tales from Makeout Point: Vinnie's Tale see *Vinnie's Tale*
Tales from the Afternoon: Little Rocks 135
Tales from the Crypt (1972 film) 126
Tales from the Crypt: Demon Knight 140
Tales of the Unusual (2000, aka *Yonimo kimyô na monogatari—Eiga no tokubetsu hen*) 164
Talking Tina (*Twilight Zone* doll) 197
The Tall Tale Heart 221
Tally, Ted 141, 210
Talmor, Jude 160
Tamahori, Lee 152
Tambasco, Antonella 185
Tamblyn, Amber 206
Tammemägi, Jason 159
Tanaka, Tatsuyuki 143
Tancharoen, Maurissa 169
Tandy, Jessica 211
Tao of the Meteor Serpent (short film) 223
Tapping, Amanda 206
Tarantino, Quentin 231, 233, 234, 252
Tareen, Semih 244
Target Practice 157
Tarkovskiy, Andrey 154
Tarver, Estes 247
Taste of Flesh (2008) 162
A Taste of Love 200
The Taste of Tea 127, 145, 188, 193
Tatchell, Terri 186
Tate, Catherine 132
Tatler, Philip 174
Tatopolous, Patrick 208
Tatt 171
Tattoo (2002 feature; dir: Schwentke) 149, 175
Taurus Studio Award 187
Taxandria (1994) 152, 184
Taxandria (2008) 136
Taxi de nuit (1998) 151
Taxidermia (2006) 148
The Taxidermist (2009 short film) 196
Taylor, Bill 213
Taylor, Dagan 143, 144
Taylor, Jim viii, 32, 35, 40, 48, 65, 78, 82, 98
Taylor, Noah 141, 232
Taylor, Richard 205, 206, 207, 233, 234
Taylor, Steven Lee 160, 226
Taylor, Vincent 214

304 Index

Tea Break (short film) 182, 201
The Tea Master 135
Tea Time (2001 short film; dir: Bogdanowitsch) 222
Teague, David 161
Teague, James 242
Teague, Lewis 153
Tears for Sale 142
Tears of Kali 182, 186, 194
Tears of the Black Tiger 194
Le Technicien 142
Technotise (year?) 214
Technotise: Edit and I (2009) 142
Teclopolis 155
Teen Agent see *If Looks Could Kill* (1991)
Teeth (2007) 163, 216
Tekkonkinkreet (aka *Tekkon Kinkreet*, aka *Tekkon kinkurîto*) 144, 229
Tel-Club 250
Teleportation (2009 short film) 214
Teles, Luís Galvão 147
Tell Him Next Year 196
Tell Tale Art 159
The Tell Tale Heart (animated film) 191, 196
The Tell-Tale Heart (2003 short film; aka *El corazón delator*; dir: Suarez) 130
The Tell-Tale Heart (2008 short film; dir: Eggers) 130
The Tell Tale Heart (short film; dir: Cohen) 123
The Tell-Tale Heart: Animated Horror Short (2010; dir: Swertfager) 196
Telluride Film Commission 115
Telluride Film Festival 21, 115
Telluride Horror Show 115
Témoin muet see *Mute Witness* (1994)
Temple, Julien 150
Temple Bar 100
Templemore-Finlayson, Amber (aka Bert) see Bert & Bertie
Le Templier (novel) 165
Le Temps du loup see *Time of the Wolf* (2003)
The Temptation of Sainthood 152
Tempus fugit (2003 TV movie) 159, 171, 175, 182
Ten see *Dix* (2008)
The Ten Steps (2004 short film) 134, 182, 193, 194, 231
Tennant, David 132, 133
Tennen shôjo Man see *Man, a Natural Girl*
Tenney, Kevin S. 176, 196
Terada, Hiroyuki 252
Terayama, Shûji 235
Terciopelo azul see *Blue Velvet*
Terezakis, Bill 139
Terminal (unproduced script) 190
The Terminator 211
Terminator 2: Judgment Day 141, 170, 186, 210
Terminator: The Sarah Connor Chronicles (TV series) 205
Terminatryx (music band) 237
Terminus (2007 short film; dir Cawood) 155
Terra incognita (short film; 2005, dir: Volkart?) 182, 188
Terrasi, Richard 196
Terraves, Mario 232
Terreur Au 3918 145
The Terrible Thing of Alpha-9! 131, 133, 191

Terror, Suzi 136, 170
Terror Enterprises 107
The Terror Factor 196
Terror Film Festival viii, 13, 28, 34, 36, 42, 66, 79, 93, 115–16, 242–44
Terror on the 3918 246
Terror Tract 127, 226
A Terrorist Ate My Brain 173
Terror'thon 116
Terry, Sammy 197
Terug Van Die Dood 238
Tesis (1996, aka *Thesis*) 128, 184
Teske, Benjamin 187
The Tesseract 231
Tessier, Éric 163, 227
Tetsuo (film series) 167
Tetsuo II: Body Hammer 152, 234, 252
Tetsuo: The Iron Man 128, 176
Texas Blood Bath Film Festival 105, 116, 125
The Texas Chainsaw Massacre (2003) 231
The Texas Chainsaw Massacre II 235
Texas FearFest 109, 116
Texas Frightmare Weekend 116
Thampanyasan, Pimwalee 177
Thanksgiving With the Kranzes 136
Tharpe, Tyler 161
That's Magic! 135
That's Not Mine Film Festival 13, 116
Théaudière, Philippe 236
Them (2006, aka *Ils*) 171, 181, 194
TheOpenPress.com 34
Theosaurology 135
There's a Werewolf in My Attic 122
There's Something Out There (2004 short film) 196
Thesis see *Tesis* (1996)
They Came Back (2004 feature, aka *Les revenants*) 148, 149, 182
They Came from Within (1975, aka *The Parasite Murders*, aka *Shivers*) 236
They Nest (2000 TV movie, aka *Eclosion*) 165
They Walk Among Us 157
They Want My Eyes 129
They're Made Out of Meat 156, 214
They're Watching Us see *Nos miran*
Thicker Than Water: The Vampire Diaries Part 1 124
Thiel, Nick 241
The Thing from Another World (CD) 198
The Thing from Another World (1951) 199
The Thing from the Cellar (2010 short film) 200
Things (feature film; year?) 238
Things II 226
The Third Cry (1974, aka *Le troisième cri*) 236
Thirst (1979 feature; dir: Hardy) 236
Thirst (2009 South Korean feature) 126, 143, 147, 228
Thirsty (2009 U.S. short film) 134, 161, 162
Thirteen Assassins see *13 Assassins*
Thir13en Ghosts 139
This Way Up (short film; 2008?) 180
Thomas, Bill 213
Thomas, Henry 148
Thomas, Jeff 158, 160
Thomas est amoureux see *Thomas in Love*
Thomas in Love (aka *Thomas est amoureux*) 127, 164, 165, 183

Thompson, Caroline 170
Thompson, Jamie 8
Thompson, Jeri Lynn 224
Thompson, Sam 122
Thompson, Timothy 214
Thomsen, Ulrich 148, 193
Thornley, Jeni 31, 254n18
Thornton, Billy Bob 152, 213
Thorpe, Ashley 130, 190
The Thousand Miracles of the Universe see *Les mille merveilles de l'univers*
The Thousand Wonders of the Universe see *Les mille merveilles de l'univers*
A Thousand Words (short film; year?) 220
Three Chinamen with a Double Bass 194
Three Days (1992) see *Trys dienos*
Three… Extremes (aka *Three: Extremes*?) 125, 231
Thrill Ride Award 106
Thriller Award (Brussels film festival) 126–27
Thriller Award (Thriller Writers) 116, 244–45
Thriller! Chiller! viii, 116, 245
Thrillerfest (Missouri film festival) 116
Thrillerfest (writers convention) 116
A Through M 173
Throw Momma from the Train 211
Thurman, Uma 206
Thy Neighbor's Wife (unproduced script) 226
Tie saam gok see *Triangle* (2007)
Tieleman, Tamar 136
Tight (2006 short film; dir: Vizcaíno) 230
Til Night 244
Tile M for Murder (2008 short film, aka *Lägg M för mord*; dir: Holmgren) 180, 187
'Till Death (dir: Hogan) 161
Tilly, Bryn 190
Tilly, Jennifer 137, 151
Tilted Love 160
Tilton, Tony vii, 109, 157
Time (dir: Campbell) 160
Time (2006, aka *Shi gan*; dir: Kim) 148, 229
Time After Time (1979) 212
Time and Again (2004 short film?; dir: Small?) 222
Time & Space (short film) 159
Time Bandits (1981) 213
Time Copy (short film) 223
Time Machine Honorary Award 231–34
Time of the Wolf (2003, aka *Le temps du loup*) 231
The Time Travelers (feature; year?) 221
Time 2 Save the World 160
Time with Nyenne 188
Timecop (1994) 209
Timecrimes (aka *Los cronocrímenes*) 143, 156, 163, 170, 186, 189, 214
Timescape 128, 152
Timmis, Conor 243
Timmy's Wish 160, 196
Tin Can Man (2007) 177
Tindall, Patti 191
The Tingler 121
Tinnell, Robert 151
Tippett, Phil 140, 208, 210, 211
Tippett Studio 139

Tirado, Ángel 131
Le Tiroir et le Corbeau 142
Titanic (1997) 208
Titra Film Award 187
Tjahjanto, Timothy 189
TL-1: Mi reino por un platillo volador 185
TL-2: La felicidad es una leyenda urbana 184
T.M.A. (aka *T.M.A.—The Missing Address*) 147, 237
To, Johnnie 144, 147, 229, 230, 231
To Be or Not to Be (dir: Matsunashi) 251
To hrima—Mia mythologia tou Skotous 150
To kako (2005 feature, aka *Evil*) 248
To mand i en sofa 152
To My Mother and Father 168
Tobin, Rick 243, 244
Toci: A Mexica Tale 223
Tod, Steven W. 187
Todd, Chris 172
Todd, Tony 88, 189
Tokyo! (2008 feature) 187
Tokyo A Go Go 250
Tokyo Godfathers 188, 231
Tokyo Gore Police 129, 143, 146, 155, 192
Tokyo Noir 148
Tôkyô zankoku keisatsu see *Tokyo Gore Police*
Tolkien, J.R.R. 169, 186
The Toll (animated short film) 172
Tollet, Olivier 185
Tombés du ciel see *Lost in Transit* (1993)
Tombstone Brides 123, 223
Tominaga, Kenji 252
Tominaga, Mia 144
Tomita, Tamlyn 223
Tomokazu 250
Tomorrow by Midnight 196
Tomorrow Never Dies 208
Tommy Bahama 23
Tomomatsu, Naoyuki 143
Tong, Kelvin 193
Tonsho, Nicolas 26
Tony (2009 feature; dir: Johnson) 227
Tony Award 1
Too Much Time 160
Tooker, Melanie 238
Toolbox Murders (2004) 138
Tooth, Owen 159
Toothnapped 219
Topless Women Talk About Their Lives 151
Tor Books 90
Torbellino de hostias 133, 228
Torchwood (TV series) 203
Torero, José Roberto 176
Tori & Rabi 193
Torloni, Christiane 148
Torment (year?) 243
Tornberg, Maria 245
Toroma Prize 252
Toronto After Dark Film Festival 21, 98, 245–46
Toronto International Film Festival 21–22, 58, 97, 246–47
Torras, Josep Maria 235
Torrens, Carles 133
Torres, Arturo Quezada 185
Torres, Gene 122
Torrez, Ellie (aka Elena Torrez) 223
Torrez, Tyger 109
Tørt og kjølig see *Cold and Dry*
Torture Device (music video) 190

Torv, Anna 203
Toss of the Coin (2002 short film) 160
Total Recall (1990) 210
Tóth, Orsi see Tóth, Orsolya
Tóth, Orsolya (aka Orsi Tóth) 148, 193
Toth, Wayne 149
Totò che visse due volte 233
Toto le héros see *Toto the Hero*
Toto the Hero 152
Tourneux, Samuel 201
Tous les hommes s'appellent Robert 142
Tovar, Lupita 137
Tower (retailer) 198
The Tower (2008 feature) 134
A Town Called Panic (2009, aka *Panique au village*) 155, 175, 180, 228
The Town of the One-Handed People (short film) 215
Toxic Avenger 18, **19**
Toy Love 149
Toy Island 198
The Toybox 159
T'Pol (character) 239, 240
Trageser, Kathy 223
The Tragic Story of Nling 246
Trail of Passion 179
Trail of the Screaming Forehead 124
Trailers from Hell (website) 197, 198
Train of Shadows (1997, aka *Tren de sombras*) 184, 233
Train Ride to Hollywood 213
Trance (1998 feature; dir: Almereyda) 233
Transfer (2003 short film; dir: Turbyne) 226
Transfer (2010 feature? dir: Lukacevic?) 214, 224
Transformers (2007) 133, 204, 216
Transformers: Revenge of the Fallen 216
Transgressions (2006 short film) 214
Transmission (2009; dir: Vranik) 170, 179
Transrexia 135, 244
Trapero, Pablo 155
Trash (dir: Kubo) 252
Trash (2010 Argentine film; dir: Réb ora) 129
Trash: Mostra Goiana de Filmes Independentes 97
Treadmill (2006) 124
Treasure (2003 short film) 160
Tredoux, Marnus 238
Tree (2007 short film; dir: Steinbeck) 220, 221
Treevenge 133, 144, 155, 189, 190, 238, 246
Tremblay, Cynthia 142
Tremblay, Frédérick 142
Tremblay, Kyla Rose 218
Tremblay, Martin 144
El tren de la bruja (2003, aka *The Spook House*) 182, 183, 201, 231, 241
Tren de sombras see *Train of Shadows* (1997)
Tren Fantasma (short film) 185
Trentacosti, Michael 226
Tres días see *Before the Fall* (2008)
Tretta, Sean 191
Trezise, Dan (aka Daniel Trezise) 214
The Triangle (2005, aka *Bryan Singer and Dean Devlin Present The Triangle*) 205
Triangle (2007 Chinese feature) 147

Tribeca Film Festival 23; Midnight Section 116
Trick or Treat (dir: Pearce) 167
Trick 'r Treat (2007; dir: Dougherty) 138, 195, 217, 246
Trieste Science Fiction Film Festival 100, 253n1
Trigon 150
Trilogy of Terror (1975) 199
The Tripper 218
Trippin' 126, 191, 223
Triptosane 130
Tristan and Isolde (1982, aka *Feuer und Schwert—Die Legende von Tristan und Isolde*) 235
Trøa, Kaja 190
Le Troisième Cri see *The Third Cry* (1974)
Trollsyn see *Second Sight* (1994)
TromaDance Film Festival viii, 15–19, Tromettes **18**; *Toxic Avenger* **19**; 35–36, 42, 49, 77–79, 93, 116
Troma's War 153
TRON (1982) 212
Troops 157
Tropezones (short film) 238
Trotman, Adam 160, 161
The Troubadour 96
Trouble see *Duplicity* (2005)
Truckers vs. Bikers 244
True Blood (TV series) 195, 215, 216
True Lies (1994) 209
True Nature 123, 130, 157, 184, 191, 195, 245
Truffe 155
Truly Madly Deeply 152
The Truman Show 169, 208
Trumbull, Douglas 212, 213, 233
Trunk or Treat 240, 243
Try a Little Tenderness 179, 187
Trys dienos (aka *Three Days*) 152
Tsai, David Kame 247
Tsai, Kuo Jung 169, 186
Tsai, Ming-liang 230, 233
Tsakpo, K. Akeseh 217
Tsao, Sam 242
TSR Audience Award 187 88
Tsuchida, Steven K. 146
Tsukamoto, Renpei 187
Tsukamoto, Shinya 127, 128, 149, 152, 167, 176, 188, 234, 252
T.T. Sindrom (aka *T.T. Syndrome*) 195
Tub (2010 short film) 130, 174
Tucker & Dale vs. Evil 125, 141, 145, 227
Tucker, Christopher 235
Tucker, Raelle 133
Tudo por um Fio 132
Tuez-moi d'abord see *Over My Dead Body* (1995)
Tufty 134
Tulin, William David 134
Tulsa International Film Festival 113
The Tumbler (2008) 177
Tumbleweed Holocaust 174
Tunzini, Guillaume 202
Tur, Marisol 203
Die Tür see *The Door* (2009)
Turan, Semra 228
Türelem see *With a Little Patience* (2007)
Turell, Bryan 161
Turken, Dana 122
Turley, Jason 178

Turn (short film?; year?) 136
Turn (2001 feature, aka *Taan*) 194
Turn It Up to 11 192
"Turn Left" (*Doctor Who* TV episode) 132
Turner, Daniel (aka Dan Turner) 159, 173, 225
Turner, Lana 236
Turner, Mike 243
Turner, Toya 134
Turno de noche 133
Tuttle, William 212, 213
Tuvalu 150, 175, 183
TV Conspiracy 159
Twelve Monkeys see *12 Monkeys*
Twentynine Palms (2003 feature; dir: Dumont) 231
Twice Upon a Yesterday (1998, aka *The Man with Rain in His Shoes*, aka *Lluvia en los zapatos*) 233
Twilight (2008) 215, 216
The Twilight Saga: Eclipse 50, 215
The Twilight Zone (book) 197
The Twilight Zone (1959–64 TV series) 170, 197
The Twilight Zone (2002–03 TV series) 199
Twilight Zone: The Movie (1983) 211
Twin Peaks 205, 252
Twin Peaks: Fire Walk with Me 210
The Twin Sisters of Sunset Street see *Les bessones del carrer de Ponent*
Twinkle Twinkle Killer Kane see *The Ninth Configuration*
Twitter.com 32–33
Two Eyes Staring 157
Two Hands 150
Two Miles Below the Surface of the Earth 243
Twohy, David N. 128
Tyler, Liv 216
Tyrants of Nazca 220
Tyrell, Bryan 158
Tyrrell, Susan 213
Tzameti (13) see *13 Tzameti*

U 43 (2004 short film) 159, 182
Ubu (1995) 233
Uchiumi, Mayumi (aka Mayumi Utusmi?) 251
Udler, Cory J. 247
Ugarek, Gary 93
The Ugliest Woman in the World (aka *La mujer más fea del mundo*) 150, 183, 194
The Ugly (1997) 151, 194, 233
The Ugly Duckling (2010 feature, aka *Gadkiy utyonok*) 227
The Ugly Swans (2006, aka *Gadkie lebedi*) 146, 181, 187, 194
Ugtv.com 157
Uian, Choi 250
Uibel, Arvid 175
Uki, Atsuya 143
Ulee's Gold 151
Ulloa, Juanma Bajo 152
Ulmer, Edgar G. *see* Edgar G. Ulmer Award
A Última Noite 132
La última polaroid 230
Ultimate Horror Fan contest **52**
UltimateFilmFest.com 34
Últimos pasajeros 184
Umbrage 92

The Umbrella Academy: Apocalypse Suite (comic book) 216
Umiko 129
Una de zombis 248
The Unborn (2009) 147
Unbreakable (2000) 90
Uncle Boonmee Who Can Recall His Past Lives 227
Unconscious (2004, aka *Inconscientes*) 193
Under My Garden 158
Under Surveillance (2006 feature; dir: Campfield) 244
Under the Bed (2007 short film; dir: Hammond) 158
Underground Horror Fest viii, 116, 247
Underground Horror Filmfest viii, 116–17, 247
The Undertaker 137
Underwood, Hamilton 226
Underworld: Evolution 217
Underworld: Rise of the Lycans 195
Unearthed (short film; year?) 219
Unfinished Business (short film; year?) 221
The Unfish (aka *Der Unfisch*) 194
The Unfun House 124, 174
The Ungodly 147
The Un-Gone 172, 214
The Unholy Sideshow 244
Unhook the Stars 151
Uninvited (2003 feature, aka *4 Inyong shiktak*) 231
The Uninvited Guest (aka *El habitante incierto*) 146, 231
Unit 30 243
The United Monster Talent Agency 130
United We Stand (2002 short film, aka *De beste går først*) 193
United We Survive 240
Universal Horror Classic Movie Archive (DVD collection) 198
Universal monsters (toys) action figures 198; busts 199; Headknockers 198; Monster Village 198
Universal Monsters Cavalcade of Horror (comic book) 198
Universal Studios 108, 110, 137, 167
Universal Studios Home Entertainment 195, 199; Legacy Series 204
The Unknown (2000 feature, aka *Det okända*) 183
Unrest (2006 feature; dir: Ipson) 156, 173, 225
Unseen (unproduced script) 126
Unspeakable: The Life & Art of Reverend Steven Johnson Leyba 122
UnstoppablePacific.com 34
Untitled: 003-Embryo (2002 short film, aka *Embryo*) 223
The Untitled Zombie Project 172
Unwelcome (2004 short film; dir: Smith) 189
Up (2009 feature) 249
Upgrade (unproduced script) 172, 224
Urania d'Argento 100, 214
Urata, Hideho 142
Urban, Karl 132
Uria, Albert 232
Uribe, Imanol 153
Urine Trouble 122
The Users Guide to Imaginary Friends (Abridged) see *Manual práctico del amigo imaginário (abreviado)*

The Usual Suspects 209
Utopiales — Festival International de Science-Fiction de Nantes 99, 179–83
Utsu-musume sayuri 250
Utterson 225
Utusmi, Mayumi *see* Uchiumi, Mayumi

V for Vendetta 133, 205, 216
Vacancy (2007 feature) 216
Vaccaro, Brenda 236
Vacchiano, Emily (aka Emily Vaughan) 173
Vadata 77, 122, 191, 238, 241
Vadeboncoeur, Maurice 133
Vadik, Mark 122, 131
The Vagrant 162
Vail, Justina 208
Vainwad *see* Despain & Vainwad
Valdemar (1975 short film; dir: Muñoz) 236
Valdemar (short film; dir: Hidalgo) 203
Valenti, Giorgio 233
Valentine (South African film; year?) 238
Valentine (2001) 139
Valentine, Richard 162
Valentino, Rudolph 78, 107
Valette, Eric 164
Valhalla Rising 147, 187
Valle, Alejandro 148
Valle, Jorge Morais 241
ValleyCon 109, 156–57
Vallier, Michael vii, 112
Valverde, María 217
Vampira 199
Vampira: The Movie 198
Vampire Film Festival viii, 117, 247
Vampire Film Series & Festival 117
Vampire Girl vs. Frankenstein Girl 143
Vampire Hunter D 127
Vampire Killers (2009, aka *Lesbian Vampire Killers*) 201
Vampirella (comic book?) 217
Vampires (1998, aka *John Carpenter's Vampires*) 139, 208
Vampires (2010; dir: Lannoo) 126, 174, 227
The Vampire's Assistant 124
Vampire's Hell 219
Vampyr (1932) 197
Vanacore, Jeffrey C. 200
Vanaja 147
Van Avermaet, Tom 129
Van Berckelaer, Yfke 123, 242, 252
Van Broekhoven, Gijs 136
Van Camp, Paul 219
Vandaag 137
Van Damme, Kaatje 228
Van Dekken, Bart 136
Van den Boom, Marc 136
Van der Woude, Jim 153
Van Diem, Mike 151
Van Diemen's Land 175, 228
Van Dien, Casper 172
Van Dormael, Jaco 152
Van Dyke, Dick 214
Van Eeden, Gideon 238
Van Hauwaert, Patrick viii, **25**–26, 28, 32, 47–49, 52, 60–63, 73, 80, 87–88, 92–93, 96, 195
Van Hees, Pieter 187, 194

Index

Van Helsing (2004) 199, 206
Van Hoytema, Hoyte 143
Vanilla County 225
Vanilla Sky 207
Vanished Acres 220, 221
The Vanished Empire 147
The Vanishing (1988) 153
Van Meenen, Karen 116
Van Passel, Frank 251
Van Rompaey, Christhope 147
Van Ronkel, Alford 169
Van Ryn, Turner 200
Van Strien, Elbert 157, 175
Van't Hul, Brian 205
Van Tongeren, Phil vii, 101
Van Tulleken, Jonathan 130
Variations for Movements 251
Vasaria Public Service Award 197
Vassdal, Kjell 151
Vassilakidis, Sophia 240
Vaughan, Emily *see* Vacchiano, Emily
Vaughn, Matthew 169
Vaugier, Emmanuelle 138
Vauth, Carsten 245
VCI Entertainment 107
Vecchi, Luca 191
The Vegan Vampire 170
Vegas & Charlie 238
Velasco, Manuela 229
Velle, François 151
Veludo, Hugo 188
Vending Machine and a Girl 251
Vendrell, Fernando 151
Venemann, Ted vii, 108–9
Venus Drowning 156
Venus Velvet 150, 183
Verboden ogen see Forbidden Eyes
Verboys, Matt 217
Het verborgen gezicht see The Hidden Face
Verboten (2008 short film) 135
Vercoutere, Marcel 213
Verduzco, Tania 228
Verhoeven, Paul 171, 211, 235
Verissimo, Fernando 96
Vermin (unproduced script) 244
Vermut, Carlos 201
Veronica Mars (2004–07 TV series) 205
Versus (2000; dir: Kitamura) 141
Vervoort, Lee 162
Vester, Paul 233
Vestido nuevo 229
Viaje a Marte see Journey to Mars (2005)
Las viandas 159
Vice Versa (1988) 210
Vicenta 227
Víctor y la máquina (aka *Victor and the Machine*) 172, 193
La victoria de Félix 229
Vicky (2010 short film) 247
Vidal 165
Vidangossy, Víctor 184
Vidas en Flamenco 231
Video Entertainment Team 137
Video Watchblog (blog) 197, 198
Video Watchdog (magazine) 198, 199
Videodrome 126, 128
Vidocq 150, 183, 232
La Vie de la mort 158
La Vie d'un chien 215
Viernes de Ánimas: El camino de las flores 185
Vierny, Sacha 233, 234

Viet-ñam 202
Vigalondo, Nacho 143, 163, 170, 175, 186, 188, 189, 214, 241
Vikaren see The Substitute (2007)
Vila, Guzmán 184, 185
Vilarasau, Emma 232
La villa seca 129
The Village (2004) 138
The Villains (short film; dir: Chang) 193
Villains (2005; dir: Cosgrove) see *Rógairí*
Villamarin, Elizabeth 218
Villazán, Núria 233
Villegas, Jessica (aka Jessica Villegas Lattuada) 186
Villeneuve, Denis 132, 133, 134, 147, 155, 201, 228
Vincent, Dennis 198
Vincent, le magnifique (aka *The Great Vincent*) 187
Vindication (2006 feature) 125, 134, 242, 243
Vine, Carl 234
Vinnie's Tale (aka *Tales from Makeout Point: Vinnie's Tale*) 248
Vinyan 158, 228
Vinzent 149
Violeta 156
Virgin Interactive 165
Virtual Dating 175, 179
Virumandi 193
Virus (short film; year?) 157
Virus (2006 short film; dir: Josefsson) 194
Virus (2010 music video) 237
Virus X (2010 feature, aka *H1N1: Virus X*) 219
The Visage 159, 222
Viscera Film Festival viii, 6, 13, **14–16**, 17, 19, 34, 36, 47, 51, 56–57, **84–85**, 106, 113, 117, 253n11
Visceral Bukowski: Inside the Sniper Landscape of L.A. Writers (book) 254n2
A Visit from the Sergeant Major with Unintended Consequences 225
Visiting Ellie 219
Visitor Q (aka *Bijitā Q*) 175
Viskocil, Joe 209
Visser, Leon 238
Vital (2004) 127, 149
Vito Power 245
Vivas, Miguel Ángel 149, 155
Vizcaíno, Sergio 230
Vlad (2003 feature) 242
Vleesdag 136
Vlog (2008 feature) 161, 245
Vogel, Fred 196
Vogel, Matthias 155, 158, 201
Vogelvrij 151
Vogt, Mary 210
Vogue Theater 6
Voice (dir: Beshir) 178
Void (short film; year?) 172
Volckman, Christian 148, 201
Volkart, Peter 188
Volkodav iz roda Serykh Psov see *Wolfhound*
Vollmar, Neele Leana 193
Voltaire, Aurelio 122, 123, 188, 240, 244
Von, Jessica 162
Von Brown, Joshua 122
Von Garnier, Katja 250

Vonnegut, Kurt, Jr. 170
Von Stoetzel, Paul 169
Von Sydow, Max 148
Von Trier, Lars 150, 152, 153, 187, 234
Voodoo Lagoon 126
Voorhees, Jason 46
Vortex 166
Vos 238
Vosloo, Arnold 137
Voss, Kurt 150
Voutas, Sam 159
Vranik, Roland 170
De Vrucht Van Uw Schoot, Vers Van de Boom 137
Vuckovic, Jovanka 197
La vuelta del malón 129
Vukotic, Dusan 154
Vulcan (city in Alberta) 240
Vysotsky, Dimitri 175

Wachowski, Andy 151, 208
Wachowski, Lana (aka Larry Wachowski) 151, 208
Wade 243
Wadleigh, Michael 141
Waffle (2010 short film) 241
Wagner, Hilary 222
Wagner, Jörg 202
Wagner, Robert 221
Wai, Ka-Fai 229
Wait Means Never 178
Waiting for Yesterday 156
Waitt, Chris 175
Wajsbrot, Alexis 196
Walas, Chris 211
Walcutt, John 235
Wald, Micha 193
Waldridge, Jeff viii, 114, 121
Walk Away (year?) 243
Walk In 172
Walken, Christopher 140
Walker, Andrew Kevin 140, 152, 209
Walker, Jeffrey 214
Walker, Jim 159
Walker, Michael 164, 175
Walker, Sam 201, 202
The Walking Dead (comic book) 215
Walking Distance (aka *Psychic Experiment?*) 237
Wall, Jordan **89**
Wallace, Cliff 138
Wallace, Michael 244
Wallace, Naomi 233
Wallace and Gromit: Curse of the Were-Rabbit 239
Wallace and Gromit in A Close Shave (1995, aka *A Close Shave*) 202
Wallander, Åsa 220
WALL-E 133, 169, 186, 204, 216, 249
Wallentin, Daniel 175
Waller, Anthony 165
Walsh, Fran 169, 186, 206
Walston, Ray 214
Walter, Tracey 211
Walton, Karen 139
Waltz, Martin *see* Gavreau, Martin
Wan, James 127, 148, 164, 201
Wang, Du Lu (aka Dulu Wang) 169, 186
Wang, Hui-Ling 169, 186
Wang, Joey 234
Wang, Shih-Li (aka Wang, Shin-Li) 236
Wang, Steve 251
Wanderlust 123

Index

Wanted (2008 feature) 216
The War of the Worlds (1953) 169, 198
War of the Worlds (2005) 205
Ward, Elizabeth 235
Ward, Roger 176
Ward, Vincent 153, 235
Ward-Lealand, Jennifer 234
Ward no 6 147
Ward 13 135, 201
WarGames (1983) 211
Warhol, Andy 66
Warlock 128
Warlords of the 21st Century see *Battletruck* (1982)
Warner Home Video 195, 198
Warrack, Christoph 159
Warren, Bill 197, 198
Warren, Gary C. 247
Warren, James 199
Wash, Tony 134
Wasielewski, Michael 243
Wasting Away (2007, aka *Aaah! Zombies!*) 200, 217, 228, 252
Watch 'Em Die see *Masacre esta noche*
Watcher (2006 short film) 173
Watchman: The Ultimate Cut (DVD) 204
Watchmen (2009) 203, 216, 249
Waters, Chad 138, 226
"The Waters of Mars" (*Doctor Who* TV episode) 132, 169
Watkins, James 147, 194, 228
Watson, Emma 133
Wattanapanich, Masha 189
Wattanapat, Nat 193
Watts, Naomi 139, 205, 207
Waxwork 128
The Wayward Cloud (2005, aka *El sabor de la sandía*, aka *Tian bian yi duo yun*) 230
We All Fall Down (2005 short film; dir: Kennedy) 225
We All Fall Down (year?; dir:?) 196, 221, 239
We Are the Night (aka *Wir sind die Nacht*) 227
We Are the Strange 144
We Are What We Are (aka *Somos lo que hay*) 142, 154, 166, 185
Weaver, Alexandra 177
Weaver, Brian 125
Weaver, Joe 167
Weaver, Sigourney 139, 140, 203, 211
Weaver, Tom 198, 199
Weaving, Hugo 133
Webber, Andrew Lloyd 231
Webber, Timothy 204
Weber, Steven 209
Webster, Kelly vii, 33, 35, 42, 50–51, 76, 80, 118
Webster, Linda vii, 105
The Wedding Night see *Bryllupsnatten* (1997)
Wedekind, Axel 167
Weed, Wyatt 162, 247
Weekend of Fear: Internationales Filmfestival für Horror, Thriller, Science Fiction & Obskure Filme viii, **40**, **46**, 50, **68**, 73, 76–77, **81**, 92, 99, 248
Weekend of Horrors 99; *see also* Fangoria's Weekend of Horrors
Weekend of Terror 101
Les Week-ends maléfiques du Comte Zaroff see *Seven Women for Satan*

Weekly Universe (website) 7, 9
Weekly World News 7
WeeklyUniverse.com *see* Weekly Universe
Weeks, Stephen 236
Weerarat, Banphot 193
Weerasethakul, Apichatpong 227
Weichsel, Jonathan 243
Weimer, Jon viii, 6, 10–11, 74
Weinberg, Coleman 122
Weiner, John 200
Weinger, Scott 210
Weinmann, Harry 161
Weintraub, Aaron 218
Weir, Peter 169
Weird Ones (1998) 161
Weirick, Ginny 161
Weiss, Darien 223
Weiss, Julie 209
Weiss, Valerie 125, 214
Wiest, Andrew 242
Weistra, Mark 137
Weisz, Martin 192, 230
Welch, Craig 233
Welcome Home, Roxy Carmichael 254n7
Welcome Stranger (2006) 177, 178
Welcome to Greensborough 178
Well-Founded Concerns 215, 220
Wells, H.G. 169
Wells, Mitchell 111
Wells, Vernon 220
Wenders, Wim 147
Wendkos, Jordan 219
Werb, Ezra 226
Werb, Mike 208
We're Closed (2007 short film) 172
Werewolf Fever 123, 200
Werewolf in a Women's Prison 124
Werewolf Trouble 196
Wertta, Iyari 185
Wes Craven's New Nightmare 140, 152
West, Jake 165, 176
Westbrook, Marie 243
Westdijk, Robert Jan 251
Westervelt, Clay 124
Weta Digital 132
Whale (animation) 136
Whaling and the Inherent Dangers Therein 135
"What Is and What Should Never Be" (*Supernatural* TV episode) 133
What Is It? (2005 feature) 230
"What the Fuck?" Award 130
Wheatley, Ben 155
Whedon, Jed 169
Whedon, Joss 137, 169, 186, 198
Whedon, Zack 169
Wheelchair Werewolf 121
Wheeler, Jonathan Grant 238
When Darkness Falls (2006; dir: Spong) 177
When Darkness Falls (unproduced script) 188
When Evil Reigns 178
When It Thunders 151
When Sally Met Frank 190
When the World Goes Dark 136
When Zombies Attack 226
Where the Dead Go 244
Where's Your Head At? (music video) 164
Wherever There Is Gold, Hell Is Nearby 243
Whigham, Shea 190

Whirity, William (aka Bill Whirity) 60, 242
Whissell, Anouk 248
White, Karl 243
White, Simon 241
White Lady Award 98, 166
White Lightnin' 142
White Rabbit (unproduced script) 172
White Room (2010 short film; dir: Chitaroni)
White Zombie (1932) 8
Whitehouse, Sacha 129
Whitelaw, Billie 153
Who Framed Roger Rabbit 170, 210
Who Killed Target 1967? 178
Why Get Married the Day the World Ends? 150, 194
Why We Had to Kill Bitch 178
Wick 199
Wick, Douglas Z. 213
Wicked City see *Yiu sau dou si* (1993)
Wicked Pixel 107
The Wicker Man (1973) 126, 198, 212
Wicki, Stephan 187
Widegren, Marcus 129
Widrich, Virgil 194
Wiest, Andrew 167
Wig (2010 feature, aka *Kazura*) 187
Wikipedia 19, 121
Wilbanks, Allen 123
Wilcox, Jason 160
Wild 6
The Wild and Wonderful Whites of West Virginia 176
The Wild Blue Yonder (2005) 145, 230
The Wild Heels 152
Wilde, Oscar 169
Wilder, Gene 170, 186
Wilderness (2006 feature) 145
Wilkins, Bob 124, 197
Wilkins, Toby 217, 218
Wilkinson, Michael 203
Wilks, Errol Anthony 167
Willard (2003) 194
William Castle Collection 197
William Wilson (2003 short film; dir: Davis) 196
Williams, Ashley C. 237
Williams, Caroline 235
Williams, Daniel 156
Williams, Jamie Renee 40–41, 242
Williams, Jerry 162
Williams, John 205, 207, 212, 213
Williams, Maxime 164
Williams, Richard 210
Williams, Robin 139, 207, 210
Williams, Steven 221
Williams, Tony 235
Williamson, Kevin 140, 209
Williamsom, Mike 201, 217
Willing, Nick 151, 165, 175
Willis Sillim's Tall Tales 222
Willow 210
Wilson, Erin 245
Wilson, Sheldon 135
Wilson, Ted 115
Wilson, Thomas F. 210
Wimer, Brian 162
Wincer, Simon 236
The Wind (2001 feature; dir: Mongillo) 226
Windcroft 162
Windigo (dir: Happyjack-McKenzie) 142

The Windigo (2000 short film; dir: Koskenmaki) 161
Windon, Stephen 126
The Window (2009 short film) 132
Window on Your Present 122
Winds of God 252
Windsor, Jason 245
Windwalker 252
Winfrey, Rob 167
Winged (1997) 161
Wingfield, Michael 124
Wings of the Dead (short film) 235
Winkler, Ken 122
Winning, David 158, 244
Winnipeg Horror Cinema viii, 98, 248
Winnipeg Short Film Massacre 98, 248–49
Winston, Max 131
Winston, Stan 140, 141, 207, 210, 211, 213, 231
Winter, Alex 166
Winterbottom, Michael 188, 231
Winter's Tale (2008) 135
Wiredprnews.com 34
Wirkola, Tommy 123, 158
The Wisdom of Crocodiles (aka *La Sagesse des crocodiles*) 127, 165, 183
Wisdom Teeth 142
Wise, Ray 124
Wise, Robert 213
The Wish (2007 short film; dir: Grillo) 244
Wisher, William, Jr. 170
Wisler, Mikel J. 243
De Wisselwachter 128, 153
Witchblade (2001–02 TV series) 207
Witchcraft (1999, aka *Myrkrahöfðinginn*) 194
The Witches (1990; dir: Roeg) 141
Witches' Night 174
The Witches of Eastwick (1987) 211
With a Little Patience (2007) 143
Witherspoon, Reese 233
WithIN see *The Cavern* (2005)
Within (2009 feature; dir: Culpepper) 85, 93, 124, 241
Within (2010 short film; dir: Mead) 199
Without/Within 220
Withoutabox.com 22, 28–32, 91, 253n13
Wittlinger, Heidi 175
Witz, Martin 234
Wizard of Darkness see *Eko Eko Azarak: Wizard of Darkness*
The Wizard of Oz (1939) 206
The Wizard of Speed and Time (1988) 213
Wo ai chu fang see *Kitchen* (1997)
Wofford, Wesley 207
Wojna swiatów — nastepne stulecie 154
Wolf (2004, aka *El Lobo*) 145, 209
Wolf, Gary K. 170
Wolf, Leonard 244
Wolfe, Matthew 122
Wolfen 141
Wolfhound (feature; year?; aka *Volkodav iz roda Serykh Psov?*) 246
Wolfman Mac 124
Wolford, Bryan vii, 6, 57–58, 108, 254n1
A Wolf's Tale see *Una storia di lupi* (2008)
Wolstencroft, Richard 95
Wolverine: Old Man Logan (comic book) 216

A Woman Who Is Beating the Earth (aka *Daichi o tataku onna*) 250
Woman's Intuition 162
Womboldt, Shane 223
Women (2000 feature, aka *Nosotras*; dir: Colell) 232
Women in Film Muse Award **19**
Women in Horror Month 105
Women of Horror Film Festival 13, 111
Wonder Award 117, 249
Wonderfest (convention) 197
Wonderful Days see *Sky Blue* (2003)
A Wonderful Life (1999 short film, aka *Quand on est amoureux c'est merveilleux*) 164
Wonderlantz (novel) 164
Wong, Barry see Jing Wong
Wong, Jing (aka Barry Wong) 251
Woo, John 176, 208
Wood, Darin 123
Wood, Ed 15, 31, 45
Wood, Elijah 206, 209
Wood, Stephanie 226
Wooden Heart 178
Woodruff, Tom, Jr. 122, 208, 210
The Woods (2006 feature; dir: McKee) 194
Woods, James 139, 208, 233
Woodward, Ed 198
Wool 100% (2006) 144
The Words and the Bees 244
Workers Club 95
Working Day (2010 short film) 129
World Horror Convention 6, 8, 10–**11**, 13, 36, 73–74, 81, 106, 253n3
World Science Fiction Convention 111
World Science Fiction Society 111
World 3-D Film Expo 199
World War Z (book) 48
World Zombie Day 197
Worldcon 111
World's Finest 157
Worlds of Wounded Clay 145
W.O.R.M. 123, 134
Worth, Nicholas 236
Worthington, Sam 203
Wozniak, Steve 222
Wrake, Run 142, 144
Wray, Fay 213
Wrecker 222
The Wrestler 147
Wretched (2007 short film; dir: Delano & Martinuzzi) 57, 238, 247
Wright, Brad 133
Wright, Edgar 125, 138
Wright, Geoffrey 232
Wright, Richard G. 151
The Wright Stuff 136
Wrightson, Bernie 168, 198
Written By (2009 short film) 188
Wrong Turn 2: Dead End 163
Wyatt, Melanee 222
Wylde, Chris 188
Wynette, Tammy 90
Wynne-Simmons, Robert 154

X (short film; year?) 215
X Fest Extreme Film Festival 102
The X-Files 50, 165, 166, 208, 209
X-Men 207
X-Men Origins: Wolverine 216
X-Men: The Last Stand 205, 216, 217
X-Mess Detritus 135, 243
X-Pression 156

X, Y (2004 feature; dir: Vitkin) 221
Xtro 154
X2 (aka *X2: X-Men United*) 206, 240

Y (short film; dir: Poltera) 159
Y (unproduced script) 189
Y que cumplas muchos más see *Happy Birthday to You?* (2006)
Y: The Last Man (comic book) 216
...ya no puedo caminar 183
Yagher, Kevin 139, 140, 141
Yajima, Yujiro 232
Yakkel, Kenny 226
Yamaguchi, Y dai 250
Yamakawa, Yoshiki 143
Yamamoto, Shunsuke 196
Yamanouchi, Daisuke 251
Yamashita, Atsuhiro see Yamashita, Nobuhiro
Yamashita, Nobuhiro (aka Atsuhiro Yamashita?) 193, 250
Yamasong 135
Yamgotchian, Alejandro viii, 119, 184
Yang, Ik-joon see Yang, Ik-june
Yang, Ik-june (aka Ik-joon Yang) 142, 155
Yard Work (2006 short film) 167
Yasuhara, Shin 251, 252
Yates, Paul Sanchez vii, 111
Yatterman 143
Ye yan see *The Banquet* (2006)
A Year in the Death of Jack Richards 159
Yeaworth, Irvin "Shorty," Jr. 105
Yeazel, Christopher Ryan 223
Yee, Chung-Man 205
Yee, Derek 145
Yelkhov, Yuri 235
Yellow Sticky Notes 143
Yellowbrickroad 188
Yennie, Ashlynn 237
Yeopgijeogin geunyeo see *My Sassy Girl* (2001)
Yesterday (2009) 129
Yesterday Was a Lie (2008) 157, 220
Yieutjib jombi see *The Neighbor Zombie* (2010)
Yim, Ho 194
Yim, Phil-Sung 147, 192, 230
Yim, Pil-Sung see Yim, Phil-Sung
The Yin Yang Master (aka *Onmyoji: The Yin Yang Master*) 188
Yip, Wai-shun see Yip, Wilson
Yip, Wilson (aka Yip, Wai-shun) 143, 187, 228
Yiu sau dou si (1993, aka *Wicked City*) 152, 234
Yo fui un Fredy Kruger adolescente 133
Yoffe, Justin **12**–**13**
Yonimo kimyô na monogatari — Eiga no tokubetsu hen see *Tales of the Unusual* (2000)
Yoru no geemu see *Night Games*
Yoshida, Daihachi 192
Yoshida, Keisuke 250
Yoshida, Kouta 250
You Are So Undead 247
You Are the Hero in This Film 194
You Make Me Feel So Dead (music video) 242
You, the Living (aka *Du levande*) 147, 187
Young, Christopher 138, 210, 233
Young, Lea Moreno see Moreno, Lea
Young, Reyna vii, 28, 32, 35, 42, 49, 66, 75, 77, 82, 89, 113, 247

Young, Shannon 225
Young Frankenstein 170, 186, 213
Young Sherlock Holmes 211
Younger & Younger 128
Youngkin, Stephen D. 198
Youngyooth, Thongkonthun 143
Your Mommy Kills Animals 144
YouTube.com 60, 72, 82, 94
Y2K: Shutdown Detected (1999 short film; dir: Gonzales) 219
Yu, Lik-wai (aka Nelson Yu Lik-wai) 231
Yu, Ronny 165, 166
Yuasa, Masaaki 145
Yubari International Fantastic Film Festival 100, 249–52
Yue, Shawn 192
Yun, Jong-chan 149
Yun, Yeo-Jong (aka Yun, Yeo-Jung) 237
Yurei 137
Yuricich, Richard 212
Yusof, Helmi 159
Yuting, Hseuh 125
Yuzna, Brian 128, 149, 165, 166, 167, 171, 175, 176, 231
Yvonne, Claudia 224

Zablocki, Raymond 169
Zach, Lucas 190
Zacherley 198, 199
Zalutsky, Sam 242
Zanette, Mariana 129
Zaramella, Juan Pablo 146
Zaror, Marko 155
Zatôichi see *The Blind Swordsman: Zatoichi*
Zazar, Lolo 150
Zbogum na dvadesetiot vek see *Goodbye, 20th Century*
Zé do Caixão *see* Coffin Joe
Zebraman see *Zeburaman*
Zeburaman (2004, aka *Zebraman*) 188
Zecevic, Dejan 195
Zelda (video game) 165
Zemeckis, Robert 169, 170, 210
Zeotrope Media 105, 125
Zéro Degree 144
Zero Population Growth (1972, aka Z.P.G.) 237
Zettell, Matt 224, 225
Zibahkhana 146
Zibolis, Alexis 220
Zimmer, Hans 139, 204
Zimmermann, Kody 126, 130, 184, 227, 245, 247
Zimmermann, Pedro 146
Zina (1986) 153
Zinema Zombie Fest 98
Zizic, M. Bogdan 236
Zmak, Wil 173
Zoic Studios 133
Z'omb D'or Award 98
Zombie, Rob 110, 137, 138, 139, 145, 197, 254n6
Zombie, Sheri Moon 137, 138, 217
Zombie American 173
Zombie Apocalypse (2008 short film) 162
Zombie Burger Attack 129
Zombie Collection (DVD set) 8
Zombie Dearest 195
Zombie Disco 111
Zombie Gets a Date 172
"Zombie Gigolo" (short story) 11
Zombie Honeymoon 138, 238, 245
Zombie Island 47, 60, 242
Zombie Jesus! 246, 252
Zombie King and the Legion of Doom 130
Zombie: le documental 133
Zombie Love (2007 short film; dir: Van Berckelaer) 47, 123, 136, 157, 162, 220, 225, 242, 252
Zombie Movie (2005 short film; dir: Stenbeck) 189, 218
Zombie Outbreak 111
Zombie Short Film Festival viii, 32, 40, 48, 65, 78, 98
The Zombie Survival Guide (book) 48
Zombiebot Film Festival 112
Zombieland 48, 138, 215, 228, 237
Zombies ...A Love Story 200
Zombies & Cigarettes 123, 200, 238
Zombies Anonymous (aka *Last Rites of the Dead*) 189
Zombies in Love 173
Zombies, Zombies, Zombies 161
ZombieWestern: It Came from the West see *It Came from the West*
Zombina and the Skeletones 76
Zombthology 162
Zomburrito 173
Zompire: The Undead Film Festival vii, 111, 117
Zone of the Dead 237
Zonnenberg, Luuk 136
Zoo (2007 feature documentary) 144, 229
Zoom Suit 222
Zophres, Mary 204
Z.P.G see *Zero Population Growth* (1972)
Zuanic, Franck 190
Zuazua, Anartz 146
Zubillaga, Haritz 194
Zuccon, Ivan 134
Zudina, Marina (aka Marina Sudina) 165
Zulawski, Andrzej 154
Zulo 148, 230
Zulueta, Iván 154
Zuni Fetish Doll 199
Zusje (1995, aka *Little Sister*) 251
Zwart water see *Two Eyes Staring*
Zwick, Edward 252
Zymet, Gregory 225

www.ingramcontent.com/pod-product-compliance
Ingram Content Group UK Ltd.
Pitfield, Milton Keynes, MK11 3LW, UK
UKHW050542150426
5217IPUK00026B/2036